289397   KT-425-234

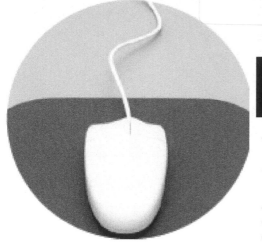

Free Online Access!

Plunkett's Airline, Hotel & Travel Industry Almanac 2017

Your purchase includes access to Book Data and Exports online

As a book purchaser, you can register for free, 1-year, 1-seat online access to the latest data for your book's industry trends, statistics and company profiles. This includes tools to export company data. Simply send us this registration form, and we will send you a user name and password. In this manner, you will have access to our continual updates during the year. Certain restrictions apply.

_____ YES, please register me for free online access. I am the actual, original purchaser. (Proof of purchase may be required.)

Customer Name _____

Title_____

Organization _____

Address _____

City_____State_____Zip_____

Country (if other than USA) _____

Phone_____Fax _____

E-mail _____

Return to: **Plunkett Research®, Ltd.**

Attn: Registration
P.O. Drawer 541737, Houston, TX 77254-1737 USA
713.932.0000 · Fax 713.932.7080 · www.plunkettresearch.com
customersupport@plunkettresearch.com

* Purchasers of used books are not eligible to register. Use of online access is subject to the terms of the end user license agreement.

PLUNKETT'S AIRLINE, HOTEL & TRAVEL INDUSTRY ALMANAC 2017

The only comprehensive
guide to travel and hospitality companies and trends

Jack W. Plunkett

Published by:
Plunkett Research®, Ltd., Houston, Texas
www.plunkettresearch.com

PLUNKETT'S
AIRLINE, HOTEL & TRAVEL INDUSTRY ALMANAC 2017

Editor and Publisher:
Jack W. Plunkett

Executive Editor and Database Manager:
Martha Burgher Plunkett

Senior Editors and Researcher:
Isaac Snider

Editors, Researchers and Assistants:
Ashley Bass
John Brucato
Gina Sprenkel
Suzanne Zarosky
Shuang Zhou

E-Commerce & Enterprise Accounts Manager:
Jillian Claire Lim

Information Technology Manager:
Seifelnaser Hamed

Video Production:
Uriel Rios

Special Thanks to:
Cruise Line Industry Association
International Air Transport Association (IATA)
Smith Travel Research
U.S. Department of Commerce: Office of Travel and Tourism
U.S. Department of Labor
U.S. Department of Transportation: Bureau of Transportation Statistics; Maritime Administration, Office of Statistical and Economic Analysis; Federal Aviation Administration. Federal Highway Administration
U.S. International Trade Administration
U.S. Travel Association
World Tourism Organization
World Travel & Tourism Council

Plunkett Research®, Ltd.
P. O. Drawer 541737, Houston, Texas 77254 USA
Phone: 713.932.0000 Fax: 713.932.7080
www.plunkettresearch.com

UCB
289397

Copyright © 2016, Plunkett Research®, Ltd. All rights reserved. Except as provided for below, you may not copy, resell, reproduce, distribute, republish, download, display, post, or transmit any portion of this book in any form or by any means, including, but not limited to, electronic, mechanical, photocopying, recording, or otherwise, without the express prior written permission of Plunkett Research, Ltd. Additional copyrights are held by other content providers, including, in certain cases, Morningstar, Inc. The information contained herein is proprietary to its owners and it is not warranted to be accurate, complete or timely. Neither Plunkett Research, Ltd. nor its content providers are responsible for any damages or losses arising from any use of this information. Market and industry statistics, company revenues, profits and other details may be estimates. Financial information, company plans or status, and other data can change quickly and may vary from those stated here. **Past performance is no guarantee of future results**.

Plunkett Research®, Ltd.
P. O. Drawer 541737
Houston, Texas 77254-1737
Phone: 713.932.0000, Fax: 713.932.7080 www.plunkettresearch.com

<u>ISBN13 #</u> 978-1-62831-416-8 (eBook Edition # 978-1-62831-741-1)

Limited Warranty and Terms of Use:

Users' publications in static electronic format containing any portion of the content of this book (and/or the content of any related Plunkett Research, Ltd. online service to which you are granted access, hereinafter collectively referred to as the "Data") or Derived Data (that is, a set of data that is a derivation made by a User from the Data, resulting from the applications of formulas, analytics or any other method) may be resold by the User only for the purpose of providing third-party analysis within an established research platform under the following conditions: (However, Users may not extract or integrate any portion of the Data or Derived Data for any other purpose.)

    a) Users may utilize the Data only as described herein. b) User may not export more than an insubstantial portion of the Data or Derived Data, c) Any Data exported by the User may only be distributed if the following conditions are met:

        i) Data must be incorporated in added-value reports or presentations, either of which are part of the regular services offered by the User and not as stand-alone products.
        ii) Data may not be used as part of a general mailing or included in external websites or other mass communication vehicles or formats, including, but not limited to, advertisements.
        iii) Except as provided herein, Data may not be resold by User.

"Insubstantial Portions" shall mean an amount of the Data that (1) has no independent commercial value, (2) could not be used by User, its clients, Authorized Users and/or its agents as a substitute for the Data or any part of it, (3) is not separately marketed by the User, an affiliate of the User or any third-party source (either alone or with other data), and (4) is not retrieved by User, its clients, Authorized Users and/or its Agents via regularly scheduled, systematic batch jobs.

<u>LIMITED WARRANTY; DISCLAIMER OF LIABILITY:</u> **While Plunkett Research, Ltd. ("PRL") has made an effort to obtain the Data from sources deemed reliable, PRL makes no warranties, expressed or implied, regarding the Data contained herein. This book and its Data are provided to the End-User "AS IS" without warranty of any kind. No oral or written information or advice given by PRL, its employees, distributors or representatives will create a warranty or in any way increase the scope of this Limited Warranty, and the Customer or End-User may not rely on any such information or advice.** <u>Customer Remedies</u>: PRL's entire liability and your exclusive remedy shall be, at PRL's sole discretion, either (a) return of the price paid, if any, or (b) repair or replacement of a book that does not meet PRL's Limited Warranty and that is returned to PRL with sufficient evidence of or receipt for your original purchase.

<u>NO OTHER WARRANTIES:</u> TO THE MAXIMUM EXTENT PERMITTED BY APPLICABLE LAW, PRL AND ITS DISTRIBUTORS DISCLAIM ALL OTHER WARRANTIES AND CONDITIONS, EITHER EXPRESSED OR IMPLIED, INCLUDING, BUT NOT LIMITED TO, IMPLIED WARRANTIES OR CONDITIONS OF MERCHANTABILITY, FITNESS FOR A PARTICULAR PURPOSE, TITLE AND NON-INFRINGEMENT WITH REGARD TO THE BOOK AND ITS DATA, AND THE PROVISION OF OR FAILURE TO PROVIDE SUPPORT SERVICES. <u>LIMITATION OF LIABILITY:</u> TO THE MAXIMUM EXTENT PERMITTED BY APPLICABLE LAW, IN NO EVENT SHALL PRL BE LIABLE FOR ANY SPECIAL, INCIDENTAL OR CONSEQUENTIAL DAMAGES WHATSOEVER (INCLUDING, WITHOUT LIMITATION, DAMAGES FOR LOSS OF BUSINESS PROFITS, BUSINESS INTERRUPTION, ABILITY TO OBTAIN OR RETAIN EMPLOYMENT OR REMUNERATION, ABILITY TO PROFITABLY MAKE AN INVESTMENT, OR ANY OTHER PECUNIARY LOSS) ARISING OUT OF THE USE OF, OR RELIANCE UPON, THE BOOK OR DATA, OR THE INABILITY TO USE THIS DATA OR THE FAILURE OF PRL TO PROVIDE SUPPORT SERVICES, EVEN IF PRL HAS BEEN ADVISED OF THE POSSIBILITY OF SUCH DAMAGES. IN ANY CASE, PRL'S ENTIRE LIABILITY SHALL BE LIMITED TO THE AMOUNT ACTUALLY PAID BY YOU FOR THE BOOK.

PLUNKETT'S AIRLINE, HOTEL & TRAVEL INDUSTRY ALMANAC 2017

CONTENTS

Continued on next page

INTRODUCTION

PLUNKETT'S AIRLINE, HOTEL & TRAVEL INDUSTRY ALMANAC, the thirteenth edition of our guide to the travel and tourism field, is designed to be used as a general source for researchers of all types.

The data and areas of interest covered are intentionally broad, ranging from the costs and effectiveness of the airline sector, to emerging technology, to an in-depth look at the major firms (which we call "THE TRAVEL 300") within the many industry sectors that make up the travel and tourism system.

This reference book is designed to be a general source for researchers. It is especially intended to assist with market research, strategic planning, employment searches, contact or prospect list creation and financial research, and as a data resource for executives and students of all types.

PLUNKETT'S AIRLINE, HOTEL & TRAVEL INDUSTRY ALMANAC takes a rounded approach for the general reader. This book presents a complete overview of the entire travel, lodging and tourism system (see "How To Use This Book"). For example, you will find trends in airline and hotel markets, along with easy-to-use charts and tables on all facets of travel in general, from growth in the cruise line industry to the number of airline passengers flying yearly.

THE TRAVEL 300 is our unique grouping of the biggest, most successful corporations in all segments of the global travel and tourism industry. Tens of thousands of pieces of information, gathered from a wide variety of sources, have been researched and are presented in a unique form that can be easily understood. This section includes thorough indexes to THE TRAVEL 300, by geography, industry, sales, brand names, subsidiary names and many other topics. (See Chapter 4.)

Especially helpful is the way in which PLUNKETT'S AIRLINE, HOTEL & TRAVEL INDUSTRY ALMANAC enables readers who have no business background to readily compare the financial records and growth plans of large travel companies and major industry groups. You'll see the mid-term financial record of each firm, along with the impact of earnings, sales and strategic plans on each company's potential to fuel growth, serve new markets and provide investment and employment opportunities.

No other source provides this book's easy-to-understand comparisons of growth, expenditures, technologies, passengers, corporations and many other items of great importance to people of all types who may be studying this, one of the largest industries in the world today.

By scanning the data groups and the unique indexes, you can find the best information to fit your personal research needs. The major growth companies in travel and tourism are profiled and then ranked using several different groups of specific criteria. Which firms are the biggest employers? Which companies earn the most profits? These things and much more are easy to find.

In addition to individual company profiles, an overview of travel markets and trends is provided. This book's job is to help you sort through easy-to-understand summaries of today's trends in a quick and effective manner.

Whatever your purpose for researching the travel and tourism field, you'll find this book to be a valuable guide. Nonetheless, as is true with all resources, this volume has limitations that the reader should be aware of:

- Financial data and other corporate information can change quickly. A book of this type can be no more current than the data that was available as of the time of editing. Consequently, the financial picture, management and ownership of the firm(s) you are studying may have changed since the date of this book. For example, this almanac includes the most up-to-date sales figures and profits available to the editors as of mid-2016. That means that we have typically used corporate financial data as of the end of 2015.

- Corporate mergers, acquisitions and downsizing are occurring at a very rapid rate. Such events may have created significant change, subsequent to the publishing of this book, within a company you are studying.

- Some of the companies in THE TRAVEL 300 are so large in scope, and in variety of business endeavors conducted within a parent organization, that we have been unable to completely list all subsidiaries, affiliations, divisions and activities within a firm's corporate structure.

- This volume is intended to be a general guide to a vast global industry. That means that researchers should look to this book for an overview and,

when conducting in-depth research, should contact the specific corporations or industry associations in question for the very latest changes and data. Where possible, we have listed contact names, toll-free telephone numbers and Internet sites for the companies, government agencies and industry associations involved so that the reader may get further details without unnecessary delay.

- Tables of industry data and statistics used in this book include the latest numbers available at the time of printing, generally through the end of 2015. In a few cases, the only complete data available was for earlier years.

- We have used exhaustive efforts to locate and fairly present accurate and complete data. However, when using this book or any other source for business and industry information, the reader should use caution and diligence by conducting further research where it seems appropriate. We wish you success in your endeavors, and we trust that your experience with this book will be both satisfactory and productive.

Jack W. Plunkett
Houston, Texas
September 2016

HOW TO USE THIS BOOK

The two primary sections of this book are devoted first to the travel industry as a whole and then to the "Individual Data Listings" for THE TRAVEL 300. If time permits, you should begin your research in the front chapters of this book. Also, you will find lengthy indexes in Chapter 4 and in the back of the book.

📹 Video Tip

For our brief video introduction to the Travel industry, see
www.plunkettresearch.com/video/travel.

THE TRAVEL INDUSTRY

Chapter 1: Major Trends Affecting the Airline, Hotel & Travel Industry.
This chapter presents an encapsulated view of the major trends that are creating rapid changes in the travel and tourism industry today.

Chapter 2: Airline, Hotel & Travel Industry Statistics.
This chapter presents in-depth statistics on spending, passengers, tourism, hotels, cruises, airlines and more.

Chapter 3: Important Airline, Hotel & Travel Industry Contacts – Addresses, Telephone Numbers and Internet Sites.
This chapter covers contacts for important government agencies, travel organizations and trade groups. Included are numerous important Internet sites.

THE TRAVEL 300

Chapter 4: THE TRAVEL 300: Who They Are and How They Were Chosen.
The companies compared in this book were carefully selected from the airline, hotel and travel industry, largely in the United States. 166 of the firms are based outside the U.S. For a complete description, see THE TRAVEL 300 indexes in this chapter.

Individual Data Listings:
Look at one of the companies in THE TRAVEL 300's Individual Data Listings. You'll find the following information fields:

Company Name:
The company profiles are in alphabetical order by company name. If you don't find the company you are seeking, it may be a subsidiary or division of one of the firms covered in this book. Try looking it up in

the Index by Subsidiaries, Brand Names and Selected Affiliations in the back of the book.

Industry Code:

Industry Group Code: An NAIC code used to group companies within like segments.

Types of Business:

A listing of the primary types of business specialties conducted by the firm.

Brands/Divisions/Affiliations:

Major brand names, operating divisions or subsidiaries of the firm, as well as major corporate affiliations—such as another firm that owns a significant portion of the company's stock. A complete Index by Subsidiaries, Brand Names and Selected Affiliations is in the back of the book.

Contacts:

The names and titles up to 27 top officers of the company are listed, including human resources contacts.

Growth Plans/ Special Features:

Listed here are observations regarding the firm's strategy, hiring plans, plans for growth and product development, along with general information regarding a company's business and prospects.

Financial Data:

Revenue (2015 or the latest fiscal year available to the editors, plus up to five previous years): This figure represents consolidated worldwide sales from all operations. These numbers may be estimates.

R&D Expense (2015 or the latest fiscal year available to the editors, plus up to five previous years): This figure represents expenses associated with the research and development of a company's goods or services. These numbers may be estimates.

Operating Income (2015 or the latest fiscal year available to the editors, plus up to five previous years): This figure represents the amount of profit realized from annual operations after deducting operating expenses including costs of goods sold, wages and depreciation. These numbers may be estimates.

Operating Margin % (2015 or the latest fiscal year available to the editors, plus up to five previous years): This figure is a ratio derived by dividing operating income by net revenues. It is a measurement of a firm's pricing strategy and operating efficiency. These numbers may be estimates.

SGA Expense (2015 or the latest fiscal year available to the editors, plus up to five previous years): This figure represents the sum of selling, general and administrative expenses of a company, including costs such as warranty, advertising, interest, personnel, utilities, office space rent, etc. These numbers may be estimates.

Net Income (2015 or the latest fiscal year available to the editors, plus up to five previous years): This figure represents consolidated, after-tax net profit from all operations. These numbers may be estimates.

Operating Cash Flow (2015 or the latest fiscal year available to the editors, plus up to five previous years): This figure is a measure of the amount of cash generated by a firm's normal business operations. It is calculated as net income before depreciation and after income taxes, adjusted for working capital. It is a prime indicator of a company's ability to generate enough cash to pay its bills. These numbers may be estimates.

Capital Expenditure (2015 or the latest fiscal year available to the editors, plus up to five previous years): This figure represents funds used for investment in or improvement of physical assets such as offices, equipment or factories and the purchase or creation of new facilities and/or equipment. These numbers may be estimates.

EBITDA (2015 or the latest fiscal year available to the editors, plus up to five previous years): This figure is an acronym for earnings before interest, taxes, depreciation and amortization. It represents a company's financial performance calculated as revenue minus expenses (excluding taxes, depreciation and interest), and is a prime indicator of profitability. These numbers may be estimates.

Return on Assets % (2015 or the latest fiscal year available to the editors, plus up to five previous years): This figure is an indicator of the profitability of a company relative to its total assets. It is calculated by dividing annual net earnings by total assets. These numbers may be estimates.

Return on Equity % (2015 or the latest fiscal year available to the editors, plus up to five previous years): This figure is a measurement of net income as a percentage of shareholders' equity. It is also called the rate of return on the ownership interest. It is a vital indicator of the quality of a company's operations. These numbers may be estimates.

Debt to Equity (2015 or the latest fiscal year available to the editors, plus up to five previous years): A ratio of the company's long-term debt to its shareholders' equity. This is an indicator of the overall financial leverage of the firm. These numbers may be estimates.

Address:

The firm's full headquarters address, the headquarters telephone, plus toll-free and fax numbers where available. Also provided is the World Wide Web site address.

Stock Ticker, Exchange: When available, the unique stock market symbol used to identify this firm's common stock for trading and tracking purposes is indicated. Where appropriate, this field may contain "private" or "subsidiary" rather than a ticker symbol. If the firm is a publicly-held company headquartered outside of the U.S., its international ticker and exchange are given.

Total Number of Employees: The approximate total number of employees, worldwide, as of 2015 (or the latest data available to the editors).

Parent Company: If the firm is a subsidiary, its parent company is listed.

Salaries/Bonuses:

(The following descriptions generally apply to U.S. employers only.)

Highest Executive Salary: The highest executive salary paid, typically a 2015 amount (or the latest year available to the editors) and typically paid to the Chief Executive Officer.

Highest Executive Bonus: The apparent bonus, if any, paid to the above person.

Second Highest Executive Salary: The next-highest executive salary paid, typically a 2015 amount (or the latest year available to the editors) and typically paid to the President or Chief Operating Officer.

Second Highest Executive Bonus: The apparent bonus, if any, paid to the above person.

Other Thoughts:

Estimated Female Officers or Directors: It is difficult to obtain this information on an exact basis, and employers generally do not disclose the data in a public way. However, we have indicated what our best efforts reveal to be the apparent number of women who either are in the posts of corporate officers or sit on the board of directors. There is a wide variance from company to company.

Hot Spot for Advancement for Women/Minorities: A "Y" in appropriate fields indicates "Yes." These are firms that appear either to have posted a substantial number of women and/or minorities to high posts or that appear to have a good record of going out of their way to recruit, train, promote and retain women or minorities. (See the Index of Hot Spots For Women and Minorities in the back of the book.) This information may change frequently and can be difficult to obtain and verify. Consequently, the reader should use caution and conduct further investigation where appropriate.

Glossary: A short list of travel industry terms.

Chapter 1

MAJOR TRENDS AFFECTING THE AIRLINE, HOTEL & TRAVEL INDUSTRY

Major Trends Affecting the Travel Industry:

1) Introduction to the Travel Industry
2) Discount Airlines Compete with Legacy Airlines, but the Differences Are Beginning to Blur
3) Major Airlines Change Strategy, Charge Fees and Boost Profits
4) Some International Airlines Cut First Class Seats and Add to Business Class/Premium Economy Now Widely Available
5) ADS-B Improves Air Traffic Control
6) Private Jet Rentals Grow in the Form of Memberships and Fractional Shares
7) Boeing and Airbus Face Waning Orders/Major Aircraft Market in China
8) New Aircraft Designs Offer Greater Passenger Comfort/More Efficient Engines
9) In Flight Wireless Takes Off
10) Air Traffic Grows/Airports Expand/Middle East and Asia Have Strong Air Traffic
11) Massive Long Term Growth in China's Travel Market/Indian Travel Market Rebounds
12) China Makes Immense Investments in Railroads, Highways & Airports
13) Online Travel Agencies (OTAs) Continue Strong Growth in Bookings/Hotels Fight to Keep Control of the Customer
14) Ecotourism, Sustainable Tourism, Adventure Tourism and Volunteerism Grow as Certification Standards Emerge
15) Hotel Occupancy, Profits and New Construction
16) Luxury Hotel Chains Expand Globally
17) What Millennials and Mobile-Savvy Consumers Want as Tourists and Travelers
18) Hotels Target Young Customers with Strategies Ranging from Micro Rooms and Hostels, to Hip Hotels that Encourage Mingling
19) Hotels Adopt Smartphones and In-Room Tablets to Deliver Services, Speed Check-In and Replace Room Keys
20) Hotel Mergers Enable Chains to Claim Market Share, Add Unique Properties
21) Localization will Drive Hotel Features, Marketing
22) Dog-Friendly Hotels Will Gain Market Share
23) "Sharing Economy" Gains Market Share in Travel with Online Sites Like Airbnb, HomeAway and Many Global Competitors
24) Cruise Industry Market Is Strong while Capacity Soars with New Ships
25) Small Cruise Ships Offer Adventure, Luxury, Intimacy or Access to More Places
26) River Cruise Lines Are Launched, with Low Capital Investment and High Fares
27) Chinese Tourism Creates Growth Opportunities for the Cruise and Hotel Industries
28) New Technologies Show Promise for Port and Airport Security
29) High Speed Passenger Trains, Including Maglev, Advance in China and Europe
30) U.S. Passenger Train Projects Receive Funding, Including Amtrak and Light Rail

1)   Introduction to the Travel Industry

📹 Video Tip

For our brief video introduction to the Travel industry, see www.plunkettresearch.com/video/travel.

The global travel industry is comprised of a wide variety of businesses, from hotels and inns to casino resorts, trains, buses, airplanes, cruise ships, tour operators and travel bookers, both online and physical. Both the United Nations and the World Travel & Tourism Council (WTTC), estimate that more than 1.3 billion tourists traveled the world during 2015. WTTC found that the global travel and tourism industry supported 108 million jobs on a direct basis in 2015. The industry generated $2.2 trillion in direct global contribution to GDP (gross domestic product).

In most parts of the world, hotels and resorts have been enjoying good to excellent occupancy rates, which enabled them to raise prices, while many new properties have been built or are under construction in promising markets. Business travel has grown substantially in recent years, while leisure travel has been generally strong worldwide. Nonetheless, when members of the European or American middle class do take a vacation, it is generally on a reduced budget. Businesses are sending more employees on trips, but keeping a tight rein on costs at the same time.

A survey by analysts at PwC forecast that 2015 U.S. hotel industry occupancy rates would be higher than at any time since 1981. ADR, average daily room rate, has also been seeing superior growth. For 2017 the study forecast an average daily revenue per available room (RevPAR) increase of 3.7%.

In the U.S., over a period of several years, major airlines cut routes and reduced the total number of seats available, partly by removing older, fuel-guzzling aircraft from service. This put the airline industry in a much more efficient operating condition. By 2015, business was so good that many airlines were adding to the number of available seats. Meanwhile, airlines have been getting a profit boost from the lower cost of fuel, thanks to declining oil prices.

U.S. airlines are also operating with much smaller staff counts recently than they were in previous years. For example, the number of employees in the U.S. scheduled airline industry plummeted from 485,000 in 2003 to 429,900 in 2016. To a large extent, airlines were able to renegotiate union contracts in recent years in order to reduce wage costs. By 2015-2016 however, unions were being much more demanding, as they could see the very high profits that airlines were generating. It is also vital to note one additional shift in airline strategy: today, they rely heavily on fees for services such as checked baggage, seats with extra legroom and on-board food.

For the near future, advanced new aircraft will bring significant changes in the global airline industry. For example, Boeing's highly advanced 787 enables international airlines to offer great enhancements to passenger comfort with extremely long intercontinental range, while the airlines benefit from a fuel efficiency boost of about 20%. Airbus competes with similarly efficient, long-haul aircraft.

Perhaps more important is the spectacular demand from global airlines for single aisle planes to replace older models that are not particularly fuel-efficient. Boeing will build a new high-efficiency version of its exceptionally popular 737, to be called the 737 MAX, which will compete with a similar offering from Airbus, an A320neo model with a new engine option. Enormous numbers of both of these aircraft will be sold over the long term.

Among international carriers, the upstart Emirates has carved out a place for itself as a major long-haul airline. It offers routes spanning the entire world with a major hub in the Middle East. Etihad is another Middle Eastern carrier that is getting rave reviews for its first class suites.

Discount airlines remain very important players in the U.S. as well as in Europe and the rest of the world. Outside the U.S., good examples include Dragonair in China and Ryanair in Europe.

E-commerce continues to play an extremely important role in the travel sector, making booking convenient for consumers and more cost-effective for travel providers. However, online travel booking sites like Orbitz and Expedia face tough competition. Airlines and hotel chains operate their own powerful online reservation systems, with rich features, multiple levels of photos and descriptions, and programs for managing frequent traveler rewards. Hotels, in particular, have been devising new strategies to win customers away from online travel agencies, offering many advantages to guests who book directly.

The cruise line business has enjoyed solid growth. Consumers see cruises as high-value package deals, and cruise ships are nearly full at all times. Some of the newest ships, such as Royal Caribbean's "Allure of the Seas" are among the largest passenger ships ever built. Approximately 12.4 million passengers sailed on cruises originating in North America during 2015, up from 12.1 million in 2014. Plunkett Research forecasted that 12.5 million would sail in 2016. The cruise industry is expanding into niche markets, including ships operated specifically for Chinese passengers, as well as more river cruises and adventure cruises.

2) Discount Airlines Compete with Legacy Airlines, but the Differences Are Beginning to Blur

For 2015, American Airlines pulled ahead of discount carrier Southwest Airlines to rank first among U.S. airlines, with 146.6 million passenger enplanements (up by 66.9% over the previous year, and boosted considerably by the inclusion of U.S. Airways' enplanements thanks to American's acquisition of U.S. Airways), followed by Southwest with 144.6 million (up 6.5%) and Delta with 138.6 million (up 7.3%). United totaled 95.3 million enplanements (up 5.5%); and JetBlue had 35.1 million (up 9.4%). These numbers include enplanements for both domestic and international flights.

Since its first flight in 1971, Southwest and its no-frills business model have enjoyed tremendous success, wooing customers based on price, not perks. For most of its history, Southwest's single-plane platform strategy (Boeing's 737) kept maintenance costs low, while its point-to-point flying system has helped to give it a solid reputation in on-time performance. (Southwest picked up some Boeing 717s when it acquired AirTran, adding a second type of aircraft for the first time in its history.)

Despite the fact that Southwest started out and made its fortune as a discount airline, it has grown to be one of the U.S.' largest carriers with expenses commensurate with its size. Some might argue that Southwest is no longer a discount airline—that its 40+ years of operations, massive size, ticket prices

and business strategy make it more of a legacy airline, albeit one without significant overseas routes.

In general terms, Southwest is facing tough competition in the form of newer discount airlines such as JetBlue. Although JetBlue has only a fraction of the fleet that Southwest boasts, it has expanded rapidly, adding new planes and entering new markets.

Both JetBlue and Southwest are making efforts to attract more business travelers. Both offer in-flight Internet access on a large portion of their fleets, which has powerful appeal to business travelers because they can work while flying. Southwest offers "business select" fares which afford business travelers to board Southwest aircraft first for priority seating for an additional charge. Additional perks included in Business Select are a complimentary beverage, additional frequent flyer credits and expedited security lines at participating airports.

As of mid-2016, Southwest was implementing technological improvements that would enable it to institute red-eye flights from the West Coast of the U.S. to markets including Baltimore, Chicago and Atlanta. It was also working on offering selected flights on a less-than-daily basis (previously, the carrier had to fly the same schedule from Sunday through Friday to all cities in its U.S. network), and the ability to cut flight schedules on days with typically slow demand such as Tuesdays and Wednesdays. The new options, which the company hopes to have fully in place by 2018, could add as much as $500 million to its annual profit.

Historically, U.S. discount carriers largely confined their operations to domestic travel, leaving international flights to the full-service airlines. However, JetBlue and Spirit are now offering tourist destinations like the Bahamas, Jamaica, Costa Rica, Aruba and the Dominican Republic, and may eventually fly even further afield. Southwest's acquisition of AirTran gave it a number of international destinations (including Jamaica, Mexico, the Dominican Republic and the Bahamas). In 2016, Southwest opened a new $100 million international terminal at Houston's Hobby Airport, which supports Southwest flights deep into Latin America. This puts Southwest in direct competition with United on vital flights to Mexico, Central America and South America.

Asian discount carriers are now offering long-haul flights. AirAsia X, for example, offers a route from Taipei to Australia, while Scoot (the discount unit of Singapore Airlines) offers flights from Singapore to Japan, Australia and India.

Keeping costs low is a challenge for long-haul flights, and carriers must rely on fuel efficient planes such as the Boeing 787 Dreamliner and the Airbus A350. The discount carriers are having to configure these planes with nine-across seating to come out ahead. Quick turnarounds are also a problem on international routes, due to more departure restrictions than domestic flights. However, growing numbers of discount airlines are taking the long-haul plunge, including Norwegian Air Shuttle which began trans-Atlantic flights in 2014. Norwegian Air's ticket prices are low while it is determined to make significant inroads to U.S. markets. As a result, legacy U.S. airlines are extremely sensitive to its plans.

The fact that major legacy airlines offer extensive global flight schedules to Asia/Pacific, South America, Europe and beyond offers an opportunity for airlines like American, Delta and United to differentiate themselves from the discount airlines, especially given the fact that their full-service domestic flights can connect smoothly with their international flights at major hubs. Legacy airlines are earning a significant portion of their net profits from international routes. Their ability to lure business travelers with first or business class seats, airline clubs and destination lounges that offer showers and changing rooms, gives them significant competitive advantage. However, with the advent of long-haul discount carrier flights, legacy airlines may have to offer economy seats at sale prices in order to maintain market share.

After a number of bankruptcies, mergers and reorganizations, legacy airlines have dramatically cut costs, especially on domestic flights, making them more competitive against Southwest than ever before. This process has included cutting the number of flights (with the net result of raising passenger load factors and efficiency on remaining flights), raising prices, developing very large revenue streams from checked baggage fees and other charges, and keeping a very tight lid on all controllable expenses. The recent merger between American Airlines and US Airways created the world's biggest airline.

Meanwhile, dozens of discount airlines, based on the Southwest model, have sprung up worldwide. Ryanair and EasyJet are setting the standard for discount operations in much of Europe. Ryanair is being especially aggressive in its cost-cutting efforts and increasing revenue by eliminating seat back pockets to lower weight and cleaning costs; eliminating airport check-in; banning checked baggage altogether; and selling 98% of its tickets via its web site.

Virgin America began service from San Francisco and Los Angeles to New York in 2007. The fact that Virgin America offers three tiers of service, including a widely admired first class section and a premium coach called "main cabin select," arguably removes this airline from the discount category. Seating areas include mood lighting, seat-back entertainment screens, electric power plugs at each seat, and a clean, modern look. In mid-2016, Alaska Airlines announced plans to acquire Virgin America for $4 billion.

Although it was launched on a true discount airline model, changes in JetBlue's strategy are moving it more into the legacy airline category and away from the discount segment. JetBlue is pushing a premium economy section. Also, the firm now has a highly competitive "Mint" business-class service on its coast-to-coast flights within the U.S., such as New York to Los Angeles. Mint cabins feature lie-flat seats.

For 2016, profitability for discount and legacy airlines alike will likely be reduced due to fare wars and falling demand, especially in Europe which was facing slower travel due to increased terrorist activity and the Brexit decision (in which a majority of British voters chose to leave the EU). As fuel prices fell in recent years, a number of airlines added flights and seats, but may have overestimated demand.

3) Major Airlines Change Strategy, Charge Fees and Boost Profits

The commercial airline industry has always been particularly vulnerable to economic and political changes. The deregulation of the U.S. airline industry in 1978 was a watershed event that led to intense price competition. Thereafter, several factors conspired to create multiple challenges for airlines. The stock market crash of 2000, the attacks on the U.S. via terrorist-controlled airliners on September 11, 2001, rapidly rising fuel costs and intense competition, among other problems, bankrupted several airlines and threatened many more with similar fates. In 2008-09 when the global economic crisis hit in earnest, global airlines were awash in losses.

Airlines around the world reduced capacity in 2010-12 in order to increase operating efficiency. Delta, for example, cut its capacity by 2% to 3% in 2012 compared to 2011. United and Southwest made similar cuts in 2011. Approximately 15% fewer commercial flights were expected in 2014 compared to 2007, with 7.8% fewer seats available. By 2015-2016, however, passenger loads and profits had risen to the point that airlines were adding seats.

With fewer flights to choose from, passengers must take those available to them. The airlines' strategy had the result of boosting passenger load ratios, leaving very few empty seats, which is a major factor in achieving efficiency and profits.

U.S. carriers have replaced smaller jets with larger ones on many routes, in a practice called upgauging. The airlines were offering 12% more total domestic seats as of mid-2015 than in 2013, but on 4.4% fewer flights. This creates many operating efficiencies, including more seats per employee and fewer landing fees. At the same time, flights have been eliminated to many small cities, which were formerly served by inefficient 50-seat regional aircraft. Analysts report that between 2010 and 2015, U.S. carriers cut the number of domestic flights made by regional jets by approximately one-third.

The plunge in oil prices beginning in late 2014, combined with high levels of passenger traffic led to unprecedented profits for airlines during 2015, and 2016 is likely to be another banner year. According to the International Air Transport Association (IATA), global aggregate profit among airlines was $35.3 billion in 2015, and was expected to reach $39.4 billion in 2016.

The greatest growth among major airlines in recent years has been in the Middle East, dominated by Emirates, followed by Etihad Airlines and Qatar Airways. Emirates, now one of the world's largest international airlines by passenger capacity, led the way with a business model that builds routes to developing countries that are often overlooked by U.S. and European carriers, and providing an alternative to local airlines. Emirates connects almost all of the world's continents through its Dubai hub.

The Air Line Pilots Association, based in the U.S., has expressed concern that U.S. carriers can't compete against rivals such as the Middle East carriers that enjoy government subsidies and financial incentives. Incentives that keep costs down included free land for airport expansion, fuel hedging contracts forgiven and nonunion workers allowed. Emirates, Qatar Airways and Etihad Airways are booming, sending more than 120 planes to American cities each week, up 300% compared to 2009. Very large new aircraft orders placed by the Middle Eastern carriers in recent years indicate their intent to continue to expand aggressively. By late 2015,

American carriers had abandoned most flights to the Middle East or India due to increasing competition.

Internet Research Tip:
The U.S. Department of Transportation operates a web site with complete information regarding U.S. airlines, their on-time ratings, consumer satisfaction ratings and much more. Visit the Aviation Consumer Protection and Enforcement Division at www.dot.gov/airconsumer.
ATWOnline offers extensive information regarding air operations, management, information technology, safety regulation and more: www.atwonline.com.
TranStats offers in depth statistics on all types of U.S. transportation, including airlines and rail, with frequent releases of the latest data. www.transtats.bts.gov.

Another shift in airline business operations is the growth in revenue from additional fees such as charges for checked bags, priority seating and food and beverages on board. IdeaWorks projected that 63 airlines would take in $59.2 billion in ancillary fee revenue during 2015, up from $49.9 billion in 2014. These fees have been a big boost to annual airline profits. Checked bag fees making up about 20% and onboard sales (food, drink, retail goods, Wi-Fi and inflight entertainment) were to account for about 30%. As of mid-2016, Southwest allowed passengers to check up to two bags at no charge, but assessed a $75 fee for each additional bag or bags weighing more than 50 pounds. JetBlue began charging passengers for checked bags in 2015, leaving Southwest as the only carrier in the U.S. to check bags at no charge.

Airlines including Delta and JetBlue are bundling fees into "upgrade packages" to make them more palatable to fliers. Delta's Comfort Plus ticket, for example, offers additional leg room in the coach cabin, early boarding and access to overhead bin space and free drinks.

New technology is paving the way for passengers to check bags themselves after printing luggage tags at home. New technologies also allow them to track bags via smartphone. Airline technology firm SITA reported in 2015 that more than one-third of global airlines are asking passengers to tag their own bags compared to 13% in 2009. By 2018, more than 75% of all airlines plan to institute the practice. Air France-KLM is releasing a small tracking device in 2015 that passengers store inside their bags, in addition to permanent bag tags the display bar codes. Airlines can change the bar codes remotely when passengers are rerouted. Qantas already had the tags as of early 2015.

Many passengers are paying for drinks, meals and even pillows and blankets. A number of airlines are charging fees of $30 or more for reserving seats in the first few rows of coach cabins (elite passengers who have achieved high status with the airlines because they travel frequently typically find many of these additional fees waived). Today, various passenger fees and charges, along with revenue-generating programs such as selling mileage awards to credit card companies, add up to an increasingly vital part of the airline business.

Mergers and acquisitions made big news in 2008 through 2013. Delta and Northwest were merged in 2008. United and Continental's merger, which resulted in one carrier flying under the United name but using Continental's logo and colors, closed in 2010. Meanwhile, British Airways (BA) and Iberia Lineas Aereas de Espana (Iberia) merged in early 2011. They now operate, along with Britain's BMI, under the corporate umbrella of International Airlines Group (IAG). American Airlines and US Airways announced a merger in late 2012, which received U.S. bankruptcy court approval in March 2013. (American had entered bankruptcy protection in 2011). The American-US Airways merger, which was finalized in December 2013, leaves four airlines (American, United, Southwest and Delta) in the U.S. controlling nearly all of the domestic market.

More and more, airlines are managing their fuel costs aggressively. For example, all new aircraft purchased by most airlines feature special upswept wing tips that are designed to reduce fuel consumption by 3% to 4%. Many airlines rely on expert market analysts for advice on when and how to purchase fuel. Results from fuel efficiency initiatives have been impressive. A 2010 World Economic forum report found that global air traffic rose 300% between 1980 and 2005, but jet fuel consumption rose only 150%. Airlines have made tremendous improvements in operating methods, while aircraft and engine manufacturers have greatly enhanced their technologies. The result is a significant drop in fuel consumption.

Like their U.S. counterparts, many global carriers have slashed costs and undertaken massive restructurings. Their efforts paid off to some extent. Global airlines are increasing their reliance on partnerships such as the Star Alliance and Oneworld Alliance. The partnerships share flight codes,

frequent flyer programs and airport lounge facilities, helping long distance travelers to cover thousands of miles as seamlessly as possible. As of late 2015, The Star Alliance network offered more than 18,500 daily flights on 28 airlines to 1,330 destinations in 192 countries.

Starting in 2010, when the global economy slowly began recovery and travel picked up, a number of airlines were re-starting growth plans including cabin refurbishment. Coach cabins have been upgraded with leather seats; many airlines are installing power ports for coach passengers and personal video-on-demand screens. Lufthansa and Southwest, among others, have installed new seats that are lighter and slimmer than those in the past. Thinner cushions on seat backs afford more space for passengers (24 inches between seat rows instead of 22.9 inches at Lufthansa, but approximately the same space as before in Southwest planes because it has added an additional row of seats to the cabin). Lighter seats reduce weight, and Southwest expects to save $10 million annually in fuel costs with the new seats.

SPOTLIGHT: Rock-It Cargo Carries Unique Air Freight Loads While Offering Unusual Services

Rock-It Cargo Limited (www.rock-itcargo.com) is a private specialty freight and logistics company that focuses on transporting expensive, fragile and unusual cargo around the world by land, sea and air. The firm was founded in London in 1978, when it provided equipment transport services for rock band the Moody Blues. Clients have included Bruce Springsteen and the E Street Band, Lady Gaga, Boeing, APR Energy, Cirque Du Soleil and the NFL. The company focuses on providing special, hands-on care to time-sensitive shipments. Its 200 employees operate from 17 offices around the world. In addition to shipping equipment for tournaments and entertainment events, Rock-It also specializes in the shipment of oversize industrial equipment.

---

4)   Some International Airlines Cut First Class Seats and Add to Business Class/Premium Economy Now Widely Available

The air travel industry's cash cow historically has been business class and first class tickets, especially those for international travel. The profits per passenger were immense at one time. This was particularly true on North Atlantic routes from New York to London. However, in recent years, fewer first class passengers were actually paying for tickets, with growing numbers cashing in frequent flyer miles to fly in the front of the plane.

Many carriers have altered strategy to emphasize business class and premium economy seats instead of first class. Two U.S. carriers, United Airlines and American Airlines, began cutting first class seats in 2012. United planned to cut one-third of its first class seats on international routes, while American was eliminating up to 90% of its international first class seats. Some non-U.S. carriers have followed suit, including Qantas Airways and Deutsche Lufthansa.

Business class tickets sell for considerably less than first class—often 50% less. While much roomier and more comfortable than coach or economy class seats, business class still takes up a lot less airplane space per passenger than first class, so more seats can be added. It is often easier for business flyers to justify the cost of business class travel than the cost of first class.

Some corporate decision makers still argue that the rest and relaxation afforded in business class cabins on airlines and in upscale hotels are worth the expense on long-distance trips, since employees are better rested and better able to do their jobs on the road. Others resist the expense and expect employees to use their own frequent flyer miles to upgrade when they want higher levels of service. Employers are likely to authorize business class travel for their staff than first class on long-haul flights.

While U.S. carriers are cutting back on first class, international airlines including Singapore Airlines, Etihad and Emirates Airlines, among others, are competing to offer new heights in luxury service. Long-haul travel, meaning flights of 12 hours or more, has been on the rise on these airlines. Singapore Airlines, Emirates and Cathay Pacific offer super long flights that cross the globe.

To make the hours in the air more bearable, all of these carriers have instituted perks such as roomier seats, expanded business class cabins, private first class seating, expanded flight crews and food and entertainment on demand. Take Singapore Airlines, for example. Its giant Airbus 380 aircraft offers private suites in first class, some with stand-alone beds rather than a seat that converts to lie flat. There are even private double-bed suites for couples. Airlines are hiring famous chefs to create ritzy in-flight menus. At Singapore Airlines, for example, an International Culinary Panel of eight celebrity chefs create menus. United Airlines works with Charlie Trotter. American Airlines boasts Maneet Chauhan, Sam Choy, Julian Barsotti and Mark Sargeant.

At British Airways, its Club World business class introduced lie-down seats that are 25% wider than before. In addition, the business class section has a Club Kitchen which offers anytime service.

First-class luxury is being taken to a new level on Emirates' flights to Dubai in the United Arab Emirates (UAE). The United Arab Emirates carrier offers 12 first class "suites," each with 5'6" louvered doors that can be closed for complete privacy while in flight. First class passengers may phone flight attendants to order food and drink, and choose from 500 channels of on-demand entertainment. First class passengers on Emirates' new Airbus 380 enjoy onboard showers, while business class customers can belly up to an in-flight bar.

Etihad raised the bar with miniature three-room suites called The Residence with a private bath with a glass sink and shower as well as dedicated butler, which began service between Dubai and London in December 2014. The flight takes about 6 hours and 55 minutes outbound from Heathrow to Dubai, and 7 hours 45 minutes of pure pampering on the return.

Emirates, Etihad and Qatar are also expanding service in business and coach class to lure more customers. Flight attendants trained as nannies entertain children from all three classes while in flight with games, crafts and face painting. Bars have been set up in business class and hot towels are being offered to passengers in coach. Emirates increased video screens in coach to 12.1 inches and offers 1,800 channels of programming.

Air France-KLM and Lufthansa are fighting back by investing about $3.48 billion in cabin upgrades in long-haul aircraft. As of mid-2015, Air France-KLM had 44 planes retrofitting with first class suites that can be enclosed.

By mid-2015, premium economy class service was available on most long-haul carriers. The class typically offers slightly larger seats than standard coach (about six inches more legroom, four to five inches more recline and one to two inches in seat width), separate bathrooms and flight attendants, larger entertainment screens and upgraded food service. The cost of premium economy is about 50% more than coach. To install the new class, Singapore Airlines takes 66 coach seats out of its A380 aircraft and installs 36 premium economy seats. Roughly 50% of passengers flying the new class pay for it themselves and 50% are corporate travelers who work for companies willing to pay the extra costs for premium economy, but unwilling to pay for Business Class.

SPOTLIGHT: Budget Transatlantic Flights

Flights linking the U.S. and Europe have long been cash cows for international airlines, especially business and first class seats. However, Norwegian Air Shuttle began offering flights in 2014 from Copenhagen to Boston, London-Gatwick to Boston and Oslo-Gardermoen to Boston for as little as $210 one-way. The carrier is able to offer extremely low fares by cramming more seats on its planes (291 on its Boeing 787s compared to the more standard 250) and keeping the planes flying from 17 to 18 hours per day instead of 15. Norwegian also flies to secondary airports where fees are lower. Icelandic carrier Wow Air offers service from London to Boston (with a stop in Reykjavik).

---

5) ADS-B Improves Air Traffic Control

A new air traffic control system that is generating headlines is the Automatic Dependent Surveillance-Broadcast (ADS-B) which commenced service in Canada in January 2009. ADS-B uses GPS information to replace radar when tracking planes. It is more accurate and faster than radar, allowing planes to travel more closely together safely. Jets flying under ADS-B surveillance need to be only five miles apart under current standards, even in remote places such as the Earth's poles or over oceans where radar coverage is not possible. ADS-B expanded in 2009 with additional receivers on the east coast of Canada and Greenland. In 2010 the Federal Aviation Administration (FAA) issued a final rule mandating ADS-B usage by January 1, 2020. The project's cost is an estimated $4.5 billion. The FAA largely completed coverage of the U.S. through 700 stations by 2014, working through contractor Exelis, Inc. The next step is for U.S. airlines to install equipment on their planes which will cost billions of dollars. The airlines have been slow to implement the installation, due to the high cost and concerns that the FAA would continue to hold up its end of the project by establishing policies and procedures and training controllers. Federal aviation regulators announced plans to exempt a number of U.S. carriers from the 2020 deadline for certain satellite-navigation upgrades. However, the FAA continues to require airlines to install ADS-B Out, a more powerful technology than the original ADS-B.

NAV CANADA, a private air traffic control service, initially installed five ground station receivers around Hudson Bay in northern Canada which had no radar coverage. By 1996, the system took control of all Canadian air traffic. Today, all 41 of Canada's air traffic towers rely on the computerized system, as do towers in eight other counties including Australia and Dubai.

Another next generation air tracking technology is Advanced Technology and Oceanic Procedures (ATOP), which has been in use at the New York, Oakland and Anchorage air traffic control centers in the U.S. since 2007. The system integrates radar and satellite tracking data supported by multiple computers onboard aircraft and on the ground. Planes report their positions every 14 minutes, and if a report is six minutes overdue or a plane veers off course, alarms sound to alert controllers. Such technology makes it much easier for pilots to gain approval to adjust flight plans due to weather or air traffic, and ATOP is credited with saving 330,000 flying miles per year and 10 million gallons of fuel thanks to greater efficiency.

The FAA is promoting another cutting-edge system called NextGen which, like ADS-B, uses GPS for navigation. Instead of pilots confirming approach and landing information by voice, they rely on computer data from NextGen, allowing maneuvers via autopilot. FAA officials claim that NextGen could achieve $2 billion in annual savings due to greater efficiencies. Costs to implement the system in ground stations and on board commercial aircraft are hefty. U.S. airlines may be required to spend approximately $20 billion by 2030 on new equipment.

Yet another system in use to aid air traffic control uses Performance-based Navigation (PBN) software such as that designed by GE Aviation (at a business unit formerly known as Naverus). The software analyzes data relating to individual aircraft performance and position in relation to other aircraft along with atmospheric data that impacts fuel consumption. GE Aviation launched a PBN project at the Jiuzhai Huanglong Airport in the Sichuan Province of China. The firm also provided technical support and assistance to Brazilian air navigation services provider DECEA to design Required Navigation Performance (RNP) flight procedures in that country.

In Europe, initiatives similar to ADS-B and PBN are under consideration. European airspace control is scattered across the members of the EU and 12 other contiguous countries. The result is that many flights zigzag around borders, adding an average of 26 miles to each flight and consuming an estimated $6.5 billion each year in costs such as fuel and wages. In early 2015, the European Aviation Safety Agency (EASA) proposed the adoption of PBN by all European airports as early as December 2018.

Another problem that the FAA is working to reduce in the U.S. is runway collision. Airport Movement Area Safety Systems (AMASS) have been installed at dozens of U.S. airports. However, while these advanced technologies are being placed at U.S. airports, many international airports, especially those in poverty-stricken countries in Africa and South America, have a long way to go in terms of airport and aircraft safety and security. Political instability and insufficient funds permit many safety breaches to pass undetected, and airplane crash rates in these countries are much higher. While many countries are doing what they can to improve safety and security, passengers continue to fly in these areas at their own risk.

6) Private Jet Rentals Grow in the Form of Memberships and Fractional Shares

Corporations continue to be conservative about major capital expenditures, including the purchase of business jets, which can cost $70 million or more for the largest long-range bizjets, and $4 million to $40 million for most other jets, depending on size and range. Many corporations have determined that they would rather rent bizjets than buy them.

Production of new, larger-cabin bizjets is underway. Bombardier's Global 5000 and 6000 offer updated cockpits, but face competition from new jets from Dassault (the Falcon 5X and 8X expected in 2017 and 2016) and Gulfstream (the G500 and G600, expected in 2018 or 2019).

The fractional ownership concept appeals to companies that need quick access to private jets but do not want the burdens of ownership. While chartering a jet from time-to-time may be appropriate for occasional users, companies that have continuous need for private jet travel find it more cost-effective and efficient to participate in fractional ownership.

Under the fractional concept, users commit to fly a given number of hours yearly. They pre-purchase the right to use one or more types of aircraft for those hours. Fractional ownership management firms then acquire, staff, maintain and operate the aircraft, keeping them ready and waiting for their user base.

Leading companies in this field include NetJets (owned by conglomerate Berkshire Hathaway), Flight Options and Flexjet. NetJets (www.netjets.com) is especially dominant in the fractional niche. Flight Options (www.flightoptions.com) is another large fractional provider. Its fleet includes Nextant 400XTs, Citation Xs and Legacy 600s. Customers wanting to make

only a modest commitment are typically sold "membership" cards. These cards are generally priced in prepaid amounts of $50,000 to $350,000. They allow the card holder to call upon aircraft on an as-needed basis, with the cost deducted from the balance remaining on the card. For example, the JetPass Card enables customers to buy as few as 25 hours of flying time. Charges work out to $5,000 to $10,000 for mid-sized jets.

Flexjet, (www.flexjet.com), offers a JetCard available in 25-hour increments. Fractional ownership and lease options are also available in 50-hour increments. Its fleet includes the Learjet 40XR, Learjet 45LXi, Phenom 300 and Learjet 75LXi aircraft in the light and super light category; Challenger 300 and Challenger 350LXi models in the super midsize category; Challenger 604 and 605 and Gulfstream G450 jets in the large category; and Gulfstream G500, Global Express and Gulfstream G650 in the ultra-long range category.

7) Boeing and Airbus Face Waning Orders/Major Aircraft Market in China

During 2015, Airbus delivered a record 635 aircraft, while Boeing delivered 762. This was big news, as these deliveries are about double the number of aircraft delivered in 2004. However, in 2016, both companies were facing slowing orders for new aircraft. Softening global economies and political unrest in a number of countries around the world are the cause.

While the new jumbojets, like the A380 and the 787 get a lot of press and admiration, perhaps more important is the demand from global airlines of all types for smaller, single-aisle planes to replace older models that are not particularly fuel-efficient. Boeing announced that it will build a new high-efficiency version of its exceptionally popular, single-aisle 737, to be called the 737 MAX. In mid-2011, American Airlines committed to buying a large quantity of the 737 MAX aircraft, leading Boeing to decide to move ahead with updated version of the 737 rather than go through the expense, delays and uncertainties of designing and launching an entirely new airliner. The aircraft will feature CFM International LEAP engines, lowered maintenance requirements and high fuel efficiency. An all-new interior design, called "Sky Interior," will have tall headroom, overhead bins that disappear into the ceiling yet carry more baggage, as well as LED lighting.

As of July 2016, Boeing had 3,278 orders for the 737 MAX, which is expected to enter service in

2017. This highly effective strategy of updating existing aircraft designs is likely to be standard operating procedure for both Airbus and Boeing for the near term. It saves on research and development investment, speeds up deliveries and enables customers to acquire advanced, fuel-efficient aircraft in a relatively short period of time.

Meanwhile, the Boeing's competition in the 737 market is the single-aisle Airbus 320neo family of jets (including the A319neo, A320neo and A321neo), which will feature high efficiency through CFM International LEAP engines or the Pratt & Whitney PW1100G PurePower engine. The result is a 15% reduction in fuel use along with two tons of additional load capacity and a boost in range of up to 500 nautical miles. As of July 2016, the A320neo family had 4,583 orders. As with Boeing's 737 MAX, this 320neo is an updating of an extremely popular aircraft that Airbus has sold for many years. The A330neo was unveiled in mid-2014, which promises to yield a 14% improvement in fuel efficiency over previous A330s, with the first deliveries in 2017. Boeing and Airbus are both enjoying strong order books and backlogs equal to several years of production.

Boeing and Airbus have been in fierce competition since 2004 when they first announced new jumbojet concepts. The success of Boeing's new fuel-efficient 787, which had its first flight in late 2009 and made its first commercial delivery in September 2011, hinges on growing demand for more frequent international flights on mid-size aircraft. To serve this market, the 787, known affectionately at Boeing as the "Dreamliner," gives airlines the ability to offer non-stop intercontinental flights between smaller regional cities, rather than just the standard flights between major cities, such as New York-London.

The Dreamliner's maximum range is 9,600 statute miles. While the 787 is not Boeing's biggest aircraft, it is the company's most fuel-efficient. The price tag is $157 million to $167 million per airplane, depending on the model. Much of the aircraft is constructed from carbon-based composite materials, which are lighter than aluminum. Today's demand for fuel efficiency positions the 787 in a favorable light. In addition to being lightweight, its composite materials are easy to mold into precise shapes. This is important for aircraft, which involve lots of curved surfaces. By using such materials, fewer pieces need to be manufactured to create a curve. Boeing promises that the materials are durable, to the extent that airlines should see 12 years of service before a

787 requires its first major maintenance overhaul (as compared to six years for an aircraft made of aluminum).

Such materials are not entirely new to Boeing's assembly line—about 11% of its 777 is already made from composite materials. Yet a commercial aircraft built primarily of composites is new. Another development is the installation of structural sensors. While diagnostic sensors that measure temperature and pressure are commonplace on aircraft, Boeing is installing multiple sensors on the 787 that allow pilots to continually monitor its structural integrity.

As of July 2016, 1,161 Dreamliners had been ordered by customers around the world—a tremendous success. The company has developed different models of the 787, with varying nautical ranges and seating capacities. The 787-8 is available with the capacity to carry 210 to 250 passengers with a range of 8,640 to 9,266 statute miles. There is also a 787-9 that carries up to 290 passengers for up to 9,600 statute miles. In addition, the 787-10 carries 323 passengers with a range of 7,020 statute miles. Another plus for the 787 is the choice of General Electric or Rolls-Royce PLC engines. Boeing designed the airplane in such a way that one engine can be swapped for the other in 24 hours as opposed to the two months required for typical aircraft. This ability is a great selling point for airlines planning ahead to times when they well might wish to sell a 787 to a rival company that uses the alternative engines.

But this strategy has its costs, too. Multiple aircraft models are expensive to design and bring to market (not to mention the cost of the 787's composite materials, which are significantly higher than aluminum). Boeing outsourced manufacturing of many of the 787's components to companies overseas, including a large number of components being manufactured in Japan. While outsourcing isn't especially new for Boeing (a significant percentage of the 777's components were made abroad), the fact that this outsourcing also includes wing manufacture in Japan is a new development. These are risky changes for a historically conservative company, and the practice initially created many unexpected headaches, including significant delays. Boeing responded effectively by acquiring a number of its suppliers, in order to gain better supply chain control, and working to establish closer relationships with its remaining outsourcers.

Boeing's 747, the original jumbo jet, took its first flight in February 1969, and the first delivery was made in December of that year. It has gone through numerous redesigns and enhancements through the years, including newer, extra-long-range models that can hold more than 500 passengers. In late 2005, Boeing announced plans to further update the 747 to compete with the A380. The newer version, called the 747-8, has 34 more seats than the 747-400, while the cargo-only version can carry 16% more load. Additional changes include a more fuel-efficient engine (the same being developed for the 787), a longer body and updated wings. The first deliveries of the 747-8 were made in October 2011.

The new 747 features a 16% improvement in fuel economy over the previous model, as well as a 30% reduction in its noise footprint. The list price for the aircraft is about $317.5 million to $319.3 million, depending on configuration.

In 2013, Boeing approached three firms, Emirates Airlines, International Consolidated Airlines Group and Japan Airlines, to become launch customers of a redesigned 777 called the 777X, expected to launch by 2020. Boeing hopes to top its record sales of the 365-seat 777-300ER, which is the best-selling twin-aisle jetliner model in history. The plane is especially suited for the extreme heat in the Middle East due to its extra-wide wings and powerful engines, making fully loaded takeoffs easier. Boeing is also capitalizing on a joint venture with Mubadala, a government-owned conglomerate in Abu Dhabi charged with diversifying the economy in the Emirates. Boeing is supplying welcome technical expertise and assistance with the venture's manufacture of advanced composite materials for jet aircraft.

Back at Airbus, the A380 represents the firm's alternative vision for the future of air travel. While Boeing's crystal ball shows an increase in demand for smaller capacity, long-haul flights between a wider range of international cities, especially in Asia and Europe, Airbus predicts that international travelers will be better served by a more centralized hub system, wherein large groups of passengers are flown in and out of fewer cities via massive jumbojets. Airbus's new A380 is well-suited for the hub model, while Boeing's aircraft could adapt to either a hub or point-to-point system.

The A380 is the world's largest passenger aircraft, and, at a price tag of $375.3 million or more, the most expensive. It holds between 555 and 800 passengers, based on single- or multiple-class models. With a range of up to 9,200 miles it can travel a great distance without refueling. The aircraft also offers good fuel efficiency. As of July 2016, Airbus had received only 319 firm orders for the A380. Sales of the giant aircraft have been slowing to the extent that Airbus announced cutting production from 27 planes per year (which it completed in 2015) to 12. The model finally showed a profit for Airbus in 2015, but only after the company slashed production costs.

Airbus has another new jet in the works, the A350 extra-wide body (sometimes called "XWB"), which will seat between 270 and 350 passengers. It is offered in three models, the A350-800, 900 and 1000. It is Airbus' answer to Boeing's 787 and its commitment to lightweight, fuel-efficient aircraft. Useful range will be as high as 8,300 nautical miles, depending on layout.

Also in January 2015, Airbus announced its first customer commitment for the A321LR, a modified version of its largest single-aisle jet, the A321. Designed to compete with Boeing's 757, it promises great fuel efficiency, cutting fuel costs by as much as 30%. The A321LR can carry 206 passengers up to 4,000 nautical miles.

As for the future, watch for intense competition between the two manufacturers to continue. Meanwhile, there will be immense, multi-trillion-dollar demand for new airliners over the long term. Boeing forecasts the global passenger and freight aircraft fleet to grow by nearly 40,000 new jetliners between 2016 and 2035, worth $5.9 trillion. Airbus' estimate is the delivery of 33,070 planes during the period, valued at $5.2 trillion (up 1.5% from its 2015 estimate).

However, some industry observers are skeptical of this rosy outlook, due to the fact that many of the world's airlines have very little capital and are relying on vast amounts of loans or leases in order to acquire aircraft. If large numbers of airlines are unable to make timely payments on these debts and leases, then future financing of airline purchases may be much harder to come by and jet sales may suffer.

Boeing and Airbus both will be facing new competition as China begins manufacturing large commercial aircraft. The Chinese government has succeeded in building its first commercial aircraft, the regional ARF-21 jet. Between 2010 and 2030, The Chinese government is fast-tracking development of its own manufacturing facilities. In late 2015, China's first big airliner, the single-aisle, 160-seat C919 jet rolled off the assembly line. Although the C919 will see its first delivery until 2018 or 2019, it is a major step in Chinese aviation. Meanwhile, China has a joint venture with Airbus for manufacture of parts for the A350 (Air China was the first airline to place firm orders for the new aircraft).

And, in 2009 the first A320 aircraft to be assembled in a new Airbus-Chinese joint venture plant in Tianjin rolled out of the factory. Another Chinese jet, the ARJ21, is a regional jet built by Comac will compete with the C919. Originally scheduled for initial delivery in 2007, the ARJ21 has run into a number of development problems. The first delivery was finally made in late 2015.

Canada's Bombardier is a North American competitor in the Airbus vs. Boeing race. In April 2016, Bombardier won a $5.6 billion order for 75 of its CSeries jets from Delta Air Lines. The CSeries promises to afford airlines a notable operating cost advantage due to its advanced engines and design. Nonetheless, production delays and cash shortages were creating great difficulties for the firm in 2015 and into early 2016. At 1,800 to 2,950 miles, depending on configuration, this new aircraft has a more modest range than competing Boeing or Airbus models. It also holds fewer passengers, with a capacity of 100 to 149 seats.

Another competitor, Brazil's Embraer, is highly competitive in smaller aircraft designed for regional airlines. Its E-175 is utilized by American Airlines in a 12 first class plus 64 economy class seat arrangement. American received the first of 60 E-175s in February 2015. Embraer's E-190 is a larger model, typically arranged with 11 first class and 88 economy seats.

Japan is also attempting to join the fray with its own jet manufacturing. Mitsubishi Heavy Industries Ltd. announced plans for the Mitsubishi Regional Jet, the MRJ90, a 96-seat that made its first flight in late 2015. Mitsubishi has financial as well as technical support from a number of major global enterprises, namely Toyota Motor Corp., Boeing and United Technologies Corp.'s Pratt & Whitney jet engines. The Regional Jet would compete with Embraer's and Bombardier's. In mid-2012, Mitsubishi won an agreement to sell 100 Regional Jets to U.S. commuter service SkyWest, Inc.

8) New Aircraft Designs Offer Greater Passenger Comfort/More Efficient Engines

An important selling point in new passenger aircraft, whether built by Airbus or Boeing, is comfort. Changes in seat configuration, window size and cabin climate are all key elements when buying new planes.

At Boeing, for example, the new 787 Dreamliner offers a new, patented eight-seats-across configuration in economy class. The three-two-three arrangement allows seats that measure 19 inches across instead of 17, which is standard on Boeing 737s and 757s. However, the plane's cabin is wide enough to fit nine seats across, allowing some buyers to configure the cabin with narrower seats and more passengers.

Windows on new aircraft models are significantly larger, as much as 65% bigger than those on older planes. The increased size allows outside views from almost any seat. Another window improvement is a film covering that can be adjusted by flight attendants to block out light during movies while still allowing passengers to see out.

Boeing and Airbus both have improved in-flight cabin humidity levels. Airbus' new A350 XWB has the ability to achieve 20% humidity while the Dreamliner offers 15%. Both are a tangible improvement of the 10% level on existing airplanes.

Meanwhile, increased entertainment and relaxation features will be featured in new aircraft at many airlines. In particular, the massive size of the A380 lends itself to designing unique areas into the plan.

The Holy Grail of airliner engineering is to save dramatic amounts of fuel, which will require significant savings in weight in both airframes and engines along with improvements in engine design. The next generation of jet engines will soon be commercialized, as the global airline industry has set high goals for fuel consumption reduction. Engine manufacturer Pratt & Whitney has designed an engine called PurePower PW 1000G that promises double-digit reductions in fuel use and emissions while reducing engine noise by as much as 50%. It will be offered on the new Airbus A320neo. The engine uses a technology called Geared Turbofan. This radical engine utilizes a gear box to vary the speeds between the fan and the turbine for more efficiency. As of July 2016, Airbus had 3,436 orders for the A320neo.

GE, in partnership with French aerospace and defense firm Safran SA, has created a new joint venture called CFM International (www.cfmaeroengines.com). It developed the LEAP engine with dramatically lower emissions, 16% fuel use reduction and much quieter operation, that was first delivered in mid-2015 to Commercial Aircraft Corporation of China (COMAC). The LEAP engines will be available on both the new Airbus A320neo and the Boeing 737 MAX. Meanwhile CFM International is working on a revolutionary design, an "open rotor" concept—something like the open propellers on non-jets, with exceptional weight savings and efficiency.

Where it can, GE is also using ceramic composites instead of metal to dramatically lighten the weight of engines and other aircraft parts. One example is an engine used in the Boeing 787 which utilizes a ceramic-composite fan case and blade, and weighs 3% less than its metal counterpart. Both Boeing and Airbus are relying more and more on composite materials to decrease weight and increase fuel efficiency. Boeing's 787 is made of 50% carbon fiber composites, while Airbus' A350 is made of 53% composites.

Boeing's new 777X features 233-foot long carbon fiber wings, with improved aerodynamics that require 15% less thrust than earlier 777 models. The wings have hydraulic actuators that fold hinged wingtips after landings, allowing the jets to use taxiways and gates in standard sizes.

9) In Flight Wireless Takes Off

Airlines in the U.S. and around the world are investing in wireless technology to provide Internet access, e-mail capability and, for non-U.S. carriers, cellphone use while in the air. Until recently, the technology necessary to provide these services was less than satisfactory and costs were prohibitively high. Today, new satellite technologies are making in-flight wireless a reality. Wi-Fi is already in use on private business jets and for commercial carrier crews. Of course, this can be very good news for airlines, as they would expect a healthy share of this money, and all airlines are keenly seeking new ways to boost revenues.

In the U.S., JetBlue Airways Corp. acquired LiveTV, LLC, a provider of entertainment as well as e-mail. JetBlue is offering the service on its flights and selling it to other carriers such as United Airlines. In addition, JetBlue has an agreement with satellite communications company ViaSat, Inc. to provide airborne terminals and services for the carrier's entire fleet of aircraft. The Viasat-1 aviation broadband network uses satellite signals to provide greater broadband capacity in-flight.

Global Eagle Entertainment ("Gee Media") acquired Row44, a provider of in-flight broadband entertainment based in Westlake Village, California, which had outfitted aircraft for Southwest Airlines, Norwegian Air Shuttle and Icelandair.

Another player in in-flight wireless is Aircell, which utilizes a network of ground antennas to transmit data for its Gogo system. Gogo is in

operation on the entire AirTran fleet and most of Delta Air Lines fleet, including its regional jets.

The challenge for in-flight wireless has been and continues to be the use of cellphones. Passengers consistently state that they absolutely do not want to be forced to listen to other passengers' cell phone calls. Limiting the services available is the answer. One technology for in-flight calls, which is provided by Geneva-based OnAir (owned by the Internet technology firm SITA), uses a low-power onboard network that captures passengers' phone signals and links them to a satellite for transmission to ground receivers. Airlines can control which services they wish to offer: text messaging, Internet access, telephone calls, etc. Some airlines may choose to define quiet times when phone calls may not be made. The firm also serves private aircraft and cruise ships.

Lufthansa is working with Panasonic to provide improved in-flight broadband service. The service, called FlyNet, could cost as much as $100,000 per airplane (which covers installing antennas and other equipment). Lufthansa is betting on the popularity of the service. However, passengers may not make phone calls on this system.

Airlines and the wireless providers are working to improve satellite connectivity, increasing speeds and making streaming live video while flying possible. Global Xpress, an in-flight wireless provider, claims transmission speeds of 50 Mbps (compared to legacy satellite Inmarsat's 500 Kbps or less).

10) Air Traffic Grows/Airports Expand/ Middle East and Asia Have Strong Air Traffic

A second Beijing Airport, Daxing, has broken ground and is expected to open by 2018. The $14 billion facility will have four runways in its first phase, and an annual capacity of 40 million passengers initially, increasing to 70 million by 2025. Much more than just an airport is planned for Daxing. An additional $13 to $14 billion will be invested in creating a massive economic and industrial region, to be centered on the airport.

In Zhengzhou, the capital of Henan Province in China, an additional "aeropolis" region is planned, with logistics facilities, research and development parks, industrial areas and exhibition halls centered on a major airport. As many as 2.6 million people are forecast to live nearby by 2025.

In Shanghai, air traffic has grown so rapidly that authorities plan to add a fourth and fifth runway to the extremely modern Pudong Airport. Airports in Guangzhou and Shenzhen will each add a third runway.

Meanwhile, Dubai's facility is benefiting from the fact that it is the home of Emirates Airlines, which is investing heavily in aircraft acquisition and international route expansion. As of early 2016, Emirates already had 72 Airbus 380s in the air, with more on the way. Dubai operates as a hub for flights to many parts of the world.

Dubai Airport's $4.5 billion Terminal 3 opened in late 2008. A further expansion of the new terminal, which opened in 2012, makes it the world's largest building with regard to floor space at 16.1 million square feet. It can accommodate 23 Airbus A380s. Another enormous new airport located nearby in the Jebel Ali area of Dubai, the $80 billion Al Maktoum International, began cargo operations in mid-2010, and when it opens for passenger traffic in the early 2020s, it is expected to be the world's largest airport with five parallel runways and an annual passenger capacity of 160 million. Nearby Abu Dhabi, home to Etihad Airways, is building a $3.2 billion new airport to open in 2017, while Qatar opened the $15.5 billion Hamad International in 2014, capable of handling 28 million passengers per year.

Large-capacity aircraft can be a logistical nightmare for airports. With up to 800 passengers on a single Airbus A380 plane, concerns about efficient loading and unloading, as well as runway and jetway issues, all come to bear. To deal with these issues, Airbus has been working with airports that it believes will handle most of the A380's traffic (among them are London-Heathrow, Dubai, Singapore, Tokyo-Narita, Frankfurt and Paris). The chief concerns are the need for additional double-decker jetways to load and unload passengers (the A380 requires a minimum of two, while some flights may need three jetways) and runway modifications to handle the added weight of the aircraft (estimated as high as 1.2 million pounds). For airlines operating the new A380, the goal is to turn around the aircraft in about 90 minutes, the same time that it takes to turn around a Boeing 747.

In 2010, Los Angeles International Airport (LAX) completed a $737 million renovation of the Tom Bradley International Terminal, including two new gates designed to accommodate new-generation A380s and 787s. Improvements continue at LAX, a facility that is vital to Southern California's economy and generates about $1.3 billion in yearly revenues on-site at the airport, as of 2016. Long-term plans

include an additional $8.5 billion in modernization aimed at better facilities for travelers, the ability to handle increased passenger counts and attempts to tame the infamous automobile traffic snarls that have long plagued the facility. Elsewhere, Atlanta's Hartsfield-Jackson Airport completed a $1.4 billion international terminal in 2012 that includes a 1.2 million square foot concourse, 12 additional gates and more than 3,500 additional parking spaces.

The CAPA Centre for Aviation reported $200 billion in 394 new airport projects underway or planned globally as of January 2016. London's Heathrow budgeted $857 million to redevelop its Terminal 3, and spent $9 billion on its new Terminal 5, which opened in 2008. It is capable of handling up to 12,000 bags per hour on its 11 miles of luggage conveyors. The airport's overall capacity has expanded to 90 million passengers per year.

Analysts are projecting significant passenger count growth at Heathrow in coming years. The British Department of Transport estimates that 320 million passengers will fly out of Britain in 2030 and 480 million by 2050. A new, third runway has been proposed for Heathrow, causing great controversy among neighbors over potential noise and air pollution. It is estimated that the runway could be in operation by 2029, enabling 260,000 additional landings yearly. However, it remains to be seen whether or not it will ever be built. Other options under consideration include adding a new, second runway to nearby Gatwick Airport, adding on to other London-area airports, or perhaps building an entirely new airport to replace Heathrow, which is very unlikely.

Private airport management companies are largely responsible for airport renovation and expansion. Notable firms include Aeroports de Paris SA, which is overseeing improvements to both Orly and Charles de Gaulle airports serving Paris, and Schiphol Group, which is in charge of the airport in Amsterdam.

BAA PLC, owned by a consortium headed by Spanish firm Grupo Ferrovial SA, formerly held Heathrow, Gatwick and Stansted airports in London; Edinburgh, Glasgow and Aberdeen airports in Scotland; and a regional airport in Southampton. BAA was under U.K. government orders to sell Gatwick and Stansted, as regulators are forcing a breakup of what they see as a monopoly. BAA complied with the October 2009 sale of Gatwick to Global Infrastructure Partners for approximately $2.31 billion, allowing BAA to pay off a significant amount of debt. BAA, now renamed Heathrow

Airport Holdings Limited, completed further upgrades at Heathrow, specifically the $3.2 billion renovation of Terminal 2 which opened in June 2014.

Dubai Aerospace Enterprise is a $15-billion consortium of oil and aerospace companies that are collectively backed by the royal family of Dubai. The enterprise hopes to build cutting-edge airport facilities throughout the Middle East and Asia.

In the U.S., the FAA sees significant need for commercial airport expansion. FAA analysts projected that the number of passengers embarking on domestic flights in the U.S. will grow from 696 million in 2015 to 848 million in 2025 and 1.01 trillion in 2034. Passengers embarking on international flights from the U.S. will grow from 89 million in 2015 to 131 million in 2025.

Some airports are sporting a wide range of new amenities, including walking paths, yoga rooms, private sleeping areas, medical clinics and improved food venues. The highest-rated airports, according to Skytrax, are Singapore Changi, Seoul Incheon and Munich Airport. Singapore Changi offers passengers five different gardens, a 3D electronics zone and the world's tallest indoor slide at 12 meters (four stories). Seoul Incheon has a 330-yard golf driving range. Munich Airport offers a recreation area, a luxury Thai restaurant with life-sized elephant statues and a five-star hotel with a tree-lined bar.

U.S. airports are also investing in improvements, but on a far less extensive scale (about $52 billion in capital improvement projects since 2008). Dallas-Fort Worth International Airport, for example, has a public yoga studio at the end of Terminal D equipped with exercise mats and instructional videos. Indianapolis International Airport offers three walking paths with signage regarding distance and average numbers of steps, two inside security and one near the ticketing area. San Francisco International Airport has a medical clinic that offers vaccinations for overseas travel, as well as treatment of symptoms of colds and allergies. For the most part, major, international American airports remain far behind the leading airports of Asia in design and amenities.

Boarding gates are also getting upgrades in a number of airports. Concession company OTG Management spent $15 million to renovate waiting areas near boarding gates in Terminal D and in Terminal C in New York's La Guardia airport. Instead of uncomfortable rows of seats, the areas now have tall seats and barstool height counters with plenty of power outlets and iPads, on which flyers can enter flight numbers to check statuses, play games and surf the Internet. The key for OTG

Management is that the iPads are also used to place orders for food and drink from nearby vendors, which is delivered right to the flyer's seat. The company planned to have 2,000 iPad stations at La Guardia, and was planning to install 2,500 iPad stations in Delta Airlines gates in Minneapolis and another 2,500 in Toronto for multiple airlines.

In the U.S., a federally-mandated Passenger Facility Charge of $4.50 has been added to every passenger who boards a plane. Airports are proposing that the fee be raised, but airlines and business travel groups oppose the idea.

New, high-tech gadgets and systems are rapidly bringing airports of the future into being, particularly in Europe and Asia. For example, at London's Gatwick Airport, beacons placed throughout the terminal identify passengers' smartphones and transmit GPS-based directions to assigned gates, including information about food and shopping venues along the way. San Francisco International Airport has 350 of the beacons installed (with plans to offer an app to assist visually impaired travelers with spoken directions) in its Terminal 2. American Airlines is installing the beacons also at Dallas-Fort Worth International Airport. In a similar vein, Virgin Atlantic's London lounge and Cathay Pacific's San Francisco lounge have beacons that recognize members as they enter and offer information about available food and drinks.

Even more futuristic is Dusseldorf's airport park in Germany where robots park cars and move them to designated spots when the drivers return. Vehicles are moved by the robots (which lift cars and trucks by the wheels) when drivers are not due back soon to less convenient locations for storage and then return them in time for pickup. SITA reports that the robots have increased garage capacity by 32% in the year they have been in operation. Dusseldorf was using three robots as of mid-2015 which cost about $250,000 each.

11) Massive, Long Term Growth in China's Travel Market/Indian Travel Market Rebounds

Decades of economic growth in both China and India are impacting business sectors around the world. Rapidly growing middle classes in both countries are beginning to travel by air in numbers never before seen, and airlines and hotel firms have seen soaring growth in the size of their markets.

Chinese citizens, according to the World Tourism Organization, made 120 million outbound trips in 2015, up from 109 million in 2014 and 97.3 million in 2013. Tourists from China spent $194 billion on travel in 2015. This is only the beginning, since only a small portion of the Chinese population have passports. Not only are the Chinese themselves traveling more, there is also a booming market in foreign business people and tourists traveling to China.

A number of hotels in the U.S. and Europe are offering special services aimed at Chinese travelers. J.W. Marriott has a Li Yu program (meaning "to serve with courtesy") while Hilton Worldwide has a Huanying ("welcome") program. These efforts may include dedicated check-in desks, television channels in Mandarin, congee rice porridge at breakfast and Chinese-labelled toiletries and do-not-disturb signs.

China Southern Airlines Co., Air China and China Eastern Airlines are ranked among the top global carriers by capacity. Chinese airlines are finding success in offering low fares to international destinations such as London and Sydney. In addition to long-haul routes, JetStar Hong Kong (a joint venture between China Eastern, Qantas and Shun Tak Holdings) offers short hops between cities in the Asia-Pacific region.

India's growing economy also boosted travel to a dramatic extent. The International Air Transport Association (IATA) forecasted that passenger numbers will grow by an average of 5.3% per year between 2012 and 2016, resulting in 500 million new passengers travelling on domestic routes and 331 million new passengers on international routes. If economic growth resumes, then this forecast growth may come close to reality. The Center for Asia Pacific Aviation raised its estimate of annual passenger traffic growth in India from 10% to 13% through 2020. Indian infrastructure, specifically runways, maintenance centers and pilots, will have to be significantly expanded to handle projected increases in traffic over the long term.

For India's hotels, ITC Hotels opened the Grand Bharat in Gurgaon with a 27-hole Jack Nicklaus golf course in 2015. The company planned another four hotels, the ITC Hotel Kolkata II in 2016, the ITC Hotel Hyderabad and the ITC Hotel Ahmedabad in 2017 and the ITC Hotel Colombo (the firm's first hotel outside of India) in 2018. Marriott Hotels had 30 properties in India by late-2015. India's luxury hotels and resorts, including the premier properties operated by Taj and Oberoi, are consistently rated at the top of the industry.

12) China Makes Immense Investments in Railroads, Highways & Airports

Some of the most ambitious transportation infrastructure investments the world has ever seen are taking place in China. This has created tremendous opportunities for global suppliers of engineering services and transportation equipment. Today, however, the equipment is, to a growing extent, being manufactured by domestic Chinese firms. For example, Chinese companies are manufacturing state of the art high speed passenger rail equipment, and the Chinese have a joint venture with Airbus to manufacture passenger aircraft within China. Meanwhile, transportation use is soaring in China, including the movement of passengers and freight by air, rail and highway.

In order to boost economic growth within the interior of the nation, China has been forced to boost investment in rail systems. During the first half of 2015, according to the China Railway Corp., the country invested more than $43.3 billion in domestic railway construction. The result was an additional 2,226 kilometers of new lines in service. A total of $128 billion was promised to rail construction for all of 2015.

The growth of high speed rail, often capable of running above 250 km per hour, has been particularly intense. The Chinese high speed rail system totaled only 8,360 km in 2010. By the beginning of 2015, it was 16,000 km, and by 2020 it is forecast to cover 25,000 km.

In March 2013, China announced the closing of its Ministry of Railways, which had accumulated $428 billion in debt and was awash with allegations of corruption. The government created of a new company, China Railway Corp. to handle commercial rail operations. Additional rail functions now fall under the jurisdiction of a new National Railway Administration under the Ministry of Transportation.

Massive highways have been constructed in China in recent years, and the truck fleet is growing. Accordingly, rail freight has significant competition from trucks in many parts of the nation.

China made headlines with regard to new rail technology thanks to a ground-breaking 1,900 km Qinghai-Tibet railway which was completed in 2006. At a cost of $3.2 billion, the line crosses some of the world's most difficult terrain with elevations of between 13,000 and 16,000 feet. Due to the high altitude, passenger cars are equipped with oxygen captured from outside air as well as personal diffusers that passengers can plug into for additional comfort. The track was constructed using specialized techniques to keep the permafrost beneath the line from thawing. These techniques include vertical pipes embedded in surrounding ground that are filled with liquid nitrogen and metal sun shades near the track to block solar radiation.

China's largest cities are now home to some of the world's newest and most advanced airports. Highways and light rail leading to the airports have also been extensively improved and modernized. A $3.8 billion expansion of the Beijing Capital International Airport officially opened in early 2008, well in time for the Summer Olympics. The expansion included a third runway and the world's largest terminal, which is 2.8 km long. The Beijing airport saw 89.9 million passengers in 2015, up from 86.1 million in 2014 and 83.7 million passengers in 2013, and ranking it the second busiest airport in the world behind Atlanta's Hartsfield-Jackson.

China's new airport development has been extremely ambitious. As of mid-2015, China had more than 60 inland airports under expansion and 30 new regional airports under construction. China's airports are expected to increase from about 200 in 2015 to 240 by 2020.

A second Beijing Airport, Daxing, broke ground in 2013 and is expected to open as soon as 2018. The $11 billion facility will have eight runways and an annual capacity of 40 million passengers initially, increasing to 70 million by 2025. In Shanghai, air traffic has grown so rapidly that authorities plan to add a fourth and fifth runway to the extremely modern Pudong Airport.

The accompanying boom for transportation providers includes a joint venture between Airbus and two of China's major aviation companies, AVIC 1 and AVIC 2. Airbus holds 51% of the venture, an assembly plant in Tianjin for the short to medium range A320 aircraft. The plant was completed in 2009, with capacity planned to grow to as many as 300 planes annually by 2016, all of which will be purchased by Chinese airlines.

Another joint venture between Airbus and AVIC built an aviation factory in Harbin, the capital of Heilongjiang Province. The plant, which opened in 2010, produces Airbus' wide-bodied A350. AVIC controls 80% of the venture with the remaining 20% held by Airbus. Meanwhile, Chinese companies are producing aircraft parts for shipment around the world.

13) Online Travel Agencies (OTAs) Continue Strong Growth in Bookings/Hotels Fight to Keep Control of the Customer

One of the biggest single changes in the travel industry has been the exceptionally rapid rise of online travel agencies, also known as OTAs. Around the globe, vast numbers of business and leisure travelers alike rely on the Internet as their primary means of gaining travel information, reserving hotels and booking air tickets. According to market research firm eMarketer, digital travel sales in America (including sales made on mobile devices) were expected to grow to $179 billion in 2015, up from $145.22 billion in 2014. On a global basis, digital travel sales were expected to rise 13.3% in 2015 over 2014, to exceed $533 billion.

Euromonitor forecast growth in online travel dollars spent at nearly 8% for 2015, in a broad view of the sector including car rental, hotel rooms, transportation and tourist attraction sales totaling more than $600 billion.

Expedia, Travelocity, Orbitz, Hotwire and Priceline (owner of Booking.com) are among the largest firms offering online travel booking services in North America.

In Europe, major online travel booking firms include EasyGroup (a holding company that owns and operates a number of travel and entertainment brands including easyCar, easyHotel and easyJet), Lastminute.com (a subsidiary of Travelocity Europe Limited) and eBookers. The numbers involved are massive.

Priceline's Booking.com offers over 600,000 properties. Other important players include China's Ctrip.com and eLong, UK-based Travelport Worldwide and India's MakeMyTrip.

In September 2015, Expedia completed its $1.3 billion acquisition of Orbitz. The merged companies could represent about 75% of U.S. online booking volume. Expedia already owned several sites, including hotels.com and Travelocity. From a U.S. travel market perspective, there will now be only two significant corporate OTA groups: Expedia and Priceline. Together, these corporate enterprises will control about 95% of the American OTA market. The two giants, Priceline and Expedia, each now have massive existing customer bases. They have enormous marketing budgets that can be used to battle competitors that might emerge. Both have extremely powerful, deeply experienced digital marketing and technology teams that may be able to out-produce and out-compete the strategies of emerging firms. They each own several respected, dominant booking brands. The firms also have reached the point of massive scale whereby they have significant clout with suppliers, and they have the potential to make their loyalty programs even more compelling and competitive due to scale.

Meanwhile, an extremely popular travel reviews and information site, TripAdvisor, has evolved into an online booking site. It is in a good position to compete head-on with Priceline and Expedia. There are even more changes in store with the online travel booking business thanks to recent entries by Google and Amazon.

SPOTLIGHT: Hotel Booking on Google, A Slam-Dunk for the Online Search Giant:

Google has invested heavily in travel-related technologies and assets as well, including the Frommer's brand of travel guides and the widely used ITA airline reservation system. Now, it has launched a hotel booking service. This strategy offers multiple advantages in addition to a new commission-based revenue stream for the search engine company.

From the consumer's point-of-view, reserving a room on Google offers greater ease of booking on mobile devices, as there is no hand-off to second or third party sites. It also means fewer screens and pages to deal with, ease of comparing hotel locations and prices and instant payment for Google Wallet users. It offers speed and convenience similar to Amazon's One-Click purchase button.

From Google's point-of-view, this new business will increase user engagement and site traffic. Users must sign in to their Google accounts to complete bookings (and therefore must establish a user account if he/she doesn't have one). This new business will also drive users to establish Google Wallet accounts and to add hotel reviews.

Google already owns substantial travel information assets, and this move into hotels is likely only a small first step into extremely promising travel industry territory. Google could easily establish travel loyalty rewards as well. Google has more opportunity in this market since Amazon shut down its hotel booking site, Amazon Destinations, in late 2015.

Consumers like the OTAs because they offer a wide choice of hotel brands, prices and locations in one view. Some sites operate as "metasearch" engines, enabling the consumer to link directly to a hotel's site for booking. The largest, however, operate as true online booking agencies.

Hotels pay from 12% to as much as 25% commission for these bookings. In addition to the fees, OTAs are causing serious alarm at hotel chains, which fear they are losing control of the loyalty of and relationship with their customers. This is due to several strategies employed by the OTAs, including continual addition of new travel planning features to their web sites and apps, as well as extremely popular loyalty points programs of their own. Hotels.com, for example, offers a free hotel night, with no restrictions, after booking 10 nights total. This is a much simpler, easier-to-use program than those offered by most chains.

Major hotel chains and airlines have invested immense sums in their own, branded Internet sites. These travel providers benefit because the use of their own online booking systems eliminates fees to middlemen and wages to human reservation agents. Encouraging travelers to book through the hotel and airline companies' own sites also gives the firms control over marketing and branding, and enables them to promote loyalty programs. Consumers benefit because they have seamless access to travel information, frequent flyer accounts and other perks. A major consideration is access to loyalty points. Hotel chains are also offering discounts through their loyalty programs. For example, Choice Hotels International offers a "member rate" of up to 10% off at some of its properties.

Most, if not all, chains have adopted aggressive online tactics and are denying awards points to customers who book their rooms through third-party sites. In addition, chains are offering "best price guarantees." For example, if a guest sees a better price at an OTA but books through the hotel chain, the hotel will give the guest another 25% off. Hotels are also boosting their digital offerings for loyalty program members who book directly with the hotels. These include smartphone apps that enable instant check-in, fast check-out, smartphone-based electronic room keys, digital concierge services and smartphone-based scheduling of hotel services and room service orders.

In most cases, hotels and OTAs have rate parity agreements in their contracts. This means that hotels may not be able to offer lower prices than those provided to the OTAs. However, the hotel chains may offer special prices to select groups of guests, such as loyalty plan members. This means that competitive advantage has to be created in some other manner, like loyalty programs, or special free perks for guests. In this regard, it's vital for hotel chains to take advantage of assets that they control. For example, Hyatt is among chains enabling direct booking guests to look at a floor plan and choose the actual room that they will stay in. Other hotels are including free meals or drinks for certain guests.

Traditional travel agencies have endured vast changes in recent years, including the growing trend among corporate travelers to use online booking services. Some travel agents have successfully repositioned themselves as "consultants," charging hourly fees for their expertise. Others specialize in providing unique knowledge about travel to out-of-the-way places such as Cambodia, French Polynesia or Africa.

The largest national travel agencies run sophisticated web sites of their own. They act as outsourced travel departments for their major corporate clients and arrange discounts for clients who purchase massive amounts of travel. For example, Carlson Wagonlit is a leading global business travel agency, with offices in more than 150 nations. Many large travel agencies that focus on leisure travelers buy hotel and aircraft space at wholesale and then create highly profitable tour packages to popular tourist destinations such as Cancun, Jamaica and Orlando.

14) Ecotourism, Sustainable Tourism, Adventure Tourism and Volunteerism Grow as Certification Standards Emerge

Ecotourism and "ecospas" are all the rage, particularly among affluent travelers seeking a soothing retreat and a respite from the daily grind back home. Ecotourism, as a philosophy used by a hotel in design, construction and operation, generally has goals that include: conservation of electricity, water and other natural resources; sensitivity to the surrounding natural environment, ecosystem, wildlife (and sometimes native peoples); use of organic ingredients in the hotel kitchen (which may include items from a hotel's own organic garden); and a peaceful, soothing environment throughout the hotel property (which may include such elements as extensive landscaping with native plants, running water, Zen-like gardens and areas that encourage contemplation, meditation and relaxation).

"Sustainable tourism" is another phrase used to describe this sector. It might be tempting to use the word "minimalist" to label some eco-properties, but the fact is that they tend to include high levels of luxurious coddling (e.g., thick towels in marble-lined bathrooms) to help justify high room rates and menu prices. Ecospas are standard features in ecofriendly hotels. At the much-touted El Monte Sagrado (www.elmontesagrado.com) in Taos, New Mexico, for example, the hotel bills itself as "the living resort," and combines water conservation and recycling efforts with spa treatments and fine dining.

Hotels involved in ecotourism are becoming touchy about the standards that should be met in order to be considered ecofriendly. Accordingly, organizations have sprung up to certify ecofriendly properties. For example, there is Costa Rica's Certification for Sustainable Tourism. Green Globe (www.greenglobe.com) is a program established in 1994 by the World Travel & Tourism Council. Australia has the Earthcheck program (www.earthcheck.org) developed by the Sustainable Tourism Cooperative Research Center. The Blue Flag campaign (www.blueflag.org) is a Danish organization that names approximately 4,000 ecofriendly beaches and marinas in 49 countries. Typically, these organizations charge fees to the hotels involved, and may require periodic on-site audits of the properties.

Europe boosted its eco-status with the January 1, 2012 implementation of the Emission Trading Scheme (ETS). Airlines flying in and out of European airports are required to purchase permits for 15% of the carbon emissions produced by their planes. Carriers are allowed 85% of their cap free of charge for the first year (the cap is set at 97% of the average aviation emissions from 2004-06). Starting in 2013, the cap decreased to 95% and free allowances were lowered to 82%. The International Air Transport Association (IATA) estimated that the measure cost $1.1 billion in 2012 and up to $3.5 billion per year by 2020. Not surprisingly, airlines in the U.S., China and Asia Pacific have strongly protested the scheme, with China threatening a trade war in which its airlines will cut orders from European manufacturer Airbus. Watch for further legal and economic wrangling through the near- and mid-term.

Another travel option gaining popularity is adventure travel that affords customers everything from rock climbing to distance cycling to white water rafting to black diamond slope skiing. Alaskan travelers on Un-Cruise Adventures' small ships are offered gentle to hard core adventure options such as whale watching or glacier hiking. Passengers regularly see brown bear, porpoises, bald eagles and humpback whales, but can also book spa appointments and enjoy gourmet meals and wines.

A new type of travel offering is "social impact travel," which include activities such as planting trees in rainforests, teaching English in schools or building water filtration systems in destinations such as Cuba and the Dominican Republic. Carnival is building its new fathom brand for Millennials and younger travelers who want to add volunteerism to their cruise experience. The 710 passenger Adonia (which is part of P&O Cruises, a Carnival subsidiary) will sail under the Fathom brand starting in 2016.

15) Hotel Occupancy, Profits and New Construction Grow

The hotel industry has been enjoying significant growth in recent years. For 2015, PricewaterhouseCoopers reported that average U.S. hotel occupancy reached 65.5% (compared to only 54.6% in 2009), and projected the rate to grow to 65.7% for 2016. Equally important, REVPAR (revenue per available room) had soared to nearly $75 by the beginning of 2015, up from only about $55 in 2009.

Marriott reported a 5.2% worldwide REVPAR increase during 2015, to reach $112.25. Average daily rates were up 4.1% on a constant dollar basis to $152.30, while occupancy increased 0.8%, over the previous year, to 73.7%. The company added 51,547 rooms worldwide during the year (including 9,590 rooms from the acquisition of Delta Hotels and Resorts). By the beginning of 2016, the firm had 270,000 rooms under development worldwide.

Companies like global hotel giants Marriott and Hilton are reporting increasing numbers of business and leisure travelers. Marriott saw strengthening in properties in Asia, Europe, the Caribbean, Latin America, and in its luxury properties around the world. Hotels in Asia particularly benefitted from strong economic growth in that region.

Improving business, rising occupancy levels and rising room rates have recently led to both the remodeling of existing properties and the construction of new hotels and motels. Lodging Econometrics estimated 742 new hotels opened in 2015 in the U.S., with another 845 hotels in the pipeline for 2016 openings and 998 for 2017.

16) Luxury Hotel Chains Expand Globally

Another interesting trend in hotels is Asian luxury chains that are building properties in Europe and the U.S. Hotel brands including Raffles Hotels & Resorts, Shangri-La Hotels and Resorts and Meritus Hotels & Resorts have been opening across Europe. For example, Shangri-La, an Asian luxury hotel chain best known for its popular properties in Singapore and Hong Kong, recently opened projects in Vienna, London and Moscow, and operates additional hotels in the Middle East, Italy, Japan, Turkey, France and Canada.

Africa has been booming, with not enough hotels to host a growing business travel market. Hoteliers have been rushing to meet the demand. By 2020, Marriott will have 50 hotels in Africa, while French firm Accor will add almost 5,000 rooms in 30 hotels between 2012 and 2016.

Hotels are competing against each other to offer the most luxurious perks. A big priority for a number of hotel chains is a great night's sleep, and firms have beefed up bed linen thread counts, instituted pillow menus and installed top-of-the-line mattresses, including the Peninsula Hotel in Manhattan which brought in ultra-expensive, handmade mattresses from Savoir Beds in London.

Perks for guests staying in presidential suites, frequent guests and those bringing their children or pets are proliferating. Signature Villa guests at the Las Ventanas al Paraiso find floating trays holding top shelf bottles of tequila in their infinity pools. Guests in the best suites at the Wequassett Resort and Golf Club in Cape Cod, Massachusetts receive free, limited edition Sperry Topsider boat shoes. Kids staying at the Jefferson Hotel in Washington, D.C. may choose from a red wagon full of toys in the lobby and find pop tarts with their names written in icing in their rooms.

Among the most luxurious and innovative hotel firms in the world are the Taj and Oberoi chains, both based in India, and the Peninsula, based in Hong Kong. Their hotels are consistently ranked among the best in the world, and offer extreme amenities for their lucky guests. Marriott has built a strong global brand with its Ritz Carlton chain, which it is growing worldwide. Its latest strategy has been to add a small number of ultra-luxury "Reserve" properties, including its exceptional hotel at Phulay Bay in Thailand, and its amazing luxury remodel of the Dorado Beach Hotel in Puerto Rico. The Ritz Carlton is so renowned for its exceptional level of personalized service that it teaches other companies how to deliver service. Competitor Four Seasons, headquartered in Toronto, Canada, has over 90 hotels worldwide.

17) What Millennials and Mobile-Savvy Consumers Want as Tourists and Travelers

At Plunkett Research, we define the Millennial cohort (Gen Y) as those people born between 1982 and 2002. (Some organizations use slightly different years.) This puts them between the ages of 13 and 33 today, totaling about 85 million in the U.S. This is the largest cohort in U.S. history—larger even than Baby Boomers. They will rapidly make up an increasingly significant share of hotel, resort and other lodging guests. Nonetheless, it's important to remember that Millennial habits and attitudes, such as deep dependence on well-curated social media pages for personal expression, are spilling over into other generations. "Millennial" may be as much a state of mind (psychographics) as a specific age cohort (demographics). Travelers of this mindset tend to see the following:

Millennial Travel Goals and Desires:

1) Unique, adventuresome, even exotic experiences that they can be proud to post to social media.
2) Reasonable prices, even bargain vacations.
3) Modest environmental impact, even eco-friendly hotels and resorts.
4) Sharing economy experiences, particularly if the sharing strategy saves money or provides an opportunity to gather with their peers. Airbnb plays well here. (Sleeping in someone's spare bedroom is not only inexpensive, it's a sharing experience to post about.) Even hostels are making a comeback.
5) Community-based experiences such as local foods and beers, even to the extent of participating in humanitarian or philanthropic projects while on vacation. The cruise and tour industries are jumping on this "social impact travel" trend—but hotels lag. Carnival is building its new Fathom brand ships for Millennials and other travelers who want to add volunteerism and authentic cultural experiences to their cruise travel. The new 710 passenger Adonia (a Carnival subsidiary) is designed for this market and will sail under the Fathom brand starting in 2016.

Millennial leisure travelers will look to gain status through posting about experiences that qualify as unique, local or authentic (in the real world). That is, travel that enables them to express who they are, where they've been and how they lead a meaningful and conscious life. A well-curated Instagram feed

may grant more status than owning a new car. Millennial business travelers will respond to unique hotel offers that enable them to post about unique experiences, foods and beverages. Hotels that create ways to drive social media postings from satisfied, fully-engaged guests will earn a superior ROI on marketing spending.

18) Hotels Target Young Customers with Strategies Ranging from Micro Rooms and Hostels, to Hip Hotels that Encourage Mingling

A few hotel companies are innovating new, cost effective room alternatives, especially in Europe and Japan, aimed at cost-conscious travelers. Busy travelers can now book tiny rooms, or "pods," that typically measure about 100 square feet (some as small as 65 square feet) in size either for the night or just a few hours to rest and freshen up. In contrast, a more traditional motel is about 300 square feet, and luxury hotel rooms are 300 to 600 square feet. Pods generally have a small bed, flat screen TV and tiny bathrooms (some offer shared bathrooms), and windows, if there are any, may open onto a corridor instead of outside. Examples of hotels offering pods are Yotel at London's Heathrow Airport (about $105 per night for a 117 square foot "premium cabin"), Pod Hotel in New York (about $139 per night for 91.5 square feet) and EasyHotel in Zurich (about $71 per night for 104 square feet). Another Pod hotel called Pod 39 in the Murray Hill area opened in New York in 2012. Hilton Hotels & Resorts introduced Tru, with 225-square foot rooms in 2016, and Marriott International is also working on a small room concept for the U.S.

The true pod business model is similar to discount airlines in that only the basics are available and low prices are of supreme importance. Pod hotels do not generally offer perks such as fitness facilities, meeting rooms or lavish room service (some do not offer food of any kind). Yet, the services they do offer can be top-of-the-line such as plasma TV screens and high-thread-count sheets. In addition to business travelers, the rooms attract vacationers looking for good deals in locations near major tourist attractions.

New hotel brands have been launched that cater largely to younger demographics. They include 1 Hotels in Miami and Manhattan; Hyatt Centric in Miami and Chicago; Moxy (part of Marriott); AC hotels from Marriott in Europe, Chicago and Miami, among others; and Graduate hotels in college towns such as Athens, Georgia and Charlottesville,

Virginia. These hotels are more affordable than high-end hotels (ranging from $70 to $399 per night) and typically feature services that appeal to Millennials such as Wi-Fi, environmentally sustainable practices, local flavor in food and décor and locations in hip neighborhoods.

A different take on the low-cost model is the youth hostel, a concept that has been around for decades, especially in Europe. Hostels are typically very low cost housing with several people to a room and communal bathrooms. Hostelling International reported that as of mid-2015, there were approximately 350 hostels in the U.S. A new partnership of private equity firm Yucaipa Cos. and New York hotel developer Sydell Group is spending $250 million to open as many as 10 low-cost properties in the U.S. over several years on a hostel business model. Its "Freehand" hostel is now open in Miami and Chicago. Affordable room rates with reasonable levels of comfort and good food are key goals.

Some hostels are attempting to go upscale with free Wi-Fi, avant garde furnishings and better security. Some offer private rooms, en suite baths, free breakfasts and concierge service. These "poshtels" include the above mentioned Freehand, Sydell Group's NoMad Hotel and Generator in London and Miami.

19) Hotels Adopt Smartphones and In-Room Tablets to Deliver Services, Speed Check-In and Replace Room Keys

By early 2016, a number of major hotel chains had already installed sophisticated web- and smartphone-based services that connect customers and rooms with reception, dining, housekeeping, and all manner of hotel services. Members of the Hilton HHonors members, for example, can check in with their smartphones and an HHonors app, making a stop at the reception desk upon arrival unnecessary. Door locks at many hotel chains around the world are being retrofitted so that they can be opened via smartphone.

Many other hotels, including the Dorchester Collection of luxury properties in Europe and the U.S. (owners of such iconic hotels as the Hotel Bel-Air and the Beverly Hills Hotel in Los Angeles), have equipped rooms with touch tablet computers. Guests use them to view in-dining menus, order room service, request housekeeping and laundry services, view local weather information and access recommendations for area attractions.

The Peninsula luxury hotel chain has long been a leader in applying connectivity and advanced technology to its rooms. A guest in one of its newer rooms may be surrounded by up to 11 different telephones (including one over the tub); electronic bedside controls for all lights, entertainment and air conditioning; and multiple ways to access the Internet.

The concept is a prime business opportunity for software and hardware manufacturers who want to target the hospitality industry. In Stuttgart, Germany, the Faunhofer Institute for Industrial Engineering and Organization is a nonprofit consultancy that is working on a FutureHotel project. FutureHotel takes the networked concept to the next level, using hallway lighting to guide guests to their rooms, pinging guests with hotel offers for dining or spa appointments or notifying them of available times for booking meeting rooms or business center facilities. See www.iao.fraunhofer.de/lang-en/component/content/article.html?id=285&Itemid=1&lang=en.

20) Hotel Mergers Enable Chains to Claim Market Share, Add Unique Properties

A combination of low interest rates (making it attractive to issue corporate debt) and a soaring travel market (climbing steadily from the end of the recent recession through early 2016) have led to very significant levels of hotel chain mergers and acquisitions. Large chains want to acquire smaller chains for any of several potential reasons. These may include building market share, moving into underserved parts of the world, purchasing unique and innovative companies that are well positioned for future growth, or simply growing the total size of the parent company.

For example, hotel giant IHG agreed to acquire Kimpton Hotels & Restaurants at the end of 2014. This gave IHG ownership of one of the most innovative and talked-about boutique, upscale chains in America. The purchase price was $430 million in cash. At the time, Kimpton operated 62 hotels and had another 17 in the pipeline. Kimpton's expertise in converting existing properties into fun, hip hotels is extraordinary. While its hotel rooms have relatively expensive rates, it offers a design that appeals perfectly to younger travelers seeking a place to stay while on business, or an exciting place for a wedding. Kimpton also is experienced in building significant new properties, as evidenced by its 2015 opening of a high rise, new hotel in downtown Austin, Texas in 2015. Kimpton operates a unique loyalty program that offers a lot to frequent travelers, and it features amenities such as cocktail or wine events in its lobbies each day. It is also 100% dog friendly. Its restaurants and bars are careful to feature locally-sourced food and drink. For example, its downtown Portland, Oregon property features wines made nearby in the Willamette Valley.

The biggest battle ever seen in the hotel industry was settled in early 2016 when Marriott beat back other suitors to agree to acquire hotel giant Starwood Hotels & Resorts. This is a major gain for Marriott, as Starwood will bring 5,500 hotels and resorts in more than 100 nations to the Marriott portfolio of properties. When completed, the merger will create the world's largest hotel chain by far. Starwood properties include Westin, W and Sheraton, as well as luxury chains St. Regis and Le Meridien.

21) Localization will Drive Hotel Features, Marketing

Travel consumers respond well to hotel properties and related marketing that feature highly localized food (think food-to-table), brews/wines/cocktails, cultural opportunities, tours (think food tours, historic tours and haunted places tours). Localization of hotel features and services will surge, particularly in crowded markets.

Hotel chain Kimpton has been a true leader in this regard. Its downtown Miami, Florida property, for example, the EPIC Hotel, is a sleek high-rise with water views. Hotel staff are uniformed in cool white (many in straw hats) and super-yachts are often moored alongside the hotel. For a different take on a waterfront hotel, the Kimpton RiverPlace Hotel in Portland, Oregon, is a laid-back mid-rise building. Uniforms are Portland casual such as the parking valets' walking shorts and vests. Umbrellas are readily-available to protect guests from Portland's rainy climate.

22) Dog-Friendly Hotels Will Gain Market Share

Marriott figured out a long time ago that allowing guests to bring their dogs is a great marketing ploy. Many other chains lag behind.

There is an important consumer/demographic trend at work here. Millennials are delaying marriage and children, but are keen on owning, and traveling with, their dogs. The same is true for the senior market. Guests don't mind paying a modest additional fee for having their dog in the room. Nonetheless, some hotels don't charge extra at all.

For example, Kimpton is 100% dog-friendly, at no extra charge. The lobby of the Kimpton in Portland, Oregon even features a chalkboard, where the names of dogs-in-residence are listed, with a big "Welcome." The Hermitage Hotel in Nashville, Tennessee has a Pampered Paws Program with a pet welcome letter at check-in, specialty pet bedding, organic welcome treats, bottled spring water, nightly pet turndown service, an in-room dining menu for pets, pet walking service and an on-call pet masseuse.

23) "Sharing Economy" Gains Market Share in Travel with Online Sites Like Airbnb, HomeAway and Many Global Competitors

One of the most remarkable growth stories in ecommerce has been the advent of new ways to book non-traditional accommodations for travelers. This "sharing economy" (also known as collaborative consumption) affords consumers the ability to rent or borrow everything from hotel rooms to cars to private homes. An early leader was VRBO, which stands for Vacation Rental by Owner, a site that allows property owners, especially owners of second homes and resort condos, to advertise their properties online to people seeking vacation accommodations. VRBO was acquired by startup HomeAway, Inc., a firm that originated when venture capital firm Austin Ventures agreed to back entrepreneur Brian Sharples in this promising business sector. The staff of Austin, Texas-based HomeAway includes many executives who were formerly at Austin-based online information company Hoovers.com. HomeAway's revenues soared from $235 million in 2012 to $379 million in 2014. HomeAway also owns Travelmob, a sharing-economy accommodations site focused on Asia. Booking.com, a major presence in online hotel room booking and a subsidiary of Priceline, has begun offering shared-space and vacation property listings on its site also.

The biggest disruptor to the hotel industry is San Francisco-based Airbnb, Inc., founded in 2008. Airbnb.com members who are willing to let travelers stay in their homes can post their information, including pricing and accommodation details. The accommodations range from a bedroom in an occupied house or apartment to a luxury apartment or condo reserved entirely for the guest. In turn, travelers may search in a given market for members who are willing to accommodate them. Airbnb is utilized in more than 34,000 cities in 192 countries. Since its founding, the company has booked over 40 million guest nights. Members are encouraged to write reviews describing the positive and/or negative aspects of their stays. These reviews are partially encouraged so that renters and travelers may view profiles and feedback before staying in homes or letting others stay in their homes, thereby reducing the risk of danger or other negative situations. The Airbnb network is also connected to Facebook, allowing members to search the social networking platform for additional information regarding certain hosts and guests. Airbnb charges room owners a 3% host fee and an additional fee of 6% to 12% per guest. The average commission is about 12% of total revenues. The typical guest stays longer, on average, than a guest in a traditional hotel. The firm has a goal of achieving $10 billion in yearly revenues by 2020.

Literally hundreds of competitors and imitators have sprung up around the world. Some are focused on particular locales, travelers or types of accommodations. For example, OneFineStay.com had raised $80 million by 2015, including a major investment from hotel firm Hyatt. It is focused on renting a curated collection of better homes and condos in major cities, including New York, Paris, Los Angeles and London.

Despite their wide popularity, room- and home-sharing sites face multiple challenges. Fraud has been a problem, with unscrupulous site members collecting fees for rentals of properties that they claim to own, but are in fact owned by others. Guest safety is a serious issue. There have been accidents, dog bites, even a guest locked into his room by a host seeking sexual favors. At most sites, there are no room inspections and no way to enforce room standards. Guest room rentals may not be covered under a homeowner's insurance policy. Likewise, such rentals may not be allowed under homeowner's association rules and municipal law. Last, but not least, the market may become saturated, with only a limited number of properties available to add to inventory.

Nonetheless, the traditional hotel industry sees room-sharing as a significant competitive threat that is already taking market share. The long-term result may be hotel chains creating their own branded sharing sites, listing both their own hotel properties and rooms or condos owned by others. Hotels may build hybrid properties as well, with apartment towers for room sharing next door to traditional hotel properties. The hotels could run the apartments to high standards, and could build oversized pools, spas and other common area facilities to be shared with guests from the apartments next door.

24) Cruise Industry Market Is Strong while Capacity Soars with New Ships

Cruise ships are a unique business model within the hospitality industry, a hotel/guest cabin side, multiple dining venues and a tour operation in one platform. The crew skills required to operate a cruise ship safely and successfully are by far the most varied within the hospitality and travel sectors. Cruise ships must have large engineering staffs, a navigation staff, housekeeping, cooking/dining/bar staff, entertainment, social directors and frequently, even casino staff. Frequently, only a small part of the crew consists of permanent employees of the cruise line, with the balance being contract workers provided by outside firms.

Cruises are particularly well-positioned for today's budget-conscious tourists, as consumers consider cruises to be fun vacation packages at reasonable prices. Parents cruising with children often bunk the entire family in one cabin, saving even more money. Baby Boomers have found cruises a cost-effective way to fulfill their travel wishes as they get older, and Millennials and Generation Xers like the party atmosphere found on some cruises.

Cruise Lines International Association (CLIA) estimated that 22.1 million passengers went on a cruise in 2014. The association expected 23 million passengers to sail in 2015.

Most cruise lines are relying on heavy marketing and competitive prices to keep occupancy rates high. High occupancy, even if it's necessary to reduce room prices to maintain that occupancy, is crucial, as cruise ships earn 20% or more of their revenue from incidentals such as on-board spa treatments, extra drinks, shore excursions and gift shop purchases. Gambling in shipboard casinos is also an important revenue generator.

To capture more revenues, cruise lines are forming their own excursion tour operations, rather than leaving this business to third parties. While consumers may get better deals if they hire their own guides and drivers, cruise lines are hoping that the convenience of one-stop shopping will attract more customers to book through their tour groups. In most cases, passengers can now book excursions on the cruise lines' web sites before they even set sail. Some ships, such as the *Queen Mary 2*, allow passengers to book excursions through channels on their in-room televisions. Cruise lines are also offering a wider variety of excursions. In addition to the standard, guided day-long bus tours, different lines, depending on the locale of ports visited, are offering helicopter tours, dog-sledding and so-called "canopy adventures," in which customers skate along cable lines in harnessed suits over treetops. Moreover, cruise lines are booking multi-day excursions and land extensions to their routes. Crystal Cruises offers trips through the rain forests of Borneo or four night excursions to Jaipur, Agra and Delhi, India. Moreover, cruise lines are spending heavily on marketing and advertising to lure customers and the agents who book the majority of cruise trips.

Among the largest ships built to-date are Royal Caribbean's $1.2 billion, 5,400 passenger *Oasis of the Seas* and sister ship *Allure of the Seas*. At 220,000 tons and 1,181 feet in length, they by far eclipse Royal Caribbean's previous behemoths, its three Freedom class ships that each weigh in at about 160,000 tons and carry about 4,300 passengers. The *Oasis* and *Allure* will be joined by a third and even bigger ship, the 227,000 ton, 5,479 passenger *Harmony of the Seas* in 2016. All three offer a plethora of revenue-generating onboard activities including multi-story water slides, ice rinks, rock climbing, carousels and themed, open-air neighborhoods in the center of the ships with gardens, restaurants, galleries and shops. An important design feature of Carnival's latest megaships is the central courtyard, with towers of rooms surrounding each side. While the courtyard gives passengers a place to stroll, shop or dine, it also enables designers to create premium interior cabins with balconies overlooking the courtyards. This is a highly desirable improvement over interior cabins on smaller, traditional ships, as such cabins sell for much lower fares since they had no views and no portholes or balconies.

New ships continue to be built. As of early 2016, 27 new cruise ships were on firm order with major shipbuilders, mostly in Europe. Major European shipyards include Fincantieri's Monfalcone yard near Trieste, Italy, Meyer Werft in Germany and Meyer Turku in Finland. Fincantieri reported that it was operating at 50% of capacity in 2009-10, was up to 70%-75% in 2015 and expected to operate at over 90% capacity by 2016-17. Meanwhile, Meyer Werft and Meyer Turku included among their projects four enormous 6,600-passenger ships for Carnival that will be the first ever ocean going ships to be powered by liquefied natural gas (LNG). Larger ships can offer greater operating efficiencies than small ships.

Some of the newer ships offer elite access to small "ship within a ship" areas featuring a concierge, 24-hour butler service and a private pool, sun deck and restaurant, in exchange for a higher fare. For example, Norwegian Cruise Line's *Norwegian Escape* (which entered service in late 2015) boasts Haven, a luxury venue open to only 275 of the ship's capacity of 5,000 passengers.

Internet Research Tip:
For extensive information about cruising and cruise lines, visit:
Cruise Lines International Association,
www.cruising.org

---

25) Small Cruise Ships Offer Adventure, Luxury, Intimacy or Access to More Places

Small cruise ships hosting anywhere between 20 and 500 passengers are a booming alternative to mega-ships such as the *Queen Mary 2* and the *Harmony of the Seas*. Although they typically have fewer restaurant/onboard activity/entertainment venue choices, they do offer higher staff-to-passenger ratios (often one staff member for every two passengers onboard small ships, compared to about one crew member to two-and-one-half or three passengers on large ships). Also, small ships can cruise into shallower waters and far smaller inlets, so that abundant wildlife might be seen or smaller ports might be enjoyed. Seattle-based Un-Cruise Adventures, for example, owns and operates the 22-passenger *Safari Quest,* from which passengers can explore the inner reaches of Alaskan coasts in kayaks, paddle boards and skiffs launched directly from the ship's stern.

With fewer passengers, there are no long lines to face in order to get on or off the ship. Passengers tend to get to know each other well, often forming lasting friendships. Future cruises reuniting former shipmates are common.

Small ship's kitchens and dining rooms are under pressure to produce delicious, memorable food that rivals the numerous dining venues found on large ships. Small ships have access to locally-sourced ingredients, while the ships' crews make extra efforts to invite passengers to join them at their tables in order to maximize a convivial atmosphere.

Top small ship cruise lines include Seabourn (a luxury line that is a wholly-owned subsidiary of Carnival Corporation), Silversea Cruises and smaller ships in the Regent Seven Seas Cruises line. Even smaller ships are owned and operated by Lindblad Expeditions (which recently purchased the Via Australis ship based in Patagonia) and Variety Cruises, based in Greece. Another small cruise line,

Hapag-Lloyd Cruises, offers a cruise that starts in Istanbul and ends in Athens, but the 516 passengers on the *Europa 2* may choose from among 20 prospective ports of call on the 10-day trip.

26) River Cruise Lines Are Launched, with Low Capital Investment and High Fares

One of the fastest growing segments in the cruise industry is river cruises, which offer smaller craft that traverse major rivers such as the Rhine in Europe; the Volga in Russia; the Yangtze in China; and the Nile in Egypt. River cruise companies such as Viking River Cruises, Uniworld River Cruises and Avalon Waterways introduced 34 new river ships in 2014 alone, and the global fleet has continued to grow. As of 2015, there were 170 river cruise ships afloat, according to CLIA, with 18 additional ships on order for 2016.

These include two new ships in the Viking River Cruises line that will sail the Mississippi River in the U.S., putting it into competition with American Cruise Lines. Crystal Cruises is also planning to begin river cruise services in March 2017. Other River cruise companies include AmaWaterways, Avalon Waterways, Tauck and Aqua Expeditions.

Onboard life on these very small ships can be quite luxurious. Uniworld's *SS Maria Theresa*, for example, surrounds its 150 passengers with $2 million in art, decorating cabin-suites of 162 to 410 square feet each. The suites boast Savoir beds, blue-marble bathrooms and French balconies.

Entertainment venues are limited, and tend to focus on cultural presentations, craft demonstrations and lectures. However, unlike large ocean-going cruise ships, Wi-Fi, meals, alcohol and most excursions are often included in the fare.

Small ships, including river cruises are a very different business model from giant cruise ships, and branching out into this business may not appeal to all major cruise lines. Consequently, both river cruises and small luxury ships are in a sector where a small competitor has an excellent chance to launch a niche business. The capital expense of building a relatively small river cruise ship is vastly less than building a major, oceangoing ship. The crews and administrative staffs are likewise vastly smaller. At the same time, revenues per cruise may be relatively small in a 400 passenger ship, compared to a giant, modern 6,000 passenger ship. Likewise, operating efficiencies may be lower in smaller ships. One of the benefits, however, is that many of the smaller cruise lines, particularly in river cruises, charge very

high fees per cruise, and thus may earn substantial profits per passenger.

27) Chinese Tourism Creates Growth Opportunities for the Cruise and Hotel Industries

The biggest potential market for cruise passenger growth is China, where the concept of cruising up until recently was almost unheard of. About 700,000 Chinese travelers went on a cruise in 2014, however, the number rose 79% from 2012 to 2014. As the Chinese middle class rapidly develops, the Asia Cruise Association expects Asian demand to triple from 2013 to 2020, reaching 3.8 million annual cruisers (1.6 million of them from China). Carnival, the world's largest cruise company and the owner of the Princess, Holland America and Cunard lines had four ships based in mainland China, starting in 2015. Norwegian Cruise Line is building a new ship, *Norwegian Joy*, which is expected to enter service in 2017 and will serve the Chinese market only. The ship will feature expanded shopping venues, a two-level racetrack, a virtual reality Galaxy Pavilion game center and an open air green space. Cruise terminals have opened or are under construction in a number of coastal cities including Shanghai, Tianjin and Xiamen.

Many challenges persist in making onboard life appealing to Chinese tastes. Alcoholic drinks, a major lure on most cruise ships, are refused or merely sampled by many Chinese. Most also prefer Chinese dining options (including chopsticks) to food from other cultures. By law, travelers cannot book an international cruise directly but must use a Chinese tour guide company. Many cruise lines are catching on quickly, however, and implementing dining venues and activities tailored to Chinese cultural norms.

As for hotels, growth in Chinese tourism is often tied to business travelers, especially for young professionals who find themselves traveling for the first time. Typical Chinese businesspeople focus on a successful image and may thereby book stays in luxury hotels, or at least in hotels with a hip image. The challenge for hotels, particularly luxury companies such as Ritz-Carlton and Four Seasons, is to establish brand awareness and loyalty on initial business trips and turn that into return trips for pleasure as well as business.

To that end, hotels are offering Mandarin translations of their web sites and apps. Conrad Hotels & Resorts offers a mobile concierge app through which Chinese travelers can order room service in Mandarin, and translating the order automatically to the local language for the hotel kitchen and service staff. Private dining rooms are being made available for Chinese businesspeople who prefer to do business over a quiet, private meal (a common business practice in China). Chinese breakfasts are appearing on menus around the world, and loyalty programs are targeting these travelers. Starwood reported that its Starwood Preferred Guest program grew 108% over less than two years within China.

28) New Technologies Show Promise for Port and Airport Security

U.S. transportation hubs continue in their efforts to keep passengers and freight safe and security costs under control. To achieve this, airports, railway stations and ports are developing new technologies and strategies. However, there are problems with disgruntled airport passengers complaining of long lines; the inconvenience of removing clothing such as jackets, belts and shoes; the frequency of selection for more thorough searches using metal detecting wands and pat downs, and more recent concerns about radiation exposure and privacy when using full body scans.

Several detection systems are already widely used at airports. Standard metal scanners are still the norm in most airports around the world. The Sentinel II, made by British security firm Smiths Detection which uses puffs of air to scan for explosives, proved too costly and too prone to break-downs and has been removed from U.S. airports.

EDS (Explosives Detection System) machines are currently in place at hundreds of U.S. airports. EDS scans bags for unusual densities, which are typical in explosive devices. ETD (Explosives-Trace-Detection) machines, installed at all U.S. airports, can detect trace particles of explosives contained in baggage.

U.S. Customs now has expedited entry kiosks at dozens of U.S. airports allowing U.S. citizens (and permanent residents) who have paid $100, passed a government background check and placed their fingerprints on file, to bypass long lines when re-entering the U.S. An additional program that is open to Trusted Travelers as well as Global Entry users, called TSA PreCheck, was launched in seven U.S. airports in October 2011.

A private firm called CLEAR operates a government-approved program that pre-checks it members and designates them as trusted travelers, enabling them to move through airport security

faster. A high level of personal information must be provided to CLEAR. CLEAR was founded using the technology assets of an earlier firm which failed and went bankrupt.

Port security is another hot issue. Industry analysts estimate that at any given time there are approximately 18 million cargo containers in circulation throughout the world, and any number of those containers could be vulnerable to terrorist activity.

Shortly after the 9/11 attacks, the U.S. government instituted a program in which all shippers sending goods to U.S. ports must deliver an electronic manifest of every container's contents to the U.S. Customs Service 24 hours before being loaded on a ship in a foreign port. The program is called the Container Security Initiative (CSI). Cargos, shippers or handlers who are deemed "high risk" by the Customs Service have their associated containers x-rayed or physically searched before loading. This works out to be between 5% and 10% of all containers to arrive at U.S. ports.

Generally, local port authorities are governmental units that own the real estate around their shipping ports. These port authorities lease real estate to terminal operators. Frequently, these terminal operators are foreign-based, and occasionally they are even owned by foreign governments. However, these terminal operators have little or nothing to do with port security, which is the focus primarily of federal agencies including the Coast Guard and U.S. Customs authorities.

Potential security risks at ports are widespread, and there is a great business opportunity here for service providers and firms that can create breakthrough security technology. While aboard ships in transit or in port, containers are hardly tamperproof—it would be easy enough for someone with ill intent to add to or alter the cargo. Physical security measures in and around U.S. ports may include Coast Guard patrols, local police patrols and port security personnel, along with security cameras and lighting. Nonetheless, ports are vast, extremely busy operations, and security measures at present are sorely taxed to provide broad coverage. Meanwhile, the huge quantity of trucks and rail cars coming and going to and from ports present another immense security risk. For example, the Ports of Los Angeles and Long Beach have, at busiest times, 11,000 trucks arriving daily.

Technology offers some hope for container security. The Hong Kong Terminal Operators Association was involved in a successful pilot program, utilizing state of the art scanners on every container entering either of two large container terminals by truck. While sitting on flatbed trucks, the containers are screened by an x-ray-like device based on gamma-rays to look for suspicious objects. Likewise, the containers are scanned for radiation. This system, known as Integrated Container Inspection System or ICIS, is offered by an American firm, Commercial Fleet Export, Inc., based in St. Louis, Missouri. ICIS can collect and integrate data from sources such as shipping records, terminal information systems and customs intelligence. Each container's identification is scanned into a database where data on container scans and inspection are used as the basis for container tracking and intelligence.

Congress requires shippers in foreign ports to scan containers that will be shipped to the U.S. for potential weapons or explosive materials. Evaluating inbound containers has finally reached a high level of success. To begin with, all containers headed to the U.S. are "screened." This involves the use of Customs officers to check manifests, shipping history and other data, including officers who are working at more than 50 ports in foreign nations. Containers considered to be high risk are then inspected physically.

At the same time, radiation detection equipment, capable of detecting materials that could be used by terrorists in "dirty bombs," is being installed in certain foreign ports, where 100% of containers will be scanned. By the end of 2015, a major portion of containers destined for the U.S. were thus scanned for radiation emissions.

Other measures to increase port safety are being developed in the private sector. Several firms, including defense contractor L-3 Communications Holdings, Inc., are developing "smart boxes" that utilize sensors in containers to scan for chemicals, nuclear materials and human heartbeats. The boxes would also contain radio frequency identification (RFID) tags which hold data about the contents of the container. The sensors will scan for any changes to the contents as listed, and set off an alarm if changes are found. The boxes are powered by batteries which, according to DHS specifications, must last for 30,000 hours before replacement. The cost for the boxes, which must fall below $50 per container according to Homeland Security rules, may be a bargain in light of the fact that the system would significantly cut down on cargo theft, which is estimated at $20 to $60 billion per year by the U.S. Department of Transportation.

Yet another promising cargo security project involves General Electric. Under this system, wireless sensors and transmitters are installed in a special box inside containers. The units collect data about container condition, security, humidity, internal temperature and radiation. They can even tell if a container has been dropped by a crane. That data is then sent to one of Globalstar's 32 satellites (Globalstar is a leading provider of satellite services), and transmitted along to a control center at GE. The goal is to cut down on theft and tampering, while increasing supply chain efficiency and reducing potential use of a container for terrorism.

29) High Speed Passenger Trains, Including Maglev, Advance in China and Europe

A number of technological advancements taking place are impacting both business and leisure travel in many parts of the world. Train travel has long been an alternative to flying, but often not a viable one if you need to get somewhere fast. A limited number of high speed trains have been in use for decades in a few places, including France and Japan. High speed trains are now changing the status quo in a growing number of locales, and new technologies are being developed.

After decades of research and testing, Maglev trains have entered the realm of popular use, albeit on a limited scale. Thanks to powerful magnetic fields, these trains float 3/8" above their tracks. Unhindered by rail friction, they can zip along at speeds up to 310 miles per hour. In some cases, such trains may be the fastest way to provide transport between locations.

In Shanghai, a maglev train serves passengers between the Pudong Airport and the City Center. The 19-mile trip takes only about eight minutes. While many are skeptical about the widespread adoption of such trains, once infrastructures are in place, traveling by maglev train may eventually become a popular option for travelers.

In Japan, engineers are working on a maglev system called electrodynamic suspension that utilizes super-cooled, superconducting electromagnets that levitate the train nearly four inches above a guideway. The technology is earmarked for use in the Chuo Shinkansen project. The train will run between Tokyo and Osaka by way of Nagoya and cost an estimated $100 billion. The first phase may be completed by 2027, with a second phase finished possibly by 2045. However, many question the need for the project due to projections that show Japan's population is expected to drop from 127 million in

2013 to 105 million in 2045. In addition, the route runs through mountainous terrain and would require the construction of numerous tunnels. If completed, supporters believe that Japan could market its technology to other countries and perhaps even provide assistance with the financing of foreign projects.

> **Internet Research Tip:**
> For a maglev video on YouTube, see:
> www.youtube.com/watch?v=weWmTldrOyo

Of course, most of today's high speed trains are not maglev, but instead take advantage of the latest advances in traditional train technologies. China is leading the world in constructing new routes that utilize such trains. For example, ultrafast trains now offer service between Beijing and Shanghai, which began running in June 2011. The trains feature first class seats that can lay flat, and a top speed of 236 mph, cutting the transit time to as little as four hours from the usual 12 hours. China's 1,428-mile route between Beijing and Guangzhou takes just eight hours, compared to the 20 hours taken by traditional trains.

The trains for China's newest routes are manufactured by domestic firms like China South Locomotive & Rolling Stock Industry (CSR) and China North Locomotive & Rolling Stock Industry. Such firms got their start largely by partnering with leading Japanese, European and North American train makers, gaining access to advanced technologies in the process. China's new routes are part of an ambitious 25,000 kilometer mile network of high speed rail to connect most major cities by 2020.

France's *Train a Grande Vitesse* (TGV) has been providing high speed rail service since 1981. Typical TGV trains, which are high speed, but not maglev, travel at 180 miles per hour, but the company has tested trains at much higher speeds. The successor to TGV trains is AGV (*Automotrice a Grande Vitesse*), which uses motors under the floors of passenger carriages instead of in separate locomotives at either end of the train and can reach a commercial speed of 222 mph. Italian operator *Nuovo Trasporto Viaggiatori* (NTV) unveiled its first fully fitted-out AGV in December 2011, the first of 25 AGV trains put into operation by the company.

By the beginning of 2015, Spain had 1,900 miles of high speed track in operation. A high speed line runs between Madrid, Seville, Malaga, Barcelona and Valencia at speeds up to 186 miles per hour. Rail passengers are enjoying quick service as well as departures and arrivals in urban centers rather than at outlying airports. Growing numbers of Spanish passengers are choosing rail over air travel.

Britain's government-sponsored firm High-speed 2 is studying high speed service between London and Birmingham in an initial phase and further service to Manchester and Leeds in a subsequent phase. Network Rail, which maintains and develops rail infrastructure, and the Association of Train Operating Companies are planning to increase capacity over the next 20 years. In addition, London's Thames-link route, general commuter lines and a number of central stations are undergoing a $9 billion expansion. (See www.gov.uk/government/organisations/high-speed-two-limited.)

Nations in the Middle East hope to enter the realm of high speed rail as well, in addition to constructing monorails and local metropolitan service. Kuwait and Qatar hope to invest $10 billion each in train projects, while the United Arab Emirates is spending $20 billion. Probably the most ambitious plan in the region is the $15 billion earmarked in Saudi Arabia to expand its rail network by a factor of five. However, these are ambitious, long-term plans that may be slowed by difficult political or economic environments.

The beneficiaries of new rail system investment will include European rail companies, which have significant expertise and experience, such as France's Alstom, the UK's Network Rail and Switzerland's ABB. However, Japanese firms will be competing fiercely for new railway design, construction and operations contracts, while GE is seeking new sales for its highly regarded locomotives. China is rapidly developing its own manufacturing of rail cars, locomotives and related equipment.

Japan has been a long-term investor in train systems. Its *Shinkansen* bullet trains form one of the fastest passenger transportation networks in the world, topping speeds of 220 mph.

Korea's Korail has a high speed network between its most populous cities, including Pusan, Seoul and Taegu. The country's first high speed train, the KTX, was built by France's Alstom and introduced in 2004. Korea then unveiled a domestically-built high speed train, the KTX-*Sancheon*, in 2010. A third project, the Hemu430X, was tested in 2012 and 2013.

30) U.S. Passenger Train Projects Receive Funding, Including Amtrak and Light Rail

The U.S. remains far behind the rest of the world in terms of high speed passenger rail. Advanced trains, boasting speeds above 200 miles per hour, are under study for routes between San Diego and Sacramento. (This route would include service between Los Angeles and San Francisco. Proponents state it could reduce annual highway traffic by 2 million cars and annual greenhouse gas emissions by 12 million tons. Critics fear that it would lose vast amounts of money.) Despite the possible advantages of regional high speed trains in the U.S., including energy efficiency, low pollution output and relief for crowded airports and highways, funding remains uncertain. Many analysts also have serious doubts that ridership could reach high enough levels to justify the investment, as America is largely an automobile-based culture. Extremely low gasoline prices in 2015-16 found even more Americans on the roadways, and may defer interest in new trains.

Voters in California have approved $10 billion in bonds to support the development of fast passenger trains. Unfortunately, the projected cost of building a high speed rail line running between Los Angeles and San Francisco ballooned from the original estimate of $36 billion in 2009 to about $68 billion as of mid-2013. In 2015, construction crews began clearing and re-routing utility lines to make way for the rail project. Many expect costs to continue to balloon and for actual utilization to be low if the project is ever completed. As of early 2016, state officials were considering moving the first segment from Burbank in Southern California to San Jose in the San Francisco Bay area.

Meanwhile, a proposed high speed line connecting Dallas and Houston, Texas was in planning as of early 2016. To be funded largely by private sources, including the government of Japan, the $10 billion Texas Central Railway would offer 90-minute service one way. The trains are to be electrically powered and have the potential to reach 205 miles per hour on a 240-mile long track. About 65% of the project's funding is to come from U.S. and Japanese sources, with the remainder from various equity investors.

A Maglev project is also proposed for the U.S. Northeastern corridor, connecting Washington, D.C. and New York City. It has a total estimated cost of $100 billion and is backed by a private company called Northeast Maglev based in Washington, D.C. As of late 2014, the line had commitments from the government of Japan for $5 billion earmarked for construction of the first leg of another $10 million for the route connecting Washington and Baltimore, Maryland.

Many leaders in various U.S. states are rejecting the thought of proceeding with high speed rail projects. These naysayers include some state governors, many state legislators and financial analysts, all concerned about potential cost overruns on construction and the further potential of long-term operating losses. Meanwhile, some observers believe that most rail projects could never be competitive with automobile travel or airline travel, in terms of costs, convenience, or both. Part of the challenge lies in the fact that the U.S. has very low population density and long distances between major cities, in contrast, for example, to the densely-populated rail corridors in Japan—one of few nations to have passenger rail systems that are financially self-sustaining.

Despite these challenges, the states of Illinois and Michigan are spending an estimated $2.1 billion in federal stimulus package funding on track upgrades, new rail cars and locomotives. New trains and infrastructure will enable speeds along certain routes to reach 110 mph, shaving about an hour off the former time needed to ride from Chicago to Detroit or St. Louis. This is a more conservative approach, improving existing railways while avoiding costly new routes. In order to accommodate higher speeds and smoother rides, old wooden railroad ties are being replaced with concrete versions, while better safety and signaling systems are being installed. Overall, federal stimulus funds made available during the recent financial crisis are helping to pay for some $12 billion in railroad improvements and planning, spanning more than 150 projects in 32 states.

Amtrak, the long-maligned federally-supported U.S. railway, posted surprising traffic gains, thanks to Acela Express, a train system that runs predominantly between major cities in the northeast with top speeds of up to 150 miles per hour. Although the Acela frequently runs behind schedule, Amtrak has seen passenger numbers surge from 2000, when average monthly ridership was approximately 1.8 million, or 21.6 million yearly. In 2015, Amtrak carried almost 30.8 million passengers (down slightly from 2013's record 31.6 million). In addition to the Acela's speed, train travel in the U.S. may be appealing to some travelers due to the increasing airline tickets. Nonetheless, the Acela has suffered many setbacks and breakdowns.

As of 2015 Amtrak operated 300 daily trains that connected 46 states, the District of Columbia and three Canadian Provinces. However, nearly all of the track that it utilizes is owned by freight railroad companies. Amtrak's own history shows how difficult it can be to make a passenger rail system financially sustainable. It has lost money every year of its existence, averaging about $1 billion in yearly losses since 2000. However, Amtrak's 2015 fiscal year results showed some improvement, with 91% of its operating costs covered by ticket sales and other revenue, up from 90% in fiscal 2014.

Amtrak hopes to expand on its success in the Northeast corridor by partnering with state governments. Since 2001, it has run a popular train from Portland Maine to Boston along a route of about 100 miles. That route, called the Downeaster, has been expanded to the north. As of early 2016, Amtrak offered service between Lynchburg, Richmond, Norfolk and Newport News, and planned to add service to Roanoke.

Meanwhile, urban light rail systems continue to expand at a modest pace in many urban centers around the U.S. Houston is slowly adding to its relatively new system, which, for a few years, has made it possible to ride from downtown to the massive event complex and sports stadium at Reliant Center as well to the Houston Medical Center, one of the largest in the world. Denver hopes to invest more than $7 billion over a ten period ending around 2022 or 2023, adding up to 122 miles of new rail to its existing 35-mile "FastTracks" system.

The growing expense and frustration of owning and operating a car in urban centers is adding to a renewed interest in commuter rail systems. Car insurance is costly, parking is expensive and hard to find, and traffic snarls and slowdowns make many commutes by car extremely inefficient.

In Florida, there is, a plan to develop a private railroad called All Aboard Florida. It would connect Miami, Ft. Lauderdale and Orlando with limited stops. The project's sponsoring companies are all owned by private equity firm Fortress Investment Group. Designed to run on existing track used by Florida East Coast Railway freight trains, the trains would run at standard speeds with the exception of a small high speed stretch where it may reach 125 mph. If the project receives state approval, completion could be as early as 2016.

SPOTLIGHT: Hyperloop

A futuristic alternative to high speed trains could be on the distant horizon thanks to a concept from Tesla Motors and SpaceX founder Elon Musk. His idea is to build a giant, above ground tube atop pylons in which a 28-passenger pod would move at speeds up to 760 mph. The solar powered pod would travel through the tube, in which fans would remove sufficient air to eliminate most of the drag that naturally slows moving objects. Musk envisions a route between Los Angeles and San Francisco, which could take as little as 30 minutes to travel. The system could cost between $6 billion and $10 billion to build, according to early estimates. The tube would be built along existing roads making construction and maintenance easier, and safety features would include pod wheels in case of system failure. By late 2015, Hyperloop Technologies (hyperlooptech.com) had raised $11.1 million in capital, and was seeking another $80 million in venture funding. The next step for the venture would be to build a prototype.

---

31) Self-Check-In Kiosks, RFID and Wireless Technologies Save Costs and Enhance Travelers' Experiences at Airlines

Most airlines offer mobile boarding passes in which the Air Transport Association's (IATA) 2D standard barcodes are stored on smartphones. Qantas offers a frequent-flyer membership card embedded with a smart chip that allows members to check-in very quickly. These passengers swipe their ID cards at airport check-in, place luggage on a conveyer belt which scans the bag for size and weight and issues a heavy-duty luggage tag (called a Q Bag Tag), and then flash the ID one last time at the gate to board without having to show a boarding pass.

A few airlines are also offering self-boarding lanes in which automated gates read boarding passes or 2D boarding codes stored on smartphones. The gates, called the SpeedBoarding Gate IER SBG, are manufactured by IER, a transportation equipment company in France.

Luggage tags are also becoming "smart." Rather than bar-coded tags that are common today, the new tags are embedded with electronic identification chips (RFID) containing information about the passenger and his or her flight. As luggage moves along the conveyor belt, scanners supplied with information about the airport's flight schedule read the luggage and forward it to the correct plane or divert it if a flight is delayed or cancelled. By incorporating RFID into baggage tags, the number of misdirected or lost bags has been reduced. Delta claimed that it previously lost as much as $100 million every year settling claims and locating misplaced luggage. In another example, at McCarran International Airport in Las Vegas, baggage was typically delivered with a painfully low level of 89% accuracy using a barcode system. A test of an RFID system resulted in 99.7% accuracy, leaving the airport eager to give the project the go-ahead. McCarran spent $125 million (75% of which was underwritten by the Transportation Security Administration) to implement the system, which assigns unique numbers used for storing data about bag owners, origins and destinations. The data is stored in centralized databases. McCarran is using disposable RFID tags provided by Motorola's Symbol unit (formerly Symbol Technologies).

A slightly different system is in place at Narita Airport outside Tokyo, Japan. Its tags are more sophisticated in that the tags themselves store data as opposed to centralized databases. Airports in Hong Kong and Philadelphia have also implemented RFID projects. Alien Technology Corp. (www.alientechnology.com) provides RFID related services at San Francisco International Airport.

The latest in baggage technology is self-service kiosks which are already installed by Alaska Air Group in dozens of airports. Elsewhere, some firms are offering luggage tags with built-in GPS units so that owners can track their luggage. Some airlines are adopting similar technology. Air France and KLM now use digital tags that are linked to passenger's frequent flyer accounts. The correct flight information is automatically uploaded to the tags, which also feature luggage tracking.

32) Aging Baby Boomers Will Cause Significant Changes in the Leisure Sector, Including Sports and Activity-Based Travel

The term "Baby Boomer" generally refers to someone born in the U.S. or Europe from 1946 to 1964. The term evolved to describe the children of soldiers and war industry workers who were involved in World War II. When those veterans and workers returned to civilian life, they started or added to families in large numbers. As a result, the Baby Boom generation is one of the largest demographic segments in the U.S., with more than 70 million surviving members as of 2016. Some Baby Boomers have already reached retirement age. In 2006, the first of the boomers reached 60, a common early

retirement age. In 2011, millions began to turn traditional retirement age (65) for the first time. Eventually, the aging of Baby Boomers will result in extremely rapid growth in the senior portion of the population.

The Baby Boom segment will have distinct requirements that should be considered by businesses that want to succeed in evolving markets. A major consideration is the fact that many boomers will attempt to reap the health benefits of exercise for the first time in years, if not for the first time in their lives. Aerobic activity will become vital to those who want to maintain healthy lifestyles, but activities and equipment must be adapted to aging bodies. For example, leaders in the bicycle marketplace are introducing a growing number of models that enable older riders to sit more upright, while leaning over less. Bicycle seats and suspension that are kinder to older bodies will sell well.

One new sport gaining popularity among Americans aged 55 and over is pickleball, a sport played on a small court using wood and graphite rackets and plastic balls. The smaller courts are easier on aging joints than tennis.

Firms that design and make equipment for high-impact or repetitive-motion sports will be striving to create equipment that is easier on older joints and muscles. For example, golf clubs or tennis rackets that have bigger sweet spots or provide more power with less effort in the stroke are logical products for this market.

Lower-impact sports and exercise will gain in favor. Swimming, power walking and day hiking should all have bright futures, as should the firms that manufacture equipment for these activities. Exercise and gym equipment makers will do well to make lines of equipment adapted to, or specifically for, older users. For example, instruction labels on gym equipment will need to have larger font sizes so that the type will be easy for older eyes to read. Softer, more ergonomic grips on weights and other gym equipment make sense. Activities that are easy for older people to enter for the first time will prosper in this market. Pilates and yoga, when taught in a manner suitable for stiffer, older bodies, could continue to boom.

Travel and tours centered on sports and recreation activities will continue to do well, especially where at least some venues are tailored to appeal to older participants. The massive number of affluent, retired consumers will be looking for healthy activities and recreation on their travels. Tours that combine cycling, hiking, walking and other activities of moderate intensity are good fits in this market, and demand will grow sharply. Tours that combine hiking or cycling with luxury accommodations or unique lodging in pristine remote settings (including the rapidly growing trend of ecotourism) will find large numbers of customers. Sporting goods manufacturers would do well to provide sponsorships and test equipment to tour operators, and should seek ways to offer seminars and sports instruction that fit neatly with the growing activity-based tour business. They will do especially well to target the 60+ age segment with marketing, products and services tailored to that group.

Tours that offer participation in cultural activities, environmental projects and educational opportunities will also enjoy soaring growth. Many travelers want to do much more than relax or shop while on tours—they want to get to know and understand the local people, help solve local problems and enrich their own lives in the process.

A select set of seniors can be extremely active and athletic. Older athletes are competing in senior and "masters" events, often setting startling records of speed and endurance. Many athletes in their 60s are either discovering exceptional ability for the first time, or nurturing and toning up athletic prowess that they haven't taken time to use in decades. Runners, tennis players, swimmers, cyclists and track and field participants well past 50, 60 and even 70 years of age are performing well (sometimes brilliantly). For example, Jeanne Daprano, a former third grade school teacher, entered masters track events for the first time in her late 40s. Recently (in her seventieth year), she became the first woman to break the seven-minute mile past age 70, running the distance in 6:46.91. At age 75, in 2012, she set world records in her age bracket for runs of 400 meters, 800 meters and one mile.

33) Private Space Vehicles Begin to Fly, Including the SpaceShipTwo, but 2014 Crash May Slow Development

While private spacecraft capable of carrying space tourists receive the most attention from the media, private firms developing systems capable of carrying commercial and scientific payloads into space are of more overall importance to the global economy and to such industries as aerospace and telecommunications. These efforts have the potential to make it easier and more cost effective to deliver satellites into Earth orbit, opening up tremendous potential for the telecommunications industry and for such services as space-based mapping of the Earth.

As of 2016, there were a small number of companies involved in the development of reusable space vehicles, led by SpaceX, Boeing, Sierra Nevada Corp. and Blue Origin, among others. All are engaged in building spacecraft to deliver cargo and astronauts to low-Earth orbit vessels such as the International Space Station (ISS).

PayPal founder Elon Musk started SpaceX (www.spacex.com), which has conducted several unmanned space test flights that connected with the ISS. Next on the SpaceX agenda is to test manned-flights on its Dragon capsule.

SpaceX is noted for its focus on developing recoverable-reusable rockets, including its Falcon9 (F9R) recoverable missile that returns to Earth and lands for reuse. The firm is also developing the "Falcon Heavy," intended to be the world's most powerful rocket. In addition, its Dragon free-flying spacecraft was the first commercial spacecraft to deliver cargo to the International Space Station and return cargo to Earth in 2012. As of early 2016, the company stated that it is profitable and has nearly 70 launches in its backlog of work, representing about $10 billion in contracts. SpaceX's revolutionary design and manufacturing have enabled it to offer dramatically lower prices for space vehicle launches.

Meanwhile, Boeing's CST-100 is intended to fly astronauts to the ISS as well. The CST-100 capsule is propelled by a United Launch Alliance Atlas 5 rocket, and the company plans a manned flight by 2017.

Sierra Nevada Corp. (www.sncorp.com) is working on a winged vehicle called the Dream Chaser that will also fly on an Atlas 5 rocket. The craft would launch vertically, but land horizontally on conventional runways, much like the Space Shuttle.

Blue Origin (www.blueorigin.com) made headlines in 2016 when its New Shepard rocket booster and space capsule vertically launched into space and then safely re-landed for the second time, proving its reusability. The company was founded in 2000 by Jeff Bezos (founder of Amazon.com).

Virgin Galactic (which is owned by Sir Richard Branson 's UK-based Virgin Group and UAE-based aabar Investments PJS) hopes to become the world's first commercial space passenger line. Its SpaceShipTwo space craft and launch vehicle WhiteKnightTwo have both been developed by Mojave-based Scaled Composites, which was founded by famed aircraft innovator Burt Rutan.

Scaled Composites initially developed SpaceShipOne, which in 2004 claimed the $10 million Ansari X Prize as the world's first privately-developed manned spacecraft. Virgin Galactic's new vehicles share much of the same basic design as this 2004 prize-winner, but are built to carry six passengers, or the equivalent scientific research payload, on sub-orbital space flights, allowing an out-of-the-seat, zero-gravity experience while offering views of the planet from the black sky of space for tourist astronauts, as well as a unique microgravity platform for researchers. Virgin Galactic commercial operations are based at Spaceport America in New Mexico, which was built with substantial funding from the State of New Mexico.

SpaceShipTwo is 60 feet long and carries a passenger cabin which is 90 inches in diameter, similar to the size of a business jet. The launch vehicle WhiteKnightTwo is capable of carrying a 35,000-pound payload to about 50,000 feet in elevation. SpaceShipTwo is then released and its own rocket motor propels it to even greater height. In April 2013, the craft performed a successful, passenger-free test flight for the first time. Virgin Galactic is also developing LauncherOne, an orbital launch vehicle for small satellites. In early 2014, the company successfully tested new liquid rocket engines for LauncherOne.

Hundreds of would-be astronauts have sent $20,000 deposits toward future flights which will start at $200,000 per person. Prior to flight, passengers will go through a two or three-day training program. The weightless part of their flight experience will last about six minutes.

Unfortunately, in October 2014, a tragic crash occurred during a test flight of SpaceShipTwo over California's Mojave Desert. It was using a recently approved engine with a new fuel mixture. The aircraft was destroyed, while one test pilot was killed and the other test pilot aboard was injured. This development could cause a serious delay to all private space vehicle efforts. However, development continues, with Virgin Galactic unveiling its new SpaceShipTwo, called Virgin Spaceship (VSS) Unity, in February 2016.

A number of other startups are also part of the private space race among the companies clustered in the Mojave Desert. XCOR Aerospace (www.xcor.com) is working on a rocket-plane vehicle called Lynx. Run by Jeff Greason (one of the Intel Pentium microprocessor engineers), XCOR is selling tickets for future trips.

Microsoft co-founder Paul Allen launched Vulcan Aerospace in April 2015 to make commercial space travel cheaper and more accessible. The new company is headed by the executive director of former Stratolaunch Systems, which initially developed a giant version of WhiteKnightTwo that will have a wingspan of 385 feet. The Stratolaunch air-launch platform is a collaboration between Scaled Composites and an established rocket manufacturer called Orbital Sciences.

Despite all the promise of reusable spacecraft and rockets, NASA announced in late 2015 that it had awarded $1.16 billion to Aerojet Rocketdyne for engines to power its Journey to Mars project. These RS-25 engines, first developed in 1970, will not be reused, but allowed to burn in the Earth's atmosphere after launch.

34) Nano Spacecraft Under Development

In April 2016, a project called Breakthrough Starshot was announced which hopes to develop a nanocraft the size of a cellphone that could fly at 20% the speed of light (more than 1,000 times faster than today's rockets and shuttles). Backed by a board of directors that includes Internet investor Yuri Milner, cosmologist Stephen Hawking and Facebook CEO Mark Zuckerberg, the $130 million project hopes to send nanocraft to the Alpha Centauri star system, which is about 40 trillion kilometers from Earth as soon as 2046. NASA's Ames Research Centre is also involved in the project.

The nanocraft will be small vehicles that carry cameras and communication equipment to send data back to Earth. The craft is expected to resemble a tiny smartchip-sized probe attached to a thin, lightweight fabric sail of about 3.5 meters in width. Although many challenges are ahead, including the engineering of the nanocraft, billions of dollars in additional funding and myriad other obstacles involved, the concept is being taken seriously by many observers.

35) The Future of Travel

Over the long term, the number of domestic and international travelers worldwide will soar. Growth in traffic at major global hubs and at airports in emerging markets will escalate accordingly. Meanwhile, the advent of the long-range Boeing 787, featuring advanced passenger comfort, long range and extreme fuel efficiency, as well as the recently launched A380 jumbo jets capable of carrying 550 to 800 passengers, will encourage even higher numbers of international travelers.

Boeing forecasts the global passenger and freight aircraft fleet to grow by nearly 40,000 new jetliners between 2016 and 2035, worth $5.9 trillion. Airbus' estimate is the delivery of 33,070 planes during the period, valued at $5.2 trillion (up 1.5% from its 2015 estimate). (The Asia Pacific markets will account for the largest share of these new aircraft, and the most popular aircraft style will remain single-aisle, highly fuel-efficient designs with advanced engines.) While there will be considerable competition from smaller aircraft manufacturers such as Embraer, most of this immense trove of revenues will go to Airbus and Boeing.

Catering to Travelers of the Near Future

- Travelers will prize dining based on farm-to-table foods, local brew pub beers and local wines on hotel restaurant menus.
- Travelers will also have more options for involvement with local communities in cultural activities, as hoteliers learn to market authentic local experiences.
- "Social Impact Travel" will grow in popularity, as vacationers use part of their time for local humanitarian and philanthropic efforts.
- Intense competition for the wealthiest travelers will continue, with ever-costlier, small luxury cruise ships, unique and exclusive tours and ultra-luxury first class suites on aircraft. Airport first-class lounges will also up the competition.
- Social media postings, online reviews and online videos will play an ever more important role. Travelers will rely on such activities to drive their travel choices. Once they begin their trips, they will spend an extraordinary amount of time posting to social media.
- Smartphones will take over more and more of routine hotel, airline and cruise line tasks, making traveling more convenient for guests. This will include the use of smartphones for room keys, rapid check-in and check-out, messaging with staff and electronic concierge services.

Source: Plunkett Research, Ltd.

New breakthroughs in passenger train technology, backed by immense investments by government transportation agencies, will change the face of train travel in many nations as ultrafast trains are introduced in high-traffic areas. Worldwide, crowded highways and expensive gasoline will slowly put more impetus on the development of new train routes.

Travelers will enjoy wider choices in local transportation once they arrive at their destinations.

Popular car-sharing services, such as ZipCar, are already establishing locations in hotel parking garages. This trend will accelerate, allowing travelers to conveniently rent a car for a few hours on an as-needed basis, instead of being forced to go to a remote car rental lot and rent a vehicle for at least one day at higher cost. The taxi business will dwindle unless it learns to compete effectively with car sharing services such as Uber. Over the long-term, driverless taxis will serve specific urban areas.

For the well-heeled and for corporations with significant travel budgets, fractional ownership of aircraft, yachts, hotel/condos and resort homes will continue to be popular. Meanwhile, one of the biggest single influences on the travel industry will be the very large numbers of Baby Boomers reaching retirement age in the U.S., along with rapidly aging populations in Europe, Japan and elsewhere. These are people who will have the time and the money to travel extensively for years and years to come.

An additional major influence on the travel industry, for now and for decades to come, is the rapid rise of millions of business professionals and members of the middle class in India, Brazil and China, Indonesia and other rapidly developing nations. The extremely rapid economic growth of those countries will continue to create immense new demand for travel services in two ways. First, business and investment professionals will be traveling more and more to and from emerging nations, promoting new deals and securing sales of goods and services. Demand for travel services, from ground transport, to business-class hotels, to train and airline service will continue to grow at a brisk pace. At the same time, rising discretionary income among middle and upper end consumers in those nations will drive the biggest boom ever seen in international tourism.

There is still plenty of room for substantial growth in the global cruise industry in the future. Ships are already being dedicated to the rapidly climbing number of Chinese tourists. Other developing markets, from Southeast Asia to South Africa, will offer similar opportunities over the long term. Specialty ships will proliferate, ranging from small, unique ultra-luxury liners, to river cruisers, to cruise lines focused on adventure cruises or cruises that focus on humanitarian projects in each locale visited.

Increased use of information technologies will be either a nuisance or a convenience to travelers, depending on their frame of reference. RFID, smart ID cards and self-check-in will proliferate in an effort to reduce the number of man hours required to handle a given number of passengers. Traveler security will become an even greater concern, leading both to new costs and taxes as well as new business opportunities for providers of technologies and services. Travelers will be exposed to an ever-growing range of technology-enhanced security and surveillance devices in a never-ending effort to thwart terrorists, thieves and crackpots.

The world of travel will grow and change rapidly. The most challenged travelers will be those seeking remote, tranquil getaways—far from the maddening, traveling hordes.

Chapter 2

AIRLINE, HOTEL & TRAVEL INDUSTRY STATISTICS

CONTENTS:

Airline, Hotel & Travel Industry Statistics and Market Size Overview

Segment	Amount	Units	Date	Source
U.S. Airline Industry				
Revenue Passenger Enplanements	814.9	Mil.	2016[1]	BTS
Revenue Departures Performed	9.1	Mil.	2016[1]	BTS
Passenger Revenue Miles	921.5	Bil.	2016[1]	BTS
Passenger Load Factor	83.3	%	2016[1]	BTS
Freight Revenue Ton Miles	6.8	Bil.	2016[1]	BTS
Average Air Fare	361	US$	2016	BTS
U.S. Rail Travel - Amtrak				
Passenger Volume	30.8	Mil.	2015[2]	Amtrak
Amtrak Revenues	3.2	Bil. US$	2015[2]	Amtrak
Amtrak Expenses	4.3	Bil. US$	2015[2]	Amtrak
Amtrak Stations	500+	Stations	2015	Amtrak
Amtrak Route Miles, Approximate	21,300+	Miles	2015	Amtrak
U. S. Lodging Industry				
Average Occupancy Rate, Forecast	65.5	%	2016	PwC
Revenue Per Available Room (RevPAR), Forecast	82.27	US$	2016	PwC
Average Daily Rate, Forecast	125.62	US$	2016	PwC
New Hotel Openings, Forecast	797	Hotels	2016	LE
New Room Openings, Forecast	90,528	Rooms	2016	LE
Lodging Industry Revenue	226.4	Bil. US$	2015	Census
Number of Hotel Properties	53,432	Units	2015	AHLA
Number of Hotel Guestrooms	5.0	Mil.	2015	AHLA
North American Cruise Industry				
Total Passengers, Sourced from North America	12.4	Mil.	2015	Carnival
Total Passengers Forecast, 2016	12.5	Mil.	2016	PRE
U.S. Travel				
Total Direct Travle Industry Spending	947.1	Bil. US$	2015	USTA
Total International Traveler Spending in the U.S.	246.2	Bil. US$	2015	ITA
Travel Trade Surplus	97.9	Bil. US$	2015	ITA
U.S. Share of World Traveler Spending	15.0	%	2014	ITA
International Visitor Arrivals to the U.S.	75.3	Mil.	2015	ITA
International Visitor Arrivals to the U.S. (Forecast)	90.3	Mil.	2020	ITA
Total Tourism-Related Employment	7.6	Mil.	Q1 2016	ITA
Travel-Generated Tax Revenue	147.9	Bil. US$	2015	USTA
World Travel				
Global Travel & Tourism Estimated Direct Contribution to GDP	2.2	Tril. US$	2015	WTTC
Global Travel & Tourism Estimated Total Contribution to GDP	7.2	Tril. US$	2015	WTTC
Percentage of Global Travel & Tourism Total Contribution to GDP	9.8%	%	2015	WTTC
Projection	10.8%	%	2026	WTTC
Global Travel & Tourism Direct Industry Employment	107.8	Mil.	2015	WTTC
International Tourism Receipts	1,232	Bil. US$	2015	UNWTO
International Tourist Arrivals	1,184	Mil.	2015	UNWTO
Global Commercial Aviation Net Profit (Estimate)	36.3	Bil. US$	2016	IATA
Global Hotel Industry Revenue	550.0	Bil. US$	2016	HM
Global Number of Hotels[3]	156,000	Units	2016	STR

[1] Represents data from May 2015 through April 2016. [2] Fiscal year data, October 2014 through September 2015. [3] Hotels with 15+ rooms in North America, 10+ rooms elsewhere.

BTS = U.S. Bureau of Transportation Statistics; PwC = PricewaterhouseCoopers; LE = Lodging Econometrics; Census = U.S. Census Bureau; AHLA = American Hotel & Lodging Association; PRE = Plunkett Research Estimate; ITA = U.S. International Trade Administration, Office of Travel and Tourism Industries; USTA = U.S. Travel Association; WTTC = World Travel & Tourism Council; UNWTO = World Tourism Organization; IATA = International Air Transport Association HM = Hotel Management; STR = STR Global.

Source: Plunkett Research,® Ltd. Copyright© 2016, All Rights Reserved
www.plunkettresearch.com

Air Carrier Traffic Statistics, U.S.: 1996-2015

(In Thousands of Ton Miles)

Year	Revenue Passenger Ton-Miles	Revenue Freight Ton-Miles	Overall Available Ton-Miles
1996	67,147,070	6,229,315	117,900,817
1997	70,545,149	6,870,796	121,775,854
1998	71,666,886	6,865,321	124,343,773
1999	75,489,431	7,420,041	131,395,095
2000	80,308,809	7,968,819	139,650,497
2001	74,612,693	6,967,291	137,615,913
2002	73,351,146	7,045,126	133,927,950
2003	75,170,112	6,515,321	134,954,795
2004	83,727,243	7,341,697	144,997,859
2005	87,946,586	7,371,274	151,413,061
2006	89,311,730	7,316,421	148,736,676
2007	91,901,919	6,873,612	152,873,956
2008	89,871,157	6,586,928	147,828,335
2009	84,529,188	5,798,871	141,132,098
2010	88,820,315	7,230,720	144,024,272
2011	90,205,855	6,910,554	146,880,568
2012	90,852,754	6,847,194	145,300,621
2013	92,219,557	6,640,943	145,534,496
2014	94,884,893	7,092,031	149,221,369
2015	98,750,126	6,971,650	156,225,784

A revenue ton-mile is one ton of revenue traffic transported one mile.

Note: Data from "Origin and Destination Survey of Airline Passenger Traffic - Table 1," a publication of the U.S. Civil Aeronautics Board, based upon a ten-percent sample. The ten-percent sample has been expanded to 100% and rounded to thousands (000). Since 2008, calculations are based on monthly figures and may not match 2007 and earlier data.

Source: U.S. Bureau of Transportation Statistics

Plunkett Research,® Ltd.

www.plunkettresearch.com

Air Carrier Traffic Statistics, U.S.:
12 Months Ended April 2016 and April 2015

	May 2015 - April 2016			May 2014 - April 2015		
	Scheduled	Non-Sched.	Total	Scheduled	Non-Sched.	Total
Revenue Passenger Enplanements (000)	809,021	5,895	814,916	770,590	5,410	776,000
Revenue Passenger Miles (000)	915,207,168	6,266,743	921,473,911	870,791,255	6,899,137	877,690,392
Available Seat Miles (000)	1,094,070,876	12,857,220	1,106,928,096	1,045,927,705	13,653,606	1,059,581,311
Passenger Load Factor (%)	83.65	48.74	83.25	83.26	50.53	82.83
Revenue Freight Ton Miles (000)	6,535,255	296,520	6,831,775	6,902,259	288,967	7,191,226
Total Revenue Ton Miles (000)	98,926,029	923,212	99,849,241	94,831,330	978,931	95,810,261
Available Ton Miles (000)	157,014,256	2,932,516	159,946,772	147,237,961	3,086,009	150,323,970
Ton Mile Load Factor (%)	63.00	31.48	62.43	64.41	31.72	63.74
Revenue Departures Performed	8,969,073	158,148	9,127,221	8,950,261	178,430	9,128,691
Revenue Aircraft Miles Flown (000)	7,268,145	72,943	7,341,088	7,101,787	75,723	7,177,510
Revenue Aircraft Hours (Airborne)	16,825,274	206,318	17,031,592	16,547,174	217,368	16,764,542

Excludes all cargo services. Includes domestic and international.

Source: U.S. Bureau of Transportation Statistics

Plunkett Research,® Ltd.

www.plunkettresearch.com

Consolidation in U.S. Airlines

Following deregulation of the U.S. airline industry in 1978, the market has gone through a period of consolidation, which has accelerated in the last decade. As of 2013, the U.S. air carrier segment consists of four dominant companies: American Airlines, United, Delta Air Lines & Southwest.

- American Airlines
    - Acquired airlines:
        - US Airways (Agreed to acquire AMR Corp., the parent company of American Airlines, out of bankruptcy in February 2013. The merger was completed in December 2013.)
        - Trans World Airlines (December 2001)
        - Reno Air (February 1999)
        - AirCal (March 1987)

- United
    - Acquired airlines:
        - Continental Airlines (October 2010)

- Delta Air Lines
    - Acquired airlines:
        - Northwest Airlines (October 2008)
        - Western (December 1986)

- Southwest
    - Acquired airlines:
        - AirTran Airways (May 2011)
        - ATA Airlines (November 2008)
        - Morris Air (December 1993)
        - Muse Air (June 1985)

Source: Plunkett Research,® Ltd. Copyright © 2016, All Rights Reserved
www.plunkettresearch.com

Annual U.S. Domestic Average Itinerary* Air Fare: 1995-2016

(In Current & Constant Dollars)

Year	2016 US$**			Current US$		
	Avg. Fare	Percent Change		Avg. Fare	Percent Change	
		From Previous Year	Cumulative From 1995		From Previous Year	Cumulative From 1995
1995	$454			$292		
1996	418	-8.0	-8.0	277	-5.3	-5.3
1997	424	1.5	-6.7	287	3.8	-1.7
1998	450	6.0	-1.1	309	7.6	5.8
1999	461	2.5	1.4	324	4.7	10.8
2000	467	1.3	2.7	339	4.7	16.0
2001	429	-8.0	-5.6	321	-5.4	9.7
2002	411	-4.1	-9.4	312	-2.6	6.9
2003	406	-1.3	-10.6	315	1.0	7.9
2004	383	-5.7	-15.7	305	-3.2	4.5
2005	373	-2.7	-17.9	307	0.6	5.2
2006	386	3.6	-15.0	329	6.9	12.4
2007	372	-3.7	-18.2	325	-1.0	11.3
2008	381	2.6	-16.1	346	6.5	18.5
2009	343	-10.1	-24.5	310	-10.4	6.2
2010	365	6.5	-19.6	336	8.3	15.0
2011	383	4.9	-15.6	364	8.3	24.5
2012	387	0.9	-14.9	375	3.0	28.3
2013	389	0.5	-14.5	382	1.9	30.7
2014	392	0.8	-13.8	391	2.5	33.9
2015	377	-3.8	-17.0	377	-3.7	29.0
2016	361	-4.2	-20.5	361	-4.2	23.6

* Fares based on domestic itinerary fares. Itinerary fares consist of round-trip fares unless the customer does not purchase a return trip. In that case, the one-way fare is included. Fares are based on the total ticket value which consists of the price charged by the airlines plus any additional taxes and fees levied by an outside entity at the time of purchase. Fares include only the price paid at the time of the ticket purchase and do not include other fees paid at the airport or onboard the aircraft. Averages do not include frequent-flyer or "zero fares" or a few abnormally high reported fares.

** Rate calculated using Bureau of Labor Statistics Consumer Price Index.

Source: U.S. Bureau of Transportation Statistics

Plunkett Research,® Ltd.

www.plunkettresearch.com

U.S. Aviation Industry Average Annual Percentage Growth Forecasts by World Region: 2016-2036

U.S. Mainline Air Carrier Enplanements % Change

World Region	2015	2016	2017	2016-36*
Domestic	5.6	5.2	2.2	1.9
International	2.4	4.4	3.8	3.6
Atlantic	-1.3	2.1	4.5	2.8
Latin America	5.1	6.2	3.8	4.3
Asia/Pacific	0.0	2.0	2.6	2.6
System	5.1	5.1	2.4	2.1

U.S. Mainline & Foreign Flag Air Carrier Passengers % Change

World Region	2015	2016	2017	2016-36*
Total U.S./Foreign Flag	4.5	3.5	3.5	3.8
Atlantic	4.0	3.5	4.4	3.7
Latin America	5.4	4.7	1.8	4.0
Asia/Pacific	3.8	2.8	4.8	3.0
Canadian Transborder	4.5	1.6	3.9	3.6

U.S. Regional Air Carrier Enplanements % Change

World Region	2015	2016	2017	2016-36*
Domestic	-0.7	0.7	2.1	1.9
International	-22.2	0.7	2.1	1.9

U.S. Commercial Air Carriers Cargo Revenue Ton Miles % Change

World Region	2015	2016	2017	2016-36*
Domestic	3.3	1.9	2.1	0.4
International	1.6	6.0	6.4	4.7
Total	2.2	4.5	4.9	3.6

All specified years are fiscal years (October 1 through September 30).

* = Average yearly percent change

Source: U.S. Federal Aviation Administration (FAA)

Plunkett Research, Ltd.

www.plunkettresearch.com

U.S. Airline Passenger Activity: 2001-2036

Fiscal Year	Revenue Passenger Enplanements (Millions)			Revenue Passenger Miles (Billions)		
	Domestic	Int'l	System	Domestic	Int'l	System
Historical						
2001	625	57	682	508	183	691
2008	681	78	759	595	234	828
2009	631	74	704	549	221	770
2010	635	77	712	555	231	786
2011	650	81	731	572	242	815
2012	654	83	737	578	244	822
2013	654	85	739	584	250	834
2014	669	88	757	600	257	857
2015^E	696	89	786	629	260	889
Forecast						
2016	726	93	819	654	266	921
2017	742	97	839	670	277	947
2018	760	101	860	688	289	977
2019	776	105	881	704	301	1,006
2020	790	109	899	719	313	1,033
2021	803	113	916	733	325	1,058
2022	814	117	931	745	337	1,083
2023	824	122	945	756	350	1,106
2024	835	126	961	768	362	1,131
2025	848	131	979	783	375	1,158
2026	863	135	998	798	388	1,186
2027	878	140	1,018	814	401	1,215
2028	895	145	1,040	833	414	1,247
2029	914	150	1,063	852	428	1,280
2030	932	155	1,087	872	442	1,314
2031	951	160	1,111	892	456	1,348
2032	971	165	1,136	913	471	1,384
2033	991	171	1,162	934	485	1,420
2034	1,011	176	1,188	956	500	1,456
2035	1,031	182	1,213	977	516	1,493
2036	1,052	188	1,240	999	532	1,531
Average Annual Growth						
2001-15	0.8%	3.3%	1.0%	1.5%	2.5%	1.8%
2015-16	4.2%	4.3%	4.2%	4.1%	2.2%	3.6%
2015-25	2.0%	3.9%	2.2%	2.2%	3.7%	2.7%
2015-36	2.0%	3.6%	2.2%	2.2%	3.5%	2.6%

Note: Values represent the sum of U.S. Mainline and Regional Air Carriers.

E = Estimate.

Source: U.S. Federal Aviation Administration
Plunkett Research, Ltd.
www.plunkettresearch.com

Total Scheduled U.S. International Passenger Traffic, U.S. Commercial Air Carriers*: 2001-2036

(Enplanements in Millions; Passenger Miles in Billions)

Fiscal Year	Revenue Passenger Enplanements				Revenue Passenger Miles			
	Atlantic	Latin America	Pacific	Total Int.	Atlantic	Latin America	Pacific	Total Int.
Historical								
2001	20	23	11	55	86	37	59	183
2008	26	39	13	78	113	61	60	234
2009	25	37	12	74	109	58	55	221
2010	25	40	13	77	109	63	59	231
2011	25	42	14	81	112	67	64	242
2012	25	44	14	83	108	70	66	244
2013	25	46	14	85	107	75	69	250
2014	25	49	14	88	108	80	69	257
2015E	25	51	14	89	107	83	71	260
Forecast								
2016	25	54	14	93	108	86	73	266
2017	26	56	15	97	113	89	75	277
2018	27	58	15	101	118	94	77	289
2019	28	61	15	105	123	99	80	301
2020	29	64	16	109	127	104	82	313
2021	30	67	16	113	132	109	84	325
2022	31	70	17	117	136	114	87	337
2023	32	73	17	121	141	120	89	350
2024	33	76	18	126	145	125	92	362
2025	33	79	18	130	149	131	95	375
2026	34	82	19	135	154	137	97	388
2027	35	86	19	140	158	143	100	401
2028	36	89	20	145	162	149	103	414
2029	37	93	20	150	167	156	106	428
2030	38	96	21	155	172	162	108	442
2031	39	100	21	160	176	169	111	456
2032	40	104	22	165	181	176	114	471
2033	41	108	22	171	186	183	117	485
2034	42	112	23	176	191	190	120	500
2035	43	116	23	182	196	197	123	516
2036	44	120	24	188	201	205	126	531
Average Annual Growth								
2001-15	1.3%	5.8%	1.5%	3.5%	1.5%	5.9%	1.3%	2.6%
2015-16	2.1%	5.9%	2.0%	4.3%	0.9%	3.5%	2.8%	2.2%
2015-25	3.1%	4.5%	2.6%	3.9%	3.4%	4.7%	2.9%	3.7%
2015-36	2.8%	4.2%	2.6%	3.6%	3.1%	4.4%	2.8%	3.5%

* Sum of U.S. mainline and regional air carriers.

E = Estimate.

Source: U.S. Federal Aviation Administration (FAA)

Plunkett Research,® Ltd.

www.plunkettresearch.com

International Visitor Arrivals to the U.S.: Selected Years, 2000-2014

(In Thousands)

By Country/ Region of Residence	2000	2011	% Chg. 2010-11	2012	% Chg. 2011-12	2013	% Chg. 2012-13	2014	% Chg. 2013-14	Chg. 2000-14	% Chg. 2000-14
Grand Total	51,237	62,700	5%	66,659	6%	69,768	5%	75,011	8%	23,774	46%
Overseas	25,975	27,883	6%	29,761	7%	32,038	8%	34,938	9%	8,963	35%
North America	25,262	34,800	4%	36,898	6%	37,730	2%	40,073	6%	14,811	59%
Canada	14,667	21,300	7%	22,699	7%	23,387	3%	23,003	-2%	8,336	57%
Mexico	10,596	13,500	0%	14,199	5%	14,343	1%	17,070	19%	6,474	61%
Latin America	5,094	5,595	7%	6,350	13%	7,131	12%	7,754	9%	2,660	52%
Argentina	534	512	17%	615	20%	686	12%	685	0%	151	28%
Brazil	737	1,508	26%	1,791	19%	2,060	15%	2,264	10%	1,527	207%
Colombia	417	497	0%	602	21%	748	24%	881	18%	464	111%
Venezuela	577	561	14%	675	20%	788	17%	616	-22%	39	7%
Europe	11,597	12,660	6%	12,478	-1%	12,895	3%	14,586	13%	2,989	26%
France	1,087	1,504	12%	1,456	-3%	1,505	3%	1,658	10%	571	53%
Germany	1,786	1,824	6%	1,876	3%	1,916	2%	2,056	7%	270	15%
Ireland	286	347	-4%	332	-4%	367	11%	NA	NA	NA	NA
Italy	612	892	6%	831	-7%	839	1%	964	15%	352	58%
Netherlands	553	601	5%	592	-1%	589	0%	642	9%	89	16%
Spain	361	700	9%	607	-13%	620	2%	708	14%	347	96%
Sweden	322	439	18%	442	1%	477	8%	552	16%	230	71%
U.K.	4,703	3,835	0%	3,763	-2%	3,835	2%	4,149	8%	-554	-12%
Asia/Pacific	8,286	8,490	5%	9,633	13%	10,514	9%	NA	NA	NA	NA
Australia	540	1,038	15%	1,122	8%	1,205	7%	1,304	8%	764	141%
China	249	1,089	36%	1,474	35%	1,807	23%	2,190	21%	1,941	780%
India	274	663	2%	724	9%	859	19%	962	12%	688	251%
Japan	5,061	3,250	-4%	3,698	14%	3,730	1%	3,620	-3%	-1,441	-28%
South Korea	662	1,145	3%	1,251	9%	1,360	9%	1,460	7%	798	121%
Taiwan	457	290	0%	290	0%	385	33%	414	8%	-43	-9%
Middle East	702	811	10%	925	14%	1,058	14%	1,226	16%	524	75%
Israel	325	303	-1%	304	0%	331	9%	NA	NA	NA	NA
Africa	295	327	4%	373	14%	439	18%	514	17%	219	74%

Note: Latin America = Caribbean, Central America and South America

NA = Not Available

Source: U.S. International Trade Administration, Office of Travel and Tourism Industries

Plunkett Research,® Ltd.

www.plunkettresearch.com

International Visitor Arrivals to the U.S., Forecast: 2014-2020

(In Thousands)

By Country/ Region of Residence	2014 Actual	2015	2016	2017	2018	2019	2020	Chg. 2014-20	% Chg. 2014-20	CAGR 2014-20
Grand Total	75,011	75,334	77,280	80,186	83,565	86,860	90,267	15,256	20.0%	3.1%
Canada	23,003	21,163	20,951	21,370	22,225	23,114	23,807	804	3.0%	0.6%
Mexico	17,070	17,923	18,461	19,199	19,967	20,566	21,183	4,114	24.0%	3.7%
Overseas	34,938	36,248	37,868	39,616	41,372	43,179	45,276	10,338	30.0%	4.4%
United Kingdom	4,149	4,440	4,617	4,709	4,757	4,852	4,949	800	19.0%	3.0%
Japan	3,620	3,548	3,512	3,547	3,583	3,619	3,655	35	1.0%	0.2%
Brazil	2,264	2,355	2,284	2,352	2,423	2,544	2,671	407	18.0%	2.8%
China	2,190	2,562	2,972	3,418	3,930	4,441	5,019	2,829	129.0%	14.8%
Germany	2,056	2,118	2,161	2,204	2,248	2,270	2,293	237	12.0%	1.8%
France	1,658	1,642	1,675	1,708	1,759	1,830	1,903	245	15.0%	2.3%
South Korea	1,460	1,664	1,748	1,817	1,872	1,928	1,986	526	36.0%	5.3%
Australia	1,304	1,369	1,410	1,453	1,511	1,571	1,650	346	27.0%	4.0%
Italy	964	954	973	983	1,012	1,043	1,074	110	11.0%	1.8%
India	962	1,087	1,163	1,221	1,283	1,347	1,414	452	47.0%	6.6%
Colombia	881	890	908	944	991	1,051	1,103	222	25.0%	3.8%
Spain	708	743	758	781	796	812	829	121	17.0%	2.7%
Argentina	685	616	585	574	574	580	585	-99	-15%	-2.6%
Netherlands	642	655	668	682	688	695	702	60	9.0%	1.5%
Venezuela	616	505	480	461	456	452	461	-155	-25%	-4.7%
Sweden	552	591	614	633	652	671	691	139	25.0%	3.8%
Switzerland	500	515	525	530	541	552	563	63	13.0%	2.0%
Taiwan	414	447	474	498	523	549	576	162	39.0%	5.7%

Note: 2015-2020 are forecasts. Some variance in data may occur due to rounding. CAGR = Compound Annual Growth Rate, the average annual rate of growth over the forecast period, including compounded growth.

Source: U.S. International Trade Administration, Office of Travel and Tourism Industries

Plunkett Research,® Ltd.

www.plunkettresearch.com

Top Destinations of U.S. Residents Traveling Abroad (Outbound): 2013-2014

(In Thousands)

2014 Rank	Country	2013	2014	% Change (14/13)
1	Mexico	20,851	25,882	24%
	Mexico (Air)	6,219	6,931	11%
2	Canada	11,478	11,515	0%
	Canada (Air)	3,221	3,410	6%
3	United Kingdom	2,640	2,832	7%
4	France	2,002	2,124	6%
5	Italy	1,799	1,908	6%
6	Germany	1,741	1,878	8%
7	Jamaica	1,799	1,385	-23%
8	Spain	1,045	1,170	12%
9	China	1,132	1,139	1%
10	India	1,045	1,077	3%
11	Japan	812	800	-2%
12	Ireland	725	708	-2%
12	Netherlands	638	708	11%
12	Philippines	580	708	22%
15	Israel	638	554	-13%
15	Switzerland	493	554	12%
17	South Korea	580	523	-10%
17	Hong Kong	551	523	-5%
19	Peru	464	492	6%
19	Austria	435	492	13%
19	Taiwan	435	492	13%
22	Brazil	406	431	6%
22	Greece	377	431	14%
24	Turkey	348	400	15%
25	United Arab Emirates	290	369	27%
26	Thailand	348	339	-3%
27	South Africa	232	246	6%
28	Singapore	203	215	6%
Subtotal to Overseas*		**29,015**	**30,780**	**6%**
Total U.S. Resident Travelers		**61,344**	**68,176**	**11%**

Note: Percentage changes based on numbers prior to rounding.

* Includes all overseas countries and Mexico air-only.

Source: U.S. International Trade Administration, Office of Travel and Tourism Industries

Plunkett Research,® Ltd.

www.plunkettresearch.com

Top 20 Countries Ranked by International Tourism, Number of Arrivals: 2006-2013

(In Thousands; Latest Year Available)

Rank (2013)	Country	2006	2007	2008	2009	2010	2011	2012	2013
	World	881,331	944,183	959,829	919,035	979,887	1,025,303	1,071,612	1,123,200
1	France	77,916	80,853	79,218	76,764	77,648	81,550	83,051	84,726
2	United States	50,977	56,135	58,007	55,103	60,010	62,821	66,657	69,768
3	Spain	58,004	58,666	57,192	52,178	52,677	56,177	57,464	60,661
4	China	49,913	54,720	53,049	50,875	55,664	57,581	57,725	55,686
5	Italy	41,058	43,654	42,734	43,239	43,626	46,119	46,360	47,704
6	Turkey	18,916	26,122	29,792	30,187	31,364	34,654	35,698	37,795
7	Germany	23,569	24,421	24,884	24,220	26,875	28,374	30,411	31,545
8	United Kingdom	30,654	30,870	30,142	28,199	28,295	29,306	29,282	31,169
9	Russian Federation	22,486	22,909	23,676	21,339	22,281	24,932	28,177	30,792
10	Thailand	13,822	14,464	14,584	14,150	15,936	19,230	22,354	26,547
11	Malaysia	17,547	20,973	22,052	23,646	24,577	24,714	25,033	25,715
12	Hong Kong SAR, China	15,821	17,154	17,319	16,926	20,085	22,316	23,770	25,661
13	Austria	20,269	20,773	21,935	21,355	22,004	23,012	24,151	24,813
14	Ukraine	18,936	23,122	25,449	20,798	21,203	21,415	23,013	24,671
15	Mexico	21,353	21,606	22,931	22,346	23,290	23,403	23,403	24,151
16	Greece	16,039	16,165	15,939	14,915	15,007	16,427	15,518	17,920
17	Canada	18,265	17,935	17,142	15,737	16,219	16,014	16,344	16,590
18	Poland	15,670	14,975	12,960	11,890	12,470	13,350	14,840	15,800
19	Macao SAR, China	10,683	12,945	10,610	10,402	11,926	12,925	13,577	14,268
20	Saudi Arabia	8,620	11,531	14,757	10,897	10,850	17,498	14,276	13,380

Note: International inbound tourists (overnight visitors) are the number of tourists who travel to a country other than that in which they have their usual residence, but outside their usual environment, for a period not exceeding 12 months and whose main purpose in visiting is other than an activity remunerated from within the country visited.

Source: The World Bank

Plunkett Research,® Ltd.

www.plunkettresearch.com

Domestic Airline Jet Fuel Prices, U.S.:
January 1986-October 2015

(Monthly Data in Dollars per Gallon)

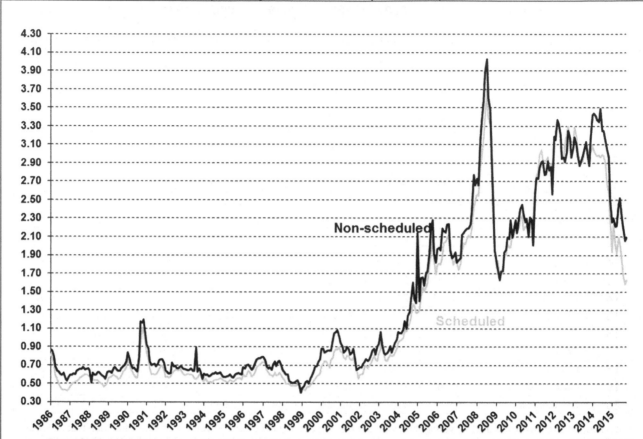

Jet Fuel Price by Type of Service	Oct-14	Oct-15
For Domestic Non-scheduled Airline Service (dollars per gallon)	$3.06	$2.09
Percent change from same month previous year	-1.0%	-31.7%
For Domestic Scheduled Airline Service (dollars per gallon)	$2.69	$1.63
Percent change from same month previous year	-11.5%	-39.4%

Notes: Jet fuel prices reported to the Bureau of Transportation Statistics differ from producer prices. Reports to BTS show the cost per gallon of fuel used by an airline during the month rather than the price charged by a producer on a single day. Fuel costs for scheduled airline services reflect contractual and storage advantages available to large buyers, while fuel costs for nonscheduled airline services reflect economic conditions for smaller buyers. Jet fuel prices also reflect seasonality due to both the seasonality of aviation and because jet fuel has similar refining requirements to heating oil. The current value is compared to the value from the same period in the previous year to account for seasonality.

Source: U.S. Bureau of Transportation Statistics

Plunkett Research,® Ltd.

www.plunkettresearch.com

Quarterly System* Operating Profit & Loss Margin for U.S. Airlines: 1st Quarter 2015-1st Quarter 2016

(Operating Profit/Loss as a Percentage of Total Operating Revenue)

1Q 2016 Rank[1]	Carrier	1Q 2015 (%)	2Q 2015 (%)	3Q 2015 (%)	4Q 2015 (%)	1Q 2016 (%)	1Q 2016 Operating Profit/Loss (Millions of US$)
1	AA-US Combined[2]	NA	NA	18.7	11.0	13.9	1,323.2
2	Delta	14.9	23.1	20.0	18.0	16.6	1,547.7
3	United	8.6	14.6	18.4	12.0	7.9	649.4
4	Southwest	17.7	21.2	23.0	20.6	19.6	943.8
5	JetBlue	16.0	17.5	20.7	20.3	21.6	348.9
6	Alaska	18.8	25.2	28.6	18.7	22.2	298.9
7	Hawaiian	13.4	16.2	24.8	19.3	17.4	95.3
8	Spirit	22.1	20.3	27.3	23.1	18.8	101.3
9	SkyWest	8.2	12.2	13.2	10.7	10.5	51.8
10	Frontier	13.5	21.4	23.7	9.8	16.9	62.2
	10-Carrier Total	**14.6**	**21.2**	**20.1**	**15.2**	**14.8**	**5,422.5**

* System = Domestic + International.

[1] Airlines are ranked by 1st quarter 2016 operating revenue.

[2] American and US Airways began combined reporting with 3Q 2015 data.

NA = Not Available

Source: U.S. Bureau of Transportation Statistics

Plunkett Research,® Ltd.

www.plunkettresearch.com

Top 10 U.S. Airlines & Airports Ranked by 2015 System* Scheduled Enplanements

(In Millions)

2015 Rank[1]	Airline Name	2015 Enplaned Passengers[1]	2014 Rank[1]	2014 Enplaned Passengers[1]	Percent Change 2014-2015[1]
1	Southwest	142.408	1	126.695	12.40%
2	Delta	114.904	2	106.220	8.18%
3	American[2]	93.280	3	66.385	40.51%
4	United	69.179	4	64.668	6.98%
5	JetBlue Airways	28.808	7	26.449	8.92%
6	SkyWest	27.840	8	25.995	7.10%
7	US Airways[2]	24.777	5	50.646	-51.08%
8	ExpressJet	23.988	6	27.968	-5.56%
9	Alaska	21.322	9	19.153	11.32%
10	Spirit	15.982	11	12.560	27.25%
2015 Rank[1]	Airport Name	2015 Enplaned Passengers[1,3]	2014 Rank[1]	2014 Enplaned Passengers[1,3]	Percent Change 2014-2015[1]
1	Atlanta	43.958	1	41.472	5.99%
2	Chicago O'Hare	30.578	2	28.114	8.76%
3	Dallas/Fort Worth	27.829	3	27.361	1.71%
4	Los Angeles	26.487	4	25.111	5.48%
5	Denver	25.158	5	24.912	0.99%
6	Charlotte	20.469	6	20.039	2.15%
7	Phoenix	20.215	7	19.223	5.16%
8	Las Vegas	19.882	8	18.687	6.39%
9	San Francisco	18.815	9	17.819	5.59%
10	Seattle	17.982	10	16.004	12.36%

Note: Percentage changes based on numbers prior to rounding.

* System = Domestic + International.

[1] 12 months ending December of each year.

[2] American and US Airways began combined reporting with 3Q 2015 data.

[3] Arrival passengers.

Source: U.S. Bureau of Transportation Statistics

Plunkett Research, Ltd.

www.plunkettresearch.com

U.S. Airline Revenue Passenger Enplanements: January 1996-April 2016

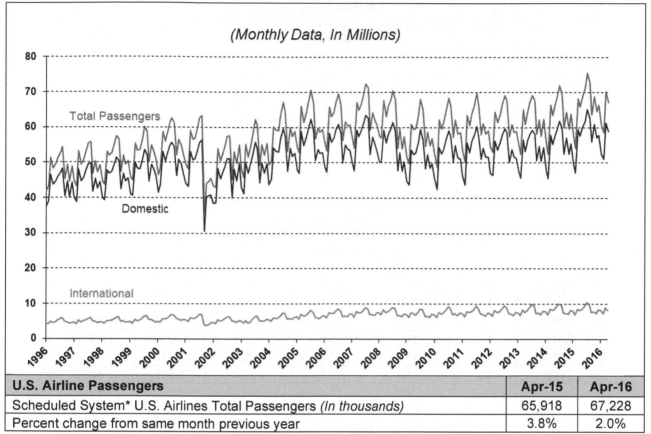

(Monthly Data, In Millions)

U.S. Airline Passengers	Apr-15	Apr-16
Scheduled System* U.S. Airlines Total Passengers *(In thousands)*	65,918	67,228
Percent change from same month previous year	3.8%	2.0%

Note: All numbers are for scheduled services.

* System = Domestic + International

Source: U.S. Bureau of Transportation Statistics

Plunkett Research,® Ltd.

www.plunkettresearch.com

Cruise Line Industry Overview, U.S.: 2009-2015

Carnival Corp.

Year	Ships	Capacity*	Passengers Carried (Thous.)	Occupancy (%)	Revenue (Mil.)	Rev. per Passenger
2015	99	216,130	10,837	104.8	15,714	1,450.0
2014	100	212,496	10,570	104.1	15,884	1,502.7
2013	101	208,302	10,061	105.1	15,456	1,536.2
2012	100	202,784	9,829	105.5	15,382	1,565.0
2011	99	195,872	9,559	106.2	15,793	1,652.2
2010	98	191,464	9,147	105.6	14,469	1,581.8
2009	93	180,746	8,519	105.5	13,460	1,580.0

Norwegian Cruise Line Holdings Ltd.

Year	Ships	Capacity*	Passengers Carried (Thous.)	Occupancy (%)	Revenue (Mil.)	Rev. per Passenger
2015	22	45,000	2,164	109.0	4,345	2,007.9
2014	21	40,000	1,933	109.0	3,126	1,617.2
2013	13	30,510	1,628	109.1	2,570	1,578.5
2012	11	26,470	1,503	107.6	2,276	1,514.4
2011	11	26,310	1,530	108.2	2,219	1,450.4
2010	11	26,310	1,404	108.7	2,012	1,433.0
2009	10	22,210	1,318	109.4	1,855	1,407.1

Royal Caribbean Cruises Ltd.

Year	Ships	Capacity*	Passengers Carried (Thous.)	Occupancy (%)	Revenue (Mil.)	Rev. per Passenger
2015	44	110,900	5,402	105.1	8,299	1,536.3
2014	43	105,750	5,150	105.6	8,074	1,567.8
2013	41	98,750	4,885	104.7	7,960	1,629.6
2012	41	98,650	4,852	104.4	7,688	1,584.5
2011	39	92,650	4,850	104.8	7,537	1,554.0
2010	40	92,300	4,586	104.3	6,753	1,472.6
2009	38	84,050	3,970	102.5	5,890	1,483.5

* Capacity is calculated based on the assumption of two passengers per cabin, though many cabins accommodate more. This is why occupancy is often more than 100%.

Source: Plunkett Research,® Ltd. Copyright © 2016, All Rights Reserved

www.plunkettresearch.com

Amtrak Ridership: January 1991-September 2015

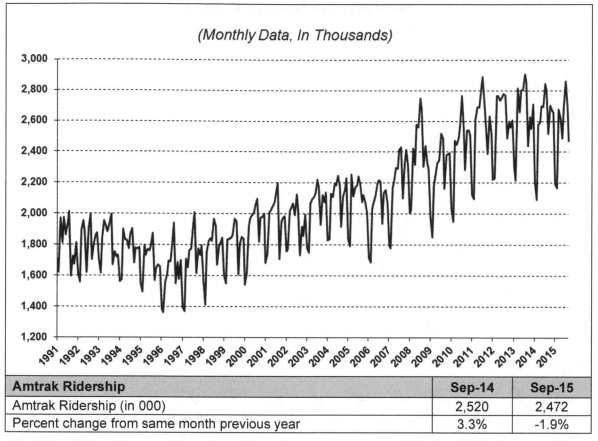

(Monthly Data, In Thousands)

Amtrak Ridership	Sep-14	Sep-15
Amtrak Ridership (in 000)	2,520	2,472
Percent change from same month previous year	3.3%	-1.9%

The National Railroad Passenger Corporation (Amtrak) officially began service in May 1971. Amtrak serves more than 500 stations in 46 states and operates over a network of more than 21,000 route miles. Ridership is highly seasonal, with July and August being the highest volume months. In 2000, Amtrak introduced high-speed rail service in the northeast U.S., which helped increase ridership.

Source: U.S. Bureau of Transportation Statistics

Plunkett Research,® Ltd.

www.plunkettresearch.com

Rail Passenger Capacity Utilization, U.S.: January 2003-August 2015

(Amtrak Passenger Load Factor; Monthly Data by Percentage)

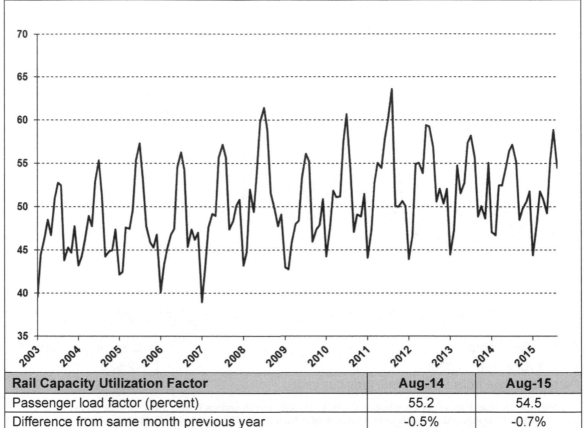

Rail Capacity Utilization Factor	Aug-14	Aug-15
Passenger load factor (percent)	55.2	54.5
Difference from same month previous year	-0.5%	-0.7%

Note: Load factor measures usage by capacity. It is calculated by dividing passenger-miles (the aggregation of trip lengths for individual passengers) by seat-miles (the sum of the products of total seats available and total miles traveled for individual trains).

Source: U.S. Bureau of Transportation Statistics

Plunkett Research,® Ltd.

www.plunkettresearch.com

Highway Vehicle Miles Traveled, U.S., Monthly:
January 1990-September 2015

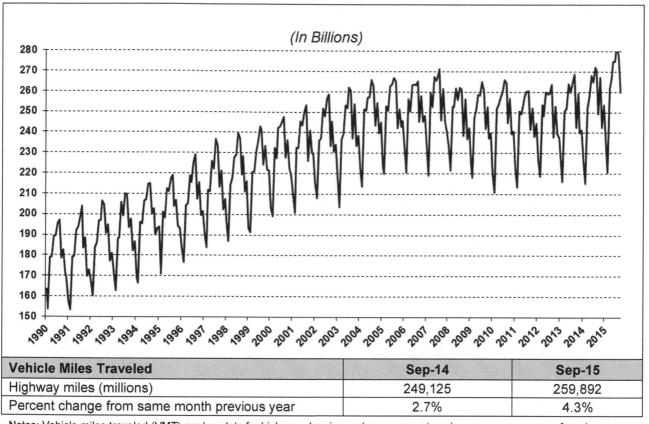

Vehicle Miles Traveled	Sep-14	Sep-15
Highway miles (millions)	249,125	259,892
Percent change from same month previous year	2.7%	4.3%

Notes: Vehicle-miles traveled (VMT) are key data for highway planning and management, and a common measure of roadway use. Along with other data, VMT are often used in estimating congestion, air quality, and potential gas-tax revenues, and can provide a general measure of the level of the nation's economic activity.

Source: U.S. Bureau of Transportation Statistics

Plunkett Research,® Ltd.

www.plunkettresearch.com

Quarterly Growth in Real Tourism Spending & Real GDP, U.S.: 2000-2016

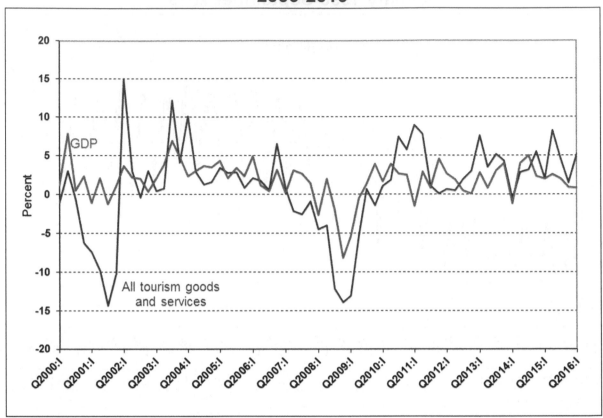

Source: U.S. Bureau of Economic Analysis

Plunkett Research,® Ltd.

www.plunkettresearch.com

Transportation Services Index, U.S.:
January 2000-September 2015

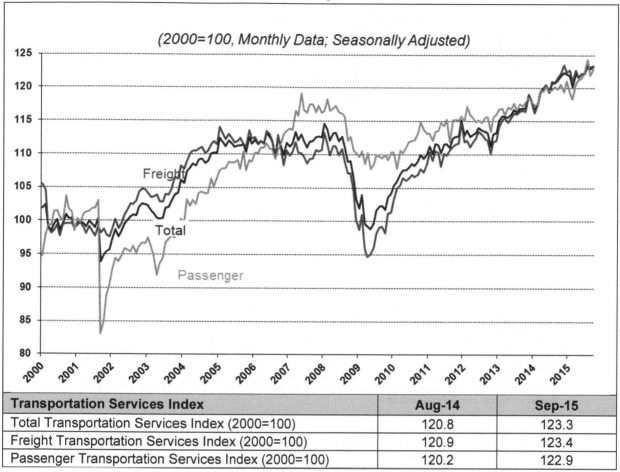

(2000=100, Monthly Data; Seasonally Adjusted)

Transportation Services Index	Aug-14	Sep-15
Total Transportation Services Index (2000=100)	120.8	123.3
Freight Transportation Services Index (2000=100)	120.9	123.4
Passenger Transportation Services Index (2000=100)	120.2	122.9

Notes: The Transportation Services Index (TSI) is a measure of the month-to-month change in the output of services provided by the for-hire transportation industry. The index can be examined together with other economic indicators to produce a better understanding of the current and future course of the economy.

Source: U.S. Bureau of Transportation Statistics

Plunkett Research,® Ltd.

www.plunkettresearch.com

Percent Change in the U.S. Transportation Services Index (TSI) from Year-to-Year: 2005-2016

(Seasonally Adjusted; 2000 = 100)

Year	Overall TSI	Percent Change	Freight TSI	Percent Change	Passenger TSI	Percent Change
2006	113.2	1.5	113.5	1.0	111.6	2.6
2007	113.0	-0.2	110.2	-2.9	119.2	6.8
2008	113.3	0.3	111.3	1.0	117.3	-1.6
2009	98.8	-12.8	95.0	-14.6	107.9	-8.0
2010	107.8	9.1	106.2	11.8	111.3	3.2
2011	110.3	2.3	108.3	2.0	114.9	3.2
2012	113.4	2.8	112.6	4.0	115.1	0.2
2013	116.1	2.4	115.6	2.7	117.1	1.7
2014	120.6	3.9	120.4	4.2	120.7	3.1
2015	122.2	1.3	122.2	1.5	122.0	1.1
2016	122.4	0.2	121.8	-0.3	123.6	1.3

Notes: TSI figures and percent changes are year-to-year, using the May TSI. Percent changes are based on numbers prior to rounding.

The Transportation Services Index (TSI) is a measure of the month-to-month changes in the output of services provided by the for-hire transportation industries. The freight transportation index consists of: for hire trucking, railroad freight services (including rail-based intermodal shipments such as containers on flat cars), inland waterways transportation, pipeline transportation (including principally petroleum and petroleum products and natural gas) and air freight. The passenger transportation index consists of local transit, intercity passenger rail and passenger air transportation. The freight index does not include international or coastal waterborne movements, private trucking, courier services or the U.S. Postal Service. The passenger index does not include intercity bus, sight seeing services, ferry services, taxi service, private automobile usage, or bicycling and other non-motorized transportation.

Source: U.S. Bureau of Transportation Statistics

Plunkett Research,® Ltd.

www.plunkettresearch.com

Estimated U.S. Accommodation Sector Quarterly Revenues: 2014-2015

(In Millions of US$; Latest Year Available)

NAICS Code[1]	Kind of business	2015	2014	4Q 2015	3Q 2015	2Q 2015	1Q 2015	4Q 2014	3Q 2014
721	**Accommodation**	**226,372**	**218,386**	**54,256**	**60,563**	**58,405**	**53,148**	**53,118**	**58,877**
7211	Traveler accommodation	219,760	211,813	53,072	58,386	56,537	51,765	51,920	56,711
7212	RV (recreational vehicle) parks and recreational camps	5,129	5,127	831	1,747	1,554	997	823	1,736
7213	Rooming and boarding houses	1,483	1,446	353	430	314	386	375	430

Estimates are based on data from the 4th Quarter 2015 Quarterly Services Report. Dollar volume estimates are published in millions of dollars; consequently, results may not be additive.

[1] For a full description of the NAICS codes used in this table, see www.census.gov/eos/www/naics/index.html

Source: U.S. Census Bureau

Plunkett Research,® Ltd.

www.plunkettresearch.com

Employment in the Airline, Hotel & Travel Industry, U.S.: 2010-May 2016

(Annual Estimates in Thousands of Employed Workers)

NAICS Code	Industry Sector	2010	2011	2012	2013	2014	2015	May-16*
Leisure & Hospitality								
721	**Accommodations**	**1759.6**	**1800.5**	**1825.1**	**1864.9**	**1894.5**	**1917.7**	**1923.7**
7211	Traveler accommodations	1,702.5	1,739.3	1,768.7	1,807.3	1,832.5	1,856.1	1,861.5
72111	Hotels & motels, except casino hotels	1,405.5	1,438.1	1,466.0	1,499.3	1,523.6	1,545.5	1,552.2
72112	Casino hotels	260.7	263.9	265.3	267.9	267.7	267.8	264.7
72119	Other traveler accommodations	36.3	37.3	37.4	40.2	41.2	42.8	44.6
721191	Bed-and-breakfast inns	15.5	15.2	14.8	15.8	16.0	16.5	16.6
721310,199	All other traveler accommodations & rooming & boarding houses	20.9	22.2	22.6	24.4	25.2	26.3	28.0
7212	RV parks & recreational camps	57.1	61.2	56.4	57.6	62.1	61.6	62.2
721211	RV parks & campgrounds	28.5	27.8	27.0	26.6	28.5	29.0	35.4
721214	Recreational & vacation camps	28.6	33.5	29.4	31.1	33.6	32.6	26.8
Professional & Business Services								
5615	**Travel arrangement & reservation services**	**185.6**	**190.4**	**191.6**	**194.5**	**196.4**	**201.2**	**205.6**
56151	Travel agencies	82.6	82.1	81.8	83.1	85.2	86.4	87.2
56152	Tour operators	23.4	24.6	24.2	25.9	26.8	27.8	29.4
56159	Other travel arrangement services	79.6	83.7	85.7	85.6	84.4	87.0	89.0
Transportation & Warehousing								
481	**Air transportation**	**458.3**	**456.9**	**459.2**	**444.3**	**444.2**	**456.3**	**471.1**
4811	Scheduled air transportation	416.5	415.5	418.0	406.0	406.4	416.5	429.9
4812	Nonscheduled air transportation	41.7	41.3	41.2	38.3	37.8	39.8	41.2
482	**Rail transportation**	**216.4**	**228.1**	**230.6**	**231.2**	**236.1**	**241.8**	**217.4**
483	**Water transportation**	**62.3**	**61.3**	**63.9**	**65.3**	**67.3**	**64.7**	**62.9**
484	**Truck transportation**	**1250.4**	**1300.5**	**1349.4**	**1382.1**	**1417.2**	**1455.3**	**1457.9**
485	**Transit & ground passenger transportation**	**429.7**	**439.9**	**440.3**	**448.5**	**466.5**	**475.4**	**494.7**
4851,2,5	Urban transit, interurban, rural & charter bus transportation	93.8	94.1	94.9	96.8	98.4	99.6	101.2
4853	Taxi & limousine service	68.3	71.6	73.6	76.8	78.8	79.2	78.9
48531	Taxi service	32.4	33.3	33.3	34.8	35.8	36.3	35.9
48532	Limousine service	35.9	38.3	40.3	42.0	43.0	42.9	43.0
4859	Other ground passenger transportation	81.6	87.6	90.2	90.8	96.1	102.4	104.1
487	**Scenic & sightseeing transportation**	**27.3**	**27.5**	**28.0**	**29.1**	**30.6**	**31.7**	**31.8**
488	**Support activities for transportation**	**542.5**	**562.2**	**579.9**	**598.3**	**625.8**	**649.4**	**648.3**
4881	Support activities for air transportation	154.1	159.1	162.5	168.8	176.7	187.0	195.5
48811	Airport operations	62.2	64.0	66.8	71.4	75.2	82.3	87.6
4884	Support activities for road transportation	80.1	81.0	86.1	88.2	93.0	93.5	91.9
4882,9	Support activities for other transportation, including rail	48.5	51.9	55.3	56.6	61.4	66.1	61.4

* Preliminary Estimate

Source: U.S. Bureau of Labor Statistics

Plunkett Research,® Ltd.

www.plunkettresearch.com

Chapter 3

IMPORTANT AIRLINE, HOTEL & TRAVEL INDUSTRY CONTACTS

Addresses, Telephone Numbers and Internet Sites

Contents:

1) Aerospace & Defense Industry Associations
2) Airline & Air Cargo Industry Associations
3) Airplane & Airport Services Organizations
4) Careers-Airlines/Flying
5) Careers-First Time Jobs/New Grads
6) Careers-General Job Listings
7) Careers-Job Reference Tools
8) Consulting Industry Associations
9) Continent & Country Guides & Information
10) Corporate Information Resources
11) Cruise Industry Associations
12) Currency Exchange
13) Economic Data & Research
14) Entertainment & Amusement Associations-General
15) Food Service Industry Associations
16) Government Agencies-Hong Kong
17) Government Agencies-India
18) Hotel, Hostel & Rental Information
19) Hotel/Lodging Associations
20) Industry Research/Market Research
21) International Regulatory Organizations
22) MBA Resources
23) Passports
24) Pilots Associations
25) Privacy & Consumer Matters
26) Railroad Associations
27) Real Estate Industry Associations
28) Restaurant Industry Associations
29) Restaurant Industry Resources
30) Spa Industry Associations
31) Trade Associations-General
32) Trade Associations-Global
33) Transport for Animals
34) Transportation Industry Associations
35) Transportation Industry Resources
36) Travel & Health
37) Travel Business & Professional Associations
38) Travel Industry Associations
39) Travel Reservations & Tickets Online
40) Travel Resources
41) Traveling for People with Disabilities
42) Travel-Local Transportation, Bus & Car Rental
43) Travel-Rail
44) Travel-Vacation Home Rental & Exchange
45) U.S. Government Agencies
46) U.S. Government Travel Sites
47) Weather Information
48) Youth Travel Associations

1) Aerospace & Defense Industry Associations

Aerospace Industries Association of Brazil
Rua Jose Alves dos Santos , 281, Ste. 203
Sao Jose dos Campos, SP 12230-081 Brazil
Phone: 55-12-3933-0657
Fax: 55-12-3931-2721
E-mail Address: *info@aiab.org.br*
Web Address: www.aiab.org.br
The Aerospace Industries Association of Brazil
(AIAB), established in 1993, is Brazil's national trade
association focused on representing and promoting
the country's aerospace sector through support of
member companies as well as through advocacy at
the legislative level.

**Aerospace Industries Association of Canada
(AIAC)**
255 Albert St., Ste. 703
Ottawa, ON K1P 6A9 Canada
Phone: 613-232-4297
Web Address: www.aiac.ca
The Aerospace Industries Association of Canada
(AIAC) is the national trade organization of Canada's
aerospace manufacturing and service sector.

**American Institute of Aeronautics and
Astronautics (AIAA)**
12700 Sunrise Valley Dr., Ste. 200
Reston, VA 20191-5807 USA
Phone: 703-264-7500
Fax: 703-264-7551
Toll Free: 800-639-2422
E-mail Address: custserv@aiaa.org
Web Address: www.aiaa.org
The American Institute of Aeronautics and
Astronautics (AIAA) is a nonprofit society aimed at
advancing the arts, sciences and technology of
aeronautics and astronautics. The institute represents
the U.S. in the International Astronautical Federation
and the International Council on the Aeronautical
Sciences.

**General Aviation Manufacturers Association
(GAMA)**
1400 K St. NW, Ste. 801
Washington, DC 20005-2485 USA
Phone: 202-393-1500
Fax: 202-842-4063
E-mail Address: bforan@gama.aero
Web Address: www.gama.aero

The General Aviation Manufacturers Association
(GAMA) is an international trade association that
represents more than 80 of the world's leading
manufacturers of general aviation aircraft, engines,
avionics and related equipment. Members also
operate aircraft fleets, fixed base operations, pilot
training and maintenance training facilities.

2) Airline & Air Cargo Industry Associations

Air Passengers Association of India
Phone: 91-044-2833-1455
Fax: 91-044-2833-1453
E-mail Address: info@air-passenger.com
Web Address: www.air-passenger.com
The Air Passengers Association of India is a
nonprofit organization dedicated to the welfare of the
air passenger. The website includes contacts to
airlines and links to industry news.

Air Transport Association of Canada (ATAC)
255 Albert St., Ste. 700
Ottawa, Ontario K1P 6A9 Canada
Phone: 613-233-7727
Fax: 613-230-8648
E-mail Address: atac@atac.ca
Web Address: www.atac.ca
The Air Transport Association of Canada (ATAC) is
an organization which supports its 230 members in
their pursuit of a safe and competitive Canadian air
transport industry that promotes Canada's commercial
airline and air freight industry.

Airlines for America (A4A)
1301 Pennsylvania Ave. NW, Ste. 1100
Washington, DC 20004 USA
Phone: 202-626-4000
E-mail Address: a4a@airlines.org
Web Address: www.airlines.org
Airlines for America (A4A), formerly the Air
Transport Association of America, is the only trade
organization for the principal U.S. airlines. ATA
creates policies and supports measures which
improve aviation safety, security and the vitality of
the aviation system.

Airports Council International (ACI)
800 Rue du Square Victoria, Ste. 1810
Montreal, Quebec H4Z 1G8 Canada
Phone: 514-373-1200
Fax: 514-373-1201

E-mail Address: aci@aci.aero
Web Address: www.aci.aero
The Airports Council International (ACI) is a
nonprofit organization that seeks to foster
cooperation among its member airports and other
partners in world aviation, including governmental,
airline and aircraft manufacturing organizations.

Airports Council International (ACI) - North America
1615 L St. NW, Ste. 300
Washington, DC 20036 USA
Phone: 202-293-8500
Fax: 202-331-1362
Toll Free: 888-424-7767
E-mail Address: memberservices@aci-na.org
Web Address: www.aci-na.org
Airports Council International (ACI) North America
represents local, regional and state governing bodies
that own and operate commercial airports throughout
the United States and Canada.

European Regions Airline Association (ERAA)
Park House, 127 Guildford Rd.
Lightwater
Surrey, GU18 5RA UK
Phone: 44-0-1276-856495
Fax: 44-0-1276-857038
E-mail Address: info@eraa.org
Web Address: www.eraa.org
The European Regions Airline Association (ERAA)
is the recognized representative body for regional air
transport throughout Europe. The group influences
regulatory and environmental conditions; facilitates
technical cooperation and advancement; and garners
public and political support.

International Air Transport Association (IATA)
800 Place Victoria
P.O. Box 113
Montreal, QC H4Z 1M1 Canada
Phone: 514-874-0202
Web Address: www.iata.org
The International Air Transport Association (IATA)
represents about 260 airlines in order to offer the
highest standards of passenger and cargo service.

Regional Airline Association (RAA)
2025 M St. NW, Ste. 800
Washington, DC 20036-3309 USA
Phone: 202-367-1170
Fax: 202-367-2170
E-mail Address: raa@raa.org

Web Address: www.raa.org
The Regional Airline Association (RAA) represents
U.S. regional airlines and the suppliers of products
and services that support the industry.

3) Airplane & Airport Services Organizations

Airnav.com
AirNav LLC
P.O. Box 20273
Atlanta, GA 30325-0273 USA
Phone: 404-975-0600
Fax: 877-392-3006
Toll Free: 877-212-2001
E-mail Address: contact@airnav.com
Web Address: www.airnav.com
Airnav.com offers information on airports,
navigation, airspace fixes and aviation fuel.

Airport Authority Hong Kong (AA)
HKIA Twr., 1 Sky Plz. Rd.
Hong Kong Int'l Airport
Lantau, Hong Kong Hong Kong
Phone: 852-2181-8888
Fax: 852-2824-0717
E-mail Address: online@hkairport.com
Web Address: www.hongkongairport.com
The Airport Authority Hong Kong (AA) is a statutory
body with a mandate to maximize the value of Hong
Kong International Airport (HKIA) for the benefit of
the territory. The site offers links to airline and flight
information, arrivals and departures, passenger
guides and transport and entertainment at HKIA.

Airports Australia
Web Address: www.airportsaustralia.com
Airports Australia offers information on Australian
airports with links to their web sites. The web site,
owned by Global Airport Marketing Pty Ltd, was
established in 1999 to promote air travel and related
businesses to worldwide travelers.

Civil Air Navigation Services Organization (CANSO)
Transpolis Schiphol Airport
Polaris Avenue 85e
Hoofddorp, JH 2132 The Netherlands
Phone: 31 23 568 5380
Fax: 31 23 568 5389
E-mail Address: info@canso.org
Web Address: www.canso.org

CANSO is a leading industry organization for the companies that provide air traffic control, worldwide. CANSO Members are responsible for supporting 85% of world air traffic.

Eurocontrol
Rue de la Fusee 96
Brussels, 1130 Belgium
Phone: 32-2-729-9011
Fax: 32-2-729-9044
E-mail Address: infocentre@eurocontrol.int
Web Address: www.eurocontrol.int
Eurocontrol is the European Union's international air control and navigation division. Its aim is to create a unified European air traffic management system. Eurocontrol has 39 member states.

GlobalAir.com
2700 Moran Ave.
Bowman Field Airport
Louisville, KY 40205 USA
Phone: 502-456-3934
Toll Free: 888-236-4309
E-mail Address: webmaster@globalair.com
Web Address: www.globalair.com
GlobalAir.com is a web site that offers information about aircraft purchasing, aviation directories, flight planning and airport facilities.

Interactive Pilot
E-mail Address: neil@pilotmall.com
Web Address: www.ipilot.com
Interactive Pilot is a personalized and easy-to-use resource tool for pilots and aviation enthusiasts, providing weather services, airport data and other information.

Landings.com
11024 Montgomery NE, Ste. 169
Albuquerque, NM 87111 USA
E-mail Address: admin@landings.com
Web Address: www.landings.com
Landings.com offers pilots news and information about the airline industry, as well as a number of forums and a flight planner.

NAV Canada
77 Metcalfe St.
Ottawa, ON K1P 5L6 Canada
Phone: 613-563-5588
Fax: 877-663-6656
Toll Free: 800-876-4693
E-mail Address: service@navcanada.ca

Web Address: www.navcanada.ca
NAV Canada is the sole provider of Canada's civil air navigation system.

4) Careers-Airlines/Flying

Aviation/Aerospace Jobs Page
920 Morgan St., Ste. T
Des Moines, IA 50309 USA
Fax: 515-243-5384
Toll Free: 800-292-7731
E-mail Address: customerservice@nationjob.com
Web Address: www.nationjob.com/aviation
The Aviation/Aerospace Jobs Page, a division of NationJob, Inc., features detailed aviation and aerospace job listings and company profiles.

AviationJobSearch.com
London Rd.
Sayers Common
West Sussex, BN6 9HS UK
Phone: 44--1273-837538
Fax: 44-1273-837549
E-mail Address: info@aviationjobsearch.com
Web Address: www.aviationjobsearch.com
AviationJobSearch.com lists jobs related to the airline industry.

Avjobs, Inc.
9609 S. University Blvd., Unit 630830
Littleton, CO 80163-3032 USA
Fax: 888-624-8691
E-mail Address: info@avjobs.com
Web Address: www.avjobs.com
Avjobs, Inc. is a group of employers dedicated to helping individuals obtain aviation, airline, aerospace and airport careers.

Flightdeck Recruitment Ltd.
15 High St., W. Mersea
Colchester, Essex CO5 8QA UK
E-mail Address: contact@flightdeckrecruitment.com
Web Address: www.flightdeckrecruitment.com
Flightdeck Recruitment Ltd. provides a link between aviation recruiters who are looking for flight deck crew and pilots or flight engineers who are seeking employment.

5) Careers-First Time Jobs/New Grads

ColleeGrad.com, Inc.
950 Tower Ln., Fl. 6
Foster City, CA 94404 USA
E-mail Address: info@quinstreet.com
Web Address: www.collegegrad.com
CollegeGrad.com, Inc. offers in-depth resources for college students and recent grads seeking entry-level jobs.

MonsterCollege
799 Market St., Ste. 500
San Francisco, CA 94103 USA
E-mail Address: info@college.monster.com
Web Address: www.college.monster.com
MonsterCollege provides information about internships and entry-level jobs, as well as career advice and resume tips, to recent college graduates.

National Association of Colleges and Employers (NACE)
62 Highland Ave.
Bethlehem, PA 18017-9085 USA
Phone: 610-868-1421
E-mail Address: customer_service@naceweb.org
Web Address: www.naceweb.org
The National Association of Colleges and Employers (NACE) is a premier U.S. organization representing college placement offices and corporate recruiters who focus on hiring new grads.

6) Careers-General Job Listings

CareerBuilder, Inc.
200 N La Salle St., Ste. 1100
Chicago, IL 60601 USA
Phone: 773-527-3600
Fax: 773-353-2452
Toll Free: 800-891-8880
Web Address: www.careerbuilder.com
CareerBuilder, Inc. focuses on the needs of companies and also provides a database of job openings. The site has over 1 million jobs posted by 300,000 employers, and receives an average 23 million unique visitors monthly. The company also operates online career centers for 140 newspapers and 9,000 online partners. Resumes are sent directly to the company, and applicants can set up a special e-mail account for job-seeking purposes. CareerBuilder is primarily a joint venture between three newspaper giants: The McClatchy Company, Gannett Co., Inc. and Tribune Company.

CareerOneStop
Toll Free: 877-872-5627
E-mail Address: info@careeronestop.org
Web Address: www.careeronestop.org
CareerOneStop is operated by the employment commissions of various state agencies. It contains job listings in both the private and government sectors, as well as a wide variety of useful career resources and workforce information. CareerOneStop is sponsored by the U.S. Department of Labor.

LaborMarketInfo (LMI)
Employment Development Dept.
800 Capitol Mall, MIC 83
Sacramento, CA 95814 USA
Phone: 916-262-2162
Fax: 916-262-2352
Web Address: www.labormarketinfo.edd.ca.gov
LaborMarketInfo (LMI) provides job seekers and employers a wide range of resources, namely the ability to find, access and use labor market information and services. It provides statistics for employment demographics on both a local and regional level, as well as career searching tools for California residents. The web site is sponsored by California's Employment Development Office.

Recruiters Online Network
E-mail Address: rossi.tony@comcast.net
Web Address: www.recruitersonline.com
The Recruiters Online Network provides job postings from thousands of recruiters, Careers Online Magazine, a resume database, as well as other career resources.

USAJOBS
1900 E St. NW, Ste. 6500
Washington, DC 20415-0001 USA
Web Address: www.usajobs.gov
USAJOBS, a program of the U.S. Office of Personnel Management, is the official job site for the U.S. Federal Government. It provides a comprehensive list of U.S. government jobs, allowing users to search for employment by location; agency; type of work; or by senior executive positions. It also has special employment sections for individuals with disabilities, veterans and recent college graduates; an information center, offering resume and interview tips and other information; and allows users to create a profile and post a resume.

7) Careers-Job Reference Tools

Vault.com, Inc.
132 W. 31st St., Fl. 17
New York, NY 10001 USA
Fax: 212-366-6117
Toll Free: 800-535-2074
E-mail Address: customerservice@vault.com
Web Address: www.vault.com
Vault.com, Inc. is a comprehensive career web site
for employers and employees, with job postings and
valuable information on a wide variety of industries.
Its features and content are largely geared toward
MBA degree holders.

8) Consulting Industry Associations

**International Society of Hospitality Consultants
(ISHC)**
411 6th St. S., Ste. 204
Naples, FL 34102 USA
Phone: 239-436-3915
E-mail Address: abelfanti@ishc.com
Web Address: www.ishc.com
The International Society of Hospitality Consultants
(ISHC) is a society dedicated to promoting the
highest quality of professional consulting standards
and practices for the hospitality industry.

9) Continent & Country Guides & Information

Africa Guide (The)
Web Address: www.africaguide.com
The Africa Guide provides travel information about
hotels, tours, employment, travel documents,
charities and cultural facts for the African continent.

Asia Travel Tips
E-mail Address: webmaster@asiatraveltips.com
Web Address: www.asiatraveltips.com
Asia Travel Tips is devoted to information about
hotels and travel throughout Asia.

China Hotel Travel Guide (Red Flag)
E-mail Address: webmaster@redflag.info
Web Address: www.redflag.info
The China Hotel Travel Guide (RedFlag) provides
hotel and travel information for China.

Countries of the World (InfoPlease)
501 Boylston St., Ste. 900

Boston, MA 02116 USA
Toll Free: 800-498-3264
Web Address: www.infoplease.com/countries.html
Countries of the World (InfoPlease) provides maps,
history, politics, statistics and other information on
countries around the world.

Countryreports.org
P.O. Box 430
Pleasant Grove, UT 84062-0430 USA
Fax: 866-300-3985
Toll Free: 866-689-0542
Web Address: www.countryreports.org
Countryreports.org offers a vast array of information
on countries around the world.

IndTravel.com
E-mail Address: admn@indtravel.com
Web Address: www.indtravel.com
IndTravel.com offers valuable resources for travelers
to India, including tips, maps, hotel discounts, links
and information on history, culture, wildlife and
cities.

Tourism Offices
1150 15th St. NW
Washington, DC 20071 USA
Phone: 202-334-6000
Fax: 202-496-3883
E-mail Address: letters@washpost.com
Web Address: www.washingtonpost.com/wp-
srv/travel/toolbox/tourismoffices.htm
The Washington Post has compiled this list of
domestic and international tourism offices.

Tourism Offices Worldwide Directory (TOWD)
E-mail Address: admin@towd.com
Web Address: www.towd.com
The Tourism Offices Worldwide Directory (TOWD)
offers information about official government tourism
offices, convention and visitors bureaus, chambers of
commerce and similar agencies that provide free,
accurate and unbiased travel information to the
public.

VirtualTourist.com, Inc.
801 Parkview Dr. N., Ste. 200
El Segundo, CA 90245 USA
E-mail Address: feedback@virtualtourist.com
Web Address: www.virtualtourist.com
VitualTourist.com, Inc. offers information for
locations around the world, posted and described by
its members.

World Factbook (The)
Central Intelligence Agency
Office of Public Affairs
Washington, DC 20505 USA
Phone: 703-482-0623
Fax: 571-204-3800
Web Address: www.cia.gov/library/publications/the-world-factbook/index.html
Published by the CIA, The World Factbook provides an array of information on every country in the world.

World Time Zones
Web Address: www.worldtimezone.com
The World Time Zones web site contains maps of the world that illustrate the various time zones. The site also has tools such as a sun clock, a world clock, a call planer, an interactive map and lists of time abbreviations.

World66.com
E-mail Address: info@world66.com
Web Address: www.world66.com
World66.com offers information on countries around the world from local editors and travelers.

10) Corporate Information Resources

bizjournals.com
120 W. Morehead St., Ste. 400
Charlotte, NC 28202 USA
Web Address: www.bizjournals.com
Bizjournals.com is the online media division of American City Business Journals, the publisher of dozens of leading city business journals nationwide. It provides access to research into the latest news regarding companies both small and large. The organization maintains 42 websites and 64 print publications and sponsors over 700 annual industry events.

Business Wire
101 California St., Fl. 20
San Francisco, CA 94111 USA
Phone: 415-986-4422
Fax: 415-788-5335
Toll Free: 800-227-0845
E-mail Address: info@businesswire.com
Web Address: www.businesswire.com
Business Wire offers news releases, industry- and company-specific news, top headlines, conference calls, IPOs on the Internet, media services and access to tradeshownews.com and BW Connect On-line

through its informative and continuously updated web site.

Edgar Online, Inc.
11200 Rockville Pike, Ste. 310
Rockville, MD 20852 USA
Phone: 301-287-0300
Fax: 301-287-0390
Toll Free: 888-870-2316
Web Address: www.edgar-online.com
Edgar Online, Inc. is a gateway and search tool for viewing corporate documents, such as annual reports on Form 10-K, filed with the U.S. Securities and Exchange Commission.

PR Newswire Association LLC
350 Hudson St., Ste. 300
New York, NY 10014-4504 USA
Fax: 800-793-9313
Toll Free: 800-776-8090
E-mail Address: MediaInquiries@prnewswire.com
Web Address: www.prnewswire.com
PR Newswire Association LLC provides comprehensive communications services for public relations and investor relations professionals, ranging from information distribution and market intelligence to the creation of online multimedia content and investor relations web sites. Users can also view recent corporate press releases from companies across the globe. The Association is owned by United Business Media plc.

11) Cruise Industry Associations

Cruise Lines International Association (CLIA)
1201 F St. NW, Ste. 250
Washington, DC 20004 USA
Phone: 202-759-9370
Fax: 202-759-9344
E-mail Address: info@cruising.org
Web Address: www.cruising.org
The Cruise Lines International Association (CLIA) is the world's largest trade organization for the cruise industry, which advocates policies and practices for encouraging safe, secure and sustainable cruise ship environment and promote cruise travel experience.

National Association of Charterboat Operators
P.O. Box 2990
Orange Beach, AL 36561 USA
Phone: 251-981-5136
Fax: 251-981-8191
E-mail Address: info@nacocharters.org

Web Address: www.nacocharters.org
NACO is a national association of charterboat owners and operators that was formed in 1991. Representing thousands of individuals all across the United States, its membership includes marine charters who provide fishing, sailing, diving, eco-tours, and other excursion vessels who carry passengers for hire.

Passenger Vessel Association (PVA)
103 Oronoco St., Ste. 200
Alexandria, VA 22314 USA
Phone: 703-518-5005
Fax: 703-518-5151
Toll Free: 800-807-8360
E-mail Address: pvainfo@passengervessel.com
Web Address: www.passengervessel.com
The Passenger Vessel Association (PVA) is a trade organization focused on issues and concerns relevant to owners and operators of passenger vessels and providers of maritime-related products and services in the U.S.

12) Currency Exchange

X-Rates.com
E-mail Address: feedback@x-rates.com
Web Address: www.x-rates.com
X-Rates.com allows visitors to view the day's currency exchange rates and to access charts demonstrating fluctuations in exchange rates of past months. Additionally, the site displays current photos of various currencies.

13) Economic Data & Research

Centre for European Economic Research (The, ZEW)
L 7, 1
Mannheim, 68161 Germany
Phone: 49-621-1235-01
Fax: 49-621-1235-224
E-mail Address: info@zew.de
Web Address: www.zew.de/en
Zentrum fur Europaische Wirtschaftsforschung, The Centre for European Economic Research (ZEW), distinguishes itself in the analysis of internationally comparative data in a European context and in the creation of databases that serve as a basis for scientific research. The institute maintains a special library relevant to economic research and provides external parties with selected data for the purpose of scientific research. ZEW also offers public events

and seminars concentrating on banking, business and other economic-political topics.

Economic and Social Research Council (ESRC)
Polaris House
North Star Ave.
Swindon, SN2 1UJ UK
Phone: 44-01793 413000
E-mail Address: esrcenquiries@esrc.ac.uk
Web Address: www.esrc.ac.uk
The Economic and Social Research Council (ESRC) funds research and training in social and economic issues. It is an independent organization, established by Royal Charter. Current research areas include the global economy; social diversity; environment and energy; human behavior; and health and well-being.

Eurostat
5 Rue Alphonse Weicker
Joseph Bech Bldg.
Luxembourg, L-2721 Luxembourg
Phone: 352-4301-33444
Fax: 352-4301-35349
E-mail Address: eurostat-pressoffice@ec.europa.eu
Web Address: www.epp.eurostat.ec.europa.eu
Eurostat is the European Union's service that publishes a wide variety of comprehensive statistics on European industries, populations, trade, agriculture, technology, environment and other matters.

Federal Statistical Office of Germany
Gustav-Stresemann-Ring 11
Wiesbaden, D-65189 Germany
Phone: 49-611-75-1
Fax: 49-611-72-4000
Web Address: www.destatis.de
Federal Statistical Office of Germany publishes a wide variety of nation and regional economic data of interest to anyone who is studying Germany, one of the world's leading economies. Data available includes population, consumer prices, labor markets, health care, industries and output.

India Brand Equity Foundation (IBEF)
Apparel House, Fl. 5
#519-22, Sector 44
Gurgaon, Haryana 122003 India
Phone: 91-124-4499600
Fax: 91-124-4499615
E-mail Address: info.brandindia@ibef.org
Web Address: www.ibef.org

India Brand Equity Foundation (IBEF) is a public-private partnership between the Ministry of Commerce and Industry, the Government of India and the Confederation of Indian Industry. The foundation's primary objective is to build positive economic perceptions of India globally. It aims to effectively present the India business perspective and leverage business partnerships in a globalizing marketplace.

National Bureau of Statistics (China)
57, Yuetan Nanjie, Sanlihe
Xicheng District
Beijing, 100826 China
Fax: 86-10-6878-2000
E-mail Address: info@gj.stats.cn
Web Address: www.stats.gov.cn/english
The National Bureau of Statistics (China) provides statistics and economic data regarding China's economy and society.

Organization for Economic Co-operation and Development (OECD)
2 rue Andre Pascal
Cedex 16
Paris, 75775 France
Phone: 33-1-45-24-82-00
Fax: 33-1-45-24-85-00
Web Address: www.oecd.org
The Organization for Economic Co-operation and Development (OECD) publishes detailed economic, government, population, social and trade statistics on a country-by-country basis for over 30 nations representing the world's largest economies. Sectors covered range from industry, labor, technology and patents, to health care, environment and globalization.

Statistics Bureau, Director-General for Policy Planning (Japan)
19-1 Wakamatsu-cho
Shinjuku-ku
Tokyo, 162-8668 Japan
Phone: 81-3-5273-2020
E-mail Address: toukeisoudan@soumu.go.jp
Web Address: www.stat.go.jp/english
The Statistics Bureau, Director-General for Policy Planning (Japan) and Statistical Research and Training Institute, a part of the Japanese Ministry of Internal Affairs and Communications, plays the central role of producing and disseminating basic official statistics and coordinating statistical work under the Statistics Act and other legislation.

Statistics Canada
150 Tunney's Pasture Driveway
Ottawa, ON K1A 0T6 Canada
Phone: 514-283-8300
Fax: 877-287-4369
Toll Free: 800-263-1136
E-mail Address: infostats@statcan.gc.ca
Web Address: www.statcan.gc.ca
Statistics Canada provides a complete portal to Canadian economic data and statistics. Its conducts Canada's official census every five years, as well as hundreds of surveys covering numerous aspects of Canadian life.

14) Entertainment & Amusement Associations-General

Airline Passenger Experience Association (APEX)
355 Lexington Ave., Fl. 15
New York, NY 10017-6603 USA
Phone: 212-297-2177
Fax: 212-370-9047
E-mail Address: info@apex.aero
Web Address: apex.aero
The Airline Passenger Experience Association (APEX), formerly the World Airline Entertainment Association (WAEA), is a worldwide network representing airlines, airline suppliers and related companies committed to excellence in inflight entertainment (IFE), communications and services.

American Association of Museums (AAM)
1575 Eye St., NW, Ste. 400
Washington, DC 20005 USA
Phone: 202-289-1818
Fax: 202-289-6578
Toll Free: 866-226-2150
E-mail Address: infocenter@aam-us.org
Web Address: www.aam-us.org
The American Association of Museums (AAM) seeks to enhance the ability of museums to serve the public interest.

International Association of Venue Managers (IAVM)
635 Fritz Dr., Ste. 100
Coppell, TX 75019-4442 USA
Phone: 972-906-7441
Fax: 972-906-7418
E-mail Address: vicki.hawarden@iavm.org
Web Address: www.iavm.org

The International Association of Venue Managers (IAVM), formerly the International Association of Assembly Managers (IAAM), is an international trade organization representing managers and suppliers of public assembly facilities, such as arenas, amphitheaters, auditoriums, convention centers/exhibit halls, performing arts venues, stadiums and university complexes.

International Special Events Society (ISES)
330 N. Wabash Ave., Ste. 2000
Chicago, IL 60611-4267 USA
Phone: 312-321-6853
Fax: 312-673-6953
Toll Free: 800-688-4737
E-mail Address: info@ises.com
Web Address: www.ises.com
The International Special Events Society (ISES) is comprised of over 7,200 professionals in over 38 countries representing special event planners and producers (from festivals to trade shows), caterers, decorators, florists, destination management companies, rental companies, special effects experts, tent suppliers, audio-visual technicians, event and convention coordinators, balloon artists, educators, journalists, hotel sales managers, specialty entertainers, convention center managers, and many more professional disciplines.

15) Food Service Industry Associations

International Flight Services Association (IFSA)
1100 Johnson Ferry Rd., Ste. 300
Atlanta, GA 30342 USA
Phone: 404-303-2969
E-mail Address: ejohnson@kellencompany.com
Web Address: www.ifsanet.com
The International Flight Services Association (IFSA), formerly the International Inflight Food Service Association, informs the public with respect to educational and career opportunities within the multi-billion-dollar inflight and railway food service industry. IFSA is managed by the Kellen Company.

16) Government Agencies-Hong Kong

GovHK
Phone: 852-183-5500
E-mail Address: enquiry@1835500.gov.hk
Web Address: www.gov.hk

GovHK is the one-stop portal of the Hong Kong Special Administrative Region (HKSAR) Government. GovHK features links to governmental agencies, information and services. It also organizes them by user groups (transport, business, trade) and subjects (education, youth, etc.).

17) Government Agencies-India

Ministry of Tourism-Gov. of India
Parliament St.
Transport Bhawan
New Delhi, 1 India
Phone: 91-11-23321380
Fax: 91-11-23710518
E-mail Address: webmaster-tour@nic.in
Web Address: www.tourism.gov.in
The Ministry of Tourism, hosted by the Government of India, includes information for travelers in India. The site provides city by city guides, information regarding airlines, hotels, railways and tour operators, locations of foreign consulates, events and a help desk.

18) Hotel, Hostel & Rental Information

AirportHotelGuide.com
Toll Free: 888-532-5115
Web Address: www.airporthotelguide.com
AirportHotelGuide.com lets travelers find airport hotels by location, covering 212 cities and more than 3,000 hotels.

19) Hotel/Lodging Associations

Alberta Hotel and Lodging Association (AHLA)
2707 Ellwood Dr. SW
Edmonton, AB T6X 0P7 Canada
Phone: 780-436-6112
Fax: 780-436-5404
Toll Free: 800-436-6112
Web Address: www.ahla.ca
The Alberta Hotel and Lodging Association (AHLA) seeks to provide an effective voice for approved travel accommodations in Alberta to both the government and the public.

American Hotel and Lodging Association
1250 I St., NW, Ste. 1100
Washington, DC 20005-3931 USA
Phone: 202-289-3100
Fax: 202-289-3199

E-mail Address: informationcenter@ahla.com
Web Address: www.ahla.com
The American Hotel and Lodging Association is a
federation of state lodging associations throughout
the U.S.

American Resort Development Association (ARDA)

1201 15th St. NW, Ste. 400
Washington, DC 20005-2842 USA
Phone: 202-371-6700
Fax: 202-289-8544
Toll Free: 855-939-1515
E-mail Address: consumer@arda-roc.org
Web Address: www.arda.org
The American Resort Development Association
(ARDA) represents the vacation ownership and resort
development industries, including timeshare owner
associations, vendors, suppliers and consultants. It
promotes the growth of industry through advocacy,
networking and business-to-business partnerships.

Asian American Hotel Owners Association (AAHOA)

1100 Abernathy Rd., Ste. 1100
Atlanta, GA 30328 USA
Phone: 404-816-5759
Fax: 404-816-6260
E-mail Address: info@aahoa.com
Web Address: www.aahoa.com
The Asian American Hotel Owners Association
(AAHOA) provides an active forum in which Asian
American hotel owners can communicate, interact
and secure their position within the hospitality
industry. Its membership consists of over 15,000
members who own more than 20,000 properties
across the U.S.

Australian Hotels Association

24 Brisbane Ave., Fl. 4
Barton, ACT 2600 Australia
Phone: 61-2-6273-4007
E-mail Address: admin@aha.org.au
Web Address: www.aha.org.au
The Australian Hotels Association seeks to protect
and develop the interests of Australia's hotel industry.

Bahamas Hotel & Tourism Association

Hotel's House
East Bay St., P.O. Box N-7799
Nassau, Bahamas
Phone: 242-502-4200
Fax: 242-502-4221

E-mail Address: bha@bahamashotels.org
Web Address: www.bhahotels.com
The Bahamas Hotel & Tourism Association seeks to
promote, increase and regulate tourism through the
cooperation, understanding and close association
among hotel owners and operators in the Bahamas.

Belgium Hotel Association

Blvd. Anspachlaan 111, B 1
Brussels, B-1000 Belgium
Phone: 32-2-513-78-14
Fax: 32-2-503-57-17
E-mail Address: y.roque@fedhorecabruxelles.be
Web Address: www.horecabruxelles.be
The Belgium Hotel Association represents members
of the hotel and catering industry in Belgium.

British Hospitality Association

Augustine House
6a Austin Friars
London, EC2N 2HA UK
Phone: 44-207-404-7744
E-mail Address: bha@bha.org.uk
Web Address: www.bha.org.uk
The British Hospitality Association represents the
hotel, restaurant and catering industry in the United
Kingdom. It promotes the interests of operators,
brands and owners across hotels, restaurants and food
service, serviced apartments, clubs and visitor
attractions.

Caribbean Hotel & Tourism Association (CHTA)

2655 Le Jeune Rd., Ste. 910
Coral Gables, FL 33134 USA
Phone: 305-443-3040
Fax: 305-675-7977
E-mail Address:
events@caribbeanhotelandtourism.com
Web Address: www.caribbeanhotelandtourism.com
The Caribbean Hotel &Tourism Association (CHTA)
is dedicated to excellence in hospitality, leadership in
marketing and sustainable growth in tourism, to the
benefit of its members and the wider Caribbean
community.

eHotelier.com

Web Address: www.ehotelier.com
eHotelier.com is an online portal dedicated to
meeting the needs of the international hoteliers'
community. Its site offers in-depth lists of industry
organizations, professional development
opportunities and industry news and insights.

European Hotel Managers Association (EHMA)
Via Nazionale 7
Rome, 00184 Italy
Phone: 39-06-481-8888
Fax: 39-06-4788-0826
E-mail Address: secretariat.ehma@ehma.com
Web Address: www.ehma.com
The European Hotel Managers Association (EHMA)
represents all hotel managers operating first-class and
luxury hotels of international repute. It is a
collaborative platform for information sharing,
professional development and networking.

**Federation of Hotel & Restaurant Associations of
India (FHRAI)**
23 Kasturba Gandhi Marg
B-82, 8th Fl., Himalaya House
New Delhi, 110 001 India
Phone: 011-40780780
Fax: 011-40780777
E-mail Address: fhrai@vsnl.com
Web Address: www.fhrai.com
The Federation of Hotel & Restaurant Associations
of India (FHRAI) is the apex body of the four
regional associations representing the hospitality
industry.

German Hotel Association
Keithstrasse 6
Berlin, 10787 Germany
Phone: 49-30-318048-0
Fax: 49-30-318048-28
E-mail Address: info@dehoga-berlin.de
Web Address: www.dehoga-berlin.de
The German Hotel Association is an organization that
represents the economic, social and professional
interests of the entire German hospitality industry.

Global Hotel Alliance
11819 Miami St., Fl. 3
Omaha, NE 68164 USA
Phone: 402-952-6668
Toll Free: 800-790-2200
E-mail Address: admin.corporate@gha.com
Web Address: www.gha.com
The Global Hotel Alliance is the world's largest
alliance of independent hotel groups, with 32 brands
and over 500 hotels across the world. The group's
web site provides destination information and tools
for customers and travel agents to book flights and
make hotel reservations.

Hotel Association of Canada (HAC)
130 Albert St., Ste. 1206
Ottawa, ON K1P 5G4 Canada
Phone: 613-237-7149
Fax: 613-237-8928
E-mail Address: info@hotelassociation.ca
Web Address: www.hotelassociation.ca
The Hotel Association of Canada (HAC) is a national
organization representing the hotel and lodging
industry in Canada, with membership comprising of
8,100 hotels, motels and resorts.

Hotel Association of India (HAI)
B-212-214 Somdutt Chamber 1
Bhikaji Cama Pl.
New Delhi, 110 066 India
Phone: 91-11-2617-1110
E-mail Address: info@hotelassociationofindia.com
Web Address: www.hotelassociationofindia.com
The Hotel Association of India (HAI) represents the
hospitality industry in India with over 300 hotels as
its members. The web site has information on the
whole spectrum of hotels and hotel groups in the
country.

Hotel Technology Next Generation
650 E. Algonquin Rd., Ste. 207
Schaumburg, IL 60173 USA
Phone: 847-303-5560
Web Address: www.htng.org
Hotel Technology Next Generation is a non-profit
trade association that facilitates the development of
next-generation, customer-centric technologies to
better meet the needs of the global hotel community.

**Hotels, Restaurants and Cafes in Europe
(HOTREC)**
111 Blvd. Anspach, Ste. 4
Brussels, B-1000 Belgium
Phone: 32-2-513-63-23
Fax: 32-2-502-41-73
E-mail Address: hotrec@hotrec.eu
Web Address: www.hotrec.eu
Hotels, Restaurants and Cafes in Europe (HOTREC)
brings together 42 national hospitality associations in
28 countries across Europe. The organization
monitors EU policies and brings the industries
concerns to EU decision-makers.

**International Hotel and Restaurant Association
(IHRA)**
42 Ave. General Guisan, Pully
Lausanne, 1009 Switzerland

Phone: 41-21-711-4283
E-mail Address: admin@ih-ra.com
Web Address: www.ih-ra.com
The International Hotel and Restaurant Association (IHRA) serves the needs of the international hospitality industry by monitoring issues that are raised by major international organizations involved in tourism.

Irish Hotels Federation (IHF)
13 Northbrook Rd.
Dublin, 6 Ireland
Phone: 353-1-497-6459
Fax: 353-1-497-4613
E-mail Address: info@ihf.ie
Web Address: www.ihf.ie
The Irish Hotels Federation (IHF) is the national organization of the hotel industry in Ireland. It represents over 1000 hotels and guesthouses and promotes and defends the interests of its members.

Japan Hotel Association (JHA)
Web Address: www.j-hotel.or.jp
The Japan Hotel Association (JHA) represents roughly 244 leading Japanese hotels and works to promote and develop the hotel industry in Japan.

Malaysian Association of Hotels
1 Ampang Ave.
C5-3, Wisma MAH, Jalan Ampang Utama 1/1,
Ampang Selangor, 68000 Malaysia
Phone: 603-4251-8477
Fax: 603-4252-8477
E-mail Address: info@hotels.org.my
Web Address: www.hotels.org.my
The Malaysian Association of Hotels seeks to unite Malaysian hotels into one representative body. The organization maintains partnership with both private and government sectors and has more than 700 members under 13 chapters.

Singapore Hotel Association (SHA)
17 Cantonment Rd.
Singapore, 089740 Singapore
Phone: 65-6513-0233
Fax: 65-6438-7170
E-mail Address: secretariat@sha.org.sg
Web Address: www.sha.org.sg
The Singapore Hotel Association's (SHA) mission is to promote the interest of its members within the hotel industry. Its membership consists of 148 hotels. The organization manages Hotel Reservations Pte

Ltd., which operates the hotel reservation counters at the airport.

Thai Hotels Association (THA)
203-209/3 Ratchadamnoen Klang Ave.
Bowonniwet, Pranakorn
Bangkok, 10200 Thailand
Phone: 66-2282-5277
Fax: 66- 2282-5278
E-mail Address: info@thaihotels.org
Web Address: www.thaihotels.org
The Thai Hotels Association (THA) is an organization of leading hotels aimed at promoting hotel industry in Thailand. It offers news, insights, latest business information to its 848 members.

20) Industry Research/Market Research

Forrester Research
60 Acorn Park Dr.
Cambridge, MA 02140 USA
Phone: 617-613-5730
E-mail Address: press@forrester.com
Web Address: www.forrester.com
Forrester Research is a publicly traded company that identifies and analyzes emerging trends in technology and their impact on business. Among the firm's specialties are the financial services, retail, health care, entertainment, automotive and information technology industries.

MarketResearch.com
11200 Rockville Pike, Ste. 504
Rockville, MD 20852 USA
Phone: 240-747-3093
Fax: 240-747-3004
Toll Free: 800-298-5699
E-mail Address: customerservice@marketresearch.com
Web Address: www.marketresearch.com
MarketResearch.com is a leading broker for professional market research and industry analysis. Users are able to search the company's database of research publications including data on global industries, companies, products and trends.

Plunkett Research, Ltd.
P.O. Drawer 541737
Houston, TX 77254-1737 USA
Phone: 713-932-0000
Fax: 713-932-7080

E-mail Address:
customersupport@plunkettresearch.com
Web Address: www.plunkettresearch.com
Plunkett Research, Ltd. is a leading provider of
market research, industry trends analysis and
business statistics. Since 1985, it has served clients
worldwide, including corporations, universities,
libraries, consultants and government agencies. At
the firm's web site, visitors can view product
information and pricing and access a large amount of
basic market information on industries such as
financial services, InfoTech, e-commerce, health care
and biotech.

STR Global (Smith Travel Research)
735 East Main St.
Hendersonville, TN 37075 USA
Phone: 615 824 8664
E-mail Address: info@str.com
Web Address: www.strglobal.com
In 2008, STR brought together Deloitte's
HotelBenchmark and The Bench to form STR
Global. STR Global offers monthly, weekly, and
daily STAR benchmarking reports to more than
38,000 hotel clients, representing nearly 5 million
rooms worldwide. STR Global and STR are now the
world's foremost sources of hotel performance trends
and will offer the definitive global hotel database and
development pipeline. STR is headquartered in
Hendersonville, TN, and STR Global is based in
London, with a satellite office in Singapore.

21) International Regulatory Organizations

International Civil Aviation Organization (ICAO)
999 University St.
Montreal, QC H3C 5 Canada
Phone: 514-954-8219
Fax: 514-954-6077
E-mail Address: icaohq@icao.int
Web Address: www.icao.int
The International Civil Aviation Organization
(ICAO) is an agency created by the United Nations
during the 1944 Convention on International Civil
Aviation in Chicago. The ICAO helps to develop
legally-binding national civil aviation regulations by
working with global industry and aviation
organizations and the 191 Signatory Stats from the
Convention to develop international Standards and
Recommended Practices (SARPs). Currently there
are over 10,000 SARPs that allow the over 100,000

daily flights to remain safe, efficient and secure
throughout all reaches of the world.

22) MBA Resources

MBA Depot
Web Address: www.mbadepot.com
MBA Depot is an online community and information
portal for MBAs, potential MBA program applicants
and business professionals.

23) Passports

American Passport Express
3340 Peachtree Rd., NE, Ste. 1800
Atlanta, GA 30326 USA
Toll Free: 800-455-5166
E-mail Address:
customerservice@americanpassport.com
Web Address: www.americanpassport.com
American Passport Express is a service that works
with the U.S. Passport Agency and foreign
consultancies to secure US passports and visas within
24 hours.

VIP Passports and Visa Services
2012 Louisiana St.
Houston, TX 77002 USA
Phone: 713-659-3767
Fax: 713-759-9119
Toll Free: 800-876-8472
E-mail Address: info@vippassports.com
Web Address: www.vippassports.com
VIP Passports and Visa Services is a 24-hour
passport and visa service that also provides birth
certificates and driving permits.

24) Pilots Associations

Aircraft Owners and Pilots Association (AOPA)
421 Aviation Way
Frederick, MD 21701 USA
Phone: 301-6959-2000
Fax: 301-695-2375
Toll Free: 800-872-2672
Web Address: www.aopa.org
The Aircraft Owners and Pilots Association, a not-
for-profit organization dedicated to general aviation,
was incorporated on May 15, 1939. Membership
totals over 400,000 private and professional pilots.

Airline Pilots Association (ALPA)
1625 Massachusetts Ave NW
Washington, DC 20036 USA
Phone: 703-689-2270
E-mail Address: media@alpa.org
Web Address: www.alpa.org
The Airline Pilots Association (ALPA) is an
association for professional airline pilots in the
United States, in Canada and internationally. ALPA
provides airline safety, security, pilot assistance,
representation and advocacy to its members.

**International Federation of Airline Pilots'
Associations (IFALPA)**
485 McGill St., Ste. 700
Montreal, Quebec H2Y 2H4 Canada
Phone: 514-419-1191
Fax: 514-419-1195
E-mail Address: ifalpa@ifalpa.org
Web Address: www.ifalpa.org
IFALPA is a non-political, non-profit making
organization which represents over 100,000 airline
pilots represented by over 100 Member Associations
from around the world. The Federation seeks to
achieve its objectives through the activities of its
component groups - elected Officers, appointed
Representatives, its expert Committees and the
Secretariat.

25) Privacy & Consumer Matters

Get Safe Online
Clifton House
Four Elms Rd.
Cardiff, CF24 1LE UK
E-mail Address: info@getsafeonline.org
Web Address: www.getsafeonline.org
Get Safe Online is a joint initiative between the U.K.
government, law enforcement, leading businesses and
the public sector. Its aim is to provide computer users
and small businesses with free, independent, user-
friendly advice that will allow them to use the
internet confidently, safely and securely. It provides
videos and online advice about such subjects as
identify theft, computer security and safe purchasing
practices for products, services and travel.

National Fraud Information Center (NFIC)
1701 K St. NW, Ste. 1200
c/o National Consumers League
Washington, DC 20006 USA
Phone: 202-835-3323
Fax: 202-835-0747

Toll Free: 800-876-7060
E-mail Address: info@nclnet.org
Web Address: www.fraud.org
The National Fraud Information Center (NFIC)
covers all types of fraud and provides information
about reporting fraud, as well as posting fraud alerts.

26) Railroad Associations

Association of American Railroads (AAR)
425 Third St., SW
Washington, DC 20024 USA
Phone: 202-639-2100
E-mail Address: media@aar.org
Web Address: www.aar.org
The Association of American Railroads (AAR) is an
industry association whose members include major
freight railroads in North America and Amtrak--the
U.S. passenger train operator. The association
represents the various interests of its railroad industry
members.

**Association of Train Operating Companies
(ATOC)**
200 Aldersgate St., Fl. 2
London, EC1A 4HD UK
Phone: 44-20-7841-8000
E-mail Address: enquiry@atoc.org
Web Address: www.atoc.org
ATOC represents Britain's passenger train companies
to the government, regulatory bodies, the media and
other opinion formers on transport policy issues.

**European Association for the Development of
Railway Transport (AEDTF)**
C/o Caisse d' Epargne des Alpes
10, rue Hebert
Grenoble, F-38000 France
E-mail Address: info@aedtf.org
Web Address: www.aedtf.org
The European Association for the Development of
Railway Transport (AEDTF) promotes the
development and maintenance of the European
railway system.

US High Speed Rail Association
10 G St. NE, Ste. 710
Washington, DC 20002 USA
Phone: 202-248-5001
E-mail Address: email@ushsr.com
Web Address: www.ushsr.com
The US High Speed Rail Association is a nonprofit
business group focused on encouraging the

development of a national high speed passenger rail system.

27) Real Estate Industry Associations

Corporate Housing Providers Association (CHPA)
9100 Purdue Rd., Ste. 200
Indianapolis, IN 46268 USA
Phone: 317-328-4631
Web Address: www.chpaonline.org
The Corporate Housing Providers Association (CHPA) is a trade association dedicated to supporting those in the corporate housing industry. The corporate housing industry, a segment of the lodging industry, provides a furnished apartment, condominium or house for rent on a short term basis, typically lasting 30 days or more. Corporate housing is usually used by those traveling for business, those relocating to a new area or those temporarily displaced.

28) Restaurant Industry Associations

American Culinary Federation (ACF)
180 Ctr. Place Way
St. Augustine, FL 32095 USA
Phone: 904-824-4468
Fax: 904-940-0741
Toll Free: 800-624-9458
E-mail Address: helpdesk@acfchefs.net
Web Address: www.acfchefs.org
The American Culinary Federation (ACF) promotes the professional image of American chefs worldwide through education among chefs at all levels, from apprentices to certified master chefs.

National Restaurant Association (NRA)
2055 L St. NW, Ste. 700
Washington, DC 20036 USA
Phone: 202-331-5900
Fax: 202-331-2429
Toll Free: 800-424-5156
Web Address: www.restaurant.org
The National Restaurant Association (NRA) is the leading business association for the restaurant industry. Its web site offers extensive industry information as well as government news, trends and membership perks.

29) Restaurant Industry Resources

Zagat Survey
76 9th Ave., Fl. 4
New York, NY 10011 USA
E-mail Address: feedback@zagat.com
Web Address: www.zagat.com
The Zagat Survey, acquired by Google in 2011, offers information, including ratings and reviews, on restaurants, hotels, nightlife and attractions throughout the U.S.

30) Spa Industry Associations

International Spa Association (ISPA)
2365 Harrodsburg Rd., Ste. A325
Lexington, KY 40504 USA
Phone: 859-226-4326
Fax: 859-226-4445
Toll Free: 888-651-4772
E-mail Address: ispa@ispastaff.com
Web Address: www.experienceispa.com
The International Spa Association (ISPA) is a leading professional organization for the spa industry. It provides educational and networking opportunities, promotes the value of the spa experience and speaks as the authoritative voice to foster professionalism and growth. ISPA represents health and wellness facilities and providers in over 70 countries.

31) Trade Associations-General

Associated Chambers of Commerce and Industry of India (ASSOCHAM)
5, Sardar Patel Marg
Chanakyapuri
New Delhi, 110 021 India
Phone: 91-11-4655-0555
Fax: 91-11-2301-7008
E-mail Address: assocham@nic.in
Web Address: www.assocham.org
The Associated Chambers of Commerce and Industry of India (ASSOCHAM) has a membership of more than 300 chambers and trade associations and serves members from all over India. It works with domestic and international government agencies to advocate for India's industry and trade activities.

BUSINESSEUROPE
168 Ave. de Cortenbergh
Brussels, 1000 Belgium
Phone: 32-2-237-65-11

Fax: 32-2-231-14-45
E-mail Address: main@businesseurope.eu
Web Address: www.businesseurope.eu
BUSINESSEUROPE is a major European trade
federation that operates in a manner similar to a
chamber of commerce. Its members are the central
national business federations of the 34 countries
throughout Europe from which they come.
Companies cannot become direct members of
BUSINESSEUROPE, though there is a support group
which offers the opportunity for firms to encourage
BUSINESSEUROPE objectives in various ways.

Ministry of External Affairs-Govt. of India
Bhawan 23-D, Janpath
New Delhi, 110 003 India
Phone: 91-11-23011127
Fax: 91-11-23013254
E-mail Address: eam@mea.gov.in
Web Address: www.mea.gov.in
The Government of India Ministry of External
Affairs website includes a list of international
organizations, trade and informational offices in India
as well as links to general information about India.

32) Trade Associations-Global

World Trade Organization (WTO)
Centre William Rappard
Rue de Lausanne 154
Geneva 21, CH-1211 Switzerland
Phone: 41-22-739-51-11
Fax: 41-22-731-42-06
E-mail Address: enquiries@wto.og
Web Address: www.wto.org
The World Trade Organization (WTO) is a global
organization dealing with the rules of trade between
nations. To become a member, nations must agree to
abide by certain guidelines. Membership increases a
nation's ability to import and export efficiently.

33) Transport for Animals

Animal Transportation Association
P.O. Box 3363
Warrenton, VA 20188 USA
E-mail Address:
info@animaltransportationassociation.org
Web Address:
www.animaltransportationassociation.org
The Animal Transportation Association is dedicated
to safe transport of animals by sea, air and land. The

website includes an online directory of professionals
involved in shipping animals as well as information
on transporting animals.

Transporting Live Animals Information
25 Cherokee Dr.
Saint Peters, MO 63376-3927 USA
Toll Free: 877-894-1960
E-mail Address: Service@traveloasis.com
Web Address: www.traveloasis.com/tranlivan.html
The Transporting Live Animals Information web site
details information on traveling with or transporting
live animals.

34) Transportation Industry Associations

**Airport Ground Transportation Association
(AGTA)**
1538 Powell Rd.
Powell, OH 43055 USA
Phone: 314-753-3432
Fax: 314-667-3850
E-mail Address: admin@agtaweb.org
Web Address: www.agtaweb.org
AGTA is an association of ground transportation
operators, airport authorities, and industry suppliers
dedicated to the continuous improvement of airport
ground transportation services for the airline
traveling public.

**Intelligent Transportation Society of America
(ITS America)**
1100 New Jersey Ave. SE, Ste. 850
Washington, DC 20003 USA
Phone: 202-484-4847
Toll Free: 800-374-8472
E-mail Address: info@itsa.org
Web Address: www.itsa.org
The Intelligent Transportation Society of America
(ITS America) is a nonprofit organization made up of
members interested in the development of intelligent
transportation systems technologies.

35) Transportation Industry Resources

**Research and Innovative Technology
Administration (RITA)**
U.S. Department of Transportation
1200 New Jersey Ave., SE
Washington, DC 20590 USA
Phone: 202-366-3492

Fax: 202-366-3759
Toll Free: 800-853-1351
E-mail Address: ritainfo@dot.gov
Web Address: www.rita.dot.gov
RITA coordinates the U.S. Department of
Transportation's research and education programs,
and is working to bring advanced technologies into
the transportation system. RITA also offers, via an
easy to use online database, vital transportation
statistics and analysis, and it supports national efforts
to improve education and training in transportation-
related fields.

36) Travel & Health

Center for Disease Control, CDC Travel
1600 Clifton Rd.
Atlanta, GA 30333 USA
Toll Free: 800-232-4636
E-mail Address: cdcinfo@cdc.gov
Web Address: wwwnc.cdc.gov/travel/
The CDC Travel section of the Center for Disease
Control's web site provides health information on
worldwide travel.

**International Association for Medical Assistance
to Travelers (IAMAT)**
1623 Military Rd., Ste. 279
Niagara Falls, NY 14304-1745 USA
Phone: 716-754-4883
Web Address: www.iamat.org
The International Association for Medical Assistance
to Travelers (IAMAT) aims to advise travelers about
health risks, the geographical distribution of diseases
and immunization requirements for all countries, as
well as to make competent medical care available to
travelers by western-trained, English-speaking
doctors.

International Travel and Health
Ave. Appia 20
Geneva, CH-1211 Switzerland
Phone: 41-22-791-2111
Fax: 41-22-791-3111
E-mail Address: hartlg@who.int
Web Address: www.who.int/ith
The International Travel and Health section of the
World Health Organization web site provides
information about health and international travel.

Travel Health Online
E-mail Address: thoeditor@shoreland.com
Web Address: www.tripprep.com

Travel Health Online provides information on health
issues related to specific destinations worldwide.

37) Travel Business & Professional Associations

American Society of Travel Agents (ASTA)
1101 King St., Ste. 200
Alexandria, VA 22314 USA
Phone: 703-739-2782
Toll Free: 800-275-2782
E-mail Address: askasta@asta.org
Web Address: www.asta.org
The American Society of Travel Agents (ASTA) is
one of the world's largest associations of travel
professionals.

**Association of Corporate Travel Executives
(ACTE)**
515 King St., Ste. 440
Alexandria, VA 22314 USA
Phone: 703-683-5322
Fax: 703-683-2720
E-mail Address: info@acte.org
Web Address: www.acte.org
The Association of Corporate Travel Executives
(ACTE) serves the specialized travel interests of
corporate purchasers and travel service suppliers
from nearly 50 countries.

Association of Retail Travel Agents (ARTA)
4320 North Miller Rd.
c/o Travel Destinations, Inc.
Scottsdale, AZ 85251-3606 USA
Fax: 866-743-2087
Toll Free: 866-369-8969
Web Address: www.arta.travel
The Association of Retail Travel Agents (ARTA) is
one of the largest nonprofit associations in North
America to exclusively represent travel agents.

**Association of Travel Marketing Executives
(ATME)**
P.O. Box 3176
West Tisbury, MA 02575 USA
Phone: 508-693-0550
Fax: 508-693-0115
E-mail Address: kzern@atme.org
Web Address: www.atme.org
The Association of Travel Marketing Executives
(ATME) is a global professional association of
senior-level travel marketing executives dedicated to

providing cutting-edge information, education and opportunities for meaningful networking with peers.

Council of Hotel and Restaurant Trainers (CHART)

741 Carleton Rd.
Westfield, NJ 07090 USA
Phone: 908.389.9277
Toll Free: 800-463-5918
E-mail Address: chart@chart.org
Web Address: www.chart.org
The Council of Hotel and Restaurant Trainers (CHART) is an association of professionals from national and international lodging and foodservice companies dedicated to training in the hospitality industry.

Hospitality Financial and Technology Professionals (HFTP)

11709 Boulder Ln., Ste. 110
Austin, TX 78726 USA
Phone: 512-249-5333
Fax: 512-249-1533
Toll Free: 800-646-4387
E-mail Address: Education@hftp.org
Web Address: www.hftp.org
Hospitality Financial and Technology Professionals (HFTP) is a organization that caters to the needs of the hospitality industry, principally to those individuals who perform accounting, financial, management or information technology activities.

Hospitality Sales and Marketing Association International (HSMAI)

7918 Jones Branch Dr., Ste. 300
McLean, VA 22102 USA
Phone: 703-506-3280
Fax: 703-506-3266
E-mail Address: info@hsmai.org
Web Address: www.hsmai.org
The Hospitality Sales and Marketing Association International (HSMAI) is an organization of sales and marketing professionals representing all segments of the hospitality industry.

Hotel Booking Agents Association (HBAA)

Chestnut Ste. Office 9
Guardian House
Godalming, Surrey GU7 2AE UK
Phone: 0845-603-3349
E-mail Address: executiveoffice@hbaa.org.uk
Web Address: www.hbaa.org.uk

The Hotel Booking Agents Association (HBAA) represents industry specialists for hotel and conference bookings in the U.K. and throughout the world, in all grades and classifications of hotels, lodges, apartments, suites and bed and breakfasts, as well as all types of conference and meeting venues.

Indian Association of Tour Operators

310 Padma Twr. II
22 Rajendra Pl.
New Delhi, 110 008 India
Phone: 91-11-25750034
Fax: 91-11-25750028
E-mail Address: iato@nda.vsnl.net.in
Web Address: www.iato.in
The Indian Association of Tour Operators website includes a list of important tourism links, a currency converting tool and travel information.

International Airlines Travel Agent Network (IATAN)

703 Waterford Way, Ste. 600
Miami, FL 33126 USA
Phone: 514-868-8858
Toll Free: 877-734-2826
E-mail Address: info@iatan.org
Web Address: www.iatan.org
The International Airlines Travel Agent Network (IATAN) seeks to promote professionalism; administer meaningful and impartial business standards; and provide cost-effective products, services and educational programs that benefit the travel industry.

International Association of Tour Managers (IATM)

397 Walworth Rd.
London, SE17 2AW UK
Phone: 44-20-7703-9154
Fax: 44-20-7703-0358
E-mail Address: iatm@iatm.co.uk
Web Address: www.iatm.co.uk
The International Association of Tour Managers (IATM) is as a forum for professional tour managers, promoting their services and representing their views at national, European Union and international levels.

International Executive Housekeepers Association (IEHA)

1001 Eastwind Dr., Ste. 301
Westerville, OH 43081-3361 USA
Phone: 614-895-7166
Fax: 614-895-1248

Toll Free: 800-200-6342
E-mail Address: excel@ieha.org
Web Address: www.ieha.org
The International Executive Housekeepers
Association (IEHA) is a professional organization for
executive housekeepers, directors of environmental
services, managers within the housekeeping or
custodial industries and suppliers of custodial goods
and services.

**International Society of Travel and Tourism
Educators (ISTTE)**
23220 Edgewater
St. Clair Shores, MI 48082 USA
Phone: 586-294-0208
Fax: 586-294-0208
E-mail Address: joannb@istte.org
Web Address: www.istte.org
The International Society of Travel and Tourism
Educators (ISTTE) is an international organization of
over 300 educators in travel, tourism and related
fields, representing all levels of educational
institutions, ranging from professional schools and
high schools to four-year colleges and graduate
institutions.

National Association for Travel Agents Singapore
120 Lower Delta Rd.
03-16 Cendex Ctr.
Singapore, 169208 Singapore
Phone: 65-6534-0187
Fax: 65-6534-4726
E-mail Address: feedback@natas.travel
Web Address: natas.travel
National Association for Travel Agents Singapore is
a membership organization which supports the travel
agents in Singapore.

National Concierge Association (NCA)
2920 Idaho Ave. N.
Minneapolis, MN 55427 USA
Phone: 612-317-2932
E-mail Address: info@ncakey.org
Web Address: www.ncakey.org
The National Concierge Association (NCA) strives to
provide networking, educational and promotional
opportunities to concierges throughout the world.

National Society of Minorities in Hospitality
6933 Commons Plz., Ste. 537
Chesterfield, VA 23832 USA
Phone: 703-549-9899
Fax: 703-997-7795

E-mail Address: hq@nsmh.org
Web Address: www.nsmh.org
The National Society of Minorities in Hospitality
strives to establish a working relationship between
the hospitality industry and minority students.

**Network of Executive Women in Hospitality, Inc.
(NEWH)**
P.O. Box 322
Shawano, WI 54166 USA
Fax: 800-693-6394
Toll Free: 800-593-6394
Web Address: www.newh.org
The Network of Executive Women in Hospitality,
Inc. (NEWH) brings together professionals from all
facets of the hospitality industry by providing
opportunities for education, professional
development and networking. Although primarily a
U.S.-based organization, NEWH does have
international chapters in Toronto and London.

Outside Sales Support Network (OSSN)
22410 68th Ave. E
Bradenton, FL 34211 USA
Phone: 941-322-9700
Fax: 941-981-1902
E-mail Address: info@ossn.com
Web Address: www.ossn.com
The Outside Sales Support Network (OSSN)
represents and supports independent travel agents,
home based travel agencies, independent contractors
and outside sales travel agents.

**Professional Association of Innkeepers
International (PAII)**
295 Seven Farms Dr., Ste. C-236
Charleston, SC 29492 USA
Phone: 856-310-1102
Fax: 856-895-0432
Toll Free: 800-468-7244
E-mail Address: jay@paii.org
Web Address: www.innkeeping.org
The Professional Association of Innkeepers
International (PAII) represents innkeepers worldwide
and acts as a forum for lodging-related issues.

Society of Incentive and Travel Executives
401 N. Michigan Ave.
Chicago, IL 60611-4267 USA
Phone: 312-321-5148
Fax: 312-527-6783
E-mail Address: site@siteglobal.com
Web Address: www.site-intl.org

The Society of Incentive and Travel Executives is a worldwide organization of business professionals dedicated to the recognition and development of motivational and performance improvement strategies in the travel industry.

The Travel Institute
945 Concord St.
Framingham, MA 01701 USA
Phone: 781-237-0280
Fax: 781-237-3860
Toll Free: 800-542-4282
E-mail Address: info@thetravelinstitute.com
Web Address: www.thetravelinstitute.com
The Travel Institute is an international nonprofit organization that educates and certifies travel industry professionals at all career stages.

Travel Agents Federation of India (TAFI)
509 The Ave., Int'l Airport Rd.
Opp Hotel Leela, Andheri (East)
Mumbai, 400 059 India
Phone: 022-28391111
Fax: 022-28255050
E-mail Address: info@tafi.in
Web Address: www.tafionline.com
The Travel Agents Federation of India (TAFI) is an organization formed to regulate the travel industry in India in accordance with sound business principles and ethics.

38) Travel Industry Associations

Association for Tourism and Leisure Education (ATLAS)
Travit
P.O. Box 3042
Arnhem, 6802-DA The Netherlands
Phone: 31-26-4452699
Fax: 31-26-4452932
E-mail Address: admin@atlas-euro.org
Web Address: www.atlas-euro.org
The Association for Tourism and Leisure Education (ATLAS) seeks to develop transnational educational initiatives in tourism and leisure.

Canadian Tourism Commission (CTC)
1055 Dunsmir St., Four Bentall Ctr., Ste. 1400
Vancouver, BC V7X 1L2 Canada
Phone: 604-638-8300
E-mail Address: pean.chantal@ctc-cct.ca
Web Address: www.corporate.canada.travel

The Canadian Tourism Commission (CTC) is a national organization whose purpose is the promotion of the Canadian tourism industry, as well as acting as a liaison between tourism companies and the Canadian government.

Central European Countries Travel Association (CECTA)
Barn Farm, Milcombe
Banbury, Oxfordshire OX15 4RU UK
Phone: 44-1295-724404
Fax: 44-1295-720089
E-mail Address: info@cecta.org
Web Address: www.cecta.org
The Central European Countries Travel Association (CECTA) brings together the collective interests of Austria, the Czech Republic, Germany, Hungary, Slovakia and Poland and their travel industries.

Convention Industry Council (CIC)
700 N. Fairfax St., Ste. 510
Alexandria, VA 22314 USA
Phone: 571-527-3116
Fax: 571-527-3105
E-mail Address: cichq@conventionindustry.org
Web Address: www.conventionindustry.org
The Convention Industry Council (CIC), founded in 1949, was established to facilitate the exchange of information between those within the meetings, conventions and exhibitions industries. Currently the CIC has 33 member organizations, representing more than 19,500 firms and over 103,500 individuals. Tools and services offered by the organization include an industry certification program, the Certified Meeting Professional (CMP); spearheading the development of accepted industry practices, the Accepted Practices Exchange (APEX) initiative; the Hall of Leaders program, recognizing industry pioneers; and the publishing of industry reference material.

Destination Marketing Association International
2025 M St. NW, Ste. 500
Washington, DC 20036 USA
Phone: 202-296-7888
Fax: 202-296-7889
E-mail Address: info@destinationmarketing.org
Web Address: www.destinationmarketing.org
The Destination Marketing Association International, formerly the International Association of Convention & Visitor Bureaus, strives to enhance the professionalism, effectiveness and image of destination management organizations worldwide. Its

members include professionals, industry partners, students and educators from roughly 15 countries.

Global Business Travel Association (GBTA)
123 N. Pitt St.
Alexandria, VA 22314 USA
Phone: 703-684-0836
Fax: 703-342-4324
E-mail Address: info@gbta.org
Web Address: www.gbta.org
The Global Business Travel Association (GBTA), formerly the National Business Travel Association, represents the interests of more than 5,000 corporate travel managers and travel service providers.

Hotel Electronic Distribution Network Association (HEDNA)
750 National Press Bldg., 529 14th St. NW
Washington, DC 20045 USA
Phone: 202-204-8400
Fax: 202-591-2445
E-mail Address: info@hedna.org
Web Address: www.hedna.org
The Hotel Electronic Distribution Network Association (HEDNA), as an association for the hotel industry, seeks to increase industry revenues and profitability from electronic distribution channels and to advance hotel electronic distribution.

International Association of Conference Centers (IACC)
243 N. Lindbergh Blvd.
St. Louis, MO 63141 USA
Phone: 314-993-8575
Fax: 314-993-8919
E-mail Address: info@iacconline.org
Web Address: www.iacconline.com
The International Association of Conference Centers (IACC) is a nonprofit, facilities-based organization founded to promote a greater awareness and understanding of the unique features of conference centers around the world.

International Council on Hotel, Restaurant and Institutional Education (I-CHRIE)
2810 N. Parham Rd., Ste. 230
Richmond, VA 23294 USA
Phone: 804-346-4800
Fax: 804-346-5009
E-mail Address: membership@chrie.org
Web Address: www.chrie.org
The International Council on Hotel, Restaurant and Institutional Education (I-CHRIE) is the global

advocate of hospitality and tourism education for schools, colleges and universities offering programs in hotel and restaurant management, foodservice management and culinary arts.

International Ecotourism Society (The, TIES)
P.O. Box 96503, #34145
Washington, DC 20090-6503 USA
Phone: 202-506-5033
Fax: 202-789-7279
E-mail Address: info@ecotourism.org
Web Address: www.ecotourism.org
The International Ecotourism Society promotes responsible travel to natural areas that conserves the environment and improves the well-being of local people by: creating an international network of individuals, institutions and the tourism industry; educating tourists and tourism professionals; influencing the tourism industry, public institutions and donors to integrate the principles of ecotourism into their operations and policies.

International Federation for IT and Travel & Tourism (IFITT)
Universitatsstr. 15
Innsbruck, A-6020 Austria
Phone: 44-1202-961517
E-mail Address: ifitt@ifitt.org
Web Address: www.ifitt.org
International Federation for IT and Travel & Tourism (IFITT) is an independent global community for the discussion, exchange and development of knowledge about the use and impact of new information and communication technologies in the travel and tourism industry.

International Festival and Events Association (IFEA)
2603 W. Eastover Terr.
Boise, ID 83706 USA
Phone: 208-433-0950
Fax: 208-433-9812
E-mail Address: beth@ifea.com
Web Address: www.ifea.com
The International Festival and Events Association (IFEA) provides professional development and fund-raising ideas to the special events industry.

International Gay and Lesbian Travel Association (IGLTA)
1201 NE 26th St., Ste. 103
Ft. Lauderdale, FL 33305 USA
Phone: 954-630-1637

Fax: 954-630-1652
E-mail Address: iglta@iglta.org
Web Address: www.iglta.com
The International Gay and Lesbian Travel Association (IGLTA) is the world's leading travel trade association committed to growing and enhancing its members' gay and lesbian tourism businesses through education, promotion and networking.

International Tourism Partnership
60 Gray's Inn Rd.
London, WC1X 8AQ UK
Phone: 44-20-7467-3600
E-mail Address: itp@iblf.org
Web Address: www.tourismpartnership.org
The International Tourism Partnership seeks to encourage the hospitality industry to make a valuable contribution to the countries and cultures in which they operate.

National Tour Association (NTA)
101 Prosperous Pl., Ste. 350
Lexington, KY 40509 USA
Phone: 859-264-6540
Fax: 859-266-6570
Toll Free: 800-682-8886
E-mail Address: NTAwashington@gmail.com
Web Address: www.ntaonline.com
The National Tour Association (NTA) is an association for travel professionals who have an interest in the packaged travel sector of the industry.

OpenTravel Alliance (OTA)
1740 Massachusetts Ave.
Boxborough, MA 01719 USA
Phone: 978-263-7606
Fax: 978-263-0696
E-mail Address: valyn.perini@opentravel.org
Web Address: www.opentravel.org
The OpenTravel Alliance (OTA) is a nonprofit organization comprised of major airlines, hoteliers, car rental companies, leisure suppliers, travel agencies, global distribution systems, technology providers and other interested parties working to create and implement industry-wide, open e-business specifications.

Pacific Asia Travel Association (PATA)
Pathumwan, 989 Rama I Rd.
Siam Twr., 28th Fl., Unit B1
Bangkok, 10330 Thailand
Phone: 66-2-658-2000

Fax: 66-2-658-2010
E-mail Address: communications@pata.org
Web Address: www.pata.org
The Pacific Asia Travel Association (PATA) is the recognized authority on Asia-Pacific travel and tourism.

Philippine Travel Agencies Association (PTAA)
12-1G EGI-Rufino Pl.
Taft cor. Sen Gil Puyat Ave.
Pasay City, 1300 Philippines
Phone: 632-552-0026
Fax: 632-552-0030
E-mail Address: ptaa@pldtdsl.net
Web Address: www.ptaa.org.ph
The Philippine Travel Agencies Association (PTAA) is the national travel association founded to foster unity in the travel industry in the Philippines and promote the welfare of its members and the traveling public.

Tourism Industry Association of Canada (TIAC)
116 Lisgar St., Ste. 600
Ottawa, ON K2P 0C2 Canada
Phone: 613-238-3883
Fax: 613-238-3878
E-mail Address: gxin@tiac.travel
Web Address: www.tiac.travel
The Tourism Industry Association of Canada (TIAC) is the national trade organization for the Canadian tourism industry, acting as a liaison between the government and the industry.

Travel and Tourism Research Association (TTRA)
5300 Lakewood Rd.
Whitehall, MI 49461 USA
Phone: 248-708-8872
Fax: 248-814-7150
E-mail Address: info@ttra.com
Web Address: www.ttra.com
The Travel and Tourism Research Association (TTRA) is a professional organization of providers and users of travel and tourism research, serving as a primary resource to the travel and tourism industry.

Travel Media Association of Canada (TMAC)
55 St. Clair Ave. W., Ste. 255
Toronto, ON M4V 2Y7 Canada
Phone: 416-934-0599
Fax: 416-967-6320
E-mail Address: info@travelmedia.ca
Web Address: www.travelmedia.ca

The Travel Media Association of Canada (TMAC) brings together Canadian travel media and tourism industry members to foster excellence, uphold ethical standards and promote professional development.

Travel Technology Initiative (TTI)
22 Green Court, The Green
Southwick, West Sussex BN42 4GS UK
Phone: 44-871-244-0747
Fax: 44-871-244-0747
E-mail Address: admin@tti.org
Web Address: www.tti.org
The Travel Technology Initiative (TTI) seeks to develop open standards for the exchange of electronic data between tour operators, airlines, ferries, hotels and rail operators.

U.S. Travel Association
1100 New York Ave. NW, Ste. 450
Washington, DC 20005-3934 USA
Phone: 202-408-8422
Fax: 202-408-1255
E-mail Address: feedback@ustravel.org
Web Address: www.ustravel.org
The U.S. Travel Association is the result of a merger between the Travel Industry Association (TIA) and the Travel Business Roundtable. It is a nonprofit association that represents and speaks for the common interests and concerns of all components of the U.S. travel industry.

United States Tour Operators Association (USTOA)
345 Seventh Ave., Ste. 1801
New York, NY 10001 USA
Phone: 212-599-6599
Fax: 212-599-6744
E-mail Address: information@ustoa.com
Web Address: www.ustoa.com
The United States Tour Operators Association (USTOA) is a professional association representing the tour operator industry.

Vacation Rental Managers Association (VRMA)
9100 Purdue Rd., Ste. 200
Indianapolis, IN 46268 USA
Phone: 317-454-8315
Fax: 317-454-8316
E-mail Address: vrma@vrma.com
Web Address: www.vrma.com
The Vacation Rental Managers Association (VRMA) is a professional trade association for the short-term property management industry.

World Tourism Organization (UNWTO)
Capitan Haya 42
Madrid, 28020 Spain
Phone: 34-91-567-8100
Fax: 34-91-571-3733
E-mail Address: omt@unwto.org
Web Address: www2.unwto.org
The World Tourism Organization (UNWTO) is a special agency of the UN that serves as a global forum for tourism policy issues and as a practical source of tourism knowledge and experience.

World Travel and Tourism Council (WTTC)
The Harlequin Bldg.
65 Southwalk St.
London, SE1 OHR UK
Phone: 44-20-7481-8007
Fax: 44-20-7488-1008
Web Address: www.wttc.org
The World Travel and Tourism Council (WTTC) is a forum for global business leaders in the travel and tourism industries.

39) Travel Reservations & Tickets Online

Expedia.com
333 108th Ave. NE
Bellevue, WA 98004 USA
Phone: 404-728-8787
Toll Free: 800-397-3342
E-mail Address: Press@expedia.com
Web Address: www.expedia.com
Expedia.com is a world leader in online travel service, through its travel products and research and planning capabilities.

Hotels.com
10440 N. Central Expy., Ste. 400
Dallas, TX 75231 USA
Phone: 214-361-7311
Toll Free: 800-246-8357
Web Address: www.hotels.com
Hotels.com is a specialized provider of discount accommodations worldwide.

Hotwire.com
655 Montgomery St., Ste. 600
San Francisco, CA 94111 USA
Phone: 415-520-1680
Toll Free: 866-468-9473
Web Address: www.hotwire.com

Hotwire.com offers travelers a quick and easy way to get better deals on airline tickets, hotel reservations and car rentals.

Kayak
55 N. Water St., Ste. 1
Norwalk, CT 06854 USA
Phone: 203-899-3100
Fax: 203-899-3125
E-mail Address: privacy-officer@kayak.com
Web Address: www.kayak.com
Kayak is a travel search engine. It searches hundreds of travel sites from all over the world to provide the information in an easy-to-use display that enables the user to refine and choose the exact result he or she wants. The user is then sent directly to the source to make a purchase.

MileageManager
1930 Frequent Flyer Pt.
Colorado Springs, CO 80915 USA
Phone: 719-597-8889
Fax: 719-597-6855
Toll Free: 800-414-1187
E-mail Address:
company@frequentflyerservices.com
Web Address: www.mileagemanager.com
MileageManager helps clients to use their airline miles to get to where they want to go. It charges a monthly subscription fee.

Orbitz.com
500 W. Madison St., Ste. 1000
Chicago, IL 60661 USA
Phone: 312-894-5000
Fax: 312-894-5001
Toll Free: 888-656-4546
E-mail Address: privacy@orbitz.com
Web Address: www.orbitz.com
Orbiz.com provides access to a variety of low fares and rates on airline tickets, rental cars, hotels, vacation packages and other travel products to be booked online.

Priceline.com
800 Connecticut Ave.
Norwalk, CT 06854 USA
Phone: 212-444-0022
Toll Free: 800-774-2354
Web Address: www.priceline.com
Priceline.com is an online travel center that allows users to name their own prices on airfare, hotels, rental cars, vacations and cruises.

Seat Guru
E-mail Address: helpfeedback@seatguru.com
Web Address: www.seatguru.com
Seat Guru provides specific information on the best and worst seating for major airlines. Its seat maps cover 700 different aircraft configurations at 100 airlines. The service is owned by TripAdvisor LLC.

Travelocity.com
3150 Sabre Dr.
Southlake, TX 76092 USA
Phone: 682-605-1000
Toll Free: 888-872-8356
Web Address: www.travelocity.com
Travelocity.com provides consumers with online tools and information for booking flights, hotels and other travel plans.

40) Travel Resources

Business Travel News
116 W. 32nd St., Fl. 14
New York, NY 10001 USA
Phone: 847-564-5941
Fax: 847-291-4816
Toll Free: 877-705-8889
E-mail Address: nbtn@omeda.com
Web Address: www.businesstravelnews.com
Business Travel News is a news and research web site for businesses that manage travel.

China National Tourist Office (CNTO)
370 Lexington Ave., Ste. 912
New York, NY 10017 USA
Phone: 1-212-760-8218
Fax: 1-212-760-8809
E-mail Address: ny@cnto.org
Web Address: www.cnto.org
The China National Tourist Office (CNTO) is the U.S. office and overseas representative of the China National Tourism Administration (CNTA) in Beijing.

Chinaculture.org
11 Huixin Dongjie, Chaoyang District
6/F, B3, Ziguang Bldg.
Beijing, 100025 China
Phone: 8610-6499-5726
Fax: 8610-8488-3500
E-mail Address: chinaculture@chinadaily.com.cn
Web Address: www1.chinaculture.org
Chinaculture.org offers broad access to up-to-date cultural news about China with information about Chinese history, culture, politics and the economy.

The site was developed under the guidance of the Ministry of Culture and offers links to travel information, art festivals and events, governmental sites and trade links relating to art and cultural exports.

Citysearch
8833 W. Sunset Blvd.
W. Hollywood, CA 90069 USA
Toll Free: 800-611-4827
E-mail Address: cscs@citysearch.com
Web Address: www.citysearch.com
Citysearch offers information on hotels, retail, professional services, restaurants, events and night life in cities around the world.

CNN, Travel
One CNN Ctr.
Atlanta, GA 30303 USA
Phone: 404-827-1500
E-mail Address: privacy.cnn@turner.com
Web Address: www.cnn.com/travel
CNN's travel site offers travel tips, columns and news stories.

Cornell Hotel and Restaurant Administration Quarterly
537 Statler Hall
Ithaca, NY 14853-6902 USA
Phone: 607-255-3025
Fax: 607-254-2922
E-mail Address: cq@sha.cornell.edu
Web Address:
www.hotelschool.cornell.edu/research/chr/pubs/quarterly/
Cornell Hotel and Restaurant Administration Quarterly is the online version of Cornell's collection of articles for hospitality managers.

Fodors, LLC
Web Address: www.fodors.com
The Fodor's web site, which is powered by Expedia.com and is from the popular travel-guide publisher, offers numerous travel resources and online guides. Fodor's is a registered trademark of Penguin Randon House.

FreeTranslation
Clivemont Rd
SDL Globe House
Maidenhead, SL6 7DY UK
Phone: 44-1628-760610
Fax: 44-1628-760611

Web Address: www.freetranslation.com
FreeTranslation provides a free service to automatically translate web pages or blocks of text through its online tools. The group also offers business quality translations in 150 languages for larger, professional projects.

Hong Kong Tourism Board
9-11/F Citicorp Ctr.
18 Whitefield Rd.
North Point, Hong Kong Hong Kong
Phone: 852-2807-6543
Fax: 852-2806-0303
E-mail Address: info@hktb.com
Web Address: www.discoverhongkong.com
The Hong Kong Tourism Board promotes Hong Kong as a travel destination. The site contains information for travelers including how to plan the trip, The site also lists attractions and events, as well as conventions and exhibition facilities.

Journal of Travel Research (JTR)
2455 Teller Rd.
Thousand Oaks, CA 91320 USA
Phone: 805-410-7763
Fax: 805-499-8096
Toll Free: 800-818-7243
E-mail Address: journals@sagepub.com
Web Address: jtr.sagepub.com
The Journal of Travel Research (JTR), a segment of SageJournals Online, comments on the latest developments in travel research and marketing that reflect the worldwide importance of tourism both economically and socially.

Lodging Magazine
385 Oxford Valley Rd., Ste. 420
Yardley, PA 19067 USA
Phone: 215-321-9662
Fax: 215-321-5124
E-mail Address: sdowney@lodgingmagazine.com
Web Address: www.lodgingmagazine.com
Lodging Magazine offers information for the global lodging industry, including subjects such as marketing, technology, food and beverages, operations, governmental affairs and finance.

Meeting News
100 Lighting Way
Secaucus, NY 07094-3626 USA
Phone: 202-902-2000
E-mail Address: lbuchanan@ntmllc.com
Web Address: www.meetingnews.com

Meeting News is an online source of news and information for meeting, convention, incentive and trade show professionals.

National Portal of India
A-Block, CGO Complex, Lodhi Rd.
Fl. 3, National Informatics Ctr.
New Delhi, 110 003 India
E-mail Address: indiaportal@gov.in
Web Address: www.india.gov.in
The National Portal of India provides information about India and includes various links to other government portals and other websites. It offers general information for citizens, visitors and businesses.

Nonrev Network (The)
Toll Free: 800-780-5733
Web Address: www.nonrev.net
The Nonrev Network is geared toward airline passengers who do not produce revenue for the airline, such as airline employees. It offers information on flights, hotels and worldwide destinations which can be of use for any traveler.

Singapore Tourism Board (STB)
Tourism Ct.
1 Orchard Spring Ln.
Singapore, Singapore
Phone: 65-6736-6622
Fax: 65-6736-9423
Toll Free: 800-736 6638
E-mail Address: feedback@stb.gov.sg
Web Address: www.stb.gov.sg
The Singapore Tourism Board (STB) is an economic development agency for one of Singapore's key service sectors - tourism. The mission of the Board is to develop and champion tourism, so as to build the sector into a key driver of economic growth for Singapore.

Travel Industry Indicators
P.O. Box 9009
St. Augustine, FL 32085 USA
Phone: 850-559-0012
E-mail Address: brianlondon@travelindicators.com
Web Address: www.travelindicators.com
Travel Industry Indicators is a monthly executive newsletter that monitors the rapidly changing travel marketplace.

Travel Weekly
100 Lighting Way
Secaucus, NJ 07094-3626 USA
Phone: 201-902-2000
Fax: 201-902-2034
E-mail Address: TWeditorial@ntmllc.com
Web Address: www.travelweekly.com
TravelWeekly.com, the web site for the Travel Weekly newspaper, offers news for the global travel industry.

41) Traveling for People with Disabilities

Society for Accessible Travel and Hospitality (SATH)
347 5th Ave., Ste. 605
New York, NY 10016 USA
Phone: 212-447-7284
Fax: 212-447-1928
E-mail Address: sathinfo@sath.org
Web Address: www.sath.org
The Society for Accessible Travel and Hospitality (SATH) is a nonprofit educational organization that actively represents travelers with disabilities.

42) Travel-Local Transportation, Bus & Car Rental

American Automobile Association (AAA)
1000 AAA Dr., Box 28
Heathrow, FL 32746 USA
Phone: 407-44-7000
Fax: 407-444-8030
Toll Free: 800-222-1134
Web Address: www.aaa.com
The American Automobile Association (AAA) offers members roadside assistance, financial services, car rental, a travel agency and a variety of other services.

American Bus Association (ABA)
111 K St. NE, Fl. 9
Washington, DC 20002 USA
Phone: 202-842-1645
Fax: 202-842-0850
E-mail Address: abainfo@buses.org
Web Address: www.buses.org
The American Bus Association (ABA), the trade association of the intercity bus industry, represents the interests of Washington, D.C.'s motor coach industry.

American Public Transportation Association (APTA)
1300 I St. NW, Ste. 1200
Washington, DC 20005 USA
Phone: 202-496-4800
Fax: 202-496-4324
E-mail Address: rsheridan@apta.com
Web Address: www.apta.com
APTA is a nonprofit international association of more than 1,500 member organizations including public transportation systems; planning, design, construction and finance firms; product and service providers; academic institutions; and state associations and departments of transportation. APTA members serve more than 90 percent of persons using public transportation in the United States and Canada.

Association of Car Rental Industry Systems Standards (ACRISS)
Priory Cottage
10 The Close, Ratton
Eastbourne, East Sussex BN20 9BW UK
Phone: 44-1323-508093
E-mail Address: info@acriss.org
Web Address: www.acriss.org
Association of Car Rental Industry Systems Standards (ACRISS) is a car rental association concerned with the development, implementation and maintenance of common standards for use when booking car rental services in Europe through automated booking systems.

International Automobile Driver's Club (IADC)
55 Grymes Hill Rd.
Staten Island, NY 10301 USA
Phone: 718-238-0623
Fax: 718-238-0623
E-mail Address: iadc.club2010@gmail.com
Web Address: www.iadc-club.com
The International Automobile Driver's Club (IADC) allows visitors to apply for an international driver's license online.

United Motorcoach Association (UMA)
113 S. West St., Fl. 4
Alexandria, VA 22314-2824 USA
Fax: 703-838-2950
Toll Free: 800-424-8262
E-mail Address: info@uma.org
Web Address: www.uma.org
The United Motorcoach Association (UMA) is North America's largest association of professional bus and motorcoach companies.

43) Travel-Rail

Amtrak
60 Massachusetts Ave., NE
Washington, DC 20002 USA
Toll Free: 800-872-7245
Web Address: www.amtrak.com
Amtrak operates a nationwide rail network, serving more than 500 destinations in 46 states on 21,000 miles of routes, with more than 20,000 employees. Its web site offers information on schedules and Amtrak vacations.

Rail Europe
44 S. Broadway, Fl. 11
White Plains, NY 10601-4411 USA
Phone: 914-681-7216
Fax: 914-681-3211
Toll Free: 800-622-8600
Web Address: www.raileurope.com
Rail Europe offers information and deals on rail, air and car travel and vacation packages.

Railpass.com
13-25 Main St., Unit 4A
Franklin, MA 02038 USA
E-mail Address: service@railpass.com
Web Address: www.railpass.com
Railpass.com offers European rail passes for sale, as well as information on European travel.

44) Travel-Vacation Home Rental & Exchange

HomeAway
Phone: 512-493-0375
E-mail Address: ebuesing@homeaway.com
Web Address: www.homeaway.com
HomeAway (www.homeaway.com) connects homeowners and property managers with travelers who seek vacation rental homes as an alternative to hotels. The site has the largest and most diverse selection of homes around the world, with more than 215,000 properties across 120 countries.

Intervac International
30 Corte San Fernando
Tiburon, CA 94920 USA
Toll Free: 800-756-4663
E-mail Address: info@intervacus.com
Web Address: www.intervac-online.com

Intervac International offers the world's largest online home exchange service, allowing members to temporarily swap lifestyles with families from over fifty countries.

45) U.S. Government Agencies

Aviation Consumer Protection Division, Department of Transportation (DOT)
1200 New Jersey Ave., SE
Washington, DC 20590 USA
Phone: 202-366-2220
Web Address: www.dot.gov/airconsumer
The Aviation Consumer Protection Division of the Department of Transportation (DOT) receives complaints from the public on aviation consumer issues, verifies compliance with aviation consumer protection requirements and makes available to the public information on pertinent consumer matters.

Bureau of Consular Affairs
2201 C St. NW
Washington, DC 20520 USA
Phone: 202-647-2492
Toll Free: 800-409-9926
E-mail Address: CAPressRequests@state.gov
Web Address: travel.state.gov
The Bureau of Consular Affairs web site is maintained by the State Department and provides travel advisories and other travel-based services, such as issuing passports and visas.

Bureau of Economic Analysis (BEA)
1441 L St. NW
Washington, DC 20230 USA
Phone: 202-606-9900
E-mail Address: customerservice@bea.gov
Web Address: www.bea.gov
The Bureau of Economic Analysis (BEA), an agency of the U.S. Department of Commerce, is the nation's economic accountant, preparing estimates that illuminate key national, international and regional aspects of the U.S. economy.

Bureau of Labor Statistics (BLS)
2 Massachusetts Ave. NE
Postal Square Building
Washington, DC 20212-0001 USA
Phone: 202-691-5200
Fax: 202-691-7890
Toll Free: 800-877-8339
E-mail Address: blsdata_staff@bls.gov
Web Address: stats.bls.gov

The Bureau of Labor Statistics (BLS) is the principal fact-finding agency for the Federal Government in the field of labor economics and statistics. It is an independent national statistical agency that collects, processes, analyzes and disseminates statistical data to the American public, U.S. Congress, other federal agencies, state and local governments, business and labor. The BLS also serves as a statistical resource to the Department of Labor.

Bureau of Transportation Statistics (BTS)
1200 New Jersey Ave. SE
Washington, DC 20590 USA
Phone: 202-366-3492
Fax: 202-366-3759
Toll Free: 800-853-1351
E-mail Address: RITAinfo@dot.gov
Web Address: www.rita.dot.gov/bts/
The Bureau of Transportation Statistics (BTS), part of the Research and Innovative Technology Administration (RITA) of the U.S. Department of Transportation (US DOT), provides comprehensive statistics on all aspects of the transportation industry.

FAA Air Traffic Control System Command Center
800 Independence Ave. SW
Washington, DC 20591 USA
Toll Free: 866-835-5322
Web Address: www.fly.faa.gov
The FAA Air Traffic Control System Command Center page from the FAA's web site shows information on flight status and delays and is updated every five minutes.

Federal Aviation Administration (FAA)
800 Independence Ave. SW
Washington, DC 20591 USA
Toll Free: 866-835-5322
Web Address: www.faa.gov
The Federal Aviation Administration (FAA) is the U.S. Government agency with primary responsibility for the safety of civil aviation. It regulates the airline industry as well as private aviation.

Federal Highway Administration (FHWA)
1200 New Jersey Ave. SE
Washington, DC 20590 USA
Phone: 202-366-4000
Toll Free: 800-424-9071
E-mail Address: hotline@oig.dot.gov
Web Address: www.fhwa.dot.gov

The Federal Highway Administration (FHWA) is the division of the Department of Transportation that provides federal financial resources and technical assistance to state and local governments for constructing, preserving and improving the national highway system.

Federal Transit Administration (FTA)
1200 New Jersey Ave. SE
Washington, DC 20590 USA
Phone: 202-366-4043
Toll Free: 866-377-8642
Web Address: www.fta.dot.gov
The Federal Transit Administration (FTA) provides financial assistance to develop new transit systems and improve, maintain, and operate existing systems.

National Transportation Safety Board (NTSB)
490 L'Enfant Plz. SW
Washington, DC 20594 USA
Phone: 202-314-6000
Web Address: www.ntsb.gov
The National Transportation Safety Board (NTSB) is an independent federal agency charged by Congress with investigating every civil aviation accident in the United States and significant accidents in other modes of transportation and issuing safety recommendations aimed at the prevention of future accidents.

Office of Airline Information (OAI)
1200 New Jersey Ave. SE
Washington, DC 20590 USA
E-mail Address: oai-support@bts.gov
Web Address:
www.rita.dot.gov/bts/sites/rita.dot.gov.bts/files/subject_areas/airline_information/sources/index.html
The Office of Airline Information (OAI) provides comprehensive financial, market and traffic statistical economic data on individual air carrier operations and the air transportation industry.

Overseas Security Advisory Council (OSAC)
U.S. Department of State
Bureau of Diplomatic Security
Washington, DC 20522-2008 USA
Phone: 571-345-2223
Fax: 571-345-2238
Web Address: www.osac.gov
The Overseas Security Advisory Council (OSAC) exists to foster the exchange of security-related information between the U.S. Government and American private-sector agencies operating abroad.

U.S. Census Bureau
4600 Silver Hill Rd.
Washington, DC 20233-8800 USA
Phone: 301-763-4636
Toll Free: 800-923-8282
Web Address: www.census.gov
The U.S. Census Bureau is the official collector of data about the people and economy of the U.S. Founded in 1790, it provides official social, demographic and economic information. In addition to the Population & Housing Census, which it conducts every 10 years, the U.S. Census Bureau numerous other surveys annually.

U.S. Customs & Border Protection (CBP)
1300 Pennsylvania Ave. NW
Washington, DC 20229 USA
Phone: 202-325-8000
Toll Free: 877-227-5511
Web Address: www.cbp.gov
The U.S. Customs & Border Protection (CBP), a part of the Department of Homeland Security, controls the import and export of all goods. Its web site contains information pertaining to international trade, trade programs, trade agreements, quotas, ports of entry, regulations and commodity status reports.

U.S. Department of Commerce (DOC)
1401 Constitution Ave. NW
Washington, DC 20230 USA
Phone: 202-482-2000
E-mail Address: TheSec@doc.gov
Web Address: www.commerce.gov
The U.S. Department of Commerce (DOC) regulates trade and provides valuable economic analysis of the economy.

U.S. Department of Labor (DOL)
200 Constitution Ave. NW
Frances Perkins Bldg.
Washington, DC 20210 USA
Toll Free: 866-487-2365
Web Address: www.dol.gov
The U.S. Department of Labor (DOL) is the government agency responsible for labor regulations.

U.S. Department of State Passport Services
2201 C St. NW
Washington, DC 20520 USA
Phone: 202-647-4000
Toll Free: 877-487-2778
E-mail Address: NPIC@state.gov

Web Address:
travel.state.gov/passport/passport_1738.html
The U.S. Department of State's Passport Services
web site offers information on applying for a U.S.
passport.

U.S. Department of Transportation (DOT)
1200 New Jersey Ave. SE
Washington, DC 20590 USA
Phone: 202-366-4000
Web Address: www.dot.gov
The U.S. Department of Transportation (DOT) is the
Government agency in charge of all aspects of the
U.S. transportation system. It has agencies dealing
with all aspects of transportation, including
highways; hazardous materials transportation;
pipelines; railroads; marine transportation; aviation;
and public transit systems, such as buses and
subways. It also has agencies researching
transportation statistics, new transportation
technologies and even the eventual impact of
environmental change on transportation. The DOT
web site has links to citizen traveler resource, as well
as resources for transportation businesses and mainly
transportation-related government grants.

**U.S. Department of Transportation (US DOT)-
Intelligent Transportation Systems (ITS)**
1200 New Jersey Ave., SE, HOIT
Washington, DC 20590 USA
Toll Free: 866-367-7487
E-mail Address: ITSHelp@dot.gov
Web Address: www.its.dot.gov
The U.S. Department of Transportation's (US DOT)
Intelligent Transportation System (ITS) program was
established to support the development of intelligent
transportation systems through the integration of
intelligent vehicles and an intelligent infrastructure.
The Federal ITS program supports the overall
advancement of ITS through investments in major
initiatives, exploratory studies and a crosscutting core
program.

U.S. Securities and Exchange Commission (SEC)
100 F St. NE
Washington, DC 20549 USA
Phone: 202-942-8088
Web Address: www.sec.gov
The U.S. Securities and Exchange Commission
(SEC) is a nonpartisan, quasi-judicial regulatory
agency responsible for administering federal
securities laws. These laws are designed to protect
investors in securities markets and ensure that they

have access to disclosure of all material information
concerning publicly traded securities. Visitors to the
web site can access the EDGAR database of
corporate financial and business information.

46) U.S. Government Travel Sites

Bureau of Consular Affairs-Travel Publications
Office of Inspector General
P.O. Box 9778
Arlington, VA 22219 USA
Phone: 202-647-3320
Toll Free: 800-409-9926
E-mail Address: oighotline@state.gov
Web Address:
travel.state.gov/travel/travel_1744.html
Bureau of Consular Affairs-Travel Publications web
site, managed by the U.S. State Department, offers
various documents covering topics ranging from
crises abroad to tips for women traveling alone.

47) Weather Information

Intellicast
400 Minuteman Rd.
Andover, MA 01810 USA
Phone: 978-983-6500
Web Address: www.intellicast.com
Intellicast provides information on current weather
and future conditions to help plan weather-sensitive
activities.

**National Weather Service - Aviation Weather
Center (AWC)**
7220 NW 101st Tetr., Rm. 118
Kansas City, MO 64153-2371 USA
E-mail Address: ncep.awc.avwx@noaa.gov
Web Address: www.aviationweather.gov
The National Weather Service's Aviation Weather
Center (AWC) enhances aviation safety by providing
weather information, forecasts and warnings.

National Weather Service (NWS)
1325 E. West Hwy.
Silver Spring, MD 20910 USA
E-mail Address: w-nws.webmaster@noaa.gov
Web Address: www.nws.noaa.gov
The National Weather Service (NWS) provides
information on weather patterns and forecasts
worldwide.

Weather Channel Online
P.O. Box 724554
Atlanta, GA 31139 USA
Web Address: www.weather.com
The Weather Channel's web site offers information
on weather by city and can be customized by the
user.

Yahoo! Weather
701 1st Ave.
Sunnyvale, CA 94089 USA
Phone: 408-349-3300
Fax: 408-349-3301
Web Address: weather.yahoo.com
The Yahoo! Weather web site allows users to search
for weather conditions worldwide by city or zip code.

48) Youth Travel Associations

GoAbroad.com
2850 McClelland Dr.
Ste. 2700
Ft. Collins, CO 80525 USA
Phone: 720-570-1702
Fax: 720-570-1703
E-mail Address: info@goabroad.com
Web Address: www.goabroad.com
Goabroad.com helps visitors find study abroad
programs, internships, language schools, college
degrees, jobs and teaching programs around the
world. It also provides a newsletter, travel guides and
assistance with TEFL certification.

**World Youth Student & Educational Travel
Confederation (WYSET)**
Keizersgracht 174-176
Amsterdam, DW 1016 The Netherlands
Phone: 31-20-421-2800
Web Address: www.wysetc.org
The World Youth Student & Educational Travel
Confederation (WYSET) is a leading global
membership association and trade forum dedicated to
the youth travel industry.

Chapter 4

THE TRAVEL 300:
WHO THEY ARE AND HOW THEY WERE CHOSEN

Includes Indexes by Company Name, Industry & Location

The companies chosen to be listed in PLUNKETT'S AIRLINE, HOTEL & TRAVEL INDUSTRY ALMANAC comprise a unique list. THE TRAVEL 300 (the actual count is 330 companies) were chosen specifically for their dominance in the many facets of travel and tourism in which they operate. Complete information about each firm can be found in the "Individual Profiles," beginning at the end of this chapter. These profiles are in alphabetical order by company name.

THE TRAVEL 300 includes leading companies from all parts of the United States as well as Europe, Asia/Pacific, Canada, Mexico and South America, and from all travel and tourism related industry segments: travel agencies; transportation carriers of all types, including major airlines, railroads and cruise lines; specialized service companies that are vital to the travel and tourism field, such as hotel management companies and online reservations firms; and many others.

Simply stated, the list contains 330 of the largest, most successful, fastest growing firms in travel and related industries in the world. To be included in our list, the firms had to meet the following criteria:

1) Generally, these are corporations based in the U.S.; however, the headquarters of 166 firms are located in other nations.

2) Prominence, or a significant presence, in travel and supporting fields. (See the following Industry Codes section for a complete list of types of businesses that are covered).

3) The companies in THE TRAVEL 300 do not have to be exclusively in the travel and tourism field.

4) Financial data and vital statistics must have been available to the editors of this book, either directly from the company being written about or from outside sources deemed reliable and accurate by the editors. A small number of companies that we would like to have included are not listed because of a lack of sufficient, objective data.

INDEX OF COMPANIES WITHIN INDUSTRY GROUPS

The industry codes shown below are based on the 2012 NAIC code system (NAIC is used by many analysts as a replacement for older SIC codes because NAIC is more specific to today's industry sectors, see www.census.gov/NAICS). Companies are given a primary NAIC code, reflecting the main line of business of each firm.

Industry Group/Company	Industry Code	2015 Sales	2015 Profits
Aerospace Product and Parts Manufacturing			
BAE Systems plc	336410	21,917,147,136	1,198,542,976
Air Traffic Control Services			
NAV Canada	488111	999,767,332	
Aircraft Components, Parts, Assemblies, Interiors and Systems Manufacturing (Aerospace)			
Spirit Aerosystems Holdings Inc	336413	6,643,899,904	788,700,032
Aircraft Engine and Engine Parts Manufacturing			
GE Aviation	336412	24,660,000,000	5,507,000,000
Rolls-Royce plc	336412	17,919,391,744	108,364,992
Aircraft Manufacturing (Aerospace), including Passenger Airliners and Military Aircraft,			
Airbus Group NV	336411	73,579,342,500	3,080,171,700
Airbus SAS	336411	52,350,594,720	2,940,771,792
Boeing Company (The)	336411	96,113,999,872	5,176,000,000
Bombardier Inc	336411	18,172,000,256	-5,346,999,808
Dassault Aviation SA	336411	4,717,890,560	159,820,352
Embraer SA	336411	5,928,099,840	69,200,000
Gulfstream Aerospace Corp	336411	8,851,000,000	1,706,000,000
Learjet Inc	336411		
Textron Inc	336411	13,422,999,552	697,000,000
Airlines, Scheduled Passenger Air Transportation			
Aer Lingus Group	481111		
Aeroflot Russian Airlines JSC	481111		
Aerolitoral SA de CV (Aeromexico Connect)	481111		
Aerovias de Mexico SA de CV (Aeromexico)	481111	2,445,533,184	63,531,960
Air Berlin plc & Co Luftverkehrs KG	481111	4,611,632,128	-504,616,416
Air Canada	481111	10,757,392,384	235,036,768
Air China Limited	481111	16,418,834,432	1,021,043,072
Air France	481111	29,638,203,650	134,207,300
Air France-KLM SA	481111	29,445,259,264	133,318,264
Air India Limited	481111	3,000,000,000	-939,434,059
Air New Zealand Ltd	481111	3,317,652,736	220,278,672
Air Wisconsin Airlines Corp	481111	1,594,340,000	106,000,000
AirAsia Berhad	481111	1,570,253,312	134,940,896
Alaska Air Group Inc	481111	5,598,000,128	848,000,000
Alitalia-Societa Aerea Italiana	481111	3,200,000,000	
All Nippon Airways Co Ltd	481111	17,040,166,912	398,064,736
Allegiant Travel Company	481111	1,262,188,032	220,374,000
American Airlines Group Inc	481111	40,989,999,104	7,609,999,872
Asiana Airlines Inc	481111	4,657,558,016	-135,970,304
Avianca Holdings SA	481111	4,361,340,928	-155,388,000

Industry Group/Company	Industry Code	2015 Sales	2015 Profits
Azul Linhas Aereas Brasileiras SA	481111	1,188,000,000	
Bangkok Airways Co Ltd	481111	562,000,000	
British Airways plc (BA)	481111	14,892,873,883	3,295,912,260
Brussels Airlines	481111		
Cathay Pacific Airways Ltd	481111	13,197,246,464	773,714,368
Ceske Aerolinie AS	481111		
China Airlines Ltd	481111	4,618,249,846	183,514,233
China Eastern Airlines Corporation Limited	481111	14,163,903,488	683,859,904
China Southern Airlines Co Ltd	481111	16,829,254,656	563,125,568
Concesionaria Vuela Compania de Aviacion SA de CV (Volaris)	481111	996,290,176	135,025,808
Delta Air Lines Inc	481111	40,704,000,000	4,526,000,128
Deutsche Lufthansa AG	481111	36,217,376,768	1,918,427,264
easyGroup	481111		
EasyJet plc	481111	6,118,052,352	715,470,080
El Al Israel Airlines Ltd	481111	2,054,040,960	106,534,000
Emirates Group (The)	481111	22,736,847,877	2,267,900,622
Endeavor Air	481111	110,650,000	-2,031,000
Etihad Airways	481111	9,000,000,000	
ExpressJet Airlines Inc	481111	1,169,923,000	
Finnair Oyj	481111	2,625,691,904	101,005,536
Frontier Airlines Inc	481111	1,604,012,260	145,512,190
GoJet Airlines LLC	481111	190,000,000	
GOL Linhas Aereas Inteligentes SA	481111	3,051,336,192	-1,392,068,352
Great Lakes Aviation Ltd	481111		
Hawaiian Airlines Inc	481111	2,317,466,880	182,646,000
Iberia Lineas Aereas de Espana SA	481111	5,171,439,818	
IndiGo (InterGlobe Aviation)	481111		
International Airlines Group (IAG)	481111	25,825,331,200	1,689,074,688
Japan Airlines Co Ltd	481111	13,373,024,256	1,530,769,536
Jet Airways India Ltd	481111	3,131,183,008	-313,168,876
JetBlue Airways Corporation	481111	6,416,000,000	677,000,000
KLM Royal Dutch Airlines	481111		
Korean Air Lines Co Ltd	481111	9,850,539,000	-480,348,000
LATAM Airlines Group SA	481111	9,740,045,312	-219,274,000
LOT Polish Airlines (Polskie Linie Lotnicze)	481111	9,354,000,000	
Malaysian Aviation Group Bhd	481111		
Martinair Holland NV	481111		
Mesa Air Group Inc	481111	1,287,000,000	
Norwegian Air Shuttle ASA	481111	2,728,287,488	29,869,552
Piedmont Airlines Inc	481111		
PT Garuda Indonesia Tbk	481111	3,470,368,768	76,480,240
Qantas Airways Ltd	481111	11,816,799,232	423,767,520
Qatar Airways	481111	9,789,067,023	445,232,671
Republic Airways Holdings Inc	481111	1,344,000,000	-27,100,000
Ryanair Holdings plc	481111	6,387,978,752	979,211,392
SAS AB	481111	4,717,065,216	113,733,024
Singapore Airlines Ltd	481111	11,537,265,664	272,690,240
SkyWest Inc	481111	3,095,563,008	117,817,000

Industry Group/Company	Industry Code	2015 Sales	2015 Profits
Southwest Airlines Co	481111	19,819,999,232	2,180,999,936
SpiceJet Ltd	481111	801,637,911	-102,328,012
Spirit Airlines Inc	481111	2,141,463,040	317,220,000
Swiss International Air Lines Ltd	481111	5,208,028,867	468,579,046
Thai Airways International PCL	481111	5,270,475,264	-376,317,536
Trans States Airlines Inc	481111		
Turk Hava Yollari AO (Turkish Airlines)	481111	10,522,000,000	1,069,000,000
United Continental Holdings Inc	481111	37,864,001,536	7,340,000,256
Virgin America Inc	481111	1,529,584,000	340,536,992
Virgin Atlantic Airways Ltd	481111	3,681,494,521	105,959,420
Virgin Australia Airlines Pty Ltd	481111	3,580,340,992	-84,297,024
Virgin Group Ltd	481111	20,146,500,000	
WestJet Airlines Ltd	481111	3,125,496,320	285,092,608
Wizz Air Hungary Airlines Ltd	481111	1,287,000,000	
XOJET Inc	481111		
Airport Related Services, Baggage Handling			
Aeroports de Paris	488119	3,294,542,848	485,820,800
Ferrovial SA	488119	10,960,343,040	813,467,392
Heathrow Airport Holdings Ltd	488119	3,615,714,620	917,084,452
Amusement and Theme Parks			
Cedar Fair LP	713110	1,235,778,048	112,222,000
Euro Disney SCA	713110	1,551,350,144	-95,130,488
Merlin Entertainments Group Plc	713110	1,668,559,744	221,952,400
Palace Entertainment Holdings Llc	713110		
Parques Reunidos SA	713110	736,197,066	22,432,459
Six Flags Entertainment Corporation	713110	1,263,938,048	154,690,000
Walt Disney Parks & Resorts	713110	16,162,000,000	3,031,000,000
Automobile Manufacturing			
Mahindra & Mahindra Limited	336111	10,718,198,784	467,389,632
Beer Manufacturing (Breweries)			
UB Group (The)	312120	635,058,972	646,489,423
Bus Systems and Services			
Arriva plc	485210	5,488,279,721	
Bus Systems and Services			
Coach USA LLC	485113	698,000,000	
FirstGroup plc	485113	7,899,807,744	98,181,296
Go-Ahead Group plc (The)	485113	4,197,772,544	68,152,440
Bus Systems and Services			
Greyhound Lines Inc	485210	986,000,000	68,500,000
National Express Group plc	485210	2,506,495,488	139,699,440
Bus Systems and Services			
Stagecoach Group plc	485113	4,183,672,320	181,870,400
Bus Systems and Services			
Trailways Transportation System Inc	485210		
Cable TV Programming, Cable Networks and Subsciption Video			
Walt Disney Company (The)	515210	52,465,000,448	8,382,000,128
Car Rental			
ADA Sa	532111	47,420,000	3,196,585

Industry Group/Company	Industry Code	2015 Sales	2015 Profits
Avis Budget Group Inc	532111	8,502,000,128	313,000,000
Dollar Thrifty Automotive Group Inc	532111	1,900,000,000	
Enterprise Holdings Inc	532111	19,400,000,000	
Hertz Global Holdings Inc	532111	10,535,000,064	273,000,000
Silvercar Inc	532111		
Sixt AG	532111	2,004,479,680	122,768,800
Car Reservations (e.g. Uber), Ticket Offices, Time Share and Vacation Club Rentals and Specialty Reservation Services			
AAA (American Automobile Association)	561599		
Amadeus IT Group SA	561599	4,420,632,576	772,722,880
Diamond Resorts Holdings LLC	561599	954,040,000	149,478,000
Interval Leisure Group Inc	561599	697,436,032	73,315,000
Leading Hotels of the World Ltd (The)	561599		
ResortQuest International Inc	561599	505,000,000	
Supranational Hotels Ltd	561599		
Tix Corporation	561599	23,421,000	16,792,000
Westgate Resorts	561599		
WorldHotels AG	561599		
WorldMark by Wyndham Inc	561599		
Wyndham Vacation Ownership	561599	2,660,000,000	
Casino Hotels and Casino Resorts			
American Casino & Entertainment Properties LLC	721120	373,067,000	12,062,000
Ameristar Casinos Inc	721120	1,275,000,000	
Boyd Gaming Corp	721120	2,199,431,936	47,234,000
Caesars Entertainment Corporation	721120	4,654,000,128	5,920,000,000
Galaxy Entertainment Group Ltd	721120	6,575,387,648	536,577,408
Kerzner International Limited	721120	400,000,000	
Las Vegas Sands Corp (The Venetian)	721120	11,688,461,312	1,966,236,032
MGM Growth Properties LLC	721120	0	-261,954,000
MGM Resorts International	721120	9,190,068,224	-447,720,000
Pinnacle Entertainment Inc	721120	2,291,847,936	48,887,000
Red Rock Resorts Inc	721120	1,352,135,040	137,658,000
Societe Anonyme des Bains de Mer et du Cercle des Etrangers a Monaco	721120	514,150,000	11,373,400
Station Casinos LLC	721120	1,352,135,000	132,504,000
Wynn Resorts Limited	721120	4,075,883,008	195,290,000
Charter Bus Services			
BostonCoach	485510	113,500,000	
Chartered Air Freight and Cargo Services			
Atlas Air Worldwide Holdings Inc	481212	1,822,658,944	7,286,000
Hf Eimskipafelag Islands	481212	549,938,768	195,943,053
Chartered Airlines (Nonscheduled Passenger Air Transportation)			
Air Partner plc	481211	250,408,187	3,649,809
Jet Aviation Management AG	481211	1,050,000,000	
NetJets Inc	481211	4,398,750,000	286,021,000
Transat AT Inc	481211		

Industry Group/Company	Industry Code	2015 Sales	2015 Profits
Commercial Real Estate Investment and Operations, Including Office Buildings, Shopping Centers, Industrial Properties and Related REITs			
Strategic Hotels & Resorts Inc	531120	1,381,600,000	
Trump Entertainment Resorts Inc	531120		
Computer Software, Accounting, Banking & Financial			
Concur Technologies Inc	511210Q	7,724,603,419	-20,571,530
Credit Card Processing, Online Payment Processing, EFT, ACH and Clearinghouses			
American Express Co	522320	32,817,999,872	5,162,999,808
Cruise Lines			
Carnival Corporation	483112	15,713,999,872	1,756,999,936
Celebrity Cruises Inc	483112	1,150,000,000	
Crystal Cruises LLC	483112	300,000,000	
Disney Cruise Line	483112	1,210,000,000	
Genting Hong Kong Limited	483112	689,953,984	2,112,686,976
MSC Cruises SA	483112	1,710,000,000	
Norwegian Cruise Line Holdings Ltd (NCL)	483112	4,345,048,064	427,136,992
Oceania Cruises	483112	835,000,000	51,886,687
Princess Cruise Lines Ltd	483112	2,985,660,000	
Royal Caribbean Cruises Ltd	483112	8,299,074,048	665,782,976
Silversea Cruises	483112		
Food Service Contractors			
Delaware North Companies Inc	722310	3,210,000,000	
Gate Gourmet Inc	722310	2,650,000,000	
HMSHost Corporation	722310	2,800,000,000	
Sodexo Inc	722310	9,200,000,000	
Hotels, Motels, Inns and Resorts (Lodging and Hospitality)			
Accor North America	721110	635,410,802	255,037,440
Accor SA	721110	6,305,502,208	275,675,072
Amanresorts International Pte Ltd (Aman Resorts)	721110	233,000,000	
Banyan Tree Holdings Limited	721110	274,756,704	-20,397,288
Barcelo Crestline Corporation	721110		
Belmond Ltd	721110	551,385,024	16,265,000
Best Western International Inc	721110	7,000,000,000	
Carlson Companies Inc	721110	3,150,000,000	
Carlson Rezidor Hotel Group	721110	1,135,234,050	
China Lodging Group Ltd	721110	870,406,336	65,808,516
Choice Hotels International Inc	721110	859,878,016	128,029,000
Club Mediterranee SA (Club Med)	721110	1,633,620,883	
Commune Hotels & Resorts LLC	721110	500,000,000	
Days Inn Worldwide Inc	721110		
Doyle Collection (The)	721110	200,000,000	
Extended Stay America Inc	721110	1,284,753,000	113,040,000
Fairmont Raffles Hotels International Inc	721110	1,000,000,000	
Four Seasons Hotels Inc	721110	4,300,000,000	
Golden Tulip Hospitality Group	721110		
Groupe du Louvre	721110	392,605,224	23,105,898

Industry Group/Company	Industry Code	2015 Sales	2015 Profits
Hilton Worldwide Inc	721110	11,271,999,488	1,404,000,000
HNA Tourism Holding (Group) Co Ltd	721110		
Homeinns Hotel Group	721110	1,029,000,000	25,800,000
Hongkong and Shanghai Hotels Ltd	721110	740,315,776	128,952,400
Hotel Properties Ltd	721110	429,044,861	60,658,066
Howard Johnson International Inc	721110		
Hyatt Hotels Corporation	721110	4,328,000,000	124,000,000
Indian Hotels Company Limited (The)	721110	623,982,656	-56,325,644
InterContinental Hotels Group plc	721110	1,803,000,064	1,222,000,000
Interstate Hotels & Resorts Inc	721110		
InTown Suites Management Inc	721110		
Jameson Inn Inc	721110		
Janus Hotels and Resorts Inc	721110		
John Q Hammons Hotels & Resorts LLC	721110	461,000,000	
Kimpton Hotel & Restaurant Group LLC	721110	1,200,000,000	
La Quinta Holdings Inc	721110	1,029,974,016	26,365,000
Loews Hotels Holding Corporation	721110	604,000,000	12,000,000
Mandarin Oriental International Ltd	721110	607,299,968	89,300,000
Marcus Corporation (The)	721110	324,267,008	23,565,000
Marriott International Inc	721110	14,485,999,616	859,000,000
Melia Hotels International SA	721110	1,963,853,696	40,645,124
Meritus Hotels & Resorts Inc	721110		
Millennium & Copthorne Hotels plc	721110	1,105,845,120	84,864,152
Morgans Hotel Group Co	721110	219,982,000	22,097,000
Movenpick Hotels & Resorts Management AG	721110	1,045,000,000	
NH Hotel Group SA	721110	1,555,342,848	1,059,767
Oakwood Worldwide	721110	860,000,000	
Oberoi Group (EIH Ltd)	721110	250,608,522	9,487,804
Ramada Worldwide Inc	721110		
Red Lion Hotels Corporation	721110	142,920,000	2,719,000
Rezidor Hotel Group AB	721110		
Ritz-Carlton Hotel Company LLC (The)	721110	2,400,000,000	
Rosewood Hotels & Resorts LLC	721110	575,000,000	
Ryman Hospitality Properties Inc	721110	1,092,124,032	111,511,000
Sands China Ltd	721110	6,820,078,080	1,459,442,048
SBE Entertainment Group LLC	721110		
Scandic Hotels AB	721110	1,494,083,703	25,843,517
Shangri-La Asia Ltd	721110	2,122,624,000	140,131,008
Shun Tak Holdings Limited	721110	568,075,520	96,026,984
Sonesta International Hotels Corp	721110		
Starwood Capital Group Global LLC	721110		
Starwood Hotels & Resorts Worldwide Inc	721110	5,762,999,808	489,000,000
Sunburst Hospitality Corporation	721110		
Super 8 Worldwide Inc	721110		
TMI Hospitality Inc	721110		
TRT Holdings Inc	721110		
TUI AG (TUI Group)	721110	22,609,422,336	384,589,312
Wyndham Worldwide Corporation	721110	5,536,000,000	612,000,000
Xanterra Parks & Resorts Inc	721110	106,000,000	

Industry Group/Company	Industry Code	2015 Sales	2015 Profits
Internet Search Engines, Online Publishing, Sharing and Consumer Services, Online Radio, TV and Entertainment Sites and Social Media			
Airbnb Inc	519130	1,425,000,000	
Ctrip.com International Ltd	519130	1,642,585,344	377,977,824
Expedia Inc	519130	6,672,316,928	764,465,024
HomeAway Inc	519130	522,800,000	
Hotels.com LP	519130		
Hotwire Inc	519130		
KAYAK Software Corporation	519130	375,000,000	8,591,807
LastMinute.com NV	519130	282,521,360	-20,253,539
MakeMyTrip Limited	519130	299,662,016	-18,252,000
Orbitz Worldwide Inc	519130	919,604,000	50,400,000
Priceline Group Inc (The)	519130	9,223,987,200	2,551,360,000
Sabre Corporation	519130	2,960,896,000	545,481,984
Sabre Travel Network	519130	2,102,792,000	751,546,000
Travelocity.com LP	519130		
Travelport Worldwide Limited	519130	2,220,999,936	16,000,000
Travelzoo Inc	519130	141,716,000	10,864,000
TripAdvisor Inc	519130	1,492,000,000	198,000,000
Irradiation Apparatus (including Medical Devices) Manufacturing			
American Science & Engineering Inc	334517	126,750,000	979,000
Limousine Service			
Carey International Inc	485320		
Movie (Motion Pictures) Theaters			
Dalian Wanda Group Co Ltd	512131	27,337,000,000	2,431,000,000
Newspaper Publishing			
Lagardere SCA	511110	8,126,765,056	83,606,368
Ocean Cargo and Deep Sea Shipping			
Mediterranean Shipping Company SA	483111	28,190,000,000	
Nippon Yusen Kabushiki Kaisha (NYK)	483111	23,885,873,152	519,919,680
Swire Pacific Ltd	483111	7,851,267,072	1,731,701,760
Other Gasoline Stations			
Bowlin Travel Centers Inc	447190	28,745,404	61,732
TravelCenters of America LLC	447190	5,850,633,216	27,719,000
Port and Harbor Operations			
TWC Enterprises Inc	488310		
Radar, Navigation, Sonar, Space Vehicle Guidance, Flight Systems and Marine Instrument Manufacturing			
Smiths Detection	334511	629,982,641	55,573,000
Railroads, Passenger and Freight, Long Distance			
Amtrak (National Railroad Passenger Corp)	482111	3,211,023,000	-1,232,686,000
Central Japan Railway Company	482111	16,630,815,744	2,553,483,776
Deutsche Bahn AG	482111	21,684,544,000	424,841,050
East Japan Railway Company	482111	27,409,801,216	1,805,577,216
Eurotunnel Group	482111	1,380,648,576	113,491,128
Guangshen Railway Co Ltd	482111	2,370,268,416	161,404,512
Keikyu Corporation	482111	3,159,596,032	107,613,824

Industry Group/Company	Industry Code	2015 Sales	2015 Profits
Kintetsu Corporation	482111	12,270,005,248	276,518,080
SNCF Reseau	482111	7,045,059,398	-11,152,105,980
Tobu Railway Co Ltd	482111	4,860,575,000	255,450,000
VIA Rail Canada Inc	482111	214,229,545	7,065,395
West Japan Railway Company	482111	13,428,963,328	666,795,968
Railroads, Short Line			
Keio Corporation	482112	4,154,254,708	150,587,647
Keisei Electric Railway Co Ltd	482112	2,196,296,218	226,493,497
MTR Corp Ltd	482112	5,377,443,840	1,675,607,424
Real Estate Rental, Leasing, Development and Management, including REITs			
DLF Limited	531100	1,139,432,448	80,478,656
gl Limited	531100	423,200,000	47,900,000
Hutchison Whampoa Properties Ltd	531100	4,385,000,000	
REITS (Real Estate Investment Trusts) - Nonresidential			
CNL Lifestyle Properties Inc	531120A	337,664,992	141,155,008
Condor Hospitality Trust Inc	531120A	57,341,000	13,125,000
FelCor Lodging Trust Inc	531120A	886,254,016	-7,428,000
Hospitality Properties Trust	531120A	1,921,904,000	166,418,000
Host Hotels & Resorts LP	531120A	5,386,999,808	558,000,000
Innkeepers USA Trust	531120A		
LaSalle Hotel Properties	531120A	1,164,358,016	135,552,000
Sunstone Hotel Investors Inc	531120A	1,249,180,032	347,355,008
RV (Recreational Vehicle) Parks and Campgrounds			
Kampgrounds of America Inc	721211		
Thousand Trails LP	721211		
Shuttle Services, Vanpool and Car Pool Operations			
SuperShuttle International Inc	485999		
Snow Ski Resorts and Skiing Related Facilities			
Booth Creek Ski Holdings Inc	713920	120,000,000	
Boyne Resorts	713920	82,000,000	
Crested Butte Mountain Resort Inc	713920		
Intrawest Resorts Holding Inc	713920	587,588,992	-6,920,000
Vail Resorts Inc	713920	1,399,923,968	114,754,000
Winter Sports Inc	713920		
Television Broadcasting			
NBCUniversal LLC	515120	26,000,000,000	5,591,000,000
Tobacco Products Manufacturing (Including Cigarettes, Cigars, e-Cigarettes and Vaporizers)			
ITC Limited	312230	5,785,230,336	1,439,524,736
Tour Operators			
AmericanTours International LLC	561520		
Holidaybreak PLC	561520	359,011,507	-4,753,459
Kuoni Reisen Holding AG	561520	3,481,520,128	-306,804,608
Pleasant Holidays LLC	561520		
Thomas Cook Group plc	561520	10,228,088,832	30,028,854

Industry Group/Company	Industry Code	2015 Sales	2015 Profits
Transportation Equipment Rental and Leasing Services, Including Aircraft, Engines, Shipping Containers and Pallets			
AerCap Holdings NV	532411	5,598,662,144	1,178,729,984
Travel Agencies			
Balboa Travel Inc	561510		
BCD Travel	561510	23,850,000,000	
Carlson Wagonlit Travel	561510	26,200,000,000	
CorpTrav Management Group	561510		
Costco Travel Inc	561510		
Flight Centre Limited	561510	1,797,847,040	195,186,400
Hogg Robinson Group North America	561510	115,346,000	12,282,071
Hogg Robinson Group plc	561510	430,979,328	19,192,354
JTB Global Marketing & Travel Inc	561510	430,000,000	
Liberty Travel Inc	561510		
Omega World Travel	561510	1,300,000,000	
Travel Leaders Group LLC	561510	290,000,000	
Uniglobe Travel International LP	561510	5,000,000,000	

ALPHABETICAL INDEX

Fairmont Raffles Hotels International Inc
FelCor Lodging Trust Inc
Ferrovial SA
Finnair Oyj
FirstGroup plc
Flight Centre Limited
Four Seasons Hotels Inc
Frontier Airlines Inc
Galaxy Entertainment Group Ltd
Gate Gourmet Inc
GE Aviation
Genting Hong Kong Limited
gl Limited
Go-Ahead Group plc (The)
GoJet Airlines LLC
GOL Linhas Aereas Inteligentes SA
Golden Tulip Hospitality Group
Great Lakes Aviation Ltd
Greyhound Lines Inc
Groupe du Louvre
Guangshen Railway Co Ltd
Gulfstream Aerospace Corp
Hawaiian Airlines Inc
Heathrow Airport Holdings Ltd
Hertz Global Holdings Inc
Hf Eimskipafelag Islands
Hilton Worldwide Inc
HMSHost Corporation
HNA Tourism Holding (Group) Co Ltd
Hogg Robinson Group North America
Hogg Robinson Group plc
Holidaybreak PLC
HomeAway Inc
Homeinns Hotel Group
Hongkong and Shanghai Hotels Ltd
Hospitality Properties Trust
Host Hotels & Resorts LP
Hotel Properties Ltd
Hotels.com LP
Hotwire Inc
Howard Johnson International Inc
Hutchison Whampoa Properties Ltd
Hyatt Hotels Corporation
Iberia Lineas Aereas de Espana SA
Indian Hotels Company Limited (The)
IndiGo (InterGlobe Aviation)
Innkeepers USA Trust
InterContinental Hotels Group plc
International Airlines Group (IAG)
Interstate Hotels & Resorts Inc
Interval Leisure Group Inc
InTown Suites Management Inc
Intrawest Resorts Holding Inc
ITC Limited
Jameson Inn Inc
Janus Hotels and Resorts Inc
Japan Airlines Co Ltd
Jet Airways India Ltd

Jet Aviation Management AG
JetBlue Airways Corporation
John Q Hammons Hotels & Resorts LLC
JTB Global Marketing & Travel Inc
Kampgrounds of America Inc
KAYAK Software Corporation
Keikyu Corporation
Keio Corporation
Keisei Electric Railway Co Ltd
Kerzner International Limited
Kimpton Hotel & Restaurant Group LLC
Kintetsu Corporation
KLM Royal Dutch Airlines
Korean Air Lines Co Ltd
Kuoni Reisen Holding AG
La Quinta Holdings Inc
Lagardere SCA
Las Vegas Sands Corp (The Venetian)
LaSalle Hotel Properties
LastMinute.com NV
LATAM Airlines Group SA
Leading Hotels of the World Ltd (The)
Learjet Inc
Liberty Travel Inc
Loews Hotels Holding Corporation
LOT Polish Airlines (Polskie Linie Lotnicze)
Mahindra & Mahindra Limited
MakeMyTrip Limited
Malaysian Aviation Group Bhd
Mandarin Oriental International Ltd
Marcus Corporation (The)
Marriott International Inc
Martinair Holland NV
Mediterranean Shipping Company SA
Melia Hotels International SA
Meritus Hotels & Resorts Inc
Merlin Entertainments Group Plc
Mesa Air Group Inc
MGM Growth Properties LLC
MGM Resorts International
Millennium & Copthorne Hotels plc
Morgans Hotel Group Co
Movenpick Hotels & Resorts Management AG
MSC Cruises SA
MTR Corp Ltd
National Express Group plc
NAV Canada
NBCUniversal LLC
NetJets Inc
NH Hotel Group SA
Nippon Yusen Kabushiki Kaisha (NYK)
Norwegian Air Shuttle ASA
Norwegian Cruise Line Holdings Ltd (NCL)
Oakwood Worldwide
Oberoi Group (EIH Ltd)
Oceania Cruises
Omega World Travel
Orbitz Worldwide Inc

Palace Entertainment Holdings Llc
Parques Reunidos SA
Piedmont Airlines Inc
Pinnacle Entertainment Inc
Pleasant Holidays LLC
Priceline Group Inc (The)
Princess Cruise Lines Ltd
PT Garuda Indonesia Tbk
Qantas Airways Ltd
Qatar Airways
Ramada Worldwide Inc
Red Lion Hotels Corporation
Red Rock Resorts Inc
Republic Airways Holdings Inc
ResortQuest International Inc
Rezidor Hotel Group AB
Ritz-Carlton Hotel Company LLC (The)
Rolls-Royce plc
Rosewood Hotels & Resorts LLC
Royal Caribbean Cruises Ltd
Ryanair Holdings plc
Ryman Hospitality Properties Inc
Sabre Corporation
Sabre Travel Network
Sands China Ltd
SAS AB
SBE Entertainment Group LLC
Scandic Hotels AB
Shangri-La Asia Ltd
Shun Tak Holdings Limited
Silvercar Inc
Silversea Cruises
Singapore Airlines Ltd
Six Flags Entertainment Corporation
Sixt AG
SkyWest Inc
Smiths Detection
SNCF Reseau
Societe Anonyme des Bains de Mer et du Cercle des
Etrangers a Monaco
Sodexo Inc
Sonesta International Hotels Corp
Southwest Airlines Co
SpiceJet Ltd
Spirit Aerosystems Holdings Inc
Spirit Airlines Inc
Stagecoach Group plc
Starwood Capital Group Global LLC
Starwood Hotels & Resorts Worldwide Inc
Station Casinos LLC
Strategic Hotels & Resorts Inc
Sunburst Hospitality Corporation
Sunstone Hotel Investors Inc
Super 8 Worldwide Inc
SuperShuttle International Inc
Supranational Hotels Ltd
Swire Pacific Ltd
Swiss International Air Lines Ltd

Textron Inc
Thai Airways International PCL
Thomas Cook Group plc
Thousand Trails LP
Tix Corporation
TMI Hospitality Inc
Tobu Railway Co Ltd
Trailways Transportation System Inc
Trans States Airlines Inc
Transat AT Inc
Travel Leaders Group LLC
TravelCenters of America LLC
Travelocity.com LP
Travelport Worldwide Limited
Travelzoo Inc
TripAdvisor Inc
TRT Holdings Inc
Trump Entertainment Resorts Inc
TUI AG (TUI Group)
Turk Hava Yollari AO (Turkish Airlines)
TWC Enterprises Inc
UB Group (The)
Uniglobe Travel International LP
United Continental Holdings Inc
Vail Resorts Inc
VIA Rail Canada Inc
Virgin America Inc
Virgin Atlantic Airways Ltd
Virgin Australia Airlines Pty Ltd
Virgin Group Ltd
Walt Disney Company (The)
Walt Disney Parks & Resorts
West Japan Railway Company
Westgate Resorts
WestJet Airlines Ltd
Winter Sports Inc
Wizz Air Hungary Airlines Ltd
WorldHotels AG
WorldMark by Wyndham Inc
Wyndham Vacation Ownership
Wyndham Worldwide Corporation
Wynn Resorts Limited
Xanterra Parks & Resorts Inc
XOJET Inc

INDEX OF HEADQUARTERS LOCATION BY STATE

To help you the firms geographically, the city and state of the headquarters of each company are in the following index.

ARIZONA
Best Western International Inc; Phoenix
Mesa Air Group Inc; Phoenix
SuperShuttle International Inc; Phoenix

CALIFORNIA
Airbnb Inc; San Francisco
AmericanTours International LLC; Los Angeles
Balboa Travel Inc; San Diego
Commune Hotels & Resorts LLC; San Francisco
Crystal Cruises LLC; Los Angeles
Hotwire Inc; San Francisco
Kimpton Hotel & Restaurant Group LLC; San Francisco
Oakwood Worldwide; Los Angeles
Palace Entertainment Holdings Llc; Newport Beach
Pleasant Holidays LLC; Westlake Village
Princess Cruise Lines Ltd; Santa Clarita
SBE Entertainment Group LLC; Los Angeles
Sunstone Hotel Investors Inc; Aliso Viejo
Tix Corporation; Studio City
Virgin America Inc; Burlingame
Walt Disney Company (The); Burbank
Walt Disney Parks & Resorts; Anaheim
XOJET Inc; Brisbane

COLORADO
Booth Creek Ski Holdings Inc; Vail
Crested Butte Mountain Resort Inc; Mt. Crested Butte
Frontier Airlines Inc; Denver
Intrawest Resorts Holding Inc; Denver
Vail Resorts Inc; Broomfield
Xanterra Parks & Resorts Inc; Greenwood Village

CONNECTICUT
KAYAK Software Corporation; Stamford
Priceline Group Inc (The); Norwalk
Starwood Capital Group Global LLC; Greenwich

DISTRICT OF COLUMBIA
Amtrak (National Railroad Passenger Corp); Washington

FLORIDA
AAA (American Automobile Association); Heathrow
Carnival Corporation; Miami
Celebrity Cruises Inc; Miami
CNL Lifestyle Properties Inc; Orlando
Disney Cruise Line; Lake Buena Vista
Hertz Global Holdings Inc; Estero
Innkeepers USA Trust; Palm Beach
Interval Leisure Group Inc; Miami
Janus Hotels and Resorts Inc; Boca Raton
Norwegian Cruise Line Holdings Ltd (NCL); Miami
Oceania Cruises; Miami
ResortQuest International Inc; Fort Walton Beach
Royal Caribbean Cruises Ltd; Miami
Spirit Airlines Inc; Miramar
Westgate Resorts; Orlando
WorldMark by Wyndham Inc; Orlando
Wyndham Vacation Ownership; Orlando

GEORGIA
Delta Air Lines Inc; Atlanta
ExpressJet Airlines Inc; Atlanta
Gulfstream Aerospace Corp; Savannah
InTown Suites Management Inc; Atlanta
Jameson Inn Inc; Smyrna

HAWAII
Hawaiian Airlines Inc; Honolulu

ILLINOIS
Boeing Company (The); Chicago
CorpTrav Management Group; Lombard
Hyatt Hotels Corporation; Chicago
Orbitz Worldwide Inc; Chicago
Strategic Hotels & Resorts Inc; Chicago
United Continental Holdings Inc; Chicago

INDIANA
Republic Airways Holdings Inc; Indianapolis

KANSAS
Learjet Inc; Wichita
Spirit Aerosystems Holdings Inc; Wichita

MARYLAND
Carey International Inc; Frederick
Choice Hotels International Inc; Rockville
HMSHost Corporation; Bethesda
Host Hotels & Resorts LP; Bethesda
LaSalle Hotel Properties; Bethesda
Marriott International Inc; Bethesda
Piedmont Airlines Inc; Salisbury
Ritz-Carlton Hotel Company LLC (The); Chevy Chase
Sodexo Inc; Gaithersburg
Sunburst Hospitality Corporation; Silver Spring

MASSACHUSSETTS
American Science & Engineering Inc; Billerica
BostonCoach; Everett
Hospitality Properties Trust; Newton
Sonesta International Hotels Corp; Newton
TripAdvisor Inc; Needham

MICHIGAN
Boyne Resorts; Petoskey

MINNESOTA
Carlson Companies Inc; Minnetonka
Carlson Rezidor Hotel Group; Minnetonka
Endeavor Air; Minneapolis
Travel Leaders Group LLC; Plymouth

MISSOURI
Enterprise Holdings Inc; St. Louis
GoJet Airlines LLC; Bridgeton
John Q Hammons Hotels & Resorts LLC; Springfield
Trans States Airlines Inc; Bridgeton

MONTANA
Kampgrounds of America Inc; Billings
Winter Sports Inc; Whitefish

NEBRASKA
Condor Hospitality Trust Inc; Norfolk

NEVADA
Allegiant Travel Company; Las Vegas
American Casino & Entertainment Properties LLC; Las Vegas
Ameristar Casinos Inc; Las Vegas
Boyd Gaming Corp; Las Vegas
Caesars Entertainment Corporation; Las Vegas
Diamond Resorts Holdings LLC; Las Vegas
Las Vegas Sands Corp (The Venetian); Las Vegas
MGM Growth Properties LLC; Las Vegas
MGM Resorts International; Las Vegas
Pinnacle Entertainment Inc; Las Vegas
Red Rock Resorts Inc; Las Vegas
Station Casinos LLC; Las Vegas
Wynn Resorts Limited; Las Vegas

NEW JERSEY
Avis Budget Group Inc; Parsippany
Coach USA LLC; Paramus
Days Inn Worldwide Inc; Parsippany
Howard Johnson International Inc; Parsippany
Liberty Travel Inc; Ramsey
Ramada Worldwide Inc; Parsippany
Super 8 Worldwide Inc; Parsippany
Wyndham Worldwide Corporation; Parsippany

NEW MEXICO
Bowlin Travel Centers Inc; Albuquerque

NEW YORK
American Express Co; New York
Atlas Air Worldwide Holdings Inc; Purchase
Delaware North Companies Inc; Buffalo
Hogg Robinson Group North America; New York
JetBlue Airways Corporation; Long Island City
Leading Hotels of the World Ltd (The); New York
Loews Hotels Holding Corporation; New York
Morgans Hotel Group Co; New York

NBCUniversal LLC; New York
Starwood Hotels & Resorts Worldwide Inc; White Plains
Travelzoo Inc; New York
Trump Entertainment Resorts Inc; Atlantic City

NORTH CAROLINA
Extended Stay America Inc; Charlotte

NORTH DAKOTA
TMI Hospitality Inc; Fargo

OHIO
Cedar Fair LP; Sandusky
GE Aviation; Cincinnati
NetJets Inc; Columbus
TravelCenters of America LLC; Westlake

OKLAHOMA
Dollar Thrifty Automotive Group Inc; Tulsa

RHODE ISLAND
Textron Inc; Providence

TENNESSEE
Ryman Hospitality Properties Inc; Nashville

TEXAS
Accor North America; Carrollton
American Airlines Group Inc; Fort Worth
FelCor Lodging Trust Inc; Irving
Greyhound Lines Inc; Dallas
HomeAway Inc; Austin
Hotels.com LP; Dallas
La Quinta Holdings Inc; Irving
Rosewood Hotels & Resorts LLC; Dallas
Sabre Corporation; Southlake
Sabre Travel Network; Southlake
Silvercar Inc; Austin
Six Flags Entertainment Corporation; Grand Prairie
Southwest Airlines Co; Dallas
Thousand Trails LP; Frisco
Travelocity.com LP; Dallas
TRT Holdings Inc; Dallas

UTAH
SkyWest Inc; St. George

VIRGINIA
Barcelo Crestline Corporation; Fairfax
Gate Gourmet Inc; Reston
Hilton Worldwide Inc; McLean
Interstate Hotels & Resorts Inc; Arlington
Omega World Travel; Fairfax
Trailways Transportation System Inc; Fairfax

INDEX OF NON-U.S. HEADQUARTERS LOCATION BY COUNTRY

FINLAND
Finnair Oyj; Helsinki-Vantaa Airport

FRANCE
Accor SA; Paris
ADA Sa; Clichy
Aeroports de Paris; Paris
Air France; Paris
Air France-KLM SA; Paris
Airbus SAS; Blagnac
Carlson Wagonlit Travel; Paris
Club Mediterranee SA (Club Med); Paris
Dassault Aviation SA; Paris
Euro Disney SCA; Paris
Eurotunnel Group; Paris
Golden Tulip Hospitality Group; Paris
Groupe du Louvre; Paris
Lagardere SCA; Paris
SNCF Reseau; Paris Cedex 13

GERMANY
Air Berlin plc & Co Luftverkehrs KG; Berlin
Deutsche Bahn AG; Berlin
Deutsche Lufthansa AG; Koeln
Sixt AG; Pullach im Isartal
TUI AG (TUI Group); Hannover
WorldHotels AG; Frankfurt

HONG KONG
Cathay Pacific Airways Ltd; Hong Kong
Galaxy Entertainment Group Ltd; Hong Kong
Genting Hong Kong Limited; Kowloon
Hongkong and Shanghai Hotels Ltd; Central
Hutchison Whampoa Properties Ltd; Hong Kong
Mandarin Oriental International Ltd; Hong Kong
MTR Corp Ltd; Kowloon
Shangri-La Asia Ltd; Quarry Bay
Shun Tak Holdings Limited; Hong Kong
Swire Pacific Ltd; Hong Kong

HUNGARY
Wizz Air Hungary Airlines Ltd; Budapest

ICELAND
Hf Eimskipafelag Islands; Reykjavik

INDIA
Air India Limited; New Delhi
DLF Limited; New Delhi
Indian Hotels Company Limited (The); Mumbai
IndiGo (InterGlobe Aviation); Gurgaon
ITC Limited; Kolkata
Jet Airways India Ltd; Mumbai
Mahindra & Mahindra Limited; Mumbai
MakeMyTrip Limited; Gurgaon
Oberoi Group (EIH Ltd); Delhi
SpiceJet Ltd; Gurgaon

UB Group (The); Bangalore

INDONESIA
PT Garuda Indonesia Tbk; Jakarta

IRELAND
Aer Lingus Group; Dublin
Ryanair Holdings plc; County Dublin

ISRAEL
El Al Israel Airlines Ltd; Lod

ITALY
Alitalia-Societa Aerea Italiana; Rome

JAPAN
All Nippon Airways Co Ltd; Tokyo
Central Japan Railway Company; Nagoya
East Japan Railway Company; Tokyo
Japan Airlines Co Ltd; Tokyo
JTB Global Marketing & Travel Inc; Tokyo
Keikyu Corporation; Tokyo
Keio Corporation; Tokyo
Keisei Electric Railway Co Ltd; Yubinbango, Ichikawa
Kintetsu Corporation; Osaka
Nippon Yusen Kabushiki Kaisha (NYK); Tokyo
Tobu Railway Co Ltd; Tokyo
West Japan Railway Company; Osaka

KOREA
Asiana Airlines Inc; Seoul
Korean Air Lines Co Ltd; Seoul

MACAU
Sands China Ltd; Baia de N. Snhora da Esparanc

MALAYSIA
AirAsia Berhad; Sepang
Malaysian Aviation Group Bhd; Subang

MEXICO
Aerolitoral SA de CV (Aeromexico Connect); Apodaca
Aerovias de Mexico SA de CV (Aeromexico); Mexico City
Concesionaria Vuela Compania de Aviacion SA de CV (Volaris); Colonia Zedec Santa Fe

MONACO
Silversea Cruises; Monte Carlo
Societe Anonyme des Bains de Mer et du Cercle des Etrangers a Monaco; Monte Carlo

NEW ZEALAND
Air New Zealand Ltd; Auckland

NORWAY
Norwegian Air Shuttle ASA; Lysaker

POLAND
LOT Polish Airlines (Polskie Linie Lotnicze); Warsaw

QATAR
Qatar Airways; Doha

RUSSIA
Aeroflot Russian Airlines JSC; Moscow

SINGAPORE
Amanresorts International Pte Ltd (Aman Resorts); Singapore
Banyan Tree Holdings Limited; Singapore
gl Limited; Singapore
Hotel Properties Ltd; Singapore
Meritus Hotels & Resorts Inc; Singapore
Singapore Airlines Ltd; Singapore

SPAIN
Amadeus IT Group SA; Madrid
Ferrovial SA; Madrid
Iberia Lineas Aereas de Espana SA; Madrid
Melia Hotels International SA; Palma de Mallorca
NH Hotel Group SA; Madrid
Parques Reunidos SA; Madrid

SWEDEN
SAS AB; Stockholm
Scandic Hotels AB; Stockholm

SWITZERLAND
Jet Aviation Management AG; Basel
Kuoni Reisen Holding AG; Zurich
Mediterranean Shipping Company SA; Geneva
Movenpick Hotels & Resorts Management AG; Baar
MSC Cruises SA; Basel
Swiss International Air Lines Ltd; Basel

TAIWAN
China Airlines Ltd; Dayuan Township, Taoyuan

THAILAND
Bangkok Airways Co Ltd; Chom Phon Chatuchak, Bangkok
Thai Airways International PCL; Bangkok

THE NETHERLANDS
AerCap Holdings NV; Schiphol
Airbus Group NV; Leiden
BCD Travel; Utrecht
KLM Royal Dutch Airlines; Amstelveen
Martinair Holland NV; Schiphol

TURKEY
Turk Hava Yollari AO (Turkish Airlines); Istanbul

UNITED ARAB EMIRATES
Emirates Group (The); Dubai
Etihad Airways; Abu Dhabi

UNITED KINGDOM
Air Partner plc; Gatwick
Arriva plc; Sunderland
BAE Systems plc; London
British Airways plc (BA); Harmondsworth
Doyle Collection (The); Dublin
easyGroup; London
EasyJet plc; Luton
FirstGroup plc; Aberdeen
Go-Ahead Group plc (The); London
Heathrow Airport Holdings Ltd; Middlesex
Hogg Robinson Group plc; Hampshire
Holidaybreak PLC; Northwich
InterContinental Hotels Group plc; Denham
International Airlines Group (IAG); Hounslow
LastMinute.com NV; Amsterdam
Merlin Entertainments Group Plc; Poole
Millennium & Copthorne Hotels plc; London
National Express Group plc; Birmingham
Rolls-Royce plc; London
Smiths Detection; Watford
Stagecoach Group plc; Perth
Supranational Hotels Ltd; London
Thomas Cook Group plc; London
Travelport Worldwide Limited; Berkshire
Virgin Atlantic Airways Ltd; Crawley
Virgin Group Ltd; London

Individual Profiles
On Each Of
THE TRAVEL 300

AAA (American Automobile Association)   www.aaa.com

NAIC Code: 561599

TYPES OF BUSINESS:

Travel Agency
Roadside Assistance
Financial Services
Insurance
Travel Guides
Automobile Repairs

BRANDS/DIVISIONS/AFFILIATES:

American Automobile Association
AAA Auto Club
AAA Motor Club
AAA Travel Services
TripTik
TourBook
1-800-AAA-HELP
www.exchangeev.aaa.com/

CONTACTS: *Note: Officers with more than one job title may be intentionally listed here more than once.*

Robert L. Darbelnet, CEO
Robert L. Darbelnet, Pres.
John Schaffer, CFO
Satish D. Mahajan, CIO
Marshall Doney, Sr. Exec. VP-Automotive & Financial Services
Mark H. Brown, Exec. VP-Publishing & Club Services
Kathleen Bower, VP-Public Affairs
Bill Sutherland, VP-Travel

GROWTH PLANS/SPECIAL FEATURES:

AAA (American Automobile Association) is a nonprofit organization that offers auto-related services to over 55 million members in North America. Founded in 1902, it operates as a national network of independent clubs that provide reciprocal services across all regions. Region-specific web sites can be accessed through AAA.com. AAA offers standard and premium AAA Auto Club and AAA Motor Club members roadside assistance, including towing, locksmith services, emergency fuel delivery, battery charging and medical assistance. The company's www.exchangeev.aaa.com/ website focuses on hybrid and electric vehicles. Even though individual clubs are divided into regions, members call for help using the same toll-free number, 1-800-AAA-HELP. Besides roadside service, AAA offers other benefits including accident insurance, car theft rewards, legal fee reimbursements, medical expense coverage, international maps, car rentals, route support and vehicle inspections. Members also receive discounts and other benefits at partner businesses, including retail outlets, travel companies, hotels and Disneyland Resorts. The company publishes TripTik maps, which provide detailed travel instructions customized to individual schedules and plans, and TourBook guides, steering members through destinations in the U.S., Canada, Mexico and the Caribbean. AAA Travel Services is one of the largest travel agencies in the U.S., operating more than 1,100 travel agencies throughout the U.S. and Canada. Agents are equipped to help customers find lodging and car rentals; book flights, cruises and packaged deals; and offer general advice and travel tips. The organization offers insurance packages that cover home ownership, other personal assets, life insurance and, of course, auto insurance, which also includes special protection in foreign countries. It also offers financial services, including AAA-branded Visa credit cards, auto loans and refinancing and the issuing of traveler's checks and currency exchange.

AAA offers employees credit union membership, travel and amusement park discounts and free AAA membership.

FINANCIAL DATA: *Note: Data for latest year may not have been available at press time.*

In U.S. $	2015	2014	2013	2012	2011	2010
Revenue						
R&D Expense						
Operating Income						
Operating Margin %						
SGA Expense						
Net Income						
Operating Cash Flow						
Capital Expenditure						
EBITDA						
Return on Assets %						
Return on Equity %						
Debt to Equity						

CONTACT INFORMATION:

Phone: 407-444-7000   Fax: 407-444-7380
Toll-Free:
Address: 1000 AAA Dr., MS 75, Heathrow, FL 32746 United States

STOCK TICKER/OTHER:

Stock Ticker: Nonprofit   Exchange:
Employees: Fiscal Year Ends: 12/31
Parent Company:

SALARIES/BONUSES:

Top Exec. Salary: $ Bonus: $
Second Exec. Salary: $ Bonus: $

OTHER THOUGHTS:

Estimated Female Officers or Directors: 1
Hot Spot for Advancement for Women/Minorities:

Accor North America
www.accorhotels.com/gb/usa/index.shtml

NAIC Code: 721110

TYPES OF BUSINESS:
Hotels

BRANDS/DIVISIONS/AFFILIATES:
Accor SA
Sofitel
Novotel
Pullman

CONTACTS:
Note: Officers with more than one job title may be intentionally listed here more than once.

Roland de Bonadona, CEO-Americas
Didier Bosc, CFO
Jeff Winslow, CIO
Didier Bosc, Chief Admin. Officer
Alan Rabinowitz, Exec. VP
Jim Amorosia, Pres.
Jeff Winslow, Chief Investment Officer
Robert Moore, Sr. VP-Technical Service

GROWTH PLANS/SPECIAL FEATURES:
Accor North America, a subsidiary of French hotel and human resources conglomerate Accor SA, operates 16 hotels with approximately 4,715 rooms across the U.S. and Canada. The firm's North American hotel chains include seven Sofitel hotels, a French luxury brand that incorporates local culture into its decor. The brand offers visitors first-rate accommodations with upscale restaurants, complete business facilities, fitness centers, fine art and antiques. The Novotel chain is another more upscale offering, which consists of a relaxed modern decor that makes it accessible to both business and leisure travelers. Novotel properties offer rooms with sitting/working areas, mid-scale restaurants and pools and golf course privileges, with eight locations in the U.S. and Canada. In addition, the firm operates one Pullman hotel, which offers upscale, executive lodging for business and leisure stays. Accor incorporates a green policy into all of its chains that consists of water-saving shower heads and faucet aerators, Energy Star program participation, power-reducing heating and cooling systems, recycled paper and soy ink for its directories, energy efficient fluorescent lighting and the use of green Ecolab products for laundry and cleaning.

FINANCIAL DATA:
Note: Data for latest year may not have been available at press time.

In U.S. $	2015	2014	2013	2012	2011	2010
Revenue	635,410,802	525,348,522	302,399,520	308,574,820	304,171,460	
R&D Expense						
Operating Income						
Operating Margin %						
SGA Expense						
Net Income	255,037,440	269,380,549	153,772,184			
Operating Cash Flow						
Capital Expenditure						
EBITDA						
Return on Assets %						
Return on Equity %						
Debt to Equity						

CONTACT INFORMATION:
Phone: 972-360-9000   Fax: 972-716-6590
Toll-Free: 800-557-3435
Address: 4001 International Pkwy., Carrollton, TX 75007 United States

STOCK TICKER/OTHER:
Stock Ticker: Subsidiary   Exchange:
Employees: 21,563   Fiscal Year Ends: 12/31
Parent Company: Accor SA

SALARIES/BONUSES:
Top Exec. Salary: $ Bonus: $
Second Exec. Salary: $ Bonus: $

OTHER THOUGHTS:
Estimated Female Officers or Directors: 1
Hot Spot for Advancement for Women/Minorities:

Sales, profits and employees may be estimates. Financial information, benefits and other data can change quickly and may vary from those stated here.

Accor SA
NAIC Code: 721110

www.accor.com

TYPES OF BUSINESS:
Hotels

BRANDS/DIVISIONS/AFFILIATES:
Ibis Budget
Ibis
Formule 1
Novotel
Sofitel
Grand Mercure Apartments
MGallery
Adagio

CONTACTS: *Note: Officers with more than one job title may be intentionally listed here more than once.*
Sebastien Bazin, CEO
Sophie Stabile, CFO
Vivek Badrinath, Deputy CEO-Mktg. & Info. Systems
Sven Boinet, Deputy CEO-Human Resources
Sven Boinet, Deputy CEO-Legal
Christophe Alaux, CEO-Hotel Svcs. France
Roland de Bonadona, CEO-Hotel Svcs. Americas
Jean-Jacques Dessors, CEO-Hotel Svcs. Mediterranean, Middle East &Africa
Michael Issenberg, CEO-Hotel Svcs. Asia Pacific
Sebastien Bazin, Chmn.
Peter Verhoeven, CEO-Hotel Svcs. Northern, Central & Eastern Europe

GROWTH PLANS/SPECIAL FEATURES:
Accor SA is a leading hotel operator, with locations around the world. Accor has over 3,900 hotels under 17 brands in 92 countries worldwide. Ibis Budget offers budget accommodations throughout Europe with services such as wireless Internet access, snacks and an all-you-can-eat breakfast. The HotelF1 and Formule 1 brands are similar to Ibis Budget, but are offered in South Africa, Australia, Brazil, Indonesia and Japan. The firm's economy offerings include Ibis and Adagio Access, which provide higher quality lodgings at modest prices. These brands can be found in North America, Europe, Australia, Asia and Africa. The company's midscale hotels include Novotel, Suite Novotel, Mama Shelter and Mercure and primarily cater to travelers in international cities or vacation locations. Extended stay capabilities are available through the Adagio brand. Accor's luxury and upscale hotels include Pullman, MGallery, The Sebel, Adagio Premium, Grand Mercure Apartments and Thalassa Sea & Spa. Brands in this category are primarily used by tourists in destination cities. Accor's premier luxury brand, Sofitel, provides guests with gourmet cuisine, specialized treatment and high quality sleeping amenities. The company derives its profits primarily from France, which alone accounts for 28% of business, with 25% coming from the rest of Europe, 26% from the Asia Pacific, 11% from the Mediterranean/Middle East/Africa and 10% from the Americas. In 2015, Accor launched its Accorhotels app for Apple Watch, available in 10 languages, which promotes top hotels and destinations and allows users to manage current bookings on Accorhotels; and sold Accor franchisee Zurich MGallery, but will continue to manage it. In February 2016, the firm acquired a 49% stake in Squarebreak, a French start-up and acquired 30% stake in Oasis Collections, a curated marketplace for private rentals.

FINANCIAL DATA: *Note: Data for latest year may not have been available at press time.*

In U.S. $	2015	2014	2013	2012	2011	2010
Revenue	6,305,502,000	6,162,016,000	6,254,661,000	6,382,329,000	6,891,876,000	6,720,145,000
R&D Expense						
Operating Income	751,327,500	680,149,100	605,581,200	594,283,100	598,802,400	148,005,900
Operating Margin %	11.91%	11.03%	9.68%	9.31%	8.68%	2.20%
SGA Expense					668,850,900	420,291,500
Net Income	275,675,100	251,948,900	142,356,800	-676,759,700	56,490,790	4,078,635,000
Operating Cash Flow	886,905,400	778,443,100	592,023,500	142,356,800	725,341,800	751,327,500
Capital Expenditure				337,814,900	437,238,700	384,137,400
EBITDA	1,113,998,000	1,042,820,000	977,290,700	960,343,400	927,578,800	628,177,600
Return on Assets %	2.75%	2.82%	1.72%	-7.69%	.32%	35.25%
Return on Equity %	6.58%	7.20%	4.75%	-19.02%	.75%	108.31%
Debt to Equity	0.72	0.76	0.67	0.54	0.45	0.48

CONTACT INFORMATION:
Phone: 33 169368080   Fax: 33 169367900
Toll-Free:
Address: 2 rue de la Mare-Neuve, Paris, 75013 France

STOCK TICKER/OTHER:
Stock Ticker: ACC N   Exchange: MEX
Employees: 190,000   Fiscal Year Ends: 12/31
Parent Company:

SALARIES/BONUSES:
Top Exec. Salary: $ Bonus: $
Second Exec. Salary: $ Bonus: $

OTHER THOUGHTS:
Estimated Female Officers or Directors: 1
Hot Spot for Advancement for Women/Minorities: Y

ADA Sa

NAIC Code: 532111

www.ada.fr

TYPES OF BUSINESS:
Automobile Rental

BRANDS/DIVISIONS/AFFILIATES:
G7 Groupe
Holiday Bikes
Via Michelin
A Vendre A Louer
ADA Box
Homebox

CONTACTS: *Note: Officers with more than one job title may be intentionally listed here more than once.*
Nicolas Rousselet, Chmn.

GROWTH PLANS/SPECIAL FEATURES:

ADA is a franchise car-rental company based in France and the French islands as well as internationally in Morocco, Luxembourg, Senegal, the Dominican Republic, Germany Canada and the U.S. As one of the largest private car-rental firms in the world, ADA has over 480 locations and offers economy-class cars, electric cars, wagons and minivans. Some agencies additionally offer commercial vehicles, such as moving vans, dump trucks, all-terrain vehicles and weight-bearing porters. Through ADA's partnership with Holiday Bikes, it also offers two-wheeled vehicles such as bicycles, motorcycles and scooters for rent at most agencies. The company's other partnerships include: ADA Box, a firm that rents storage space to customers; A Vendre A Louer, a provider of real estate classified ads on the internet; and Homebox, which rents storage boxes that are located within the company's secure facility. In addition, most of the firm's agencies offer special equipment, such as baby and child seats, boosters, GPS systems and snow chains. The company offers supplemental insurance. The company operates in-terminal locations in nearly all of the major airports in France, including Ajaccio, Bastia, Bordeaux, Brest, Lorient, Lyon, Marseille, Montpellier, Nantes, Nice, Paris Orly, Paris Roissy Charles de Gaulle, Perpignan, Toulouse, Guadeloupe, Guyana and La Reunion. ADA also has agencies at all major railway stations in France. ADA customers can locate the agency of their choice through the company's partnership with Via Michelin, a map, route planner and travel guide service for the U.S. and Europe. ADA is a subsidiary of the G7 Groupe, a global holding company with several subsidiaries. These include Europe's largest taxi company, a software company and numerous real estate holdings.

FINANCIAL DATA: *Note: Data for latest year may not have been available at press time.*

In U.S. $	2015	2014	2013	2012	2011	2010
Revenue	47,420,000	50,529,848	39,164,539	115,410,451	132,701,000	
R&D Expense						
Operating Income						
Operating Margin %						
SGA Expense						
Net Income	3,196,585	3,627,812	2,690,608			
Operating Cash Flow						
Capital Expenditure						
EBITDA						
Return on Assets %						
Return on Equity %						
Debt to Equity						

CONTACT INFORMATION:
Phone: 41-27-46-00 Fax: 47-39-17-65
Toll-Free:
Address: 22-28 rue Henri Barbusse, Clichy, 92585 France

STOCK TICKER/OTHER:
Stock Ticker: ALADA Exchange: Paris
Employees: 101 Fiscal Year Ends: 12/31
Parent Company: G7 Groupe

SALARIES/BONUSES:
Top Exec. Salary: $ Bonus: $
Second Exec. Salary: $ Bonus: $

OTHER THOUGHTS:
Estimated Female Officers or Directors:
Hot Spot for Advancement for Women/Minorities:

Sales, profits and employees may be estimates. Financial information, benefits and other data can change quickly and may vary from those stated here.

Aer Lingus Group
NAIC Code: 481111

www.aerlingus.com

TYPES OF BUSINESS:
Airline
Air Cargo

BRANDS/DIVISIONS/AFFILIATES:
International Airlines Group SA

GROWTH PLANS/SPECIAL FEATURES:
Aer Lingus Group is a is an Irish airline, with operating bases in Belfast City, Cork and Shannon, Ireland. Aer Lingus has codeshare agreements with Oneworld, Star Alliance and SkyTeam members, as well as interline agreements with Etihad Airways, JetBlue Airways and United Airlines. The firm has a hybrid business model, operating a mixed-fare service on its European and North African routes, as well as full-service, two-class flights on its transatlantic routes. The airline flies to 82 destinations via a fleet of 46 aircraft. Aer Lingus' fleet includes Airbus A330-300 and A330-200 aircrafts, Boeing 767 and 757 aircraft, Airbus A321, A320 and A319 aircraft, as well as ATR aircraft. In September 2015, the firm was acquired by International Airlines Group SA, becoming its wholly-owned subsidiary.

CONTACTS: Note: Officers with more than one job title may be intentionally listed here more than once.
Stephen Kavanagh, CEO
Ravindra Simhambhatla, CTO
Donal Moriarty, Corp. Sec.
Derek Abbey, Dir.-Investor Rel.

FINANCIAL DATA: Note: Data for latest year may not have been available at press time.

In U.S. $	2015	2014	2013	2012	2011	2010
Revenue		1,758,985,000	1,610,118,000	1,574,154,000	1,455,552,000	1,373,372,000
R&D Expense						
Operating Income		-122,435,900	49,474,640	48,116,600	97,469,210	24,343,010
Operating Margin %		-6.96%	3.07%	3.05%	6.69%	1.77%
SGA Expense		475,167,800	366,434,300	354,446,900	112,566,900	122,782,700
Net Income		-108,235,200	38,513,160	38,444,240	80,436,100	48,619,360
Operating Cash Flow		197,556,200	114,189,400	133,850,400	87,356,230	44,440,180
Capital Expenditure		62,453,960	38,303,020	46,471,580	35,624,220	907,242
EBITDA		-10,532,140	153,572,500	154,379,200	209,004,600	151,753,500
Return on Assets %		-5.39%	1.93%	1.88%	3.91%	2.43%
Return on Equity %		-12.66%	4.04%	4.07%	8.68%	5.71%
Debt to Equity		0.45	0.42	0.58	0.64	0.59

CONTACT INFORMATION:
Phone: 353 18868022   Fax: 353 18863832
Toll-Free:
Address: Dublin Airport, Dublin, Ireland

STOCK TICKER/OTHER:
Stock Ticker: AELGF   Exchange: GREY
Employees: 3,766   Fiscal Year Ends: 12/31
Parent Company: International Airlines Group SA

SALARIES/BONUSES:
Top Exec. Salary: $ Bonus: $
Second Exec. Salary: $ Bonus: $

OTHER THOUGHTS:
Estimated Female Officers or Directors: 2
Hot Spot for Advancement for Women/Minorities: Y

AerCap Holdings NV

NAIC Code: 532411

www.aercap.com

TYPES OF BUSINESS:

Commercial Air, Rail, and Water Transportation Equipment Rental and Leasing
Engine Leasing
Aircraft Parts
Maintenance/Repair Services
Asset Management Services

BRANDS/DIVISIONS/AFFILIATES:

International Lease Finance Corporation
AeroTurbine Inc

CONTACTS: Note: Officers with more than one job title may be intentionally listed here more than once.

Aengus Kelly, CEO
Wouter den Dikken, COO
Keith Helming, CFO
Edward O'Byrne, CIO
Joe Venuto, CTO
Paul Rofe, Treas.
Edward OByrne, Chief Investment Officer
Tom Kelly, CEO-AerCap Ireland Ltd.
Pieter Korteweg, Chmn.

GROWTH PLANS/SPECIAL FEATURES:

AerCap Holdings NV is a global aviation company that provides solutions for business airlines as well as third-party management services for commercial aircraft owners. The firm also maintains several certified repair stations, through which it provides maintenance, overhaul and disassembly services for aircraft and engines. Headquartered in Amsterdam, the firm also has international offices in Ireland, the UAE, China, Singapore and the U.S. AerCap's portfolio consists of more than 1,300 aircraft, owned and managed, as well as an order book of 458 new aircraft on contract. The company operates in three divisions: leasing & trading, asset management and AeroTurbine. The leasing & trading division focuses on managing leases, sales and leasebacks of new and used aircraft, as well as aircraft trading. AerCap leases most of its aircraft under operating leases to 89 commercial airlines and cargo operator customers in more than 48 countries. Its current fleet includes two types of aircraft, narrowbodies and widebodies, which consist of products from the Airbus and Boeing families. Through aircraft trading the firm is involved in acquisition and sale of aircraft and aircraft equipment. The firm's asset management services for aircraft owners, financiers and investors include remarketing, purchasing and selling aircraft; technical and contract management; financial engineering; and securitization services. AerCap also removes and remodels engines, deconstructs old airframes and then sells dissembled parts. The AeroTurbine segment operates through wholly owned subsidiary, AeroTurbine, Inc., and offers airframe and engine components, aircraft engines as well as comprehensive fleet management solutions. In 2014, AerCap acquired International Lease Finance Corporation, an international leaser and remarketer of commercial aircraft.

FINANCIAL DATA: Note: Data for latest year may not have been available at press time.

In U.S. $	2015	2014	2013	2012	2011	2010
Revenue	5,598,662,000	3,874,766,000	1,050,066,000	972,520,000	1,093,923,000	1,834,461,000
R&D Expense						
Operating Income	2,481,918,000	1,846,039,000	563,275,000	151,965,000	230,051,000	513,557,000
Operating Margin %	44.33%	47.64%	53.64%	15.62%	21.02%	27.99%
SGA Expense	962,634,000	490,193,000	149,061,000	164,564,000	191,247,000	188,330,000
Net Income	1,178,730,000	810,447,000	292,410,000	163,655,000	172,224,000	207,573,000
Operating Cash Flow	3,360,040,000	2,296,699,000	694,878,000	644,414,000	621,556,000	582,369,000
Capital Expenditure	2,772,110,000	2,088,444,000	1,996,159,000	1,074,781,000	810,236,000	2,088,974,000
EBITDA	4,331,628,000	2,997,442,000	883,596,000	809,822,000	924,711,000	854,943,000
Return on Assets %	2.68%	3.04%	3.24%	1.85%	1.84%	2.53%
Return on Equity %	14.54%	15.75%	12.86%	7.44%	7.67%	11.96%
Debt to Equity	3.57	3.86	2.57	2.73	2.68	3.02

CONTACT INFORMATION:

Phone: 31 206559655   Fax: 31 206559100
Toll-Free:
Address: AerCap House, Stationsplein 965, Schiphol Airport, Schiphol, 1117 CE Netherlands

STOCK TICKER/OTHER:

Stock Ticker: AER
Employees: 332
Parent Company:

Exchange: NYS
Fiscal Year Ends: 12/31

SALARIES/BONUSES:

Top Exec. Salary: $ Bonus: $
Second Exec. Salary: $ Bonus: $

OTHER THOUGHTS:

Estimated Female Officers or Directors:
Hot Spot for Advancement for Women/Minorities:

Sales, profits and employees may be estimates. Financial information, benefits and other data can change quickly and may vary from those stated here.

Aeroflot Russian Airlines JSC

www.aeroflot.ru/cms/en

NAIC Code: 481111

TYPES OF BUSINESS:

Airline
Air Cargo
Intermodal Shipping & Logistics Services

BRANDS/DIVISIONS/AFFILIATES:

Aurora Airline
Pobeda Airlines LLC
Rossiya Airline JSC

CONTACTS: Note: Officers with more than one job title may be intentionally listed here more than once.

Vitaly Gennadevich Savelev, CEO
Shamil Ravilyevich Kurmashov, CFO
Yury Ilyich Belykh, Head-Aviation & Technical Section
Vladimir Nikolavich Antonov, CEO-Prod.
Igor Petrovich Chalik, Dir.-Oper. Dept.
Vitaly Gennadevich Saveliev, Chmn.

GROWTH PLANS/SPECIAL FEATURES:

Aeroflot Russian Airlines JSC is a Russian air carrier. It offers service to 129 destinations to 52 countries around the world, including numerous routes connecting Russia with the CIS (Commonwealth of Independent States) and Baltic nations. In addition, Aeroflot provides direct service to Moscow from four U.S. cities. With a fleet of 165 aircraft, including 29 narrow-body regional aircraft (SSJ100s), 105 narrow-body medium-range aircraft (Boeing 737s and Airbus 320s, 321s) and 31 wide-body long haul aircraft (Boeing 737s, 777s). The company has numerous code-sharing agreements with airlines operating in Eastern Europe and Asia. Aeroflot is a member of the SkyTeam Alliance, whose other members include Delta Airlines, Air France, Continental and Korean Air, among others. The Russian government currently owns 51% of the firm, with legal entities and individuals owning the remaining 49%. Aeroflot subsidiaries include 51%-owned Aurora Airline, a Russian far east air carrier; Pobeda Airlines LLC, a Russian low-cost airline; and Rossiya Airline JSC, a Russian airline headquartered in Saint Petersburg, with its hub at Pulkovo Airport. In March 2016, the firm merged the operations of subsidiaries Rossiya Airlines and Donavia.

FINANCIAL DATA: Note: Data for latest year may not have been available at press time.

In U.S. $	2015	2014	2013	2012	2011	2010
Revenue		4,350,651,000	4,712,434,000	3,877,779,000	2,698,545,000	2,072,614,000
R&D Expense						
Operating Income		176,752,900	320,586,000	170,442,900	194,842,800	239,636,800
Operating Margin %		4.06%	6.80%	4.39%	7.22%	11.56%
SGA Expense		369,631,400				
Net Income		-242,682,400	129,833,500	105,829,900	246,526,600	121,497,900
Operating Cash Flow		564,345,100	468,834,500	257,594,200	187,817,800	354,752,700
Capital Expenditure		431,702,000	71,441,930	79,622,620	64,328,730	56,286,340
EBITDA		11,262,750	493,233,000	298,668,200	527,174,500	334,599,000
Return on Assets %		-6.34%	4.13%	3.74%	10.85%	6.56%
Return on Equity %		-54.47%	14.47%	13.28%	40.87%	26.82%
Debt to Equity			1.19	1.05	1.13	1.66

CONTACT INFORMATION:

Phone: 7 4952584089   Fax: 7 4995006760
Toll-Free:
Address: 10 Arbat St., Moscow, 119002 Russia

SALARIES/BONUSES:

Top Exec. Salary: $ Bonus: $
Second Exec. Salary: $ Bonus: $

STOCK TICKER/OTHER:

Stock Ticker: AERAY   Exchange: GREY
Employees: 29,548   Fiscal Year Ends: 12/31
Parent Company:

OTHER THOUGHTS:

Estimated Female Officers or Directors:
Hot Spot for Advancement for Women/Minorities:

Sales, profits and employees may be estimates. Financial information, benefits and other data can change quickly and may vary from those stated here.

Aerolitoral SA de CV (Aeromexico Connect) aeromexico.com/en/us
NAIC Code: 481111

TYPES OF BUSINESS:
Regional Airline
Travel Reservations

BRANDS/DIVISIONS/AFFILIATES:
Grupo Aeromexico
AeroMexico Connect

CONTACTS: Note: Officers with more than one job title may be intentionally listed here more than once.
Raul Saenz, CEO
Juan Rodriguez Castaneda, Chief Corp. & Industrial Affairs Officer
Claudia Contreras Chavez-Peon, Chief Customer Experience Officer
Sergio Alfonso Allard Barroso, Chief Commercial Officer

GROWTH PLANS/SPECIAL FEATURES:
Aerolitoral SA de CV, operating as AeroMexico Connect, is a Mexican regional airline. The company's services include ground transportation, in flight dining and entertainment, extended schedule, holiday destinations, check-in and reservations. The company also provides charter services for corporate travelers and groups. The company makes more than 300 daily flights. The company's 63 aircraft comprise an all-Embraer fleet of ERJ-145s, E170s, E175s and E190s. The company's corporate service accommodates the travel needs of small- to medium-sized businesses, offering last minute adjustments on itineraries, lines of credit, preferential treatment for high demand travel dates and reward travel tickets. The firm is a member of SkyTeam, a global airline alliance that offers more than 15,000 daily flights to over 1,000 destinations worldwide, VIP airport lounges and frequent flier miles to customers. In addition, the company provides vacation packages, car rental, hotel reservations and activities. Aerolitoral is a wholly-owned subsidiary of Grupo Aeromexico.

FINANCIAL DATA: Note: Data for latest year may not have been available at press time.

In U.S. $	2015	2014	2013	2012	2011	2010
Revenue						
R&D Expense						
Operating Income						
Operating Margin %						
SGA Expense						
Net Income						
Operating Cash Flow						
Capital Expenditure						
EBITDA						
Return on Assets %						
Return on Equity %						
Debt to Equity						

CONTACT INFORMATION:
Phone: 52-55-9132-4567   Fax:
Toll-Free: 800-021-4000
Address: Carretera Miguel Aleman, Km 22.8, Apodaca, NL 66600 Mexico

STOCK TICKER/OTHER:
Stock Ticker: Subsidiary   Exchange:
Employees: Fiscal Year Ends: 12/31
Parent Company: Grupo Aeromexico

SALARIES/BONUSES:
Top Exec. Salary: $ Bonus: $
Second Exec. Salary: $ Bonus: $

OTHER THOUGHTS:
Estimated Female Officers or Directors: 1
Hot Spot for Advancement for Women/Minorities:

Aeroports de Paris

NAIC Code: 488119

www.aeroportsdeparis.fr

TYPES OF BUSINESS:

Airports, Civil, Operation and Maintenance

BRANDS/DIVISIONS/AFFILIATES:

Charles de Gaulle
Le Bourget
Orly
Le Bourget
Aeroports de Paris Management
ADP Ingeierie
Hub One
Hub Safe

CONTACTS: Note: Officers with more than one job title may be intentionally listed here more than once.

Augustin de Romanet, CEO
Francois Rubichon, COO
Pascal Bourgue, Dir.-Mktg. & Retail
Catherine Benet, Dir.-Human Resources
Laurent Galzy, Exec. Dir.-Admin.
Bernard Cathelain, Exec. Dir.-Dev. & Planning
Pascal Bourgue, Dir.-Comm.
Laurent Galzy, Exec. Dir.-Finance
Franck Goldnadel, Managing Dir.-Charles de Gaulle Airport
Franck Mereyde, Managing Dir.-Orly Airport
Francois Cangardel, Dir.-Real Estate
Augustin de Romanet, Chmn.

GROWTH PLANS/SPECIAL FEATURES:

Aeroports de Paris (ADP) is a leading European airport management company. Major activities include airport operations, retail and real estate. ADP owns and operates one heliport and 13 airports in and around Paris, including Charles de Gaulle, Le Bourget and Orly. The company's other 10 airfields are Chavenay-Villepreux, Chelles-le-Pin, Coulommiers-Voisins, Etampes-Mondesir, Lognes-Emerainville, Meaux-Esbly, Persan-Beaumont, Pontoise-Cormeilles-en-Vexin, Saint-Cyr-l'Ecole and Toussus-le-Noble. The firm collectively serves over 95.4 million passengers annually. The company manages 34 airports directly or indirectly, serving more than 250 million passengers in 2015. ADP provides airlines, passengers and freight & mail operators quality facilities and services tailored to their needs. Wholly-owned subsidiaries of the firm include Aeroports de Paris Management, which operates, manages and develops foreign airports outside of Paris; ADP Ingenierie, a provider of airport architecture and engineering in France and abroad; Hub One, a provider of telecommunications, radio communications, as well as mobility and traceability solutions; and Hub Safe (formerly Alyzia Surete), providing airport security service. Moreover, ADP owns a 49% stake in TAV Construction, a building company based in Turkey; and 38%-owned TAV Airports, an airport management firm based in Turkey. ADP's retail operations includes overseeing the business activities of shops, restaurants, parking, car rental companies and other rentals in the airport terminals. Real estate activities include the maintenance of aircraft hangars, cargo terminals and other industrial areas at the airports, as well as offices, hotels, shops and business/logistics locations.

FINANCIAL DATA: Note: Data for latest year may not have been available at press time.

In U.S. $	2015	2014	2013	2012	2011	2010
Revenue	3,294,543,000	3,153,316,000	3,112,029,000	2,983,222,000	2,826,250,000	3,094,571,000
R&D Expense						
Operating Income	889,165,100	824,765,600	741,759,100	725,441,200	736,075,100	612,624,500
Operating Margin %	26.98%	26.15%	23.83%	24.31%	26.04%	19.79%
SGA Expense						
Net Income	485,820,800	454,186,000	344,300,100	385,541,800	392,087,900	339,369,600
Operating Cash Flow	1,133,205,000	1,031,522,000	919,179,800	1,034,245,000	972,101,400	890,380,700
Capital Expenditure	594,283,100	459,835,000	501,438,200	730,503,900	775,295,400	565,762,000
EBITDA	1,439,385,000	1,324,144,000	1,250,520,000	1,202,675,000	1,273,290,000	1,180,581,000
Return on Assets %	4.25%	4.13%	3.20%	3.74%	4.05%	3.68%
Return on Equity %	10.61%	10.30%	8.06%	9.30%	9.93%	9.04%
Debt to Equity	1.06	1.02	0.95	0.93	0.83	

CONTACT INFORMATION:

Phone: 33-1-43-35-70-00   Fax: 33-1-43-35-74-27
Toll-Free:
Address: 291 Blvd. Raspail, Paris, 75014 France

STOCK TICKER/OTHER:

Stock Ticker: AEOXF   Exchange: GREY
Employees: 8,966   Fiscal Year Ends: 12/31
Parent Company:

SALARIES/BONUSES:

Top Exec. Salary: $ Bonus: $
Second Exec. Salary: $ Bonus: $

OTHER THOUGHTS:

Estimated Female Officers or Directors: 1
Hot Spot for Advancement for Women/Minorities: Y

Aerovias de Mexico SA de CV (Aeromexico) www.aeromexico.com

NAIC Code: 481111

TYPES OF BUSINESS:

International Airline
Flight Services
Cargo Services
Maintenance & Engineering Services

BRANDS/DIVISIONS/AFFILIATES:

AeroMexico
AeroMexico Connect
AeroMexico Contigo
AeroMexico MRO
Aeromexico Express

CONTACTS: *Note: Officers with more than one job title may be intentionally listed here more than once.*

Andres Conesa Labastida, CEO
Corneel Koster, COO
Ricardo Sanchez Baker, CFO
Juan Rodriguez Castaneda, Chief Corp. & Industrial Affairs Officer
Claudia Contreras Chavez-Peon, Chief Mktg. Officer & Customer Experience
Javier Arrigunaga, Chmn.

GROWTH PLANS/SPECIAL FEATURES:

Aerovias de Mexico SA de CV (AeroMexico) is a leading airline company in Mexico. AeroMexico, its major transcontinental airline, operates over 600 flights daily to destinations in Mexico, the U.S., Canada, Europe, Asia and Central and South America. From its hub in Mexico City International Airport, the airline currently flies to 45 domestic destinations and 32 international destinations. The company carries on average over 14 million passengers per year. Its fleet consists of 120 aircraft comprised of Boeing 787, 777 and 737 jetliners and next-generation Embraer 145, 170, 175 and 190 models. Subsidiary AeroMexico Connect is a holding company whose subsidiaries provide commercial aviation services in Mexico, as well as the promotion of passenger loyalty programs. AeroMexico MRO, the firm's maintenance and engineering division, operates two maintenance facilities in Mexico, which offer heavy maintenance checks; application of airworthiness directives and service bulletins; modifications to engines, systems and other components; installation of GPS, TCAS (traffic collision avoidance system), radar, windshear, winglets, heaters and blankets; and interior modifications. Aeromexico Contigo is the firm's current brand for its USA-Mexico flights. Aeromexico Express is a commuter airline based in Monterey, and is a partnership with Aeromar. AeroMexico has an expanded codeshare network as a member of the Delta Alliance. The firm is also a founding member of the SkyTeam global airline alliance.

FINANCIAL DATA: *Note: Data for latest year may not have been available at press time.*

In U.S. $	2015	2014	2013	2012	2011	2010
Revenue	2,445,533,000	2,225,601,000	2,183,845,000	2,168,448,000	1,962,371,000	1,538,863,000
R&D Expense						
Operating Income	166,097,600	92,054,540	131,716,200	133,213,900	187,897,700	148,190,700
Operating Margin %	6.79%	4.13%	6.03%	6.14%	9.57%	9.62%
SGA Expense	255,764,000	268,411,200	298,601,600	279,672,500	193,959,600	100,187,000
Net Income	63,531,960	42,922,120	59,202,840	72,483,100	114,062,000	130,527,200
Operating Cash Flow	237,494,500	140,120,600	172,532,100	127,317,300	163,553,500	78,767,220
Capital Expenditure	199,698,000	143,998,900	141,293,400	167,271,500	124,697,900	17,964,260
EBITDA	258,376,600	185,014,200	216,886,000	212,800,500	226,982,400	185,472,900
Return on Assets %	2.63%	2.22%	3.57%	5.30%	11.71%	18.53%
Return on Equity %	11.59%	8.98%	13.95%	21.36%	88.01%	
Debt to Equity	1.48	1.13	0.95	0.72	0.43	

CONTACT INFORMATION:

Phone: 52 5591324000   Fax:
Toll-Free:
Address: Paseo de la Reforma, 445, Mexico City, 06500 Mexico

STOCK TICKER/OTHER:

Stock Ticker: AEROMEX   Exchange: MEX
Employees: Fiscal Year Ends:
Parent Company:

SALARIES/BONUSES:

Top Exec. Salary: $ Bonus: $
Second Exec. Salary: $ Bonus: $

OTHER THOUGHTS:

Estimated Female Officers or Directors: 1
Hot Spot for Advancement for Women/Minorities:

Sales, profits and employees may be estimates. Financial information, benefits and other data can change quickly and may vary from those stated here.

Air Berlin plc & Co Luftverkehrs KG

www.airberlin.com

NAIC Code: 481111

TYPES OF BUSINESS:

Airline

BRANDS/DIVISIONS/AFFILIATES:

Niki
Belair
Luftfahrtgesellschaft Walter mgH (LGW)

GROWTH PLANS/SPECIAL FEATURES:

Air Berlin PLC & Co. Luftverkehrs KG is one of Germany's leading airlines. It maintains hubs at Berlin Tegel Airport and Dusseldorf Airport, and operates a route network that includes a total of 17 German cities, some European metropolitan and several leisure destinations in Southern Europe and North Africa. Air Berlin also provides intercontinental services to destinations in the Caribbean and the Americas. The company's fleet include 130 aircraft, featuring Airbus 319s, 320s, 321s and 330s, as well as Bombardier Dash 8s. In 2016, the firm phased out its Boeing 737 aircraft, except for five in which TUIfly will operate until 2019. Air Berlin announced plans to focus on their short- and mid-haul fleet on the Airbus 320 family in order to restructure and cut costs. Air Berlin is a member of the Oneworld alliance, and owns subsidiaries Niki, an Australian low-cost airline; Belair, a Swiss airline; and LGW (Luftfahrtgesellschaft Walter mbH), a German regional airline.

CONTACTS: Note: Officers with more than one job title may be intentionally listed here more than once.

Stefan Pichler, CEO
Jean Christoph Debus, COO
Ulf Huettmeyer, CFO
Martina Niemann, Chief Human Resources Officer
Uwe Berlinghoff, Dir.-Corp. Comm.
Ingolf T. Hegner, Head-Investor Rel.
Hans-Joachim Korber, Chmn.

FINANCIAL DATA: Note: Data for latest year may not have been available at press time.

In U.S. $	2015	2014	2013	2012	2011	2010
Revenue	4,611,632,000	4,700,208,000	4,685,113,000	4,871,399,000	4,776,091,000	4,206,958,000
R&D Expense						
Operating Income	-346,800,400	-331,902,600	-261,982,800	79,259,970	-279,092,700	-10,553,610
Operating Margin %	-7.52%	-7.06%	-5.59%	1.62%	-5.84%	-.25%
SGA Expense	540,929,800					3,025,099,000
Net Income	-504,616,400	-425,566,600	-356,470,500	7,697,435	-307,126,900	-109,771,800
Operating Cash Flow	-268,782,000	-392,255,100	-193,264,000	-252,893,500	-221,349,000	-15,976,730
Capital Expenditure				61,454,070	198,626,100	66,212,860
EBITDA	-336,941,600	-222,366,900	-165,732,700	163,030,200	-214,877,400	75,203,930
Return on Assets %	-28.70%	-20.59%	-15.37%	.30%	-11.73%	-4.06%
Return on Equity %				3.54%	-71.62%	-17.42%
Debt to Equity				6.82	3.71	1.60

CONTACT INFORMATION:

Phone: 49-30-3434-1590   Fax: 49-30-3434-1599
Toll-Free:
Address: Saatwinkler Damm 42-43, Berlin, D-13627 Germany

STOCK TICKER/OTHER:

Stock Ticker: AIBEF
Employees: 8,440
Parent Company:

Exchange: GREY
Fiscal Year Ends: 12/31

SALARIES/BONUSES:

Top Exec. Salary: $ Bonus: $
Second Exec. Salary: $ Bonus: $

OTHER THOUGHTS:

Estimated Female Officers or Directors: 2
Hot Spot for Advancement for Women/Minorities: Y

Sales, profits and employees may be estimates. Financial information, benefits and other data can change quickly and may vary from those stated here.

Air Canada

NAIC Code: 481111

TYPES OF BUSINESS:

Airline

BRANDS/DIVISIONS/AFFILIATES:

Air Canada Cargo
AC Jetz
Air Canada Vacations

CONTACTS: Note: Officers with more than one job title may be intentionally listed here more than once.

Calin Rovinescu, CEO
Amos Kazzaz, Vice President, Divisional
Michael Rousseau, CFO
Lise Fournel, Chief Information Officer
Chris Isford, Controller
Klaus Goersch, COO
David Richardson, Director
David J. Shapiro, Other Executive Officer
Benjamin M. Smith, President, Divisional
Craig Landry, President, Divisional
Carolyn Hadrovic, Secretary
Kevin Howlett, Senior VP, Divisional
Richard Steer, Vice President, Divisional
Alan Butterfield, Vice President, Divisional
Lucie Guillemette, Vice President, Divisional
Priscille LeBlanc, Vice President, Divisional
Yves Dufresne, Vice President, Divisional

GROWTH PLANS/SPECIAL FEATURES:

Air Canada is Canada's largest domestic, full service airline as well as a leading provider of scheduled passenger services in the regional Canadian market, the Canada-USA transborder market and the international market to and from Canada. Air Canada and its affiliates provide direct passenger service to more than 190 destinations on five continents, carrying more than 38 million passengers. It offers direct service to 64 Canadian cities, 52 USA destinations and 78 cities in the Europe, Central America, South America, the Middle East, Asia, Australia, the Caribbean and Mexico. Through capacity purchase agreements, Air Canada operates express flights through Jazz Aviation LP, Sky Regional Airlines Inc., Air Georgian Ltd. and Exploits Valley Air Services. The firm operates most of its flights from hubs in Toronto, Montreal, Vancouver and Calgary. Air Canada's fleet of 404 aircraft consists of Boeing 777s, 787s and 767s; Airbus A330s, A321s, A320s and A319s; Embraer 175s and 190s; CRJ 705s, 100s and 200s; Dash8 100s, 300s and 400s; and Beechcrafts 1900s. Air Canada is a founding member of the world's largest air transportation network, Star Alliance, which currently includes 28 international airline members. Other operations conducted by the company include AC Jetz, a specialty charter service for professional sports teams, corporate travelers and executive groups; Air Canada Vacations, a tour operator offering travel packages and cruises; and Air Canada Cargo, offering direct cargo service to more than 150 destinations worldwide.

Employee benefits include life and accident insurance plans.

FINANCIAL DATA: Note: Data for latest year may not have been available at press time.

In U.S. $	2015	2014	2013	2012	2011	2010
Revenue	10,757,390,000	10,295,080,000	9,604,704,000	9,401,471,000	9,007,416,000	8,366,688,000
R&D Expense						
Operating Income	1,160,446,000	632,194,600	480,157,600	338,980,400	138,850,100	280,027,300
Operating Margin %	10.78%	6.14%	4.99%	3.60%	1.54%	3.34%
SGA Expense	4,723,231,000	3,849,018,000	3,707,841,000	3,567,439,000	3,422,384,000	3,118,310,000
Net Income	235,036,800	77,569,890	4,654,194	98,513,760	-197,003,200	02,999,700
Operating Cash Flow	1,560,706,000	729,932,700	567,035,900	503,428,600	454,559,600	670,203,800
Capital Expenditure	1,407,894,000	1,164,324,000	746,222,300	358,372,900	170,653,800	91,532,470
EBITDA	1,016,941,000	729,157,000	722,175,700	892,829,500	619,007,700	946,352,600
Return on Assets %	2.54%	.99%	.06%	1.35%	-2.52%	1.02%
Return on Equity %						6.71%
Debt to Equity	451.53					2.27

CONTACT INFORMATION:

Phone: 514 422-5000   Fax: 514 422-0296
Toll-Free: 888-247-2262
Address: 7373 Cote-Vertu Blvd. W., Saint-Laurent, QC H4S 1Z3 Canada

STOCK TICKER/OTHER:

Stock Ticker: AC   Exchange: TSE
Employees: 23,600   Fiscal Year Ends: 12/31
Parent Company:

SALARIES/BONUSES:

Top Exec. Salary: $ Bonus: $
Second Exec. Salary: $ Bonus: $

OTHER THOUGHTS:

Estimated Female Officers or Directors: 7
Hot Spot for Advancement for Women/Minorities: Y

Sales, profits and employees may be estimates. Financial information, benefits and other data can change quickly and may vary from those stated here.

Air China Limited

NAIC Code: 481111

TYPES OF BUSINESS:

Airline
Aircraft Maintenance
Air Cargo

BRANDS/DIVISIONS/AFFILIATES:

Air China Cargo Co Ltd
Air Macau Co Ltd
Shenzhen Airlines Co Ltd
Shandong Airlines Co Ltd
Dalian Airlines Co Ltd
Beijing Airlines
China National Aviation Holding Co

CONTACTS: *Note: Officers with more than one job title may be intentionally listed here more than once.*

Cai Jianjiang, Pres.
Rao Xinyu, Co-Corp. Sec.
Wang Yinxiang, Vice Chmn.
Fan Cheng, Sr. VP
Tam Shuit Mui, Co-Corp. Sec.
Wang Changshun, Chmn.

GROWTH PLANS/SPECIAL FEATURES:

Air China Limited, headquartered in Beijing, is one of China's three national airline companies, along with China Eastern and China Southern. China National Aviation Holding Co. controls 51% of the company's outstanding stock. Air China, together with its subsidiaries, carries over 70 million passengers and more than 1.4 million tons of freight. The airline carries passengers and cargo via 360 domestic and international routes, including 100 international routes, 15 regional routes and 245 domestic routes. Air China serves 174 cities in 40 countries and regions. The company's in-service fleet consists of 382 aircraft (Airbus 319s, 320s, 321s and 330s, Boeing 737s, 747s, 777s and 787s), with 175 Airbus, Boeing and Comac aircraft on order as of July 2016. In addition, Air China provides specialty flight services for Chinese leaders and visiting leaders from foreign countries. Through the firm's membership in the Star Alliance, a code-sharing partnership that includes Air Macau, El Al, Hawaiian Airlines, Tibet Airlines, Virgin Atlantic and more. Air China also has an ongoing partnership with Cathay Pacific Airways, which handles sales to Air China passengers in Hong Kong, Macao and Taiwan, while the company is responsible for Cathay Pacific sales in mainland China. The firm holds interests in Air China Cargo Co. Ltd. (51%), Air Macau Co. Ltd. (66.9%), Shenzhen Airlines Co. Ltd. (51%), Shandong Airlines Co. Ltd. (51%), Dalian Airlines Co. Ltd. (80%) and Beijing Airlines (51%).

FINANCIAL DATA: *Note: Data for latest year may not have been available at press time.*

In U.S. $	2015	2014	2013	2012	2011	2010
Revenue	16,418,830,000	15,800,330,000	14,715,460,000	15,048,920,000	14,641,730,000	12,203,470,000
R&D Expense						
Operating Income	1,257,054,000	590,452,100	596,783,200	858,387,200	1,379,203,000	2,150,055,000
Operating Margin %	7.65%	3.73%	4.05%	5.70%	9.41%	17.61%
SGA Expense	1,533,136,000	1,605,618,000	1,548,394,000	1,518,202,000	1,481,410,000	1,182,242,000
Net Income	1,021,043,000	570,117,600	500,213,000	745,816,300	1,126,983,000	1,840,114,000
Operating Cash Flow	4,786,071,000	2,641,211,000	2,628,138,000	1,871,883,000	3,261,725,000	2,964,389,000
Capital Expenditure	1,149,324,000	2,084,710,000	3,377,686,000	2,305,697,000	3,394,419,000	2,611,204,000
EBITDA	3,774,301,000	2,948,050,000	2,768,178,000	2,966,219,000	3,176,799,000	3,733,702,000
Return on Assets %	3.20%	1.82%	1.69%	2.75%	4.55%	9.34%
Return on Equity %	11.86%	6.97%	6.33%	10.16%	16.91%	37.23%
Debt to Equity	0.81	0.90	0.78	0.83	0.84	0.98

CONTACT INFORMATION:

Phone: 471-6964103   Fax: 471-6959152
Toll-Free:
Address: 1F, Air China Bldg, 96 Zhelimu Rd, Beijing, Beijing 101312 China

STOCK TICKER/OTHER:

Stock Ticker: AIRYY
Employees: 68,553
Parent Company:

Exchange: PINX
Fiscal Year Ends: 12/31

SALARIES/BONUSES:

Top Exec. Salary: $ Bonus: $
Second Exec. Salary: $ Bonus: $

OTHER THOUGHTS:

Estimated Female Officers or Directors: 3
Hot Spot for Advancement for Women/Minorities: Y

Air France
NAIC Code: 481111

www.airfrance.com

TYPES OF BUSINESS:
Airline-Global
Airlines-Regional
Air Freight
Air Transportation Consulting
Airline Catering & Cleaning
Aircraft Maintenance

BRANDS/DIVISIONS/AFFILIATES:
Air France-KLM SA
HOP!
Servair
Regional
Air France Consulting
City Jet
Transavia France

CONTACTS: Note: Officers with more than one job title may be intentionally listed here more than once.
Frederic Gagey, CEO
Franck Terner, Exec. VP-Eng. & Maintenance
Adeline Challon-Kemoun, Sr. VP-Comm.
Alain Malka, Exec. VP-Air France Cargo
Christian Boireau, Exec. VP-Commercial France
Bruno Matheu, Chief Officer-Long-Haul Passenger Activity
Eric Schramm, Exec. VP-Flight Oper.
Frederic Gagey, Chmn.

GROWTH PLANS/SPECIAL FEATURES:
Air France, a subsidiary of Air France-KLM SA, is one of the world's largest airlines in terms of international passenger traffic. Air France created Air France-KLM as a holding company after it acquired KLM Royal Dutch Airlines (KLM); KLM and Air France continue to operate independently. Air France, with a fleet of 344 planes, offers flights to destinations around the world. The firm's core segments include passenger transport, cargo and aircraft maintenance. Passenger transport comprises the firm's core activity in terms of revenue, transporting over 77 million passengers to more than 100 countries, annually. The cargo segment transports 1.3 million tons of cargo to 255 destinations, via 13 freighters on a yearly basis. Aircraft maintenance strives to ensure flight safety, manage aircraft operations and keep costs down. Under the Air France brand, this division provides maintenance services and solutions to 150 customer airlines throughout the world, representing over 1,300 aircraft. The firm's primary maintenance sites include Paris-Charles-de-Gaulle, Orly, Toulouse Blagnac, Le Bourget and Villeneuve-le-Roi. HOP! is a regional subsidiary between regional airline subsidiaries Brit Air, Regional and Airlinair, which offers daily flights to 50 French and European destinations. Other subsidiaries include Servair, offering catering, cleaning and consulting services; Regional, a regional airline that offers service between France and Europe; Air France Consulting, which provides a variety of research, planning, training and financial services to third-party airlines; City Jet, an Irish regional airline; and Transavia France, a regional airline that offers charter flights to various countries around the Mediterranean basin. Air France is also a founding member of global airline alliance, SkyTeam. On January 14, 2016, the firm retired its last Boeing 747-400 with a special scenic flight, having operated the 747 in several variants since 1970.

FINANCIAL DATA: Note: Data for latest year may not have been available at press time.

In U.S. $	2015	2014	2013	2012	2011	2010
Revenue	29,638,203,650	26,733,244,044	28,924,401,664	29,070,610,432	27,657,256,960	23,800,293,376
R&D Expense						
Operating Income						
Operating Margin %						
SGA Expense						
Net Income	134,207,300	-202,796,430	-2,070,724,224	-1,351,014,272	-916,921,600	-1,766,972,672
Operating Cash Flow						
Capital Expenditure						
EBITDA						
Return on Assets %						
Return on Equity %						
Debt to Equity						

CONTACT INFORMATION:
Phone: 33 141567800   Fax: 33 141567029
Toll-Free: 800-237-2747
Address: 45 rue de Paris, Paris, 95747 France

STOCK TICKER/OTHER:
Stock Ticker: Subsidiary   Exchange:
Employees: 106,933   Fiscal Year Ends: 12/31
Parent Company: Air France-KLM SA

SALARIES/BONUSES:
Top Exec. Salary: $ Bonus: $
Second Exec. Salary: $ Bonus: $

OTHER THOUGHTS:
Estimated Female Officers or Directors: 4
Hot Spot for Advancement for Women/Minorities: Y

Air France-KLM SA

www.airfranceklm.com

NAIC Code: 481111

TYPES OF BUSINESS:

Airlines-International
Airlines-Regional
Frequent Flyer Program
Cargo Services
In-flight Catering
Aircraft Maintenance

BRANDS/DIVISIONS/AFFILIATES:

Flying Blue
Regional
Brit Air
Servair
Air France Consulting
Societe Air France
KLM Cityhopper
Martinair

CONTACTS: Note: Officers with more than one job title may be intentionally listed here more than once.

Alexandre de Juniac, CEO
Philippe Calavia, CFO
Pieter Bootsman, Exec. VP-Commercial Mktg.-Passenger Bus.
Wim Kooijman, Exec. VP-Human Resources
Jean-Chirstophe Lalanne, Exec. VP-IT
Franck Terner, Exec. VP-Eng. & Maintenance
Guy Zacklad, Group Exec. Sec.
Bram Graber, Exec. VP-Strategy-Passenger Bus.
Francois Brousse, Sr. VP-Corp. Comm.
Frederic Gagey, CEO
Camiel Eurlins, CEO
Alain Bassil, COO-Air France
Pieter Elbers, COO-KLM
Alexandre de Juniac, Chmn.
Erik Varwijk, Exec. VP-Intl & the Netherlands
Erik Varwijk, Exec. VP-Cargo

GROWTH PLANS/SPECIAL FEATURES:

Air France-KLM SA is a holding company for French airline Air France and Dutch carrier KLM. The firm also oversees a joint frequent flyer program called Flying Blue, which offers cargo transportation services and operates a maintenance business. Passenger transport is Air France-KLM's primary operating segment. Air France's subsidiaries include Regional, a regional carrier serving 20 destinations; Brit Air, a regional airline; Servair, an in-flight catering provider; and Air France Consulting, specializing in aerospace management and engineering services. KLM subsidiaries include Societe Air France and regional carriers KLM Cityhopper and Martinair. Air France-KLM jointly flies more than 89 million passengers annually, operating out of hubs such as Paris-Charles de Gaulle and Amsterdam-Schiphol. In total, the firm operates up to 2,200 daily flights via 534 aircraft that fly to 320 destinations in 114 countries. The company's top regions/networks are Europe, the Americas, Asia, Africa-Middle East and Caribbean and Indian Ocean. Air France-KLM is a member of SkyTeam, a leading airline alliance, which also includes Delta Airlines, Continental Airlines and Northwest Airlines.

FINANCIAL DATA: Note: Data for latest year may not have been available at press time.

In U.S. $	2015	2014	2013	2012	2011	2010
Revenue	29,445,260,000	28,145,970,000	28,832,900,000	28,978,650,000	26,688,510,000	
R&D Expense						
Operating Income	1,259,745,000	848,491,600	-256,468,200	-994,237,900	1,001,017,000	
Operating Margin %	4.27%	3.01%	-.88%	-3.43%	3.75%	
SGA Expense		982,939,800				
Net Income	133,318,300	-223,703,500	-2,064,174,000	-1,346,740,000	692,577,100	
Operating Cash Flow	2,146,650,000	1,143,374,000	1,670,998,000	961,473,300	1,525,251,000	
Capital Expenditure	1,860,807,000	1,616,766,000	1,339,962,000	1,663,089,000	2,397,469,000	
EBITDA	2,389,561,000	2,797,424,000	1,907,129,000	1,231,499,000	2,901,367,000	
Return on Assets %	.50%	-.81%	-6.90%	-4.35%	2.16%	
Return on Equity %		-25.20%	-50.99%	-21.74%	10.03%	
Debt to Equity	31.37		3.83	1.94	1.31	

CONTACT INFORMATION:

Phone: 33 141567800   Fax: 33 141567029
Toll-Free:
Address: 45 rue de Paris, Paris, 95 747 France

STOCK TICKER/OTHER:

Stock Ticker: AFLYY   Exchange: PINX
Employees: 94,666   Fiscal Year Ends: 12/31
Parent Company:

SALARIES/BONUSES:

Top Exec. Salary: $ Bonus: $
Second Exec. Salary: $ Bonus: $

OTHER THOUGHTS:

Estimated Female Officers or Directors: 5
Hot Spot for Advancement for Women/Minorities: Y

Air India Limited

NAIC Code: 481111

www.airindia.in

TYPES OF BUSINESS:

Airline-Global
Airline-Regional
Low-Fare Airline
Hotels

BRANDS/DIVISIONS/AFFILIATES:

Flying Returns
Centaur Hotels Corporation of Air India Ltd

CONTACTS: Note: Officers with more than one job title may be intentionally listed here more than once.

Ashwani Lohani, Managing Dir.
V. Hejmadi, Director-Finance
N.K. Jain, Exec. Dir.-Personnel
Pankaj Srivastava, Dir.-Commercial
S. Venkat, Dir.-Finance
Ashwani Lohani, Chmn.

GROWTH PLANS/SPECIAL FEATURES:

Air India Limited was formed when the Indian government merged its two former air carriers, Air India (AI), currently serving international routes, and Indian Airlines, serving domestic routes. Its fleet, totaling over 120 passenger aircraft, consists of Boeing, Airbus, ATR and CRJ models. The firm's fleet also supports the cargo operations of Air India Cargo. The company's cargo services are equipped to carry a variety of commodities, including postal mail; odd-sized cargo, such as livestock; dangerous goods, such as flammable and radioactive substances; and sentimental shipments, consisting of mortal remains. Air India's international operations cover 34 destinations across the USA, Europe, Australia, Far-East and South-East Asia and the Gulf. The firm recently added the B787 Dreamliner to its fleet. Through codeshare arrangements with international carriers, it offers an increased network of international destinations. Its frequent flyer program, Flying Returns, has over one million members. In addition, Air India has on-the-ground operations, which are managed by the Centaur Hotels Corporation of Air India Ltd., providing lodging accommodations for passengers. The company is a member of the Star Alliance, an alliance of over 27 of the leading airlines in the world.

FINANCIAL DATA: Note: Data for latest year may not have been available at press time.

In U.S. $	2015	2014	2013	2012	2011	2010
Revenue	3,000,000,000	2,855,871,051	2,404,070,375	2,200,895,383	2,103,688,391	2,899,320,000
R&D Expense						
Operating Income						
Operating Margin %						
SGA Expense						
Net Income	-939,434,059	-1,130,971,790	-821,324,110	-1,130,971,790	-1,027,054,909	-1,233,050,000
Operating Cash Flow						
Capital Expenditure						
EBITDA						
Return on Assets %						
Return on Equity %						
Debt to Equity						

CONTACT INFORMATION:

Phone: 91-22-2279-6666   Fax: 91-22-2202-1096
Toll-Free: 800-180-1407
Address: Airlines House, 113, Gurudwara Rakabganj Road, New Delhi, 110 001 India

STOCK TICKER/OTHER:

Stock Ticker: Government-Owned
Employees: 23,044
Parent Company:

Exchange:
Fiscal Year Ends: 03/31

SALARIES/BONUSES:

Top Exec. Salary: $ Bonus: $
Second Exec. Salary: $ Bonus: $

OTHER THOUGHTS:

Estimated Female Officers or Directors:
Hot Spot for Advancement for Women/Minorities: Y

Air New Zealand Ltd

NAIC Code: 481111

TYPES OF BUSINESS:

Airline
Aircraft Engineering
Cargo Carrier
Maintenance
Consulting Services

BRANDS/DIVISIONS/AFFILIATES:

Air New Zealand Engineering Services
Air New Zealand Consulting
Air New Zealand Holidays
Air New Zealand Cargo
TAE
Christchurch Engine Centre
Mount Cook Airline
Zeal320

CONTACTS: Note: Officers with more than one job title may be intentionally listed here more than once.

Christopher Luxon, CEO
Bruce Parton, COO
Rob McDonald, CFO
Mike Tod, CMO
Lorraine Murphy, Chief People Officer
Vanessa Stoddart, Gen. Mgr.-Tech. Oper.
John Blair, General Counsel
David Morgan, Gen. Mgr.-Airline Oper. & Safety
Stephen Jones, Gen. Mgr.-Strategy
Mike Tod, Gen. Mgr.-Corp. Comm.
George Roger Wayne France, Deputy Chmn.
Norm Thompson, Deputy CEO
Bruce Parton, Gen. Mgr.-Shorthaul Airlines
Christopher Luxon, CEO Designate
Antony Carter, Chmn.

GROWTH PLANS/SPECIAL FEATURES:

Air New Zealand Ltd. (ANZ) is a domestic and international airline that transports passengers and cargo throughout New Zealand and the Pacific Islands, as well as to North America, Australia, South America, the U.K. and Asia. The group also operates in areas including travel booking systems, travel wholesaling, aircraft engineering, ground handling services, retailing services, aircraft consulting and aircraft training. The Air New Zealand Engineering Services division provides aircraft, airmotive & component maintenance, repair & overhaul services, including full maintenance system & configuration management, reliability data, cost control and status reporting. The consulting division markets a range of airline management services including integrity & risk reviews, network & fleet analysis, market analysis & planning, quality management, emergency planning, schedule management, executive leasing and airports & airways reviews. The airline owns and leases a fleet of 105 aircraft, including Boeing and Airbus jets and Beech, Aerospatiale and Bombardier turbo-props. As a member of the Star Alliance, ANZ maintains code-share agreements with airlines including Lufthansa and United. Additionally, the firm's operations subsidiaries include Air New Zealand Consulting, Air New Zealand Holidays and Air New Zealand Cargo. Its technical subsidiaries include: Air New Zealand Engineering Services, TAE, Christchurch Engine Centre (50% owned) and Altitude Aerospace Interiors. Its four wholly owned subsidiary airlines include: Air Nelson, Eagle Airways, Mount Cook Airline and Zeal320. In conjunction with these subsidiaries, the firm operates over 300 domestic flights in New Zealand every day as well as in international cities. In 2015, ANZ sold its Safe Air engineering subsidiary.

FINANCIAL DATA: Note: Data for latest year may not have been available at press time.

In U.S. $	2015	2014	2013	2012	2011	2010
Revenue	3,317,653,000	3,121,408,000	2,959,641,000	2,670,646,000	2,549,716,000	2,500,984,000
R&D Expense						
Operating Income	354,332,100	109,585,100	198,676,700	94,124,930	64,021,910	93,338,740
Operating Margin %	10.68%	3.51%	6.71%	3.52%	2.51%	3.73%
SGA Expense	1,038,745,000	1,011,718,000	860,718,500	786,360,200	768,262,900	767,726,600
Net Income	220,278,700	185,234,200	116,642,400	42,296,650	47,575,910	50,687,260
Operating Cash Flow	740,998,600	516,110,500	480,669,300	281,183,300	273,708,300	206,457,900
Capital Expenditure	753,124,000	455,308,500	273,020,200	371,138,200	468,123,500	267,653,500
EBITDA	662,856,900	624,281,600	485,796,500	319,905,600	270,771,600	301,651,000
Return on Assets %	5.06%	4.79%	3.40%	1.37%	1.66%	1.70%
Return on Equity %	16.64%	14.89%	10.76%	4.48%	5.13%	5.19%
Debt to Equity	1.05	0.82	0.80	0.91	0.73	0.57

CONTACT INFORMATION:

Phone: 64 93755998   Fax: 64 93755990
Toll-Free: 800-242-3038
Address: 185 Fanshawe St., Auckland, 1010 New Zealand

STOCK TICKER/OTHER:

Stock Ticker: ANZFF   Exchange: GREY
Employees: 10,336   Fiscal Year Ends: 06/30
Parent Company:

SALARIES/BONUSES:

Top Exec. Salary: $ Bonus: $
Second Exec. Salary: $ Bonus: $

OTHER THOUGHTS:

Estimated Female Officers or Directors: 2
Hot Spot for Advancement for Women/Minorities:

Air Partner plc

NAIC Code: 481211

www.airpartner.com

TYPES OF BUSINESS:

Charter Aircraft
Express Freight Service

BRANDS/DIVISIONS/AFFILIATES:

JetCard
CharterPLUS

CONTACTS: Note: Officers with more than one job title may be intentionally listed here more than once.

Mark Briffa, CEO
Neil J. Morris, CFO
Graeme Manning, Corp. Sec.
Richard Everitt, Chmn.

GROWTH PLANS/SPECIAL FEATURES:

Air Partner plc is one of the largest aircraft charter companies in the world, with 20 offices throughout North America, Europe, Asia and the Middle East. The company provides executive charter service, commercial aircraft, private jet services and urgent and outsize freight service. In addition, Air Partner provides clients with instant access to chartered aircraft services 24 hours a day. Moreover, the firm offers specialty services for royalty, government, military, group charter, emergency planning, celebrity tours and crisis and relief flights. The company also offers carbon-neutral flights, with optional carbon offset costs offered standard in any proposal. These additional costs are invested in carbon-neutral projects that have included heat recovery in China, hydraulic power in China, solar generation in India and agricultural methane capture in Germany. Air Partner's freight operations are supported by specialist freight teams in nine of its 21 worldwide locations based at its U.K. headquarters and in France, Germany, Japan, Dubai, Hong Kong, Turkey, the USA and Italy. The firm's membership program, JetCard, offers members greater flexibility in the type of aircraft chartered as well as flight credit benefits and account management services. Air Partner's CharterPLUS service, designed for corporate clients and group travel organizers, provides added financial protection for booked charter flights. Air Partner has been granted a Royal Warrant by Queen Elizabeth II of England, becoming the first aviation company to receive this honor. The warrant entitles the airline to display the Royal Arms together with the words By Appointment.

FINANCIAL DATA: Note: Data for latest year may not have been available at press time.

In U.S. $	2015	2014	2013	2012	2011	2010
Revenue	250,408,187	336,452,653	359,700,000	371,100,000	459,800,000	375,000,000
R&D Expense						
Operating Income						
Operating Margin %						
SGA Expense						
Net Income	3,649,809	5,712,709	4,100,000	4,900,000	6,600,000	-2,800,000
Operating Cash Flow						
Capital Expenditure						
EBITDA						
Return on Assets %						
Return on Equity %						
Debt to Equity						

CONTACT INFORMATION:

Phone: 44-1293-844-888   Fax: 44-1293-536-810
Toll-Free: 888-247-7278
Address: 2 City Place, Beehive Ring Road, Gatwick, West Sussex RH6 0PA United Kingdom

STOCK TICKER/OTHER:

Stock Ticker: AIR
Employees: 196
Parent Company:

Exchange: London
Fiscal Year Ends: 01/31

SALARIES/BONUSES:

Top Exec. Salary: $ Bonus: $
Second Exec. Salary: $ Bonus: $

OTHER THOUGHTS:

Estimated Female Officers or Directors:
Hot Spot for Advancement for Women/Minorities:

Sales, profits and employees may be estimates. Financial information, benefits and other data can change quickly and may vary from those stated here.

Air Wisconsin Airlines Corp

NAIC Code: 481111

TYPES OF BUSINESS:

Regional Airline
Ground Handler

BRANDS/DIVISIONS/AFFILIATES:

US Airways Express

CONTACTS: *Note: Officers with more than one job title may be intentionally listed here more than once.*

Christine Deister, CEO
Bob Frisch, COO
James P. Rankin, Pres.
Stan Petersen-Gauthier, CFO
Bob Frisch, VP-Flight Oper.
Stan Petersen-Gauthier, VP-Finance
Janet Huculak, VP-Strategic Sourcing

GROWTH PLANS/SPECIAL FEATURES:

Air Wisconsin Airlines Corp. is a privately-held regional airline that partners with US Airways and United Airlines. Based in Appleton, Wisconsin, Air Wisconsin schedules nearly 500 departures per day and serves 70 cities in 26 states in the U.S., located predominately in the Northeast, Southeast and Midwest regions as well as three provinces in Canada. The firm carries approximately 6 million passengers annually, making it one of the largest privately-held regional airlines in the country. The company's maintenance bases are located in Wisconsin, Pennsylvania, Virginia and South Carolina. The firm provides flying services as US Airways Express on 71 small Canadair regional jets, each with 50 seats, at a maximum speed of 530 miles per hour and an altitude ceiling of 41,000 feet. Air Wisconsin also performs ground-handling services for several carriers in 15 locations, including United Airlines' United Express hub operation at Washington Dulles International Airport. It primarily transports customers from large and small towns to larger destinations and connections.

The firm offers employees 401(k); travel privileges; flexible spending accounts; sick leave; and medical, dental, life and short-term disability insurance.

FINANCIAL DATA: *Note: Data for latest year may not have been available at press time.*

In U.S. $	2015	2014	2013	2012	2011	2010
Revenue	1,594,340,000	1,709,000,000	1,807,000,000	1,668,509,000	1,320,800,000	589,158,000
R&D Expense						
Operating Income						
Operating Margin %						
SGA Expense						
Net Income	106,000,000	72,900,000	55,000,000			
Operating Cash Flow						
Capital Expenditure						
EBITDA						
Return on Assets %						
Return on Equity %						
Debt to Equity						

CONTACT INFORMATION:

Phone: 920-739-5123   Fax: 920-739-1325
Toll-Free:
Address: W6390 Challenger Dr., Ste. 203, Appleton, WI 54914 United States

STOCK TICKER/OTHER:

Stock Ticker: Private
Employees: 1,500
Parent Company:

Exchange:
Fiscal Year Ends: 05/31

SALARIES/BONUSES:

Top Exec. Salary: $ Bonus: $
Second Exec. Salary: $ Bonus: $

OTHER THOUGHTS:

Estimated Female Officers or Directors: 2
Hot Spot for Advancement for Women/Minorities: Y

Sales, profits and employees may be estimates. Financial information, benefits and other data can change quickly and may vary from those stated here.

AirAsia Berhad

NAIC Code: 481111

www.airasia.com

TYPES OF BUSINESS:

Airline

BRANDS/DIVISIONS/AFFILIATES:

Air Asia
AirAsia Indonesia
Thai AirAsia
Philippines AirAsia
AirAsia India
AirAsia Go Holiday Sdn Bhd
AirAsiaGo
Air Asia Red Tix

CONTACTS: Note: Officers with more than one job title may be intentionally listed here more than once.

Aireen Omar, CEO
Lau Kin Choy, Regional Head-Tech, Innovation & Commercial
Anaz Tajuddin, Regional Head-Eng.
Amir Faezal bin Zakaria, Regional Head-Legal & Compliance
Adrian Jenkins, Regional Head-Flight Oper.
Ashok Kumar, Regional Head-Strategy, Airport & Planning
Dany Bolduc, Gen. Mgr.-iVentures
Chin Nyok San, Regional Head-Bus. Dev.
Terri Chin, Regional Head-Quality & Assurance
Kamarudin Bin Meranun, Chmn.

GROWTH PLANS/SPECIAL FEATURES:

AirAsia Berhad is the operating company for AirAsia, a short-haul discount airline based in Malaysia. Together with its minority-owned affiliates AirAsia Indonesia, Thai AirAsia, Philippines AirAsia and AirAsia India, company carries more than 45 million passengers annually. The airlines operate a fleet of 188 aircraft that travel to 100 destinations, offering nearly 3,500 flights per week. Its fleet includes Airbus 330s, with 330neos and 350s currently on order for a 2018 delivery. Costs are kept low by selling paperless tickets over the Internet, streamlining operations, using a point-to-point network, keeping luxury travel services to a minimum and fast aircraft turnaround. Through wholly-owned subsidiary AirAsia Go Holiday Sdn Bhd, the carrier offers AirAsiaGo, an online program in which customers may book holiday packages and special promotions. AirAsia Red Tix provides online tickets to music concerts, theater shows and sporting events. Sister airlines AirAsia X, Thai AirAsia X and Indonesia AirAsia X are medium- and long-haul operations of the AirAsia brand. These airlines can also provide cargo transport services.

FINANCIAL DATA: Note: Data for latest year may not have been available at press time.

In U.S. $	2015	2014	2013	2012	2011	2010
Revenue	1,570,253,000	1,350,358,000	1,274,578,000	1,233,255,000	1,120,815,000	984,415,000
R&D Expense						
Operating Income	507,815,300	212,833,700	252,050,800	256,474,800	289,861,900	266,035,300
Operating Margin %	32.33%	15.76%	19.77%	20.79%	25.86%	27.02%
SGA Expense						
Net Income	134,940,900	20,654,270	90,291,730	456,624,400	138,464,100	264,651,400
Operating Cash Flow	549,528,300	75,308,180	239,649,400	337,843,700	350,047,100	403,720,900
Capital Expenditure	153,072,600	519,782,800	565,984,600	474,078,000	179,288,600	461,782,500
EBITDA	398,423,900	392,232,600	400,970,700	397,894,100	432,568,200	401,859,600
Return on Assets %	2.57%	.43%	2.09%	11.94%	4.09%	8.61%
Return on Equity %	12.01%	1.73%	6.64%	36.85%	14.46%	33.90%
Debt to Equity	2.29	2.29	1.80	1.23	1.78	2.00

CONTACT INFORMATION:

Phone: 60 321719222   Fax:
Toll-Free:
Address: Terminal Jalan KLIA S3, Kuala Lumpur Int'l Airport, Sepang, 64000 Malaysia

STOCK TICKER/OTHER:

Stock Ticker: AIABF   Exchange: GREY
Employees: 6,304   Fiscal Year Ends:
Parent Company:

SALARIES/BONUSES:

Top Exec. Salary: $ Bonus: $
Second Exec. Salary: $ Bonus: $

OTHER THOUGHTS:

Estimated Female Officers or Directors: 3
Hot Spot for Advancement for Women/Minorities: Y

Sales, profits and employees may be estimates. Financial information, benefits and other data can change quickly and may vary from those stated here.

Airbnb Inc

NAIC Code: 519130

TYPES OF BUSINESS:
Online Homestay Reservations

BRANDS/DIVISIONS/AFFILIATES:
Airbnb.com

CONTACTS: Note: Officers with more than one job title may be intentionally listed here more than once.
Brian Chesky, CEO
Laurence A. Tosi, CFO
Nathan Blecharczyk, CTO

GROWTH PLANS/SPECIAL FEATURES:
Airbnb, Inc., founded in 2008, operates a social networking site for travelers and those who have spare housing space. Through Airbnb.com, members who are willing to let travelers stay in their homes, guest houses, resort properties and other accommodations can post their information, including pricing, photos and amenities. In turn, travelers may search in a given market for members who are willing to accommodate them. Airbnb offers more than 2 million listings in 192 countries. Since its founding, the company has booked over 60 million guest nights. Members are encouraged to write reviews describing the positive and/or negative aspects of their stays. These reviews are partially encouraged so that renters and travelers may view profiles and feedback before staying in homes or letting others stay in their homes, thereby reducing the risk of danger or other negative situations. The Airbnb network is also connected to Facebook, allowing members to search the social networking platform for additional information regarding certain hosts and guests. Airbnb charges room owners a 3% host fee and an additional fee of 6% to 12% per guest. The average commission is about 12% of total revenues. The typical guest stays longer, on average, than a guest in a typical hotel. The firm has a goal of achieving $10 billion in yearly revenues by 2020.

FINANCIAL DATA: Note: Data for latest year may not have been available at press time.

In U.S. $	2015	2014	2013	2012	2011	2010
Revenue	1,425,000,000	900,000,000	264,000,000	132,000,000	120,000,000	80,000,000
R&D Expense						
Operating Income						
Operating Margin %						
SGA Expense						
Net Income						
Operating Cash Flow						
Capital Expenditure						
EBITDA						
Return on Assets %						
Return on Equity %						
Debt to Equity						

CONTACT INFORMATION:
Phone: 415-728-0000   Fax:
Toll-Free:
Address: 888 Brannan St., Fl. 4, San Francisco, CA 94107 United States

STOCK TICKER/OTHER:
Stock Ticker: Private   Exchange:
Employees: 4,175   Fiscal Year Ends: 12/31
Parent Company:

SALARIES/BONUSES:
Top Exec. Salary: $ Bonus: $
Second Exec. Salary: $ Bonus: $

OTHER THOUGHTS:
Estimated Female Officers or Directors:
Hot Spot for Advancement for Women/Minorities:

Airbus Group NV

www.airbusgroup.com

NAIC Code: 336411

TYPES OF BUSINESS:

Aircraft Manufacturing
Helicopter Manufacturing
Transport Aircraft
Military Aircraft
Defense Communications Systems
Satellites
Space Systems
Maintenance Services

BRANDS/DIVISIONS/AFFILIATES:

Dassault Aviation SA

CONTACTS: Note: Officers with more than one job title may be intentionally listed here more than once.

Thomas Enders, CEO
Tom Williams, COO
Harald Wilhelm, CFO
Marwan Lahoud, Chief Mktg. Officer
Thierry Baril, Chief Human Resources Officer
Jean Botti, CTO
Marwan Lahoud, Chief Strategy Officer
Fabrice Bregier, CEO-Airbus
Bernhard Gerwert, CEO-Airbus Defense & Space
Guillaume Faury, CEO-Airbus Helicopters
Francois Auque, Exec. VP-Space Systems
Denis Ranque, Chmn.

GROWTH PLANS/SPECIAL FEATURES:

Airbus Group NV is a leading developer of aerospace and defense products and technologies worldwide. It was formed from the combination of several European aerospace companies, including DaimlerChrysler Aerospace (Germany), Aerospatiale Matra (France) and Construcciones Aeronauticas SA (Spain). The company operates through three major divisions: Airbus, Airbus defense & space and Airbus helicopters. Airbus manufactures commercial aircraft, capturing roughly half of all commercial airliner orders. Airbus's latest projects include the model A380, one of the largest commercial jets available with space for 555 passengers divided between two levels of seating; the A320neo (new engine option), featuring new engines and large wingtip devices that result in a 15% fuel-burn reduction, an annual CO2 reduction of 3,600 tons per aircraft; and the A350 XWB, a fuel efficient model that can transport 250-400 passengers. Airbus defense & space consists of the firm's military aircraft, including the Eurofighter and A330MRTT; space systems, which include telecom and observation satellites and launchers; communication, intelligence & security (CIS), including cyber security and defense systems; and electronics operations. Airbus helicopters offers one of the largest ranges of civil and military helicopters. The company's helicopter models range from the EC120 light helicopter to the EC225 Super Puma, as well as from the AS550 C3 Fennec to the Tiger on the military side. Its X3 high-speed hybrid helicopter combines vertical take-off and landing capabilities with a fast cruise speed of more than 255 knots, and the X4 rotocraft is currently underway, and will offer enhanced fuel efficiency and lower sound levels. In May 2015, the firm sold a 17.5% stake in Dassault Aviation SA. It currently still owns around 23%. In December of same year, the firm agreed to acquire Navtech group of companies, a leading global provider of flight operations solutions.

FINANCIAL DATA: Note: Data for latest year may not have been available at press time.

In U.S. $	2015	2014	2013	2012	2011	2010
Revenue	73,579,342,500	67,999,470,695	62,967,291,904	60,017,422,336	52,204,961,792	48,617,517,056
R&D Expense						
Operating Income						
Operating Margin %						
SGA Expense						
Net Income	3,080,171,700	2,624,195,145	1,556,755,072	1,304,911,488	1,101,948,800	607,825,216
Operating Cash Flow						
Capital Expenditure						
EBITDA						
Return on Assets %						
Return on Equity %						
Debt to Equity						

CONTACT INFORMATION:

Phone: 31 715245600   Fax: 31 715232807
Toll-Free:
Address: PO Box 32008, Leiden, 2303 Netherlands

STOCK TICKER/OTHER:

Stock Ticker: AIR   Exchange: Paris
Employees: 138,622   Fiscal Year Ends: 12/31
Parent Company:

SALARIES/BONUSES:

Top Exec. Salary: $ Bonus: $
Second Exec. Salary: $ Bonus: $

OTHER THOUGHTS:

Estimated Female Officers or Directors: 1
Hot Spot for Advancement for Women/Minorities:

Sales, profits and employees may be estimates. Financial information, benefits and other data can change quickly and may vary from those stated here.

Airbus SAS

NAIC Code: 336411

TYPES OF BUSINESS:

Aircraft Manufacturing
Commercial Aircraft
Military Aircraft

BRANDS/DIVISIONS/AFFILIATES:

Airbus China
Airbus Group NV
Airbus Americas
Airbus Japan
A350 XWB
A380
A320
A320neo

CONTACTS: Note: Officers with more than one job title may be intentionally listed here more than once.

Fabrice Bregier, CEO
Thomas Charles Williams, COO
Harald Wilhelm, CFO
Charles Champion, Exec. VP-Eng.
John Leahy, COO-Customers
Domingo Urena-Raso, Head-Airbus Military
Tom Williams, Exec. VP-Programs
Eric Chen, Pres., Airbus China
Klaus Richter, Exec. VP-Procurement

GROWTH PLANS/SPECIAL FEATURES:

Airbus SAS (Airbus), a subsidiary of Airbus Group NV, competes head-to-head with Boeing in the military, freighter and commercial aircraft sector. Airbus's single-aisle and wide-body jets have capacities ranging from 100 to 1,000 passengers. The firm maintains over 150 field sites around the globe, production facilities in Europe, engineering and sales locations in North America, sales and customer support centers in Japan and China and a joint engineering center in Russia with Kaskol. Subsidiaries include Airbus Americas, Airbus China and Airbus Japan. The firm's A380 jumbo jet model, with a capacity of up to 853 passengers, burns less fuel per seat than today's largest aircraft. The A350 XWB family of aircraft, designed to compete with the new high-efficiency Boeing 787, have seating capacities ranging from 280-1,000 and offer greater fuel burn efficiency and reduced CO2 emissions. The company's freight and cargo business unit houses its freighter aircraft production and supports the passenger-to-cargo conversions of its jetliners. In 2015, the firm announced that more than 12,300 Airbus A320 family aircraft had been ordered, and more than 6,800 delivered to more than 400 customers and operators worldwide, making it the world's best-selling single-aisle aircraft family. The A320neo family incorporates the latest technologies, including new generation engines and Sharklet wing tip devices, which together deliver more than 15 percent in fuel savings and aims to deliver 20 percent by 2020. Airbus has more than 4,400 A320neo family orders from nearly 80 customers.

FINANCIAL DATA: Note: Data for latest year may not have been available at press time.

In U.S. $	2015	2014	2013	2012	2011	2010
Revenue	52,350,594,720	48,268,962,000	58,249,000,000	50,998,600,000	42,863,400,000	39,725,300,000
R&D Expense						
Operating Income						
Operating Margin %						
SGA Expense						
Net Income	2,940,771,792	2,649,823,912	2,370,740,000	1,625,420,000	756,192,000	
Operating Cash Flow						
Capital Expenditure						
EBITDA						
Return on Assets %						
Return on Equity %						
Debt to Equity						

CONTACT INFORMATION:

Phone: 33-5-61-93-33-33   Fax: 33-5-61-93-49-55
Toll-Free:
Address: 1 Rond Point Maurice Bellonte, Blagnac, 31707 France

STOCK TICKER/OTHER:

Stock Ticker: Subsidiary
Employees: 74,000
Parent Company: Airbus Group NV

Exchange:
Fiscal Year Ends: 12/31

SALARIES/BONUSES:

Top Exec. Salary: $ Bonus: $
Second Exec. Salary: $ Bonus: $

OTHER THOUGHTS:

Estimated Female Officers or Directors:
Hot Spot for Advancement for Women/Minorities:

Alaska Air Group Inc

NAIC Code: 481111

www.alaskaair.com

TYPES OF BUSINESS:

Airlines
Air Cargo

BRANDS/DIVISIONS/AFFILIATES:

Alaska Airlines Inc
Horizon Air Industries Inc

CONTACTS: Note: Officers with more than one job title may be intentionally listed here more than once.

Bradley Tilden, CEO
Brandon Pedersen, CFO
Christopher Berry, Chief Accounting Officer
Benito Minicucci, COO, Subsidiary
David Campbell, COO, Subsidiary
Kyle Levine, General Counsel
Andrew Harrison, Other Executive Officer
Shannon Alberts, Secretary
Joseph Sprague, Senior VP, Divisional

GROWTH PLANS/SPECIAL FEATURES:

Alaska Air Group, Inc., through its operating subsidiaries Alaska Airlines, Inc. (Alaska) and Horizon Air Industries, Inc. (Horizon), provides passenger air service to more than 32 million passengers per year to over 100 destinations. The firm also provides freight and mail services, primarily to and within Alaska and on the West Coast. Alaska, founded in 1932, operates a fleet of passenger jets and contracts with Horizon, SkyWest Airlines, Inc. and Peninsula Airways, Inc. for regional capacity. Alaska operates an all-Boeing 737 fleet and Horizon operates and all-Bombardier Q400 turboprop fleet. Alaska offers north/south service within the western USA, Canada and Mexico as well as passenger and dedicated cargo services to and within Alaska. It also provides long-haul east/west service to Hawaii and cities in the mid-continental and eastern USA, primarily from Seattle, where it has its largest concentration of departures. Alaska's leading airports are Seattle and Portland. Horizon is the largest regional airline in the Pacific Northwest, representing 90% of Air Group's regional revenue. The subsidiary serves a number of cities in the USA, Canada and Mexico. Horizon's leading airports are within the West Coast and Pacific Northwest regions. New routes in 2015 included Seattle to Milwaukee, Oklahoma City and Washington D.C.; from Las Vegas to Mammoth Lakes; from San Diego to Kona; and from Portland to St. Louis. In April 2016, the firm agreed to acquire Virgin America, Inc. for $2.6 billion.

Both Alaska and Horizon airlines offer employee benefits such as flight privileges, personal time off, health coverage, a 401(k) plan, a profit sharing plan and performance rewards.

FINANCIAL DATA: Note: Data for latest year may not have been available at press time.

In U.S. $	2015	2014	2013	2012	2011	2010
Revenue	5,598,000,000	5,368,000,000	5,156,000,000	4,657,000,000	4,317,800,000	3,832,300,000
R&D Expense						
Operating Income	1,298,000,000	962,000,000	838,000,000	532,000,000	448,900,000	471,600,000
Operating Margin %	23.18%	17.92%	16.25%	11.42%	10.39%	12.30%
SGA Expense	1,585,000,000	1,705,000,000	1,591,000,000	1,653,000,000	1,237,700,000	1,219,900,000
Net Income	848,000,000	605,000,000	508,000,000	316,000,000	244,500,000	251,100,000
Operating Cash Flow	1,584,000,000	1,030,000,000	981,000,000	753,000,000	696,000,000	553,700,000
Capital Expenditure	831,000,000	694,000,000	566,000,000	518,000,000	387,400,000	183,000,000
EBITDA	1,640,000,000	1,297,000,000	1,121,000,000	842,000,000	727,900,000	744,700,000
Return on Assets %	13.33%	10.00%	8.95%	5.90%	4.78%	5.02%
Return on Equity %	37.37%	29.11%	29.44%	24.36%	21.46%	25.39%
Debt to Equity	0.23	0.32	0.37	0.61	0.93	1.18

CONTACT INFORMATION:

Phone: 206 392-5040   Fax:
Toll-Free: 800-252-7522
Address: 19300 Pacific Highway South, Seattle, WA 98188 United States

STOCK TICKER/OTHER:

Stock Ticker: ALK
Employees: 15,143
Parent Company:

Exchange: NYS
Fiscal Year Ends: 12/31

SALARIES/BONUSES:

Top Exec. Salary: $454,254   Bonus: $
Second Exec. Salary: $390,769   Bonus: $

OTHER THOUGHTS:

Estimated Female Officers or Directors: 13
Hot Spot for Advancement for Women/Minorities: Y

Sales, profits and employees may be estimates. Financial information, benefits and other data can change quickly and may vary from those stated here.

Alitalia-Societa Aerea Italiana

www.alitalia.com

NAIC Code: 481111

TYPES OF BUSINESS:

Airline
Pilot Technical Training Services

BRANDS/DIVISIONS/AFFILIATES:

CAI-Compagnia Aera Italian SpA
Etihad Airways

CONTACTS: *Note: Officers with more than one job title may be intentionally listed here more than once.*

Silvano Cassano, CEO
Rita Ciccone, Head-Legal
Marco Sansavini, Chief Strategy Officer
Antonio Perno, Head-Auditing
Luca Cordero di Montezemolo, Chmn.

GROWTH PLANS/SPECIAL FEATURES:

Alitalia-Societa Aerea Italiana is Italy's largest airline. The company began operations in 2015, after acquiring the operational activities of Alitalia-Compagnia Aerea Italiana, now named CAI-Compagnia Aerea Italian SpA. CAI has a 51% controlling stake in Alitalia, and the remaining 49% are owned by Etihad Airways, the national airline of the United Arab Emirates. Alitalia's fleet comprises 122 aircraft, including 24 long-haul Boeing 777s and 14 Airbus A330s; 78 medium-haul Airbus 319s, 320s and 321s; and 20 regional Embraer 175s and 190s. During 2015, Alitalia carried 22.9 million passengers, offering 97 destinations of which 27 are in Italy and 75 for the rest of the world. Alitalia collaborates with Etihad Airways Partners: airberlin, Air Serbia, Air Seychelles, Etihad Airways, Etihad Regional (operated by Darwin Airline), Jet Airways and NIKI. Moreover, Alitalia is a member of the SkyTeam alliance. Alitalia operates in both passenger and cargo transportation, as well as a training center for its crew.

FINANCIAL DATA: *Note: Data for latest year may not have been available at press time.*

In U.S. $	2015	2014	2013	2012	2011	2010
Revenue	3,200,000,000	3,179,650,000	4,100,000,000	4,633,185,540	4,483,644,772	4,155,709,025
R&D Expense						
Operating Income						
Operating Margin %						
SGA Expense						
Net Income		-40,133,009	-51,141,377			
Operating Cash Flow						
Capital Expenditure						
EBITDA						
Return on Assets %						
Return on Equity %						
Debt to Equity						

CONTACT INFORMATION:

Phone: 39-06-6563-1   Fax: 39-06-6562-2300
Toll-Free:
Address: Piazza Almerico da Schio - Palazzina RPU, Rome, 00054 Italy

STOCK TICKER/OTHER:

Stock Ticker: Private   Exchange:
Employees: 14,036   Fiscal Year Ends: 12/31
Parent Company: CAI-Compagnia Aerea Italian SpA

SALARIES/BONUSES:

Top Exec. Salary: $ Bonus: $
Second Exec. Salary: $ Bonus: $

OTHER THOUGHTS:

Estimated Female Officers or Directors: 1
Hot Spot for Advancement for Women/Minorities:

All Nippon Airways Co Ltd

NAIC Code: 481111

www.ana.co.jp

TYPES OF BUSINESS:

Airline
Aircraft Equipment Maintenance
Travel Services
Trading & Sales
Information Systems Services

BRANDS/DIVISIONS/AFFILIATES:

ANA Sales Co Ltd
ANA Hallo Tour
ANA Sky Holiday

CONTACTS: Note: Officers with more than one job title may be intentionally listed here more than once.

Osamu Shinobe, CEO
Osamu Shinobe, Pres.
Akira Okada, Exec. VP-Cargo Mktg. & Svcs.
Hiroyuki Kunibu, Sr. VP-Human Resources
Keisuke Okada, Sr. Exec. VP-IT Strategy & Innovation
Hiroyuki Ito, Sr. Exec. VP-Eng.
Tetsuo Fukuda, Exec. VP-Gen. Admin.
Koichi Uchizono, Exec. VP-Oper.
Tetsuo Fukuda, Exec. VP-Corp. Planning
Kiyoshi Tonomoto, Exec. VP-Investor Rel.
Kiyoshi Tonomoto, Exec. VP-Finance & Acct.
Takashi Shiki, Pres., ANA Sales Co., Ltd.
Hiroki Izumi, Pres., ANA Wings Co., Ltd.
Katsuya Kato, Pres., ANA Airport Svcs. Co., Ltd.
Miyoshi Ozawa, Pres., ANA Air Svcs. Tokyo Co. Ltd.
Shinichiro Ito, Chmn.
Keisuke Okada, Sr. Exec. VP-Intl Affairs & Alliances
Hayao Hora, Sr. Exec. VP-Purchasing & Facilities

GROWTH PLANS/SPECIAL FEATURES:

All Nippon Airways Co. Ltd. (ANA) is one of the leading domestic passenger carriers in Japan. ANA and its subsidiaries and affiliates comprise three business segments: air transportation, travel services and other businesses. The primary segment, air transportation, is involved with domestic and international flights as well as passenger services, cargo and airmail transportation. The company has a fleet of 195 aircraft and serves domestic and international passengers. Its cargo and mail operations use available space on passenger flights as well as space on 12 cargo freighters. It offers domestic flights on six routes daily and international flights on 18 routes weekly. Other ANA companies provide aircraft maintenance, aircraft handling services and reservation and information services. The travel services segment develops and sells the company's consumer products. ANA Sales Co. Ltd. sells ANA's air transportation services and travel packages under brand names ANA Hallo Tour and ANA Sky Holiday. Internationally, the segment provides local services to customers who purchased travel packages in Japan. The other businesses run by ANA include communications, trading and sales, real estate, information systems, building management, ground transportation and distribution, aircraft equipment maintenance, spare parts sales, logistics and other services. ANA is a member of the Star Alliance, one of the world's largest airline alliances.

FINANCIAL DATA: Note: Data for latest year may not have been available at press time.

In U.S. $	2015	2014	2013	2012	2011	2010
Revenue	17,040,170,000	15,921,920,000	14,754,070,000	14,037,270,000	13,501,730,000	
R&D Expense						
Operating Income	910,366,500	656,224,500	1,032,550,000	964,874,600	674,344,200	
Operating Margin %	5.34%	4.12%	6.99%	6.87%	4.99%	
SGA Expense	1,070,758,000	887,155,100	789,406,700	752,958,700	761,938,900	
Net Income	398,064,700	178,351,900	415,756,700	280,257,400	228,971,500	
Operating Cash Flow	2,057,392,000	1,990,214,000	1,722,418,000	2,132,247,000	2,027,657,000	
Capital Expenditure	2,731,885,000	1,827,267,000	1,618,553,000	1,957,963,000	2,105,317,000	
EBITDA	2,227,181,000	1,901,764,000	2,116,455,000	2,011,626,000	1,718,599,000	
Return on Assets %	1.75%	.87%	2.08%	1.43%	1.23%	
Return on Equity %	5.08%	2.49%	6.55%	5.27%	4.69%	
Debt to Equity	0.76	0.86	0.98	1.52	1.52	

CONTACT INFORMATION:

Phone: 81 367351001   Fax: 81 367351005
Toll-Free:
Address: Shiodome-City Ctr., 1-5-2, Higashi-Shimbashi, Minato-ku, Tokyo, 144-8525 Japan

STOCK TICKER/OTHER:

Stock Ticker: ALNPF   Exchange: GREY
Employees: 32,578   Fiscal Year Ends: 03/31
Parent Company:

SALARIES/BONUSES:

Top Exec. Salary: $ Bonus: $
Second Exec. Salary: $ Bonus: $

OTHER THOUGHTS:

Estimated Female Officers or Directors:
Hot Spot for Advancement for Women/Minorities:

Sales, profits and employees may be estimates. Financial information, benefits and other data can change quickly and may vary from those stated here.

Allegiant Travel Company

NAIC Code: 481111

TYPES OF BUSINESS:

Airline
Packaged Vacations
Air Service

BRANDS/DIVISIONS/AFFILIATES:

Allegiant.com

CONTACTS: *Note: Officers with more than one job title may be intentionally listed here more than once.*

Maurice Gallagher, CEO
Scott Sheldon, CFO
Gregory Anderson, Chief Accounting Officer
Jude Bricker, Senior VP, Divisional
Scott Allard, Senior VP

GROWTH PLANS/SPECIAL FEATURES:

Allegiant Travel Company is an airline focused on providing travel related services and products to underserved U.S. cities. The company sells air travel both on a stand-alone basis and bundled with hotel rooms, rental cars and other travel-related services, such as attractions and hotel shuttle services, from third-party operators. Additionally, the firm sells air transportation using fixed-fee flying arrangements, with a majority of its arrangements taking place through affiliates of Peppermill Resorts, Inc. Allegiant's popular destinations that are serviced include Las Vegas, Nevada; Orlando, Florida; Phoenix, Arizona; Tampa/St. Petersburg, Florida; Los Angeles, California; Ft. Lauderdale, Florida; West Palm Beach, Florida; Punta Gorda, Florida; the San Francisco Bay Area, California; Honolulu and Maui, Hawaii; and Palm Springs, California. Allegiant additionally provides service on a seasonal basis to San Diego, California, Myrtle Beach, South Carolina, New Orleans, Louisiana and Jacksonville, Florida. The company also has authority for charter service to Canada and Mexico. Its fleet consists of McDonnell Douglas MD-80/MD-83/MD-88, Boeing 757 and Airbus 319/320 aircraft. The company maintains full control over its inventory and distributes its product through its web site, Allegiant.com; its call center; and at its airport ticket counters. The firm markets its services through advertising and promotions in newspapers, magazines, television, radio and targeted public relations and promotional efforts. The company, headquartered in Las Vegas, Nevada, maintains operational bases at airports located in Florida, Arizona, Nevada, California, South Carolina, Hawaii and Washington.

Employee benefits include employee discounts on company products and services, 401(k) and retirement planning, health care insurance and development training through Allegiant University.

FINANCIAL DATA: *Note: Data for latest year may not have been available at press time.*

In U.S. $	2015	2014	2013	2012	2011	2010
Revenue	1,262,188,000	1,137,046,000	996,150,000	908,719,000	779,117,000	663,641,000
R&D Expense						
Operating Income	371,702,000	157,345,000	154,737,000	132,304,000	85,444,000	104,656,000
Operating Margin %	29.44%	13.83%	15.53%	14.55%	10.96%	15.77%
SGA Expense	319,126,000	221,837,000	235,542,000	152,517,000	139,761,000	155,429,000
Net Income	220,374,000	86,689,000	92,273,000	78,597,000	49,398,000	65,702,000
Operating Cash Flow	365,367,000	269,781,000	196,888,000	176,772,000	129,911,000	97,956,000
Capital Expenditure	252,686,000	279,418,000	177,516,000	105,084,000	86,582,000	98,499,000
EBITDA	471,326,000	241,745,000	225,437,000	190,889,000	128,664,000	140,819,000
Return on Assets %	16.93%	7.99%	10.67%	10.44%	8.17%	13.12%
Return on Equity %	68.25%	25.93%	23.77%	20.90%	15.21%	22.28%
Debt to Equity	1.62	1.84	0.56	0.34	0.39	0.03

CONTACT INFORMATION:

Phone: 702 851-7300　　　Fax: 702 256-7209
Toll-Free:
Address: 1201 North Town Center Drive, Las Vegas, NV 89144 United States

STOCK TICKER/OTHER:

Stock Ticker: ALGT　　　　　　　Exchange: NAS
Employees: 2,846　　　　　　　　Fiscal Year Ends: 12/31
Parent Company:

SALARIES/BONUSES:

Top Exec. Salary: $　　　　　Bonus: $2,926,633
Second Exec. Salary: $195,000　　Bonus: $633,805

OTHER THOUGHTS:

Estimated Female Officers or Directors: 1
Hot Spot for Advancement for Women/Minorities:

Sales, profits and employees may be estimates. Financial information, benefits and other data can change quickly and may vary from those stated here.

Amadeus IT Group SA

www.amadeus.com

NAIC Code: 561599

TYPES OF BUSINESS:

Reservation Services
Online Travel Services
Corporate Travel Software-Hosted

BRANDS/DIVISIONS/AFFILIATES:

Amadeus Altea Suite
Altea Reservation
Altea Inventory
Altea Departure Control
Altea eCommerce
Amadeus.net
CheckMyTrip.com
Amadeus IT Holding SA

CONTACTS: Note: Officers with more than one job title may be intentionally listed here more than once.

Luis Maroto, CEO
Luis Maroto, Pres.
Ana de Pro, CFO
Sabine Hansen Peck, Sr. VP-Communications & Branding
Sabine Hansen Peck, Sr. VP- Human Resources
Herve Couturier, Exec. VP-R&D
Denis Lacroix, VP-Product Dev. & Sales
Tomas Lopez Fernebrand, General Counsel
Eberhard Haag, Exec. VP-Global Oper.
Alex Luzarraga, VP-Corp. Strategy
Denis Lacroix, VP-e-commerce Platforms
Francisco Perez-Lozao Ruter, Sr. VP-New Bus.
Julia Sattel, VP-Airline IT
Claude Giafferri, VP
Petra Euler, Managing Dir.- Amadeus Germany
Jose Antonio Tazon Gargia, Chmn.
David Brett, Pres., Amadeus Asia Pacific
Holger Taubmann, Sr. VP-Dist.

GROWTH PLANS/SPECIAL FEATURES:

Amadeus IT Group SA operates one of the largest travel reservation and ticketing systems in the world. The company operates in two segments: service distribution and IT solutions. The distribution segment provides travel distribution services in Europe, the Middle East, Africa, the Asia Pacific region and South and Central America. Its service distribution network includes access to over 711 airlines, 30 car rental companies, over 110,000 hotels, 50 ferry & cruise lines, 207 tour operators, 95 rail operators and 24 travel insurance companies. The IT solutions segment features the Amadeus Altea Suite, a customer management suite that focuses on inventory management, departure control and sales and reservations. It consists of three modules: Altea Reservation, which enables customers to manage bookings, fare prices and ticketing through a single interface; Altea Inventory, which permits airlines to create and manage schedules, seat capacity and associated fares; and Altea Departure Control, which covers flight departure aspects, including check-in, boarding passes and gate control. In addition, the firm offers Altea eCommerce, a suite of solutions that seeks to improve airline e-commerce sales and support processes. Amadeus also operates Amadeus.net, a travel planning tool used to help customers find flights, hotels and car rentals, and CheckMyTrip.com, a service that allows people to check the status of their itineraries. The company operates as a subsidiary of Amadeus IT Holding SA.

FINANCIAL DATA: Note: Data for latest year may not have been available at press time.

In U.S. $	2015	2014	2013	2012	2011	2010
Revenue	4,420,633,000	3,861,357,000	3,506,613,000	3,288,132,000	3,117,252,000	2,930,277,000
R&D Expense						
Operating Income	1,189,690,000	1,079,725,000	1,003,284,000	940,586,400	939,132,300	352,371,500
Operating Margin %	26.91%	27.96%	28.61%	28.60%	30.12%	12.02%
SGA Expense						
Net Income	772,722,900	713,475,300	635,686,400	561,210,000	824,955,300	154,561,100
Operating Cash Flow	1,438,189,000	1,227,613,000	1,156,031,000	1,120,029,000	1,107,285,000	791,156,900
Capital Expenditure	621,499,300	483,018,800	464,557,700	394,154,300	353,238,000	285,080,800
EBITDA	1,673,427,000	1,495,620,000	1,348,985,000	1,249,561,000	1,254,926,000	789,576,300
Return on Assets %	10.38%	10.89%	10.63%	9.74%	14.06%	2.51%
Return on Equity %	33.25%	34.32%	33.42%	35.57%	72.10%	57.18%
Debt to Equity	0.56	0.83	0.77	1.00	1.59	3.80

CONTACT INFORMATION:

Phone: 34 915820100   Fax: 34 915820188
Toll-Free:
Address: Salvador de Madariaga 1, Madrid, 28027 Spain

STOCK TICKER/OTHER:

Stock Ticker: AMADF   Exchange: PINX
Employees: 11,037   Fiscal Year Ends: 12/31
Parent Company:

SALARIES/BONUSES:

Top Exec. Salary: $ Bonus: $
Second Exec. Salary: $ Bonus: $

OTHER THOUGHTS:

Estimated Female Officers or Directors: 4
Hot Spot for Advancement for Women/Minorities: Y

Sales, profits and employees may be estimates. Financial information, benefits and other data can change quickly and may vary from those stated here.

American Casino & Entertainment Properties LLC

acepllc.com/InvestorRelations/Investor

NAIC Code: 721120

TYPES OF BUSINESS:

Casino Hotel Properties
Retail Outlets
Restaurants
Recreational Vehicle Park

BRANDS/DIVISIONS/AFFILIATES:

Stratosphere Casino Hotel & Tower
Arizona Charlie's Decatur
Arizona Charlie's Boulder
Aquarius Casino Resort
Whitehall Street Real Estate Fund
Goldman Sachs Group

CONTACTS: *Note: Officers with more than one job title may be intentionally listed here more than once.*

Frank V. Riolo, CEO
Ned Martin, CFO
Phyllis A. Gilland, General Counsel
Paul Hobson, Gen. Mgr.-Stratosphere Casino, Hotel & Tower
Ronald P. Lurie, Exec. VP
Mark Majetich, Sr. VP
Sean Hammond, Gen. Mgr.-Aquarius Casino Resort

GROWTH PLANS/SPECIAL FEATURES:

American Casino & Entertainment Properties LLC (ACEP), a wholly-owned subsidiary of the Goldman Sachs Group affiliate Whitehall Street Real Estate Fund, is a holdings company that operates four gaming and entertainment properties across Nevada. The firm's entertainment properties consist of the Stratosphere Tower Hotel & Casino, a mixed-use resort destination on the Las Vegas Strip; Arizona Charlie's Decatur and Arizona Charlie's Boulder, two casinos also located in Las Vegas; and the Aquarius Casino Resort in Laughlin, Nevada, south of Las Vegas. The Stratosphere is the firm's flagship property, featuring 2,427 hotel rooms, 80,000 square feet of casino space and 110,000 square feet of retail space as well as a revolving restaurant, a roller coaster and the Stratosphere Tower, the tallest freestanding observation tower in the U.S. The Arizona Charlie's Decatur and Arizona Charlie's Boulder are off-Strip full-service casinos and restaurants featuring slot machines, game tables, poker lounges and various other gaming features. Arizona Charlie's Boulder also features a recreational vehicle (RV) park offering amenities such as game and exercise rooms, a swimming pool and shower and laundry facilities. The Aquarius Casino Resort features a 57,070-square-foot casino and 1,907 hotel rooms, including 90 suites and seven restaurants. The Aquarius also maintains 35,000 square feet of rentable meeting space, indoor and outdoor entertainment facilities and a wedding chapel.

FINANCIAL DATA: *Note: Data for latest year may not have been available at press time.*

In U.S. $	2015	2014	2013	2012	2011	2010
Revenue	373,067,000	351,100,000	337,400,000	339,729,000	341,890,000	336,838,000
R&D Expense						
Operating Income						
Operating Margin %						
SGA Expense						
Net Income	12,062,000	6,980,000	-15,100,000	-15,798,000	-20,264,000	-36,747,000
Operating Cash Flow						
Capital Expenditure						
EBITDA						
Return on Assets %						
Return on Equity %						
Debt to Equity						

CONTACT INFORMATION:

Phone: 702-380-7777   Fax: 702-383-4734
Toll-Free:
Address: 2000 S. Las Vegas Blvd., Las Vegas, NV 89104 United States

STOCK TICKER/OTHER:

Stock Ticker: Private   Exchange:
Employees: 4,300   Fiscal Year Ends: 12/31
Parent Company: Whitehall Street Real Estate Funds

SALARIES/BONUSES:

Top Exec. Salary: $ Bonus: $
Second Exec. Salary: $ Bonus: $

OTHER THOUGHTS:

Estimated Female Officers or Directors: 1
Hot Spot for Advancement for Women/Minorities: Y

American Express Co

www.americanexpress.com

NAIC Code: 522320

TYPES OF BUSINESS:

Credit Card Processing and Issuing
Travel-Related Services
Lending & Financing
Transaction Services
Bank Holding Company
International Banking Services
Expense Management
Magazine Publishing

BRANDS/DIVISIONS/AFFILIATES:

American Express Travel Related Services Co Inc
American Express Bank FSB
American Express Centurion Bank

CONTACTS: Note: Officers with more than one job title may be intentionally listed here more than once.

Kenneth Chenault, CEO
James Bush, President, Divisional
Jeffrey Campbell, CFO
Marc Gordon, Chief Information Officer
Paul Fabara, Chief Risk Officer
Linda Zukauckas, Controller
Michael ONeill, Executive VP, Divisional
Laureen Seeger, Executive VP
L. Cox, Other Executive Officer
Anre Williams, President, Divisional
Ashwini Gupta, President, Divisional
Douglas Buckminster, President, Divisional
Susan Sobbott, President, Divisional
Carol Schwartz, Secretary
Stephen Squeri, Vice Chairman

GROWTH PLANS/SPECIAL FEATURES:

American Express Co. (AmEx), a bank holding company, is a leading global payments and travel firm. Its principal products are charge and credit payment card products and travel-related services. The firm primarily operates through subsidiary American Express Travel Related Services Company, Inc. AmEx's business is organized into four main segments: U.S. card services, international card services, global commercial services and global network & merchant services. The U.S. card services segment operates through AmEx's USA banking subsidiaries American Express Centurion Bank and American Express Bank, FSB. The division provides a wide array of card products and services to consumers and small businesses in the USA. The firm's international card services division offers these services in countries worldwide. The global commercial services segment offers expense management services to firms and organizations worldwide. Its products and services include corporate purchasing cards, corporate cards, corporate meeting cards, buyer initiated payment programs and business travel accounts. The global network & merchant services division operates a global general-purpose charge and credit card network for both proprietary and issued cards; manages merchant services internationally, which includes signing merchants to accept cards and processing and settling card transactions for those merchants; and offers merchants point-of-sale (POS), servicing/settlement and marketing/information products and services. In June 2016, the 16-year partnership between American Express and Costco dissolved, with Costco no longer accepting American Express credit cards.

FINANCIAL DATA: Note: Data for latest year may not have been available at press time.

In U.S. $	2015	2014	2013	2012	2011	2010
Revenue	32,818,000,000	34,292,000,000	32,974,000,000	31,582,000,000	29,962,000,000	27,819,000,000
R&D Expense						
Operating Income	7,938,000,000	8,991,000,000	7,888,000,000	6,451,000,000	6,956,000,000	5,964,000,000
Operating Margin %	24.18%	26.21%	23.92%	20.42%	23.21%	21.43%
SGA Expense	16,099,000,000	17,168,000,000	16,458,000,000	16,568,000,000	16,182,000,000	14,210,000,000
Net Income	5,163,000,000	5,885,000,000	5,359,000,000	4,482,000,000	4,935,000,000	4,057,000,000
Operating Cash Flow	10,972,000,000	10,990,000,000	8,547,000,000	7,082,000,000	10,475,000,000	9,287,999,000
Capital Expenditure	1,341,000,000	1,195,000,000	1,006,000,000	1,053,000,000	1,109,000,000	887,000,000
EBITDA						
Return on Assets %	3.16%	3.73%	3.49%	2.92%	3.28%	2.95%
Return on Equity %	24.49%	29.07%	27.92%	23.78%	28.18%	26.15%
Debt to Equity	2.32	2.80	2.83	3.12	3.16	4.09

CONTACT INFORMATION:

Phone: 212 640-2000   Fax: 212 640-2458
Toll-Free: 800-528-4800
Address: 200 Vesey St., World Financial Ctr., New York, NY 10285
United States

STOCK TICKER/OTHER:

Stock Ticker: AXP
Employees: 54,800
Parent Company:

Exchange: NYS
Fiscal Year Ends: 12/31

SALARIES/BONUSES:

Top Exec. Salary:
$1,000,000
Second Exec. Salary:
$800,000

Bonus: $4,850,000

Bonus: $3,858,000

OTHER THOUGHTS:

Estimated Female Officers or Directors: 4

Hot Spot for Advancement for Women/Minorities: Y

American Science & Engineering Inc

www.as-e.com

NAIC Code: 334517

TYPES OF BUSINESS:

X-Ray Inspection Solutions
Security Systems
Radiation Detection Technology
Maintenance, Warranty & Research Services
Engineering & Training Services

BRANDS/DIVISIONS/AFFILIATES:

Z Backscatter
Sentry Portal
Omniview Gantry
Z Portal
Mini Z
AS&E
Gemini
SmartCheck

CONTACTS: *Note: Officers with more than one job title may be intentionally listed here more than once.*

Charles Dougherty, CEO
Hamilton Helmer, Director
Michael Muscatello, General Counsel
Michael Tropeano, Senior VP, Divisional
Lanning Levine, Senior VP, Divisional
Diane Basile, Treasurer
Laura Berman, Vice President, Divisional
David Hack, Vice President, Divisional

GROWTH PLANS/SPECIAL FEATURES:

American Science & Engineering, Inc. (AS&E) develops, manufactures, markets and sells X-ray inspection and other detection products for homeland security and other targeted markets. The company also provides maintenance, warranty, engineering and training services related to these products. AS&E's X-ray imaging products utilize several technologies, including traditional transmission X-ray technology, its proprietary Z Backscatter technology and Radioactive Threat Detection (RTD) capability. The Z Backscatter technology creates photo-quality X-ray images that highlight organic threats and contraband such as explosives, plastic weapons and drugs. The RTD technology is capable of detecting radioactive materials in vehicles. AS&E technologies are incorporated into systems such as the Sentry Portal, OmniView Gantry, Z Portal, Mini Z, AS&E, Gemini and SmartCheck. The Z Backscatter Van (ZBV) is a screening system built into a commercially available delivery van, which allows operators to conduct X-ray imaging of suspect vehicles, highlighting organic materials such as plastic explosives. AS&E's products are used to inspect parcels, baggage, vehicles, pallets, cargo containers and people, and are sold in the U.S. and throughout the world to a variety of customers, including port and border security authorities, aviation security agencies, law enforcement agencies, military organizations and high threat commercial and government facilities. Customers use the firm's products to help combat terrorism, trade fraud, drug trafficking, weapons smuggling and illegal immigration as well as for military force protection and general facility security.

Employee benefits include medical, dental and vision coverage; flexible spending accounts; disability insurance; life insurance; a 401(k); and an employee assistance program

FINANCIAL DATA: *Note: Data for latest year may not have been available at press time.*

In U.S. $	2015	2014	2013	2012	2011	2010
Revenue	126,750,000	190,249,000	186,680,000	203,552,000	278,576,000	
R&D Expense	23,390,000	22,089,000	23,618,000	25,544,000	22,619,000	
Operating Income	1,165,000	22,756,000	26,268,000	31,949,000	64,444,000	
Operating Margin %	.91%	11.96%	14.07%	15.69%	23.13%	
SGA Expense	32,707,000	31,805,000	29,533,000	35,624,000	42,139,000	
Net Income	979,000	15,117,000	17,454,000	21,422,000	42,817,000	
Operating Cash Flow	-11,136,000	32,546,000	31,157,000	51,019,000	33,204,000	
Capital Expenditure	2,580,000	1,821,000	3,618,000	5,211,000	5,304,000	
EBITDA	5,630,000	28,089,000	31,625,000	38,317,000	69,946,000	
Return on Assets %	.42%	5.52%	5.75%	6.47%	13.45%	
Return on Equity %	.56%	7.52%	7.53%	8.16%	17.55%	
Debt to Equity			0.01	0.01	0.02	

CONTACT INFORMATION:

Phone: 978 262-8700   Fax: 978 262-8804
Toll-Free: 800-225-1608
Address: 829 Middlesex Turnpike, Billerica, MA 01821 United States

STOCK TICKER/OTHER:

Stock Ticker: ASEI
Employees: 245
Parent Company:

Exchange: NAS
Fiscal Year Ends: 03/31

SALARIES/BONUSES:

Top Exec. Salary: $566,000   Bonus: $
Second Exec. Salary: $307,000   Bonus: $

OTHER THOUGHTS:

Estimated Female Officers or Directors: 1
Hot Spot for Advancement for Women/Minorities:

Sales, profits and employees may be estimates. Financial information, benefits and other data can change quickly and may vary from those stated here.

AmericanTours International LLC

www.americantours.com

NAIC Code: 561520

TYPES OF BUSINESS:

Tours

BRANDS/DIVISIONS/AFFILIATES:

DriveAmerica
City Breaks
Cuba by ATI

CONTACTS: Note: Officers with more than one job title may be intentionally listed here more than once.

Noel Irwin-Hentschel, CEO
Michael Fitzpatrick, Pres. & Co-Founder
Michael Fitzpatrick, Pres.
Stephen Shelley, VP-IT
Kathy Dodge, Sr. VP
Eric Thomas, VP-ATI South

GROWTH PLANS/SPECIAL FEATURES:

AmericanTours International LLC (ATI) is one of the largest inbound tour operators in the U.S., with offices in California, Florida, New York, Hawaii and Beijing. The firm focuses on foreign travelers staying in the U.S. for business. ATI is also the preferred travel provider for members of the American Automobile Association (AAA). Its tours can be reserved through company offices, participating travel agents or directly through certain participating companies. ATI's tours feature Hawaii, Canada and the eastern and western U.S. The firm offers tours by motorcoach, car, plane and cruise line (through Holland America). Escorted motorcoach tours include Eastern Discovery, Western Discovery and New England and Atlantic Canada. The firm also offers self-drive car tours, called DriveAmerica tours. The company also offers City Breaks packs, which combine hotel reservations with popular local attractions. The firm additionally offers special group trip planning services, encompassing anywhere from 20 to 2,000 people. Moreover, the company's Cuba by ATI service has been sending Americans to Cuba since 2009, when it first received the Travel Service Provider license from the U.S. Treasury Department's Office of Foreign Assets Control. Cuba by ATI makes individual and group travel easy as a one-stop-shop for hotel accommodations, ground transportation, international & domestic air ticketing, access to attractions and special event planning.

FINANCIAL DATA: Note: Data for latest year may not have been available at press time.

In U.S. $	2015	2014	2013	2012	2011	2010
Revenue						
R&D Expense						
Operating Income						
Operating Margin %						
SGA Expense						
Net Income						
Operating Cash Flow						
Capital Expenditure						
EBITDA						
Return on Assets %						
Return on Equity %						
Debt to Equity						

CONTACT INFORMATION:

Phone: 310-641-9953   Fax: 310-216-5807
Toll-Free:
Address: 6053 W. Century Blvd., Los Angeles, CA 90045 United States

STOCK TICKER/OTHER:

Stock Ticker: Private
Employees: 225
Parent Company:

Exchange:
Fiscal Year Ends: 12/31

SALARIES/BONUSES:

Top Exec. Salary: $ Bonus: $
Second Exec. Salary: $ Bonus: $

OTHER THOUGHTS:

Estimated Female Officers or Directors: 3
Hot Spot for Advancement for Women/Minorities: Y

Sales, profits and employees may be estimates. Financial information, benefits and other data can change quickly and may vary from those stated here.

Ameristar Casinos Inc
www.ameristar.com

NAIC Code: 721120

TYPES OF BUSINESS:
Casino Resorts
Casino Management

BRANDS/DIVISIONS/AFFILIATES:
Pinnacle Entertainment Inc
Ameristar Kansas City
Ameristar St. Charles
Ameristar Council Bluffs
Ameristar Vicksburg
Horseshu Hotel & Casino
Ameristar Black Hawk
Ameristar Casino Hotel East Chicago

CONTACTS: Note: Officers with more than one job title may be intentionally listed here more than once.
Anthony Sanfilippo, CEO-Pinnacle Entertainment
Neil Walkoff, Exec. VP-Oper.-Pinnacle Entertainment
Carlos Ruisanchez, CFO
Christina Donelson, Sr.VP-Human Resources-Pinnacle Entertainment
Jim Frank, Sr. VP

GROWTH PLANS/SPECIAL FEATURES:
Ameristar Casinos, Inc., a subsidiary of Pinnacle Entertainment, is a gaming and entertainment company that develops, owns and operates eight casino facilities. Its properties include Ameristar St. Charles and Ameristar Kansas City in Missouri; Ameristar Vicksburg in Mississippi; Ameristar Council Bluffs in southwestern Iowa; Ameristar Black Hawk in Denver, Colorado; Ameristar Casino Hotel East Chicago; and Cactus Pete's Resort Casino and Horseshu Hotel & Casino, both near the Idaho border in Jackpot, Nevada. The casinos typically offer slot machines and a variety of table games, including blackjack, craps, roulette, baccarat and numerous live poker variations such as Texas Hold 'Em and Pai Gow. In addition, some locations offer sports book wagering. The casinos also offer a variety of casual dining and upscale restaurants, sports bars and private clubs for Star Awards members. Ameristar St. Charles offers two ballrooms for its guests, five meeting rooms and an executive board room. Ameristar Kansas City features an 18-screen movie theater, a 4,280 square foot arcade and an activity center called Kids Quest. Ameristar Vicksburg is a permanently docked riverboat casino located on the Mississippi River, while Ameristar Council Bluffs offers a cruising riverboat casino that travels down the Missouri River. The East Chicago property is a 56,000 square foot complex that features a 550-seat ballroom. Cactus Pete's features an outdoor amphitheater, arcades, an 18-hole golf course and tennis courts. Horseshu Hotel & Casino, located across the street from Cactus Pete's, is an old-western style casino, and includes onsite amenities such as a grocery store, gas station and garage.

The firm offers employees medical, dental and vision insurance; prescription drug coverage; a 401(k); life & disability insurance; flexible spending accounts; an employee assistance program; and tuition reimbursement.

FINANCIAL DATA: Note: Data for latest year may not have been available at press time.

In U.S. $	2015	2014	2013	2012	2011	2010
Revenue	1,275,000,000	775,381,800	425,800,000	1,195,220,992	1,214,505,984	1,189,282,048
R&D Expense						
Operating Income						
Operating Margin %						
SGA Expense						
Net Income		203,332,800	109,300,000			
Operating Cash Flow						
Capital Expenditure						
EBITDA						
Return on Assets %						
Return on Equity %						
Debt to Equity						

CONTACT INFORMATION:
Phone: 702-567-7000 Fax:
Toll-Free:
Address: 3773 Howard Hughes Pkwy., Ste. 490S, Las Vegas, NV 89169 United States

STOCK TICKER/OTHER:
Stock Ticker: Subsidiary   Exchange:
Employees: 7,115   Fiscal Year Ends: 12/31
Parent Company: Pinnacle Entertainment Inc

SALARIES/BONUSES:
Top Exec. Salary: $ Bonus: $
Second Exec. Salary: $ Bonus: $

OTHER THOUGHTS:
Estimated Female Officers or Directors: 1
Hot Spot for Advancement for Women/Minorities: Y

Amtrak (National Railroad Passenger Corp)   www.amtrak.com

NAIC Code: 482111

TYPES OF BUSINESS:
Line-Haul Railroads
Railroad Maintenance

BRANDS/DIVISIONS/AFFILIATES:
National Railroad Passenger Corp (The)

CONTACTS: *Note: Officers with more than one job title may be intentionally listed here more than once.*
Joseph H. Boardman, CEO
D. J. Stadtler, VP-Operations
Gerald Sokol, Jr., CFO
Matt Hardison, CMO
Barry Melnkovic, Chief People Officer
Jason Molfetas, CIO
Emmett Fremaux, VP-Prod. Mgmt.
Eleanor Acheson, General Counsel
DJ Stadltler, VP-Oper.
Joseph McHugh, VP-Corp. Comm. & Gov't Affairs
Theodore Alves, Inspector Gen.
Stephen Gardner, VP-NEC Infrastructure & Investment Dev.
Polly Hanson, Chief of Police
Anthony R. Coscia, Chmn.

GROWTH PLANS/SPECIAL FEATURES:
Amtrak (officially The National Railroad Passenger Corp.) is a government-owned passenger rail line and the country's largest provider of contract-commuter service. Its route system covers 21,000 route miles in 46 States, Washington, D.C and three Canadian provinces, stopping at more than 500 stations. The busiest stations are located in New York City, Philadelphia, Washington, D.C., Chicago and Los Angeles. During 2015, the firm carried nearly 31 million passengers and collected nearly $2 billion in ticket revenue. The organization also owns and maintains more than 100 station facilities, 18 tunnels and 1,414 bridges. Amtrak operates over 1,360 railroad cars including sleeper, coach, first-class, business-class, dormitory, crew, lounge and dining cars as well as baggage and mail cars. Amtrak contracts with 13 state transportation agencies or commuter agencies for use of facilities and assets or for delivery of commuter services. These agencies include Maryland Area Regional Commuter, Connecticut's Shore Line East and Califronia's Metrolink. Additionally, the firm conducts maintenance for the Sound Transit System in Seattle, dispatching for the South Florida Regional Transportation Authority Tri-Rail service and dispatching and maintenance for the Massachusetts Bay Transportation Authority. Amtrak is largely owned by the U.S. Department of Transportation and is subsidized by the federal government.

FINANCIAL DATA: *Note: Data for latest year may not have been available at press time.*

In U.S. $	2015	2014	2013	2012	2011	2010
Revenue	3,211,023,000	3,235,600,000	2,990,800,000	2,866,300,000	2,706,800,000	2,513,384,000
R&D Expense						
Operating Income						
Operating Margin %						
SGA Expense						
Net Income	-1,232,686,000	-1,082,612,000	-1,275,600,000	-1,255,000,000	-1,342,000,000	-1,208,396,000
Operating Cash Flow						
Capital Expenditure						
EBITDA						
Return on Assets %						
Return on Equity %						
Debt to Equity						

CONTACT INFORMATION:
Phone: 202-906-3000   Fax: 202-906-3306
Toll-Free:
Address: 60 Massachusetts Ave. NE, Washington, DC 20002 United States

STOCK TICKER/OTHER:
Stock Ticker: Government-Owned   Exchange:
Employees: 20,899   Fiscal Year Ends: 09/30
Parent Company:

SALARIES/BONUSES:
Top Exec. Salary: $ Bonus: $
Second Exec. Salary: $ Bonus: $

OTHER THOUGHTS:
Estimated Female Officers or Directors: 3
Hot Spot for Advancement for Women/Minorities: Y

Sales, profits and employees may be estimates. Financial information, benefits and other data can change quickly and may vary from those stated here.

Arriva plc

NAIC Code: 485210

www.arriva.co.uk

TYPES OF BUSINESS:

Bus Services
Rail Service
Bus Distribution

BRANDS/DIVISIONS/AFFILIATES:

Deutsche Bahn AG
Arriva Trains Wales
Trenau Arriva Cymru
CrossCountry Rail
KM SpA

CONTACTS: Note: Officers with more than one job title may be intentionally listed here more than once.

Manfred Rudhart, CEO
Martin Hibbert, CFO
Mark Bowd, Group Dir.-Eng.
Chris Applegarth, Dir.-Legal & Commercial Svcs.
Mark Yexley, Dir.-Oper. & Commercial-U.K. Bus.
Piers Marlow, Dir.-Bus. Dev.
Simon Craven, Dir.-Comm.
Peter Telford, Dir.-Finance & Bus. Dev.-U.K. Bus.
Marco Piuri, Managing Dir.-Italy & Iberia
Mike Cooper, Managing Dir.-Mainland Europe
Bob Holland, Managing Dir.-U.K.
Thomas Oster, Managing Dir.-Denmark
Anne Hettinga, Managing Dir.-Netherlands

GROWTH PLANS/SPECIAL FEATURES:

Arriva plc, based in the U.K., is one of Europe's leading passenger transport service providers. The company is a subsidiary of Deutsche Bahn AG. With a fleet numbering over 20,000 vehicles, the firm provides more than 2.2 billion passenger journeys each year to riders in countries including the Czech Republic, Denmark, Hungary, Italy, Malta, the Netherlands, Poland, Portugal, Slovakia, Spain, Sweden and the U.K. Its fleet of vehicles includes buses, trains, commuter coaches and water buses as well as airport-related transport services and bus and coach distribution. Arriva is the largest private bus operator in Denmark, representing nearly 50% of the bus services within Copenhagen, and is one of the largest bus operators in London, where it runs over 1,400 buses via 13 depots. The company's other U.K. operations include bus services in the Northeast, Northwest and Southeast of England as well as Yorkshire, the Midlands, the Shires, Scotland and Wales. It also operates Arriva Trains Wales/Trenau Arriva Cymru, an integrated rail franchise throughout Wales and the border countries with 139 trains covering a route of over 1,000 miles; and the CrossCountry Rail franchise, covering approximately 1,478 route miles and serving over 240 stations across the U.K. In 2015, the firm announced plans to begin operating a service between The Hague, Netherlands and Brussels, Belgium. That same year, the Province of Limburg, the southernmost of the 12 provinces of the Netherlands, contracted Arriva to provide the entire public transport (busses and 4 regional rail lines) in Limburg from 2016 up to 2031. In 2016, the firm acquired a further 51% stake in Cremona bus operator, KM SpA, now owning 100% of the company, which has a fleet of 100 buses.

FINANCIAL DATA: Note: Data for latest year may not have been available at press time.

In U.S. $	2015	2014	2013	2012	2011	2010
Revenue	5,488,279,721	5,469,278,280	4,654,430,000	4,183,419,500	4,350,570,000	4,359,714,000
R&D Expense						
Operating Income						
Operating Margin %						
SGA Expense						
Net Income						
Operating Cash Flow						
Capital Expenditure						
EBITDA						
Return on Assets %						
Return on Equity %						
Debt to Equity						

CONTACT INFORMATION:

Phone: 44-191-520-4000   Fax: 44-191-520-4001
Toll-Free:
Address: Admiral Way, Doxford Int'l Bus. Park, Sunderland, SR3 3XP United Kingdom

STOCK TICKER/OTHER:

Stock Ticker: Subsidiary
Employees: 46,484
Parent Company: Deutsche Bahn AG

Exchange:
Fiscal Year Ends: 12/31

SALARIES/BONUSES:

Top Exec. Salary: $ Bonus: $
Second Exec. Salary: $ Bonus: $

OTHER THOUGHTS:

Estimated Female Officers or Directors: 2
Hot Spot for Advancement for Women/Minorities:

Sales, profits and employees may be estimates. Financial information, benefits and other data can change quickly and may vary from those stated here.

Asiana Airlines Inc

NAIC Code: 481111

TYPES OF BUSINESS:

Air Passenger Transportation
Air Cargo Shipping
Construction & Engineering Services
Ground Handling Services
Catering & Food Services
Logo & E-business Services

BRANDS/DIVISIONS/AFFILIATES:

Asiana Club
Kumho Asiana Group
Asiana IDT
Asiana Value Enhancement Purchasing System (AVEPS)
AAS Airport Services Inc
Star Alliance

CONTACTS: Note: Officers with more than one job title may be intentionally listed here more than once.

Soo-Cheon Kim, CEO
Kim Mi-Hyeong, VP
Han Chang-Soo, Sr. Managing Dir.
Ryu Gwang-Hui, Sr. Managing Dir.
Han Tae-Geun, Sr. Managing Dir.

GROWTH PLANS/SPECIAL FEATURES:

Asiana Airlines, Inc. is a Korean airline company that primarily provides passenger air service. Its other capabilities include air cargo shipping services, construction and engineering, ground handling, catering and food services, communications services and logo and e-business services. Asiana Airlines operates a fleet of 83 aircraft, servicing 10 domestic passenger routes, 88 international passenger routes and 25 international cargo routes. The company has a code share program with 26 international airlines, including Continental Airlines, United, US Airways, Air Canada, All Nippon Airways, Air China, Qatar Airways and South African Airways. Asiana Airlines provides various travel packages composed of its flights and hotel reservations, and it also offers a frequent flyer program to the members of its Asiana Club and Star Alliance members. Asiana Airlines is affiliated with Kumho Asiana Group, a conglomeration of companies that are involved in a diverse range of business, from ground transportation, aviation and tires to human resources, cultural foundations, finance, construction and chemicals. The company is also affiliated with Asiana IDT, an information system services company that serves the air transportation, financial services, manufacturing and construction sectors. In addition, its AAS Airport Services, Inc. subsidiary supplies ground handling, cargo handling, fuel supply handling and catering services. The company created the Asiana Value Enhancement Purchasing System (AVEPS) to facilitate purchases from its ground handling operations.

FINANCIAL DATA: Note: Data for latest year may not have been available at press time.

In U.S. $	2015	2014	2013	2012	2011	2010
Revenue	4,657,558,000	4,969,329,000	4,889,336,000	5,045,748,000	4,770,942,000	4,539,698,000
R&D Expense						
Operating Income	8,373,256	37,791,740	-55,118,660	118,612,600	307,297,600	547,679,400
Operating Margin %	.17%	.76%	-1.12%	2.35%	6.44%	12.06%
SGA Expense	318,462,200	314,713,700	303,894,800	307,871,700	315,024,900	384,199,200
Net Income	-135,970,300	-85,229,460	-128,065,400	45,295,060	14,696,720	196,110,000
Operating Cash Flow	314,011,800	292,585,800	199,418,000	256,942,000	563,249,200	665,067,700
Capital Expenditure	217,699,500	288,135,500	340,060,300	341,434,900	231,030,800	183,033,200
EBITDA	293,981,300	307,421,300	212,314,100	435,237,300	399,498,200	673,280,100
Return on Assets %	-2.26%	-1.51%	-2.44%	.92%	.29%	3.74%
Return on Equity %	-21.26%	-11.82%	-16.34%	5.79%	1.80%	25.21%
Debt to Equity	4.57	3.61	3.36	2.42	1.67	2.00

CONTACT INFORMATION:

Phone: 82-2-2669-8000   Fax: 82-2-2669-4280
Toll-Free:
Address: 443-83 Ojeong-ro, Gangseo-gu, Seoul, 157-731 South Korea

STOCK TICKER/OTHER:

Stock Ticker: ASAIF
Employees: 9,125
Parent Company:

Exchange: GREY
Fiscal Year Ends: 12/31

SALARIES/BONUSES:

Top Exec. Salary: $ Bonus: $
Second Exec. Salary: $ Bonus: $

OTHER THOUGHTS:

Estimated Female Officers or Directors:
Hot Spot for Advancement for Women/Minorities:

Sales, profits and employees may be estimates. Financial information, benefits and other data can change quickly and may vary from those stated here.

Atlas Air Worldwide Holdings Inc

www.atlasair.com

NAIC Code: 481212

TYPES OF BUSINESS:

Air Freight-Charter
Military & Commercial Aircraft Charter

BRANDS/DIVISIONS/AFFILIATES:

Atlas Air Inc
Polar Air Cargo Worldwide Inc
Titan
Southern Air Holdings Inc

CONTACTS: Note: Officers with more than one job title may be intentionally listed here more than once.

William Flynn, CEO
Spencer Schwartz, CFO
Frederick Mccorkle, Chairman of the Board
Keith Mayer, Chief Accounting Officer
John Dietrich, COO
Michael Steen, Executive VP
Adam Kokas, General Counsel

GROWTH PLANS/SPECIAL FEATURES:

Atlas Air Worldwide Holdings, Inc. is an aviation holding company that manages and operates one of the world's largest fleet of 747 Boeing all-cargo aircraft. The firm operates through two subsidiaries: wholly-owned Atlas Air, Inc., an airline that provides aircraft, crew, maintenance and insurance (ACMI) services for other airlines globally; and 51%-owned Polar Air Cargo Worldwide, Inc., which provides airport-to-airport freight services in the Middle East, Australia, Europe, Asia and North and South America. The company has four operating divisions: ACMI, air mobility command (AMC) charter, commercial charter and dry leasing. The core of Atlas's business has been providing cargo aircraft outsourcing services to customers on an ACMI basis in exchange for guaranteed minimum revenues at predetermined levels of operation for defined periods of time. The AMC Charter business primarily provides full planeload passenger and cargo aircraft to the AMC. The firm participates in the U.S. Civil Reserve Air Fleet (CRAF) Program under contracts with the AMC, which typically cover a one-year period. Atlas has made a substantial number of its aircraft available for use by the U.S. Military in support of their operations. The commercial charter business segment provides full planeload cargo and passenger capacity to customers for one or more flights based on a specific origin and destination. The commercial charter is generally booked on a short-term, as-needed, basis. In addition, Atlas provides limited airport-to-airport cargo services to select markets, including several cities in South America. Finally, the dry leasing business is operated by several wholly-owned subsidiaries, collectively referred to as Titan. Titan provides cargo and passenger aircraft, as well as engine leasing solutions in which the customer operates and is responsible for insurance and maintaining the flight equipment. In April 2016, the firm acquired Southern Air Holdings, Inc. for $110 million.

FINANCIAL DATA: Note: Data for latest year may not have been available at press time.

In U.S. $	2015	2014	2013	2012	2011	2010
Revenue	1,822,659,000	1,799,198,000	1,656,900,000	1,646,032,000	1,398,216,000	1,337,774,000
R&D Expense						
Operating Income	123,505,000	175,972,000	186,790,000	226,491,000	151,100,000	227,886,000
Operating Margin %	6.77%	9.78%	11.27%	13.75%	10.80%	17.03%
SGA Expense	454,127,000	79,199,000	61,420,000	56,461,000	44,037,000	34,338,000
Net Income	7,286,000	106,757,000	93,837,000	129,927,000	96,083,000	141,810,000
Operating Cash Flow	372,887,000	273,145,000	305,000,000	258,497,000	142,958,000	280,543,000
Capital Expenditure	272,088,000	544,319,000	602,947,000	552,036,000	801,642,000	70,002,000
EBITDA	226,113,000	331,672,000	300,802,000	323,274,000	218,786,000	291,124,000
Return on Assets %	.17%	2.73%	2.73%	4.68%	4.44%	7.71%
Return on Equity %	.50%	7.80%	7.21%	10.72%	8.79%	14.67%
Debt to Equity	1.19	1.25	1.16	0.89	0.59	0.37

CONTACT INFORMATION:

Phone: 914 701-8000   Fax: 914 701-8001
Toll-Free:
Address: 2000 Westchester Ave., Purchase, NY 10577 United States

STOCK TICKER/OTHER:

Stock Ticker: AAWW   Exchange: NAS
Employees: 1,998   Fiscal Year Ends: 12/31
Parent Company:

SALARIES/BONUSES:

Top Exec. Salary: Bonus: $
$1,035,040
Second Exec. Salary: Bonus: $
$665,026

OTHER THOUGHTS:

Estimated Female Officers or Directors: 2

Hot Spot for Advancement for Women/Minorities:

Sales, profits and employees may be estimates. Financial information, benefits and other data can change quickly and may vary from those stated here.

Avianca Holdings SA

NAIC Code: 481111

www.aviancaholdings.com

TYPES OF BUSINESS:

Airline

BRANDS/DIVISIONS/AFFILIATES:

Aerovias del Continente Americano
Tampa Cargo SA
Aerolineas Galapagos SA
TACA International Airlines
Islena de Inversiones CA de CV
Transmerican Airlines SA
Servicios Aereos Nacionales SA
Aerotaxis La Costena

CONTACTS: Note: Officers with more than one job title may be intentionally listed here more than once.

Fabio Villegas Ramirez, CEO
Estuardo Ortiz, COO
Gerardo Grajales, CFO
Elisa Murgas, Sec.
German Efromovich, Chmn.

GROWTH PLANS/SPECIAL FEATURES:

Avianca Holdings SA, operating out of Panama, is the holding company for a number of airlines flying both locally and internationally, and operates as both cargo and passenger airlines. Airlines which the company owns include Aerovias del Continente Americano, Tampa Cargo SA, Aerolineas Galapagos SA, TACA International Airlines, Transmerican Airlines SA, Servicios Aereos Nacionales SA, Aerotaxis La Costena and Islena de Inversiones CA de CV. All airlines operate under the single banner of the Avianca trademark. During 2015, the company transported over 10 million passengers to Latin America, Europe, North America, the Middle East, Asia Pacific and Africa. Tampa Cargo carrys cargo through passenger fleet aircraft bellies and parcels and goods through business unit Deprisa. Avianca has a fleet of over 181 aircraft, flying to 100 destinations in 25 countries. Through its codeshare agreements with Star Alliance member airlines, Avianca can reach 1,200 destinations in 193 countries. In addition to airline operations, the company is also engaged in tourism, engineering, maintenance and specialized maintenance services.

FINANCIAL DATA: Note: Data for latest year may not have been available at press time.

In U.S. $	2015	2014	2013	2012	2011	2010
Revenue	4,361,341,000	4,703,571,000	4,609,604,000	4,269,656,000	3,794,428,000	
R&D Expense						
Operating Income	218,816,000	279,468,000	384,931,000	280,898,000	202,383,000	
Operating Margin %	5.01%	5.94%	8.35%	6.57%	5.33%	
SGA Expense	1,455,054,000	1,496,639,000	1,516,692,000	1,374,212,000	1,246,853,000	
Net Income	-155,388,000	129,270,000	248,821,000	35,141,000	99,876,000	
Operating Cash Flow	363,002,000	257,130,000	544,642,000	391,226,000	330,312,000	
Capital Expenditure	173,511,000	159,995,000	291,428,000	386,248,000	221,803,000	
EBITDA	291,661,000	511,423,000	578,191,000	347,154,000	360,975,000	
Return on Assets %	-2.22%	2.26%	5.23%	.84%	2.63%	
Return on Equity %	-11.25%	11.01%	26.37%	4.75%	16.79%	
Debt to Equity	2.33	2.32	1.67	2.18	1.81	

CONTACT INFORMATION:

Phone: 57-1-587-7700   Fax:
Toll-Free:
Address: Avenida Calle 26 #59-15, Bogota, F8 Colombia

STOCK TICKER/OTHER:

Stock Ticker: AVH   Exchange: NYS
Employees: 20,545   Fiscal Year Ends: 12/31
Parent Company: Synergy Group Corp

SALARIES/BONUSES:

Top Exec. Salary: $ Bonus: $
Second Exec. Salary: $ Bonus: $

OTHER THOUGHTS:

Estimated Female Officers or Directors: 1
Hot Spot for Advancement for Women/Minorities:

Sales, profits and employees may be estimates. Financial information, benefits and other data can change quickly and may vary from those stated here.

Avis Budget Group Inc

NAIC Code: 532111

TYPES OF BUSINESS:

Automobile Rental
Franchising
Truck Rental

BRANDS/DIVISIONS/AFFILIATES:

Avis
Budget
ZipCar
Payless
Apex
Maggiore Group

CONTACTS: *Note: Officers with more than one job title may be intentionally listed here more than once.*

Larry De Shon, CEO
David Wyshner, CFO
Ronald Nelson, Chairman of the Board
David Calabria, Chief Accounting Officer
W. Deaver, Executive VP
Michael Tucker, Executive VP
Edward Linnen, Executive VP
Joseph Ferraro, President, Divisional
Mark Servodidio, President, Divisional
Jean Sera, Secretary
Bryon Koepke, Senior VP

GROWTH PLANS/SPECIAL FEATURES:

Avis Budget Group, Inc. (ABG) operates in the global vehicle rental industry through Avis, Budget, Zipcar, Payless and Apex. Avis is a rental car supplier to the premium commercial and leisure segments of the travel industry. Budget is a rental car supplier to the price-conscious segments of the travel industry. Its fleet of approximately 21,000 Budget trucks are rented through a network of approximately 1,000 dealer-operated and 450 company-operated locations throughout the continental USA. Zipcar is the world's leading car sharing company, with nearly 1 million members in the USA, Canada and Europe. Payless is a rental car supplier comprised of 200 vehicle rental locations worldwide. These include 80 company-operated locations and 100 locations operated by licensees. Apex operates in New Zealand and Australia via 20 locations. ABG's operations include approximately 11,000 car and truck rental locations in the USA, Canada, Australia, New Zealand, Latin America, the Caribbean and parts of Asia, with a fleet of more than 580,000 vehicles. It completed more than 38 million vehicle rental transactions worldwide in 2015. The company operates in three segments: North America, which provides car rentals in the USA, vehicle rentals in Canada, and operates ABG's car sharing business in North America; international, which provides and licenses ABG's brands to third parties for vehicle rentals and ancillary products and services primarily in Europe, the Middle East, Asia, South America, Central America, the Caribbean, Australia and New Zealand, and also operates ABG's car sharing business in select markets; and truck rental, which provides truck rentals and ancillary products and services to consumers and commercial users in the USA. In 2015, the firm acquired Maggiore Group, Italy's fourth-largest vehicle rental business.

The company offers its employees medical, dental and vision coverage; life insurance; flexible spending accounts; short-and long-term disability, AD&D; and 401(k).

FINANCIAL DATA: *Note: Data for latest year may not have been available at press time.*

In U.S. $	2015	2014	2013	2012	2011	2010
Revenue	8,502,000,000	8,485,000,000	7,937,000,000	7,357,000,000	5,900,000,000	5,185,000,000
R&D Expense						
Operating Income	974,000,000	978,000,000	589,000,000	300,000,000	36,000,000	124,000,000
Operating Margin %	11.45%	11.52%	7.42%	4.07%	.61%	2.39%
SGA Expense	1,093,000,000	1,080,000,000	1,070,000,000	959,000,000	1,011,000,000	583,000,000
Net Income	313,000,000	245,000,000	16,000,000	290,000,000	-29,000,000	54,000,000
Operating Cash Flow	2,584,000,000	2,579,000,000	2,253,000,000	1,889,000,000	1,578,000,000	1,640,000,000
Capital Expenditure	12,127,000,000	12,057,000,000	11,051,000,000	11,199,000,000	8,724,000,000	8,092,000,000
EBITDA	2,750,000,000	3,059,000,000	2,552,000,000	2,461,000,000	2,031,000,000	3,190,000,000
Return on Assets %	1.80%	1.47%	.10%	2.06%	-.24%	.52%
Return on Equity %	56.70%	34.12%	2.09%	49.61%	-7.05%	17.08%
Debt to Equity	28.00	17.30	13.80	12.75	21.19	17.09

CONTACT INFORMATION:

Phone: 973 496-4700   Fax: 212 413-1924
Toll-Free:
Address: 6 Sylvan Way, Parsippany, NJ 07054 United States

STOCK TICKER/OTHER:

Stock Ticker: CAR   Exchange: NAS
Employees: 30,000   Fiscal Year Ends: 12/31
Parent Company:

SALARIES/BONUSES:

Top Exec. Salary: Bonus: $
$1,244,521
Second Exec. Salary: Bonus: $
$748,836

OTHER THOUGHTS:

Estimated Female Officers or Directors: 2

Hot Spot for Advancement for Women/Minorities:

Sales, profits and employees may be estimates. Financial information, benefits and other data can change quickly and may vary from those stated here.

Azul Linhas Aereas Brasileiras SA

www.voeazul.com.br

NAIC Code: 481111

TYPES OF BUSINESS:

Regional Airline
Air Cargo
Bus Services

BRANDS/DIVISIONS/AFFILIATES:

Azul Cargo
TRIP Linhas Aereas

CONTACTS: Note: Officers with more than one job title may be intentionally listed here more than once.

David Neeleman, CEO
Pedro Janot, Pres.
David Neeleman, Chmn.

GROWTH PLANS/SPECIAL FEATURES:

Azul Linhas Aereas Brasileiras SA (Azul Brazilian Airlines) is a low-cost airline based in Brazil. The airline serves 102 destinations within the country by air and additional destinations by bus lines. Azul's fleet currently consists of 139 aircraft. The company's aircraft feature only economy-class seating and typically have high load rates. The firm's hub is located at the Viracopos-Campinas International Airport in Campinas, Sao Paulo. Azul currently only offers scheduled flights in Brazil. Azul's destinations include Belo Horizonte, Brasilia, Campinas, Campo Grande, Cuiaba, Curitiba, Florianopolis, Fortaleza, Goiania, Maceio, Manaus, Maringa, Natal, Navegantes, Porto Alegre, Porto Seguro, Rio de Janeiro, Recife, Salvador da Bahia, Sao Paulo and Vitoria. International destinations, such as Buenos Aires and San Carlos de Bariloche in Argentina, are available via chartered services. Wholly-owned TRIP Linhas Aereas is a regional carrier in Brazil. In select markets, the firm offers a free shuttle service from points around the city to the airport. Additionally, its cargo division, Azul Cargo, provides air freight and delivery and transfer services along its destination route.

FINANCIAL DATA: Note: Data for latest year may not have been available at press time.

In U.S. $	2015	2014	2013	2012	2011	2010
Revenue	1,188,000,000	1,474,200,000	1,326,780,000			
R&D Expense						
Operating Income						
Operating Margin %						
SGA Expense						
Net Income						
Operating Cash Flow						
Capital Expenditure						
EBITDA						
Return on Assets %						
Return on Equity %						
Debt to Equity						

CONTACT INFORMATION:

Phone: 55-11-4003-3255   Fax:
Toll-Free: 1-844-499-2985
Address: 939 Edif. C. Branco Office Park, Barueri, 06455-040 Brazil

STOCK TICKER/OTHER:

Stock Ticker: Private   Exchange:
Employees: 4,500   Fiscal Year Ends: 12/31
Parent Company:

SALARIES/BONUSES:

Top Exec. Salary: $ Bonus: $
Second Exec. Salary: $ Bonus: $

OTHER THOUGHTS:

Estimated Female Officers or Directors:
Hot Spot for Advancement for Women/Minorities:

Sales, profits and employees may be estimates. Financial information, benefits and other data can change quickly and may vary from those stated here.

BAE Systems plc

NAIC Code: 336410

www.baesystems.com

TYPES OF BUSINESS:

Defense and Aerospace Systems
Military Vehicles
Military Aircraft
Naval Vessels & Submarines
Satellite Manufacturing
Electronic Systems
Advanced Materials & Technologies
Security & Surveillance Technology

BRANDS/DIVISIONS/AFFILIATES:

BAE Systems Applied Intelligence
BAE Systems Saudi Arabia
BAE Systems Australia
BAE Systems India
BAE Systems Inc

CONTACTS: Note: Officers with more than one job title may be intentionally listed here more than once.

Ian King, CEO
Peter Lynas, CFO
Lynn C. Minella, Dir.-Human Resources
Phillip Bramwell, General Counsel
Alan Garwood, Dir.-Bus. Dev.
Claire Divver, Dir.-Comm.
Nigel Whitehead, Managing Dir.-Programs & Support
Tom Arseneault, COO-BAE Systems, Inc.
Kevin Taylor, Dir.-Strategy
Jerry Demuro, CEO
Roger Carr, Chmn.
Guy Griffiths, Managing Dir.-Intl

GROWTH PLANS/SPECIAL FEATURES:

BAE Systems plc is an aerospace and defense firm involved in the research, development, engineering and manufacture of military vehicles, aircraft, naval vessels and submarines, satellites, surveillance systems and security technology. The company operates in seven business groups. Defense designs, develops, manufactures and integrates defense systems and equipment. Its products include advanced materials, artillery, combat aircraft/vehicles, commercial aircraft, communications, amphibious, avionics and critical infrastructure. Electronics & systems integration provides flight and engine controls, electronic warfare and night vision systems, surveillance and reconnaissance sensors, secure networked communications equipment and energy management systems. Cyber & intelligence collects, manages and uses information to protect and enhance critical assets, provide intelligence and strengthen resilience in today's operating environment. Consultancy services works with its customers to better understand their challenges and to develop and implement business strategies, initiatives and best practice solutions that increase business performance. IT & information systems provide IT operations and business solutions, comprehensive analysis and threat assessments to a wide range of customers. Military & technical services consists of maintenance, modernization, supply chain, training, engineering and information, facilities, energy and availability services. Security delivers effective, custom built and innovative solutions to help address a range of security issues. BAE's primary markets include Australia, Saudi Arabia, India, the U.K. and the U.S. Subsidiaries include BAE Systems Applied Intelligence and BAE Systems Australia/India/Saudi Arabia.

U.S. subsidiary BAE Systems, Inc. offers employees medical, dental and vision coverage; a flexible spending account; life, voluntary home and auto, disability and long-term care insurance; a 401(k); transit benefits; and wellness programs.

FINANCIAL DATA: Note: Data for latest year may not have been available at press time.

In U.S. $	2015	2014	2013	2012	2011	2010
Revenue	21,917,150,000	20,145,440,000	22,017,680,000	23,284,110,000	23,200,550,000	27,391,540,000
R&D Expense					1,500,137,000	1,694,672,000
Operating Income	1,961,015,000	1,697,283,000	1,052,315,000	2,141,188,000	2,062,852,000	2,090,269,000
Operating Margin %	8.94%	8.42%	4.77%	9.19%	8.89%	7.63%
SGA Expense						
Net Income	1,198,543,000	966,145,700	219,341,200	1,394,383,000	1,618,947,000	1,373,494,000
Operating Cash Flow	819,918,300	873,447,900	-143,616,300	2,837,074,000	629,300,300	1,255,989,000
Capital Expenditure	539,213,800	420,403,900	351,207,000	524,852,100	500,045,700	557,492,200
EBITDA	2,252,164,000	2,240,413,000	2,874,936,000	2,904,965,000	3,177,836,000	3,278,367,000
Return on Assets %	4.60%	3.74%	.80%	4.70%	5.26%	4.24%
Return on Equity %	38.00%	28.33%	4.73%	26.83%	25.90%	21.20%
Debt to Equity	1.26	1.55	0.74	0.79	0.63	0.40

CONTACT INFORMATION:

Phone: 44 1252373232   Fax: 44 1252383991
Toll-Free:
Address: 6 Carlton Gardens, London, SW1Y 5AD United Kingdom

STOCK TICKER/OTHER:

Stock Ticker: BAESF   Exchange: PINX
Employees: 82,500   Fiscal Year Ends: 12/31
Parent Company:

SALARIES/BONUSES:

Top Exec. Salary: $ Bonus: $
Second Exec. Salary: $ Bonus: $

OTHER THOUGHTS:

Estimated Female Officers or Directors: 4
Hot Spot for Advancement for Women/Minorities: Y

Sales, profits and employees may be estimates. Financial information, benefits and other data can change quickly and may vary from those stated here.

Balboa Travel Inc

www.balboa.com

NAIC Code: 561510

TYPES OF BUSINESS:

Travel Agency
Corporate Travel Planning
Meeting & Event Planning
Consulting Services
Vacation Planning Services

BRANDS/DIVISIONS/AFFILIATES:

Balboa Meetings and Incentives
Balboa Vacations

CONTACTS: Note: Officers with more than one job title may be intentionally listed here more than once.

Denise Jackson, CEO
John Cruse, COO
Denise Jackson, Pres.
Tina Gilmore, Dir.-Mktg. & Airline Rel.
Bill Russell, Sr. VP-IT
Leigh Kramer, VP-Strategic Bus. Dev.
Kellie Dyer, Dir.-Implementation & Online Prod. Solutions
Inez Reynolds, Sr. VP-Finance & Data Solutions
John Cruse, Exec. VP-Corp. Travel Solutions
Mary Alice Gonsalves, Treas.
Jill Valentine, VP-Global Solutions
Stephen Thomas-Schulere, Sr. VP-Strategic Solutions
Jose G. da Rosa, Chmn.

GROWTH PLANS/SPECIAL FEATURES:

Balboa Travel, Inc., founded in 1969 as the travel agent for the international tuna fishing industry, is an international travel agency specializing in corporate travel. The company was one of the first travel agencies to automate its services, and it continues to offer its clients a full range of technological offerings for travel management and planning. The company's corporate travel services include a variety of online booking tools and resources; negotiation assistance for arranging corporate air, car and hotel programs; an international rate desk; and 24-hour-a-day emergency service. Balboa is a member of BCD Travel's affiliate program, which is a search engine for hotels. In addition, Balboa offers consulting services to clients wishing to develop a travel expense management system or corporate travel policy, and it helps companies meet budgets and save money on travel expenditures through its account management services. The firm owns and operates Balboa Meetings and Incentives, which offers full service capabilities in the areas of incentive program development, product launches, event planning, merchandise awards, customer appreciation programs, group travel and meetings. Balboa Vacations offers vacation planning services including wholesale tour rates, group cruise discounts and last-minute packages.

Balboa offers employees a benefits package that includes a 401(k) plan as well as travel industry benefits.

FINANCIAL DATA: Note: Data for latest year may not have been available at press time.

In U.S. $	2015	2014	2013	2012	2011	2010
Revenue						
R&D Expense						
Operating Income						
Operating Margin %						
SGA Expense						
Net Income						
Operating Cash Flow						
Capital Expenditure						
EBITDA						
Return on Assets %						
Return on Equity %						
Debt to Equity						

CONTACT INFORMATION:

Phone: 858-678-3300   Fax: 858-678-3399
Toll-Free: 800-359-8773
Address: 5414 Oberlin Dr., Ste. 300, San Diego, CA 92121 United States

STOCK TICKER/OTHER:

Stock Ticker: Private   Exchange:
Employees: Fiscal Year Ends: 06/30
Parent Company:

SALARIES/BONUSES:

Top Exec. Salary: $ Bonus: $
Second Exec. Salary: $ Bonus: $

OTHER THOUGHTS:

Estimated Female Officers or Directors: 9
Hot Spot for Advancement for Women/Minorities: Y

Bangkok Airways Co Ltd

NAIC Code: 481111

TYPES OF BUSINESS:

Regional Commuter Airlines
Airport Operations
Restaurant
Spa
Souvenir Shop
Rice Cultivation

BRANDS/DIVISIONS/AFFILIATES:

Samui Airport
Sukhothai Airport
Trat Airport

CONTACTS: Note: Officers with more than one job title may be intentionally listed here more than once.

Prasert Prasarttong-Osoth, CEO
Puttipong Prasarttong-Osoth, Pres.
Thavatvong Thanasumitra, Sr. Exec. VP-Finance

GROWTH PLANS/SPECIAL FEATURES:

Bangkok Airways Co. Ltd. is a regional airline operating out of Thailand. Bangkok Airways has a fleet of 33 aircraft serving 11 domestic and 13 international destinations. The company's fleet consists of eight Airbus 320s, 12 Airbus 319s, seven ATR 72-500s and six ATR 72-600s. Some of its destinations include Japan, China, Malaysia, Vietnam, Laos and Cambodia as well as nearly all the major resort locations in Thailand. Besides flight operations, the firm owns and operates three airports: Samui Airport, Sukhothai Airport and Trat Airport, which serve as regional hubs for the airlines. All three airports feature open-air terminals, reflecting both the aesthetic of the surrounding environment and the architecture of the local Thai culture. Built in 1982, Samui Airport was designed to blend in to the natural flora of the beach resort at Koh Samui, featuring an open-air Thai restaurant. Other amenities include a spa featuring Thai message and a souvenir shop. It also houses a customs and immigration facility and a post office. As a hub, Samui mainly serves northern Thailand. Sukhothai Airport, which opened in 1996, is located in Sukhothai, the ancient capital of Thailand, and its terminals are built in the style of Siamese pagodas. Bangkok Airways grows organic rice in the paddies surrounding the airport, which it serves during in-flight meals. This airport serves as the airline's domestic hub for international flights in the Mekong River area. The Trat Province airport opened in 2002, and serves as a hub for eastern Thailand, including the Koh Chang island resort and other islands. The airlines operation base is the Suvarnabhumi International Airport.

FINANCIAL DATA: Note: Data for latest year may not have been available at press time.

In U.S. $	2015	2014	2013	2012	2011	2010
Revenue	562,000,000	553,271,951	525,000,000	520,000,000	400,992,816	266,294,273
R&D Expense						
Operating Income						
Operating Margin %						
SGA Expense						
Net Income		8,750,503				
Operating Cash Flow						
Capital Expenditure						
EBITDA						
Return on Assets %						
Return on Equity %						
Debt to Equity						

CONTACT INFORMATION:

Phone: 66-2-265-5678   Fax: 66-2-265-5522
Toll-Free:
Address: Vibhavadirangsit Road 99 Mu 14, Chom Phon Chatuchak, Bangkok, 10900 Thailand

STOCK TICKER/OTHER:

Stock Ticker: Subsidiary   Exchange:
Employees: Fiscal Year Ends:
Parent Company: Bangkok Airways Public Company Limited

SALARIES/BONUSES:

Top Exec. Salary: $ Bonus: $
Second Exec. Salary: $ Bonus: $

OTHER THOUGHTS:

Estimated Female Officers or Directors:
Hot Spot for Advancement for Women/Minorities:

Banyan Tree Holdings Limited

NAIC Code: 721110

www.banyantree.com

TYPES OF BUSINESS:

Hotels & Resorts
Spas
Fine Art Galleries
Design Services

BRANDS/DIVISIONS/AFFILIATES:

Architrave
Angsana
Cassia
Banyan Tree
Banyan Tree Management Academy
Canopy Marketing Group Ptd Ltd
Banyan Tree Residences
Banyan Tree Hotels & Resorts

CONTACTS: Note: Officers with more than one job title may be intentionally listed here more than once.

Chiang See Ngoh Claire, Managing Dir.
Eddy See Hock Lye, CFO
Claire Chiang, Managing Dir.-Retail Oper.
Ho KwonCjan, Chief Group Designer
Shankar Chandran, Managing Dir.-Spa Oper.
Dharmali Kusumadi, Managing Dir.-Design Svcs.
Ho KwonPing, Exec. Chmn.

GROWTH PLANS/SPECIAL FEATURES:

Banyan Tree Holdings Limited, operating as Banyan Tree Hotels & Resorts, is a Singapore-based hospitality company that develops, manages, operates and invests in resorts, hotels, spas and other properties across 27 countries. The company's portfolio includes more than 30 hotels and resorts, 60 spas, 80 retail galleries and two golf course clubs. All employees are trained at the Banyan Tree Management Academy, which is centrally located in Phuket, Thailand. Banyan Tree's operations are divided into several segments: hotel management & investment, in which it owns and manages luxury hotels under its Angsana, Cassia, Dhawa and Banyan Tree brands as well as hotels that are managed by other operators; Canopy Marketing Group Ptd Ltd., a wholly-owned subsidiary that provides marketing insights on global niche markets such as hotels, resorts, spas, and gallery as well as residential ownership; spa operations, which oversees its more than 60 spa outlets worldwide; gallery operations, which oversees its more than 80 stores worldwide; hotel residences, which are sold under the Banyan Tree Residences brand name; property sales, which are properties not part of hotel operations and sold by subsidiary Laguna Resorts and Hotels; design and other services, which comprises subsidiary Architrave, Bayan's in-house architectural arm, and other services comprise the firm's golf course clubs; and Real Estate Hospitality Funds, which was set up to tap private equity and other sources of investments in order to provide a cost effective structure to fund the group's future developments. The majority of Banyan Tree's properties and operations are located in the Asia Pacific region and Mexico, with destinations in Bahrain, China, Indonesia, Korea, Maldives, Seychelles, Thailand and the UAE.

FINANCIAL DATA: Note: Data for latest year may not have been available at press time.

In U.S. $	2015	2014	2013	2012	2011	2010
Revenue	274,756,700	242,646,100	263,978,800	250,836,500	244,221,900	226,292,900
R&D Expense						
Operating Income	4,671,090	21,629,180	38,276,700	34,454,290	15,340,030	46,747,960
Operating Margin %	1.70%	8.91%	14.49%	13.73%	6.28%	20.65%
SGA Expense	66,380,320	56,929,920	83,656,380	50,307,980	73,141,620	51,103,290
Net Income	-20,397,290	759,738	13,449,950	11,016,570	2,227,329	11,631,770
Operating Cash Flow	-82,070,940	-24,312,350	-4,212,282	22,950,010	-5,710,263	8,320,795
Capital Expenditure	17,549,570	16,408,110	13,127,530	19,865,840	20,288,330	13,463,290
EBITDA	24,701,480	40,419,530	56,975,140	57,793,430	31,685,880	81,839,680
Return on Assets %	-1.78%	.07%	1.30%	1.08%	.11%	1.12%
Return on Equity %	-4.90%	.18%	3.31%	2.74%	.29%	3.04%
Debt to Equity	1.02	0.78	0.60	0.56	0.57	0.33

CONTACT INFORMATION:

Phone: 65 6849-5888   Fax: 65 6462-2463
Toll-Free: 800-591-0439
Address: 211 Upper Bukit Timah Rd., Singapore, 588182 Singapore

STOCK TICKER/OTHER:

Stock Ticker: BYNEF   Exchange: GREY
Employees: Fiscal Year Ends: 12/31
Parent Company:

SALARIES/BONUSES:

Top Exec. Salary: $ Bonus: $
Second Exec. Salary: $ Bonus: $

OTHER THOUGHTS:

Estimated Female Officers or Directors: 3
Hot Spot for Advancement for Women/Minorities: Y

Sales, profits and employees may be estimates. Financial information, benefits and other data can change quickly and may vary from those stated here.

Barcelo Crestline Corporation

NAIC Code: 721110

www.crestlinehotels.com

TYPES OF BUSINESS:

Hotels

BRANDS/DIVISIONS/AFFILIATES:

Barcelo Corporacion Empresarial SA
Crestline Hotels & Resorts LLC

GROWTH PLANS/SPECIAL FEATURES:

Barcelo Crestline Corporation is a leading independent hospitality management company. It is a privately-owned subsidiary of Barcelo Corporacion Empresarial SA (based in Palma de Mallorca, Spain). Through its operating company and wholly-owned subsidiary Crestline Hotels & Resorts, LLC (Crestline), the firm manages properties including 106 hotels, resorts and conference and convention centers with nearly 15,700 rooms in 28 states and Washington, D.C. Crestline operates five private-label hotels, with the remainder falling under brand lines such as Starwood, Marriott, InterContinental Hotels Group, Hyatt and Hilton. It generally acquires boutique or premium branded limited-service hotels, or first class, full-service hotels located in either suburban or urban markets.

CONTACTS: Note: Officers with more than one job title may be intentionally listed here more than once.

James Carroll, CEO
James Carroll, Pres.
Pam Siegler, CFO
Vicki Denfeld, Exec. VP-Sales & Mktg.
Jerry Galindo, VP-IT
Pierre Donahue, General Counsel
Ed Hoganson, Exec. VP-Bus. Dev.
Ed Hoganson, Exec. VP-Finance
Carolee Moore, VP-Sales & Mktg.
Pan Siegler, VP-Hotel Accounting & Finance
Bruce Wardinski, Chmn.

FINANCIAL DATA: Note: Data for latest year may not have been available at press time.

In U.S. $	2015	2014	2013	2012	2011	2010
Revenue						
R&D Expense						
Operating Income						
Operating Margin %						
SGA Expense						
Net Income						
Operating Cash Flow						
Capital Expenditure						
EBITDA						
Return on Assets %						
Return on Equity %						
Debt to Equity						

CONTACT INFORMATION:

Phone: 571-529-6000   Fax: 571-529-6050
Toll-Free:
Address: 3950 University Dr., Ste. 301, Fairfax, VA 22030 United States

STOCK TICKER/OTHER:

Stock Ticker: Subsidiary   Exchange:
Employees: 3,677   Fiscal Year Ends: 12/31
Parent Company: Barcelo Corporacion Empresarial SA

SALARIES/BONUSES:

Top Exec. Salary: $ Bonus: $
Second Exec. Salary: $ Bonus: $

OTHER THOUGHTS:

Estimated Female Officers or Directors: 4
Hot Spot for Advancement for Women/Minorities: Y

Sales, profits and employees may be estimates. Financial information, benefits and other data can change quickly and may vary from those stated here.

BCD Travel

NAIC Code: 561510

TYPES OF BUSINESS:

Travel Agency
Travel Consulting
Meeting Planning & Services

BRANDS/DIVISIONS/AFFILIATES:

BCD Holdings
Advito
BCD Travel Management
BCD Meetings & Incentives
BCD Leisure Services
World Travel Service Inc

CONTACTS: Note: Officers with more than one job title may be intentionally listed here more than once.

John Snyder, CEO
David Coppens, COO
John Snyder, Pres.
Stephan Baars, CFO
Louise Miller, Exec. VP-Sales & Mktg.
Christian Dahl, Sr. VP-Talent Mgmt. & Global Human Resources
Russell Howell, Exec. VP-IT
Russ Howell, Exec. VP-Global Tech.
Scott Graf, Pres., BCD Meetings & Incentives
Mike Janssen, Pres., Americas
Greg O'Neil, Pres., Asia Pacific
Rose Collazo Stratford, Exec. VP-Global Supplier Rel. & Strategic Sourcing
Ilona De March, Pres., EMEA

GROWTH PLANS/SPECIAL FEATURES:

BCD Travel, a wholly-owned subsidiary of BCD Holdings, is a world leader in delivering corporate travel management products. BCD operates in 110 countries in over 1,500 locations across six continents. Its integrated and global technology infrastructure provides analysis of travel data, allowing corporations to set foundations for efficiency and return on travel investments. Its business lines include traditional and online corporate travel management, Advito, meetings and incentives and leisure services. BCD Travel Management provides complete planning services for multiple stages of a trip and is designed to reduce the costs and possible risks that a traveler may encounter. The company provides traveler tracking services, carbon offsetting and, if necessary, medical repatriation. The firm's consulting business, Advito, offers advice from an independent consulting organization with industry knowledge and close ties to a leading travel management company. BCD Meetings & Incentives offers a range of services, from turnkey registration tools to travel planning and operations management. Companies can use these programs to coordinate business enhancing meetings or simply to reward employees. BCD Leisure Services offers planned employee travel events, which are usually used as benefits. In 2015, the firm acquired Knoxville, Tennessee-based World Travel Service, Inc., a corporate travel agency.

FINANCIAL DATA: Note: Data for latest year may not have been available at press time.

In U.S. $	2015	2014	2013	2012	2011	2010
Revenue	23,850,000,000	24,200,000,000				
R&D Expense						
Operating Income						
Operating Margin %						
SGA Expense						
Net Income						
Operating Cash Flow						
Capital Expenditure						
EBITDA						
Return on Assets %						
Return on Equity %						
Debt to Equity						

CONTACT INFORMATION:

Phone: 31-20-562-1800   Fax: 27-11-361-3636
Toll-Free:
Address: Europalaan 400, Utrecht, 3526 Netherlands

STOCK TICKER/OTHER:

Stock Ticker: Subsidiary   Exchange:
Employees: 11,000   Fiscal Year Ends: 12/31
Parent Company: BCD Holdings

SALARIES/BONUSES:

Top Exec. Salary: $ Bonus: $
Second Exec. Salary: $ Bonus: $

OTHER THOUGHTS:

Estimated Female Officers or Directors: 4
Hot Spot for Advancement for Women/Minorities: Y

Boeing Company (The)

NAIC Code: 336411

TYPES OF BUSINESS:

Aircraft Manufacturing
Aerospace Technology & Manufacturing
Military Aircraft
Satellite Manufacturing
Communications Products & Services
Air Traffic Management Technology
Financing Services
Research & Development

BRANDS/DIVISIONS/AFFILIATES:

Boeing 777
Boeing 737
Boeing 787 Dreamliner
Boeing Capital Corporation
Boeing 747-8

CONTACTS: Note: Officers with more than one job title may be intentionally listed here more than once.

Michael Lohr, Assistant General Counsel
Thomas Downey, Senior VP, Divisional
Christopher Chadwick, CEO, Divisional
Raymond Conner, CEO, Divisional
Gregory Smith, CFO
Robert Verbeck, Chief Accounting Officer
John Tracy, Chief Technology Officer
Dennis Muilenburg, Director
J. Luttig, Executive VP
Bertrand-Marc Allen, President, Subsidiary
Anthony Parasida, Senior VP, Divisional
Timothy Keating, Senior VP, Divisional
Diana Sands, Senior VP, Divisional
Heidi Capozzi, Vice President, Divisional

GROWTH PLANS/SPECIAL FEATURES:

The Boeing Company is one of the world's major aerospace firms. The company operates in the following segments: commercial airplanes; defense, space & security (BDS), which is further subdivided into Boeing military aircraft (BMA), network & space systems (N&SS) and global services & support (GS&S); and Boeing Capital Corporation (BCC). The commercial airplanes segment develops, produces and markets commercial jet aircraft and related support services. Its family of jet aircraft includes the 737 narrow-body model, the 767 and 777 wide-body models, the 787 Dreamliner and the 747-8 intercontinental and freighter models. The BDS BMA subdivision is focused on the development of military aircraft and precision engagement as well as mobility products and services. The N&SS subdivision provides products and services to assist customers in transforming operations through network integration, intelligence and surveillance systems, communications and space exploration. The GS&S subdivision is engaged in operations, maintenance and logistics support functions for military platforms. BCC provides financing to commercial aircraft customers. In 2015, the company signed the second phase of a performance-based contract with the U.S. Defense Logistics Agency that reduces combat logistics support costs while enhancing warfighter readiness. As a result, Boeing will provide support for 11 different aircraft including the F/A-18 Super Hornet, AH-64 Apache, AV-8B Harrier, B-52 Stratofortress and C-17 Globemaster III. Also in 2015, the firm won the contract to sustain the Minuteman III intercontinental ballistic missile (ICBM) guidance system for the U.S. Air Force.

The company offers its employees benefits including medical, dental, life, AD&D and disability insurance; flexible spending accounts; pension and retirement savings plans; tuition assistance; and onsite and on-the-job training.

FINANCIAL DATA: Note: Data for latest year may not have been available at press time.

In U.S. $	2015	2014	2013	2012	2011	2010
Revenue	96,114,000,000	90,762,000,000	86,623,000,000	81,698,000,000	68,735,000,000	64,306,000,000
R&D Expense	3,331,000,000	3,047,000,000	3,071,000,000	3,298,000,000	3,918,000,000	4,121,000,000
Operating Income	7,443,000,000	7,473,000,000	6,562,000,000	6,311,000,000	5,844,000,000	4,971,000,000
Operating Margin %	7.74%	8.23%	7.57%	7.72%	8.50%	7.73%
SGA Expense	3,525,000,000	3,767,000,000	3,956,000,000	3,717,000,000	3,408,000,000	3,644,000,000
Net Income	5,176,000,000	5,446,000,000	4,585,000,000	3,900,000,000	4,018,000,000	3,307,000,000
Operating Cash Flow	9,363,000,000	8,858,000,000	8,179,000,000	7,508,000,000	4,023,000,000	2,952,000,000
Capital Expenditure	2,450,000,000	2,236,000,000	2,238,000,000	1,710,000,000	1,713,000,000	1,127,000,000
EBITDA	9,263,000,000	9,376,000,000	8,462,000,000	8,184,000,000	7,551,000,000	6,750,000,000
Return on Assets %	5.34%	5.67%	5.05%	4.61%	5.40%	5.06%
Return on Equity %	68.95%	46.21%	44.20%	83.13%	127.94%	135.14%
Debt to Equity	1.37	0.93	0.54	1.52	2.85	4.14

CONTACT INFORMATION:

Phone: 312 544-2000   Fax:
Toll-Free:
Address: 100 N. Riverside Plz., Chicago, IL 60606 United States

STOCK TICKER/OTHER:

Stock Ticker: BA   Exchange: NYS
Employees: 165,500   Fiscal Year Ends: 12/31
Parent Company:

SALARIES/BONUSES:

Top Exec. Salary: Bonus: $
$1,719,962
Second Exec. Salary: Bonus: $
$1,354,269

OTHER THOUGHTS:

Estimated Female Officers or Directors: 7

Hot Spot for Advancement for Women/Minorities: Y

Sales, profits and employees may be estimates. Financial information, benefits and other data can change quickly and may vary from those stated here.

Bombardier Inc

NAIC Code: 336411

www.bombardier.com

TYPES OF BUSINESS:

Aircraft Manufacturing
Railway Vehicles & Equipment
Business, Passenger & Civil Aircraft
Jet Leasing & Charters
Railroad Car Leasing & Management
Amphibious Aircraft

BRANDS/DIVISIONS/AFFILIATES:

Learjet
Challenger
Global
Flexjet
Bombardier Aerospace
Bombardier Transportation

CONTACTS: *Note: Officers with more than one job title may be intentionally listed here more than once.*

Alain Bellemare, CEO
Daniel Desjardins, Senior VP
John Di Bert, CFO
Laurent Beaudoin, Chairman Emeritus
Pierre Beaudoin, Chairman of the Board
J. R. Bombardier, Director
Jean-Louis Fontaine, Director
Nico Buchholz, Other Executive Officer
FranCois Caza, Other Executive Officer
Laurent Troger, President, Divisional
Jean Seguin, President, Divisional
Frederick Cromer, President, Divisional
David Coleal, President, Divisional
John Macdonald, Senior VP, Divisional

GROWTH PLANS/SPECIAL FEATURES:

Bombardier, Inc. is a diversified manufacturer with operations in commercial aircraft, business jets and rail transportation equipment, systems and services. Through its aerospace division, Bombardier Aerospace, the company is one of the largest producers of commercial aircraft, specialty aircraft and business jets in the world. Its business aircraft include the Learjet, Challenger and Global models. Bombardier also offers business jet leases and charter services, in part through SkyJet. In addition, the aerospace division provides defense services, including fleet management and aviation training management. The firm also makes multi-role amphibious aircraft, suitable for tasks such as forest-fire fighting, maritime surveillance, search and rescue and utility transport. Through the Flexjet program, Bombardier offers whole aircraft ownership and management, fractional jet ownership, jet cards and charter brokerage services. The company's transportation division, Bombardier Transportation, is one of the world's largest producers of railway vehicles and equipment, with approximately 63 production sites and more than 18 service centers across 26 countries. It covers a full range of products and services, which the firm divides into six categories: propulsion and controls, including products for applications such as trolley buses and freight locomotives; bogies, which includes all products for application on rail vehicles; rail vehicles, which includes monorails, advanced rapid transit and commuter trains; transportation systems, which provide customized transportation system solutions; general fleet servicing; and rail control solutions. In early 2015, the firm sold five Q400 NextGen aircraft and agreed to sell up to 23 Q400 NextGen aircraft. It also launched a new extended service program for Dash 8-300 aircraft, extending the turboprop from 80,000 flight cycles to 120,000.

FINANCIAL DATA: *Note: Data for latest year may not have been available at press time.*

In U.S. $	2015	2014	2013	2012	2011	2010
Revenue	18,172,000,000	20,111,000,000	18,151,000,000	16,768,000,000	17,712,000,000	19,366,000,000
R&D Expense	355,000,000	347,000,000	293,000,000	299,000,000	193,000,000	141,000,000
Operating Income	405,000,000	872,000,000	923,000,000	695,000,000	1,050,000,000	1,098,000,000
Operating Margin %	2.22%	4.33%	5.08%	4.14%	5.92%	5.66%
SGA Expense	1,213,000,000	1,358,000,000	1,417,000,000	1,443,000,000	1,369,000,000	1,453,000,000
Net Income	-5,347,000,000	-1,260,000,000	564,000,000	588,000,000	755,000,000	698,000,000
Operating Cash Flow	20,000,000	847,000,000	1,380,000,000	1,348,000,000	1,678,000,000	552,000,000
Capital Expenditure	1,879,000,000	1,982,000,000	2,357,000,000	2,140,000,000	1,094,000,000	805,000,000
EBITDA	-4,591,000,000	-286,000,000	1,433,000,000	1,665,000,000	1,597,000,000	1,692,000,000
Return on Assets %	-21.26%	-4.42%	2.04%	2.28%	3.37%	3.27%
Return on Equity %		-142.05%	33.07%	44.17%	20.73%	25.14%
Debt to Equity			3.36	4.02	1.18	1.24

CONTACT INFORMATION:

Phone: 514 861-9481   Fax: 514 861-7053
Toll-Free:
Address: 800 Rene-Levesque Blvd. W., Montreal, QC H3B 1Y8 Canada

STOCK TICKER/OTHER:

Stock Ticker: BBD.A
Employees: 70,900
Parent Company:

Exchange: TSE
Fiscal Year Ends: 12/31

SALARIES/BONUSES:

Top Exec. Salary: $ Bonus: $
Second Exec. Salary: $ Bonus: $

OTHER THOUGHTS:

Estimated Female Officers or Directors: 3
Hot Spot for Advancement for Women/Minorities: Y

Sales, profits and employees may be estimates. Financial information, benefits and other data can change quickly and may vary from those stated here.

Booth Creek Ski Holdings Inc

www.boothcreek.com

NAIC Code: 713920

TYPES OF BUSINESS:

Ski Resorts
Golf Courses
Event Hosting
Summer Recreation

BRANDS/DIVISIONS/AFFILIATES:

Sierra-at-Tahoe Snowsports Resort
Booth Creek Resorts
CNL Lifestyle Properties

CONTACTS: Note: Officers with more than one job title may be intentionally listed here more than once.

George N. Gillett, Jr., CEO
Christopher P. Ryman, Pres.
Jeffrey J. Joyce, Pres.-Finance
Timothy H. Beck, Exec. VP-Planning
Brian Pope, Principal Acct. Officer

GROWTH PLANS/SPECIAL FEATURES:

Booth Creek Ski Holdings, Inc., doing business as Booth Creek Resorts, is a business management company. It specializes in ski resort operations and administration as well as the advertising and marketing of those resorts. The company currently owns Sierra-at-Tahoe Snowsports Resort in Lake Tahoe, California. This resort operates under a long-term lease agreement with real estate investment trust CNL Lifestyle Properties. It provides a full range of services, such as equipment rentals, skiing lessons and restaurants. In addition to alpine skiing and snowboarding, Booth Creek's resorts offer opportunities for cross-country skiing, tubing, snowmobiling and snowshoeing. Sierra-at-Tahoe Snowsports Resort receives approximately 500 inches of annual snowfall; its mountain has roughly 2,200 vertical feet on which to ski. Its most popular runs include West Bowl, Grandview and Huckleberry Canyon.

FINANCIAL DATA: Note: Data for latest year may not have been available at press time.

In U.S. $	2015	2014	2013	2012	2011	2010
Revenue	120,000,000	110,000,000	116,000,000	115,000,000		
R&D Expense						
Operating Income						
Operating Margin %						
SGA Expense						
Net Income						
Operating Cash Flow						
Capital Expenditure						
EBITDA						
Return on Assets %						
Return on Equity %						
Debt to Equity						

CONTACT INFORMATION:

Phone: 530-550-5100   Fax: 530-550-5116
Toll-Free:
Address: 950 Red Sand Stone Rd., #43, Vail, CO 81657 United States

STOCK TICKER/OTHER:

Stock Ticker: Subsidiary   Exchange:
Employees: 509   Fiscal Year Ends: 10/31
Parent Company: Booth Creek Management Corp

SALARIES/BONUSES:

Top Exec. Salary: $ Bonus: $
Second Exec. Salary: $ Bonus: $

OTHER THOUGHTS:

Estimated Female Officers or Directors: 1
Hot Spot for Advancement for Women/Minorities:

Sales, profits and employees may be estimates. Financial information, benefits and other data can change quickly and may vary from those stated here.

BostonCoach

www.bostoncoach.com

NAIC Code: 485510

TYPES OF BUSINESS:

Charter Buses
Airport Transport
Chauffeured Cars
Event Planning

BRANDS/DIVISIONS/AFFILIATES:

Marcou Transportation Group

CONTACTS:
Note: Officers with more than one job title may be intentionally listed here more than once.

Scott Solombrino, CEO
Lisa Censullo, VP
Larry Moulter, Pres.

GROWTH PLANS/SPECIAL FEATURES:

BostonCoach, owned by Marcou Transportation Group, is a leading provider of ground transportation services. Through an affiliate network of chauffer and group transportation, the firm serves thousands of cities across 37 countries. The company offers sedans, limousines, vans, SUVs, business-class vans and motor coaches for transfers, with a total fleet of more than 21,000 vehicles worldwide. Other services include event planning, group transportation, transfer services and road show services. The firm also offers shuttle services, including vehicle provision, route mapping and operation management. Moreover, BostonCoach allows customers to reserve transportation online as well as get a transportation price quote or plan a group transport. The company is the transportation partner for nearly 60% of the Fortune 500, and 85% of the Fortune 100, with experience in developing tailor-made transportation programs for medical, high-tech, financial, consulting, legal and entertainment industries.

BostonCoach offers its employees benefits including tuition reimbursement, a medical and dental plan, mass transit subsidies, life insurance and a 401(k) plan. Chauffer employees also receive 60 hours of classroom and on-the-road training.

FINANCIAL DATA:
Note: Data for latest year may not have been available at press time.

In U.S. $	2015	2014	2013	2012	2011	2010
Revenue	113,500,000	112,000,000	110,000,000	105,000,000	100,000,000	83,000,000
R&D Expense						
Operating Income						
Operating Margin %						
SGA Expense						
Net Income						
Operating Cash Flow						
Capital Expenditure						
EBITDA						
Return on Assets %						
Return on Equity %						
Debt to Equity						

CONTACT INFORMATION:

Phone: 617-563-8600   Fax: 617-563-0037
Toll-Free:
Address: 69 Norman St., Everett, MA 02140 United States

STOCK TICKER/OTHER:

Stock Ticker: Subsidiary   Exchange:
Employees: 560   Fiscal Year Ends: 12/31
Parent Company: Marcou Transportation Group

SALARIES/BONUSES:

Top Exec. Salary: $ Bonus: $
Second Exec. Salary: $ Bonus: $

OTHER THOUGHTS:

Estimated Female Officers or Directors:
Hot Spot for Advancement for Women/Minorities:

Sales, profits and employees may be estimates. Financial information, benefits and other data can change quickly and may vary from those stated here.

Bowlin Travel Centers Inc

www.bowlintc.com

NAIC Code: 447190

TYPES OF BUSINESS:

Convenience Stores
Gas Stations
Gift Shops
Outdoor Advertising

BRANDS/DIVISIONS/AFFILIATES:

Thing (The)
Butterfield Station
Bowlin's Running Indian

CONTACTS: *Note: Officers with more than one job title may be intentionally listed here more than once.*

Michael L. Bowlin, CEO
Michael L. Bowlin, Pres.
Nina J. Pratz, CFO
William J. McCabe, Sr. VP-Mgmt. Info. Systems
Kim D. Stake, Chief Admin. Officer
William J. McCabe, Sec.
William J. McCabe, Treas.
Michael L. Bowlin, Chmn.

GROWTH PLANS/SPECIAL FEATURES:

Bowlin Travel Centers, Inc. operates 10 full-service travel centers and five restaurants located along well-traveled interstate highways in New Mexico and Arizona. The company's travel centers offer brand-name food and gasoline as well as a variety of Southwestern merchandise. The firm operates five full-service restaurants under the Dairy Queen/Brazier or Dairy Queen trade names, as well as one Subway restaurant at its Picacho, Arizona location. All of the company's travel centers sell convenience store food such as chips, nuts, cookies and prepackaged sandwiches along with a variety of bottled and canned drinks. In addition to the Southwestern merchandise it purchases from Native American tribes, the firm also imports items from Mexico, including handmade blankets, earthen pottery and wood items. Additional goods, novelties and imprinted merchandise are imported from several Pacific Rim countries. Bowlin is an authorized ExxonMobil distributor and sells ExxonMobil gas at five of its New Mexico travel centers. Due to a supply agreement with Arizona Fuel Distributors, LLC, all of Bowlin's Arizona locations offer Shell gasoline. The company operates its travel centers under a number of its own trademarks, including The Thing, Butterfield Station and Bowlin's Running Indian.

Bowlin offers employee benefits such as sales commissions, onsite housing and a merchandise/restaurant discount.

FINANCIAL DATA: *Note: Data for latest year may not have been available at press time.*

In U.S. $	2015	2014	2013	2012	2011	2010
Revenue					26,085,640	23,045,530
R&D Expense						
Operating Income					-28,819	-253,988
Operating Margin %					- .11%	-1.10%
SGA Expense					7,778,437	7,389,744
Net Income					-36,622	-189,851
Operating Cash Flow					727,632	931,169
Capital Expenditure					1,826,734	559,735
EBITDA					1,202,885	911,763
Return on Assets %					- .19%	- .99%
Return on Equity %					- .30%	-1.52%
Debt to Equity					0.43	0.35

CONTACT INFORMATION:

Phone: 505 266-5985   Fax: 505 266-7821
Toll-Free: 800-716-8413
Address: 150 Louisiana Blvd. NE, Albuquerque, NM 87108 United States

STOCK TICKER/OTHER:

Stock Ticker: BWTL   Exchange: PINX
Employees: 139   Fiscal Year Ends: 01/31
Parent Company:

SALARIES/BONUSES:

Top Exec. Salary: $ Bonus: $
Second Exec. Salary: $ Bonus: $

OTHER THOUGHTS:

Estimated Female Officers or Directors: 2
Hot Spot for Advancement for Women/Minorities:

Sales, profits and employees may be estimates. Financial information, benefits and other data can change quickly and may vary from those stated here.

Boyd Gaming Corp

www.boydgaming.com

NAIC Code: 721120

TYPES OF BUSINESS:

Casinos & Hotels
Casino Management

BRANDS/DIVISIONS/AFFILIATES:

California Hotel & Casino
Borgata Hotel Casino & Spa
Blue Chip Hotel and Casino
Delta Downs Racetrack and Casino
Gold Coast Hotel and Casino
Fremont Hotel & Casino
IP Casino Resort Spa
Eldorado Casino

CONTACTS: *Note: Officers with more than one job title may be intentionally listed here more than once.*

William Boyd, Chairman of the Board
Anthony McDuffie, Chief Accounting Officer
Marianne Johnson, Director
William Boyd, Director
Theodore Bogich, Executive VP, Divisional
Stephen Thompson, Executive VP, Divisional
Josh Hirsberg, Executive VP
Keith Smith, President
Brian Larson, Secretary

GROWTH PLANS/SPECIAL FEATURES:

Boyd Gaming Corp. is a multi-jurisdictional gaming company and one of the country's leading casino operators. It currently owns and operates 22 casinos (21 wholly-owned) totaling over 1.2 million square feet and housing 29,736 slot machines, 757 table games and 11,391 hotel rooms. The firm divides its properties into five segments: Las Vegas local, downtown Las Vegas, Midwest & South, peninsula and Borgata. The Las Vegas local properties include The Orleans Hotel and Casino, Sam's Town Hotel & Gambling Hall, Gold Coast Hotel and Casino, Eldorado Casino, Jokers Wild Casino and Suncoast Hotel and Casino. Downtown Las Vegas facilities consist of the Fremont Hotel & Casino; California Hotel & Casino; and Main Street Casino, Brewery and Hotel. The Midwest & South properties include IP Casino Resort Spa, Sam's Town Hotel and Gambling Hall, Delta Downs Racetrack and Casino & Hotel, Sam's Town Hotel and Casino, Treasure Chest Casino, Par-a-Dice Hotel and Casino and Blue Chip Hotel and Casino. The peninsula properties include Diamond Jo Dubuque, Diamond Jo Worth, Evangeline Downs Racetrack and Casino, Amelia Belle Casino and Kansas Star Casino. The Borgata property includes Borgata Hotel Casino & Spa. Additionally, Boyd owns and operates a travel agency and an insurance company that underwrites travel-related insurance, each located in Hawaii.

Boyd Gaming offers its employees pharmacy, life, short-term disability, medical, dental and vision coverage; flexible spending accounts; and a 401(k).

FINANCIAL DATA: *Note: Data for latest year may not have been available at press time.*

In U.S. $	2015	2014	2013	2012	2011	2010
Revenue	2,199,432,000	2,701,319,000	2,894,438,000	2,487,426,000	2,336,238,000	2,140,899,000
R&D Expense						
Operating Income	344,623,000	251,516,000	278,301,000	-854,875,000	233,104,000	183,938,000
Operating Margin %	15.66%	9.31%	9.61%	-34.36%	9.97%	8.59%
SGA Expense	406,268,000	509,904,000	562,507,000	670,202,000	604,099,000	571,680,000
Net Income	47,234,000	-53,041,000	-80,264,000	-908,865,000	-3,854,000	10,310,000
Operating Cash Flow	339,846,000	322,859,000	277,035,000	142,445,000	253,510,000	285,070,000
Capital Expenditure	131,170,000	149,374,000	144,520,000	125,974,000	87,224,000	87,477,000
EBITDA	471,768,000	493,546,000	506,749,000	-639,511,000	439,796,000	394,898,000
Return on Assets %	1.06%	-1.03%	-1.32%	-14.88%	-.06%	.20%
Return on Equity %	9.98%	-11.68%	-20.74%	-120.70%	-.32%	.87%
Debt to Equity	6.37	7.83	9.26	15.89	2.78	2.68

CONTACT INFORMATION:

Phone: 702 792-7200   Fax: 702 792-7266
Toll-Free:
Address: 3883 Howard Hughes Pkwy., 9th Fl., Las Vegas, NV 89169
United States

STOCK TICKER/OTHER:

Stock Ticker: BYD   Exchange: NYS
Employees: 18,290   Fiscal Year Ends: 12/31
Parent Company:

SALARIES/BONUSES:

Top Exec. Salary: Bonus: $250,000
$1,040,000
Second Exec. Salary: Bonus: $
$1,275,000

OTHER THOUGHTS:

Estimated Female Officers or Directors: 3

Hot Spot for Advancement for Women/Minorities: Y

Boyne Resorts

NAIC Code: 713920

TYPES OF BUSINESS:

Ski Resorts
Golf Courses
Real Estate Development
Retail Operations
Indoor Waterpark
Spas
Restaurants

BRANDS/DIVISIONS/AFFILIATES:

Boyne Highlands Resort
Boyne Mountain Resort
Inn at Bay Harbor (The)
Bay Harbor Golf Club
Crooked Tree Golf Club
Avalanche Bay Indoor Waterpark
Boyne Realty

GROWTH PLANS/SPECIAL FEATURES:

Boyne Resorts are year-round Michigan-based mountain resorts known for skiing, golf and spas. The resorts include retail stores and real estate opportunities based in Lower Northern Michigan. Boyne's ski resorts include Boyne Highlands Resort in Harbor Springs, and Boyne Mountain Resort in Boyne Falls. In addition to its skiing operations there is The Inn at Bay Harbor, a Renaissance Lake Michigan spa resort in Bay Harbor; Bay Harbor Golf Club and Crooked Tree Golf Club, which are golf resorts; Avalanche Bay Indoor Waterpark, which features water rides and slides, as well as lodging and party packages; Boyne Country Sports, retail stores offering backpacks, apparel, ski/snowboard/golf equipment, footwear and travel gear; and Boyne Realty, a real estate firm.

CONTACTS: Note: Officers with more than one job title may be intentionally listed here more than once.

Stephen Kircher, Pres., Eastern Oper.
John Kircher, Pres., Western Oper.
Ed Grice, Pres., Boyne Mountain Resort
Brad Keen, Pres., Boyne Highlands Resort
Kathrynn Kircher, Principal - Boyne Design Group
Amy Kircher Wright, Chmn.

FINANCIAL DATA: Note: Data for latest year may not have been available at press time.

In U.S. $	2015	2014	2013	2012	2011	2010
Revenue	82,000,000	80,000,000	82,000,000	80,800,000		
R&D Expense						
Operating Income						
Operating Margin %						
SGA Expense						
Net Income						
Operating Cash Flow						
Capital Expenditure						
EBITDA						
Return on Assets %						
Return on Equity %						
Debt to Equity						

CONTACT INFORMATION:

Phone: 231-549-6000   Fax: 231-439-4786
Toll-Free:
Address: 3951 Charlevoix Ave, Petoskey, MI 49770 United States

STOCK TICKER/OTHER:

Stock Ticker: Private   Exchange:
Employees: 5,500   Fiscal Year Ends: 12/31
Parent Company:

SALARIES/BONUSES:

Top Exec. Salary: $ Bonus: $
Second Exec. Salary: $ Bonus: $

OTHER THOUGHTS:

Estimated Female Officers or Directors: 2
Hot Spot for Advancement for Women/Minorities:

Sales, profits and employees may be estimates. Financial information, benefits and other data can change quickly and may vary from those stated here.

British Airways plc (BA)

NAIC Code: 481111

TYPES OF BUSINESS:
Airline
Travel Services
Data Management
Travel Software

BRANDS/DIVISIONS/AFFILIATES:
International Airlines Group
Qatar Airlines
OpenSkies
BA City Flyer

CONTACTS: *Note: Officers with more than one job title may be intentionally listed here more than once.*
Alejandro Cruz de Llano, CEO
Garrett Copeland, COO
Stephen William Lawrence Gunning, CFO
Andy Lord, Dir.-Oper.
Lynne Embleton, Dir.-Strategy & Bus. Units

GROWTH PLANS/SPECIAL FEATURES:
British Airways plc (BA) is an international passenger airline company with flights to 188 destinations. The airline is based out of London's Heathrow airport and has a hub in Gatwick airport as well. The airline flies approximately 43 million passengers annually and carries cargo to destinations in Europe, the Americas and throughout the world. BA's 293 aircraft fleet consists of Airbus 318s, 319s, 320s, 321s and 380s; Boeing 747s, 757s, 767s, 777s and 787s; and Ebraer 170s and 190s. The firm is a member of the oneworld alliance, which offers 1,000 destinations through a global network of airlines that include American Airlines, Cathay Pacific, Finnair, Iberia, Japan Airlines, Lan Airlines, Qantas, Royal Jordanian and S7 Airlines. OpenSkies, the firm's subsidiary airline, was created to take advantage of the aviation agreement which enables airlines to fly between any destination in the EU and the U.S. The carrier offers transportation between Paris and New York City as well as to Newark, New Jersey. The company's other wholly-owned subsidiary BA City Flyer operates domestically in the U.K. In 2015, Qatar Airlines purchased a 10% stake in International Airlines Group, BA's parent.

The company offers its employees reduced airfare, travel discounts, pension, profit sharing and health care plans, sports and social amenities, opportunities to join British Airways clubs and subsidized staff restaurants.

FINANCIAL DATA: *Note: Data for latest year may not have been available at press time.*

In U.S. $	2015	2014	2013	2012	2011	2010
Revenue	14,892,873,883	17,377,971,857	19,207,837,800	16,971,000,000	12,931,700,000	10,593,200,000
R&D Expense						
Operating Income						
Operating Margin %						
SGA Expense						
Net Income	3,295,912,260	1,040,987,818	421,140,370	365,227,000	870,139,000	-563,189,000
Operating Cash Flow						
Capital Expenditure						
EBITDA						
Return on Assets %						
Return on Equity %						
Debt to Equity						

CONTACT INFORMATION:
Phone: 0844-493-0748   Fax: 212-251-6767
Toll-Free: 800-255-5305
Address: Waterside HBA3, Harmondsworth, UB7 0GB United Kingdom

STOCK TICKER/OTHER:
Stock Ticker: Subsidiary
Employees: 43,213
Parent Company: International Airlines Group (IAG)

Exchange:
Fiscal Year Ends: 12/31

SALARIES/BONUSES:
Top Exec. Salary: $ Bonus: $
Second Exec. Salary: $ Bonus: $

OTHER THOUGHTS:
Estimated Female Officers or Directors: 2
Hot Spot for Advancement for Women/Minorities: Y

Brussels Airlines

www.brusselsairlines.com

NAIC Code: 481111

TYPES OF BUSINESS:

International Airline
Cargo
Charter Services

BRANDS/DIVISIONS/AFFILIATES:

SN Airholding
Deutsche Lufthansa AG
Brussels Airline Cargo

CONTACTS: *Note: Officers with more than one job title may be intentionally listed here more than once.*

Bernard Gustin, CEO
Jan De Raeymaeker, CFO
Lars Redeligx, Chief Commercial Officer
Etienne Davignon, Chmn.

GROWTH PLANS/SPECIAL FEATURES:

Brussels Airlines is a leading Belgian airline. It serves business and leisure travelers to 76 destinations throughout Europe and Africa, a direct transatlantic service to New York and, through agreements with intercontinental partners, flights to certain locations in the Middle East, China, Thailand, India and Canada. The firm transports more than 7.5 million passengers annually. In addition to basic passenger services, Brussels Airlines also markets cargo shipping services in Europe and Africa and charter plane services in Europe, the Mediterranean Basin (including North Africa) and parts of Russia. Subsidiary Brussels Airlines Cargo provides freight transportation, transporting more than 41,000 tons of cargo in 2015 between Europe and Africa, Europe and the U.S. and within Europe alone. The company maintains a fleet of 46 aircraft, including 12 AVRO RJ100s, 23 Airbus A319/A320s, eight Airbus A330s and three Bombardier DH8s. The firm is a partner of Star Alliance, a global airline network that provides more than 1,200 destinations throughout 193 countries. The company is controlled by SN Airholding, a private holding firm that is 45%-owned by Deutsche Lufthansa AG.

FINANCIAL DATA: *Note: Data for latest year may not have been available at press time.*

In U.S. $	2015	2014	2013	2012	2011	2010
Revenue						
R&D Expense						
Operating Income						
Operating Margin %						
SGA Expense						
Net Income						
Operating Cash Flow						
Capital Expenditure						
EBITDA						
Return on Assets %						
Return on Equity %						
Debt to Equity						

CONTACT INFORMATION:

Phone: 32-2-754-1906   Fax:
Toll-Free:
Address: 100-102, Ave. des Saisons, Box 30, Brussels, 1050 Belgium

STOCK TICKER/OTHER:

Stock Ticker: Subsidiary   Exchange:
Employees: 3,500   Fiscal Year Ends:
Parent Company: SN Airholding

SALARIES/BONUSES:

Top Exec. Salary: $ Bonus: $
Second Exec. Salary: $ Bonus: $

OTHER THOUGHTS:

Estimated Female Officers or Directors:
Hot Spot for Advancement for Women/Minorities:

Sales, profits and employees may be estimates. Financial information, benefits and other data can change quickly and may vary from those stated here.

Caesars Entertainment Corporation

www.caesars.com

NAIC Code: 721120

TYPES OF BUSINESS:

Casino Hotels
Dockside & Riverboat Casinos
Racing Venues
Casino Management
Online Games

BRANDS/DIVISIONS/AFFILIATES:

Harrah's
Caesers
Caesars Entertainment UK
Horseshoe
World Series of Poker
Caesars Interactive Entertainment Inc
Bally's Las Vegas
Flamingo Las Vegas

CONTACTS: Note: Officers with more than one job title may be intentionally listed here more than once.

Mark Frissora, CEO
Eric Hession, CFO
Gary Loveman, Chairman of the Board
Gregory Miller, Executive VP, Divisional
Mary Thomas, Executive VP, Divisional
Richard Broome, Executive VP, Divisional
Janis Jones, Executive VP, Divisional
Les Ottolenghi, Executive VP
Timothy Donovan, Executive VP
Scott Wiegand, Other Corporate Officer
Steven Tight, President, Divisional
Thomas Jenkin, President, Divisional
Robert Morse, President, Divisional
Keith Causey, Senior VP

GROWTH PLANS/SPECIAL FEATURES:

Caesars Entertainment Corporation is one of the largest gaming companies in the world. The firm owns or manages 50 casinos in 14 U.S. states and five countries throughout the world. It operates casino entertainment facilities primarily under the Harrah's, Caesars, and Horseshoe brands in the U.S., including land-based casinos, riverboat or dockside casinos, casino clubs and several racing venues. In Las Vegas alone, the firm owns Caesars Palace, Harrah's Las Vegas, Rio All-Suite Hotel & Casino, Bally's Las Vegas, Flamingo Las Vegas, Paris Las Vegas, Planet Hollywood Resort and Casino, The Quad Resort & Casino and Bill's Gamblin' Hall & Saloon. In addition, the firm owns Caesars Entertainment UK family of casinos. Besides casinos, the firm's properties generally include hotel and convention space, restaurants and non-gaming entertainment facilities. Its facilities contain an aggregate 1.48 million square feet of gaming space and over 15,700 hotel rooms. Through its subsidiary Caesars Interactive Entertainment, Inc., the company owns and operates the World Series of Poker tournament and develops online games, both real money wagered and play-for-fun games. Other subsidiaries are Caesars Entertainment Resort Properties and Caesars Growth Partners, LLC. Caesars was purchased in 2008 for about $30 billion by two private equity companies. Much of the purchase was funded by debt. In January 2015, the company filed a complex bankruptcy for its main operating company in attempt to eliminate much of its vast debts and reduce interest expenses.

FINANCIAL DATA: Note: Data for latest year may not have been available at press time.

In U.S. $	2015	2014	2013	2012	2011	2010
Revenue	4,654,000,000	8,516,000,000	8,559,700,000	8,586,700,000	8,834,500,000	8,818,600,000
R&D Expense						
Operating Income	573,000,000	-452,000,000	-2,234,600,000	-313,400,000	875,500,000	532,300,000
Operating Margin %	12.31%	-5.30%	-26.10%	-3.64%	9.91%	6.03%
SGA Expense	1,485,000,000	2,588,000,000	2,347,600,000	2,316,300,000	2,271,300,000	2,204,700,000
Net Income	5,920,000,000	-2,783,000,000	-2,948,200,000	-1,497,500,000	-687,600,000	-831,100,000
Operating Cash Flow	120,000,000	-735,000,000	-109,400,000	26,500,000	123,100,000	170,800,000
Capital Expenditure	350,000,000	998,000,000	726,300,000	507,700,000	305,900,000	177,200,000
EBITDA	7,091,000,000	132,000,000	-1,464,100,000	751,200,000	1,830,100,000	1,873,800,000
Return on Assets %	33.13%	-11.54%	-11.19%	-5.29%	-2.40%	-2.88%
Return on Equity %				-503.36%	-52.10%	-234.14%
Debt to Equity	6.86				19.62	11.50

CONTACT INFORMATION:

Phone: 702 407-6000   Fax: 702 407-6037
Toll-Free: 800-318-0047
Address: 1 Caesars Palace Dr., Las Vegas, NV 89109 United States

STOCK TICKER/OTHER:

Stock Ticker: CZR   Exchange: NAS
Employees: 68,000   Fiscal Year Ends: 12/31
Parent Company:

SALARIES/BONUSES:

Top Exec. Salary: $1,900,000   Bonus: $
Second Exec. Salary: $1,599,231   Bonus: $

OTHER THOUGHTS:

Estimated Female Officers or Directors: 2

Hot Spot for Advancement for Women/Minorities: Y

Sales, profits and employees may be estimates. Financial information, benefits and other data can change quickly and may vary from those stated here.

Carey International Inc

NAIC Code: 485320

www.carey.com

TYPES OF BUSINESS:

Chauffeured Vehicle Service

BRANDS/DIVISIONS/AFFILIATES:

Mobile Operations Center
Carey Rewards Club
Carey Alliance Netowrk
Embarque

CONTACTS: *Note: Officers with more than one job title may be intentionally listed here more than once.*

Gary L. Kessler, CEO
Gary L. Kessler, Pres.
Mitchell J. Lahr, CFO
Eugene S. Willard, Sr. VP-Tech.
Diane M. Ennist, General Counsel
Sally A. Snead, Sr. VP-Oper.
Eugene S. Willard, Sr. VP-Planning & Strategy
Scott F. Ziegler, Chief Acct. Officer
David F. Ng, VP-Global Accounts
Louis A. Tessier, VP-Treasury & Risk Mgmt.
Frank A. Scaravaglione, VP-Travel Industry Sales
Joel J. Barch, VP-Customer Experience
Nicholas J. Riley, VP-Int'l Network

GROWTH PLANS/SPECIAL FEATURES:

Carey International, Inc. provides chauffeured vehicle service through wholly-owned and operated companies, licensees and affiliates, covering more than 1000 cities worldwide. The firm's wholly-owned subsidiaries operate in large metropolitan markets, including Boston, Chicago, Detroit, Indianapolis, Los Angeles, New York, London, Paris, San Francisco and Washington, D.C. The company's fleet consists of chauffeured sedans, limousines, vans, sport utility vehicles, minibuses and motor coaches. Some Carey vehicles are specially designed for extra legroom, and all vehicles are equipped with wireless Internet access. Certain vehicles come with the Mobile Operations Center option, which include cell phones, two-way radios, computers, fax machines and copiers. Additional optional features include DVD players, satellite radios and reading lamps. Carey provides services for airport pick-ups & drop-offs, inter-office transfers, business meetings, conventions, promotional tours and sightseeing, special events and leisure travel. In addition, the company provides Internet reservations through its e-Reservation Center. The company also operates a Meetings & Events division, allowing planners to coordinate all aspects of corporate group transportation. Carey offers the Carey Rewards Club, a loyalty program that allows customers to accrue points through business with the company and redeem them for varying rewards, including merchandise and travel awards. The company also partners with the Carey Alliance Network, a branded network of affiliated companies that operates in areas not directly serviced by Carey. Subsidiary Embarque offers chauffeur services exclusively from carbon-offsetting vehicles approved by the Environmental Protection Agency.

FINANCIAL DATA: *Note: Data for latest year may not have been available at press time.*

In U.S. $	2015	2014	2013	2012	2011	2010
Revenue						
R&D Expense						
Operating Income						
Operating Margin %						
SGA Expense						
Net Income						
Operating Cash Flow						
Capital Expenditure						
EBITDA						
Return on Assets %						
Return on Equity %						
Debt to Equity						

CONTACT INFORMATION:

Phone: 202-895-1200   Fax: 202-895-1269
Toll-Free: 800-930-1490
Address: 7445 New Technology Way, Frederick, MD 20016 United States

STOCK TICKER/OTHER:

Stock Ticker: Private   Exchange:
Employees: 1,206   Fiscal Year Ends:
Parent Company:

SALARIES/BONUSES:

Top Exec. Salary: $ Bonus: $
Second Exec. Salary: $ Bonus: $

OTHER THOUGHTS:

Estimated Female Officers or Directors: 4
Hot Spot for Advancement for Women/Minorities: Y

Carlson Companies Inc

www.carlson.com

NAIC Code: 721110

TYPES OF BUSINESS:

Hotels & Resorts
Travel Agencies & Services
Marketing Services
Restaurant Chains
Online Travel Services
Business & Government Travel Management

BRANDS/DIVISIONS/AFFILIATES:

Radisson
Park Plaza
Park Inn by Radisson
Country Inns & Suites by Carlson
Hotel Quorvus
Rezidor Hotel Group
Carlson Wagonlit Travel
CWT Meetings & Events

CONTACTS: Note: Officers with more than one job title may be intentionally listed here more than once.

David P. Berg, CEO
Trey Hall, CFO
Cindy Rodahl, VP-Human Resources & Comm.
William A. Van Brunt, General Counsel
Brad Hall, Treasurer
Thorsten Kirschke, Pres., Carlson Rezidor Hotel Group, Americas
Gordon McKinnon, Chief Branding Officer
Diana L. Nelson, Chmn.
Simon Barlow, Pres., Carlson Rezidor Hotel Group, Asia Pacific

GROWTH PLANS/SPECIAL FEATURES:

Carlson Companies, Inc. is an integrated travel and hospitality company with operations in hotels, restaurants and corporate travel management. The company operates over 1,400 hotels in more than 150 countries. Its brand portfolio spans mid-priced properties to full-service premium and luxury hotels and resorts; these include Radisson, Radisson Red and Radisson Blu, which together comprise 448 locations with over 99,000 rooms; Park Plaza, comprising 46 operating locations and eight in development; Park Inn by Radisson, 142 locations with more than 26,000 rooms; Country Inns & Suites by Carlson, 473 and 55 under development locations; and Hotel Quorvus, with three properties in operation. Carlson also owns a majority share in Rezidor Hotel Group (50.3%). The firm's travel management division, which is comprised of wholly-owned Carlson Wagonlit Travel (CWT), offers corporate clients business travel management programs with the objective of maximizing productivity while minimizing cost. Through CWT Meetings & Events, it provides numerous events and meetings management services, annually delivering over 40,000 events for its clients. In April 2016, the firm agreed to be acquired by HNA Tourism Group Co. Ltd.

FINANCIAL DATA: Note: Data for latest year may not have been available at press time.

In U.S. $	2015	2014	2013	2012	2011	2010
Revenue	3,150,000,000	4,400,000,000	4,400,000,000	4,500,000,000	4,130,000,000	3,900,000,000
R&D Expense						
Operating Income						
Operating Margin %						
SGA Expense						
Net Income						
Operating Cash Flow						
Capital Expenditure						
EBITDA						
Return on Assets %						
Return on Equity %						
Debt to Equity						

CONTACT INFORMATION:

Phone: 763-212-5000   Fax: 763-212-2219
Toll-Free:
Address: 701 Carlson Pkwy., Minnetonka, MN 55305 United States

STOCK TICKER/OTHER:

Stock Ticker: Private   Exchange:
Employees: 110,000   Fiscal Year Ends: 12/31
Parent Company:

SALARIES/BONUSES:

Top Exec. Salary: $ Bonus: $
Second Exec. Salary: $ Bonus: $

OTHER THOUGHTS:

Estimated Female Officers or Directors: 6
Hot Spot for Advancement for Women/Minorities: Y

Sales, profits and employees may be estimates. Financial information, benefits and other data can change quickly and may vary from those stated here.

Carlson Rezidor Hotel Group

NAIC Code: 721110

TYPES OF BUSINESS:
Hotels & Resorts

BRANDS/DIVISIONS/AFFILIATES:
HNA Tourism Holding (Group) Co Ltd
Radisson Hotels & Resorts
Park Plaza Hotels & Resorts
Country Inns & Suites By Carlson
Park Inn Hotels
Quorvus
Carlson Wagonlit Travel
HNA Group Co Ltd

CONTACTS: Note: Officers with more than one job title may be intentionally listed here more than once.
David P. Berg, CEO
Trudy Rautio, Pres.
William A. Van Brunt, General Counsel
Tony Pellegrin, Sr. VP-Corp. Dev.
Cindy Rodahl, Exec. VP-Comm.
Brad Hall, Treas.
Diana L. Nelson, Chmn.

GROWTH PLANS/SPECIAL FEATURES:
Carlson Rezidor Hotel Group, a subsidiary of HNA Tourism Holding (Group) Co., Ltd., is one of the world's leading hotel franchisors. The firm includes more than 1,400 locations in over 110 countries and territories. Specific brands include Radisson Hotels & Resorts, Park Plaza Hotels & Resorts, Park Inn Hotels, Country Inns & Suites By Carlson and Quorvus. The company's Radisson chain owns 500 full-service hotels at locations throughout North America, Latin America, Asia Pacific, Europe, the Middle East and Africa. Radisson Hotels offer pre-arrival online check-in, a fitness center and free high-speed Internet access. The firm's 48 Park Plaza Hotels include restaurants, meeting rooms, catering, suites and recreational facilities. The Park Inn is the company's economy brand with approximately 211 hotels in operation and under development worldwide. Country Inns & Suites By Carlson is a mid-tier lodging chain with more than 470 locations in the Americas, Europe and India. Specialty services include an in-hotel Read It and Return Lending Library in which guests can borrow a book and return it on their next stay. Quorvus has two hotels in operation in Edinburgh and Kuwait. It is a stylish and contemporary hotel that utilizes the intimate and eclectic creative vision of Rosita Missoni. Quorvus has a hotel in London currently under development. The firm offers a Club Carlson rewards program, which allow clients to accumulate award points towards flights, hotel stays and other bonuses. Other business operations of the company include Carlson Wagonlit Travel (CWT), a business travel management service. In April 2016, Carlson Companies, Inc. sold the Carlson Rezidor Hotel Group to China's HNA Tourism Holding (Group) Co., Ltd., itself a subsidiary of HNA Group Co., Ltd.

FINANCIAL DATA: Note: Data for latest year may not have been available at press time.

In U.S. $	2015	2014	2013	2012	2011	2010
Revenue	1,135,234,050	1,067,256,645	7,500,000,000	7,200,000,000	7,000,000,000	6,500,000,000
R&D Expense						
Operating Income						
Operating Margin %						
SGA Expense						
Net Income						
Operating Cash Flow						
Capital Expenditure						
EBITDA						
Return on Assets %						
Return on Equity %						
Debt to Equity						

CONTACT INFORMATION:
Phone: 763-212-5000   Fax:
Toll-Free:
Address: 701 Carlson Pkwy., Minnetonka, MN 55305 United States

STOCK TICKER/OTHER:
Stock Ticker: Subsidiary   Exchange:
Employees: 90,000   Fiscal Year Ends: 12/31
Parent Company: HNA Group Co Ltd

SALARIES/BONUSES:
Top Exec. Salary: $ Bonus: $
Second Exec. Salary: $ Bonus: $

OTHER THOUGHTS:
Estimated Female Officers or Directors: 6
Hot Spot for Advancement for Women/Minorities: Y

Sales, profits and employees may be estimates. Financial information, benefits and other data can change quickly and may vary from those stated here.

Carlson Wagonlit Travel

www.carlsonwagonlit.com

NAIC Code: 561510

TYPES OF BUSINESS:

Travel Agency
Expense Management
Consulting

BRANDS/DIVISIONS/AFFILIATES:

Carlson Companies Inc
CWT Program Management Center
Carlson Marketing
CWT Travel Management Institute
CWT Vision
Ormes

CONTACTS: *Note: Officers with more than one job title may be intentionally listed here more than once.*

Kurt Ekert, CEO
Douglas Anderson, Pres.
Martine Gerow, Exec. VP
David Moran, Exec. VP- Human Resources
Andrew Jordan, Exec. VP-IT
Andrew Winterton, Pres., Prod. & Suppliers
Jerry Hogan, General Counsel
David Moran, Exec. VP-Enterprise Strategy
Berthold Trenkel, Exec. VP-Traveler & Transactions Svcs.
Cathy Voss, Exec. VP-Global Program Solutions
Hakan Ericsson, Pres., Americas
Andrew Waller, Pres., EMEA
Kelly Kuhn, Pres., Asia-Pacific

GROWTH PLANS/SPECIAL FEATURES:

Carlson Wagonlit Travel (CWT) is one of the largest travel agencies in the world. The firm is wholly-owned by Carlson Companies, Inc. With locations in over 150 countries, CWT caters primarily to corporations and other business travelers. The company provides products and services in a variety of areas. For its traveler and transaction services category, CWT has continuously trained counselors as well as an online travel portal. Its traveler services include an application for accessing travel information from a user's smartphone; VIP traveler services; and Visa, currency and insurance provisions. For its program services, CWT has developed the CWT Program Management Center, a web-based multilingual resource for travel management and research. For its meetings and events category, CWT has nearly 40,000 meetings and events professionals in almost 200 countries, and it also partners with marketing services firms such as Carlson Marketing. Through tracking reports, destination intelligence, travel alerts and incident reporting, CWT's safety and security category informs companies of potential risks and is capable of assisting travelers in the event of a crisis. The recently created CWT energy services division specializes in providing transportation and travel services to the energy, oil and gas, drilling and exploration and marine services industries. Additionally, the CWT Travel Management Institute conducts research on travel management and publishes its findings in the quarterly CWT Vision. CWT has 54 wholly-owned/joint ventures/minority holdings worldwide. In 2015, CWT acquired Ormes, an agency that specializes in corporate meetings and events. In January 2016, the firm sold subsidiary Havas Voyages to Marietton Group.

FINANCIAL DATA: *Note: Data for latest year may not have been available at press time.*

In U.S. $	2015	2014	2013	2012	2011	2010
Revenue	26,200,000,000	27,300,000,000	26,900,000,000	27,700,000,000	28,000,000,000	24,300,000,000
R&D Expense						
Operating Income						
Operating Margin %						
SGA Expense						
Net Income						
Operating Cash Flow						
Capital Expenditure						
EBITDA						
Return on Assets %						
Return on Equity %						
Debt to Equity						

CONTACT INFORMATION:

Phone: 33-01-41-33600   Fax:
Toll-Free:
Address: 31 rue du Colonel Pierre Avia, Paris, 75015 France

STOCK TICKER/OTHER:

Stock Ticker: Subsidiary   Exchange:
Employees: 20,000   Fiscal Year Ends: 12/31
Parent Company: Carlson Companies Inc

SALARIES/BONUSES:

Top Exec. Salary: $ Bonus: $
Second Exec. Salary: $ Bonus: $

OTHER THOUGHTS:

Estimated Female Officers or Directors: 3
Hot Spot for Advancement for Women/Minorities: Y

Carnival Corporation   www.carnival.com

NAIC Code: 483112

TYPES OF BUSINESS:

Cruise Line
On-Board Casinos
Tours
Resort Hotels

BRANDS/DIVISIONS/AFFILIATES:

Carnival Cruise Lines
Princess Cruises
Holland America Line
Seabourn Cruise Line
Costa Cruises
P&O Cruises
Cunard
AIDA Cruises

CONTACTS: *Note: Officers with more than one job title may be intentionally listed here more than once.*

David Noyes, CEO, Geographical
Michael Thamm, CEO, Subsidiary
Stein Kruse, CEO, Subsidiary
Arnold Donald, CEO
David Bernstein, CFO
Micky Arison, Chairman of the Board
Larry Freedman, Chief Accounting Officer
Josh Leibowitz, Chief Strategy Officer
Alan Buckelew, COO
Arnaldo Perez, Secretary

GROWTH PLANS/SPECIAL FEATURES:

Carnival Corporation is a leading provider of cruises and vacation packages to destinations worldwide. The firm is linked with its sister company Carnival plc. The firm divides its cruise brands into two segments: North America, which includes Carnival Cruise Lines, Princess Cruises, Holland America Line and Seabourn Cruise Line; and Europe, Australia & Asia (EAA), comprised of Costa Cruises, P&O Cruises, Cunard and AIDA Cruises. In total, the company operated 99 ships and 10.8 million guests in 2015. Carnival Cruise Lines operates 24 ships and is based in North America. Princess is a global cruise and tour company operating 18 ships. Holland America Line serves the industry's premium segment, with 13 ships sailing to all seven continents. Seabourn offers luxury cruises on its three luxury yachts. Costa Cruises is a leading cruise company in Europe, Spain and South America, operating a modern fleet of 15 ships. P&O Cruises, which operates from the U.K. and Australia, sails to destinations in the Caribbean, South America, Scandinavia, the Mediterranean and Atlantic Islands as well as Round the World cruises. Cunard operates the Queen Mary 2, Queen Elizabeth and Queen Victoria ships. AIDA operates in the German-speaking cruise market via a fleet of 10 ships. The company also owns Holland America Princess Alaska Tours, a leading tour operator in Alaska and the Canadian Yukon, offering lodging (at 11 owned hotels and lodges), chartered motorcoaches, rail cars, luxury day boats and sightseeing packages. In 2016, the firm commenced operations of its new brand called fathom Cruise Line, a social travel category that offers consumers meaningful impact travel experiences to work alongside locals as they tackle community needs.

FINANCIAL DATA: *Note: Data for latest year may not have been available at press time.*

In U.S. $	2015	2014	2013	2012	2011	2010
Revenue	15,714,000,000	15,884,000,000	15,456,000,000	15,382,000,000	15,793,000,000	14,469,000,000
R&D Expense						
Operating Income	2,574,000,000	1,792,000,000	1,352,000,000	1,642,000,000	2,255,000,000	2,347,000,000
Operating Margin %	16.38%	11.28%	8.74%	10.67%	14.27%	16.22%
SGA Expense	2,067,000,000	2,054,000,000	1,879,000,000	1,720,000,000	1,717,000,000	1,614,000,000
Net Income	1,757,000,000	1,236,000,000	1,078,000,000	1,298,000,000	1,912,000,000	1,978,000,000
Operating Cash Flow	4,545,000,000	3,430,000,000	2,834,000,000	2,999,000,000	3,766,000,000	3,818,000,000
Capital Expenditure	2,294,000,000	2,583,000,000	2,149,000,000	2,332,000,000	2,696,000,000	3,579,000,000
EBITDA	3,642,000,000	3,168,000,000	2,979,000,000	3,165,000,000	3,799,000,000	3,773,000,000
Return on Assets %	4.46%	3.10%	2.72%	3.33%	5.02%	5.32%
Return on Equity %	7.31%	5.06%	4.44%	5.43%	8.16%	8.77%
Debt to Equity	0.31	0.30	0.32	0.29	0.33	0.34

CONTACT INFORMATION:

Phone: 305 599-2600   Fax: 305 471-4700
Toll-Free:
Address: 3655 NW 87th Ave., Miami, FL 33178 United States

STOCK TICKER/OTHER:

Stock Ticker: CCL   Exchange: NYS
Employees: 12,900   Fiscal Year Ends: 11/30
Parent Company:

SALARIES/BONUSES:

Top Exec. Salary: Bonus: $
$1,000,000
Second Exec. Salary: Bonus: $
$825,000

OTHER THOUGHTS:

Estimated Female Officers or Directors: 1

Hot Spot for Advancement for Women/Minorities: Y

Sales, profits and employees may be estimates. Financial information, benefits and other data can change quickly and may vary from those stated here.

Cathay Pacific Airways Ltd

www.cathaypacific.com

NAIC Code: 481111

TYPES OF BUSINESS:

Airline
Cargo Services
Flight Catering
Laundry Services
Travel Agency

BRANDS/DIVISIONS/AFFILIATES:

Swire Pacific Ltd
Hong Kong Dragon Airlines Limited
Cathay Pacific Catering Services (HK) Limited
Cathay Holidays Limited
Hong Kong Airport Services Limited
Vogue Laundry Service Limited
Cathay Pacific Services Limited
Air Hong Kong

CONTACTS:
Note: Officers with more than one job title may be intentionally listed here more than once.

Ivan Chu, CEO
Rupert Bruce Hogg, COO
Martin James Murray, CFO
Christopher Gibbs, Dir.-Eng.
Richard Hall, Dir.-Flight Oper.
James Barrington, Dir.-Corp. Dev.
Martin Murray, Dir.-Finance
Philippe de Gentile-Williams, Dir.-Service Delivery
Chitty Cheung, Dir.-Corp. Affairs
John Slosar, Chmn.
Nick Rhodes, Dir.-Cargo

GROWTH PLANS/SPECIAL FEATURES:

Cathay Pacific Airways Ltd., a Hong Kong-based airline that is 40% owned by Swire Pacific Ltd., flies to 162 locations in 42 countries and territories. Its fleet of 145 wide-body aircraft includes both Boeing and Airbus aircraft and has an average age of 8.5 years. The airline is a member of the oneworld alliance and has code-share agreements with 15 airlines, including American Airlines, Japan Airlines, Qantas, Finnair and British Airways. Wholly-owned subsidiary airline, Hong Kong Dragon Airlines Limited (branded as Cathay Dragon), offers flights to 44 destinations across Mainland China and Asia. Both Cathay Dragon and Cathay Pacific provide cargo services throughout their flight networks. The firm also operates five additional wholly-owned subsidiaries: Cathay Pacific Catering Services (HK) Limited, servicing 30 airlines and producing 80,000 meals daily; Cathay Holidays Limited, a tour subsidiary that offers hotel and travel packages; Cathay Pacific Services Limited, recently awarded a 20 year contract to build and service a terminal at Hong Kong International Airport; Hong Kong Airport Services Limited, a ramp handling companies in Hong Kong; and Vogue Laundry Service Limited, which provides laundering and dry-cleaning services to airlines and hotels. Additionally, the company owns 20.13% of Air China, 49% of Air China Cargo and 60% of Air Hong Kong.

Employees are offered medical and dental coverage, retirement plans and various insurance plans, staff facilities and company transportation in Hong Kong and discounted airline travel.

FINANCIAL DATA:
Note: Data for latest year may not have been available at press time.

In U.S. $	2015	2014	2013	2012	2011	2010
Revenue	13,197,250,000	13,667,790,000	12,957,650,000	12,814,770,000	12,689,690,000	11,544,340,000
R&D Expense						
Operating Income	859,338,800	571,903,900	484,861,000	230,566,900	709,238,200	1,425,311,000
Operating Margin %	6.51%	4.18%	3.74%	1.79%	5.58%	12.34%
SGA Expense	102,904,000	103,033,000	99,938,110	100,196,000	102,001,300	94,908,970
Net Income	773,714,400	406,200,100	337,855,300	118,120,400	709,367,200	1,835,379,000
Operating Cash Flow	2,062,594,000	1,326,275,000	1,634,601,000	959,405,800	1,802,755,000	2,269,433,000
Capital Expenditure	1,699,464,000	1,910,817,000	2,647,909,000	2,704,776,000	2,270,852,000	1,070,176,000
EBITDA	2,800,459,000	2,286,584,000	2,082,323,000	1,738,923,000	2,269,691,000	3,118,832,000
Return on Assets %	3.48%	1.83%	1.60%	.62%	4.14%	11.79%
Return on Equity %	12.04%	5.49%	4.36%	1.62%	9.99%	29.49%
Debt to Equity	1.04	1.06	0.90	0.89		

CONTACT INFORMATION:

Phone: 852 27471888   Fax: 852 25601411
Toll-Free:
Address: One Pacific Place, 88 Queensway, Hong Kong, Hong Kong

STOCK TICKER/OTHER:

Stock Ticker: CPCAF   Exchange: PINX
Employees: 32,900   Fiscal Year Ends: 12/31
Parent Company:

SALARIES/BONUSES:

Top Exec. Salary: $ Bonus: $
Second Exec. Salary: $ Bonus: $

OTHER THOUGHTS:

Estimated Female Officers or Directors: 2
Hot Spot for Advancement for Women/Minorities:

Sales, profits and employees may be estimates. Financial information, benefits and other data can change quickly and may vary from those stated here.

Cedar Fair LP

NAIC Code: 713110

www.cedarfair.com

TYPES OF BUSINESS:

Amusement Parks
Water Parks
Hotels
Camping
Marina

BRANDS/DIVISIONS/AFFILIATES:

Cedar Point
Knott's Berry Farm
Dorney Park & Wildwater Kingdom
Valleyfair
Kings Island
Kings Dominion
Carowinds
Castaway Bay Indoor Waterpark Resort

CONTACTS: Note: Officers with more than one job title may be intentionally listed here more than once.

Matthew Ouimet, CEO
Brian Witherow, CFO
Eric Affeldt, Chairman of the Board
David Hoffman, Chief Accounting Officer
Kelley Semmelroth, Chief Marketing Officer
Richard Zimmerman, COO
H. Bender, Executive VP, Divisional
Duffield Milkie, General Counsel
Robert Decker, Senior VP, Divisional
Craig Freeman, Senior VP, Divisional

GROWTH PLANS/SPECIAL FEATURES:

Cedar Fair LP owns and operates 11 amusement parks, three outdoor water parks, one indoor water park and five hotels. These include Cedar Point, in Sandusky, Ohio; Knott's Berry Farm, in Buena Park, California; Dorney Park & Wildwater Kingdom, in South Whitehall Township, Pennsylvania; Valleyfair, in Shakopee, Minnesota; Worlds of Fun, in Kansas City, Missouri; Wildwater Kingdom, in Aurora, Ohio; Michigan's Adventure, near Muskegon, Michigan; Kings Island near Cincinnati, Ohio; Kings Dominion near Richmond, Virginia; Carowinds in Charlotte, North Carolina; Great America located in Santa Clara, California; Canada's Wonderland near Toronto, Canada; and Castaway Bay Indoor Waterpark Resort in Sandusky, Ohio. Two of the outdoor water parks are located adjacent to Cedar Point and Knott's Berry Farm, and the third is Wildwater Kingdom located in Aurora, Ohio. Cedar Point's only year-round hotel is Castaway Bay, an indoor water park resort. Castaway Bay features a tropical Caribbean theme with 237 hotel rooms centered around a 38,000-square-foot indoor water park. The park's largest hotel, the Hotel Breakers, has more than 600 guest rooms. Located near the Causeway entrance to the park is Breakers Express, a 350-room, limited-service seasonal hotel. Cedar Point also features the Sandcastle Suites Hotel, which features 187 suites, a courtyard pool and tennis courts. The park also owns and operates the Cedar Point Marina, Castaway Bay Marina and Camper Village. Additionally, the company has a management contract for Gilroy Gardens Family Theme Park in Gilroy, California.

FINANCIAL DATA: Note: Data for latest year may not have been available at press time.

In U.S. $	2015	2014	2013	2012	2011	2010
Revenue	1,235,778,000	1,159,605,000	1,134,572,000	1,068,454,000	1,028,472,000	977,592,000
R&D Expense						
Operating Income	295,331,000	278,332,000	301,761,000	232,642,000	238,768,000	153,729,000
Operating Margin %	23.89%	24.00%	26.59%	21.77%	23.21%	15.72%
SGA Expense	171,490,000	156,864,000	152,412,000	138,311,000	140,426,000	134,001,000
Net Income	112,222,000	104,215,000	108,204,000	202,432,000	144,316,000	-31,567,000
Operating Cash Flow	342,217,000	337,103,000	324,457,000	285,933,000	218,177,000	182,115,000
Capital Expenditure	175,865,000	166,719,000	120,448,000	96,232,000	90,190,000	71,706,000
EBITDA	346,894,000	334,672,000	354,005,000	370,539,000	364,985,000	248,759,000
Return on Assets %	5.56%	5.14%	5.35%	4.93%	3.47%	-1.49%
Return on Equity %	146.47%	88.56%	72.52%	63.66%	48.77%	-23.82%
Debt to Equity	27.30	16.20	10.92	9.62	9.70	11.51

CONTACT INFORMATION:

Phone: 419 626-0830   Fax: 419 627-2234
Toll-Free:
Address: 1 Cedar Point Dr., Sandusky, OH 44870 United States

STOCK TICKER/OTHER:

Stock Ticker: FUN   Exchange: NYS
Employees: 2,000   Fiscal Year Ends: 12/31
Parent Company:

SALARIES/BONUSES:

Top Exec. Salary: $961,840   Bonus: $
Second Exec. Salary: Bonus: $
$570,723

OTHER THOUGHTS:

Estimated Female Officers or Directors: 3
Hot Spot for Advancement for Women/Minorities: Y

Celebrity Cruises Inc

www.celebritycruises.com

NAIC Code: 483112

TYPES OF BUSINESS:

Cruise Lines

BRANDS/DIVISIONS/AFFILIATES:

Royal Caribbean Cruises Ltd
Celebrity Millenium
Celebrity Xpeditions
EDGE

CONTACTS: Note: Officers with more than one job title may be intentionally listed here more than once.

Lisa Lutoff-Perlo, CEO

GROWTH PLANS/SPECIAL FEATURES:

Celebrity Cruises, Inc., a subsidiary of Royal Caribbean Cruises Ltd., is a luxury cruise line based in Miami, Florida. The firm operates 10 ships with an aggregate capacity of approximately 24,800 berths. Its cruise itineraries range from two to 18 nights and include destinations in Alaska, Asia, Australia, Bermuda, Canada, the Caribbean, Europe, Hawaii, New England, New Zealand, the Panama Canal, the U.S. Pacific Coast and South America. Celebrity Cruises is positioned within the premium segment of the cruise vacation industry. Its ships feature a high staff-to-guest ratio, fine dining, personalized service, spa facilities and multiple onboard activities and entertainment options. The firm's Celebrity Millenium ships consist of gas turbine engines, which reduce exhaust emissions by up to 95% over traditional propulsion systems, and each boast original paneling and artifacts from the famed transatlantic luxury liners after which they are named. Adventure cruises to the Galapagos, through Celebrity Xpeditions, offers travelers once-in-a-lifetime opportunities to explore new and exotic settings as well as providing a series of premium excursion options on select itineraries. In December 2014, the firm ordered a new class of vessels from French shipbuilder STX France, comprising two 2,900-guest, 117,000-gross-registered-ton ships, developed under the project name EDGE, which will deliver small ship itineraries with large ship amenities. The first EDGE vessel is expected to be delivered in 2018, and the second in 2020. During 2015, Celebrity's oldest ship, Century, departed the fleet.

FINANCIAL DATA: Note: Data for latest year may not have been available at press time.

In U.S. $	2015	2014	2013	2012	2011	2010
Revenue	1,150,000,000	1,100,000,000	1,000,000,000	999,443,000	924,003,000	945,748,000
R&D Expense						
Operating Income						
Operating Margin %						
SGA Expense						
Net Income						
Operating Cash Flow						
Capital Expenditure						
EBITDA						
Return on Assets %						
Return on Equity %						
Debt to Equity						

CONTACT INFORMATION:

Phone: 305-539-6000   Fax:
Toll-Free: 800-647-2251
Address: 1050 Caribbean Way, Miami, FL 33132 United States

STOCK TICKER/OTHER:

Stock Ticker: Subsidiary   Exchange:
Employees: Fiscal Year Ends: 12/31
Parent Company: Royal Caribbean Cruises Ltd

SALARIES/BONUSES:

Top Exec. Salary: $ Bonus: $
Second Exec. Salary: $ Bonus: $

OTHER THOUGHTS:

Estimated Female Officers or Directors:
Hot Spot for Advancement for Women/Minorities:

Central Japan Railway Company

NAIC Code: 482111

www.jr-central.co.jp

TYPES OF BUSINESS:

Line-Haul Railroads
Travel Agency Services
Retail Operations
Real Estate Sales & Leasing
Construction Services
Food & Beverage Sales
Insurance Agency Services
Hotel Operation

BRANDS/DIVISIONS/AFFILIATES:

JR Central
Chuo Shinkansen
JR West
JR Tokai Tours
JR Tokai Real Estate Co
JR Tokai Bus Co
Tokai Transport Services Co
JR Information Systems Co

CONTACTS: Note: Officers with more than one job title may be intentionally listed here more than once.

Koei Tsuge, Pres.
Tsutomu Morimura, Exec. VP
Koei Tsuge, Exec. VP
Shin Kaneko, Exec. VP
Naotoshi Yoshikawa, Exec. VP
Yoshiyukui Kasai, Chmn.

GROWTH PLANS/SPECIAL FEATURES:

Central Japan Railway Company, also known as JR Central, operates primarily in Tokaido Shinkansen, the main transportation artery linking Japan's principal metropolitan areas of Tokyo, Nagoya and Osaka. The company also operates a network of 13 conventional lines centered in the Nagoya and Shizuoka areas. JR Central has 405 stations that form an integrated network with the Tokaido Shinkansen station, which has a line running to Tokyo using new trains with a top speed of 167 mph. In total, the firm operates around 1,225 miles of track and manages 4,890 rolling stock cars. Chuo Shinkansen, one of the company's top projects in development, is a transport system of superconducting magnetically levitated trains with an estimated maximum operating speed of over 300 mph. The technology being researched and developed by JR Central to support its Chuo Shinkansen system is the Superconducting Maglev system. The Maglev test line runs about 11 miles. In collaboration with JR West, JR Central also developed the Shinkansen rolling stock Series N700, which conserves energy by reducing body weight and running resistance with its body inclining system. Although transportation accounts for the vast majority of JR Central's total revenue, the firm is also involved in retail operations and real estate, among other sectors. The company has 39 subsidiaries, all based in Japan, including JR Tokai Tours, JR Tokai Real Estate Co., JR Tokai Bus Co., Tokai Transport Services Co., JR Tokai Information Systems Co., JR Tokai Construction Co. and JR Tokai Hotels Co.

FINANCIAL DATA: Note: Data for latest year may not have been available at press time.

In U.S. $	2015	2014	2013	2012	2011	2010
Revenue	16,630,820,000	16,434,420,000	15,765,850,000	15,000,180,000	14,948,020,000	
R&D Expense						
Operating Income	5,038,069,000	4,918,870,000	4,237,942,000	3,704,686,000	3,474,223,000	
Operating Margin %	30.29%	29.93%	26.88%	24.69%	23.24%	
SGA Expense						
Net Income	2,553,484,000	2,586,352,000	2,024,017,000	1,353,551,000	1,351,751,000	
Operating Cash Flow	5,676,612,000	5,375,788,000	5,095,014,000	4,452,076,000	5,190,584,000	
Capital Expenditure	2,015,106,000	2,067,228,000	2,719,464,000	2,886,877,000	2,792,003,000	
EBITDA	7,444,140,000	7,551,485,000	6,520,566,000	6,167,293,000	5,881,308,000	
Return on Assets %	5.08%	4.91%	3.82%	2.53%	2.55%	
Return on Equity %	13.99%	15.65%	14.10%	10.50%	11.61%	
Debt to Equity	0.63	0.74	0.98	1.17	1.34	

CONTACT INFORMATION:

Phone: 81 525642620   Fax:
Toll-Free:
Address: JR Central Towers 1-1-4, Meieki, Nakamura-ku, Nagoya, Aichi Prefecture 450-6101 Japan

STOCK TICKER/OTHER:

Stock Ticker: CJPRY   Exchange: PINX
Employees: 18,231   Fiscal Year Ends: 03/31
Parent Company:

SALARIES/BONUSES:

Top Exec. Salary: $ Bonus: $
Second Exec. Salary: $ Bonus: $

OTHER THOUGHTS:

Estimated Female Officers or Directors:
Hot Spot for Advancement for Women/Minorities:

Sales, profits and employees may be estimates. Financial information, benefits and other data can change quickly and may vary from those stated here.

Ceske Aerolinie AS

NAIC Code: 481111

TYPES OF BUSINESS:

Airline
Charter Flights
Ground Services & Aircraft Maintenance
Travel Agency
Travel-Related IT Products

BRANDS/DIVISIONS/AFFILIATES:

Czech Airlines
CSA Services sro
Czech Airlines Cargo
Czech Airlines Handling
Czech Airlines Technics
Korean Air
Travels Service
Czech Aeroholding

CONTACTS: *Note: Officers with more than one job title may be intentionally listed here more than once.*

Martin Stolba, COO
Philippe Moreels, Pres.
Marek Tybl, VP-Flight Oper.
Jana Viskova, Press Officer
Jozef Sincak, Chmn.

GROWTH PLANS/SPECIAL FEATURES:

Ceske Aerolinie AS (CSA), also known as Czech Airlines, is the national airline of the Czech Republic. It carries 5 million passengers per year and maintains a fleet of 17 airplanes, which it obtains from manufacturers Airbus and ATR aircraft. It flies Airbus jets for medium- and long-haul flights and ATR aircraft for shorter trips. Cooperating with other airlines, including its membership in the SkyTeam Alliance, CSA flies to 40 destinations in 23 countries. The firm provides other services through its subsidiaries. CSA Services s.r.o. supplies call center services for CSA's customer relations programs. Czech Airlines Cargo provides transportation of airmail on Czech Airlines flights. Czech Airlines Handling provides passenger ticketing, baggage loading and cargo and mail handling. Last, Czech Airlines Technics provides aircraft maintenance and repair services. The company recently began a reorganization process as part of a transformation to a holding structure. CSA's shareholding structure is as follows: Korean Air 44%, Travel Service 34%, Czech Aeroholding 19.74% and Ceska Pojistovna 2.26%.

FINANCIAL DATA: *Note: Data for latest year may not have been available at press time.*

In U.S. $	2015	2014	2013	2012	2011	2010
Revenue						
R&D Expense						
Operating Income						
Operating Margin %						
SGA Expense						
Net Income						
Operating Cash Flow						
Capital Expenditure						
EBITDA						
Return on Assets %						
Return on Equity %						
Debt to Equity						

CONTACT INFORMATION:

Phone: 420-239-007-007   Fax: 420-224-314-273
Toll-Free:
Address: Jana Kaspara 1069/1, Prague, 160 08 Czech Republic

STOCK TICKER/OTHER:

Stock Ticker: Government-Owned   Exchange:
Employees: Fiscal Year Ends: 12/31
Parent Company:

SALARIES/BONUSES:

Top Exec. Salary: $ Bonus: $
Second Exec. Salary: $ Bonus: $

OTHER THOUGHTS:

Estimated Female Officers or Directors: 1
Hot Spot for Advancement for Women/Minorities:

Sales, profits and employees may be estimates. Financial information, benefits and other data can change quickly and may vary from those stated here.

China Airlines Ltd

www.china-airlines.com

NAIC Code: 481111

TYPES OF BUSINESS:

Airline
Aircraft Maintenance & Repair Services

BRANDS/DIVISIONS/AFFILIATES:

Cal-Asia Investment Inc
CAL Park
Hua Hsia Company Limited
Taiwan Aircraft Maintenance & Engineering Co
Mandarin Airlines
Tigerair Taiwan
China Pacific Laundry Services Ltd
Taiwan Air Cargo Limited

CONTACTS: *Note: Officers with more than one job title may be intentionally listed here more than once.*

Yu-Hern Chang, Pres.
Deji Liang, Deputy Gen. Mgr.-Eng. & Repair
Liangzhong Han, Gen. Mgr.-Finance
Binghuang Shi, Deputy Gen. Mgr.-Service
Nalheng Liu, Deputy Gen. Mgr.-Freight
Huang-Hsiang Sun, Chmn.

GROWTH PLANS/SPECIAL FEATURES:

China Airlines Ltd. provides passenger and freight air service. It operates a fleet of approximately 82 aircrafts, which consists of 64 passenger jets and 18 freighters. In addition, the airlines have 10 aircraft that are stored, and 14 on order and expected to be delivered between 2016-2018. The company flies to 118 destinations in 33 countries in Europe, Asia, the Americas and Oceania. China Airlines' destinations include Amsterdam, Rome, Tokyo, Hong Kong, Bangkok, Hanoi, New Delhi, Honolulu, Los Angeles, New York, San Francisco, Atlanta, Sydney and Frankfurt. The carrier has a total of 13 subsidiaries and joint venture companies. Its fully-owned subsidiaries include Cal-Asia Investment, Inc., CAL Park, Hua Hsia Company Limited and Taiwan Aircraft Maintenance & Engineering Co. Majority-owned firms include Mandarin Airlines (93.99%), Tigerair Taiwan (80%), China Pacific Laundry Services Ltd. (55%), Taiwan Air Cargo Terminals Limited (54%), China Pacific Catering Services Ltd. and Dynasty Holidays (51%).

Employees are offered medical insurance, discounted tickets and retirement benefits.

FINANCIAL DATA: *Note: Data for latest year may not have been available at press time.*

In U.S. $	2015	2014	2013	2012	2011	2010
Revenue	4,618,249,846	4,826,766,692	4,482,853,527	4,425,095,567	4,344,170,000	5,115,745,000
R&D Expense						
Operating Income						
Operating Margin %						
SGA Expense						
Net Income	183,514,233	-23,846,669	-40,561,215	-13,308,153		386,630,000
Operating Cash Flow						
Capital Expenditure						
EBITDA						
Return on Assets %						
Return on Equity %						
Debt to Equity						

CONTACT INFORMATION:

Phone: 886-3-399-8888   Fax: 866-2-2514-6005
Toll-Free: 800-2275-118
Address: No. 1 Hangzhan S. Rd, Dayuan Township, Taoyuan, 33758 Taiwan

STOCK TICKER/OTHER:

Stock Ticker: 2610.TW   Exchange: Taipei
Employees: 11,154   Fiscal Year Ends: 12/31
Parent Company:

SALARIES/BONUSES:

Top Exec. Salary: $ Bonus: $
Second Exec. Salary: $ Bonus: $

OTHER THOUGHTS:

Estimated Female Officers or Directors:
Hot Spot for Advancement for Women/Minorities:

Sales, profits and employees may be estimates. Financial information, benefits and other data can change quickly and may vary from those stated here.

China Eastern Airlines Corporation Limited www.ceair.com

NAIC Code: 481111

TYPES OF BUSINESS:
Airline
Cargo & Mail

BRANDS/DIVISIONS/AFFILIATES:
China Cargo Airlines
China United Airlines Co Ltd
Shanghai Airlines

CONTACTS: Note: Officers with more than one job title may be intentionally listed here more than once.
Ma Xulun, Pres.
Wu Yongliang, CFO
Wang Jian, Sec.
Tang Bing, VP
Shu Mingjiang, VP
Li Yangmin, VP
Tian Liuwen, VP
Liu Shaoyong, Chmn.

GROWTH PLANS/SPECIAL FEATURES:
China Eastern Airlines Corporation Limited (CE Airlines) is one of the three largest air carriers in China and the primary air carrier serving Shanghai. In 2015, the firm carried over 80 million passengers and more than 7 million tons of cargo and mail. Its fleet currently consists of 433 aircraft, comprising Airbus 319s, 320s, 321s, 330s and 350s, as well as Boeing 737s and 777s. Orders for A320s, A320neo, A350s, B-737s, 777s and Comac C919s are scheduled to be delivered between 2017 and 2022. The firm operates primarily from Shanghai's Hongqiao Airport and Pudong International Airport. CE Airlines serves a route network that covers 1,052 domestic and foreign destinations in 177 countries through its membership in the SkyTeam Alliance. The company's most heavily traveled domestic routes link Shanghai to China's large commercial and business centers, such as Beijing, Guangzhou and Shenzhen. CE Airlines covers most major cities between Mainland China and Hong Kong, operating both passenger and cargo flights. Subsidiary China Cargo Airlines is a cargo airline with its head office in Hongqiao International Airport; China United Airlines Co. Ltd. is a budget airline headquartered in Beijing; and Shanghai Airlines is headquartered in Shanghai. The firm operates nearly 1,000 international flights per week, serving more than 60 cities, primarily linking Shanghai to major cities in Asian and Southeast Asian countries and certain European, USA and Australian cities.

FINANCIAL DATA: Note: Data for latest year may not have been available at press time.

In U.S. $	2015	2014	2013	2012	2011	2010
Revenue	14,163,900,000	13,593,540,000	13,711,920,000	13,109,390,000	12,580,580,000	11,223,670,000
R&D Expense						
Operating Income	1,902,961,000	913,119,500	237,603,900	637,300,700	628,927,100	858,698,000
Operating Margin %	13.43%	6.71%	1.73%	4.86%	4.99%	7.65%
SGA Expense	4,132,250,000	3,322,682,000	3,657,207,000	3,734,719,000	3,488,969,000	3,404,588,000
Net Income	683,859,900	513,987,700	357,616,500	445,201,500	689,698,000	747,315,400
Operating Cash Flow	3,666,496,000	1,853,370,000	1,628,855,000	1,901,809,000	2,053,392,000	1,603,950,000
Capital Expenditure	1,314,060,000	878,451,700	274,637,600	926,706,200	809,170,700	983,201,400
EBITDA	2,811,860,000	2,299,078,000	1,807,537,000	1,848,967,000	2,000,030,000	2,061,610,000
Return on Assets %	2.49%	2.22%	1.79%	2.47%	4.19%	5.66%
Return on Equity %	13.46%	11.99%	9.52%	13.72%	25.85%	60.07%
Debt to Equity	1.99	2.15	1.76	1.84	2.05	2.64

CONTACT INFORMATION:
Phone: 86 2162686268   Fax: 86 2162686116
Toll-Free:
Address: Kong Gang San Lu, No. 92, Shanghai, 200335 China

STOCK TICKER/OTHER:
Stock Ticker: CEA   Exchange: NYS
Employees: 69,849   Fiscal Year Ends: 12/31
Parent Company: China Eastern Air Holding Co

SALARIES/BONUSES:
Top Exec. Salary: $193,386   Bonus: $
Second Exec. Salary: Bonus: $
$108,978

OTHER THOUGHTS:
Estimated Female Officers or Directors: 1
Hot Spot for Advancement for Women/Minorities:

Sales, profits and employees may be estimates. Financial information, benefits and other data can change quickly and may vary from those stated here.

China Lodging Group Ltd

NAIC Code: 721110

TYPES OF BUSINESS:

Hotels & Resorts

BRANDS/DIVISIONS/AFFILIATES:

HanTing Hotels
JI Hotel
HanTing Hi Inn
HuaZhu Club
Starway Hotel
Joya Hotel
HuaZhu Hotel Group
Elan Hotel

CONTACTS: *Note: Officers with more than one job title may be intentionally listed here more than once.*

Jenny Zhang, CEO
Yunhang Xie, COO
Hui Chen, CFO
Min (Jenny) Zhang, Chief Strategy Officer
Qi Ji, Exec. Chmn.

GROWTH PLANS/SPECIAL FEATURES:

China Lodging Group Ltd. is a China-based holding group active in China's hospitality sector. The firm conducts operations through HuaZhu Hotel Group, a leading chain of economy hotels with 2,763 hotels in 352 cities. China Lodging employs a lease-and-operate model, which is used to directly operate hotels in prime locations, and a franchise-and-manage model, which is used to expand network coverage. The firm's primary brands are HanTing Hotels, with 1,648 existing hotels and 374 under development; HanTing Hi Inn, with 158 hotels and 109 under development; JI Hotel, with 117 hotels and 76 under development; Starway Hotel, with 55 hotels, and an additional 45 leased; Elan Hotel, with 13 hotels and 65 under development; and three Joya Hotels with two under development. The economy hotels of HanTing Hotel and HanTing Hi Inn are targeted towards value-conscious travelers and workers or to appeal to the younger, budget conscious traveler. The midscale hotels of JI Hotel and Starway Hotel are geared more towards the older, experienced traveler and the middle class who want both a good value and a good location. The Joya Hotel will be the firm's upscale or premium hotel brand and is geared towards very affluent, elite travelers who seek a low-key yet elegant experience. The firm's HuaZhu Club rewards program has over 15 million members, who represent 80% of its room nights sold. The company hopes to harness rapidly growing levels of middle-class leisure travelers with increasing amounts of disposable income in China to help fuel its growth.

FINANCIAL DATA: *Note: Data for latest year may not have been available at press time.*

In U.S. $	2015	2014	2013	2012	2011	2010
Revenue	870,406,300	748,331,100	628,335,500	486,031,500	339,080,700	262,042,400
R&D Expense						
Operating Income	90,611,660	58,688,660	57,359,220	33,120,250	16,150,070	38,633,020
Operating Margin %	10.41%	7.84%	9.12%	6.81%	4.76%	14.74%
SGA Expense	103,167,700	107,905,500	95,588,000	83,035,700	66,187,450	45,518,020
Net Income	65,808,520	46,326,420	42,182,860	26,360,640	17,308,570	32,520,120
Operating Cash Flow	263,727,400	219,163,000	161,306,100	107,880,100	69,145,660	70,711,170
Capital Expenditure	97,829,500	141,888,500	162,326,200	150,968,000	118,086,000	61,027,600
EBITDA	196,124,300	148,883,200	128,493,000	87,735,140	57,381,680	68,322,220
Return on Assets %	6.29%	5.40%	5.88%	4.45%	3.49%	9.32%
Return on Equity %	13.13%	10.18%	10.59%	7.42%	5.26%	14.34%
Debt to Equity						

CONTACT INFORMATION:

Phone: 86 2161959595   Fax:
Toll-Free:
Address: 2266 Hongqiao Rd., Changning District, Shanghai, 200336 China

STOCK TICKER/OTHER:

Stock Ticker: HTHT   Exchange: NAS
Employees: 15,551   Fiscal Year Ends: 12/31
Parent Company:

SALARIES/BONUSES:

Top Exec. Salary: $ Bonus: $
Second Exec. Salary: $ Bonus: $

OTHER THOUGHTS:

Estimated Female Officers or Directors: 3
Hot Spot for Advancement for Women/Minorities: Y

China Southern Airlines Co Ltd

www.csair.com

NAIC Code: 481111

TYPES OF BUSINESS:

Airline
Air Cargo & Mail Services

BRANDS/DIVISIONS/AFFILIATES:

China Southern Air Holding Company
Xiamen Airlines
Shantou Airlines
Zhuhai Airlines
Chongqing Airlines
Guizhou Airlines
Guangzhou Nanland Air Catering Co Ltd
China Southern West Australian Flying College

CONTACTS: Note: Officers with more than one job title may be intentionally listed here more than once.

Tan Wan Geng, CEO
Zhang Zi Fang, COO
Tan Wangeng, Pres.
Yuan Xifan, Chief Eng.
Chen Wei Hua, General Counsel
Su Liang, Chief Economist
Xie Bing, Corp. Sec.
Wang Chang Shun, Chmn.

GROWTH PLANS/SPECIAL FEATURES:

China Southern Airlines Co., Ltd. (CSA) provides commercial airline services throughout China, Hong Kong and Macau, Southeast Asia and other parts of the world. The airline, which is 51.99%-owned by China Southern Air Holding Company (CSAHC), carried more than 1 billion passengers in 2015. It offers flights to 257 destinations in 40 countries and regions across the world, with a fleet of more than 660 aircraft. CSA's central hubs are situated in Guangzhou and Beijing. The company conducts a portion of its airline operations through its five airline subsidiaries: Xiamen Airlines, Shantou Airlines, Zhuhai Airlines, Chongqing Airlines and Guizhou Airlines. Other than the Xiamen and Chongqing airlines, CSA's businesses and operations are conducted under the China Southern name in both Chinese and English. An additional subsidiary, Guangzhou Nanland Air Catering Co. Ltd. (55%-owned), provides in-flight meals, snacks, drinks and related services for all of the company's flights originating in Guangzhou and substantially all other flights departing from Guangzhou Baiyun Airport. The company has a pilot training program in cooperation with the Beijing University of Aeronautics and Astronautics whereby trainees have two years of theoretical training, then receive flight training at China Southern West Australian Flying College Pty Ltd. CSA is also a part of SkyTeam, a global alliance of member airlines with over 1,000 destinations. The firm's fleet are comprised of Boeing 737, 747, 757, 777 and 787 aircraft, as well as Airbus 320, 330 and 380 aircraft, with an average age of 6.3 years.

FINANCIAL DATA: Note: Data for latest year may not have been available at press time.

In U.S. $	2015	2014	2013	2012	2011	2010
Revenue	16,829,250,000	16,366,820,000	14,853,940,000	14,999,700,000	13,625,200,000	11,530,060,000
R&D Expense						
Operating Income	2,025,503,000	715,663,900	227,601,600	768,569,900	656,125,700	875,738,600
Operating Margin %	12.03%	4.37%	1.53%	5.12%	4.81%	7.59%
SGA Expense	1,404,196,000	1,515,435,000	1,522,971,000	1,428,162,000	1,400,880,000	1,178,856,000
Net Income	563,125,600	267,846,400	414,506,200	394,760,700	917,942,800	873,477,600
Operating Cash Flow	3,577,415,000	2,045,400,000	1,462,529,000	1,764,139,000	1,892,711,000	1,724,647,000
Capital Expenditure	1,829,706,000	1,303,660,000	1,855,179,000	2,371,428,000	3,020,318,000	2,030,176,000
EBITDA	3,059,659,000	4,056,886,000	2,204,872,000	2,178,343,000	2,356,958,000	2,485,530,000
Return on Assets %	1.98%	1.00%	1.78%	1.92%	5.06%	5.62%
Return on Equity %	9.99%	6.07%	8.18%	0.05%	20.00%	31.20%
Debt to Equity	1.67	2.40	1.99	1.50	1.33	1.67

CONTACT INFORMATION:

Phone: 773-601-8800   Fax: 773-601-8866
Toll-Free:
Address: 278 Ji Chang Rd., Guangzhou, 510405 China

STOCK TICKER/OTHER:

Stock Ticker: ZNH   Exchange: NYS
Employees: 82,132   Fiscal Year Ends:
Parent Company: China Southern Air Holding Co

SALARIES/BONUSES:

Top Exec. Salary: $95,864   Bonus: $
Second Exec. Salary: $67,979   Bonus: $

OTHER THOUGHTS:

Estimated Female Officers or Directors:
Hot Spot for Advancement for Women/Minorities:

Sales, profits and employees may be estimates. Financial information, benefits and other data can change quickly and may vary from those stated here.

Choice Hotels International Inc   www.choicehotels.com

NAIC Code: 721110

TYPES OF BUSINESS:

Hotels
Motels
Suites
Franchising

BRANDS/DIVISIONS/AFFILIATES:

Econo Lodge
MainStay Suites
Rodeway Inn
Quality Inn
Clarion Hotels
Comfort Inn
Sleep Inn
Comfort Suites

CONTACTS: Note: Officers with more than one job title may be intentionally listed here more than once.

Stephen Joyce, CEO
Stewart Bainum, Chairman of the Board
Scott Oaksmith, Chief Accounting Officer
Patrick Pacious, COO
Simone Wu, General Counsel
David Pepper, Senior VP, Divisional
Patrick Cimerola, Senior VP, Divisional

GROWTH PLANS/SPECIAL FEATURES:

Choice Hotels International, Inc. is one of the world's largest franchisers of hotel properties. It has 6,300 hotels open and 638 hotels under development in 50 states, Washington, D.C. and over 35 foreign countries and territories around the globe, with over 500,000 rooms worldwide. The firm's 11 proprietary brand names include Comfort Inn, Comfort Suites, Sleep Inn, Quality Inn, Clarion Hotels, Econo Lodge, Rodeway Inn, MainStay Suites, Suburban Extended Stay Hotel, Cambria Suites and Ascend Collection. Choice Hotel's business is based on franchise revenues that consist of initial fees and ongoing royalty fees. The company also collects marketing and reservation fees to support centralized activities. The firm's largest brand is Comfort Inn, which provides mid-scale rooms without food and beverage service, targeted primarily to business and leisure travelers. The Comfort Inn, Comfort Suites and Sleep Inn brands compete in the limited-service midscale without food and beverage market; the Quality Inn and Clarion Hotel brands compete primarily in the full-service midscale with food and beverage market; the Econo Lodge and Rodeway Inn brands compete in the limited-service economy market; the MainStay brand and the Extended Stay Hotel brands compete in the extended stay market; the Ascend Collection represents individual properties that are historic, boutique and/or unique and desire to retain their independent brand identity but have access to Choice's marketing and distribution channels. To support its hotel operations, Choice Hotels maintains call centers, proprietary web sites and global distribution systems to help deliver customers to franchisees through multiple channels.

The firm offers employees a 401(k) plan; an employee stock purchase plan; medical, dental, vision and prescription coverage; life and AD&D insurance; flexible spending accounts; long-term care coverage; an employee assistance program; paid leave; tuition

FINANCIAL DATA: Note: Data for latest year may not have been available at press time.

In U.S. $	2015	2014	2013	2012	2011	2010
Revenue	859,878,000	757,970,000	724,307,000	691,509,000	638,793,000	596,076,000
R&D Expense						
Operating Income	225,319,000	214,568,000	194,494,000	193,142,000	171,863,000	160,762,000
Operating Margin %	26.20%	28.30%	26.85%	27.93%	26.90%	26.97%
SGA Expense	134,254,000	121,418,000	113,567,000	101,852,000	106,404,000	94,540,000
Net Income	128,029,000	123,160,000	112,601,000	120,687,000	110,396,000	107,441,000
Operating Cash Flow	159,872,000	183,891,000	152,040,000	161,020,000	134,844,000	144,935,000
Capital Expenditure	27,765,000	20,946,000	31,524,000	15,443,000	10,924,000	24,368,000
EBITDA	238,360,000	224,609,000	208,924,000	204,583,000	179,020,000	173,233,000
Return on Assets %	18.63%	20.74%	21.43%	25.18%	25.69%	28.58%
Return on Equity %						
Debt to Equity						

CONTACT INFORMATION:

Phone: 301 592-5000   Fax: 301 592-6269
Toll-Free:
Address: 1 Choice Hotels Cir., Ste. 400, Rockville, MD 20850 United States

STOCK TICKER/OTHER:

Stock Ticker: CHH   Exchange: NYS
Employees: 1,331   Fiscal Year Ends: 12/31
Parent Company:

SALARIES/BONUSES:

Top Exec. Salary: $998,462   Bonus: $249,970
Second Exec. Salary: $549,142   Bonus: $67,498

OTHER THOUGHTS:

Estimated Female Officers or Directors: 2
Hot Spot for Advancement for Women/Minorities: Y

Sales, profits and employees may be estimates. Financial information, benefits and other data can change quickly and may vary from those stated here.

Club Mediterranee SA (Club Med)

www.clubmed-corporate.com

NAIC Code: 721110

TYPES OF BUSINESS:

Resort Hotels
Tour Marketing/Packaging
Cruises
Seminars, Conventions & Event Planning
Licensed Apparel Products

BRANDS/DIVISIONS/AFFILIATES:

Club Med
Club Med Decouverte
Club Med 2
Club Med Villas & Chalets
Fosun International Ltd

CONTACTS: *Note: Officers with more than one job title may be intentionally listed here more than once.*

Henri G. dEstaing, CEO
Michel Wolfovski, CFO
Sylvain Rabuel, VP-Sales & Mktg., France, Benelux & Switzerland
Sylvie Brisson, VP-Human Resources
Patrick Calvet, VP-Villages Europe-Africa
Laure Baume, CEO-New Markets Europe-Africa
Olivier Horps, VP-Greater China
Xavier Mufraggi, VP-North America
Henri G. dEstaing, Chmn.
Janyck Daudet, VP-Latin America

GROWTH PLANS/SPECIAL FEATURES:

Club Mediterranee SA (Club Med) is an international operator of resort hotels and tours, with operations in over 40 countries worldwide. Club Med is known for being the originator of all-inclusive vacations packages, which group fees for every meal, drink, activity and amenity into one price. The core business of the company is the operation of vacation villages and resorts organized like small towns. These villages and villas include streets with shops and houses and feature a large number of luxury accommodations in hand-picked locations. The company operates approximately 70 properties, concentrated in equatorial locations, including the Caribbean, Southeast Asia and the Mediterranean, as well as several ski resorts. In addition, the firm offers Club Med Decouverte, a tour guide service that takes small groups to places such as Phuket and Cancun Yucatan, as well as weekend getaways to Venice, Istanbul and other well-known cities. It also operates Club Med 2, a luxury sailing ship in the Mediterranean. Club Med organizes corporate events, weddings and other events at its villages and other venues. Besides vacation packages, the company sells licensed products such as sportswear and children's clothing. Through Club Med Villas & Chalets, it offers freehold real estate at its villas on the island of Mauritius and its chalet apartments in the French Alps. In February 2015, Chinese conglomerate Fosun International, Ltd. gained a controlling interest in Club Med. The firm plans to open seven new resorts between 2015 and 2018.

FINANCIAL DATA: *Note: Data for latest year may not have been available at press time.*

In U.S. $	2015	2014	2013	2012	2011	2010
Revenue	1,633,620,883	1,489,601,792	1,513,246,208	1,555,161,472	1,514,320,896	1,449,836,032
R&D Expense						
Operating Income						
Operating Margin %						
SGA Expense						
Net Income		-12,896,985	-11,822,236	1,074,749	2,149,498	-15,046,483
Operating Cash Flow						
Capital Expenditure						
EBITDA						
Return on Assets %						
Return on Equity %						
Debt to Equity						

CONTACT INFORMATION:

Phone: 33 153353553   Fax: 33 153353616
Toll-Free:
Address: 11 Rue de Cambrai, Paris, 75957 France

STOCK TICKER/OTHER:

Stock Ticker: Subsidiary   Exchange:
Employees: 12,811   Fiscal Year Ends: 12/31
Parent Company: Fosun International Ltd

SALARIES/BONUSES:

Top Exec. Salary: $ Bonus: $
Second Exec. Salary: $ Bonus: $

OTHER THOUGHTS:

Estimated Female Officers or Directors: 6
Hot Spot for Advancement for Women/Minorities: Y

CNL Lifestyle Properties Inc

NAIC Code: 0

www.cnllifestylereit.com/index.stml

TYPES OF BUSINESS:

Real Estate Investment Trust
Retail, Hotel & Entertainment Properties
Commercial Financing
Investment Advisory Services
Real Estate Development & Management
Health Care & Assisted Living Properties
Industrial Properties

BRANDS/DIVISIONS/AFFILIATES:

CONTACTS: Note: Officers with more than one job title may be intentionally listed here more than once.

Thomas K. Sittema, CEO
Tracy G. Schmidt, CFO
Lisa A. Schultz, Chief Svcs. Officer
Holly Greer, General Counsel
Lisa A. Schultz, Chief Comm. Officer
Andy Hyltin, Pres., Fund Mgmt.
Jeffrey R. Shafer, Pres., CNL Securities Corp.
Paul Ellis, Pres., CNL Commercial Real Estate
Stephen H. Mauldin, Pres., Fund Mgmt.
James M. Seneff, Jr., Chmn.

GROWTH PLANS/SPECIAL FEATURES:

CNL Lifestyle Properties, Inc. (CNL) is a real estate investment trust (REIT) that invests in income-producing properties with a focus on lifestyle-related industries. It acquires properties and leases them on a long-term, triple-net lease basis or engages qualified third-party managers to operate properties on its behalf. CNL invests in properties with the potential for long-term revenue generation. The company's current portfolio consists of 49 properties. CNL also monitors lifestyle trends driven by demographics, develops relationships with industry leaders and invests in income-producing properties. These properties are diversified by geography, operator and lifestyle sector. CNL's investments include properties such as ski and mountain, attraction sites, senior housing and marinas.

Employees of the firm receive a 401(k) plan; educational assistance; adoption assistance; flexible spending accounts; and medical, prescription, hospitalization, dental, vision, disability and life insurance.

FINANCIAL DATA: Note: Data for latest year may not have been available at press time.

In U.S. $	2015	2014	2013	2012	2011	2010
Revenue	337,665,000	373,295,000	512,801,000	481,279,000	420,071,000	300,023,000
R&D Expense						
Operating Income	-109,691,000	-10,378,000	-229,843,000	-12,795,000	4,132,000	-58,491,000
Operating Margin %	-32.48%	-2.78%	-44.82%	-2.65%	.98%	-19.49%
SGA Expense	25,976,000	27,298,000	33,947,000	33,200,000	31,735,000	26,294,000
Net Income	141,155,000	-92,144,000	-252,539,000	-76,073,000	-69,610,000	-81,889,000
Operating Cash Flow	62,643,000	126,934,000	135,480,000	76,726,000	83,064,000	79,776,000
Capital Expenditure	49,272,000	207,505,000	315,015,000	259,825,000	192,037,000	140,530,000
EBITDA	46,896,000	132,195,000	-292,000	138,034,000	135,591,000	104,611,000
Return on Assets %	8.51%	-3.69%	-8.95%	-2.60%	-2.50%	-3.06%
Return on Equity %	14.37%	-7.29%	-16.39%	-4.22%	-3.64%	-4.24%
Debt to Equity	0.23	0.74	0.84	0.60	0.48	0.31

CONTACT INFORMATION:

Phone: 866-650-0650   Fax: 877-694-1116
Toll-Free: 800-522-3863
Address: 450 S. Orange Ave., Orlando, FL 32801-3336 United States

STOCK TICKER/OTHER:

Stock Ticker: CLLY   Exchange: GREY
Employees: Fiscal Year Ends: 12/31
Parent Company:

SALARIES/BONUSES:

Top Exec. Salary: $ Bonus: $
Second Exec. Salary: $ Bonus: $

OTHER THOUGHTS:

Estimated Female Officers or Directors: 3
Hot Spot for Advancement for Women/Minorities: Y

Coach USA LLC

www.coachusa.com

NAIC Code: 485113

TYPES OF BUSINESS:

Bus Services
City Sightseeing Tours
Charter Services
Motorcoach Tours

BRANDS/DIVISIONS/AFFILIATES:

Stagecoach Group plc
Gray Line New York Sightseeing
Chicago Trolley & Double Decker Co
usmegabus.com

CONTACTS: *Note: Officers with more than one job title may be intentionally listed here more than once.*

Dale Moser, CEO
Dale Moser, Pres.

GROWTH PLANS/SPECIAL FEATURES:

Coach USA LLC, a subsidiary of U.K.-based Stagecoach Group plc, is a bus service provider in the U.S. and Canada. The company, through more than 20 subsidiaries in North America, operates bus routes, motorcoach tours, charters and city sightseeing tours. The local companies owned by Coach USA are independently managed and operated to meet the needs of the communities they serve. Coach USA is active primarily in the Northeast U.S., the North central U.S. and Canada. In the Northeast region, the company covers New York, New Jersey and Pennsylvania. Services offered in the region include commuter and local bus services, Newark Airport express shuttle services and charter and contract services. It also offers hop-on-hop-off double-decker sightseeing bus tours of New York through subsidiary Gray Line New York Sightseeing. In the North central region, Coach USA covers seven states, serving cities such as Chicago and Milwaukee. Services offered in the region include charter and contract services, Chicago Airport bus service and a school bus business in Milwaukee. The firm also operates hop-on-hop-off double-decker sightseeing bus tours of Chicago through subsidiary Chicago Trolley & Double Decker Co. The company covers Quebec and Ontario in Canada with services primarily consisting of scheduled service and chartered service as well as a number of sightseeing bus tours and contract services. Coach USA also operates a megabus service in the North East and Central regions of the U.S. and Canada through usmegabus.com.

FINANCIAL DATA: *Note: Data for latest year may not have been available at press time.*

In U.S. $	2015	2014	2013	2012	2011	2010
Revenue	698,000,000	657,157,952	518,830,000	470,000,000	461,000,000	
R&D Expense						
Operating Income						
Operating Margin %						
SGA Expense						
Net Income		38,000,000	21,100,000			
Operating Cash Flow						
Capital Expenditure						
EBITDA						
Return on Assets %						
Return on Equity %						
Debt to Equity						

CONTACT INFORMATION:

Phone: 201-225-7500   Fax: 201-225-7590
Toll-Free:
Address: 160 S. Route 17 N., Paramus, NJ 07652 United States

STOCK TICKER/OTHER:

Stock Ticker: Subsidiary   Exchange:
Employees: 5,000   Fiscal Year Ends: 04/30
Parent Company: Stagecoach Group plc

SALARIES/BONUSES:

Top Exec. Salary: $ Bonus: $
Second Exec. Salary: $ Bonus: $

OTHER THOUGHTS:

Estimated Female Officers or Directors:
Hot Spot for Advancement for Women/Minorities:

Commune Hotels & Resorts LLC

www.communehotels.com

NAIC Code: 721110

TYPES OF BUSINESS:

Hotels
Day Spas
Restaurants
Hospitality Consulting
Condominium Management

BRANDS/DIVISIONS/AFFILIATES:

Joie de Vivre Hotels
Thompson Hotels
tommie
Alila
Chicago Athletic Assoc
Hotel Rex
Phoenix Hotel
Hotel Tomo

CONTACTS: Note: Officers with more than one job title may be intentionally listed here more than once.

Niki Leondakis, CEO
Rick Colangelo, Exec. VP-Oper.
Jennifer Foley Shields, VP-Comm. & Special Projects
Karolina Kiebowicz, Sr. Dir-Public Rel.
John Pritzker, Chmn.

GROWTH PLANS/SPECIAL FEATURES:

Commune Hotels & Resorts operates through the hotel brands Joie de Vivre Hotels (JdV), Thompson Hotels, tommie, Alila and Chicago Athletic Assoc. JdV's properties include over 30 hotels throughout California as well as a location in Scottsdale, Arizona, 2 in Honolulu and Chicago. JdV hotels each target a niche audience by embodying a particular lifestyle or theme, such as arts & literature featured at the Hotel Rex; rock and roll at the Phoenix Hotel; or Japanese pop-culture at Hotel Tomo. It also owns and operates the Kabuki Springs & Spa in San Francisco, Spa Vitale at Hotel Vitale, Spa Aiyana in Carmel Valley Ranch and a spa located in the Ventana Inn near Big Sur. Thompson Hotels offer luxury boutique accommodations in 10 domestic and international locations, catering to a chic, urban, bohemian clientele. Thompson's domestic hotels include locations in New York, Los Angeles, Nashville, Seattle, Chicago and Miami; international locations are represented by the Belgraves in London, U.K.; Thompson Toronto in Toronto, Canada; The Cape in Los Cabos, Mexico; and the Thompson Playa in Playa Del Carmen, Mexico. tommie is a youthful, micro-lifestyle hotel brand located in Los Angeles and New York City. Tommie hotels combine the playfulness of JdV with the sophistication of the Thompson. Alila hotels provide a combination of design luxury in unique locations, including private space and personalized hospitality, along with natural cultural elements. Alila hotels are located in China, Indonesia, India and Oman. Chicago Athletic Assoc. opened in 2015 on Michigan Avenue, and features a hotel, views of Millennium Park, restaurant and nightlife talents. In January 2016, the firm announced a planed merger with Colorado based Destination Hotels.

FINANCIAL DATA: Note: Data for latest year may not have been available at press time.

In U.S. $	2015	2014	2013	2012	2011	2010
Revenue	500,000,000	490,000,000	475,000,000	450,000,000	328,000,000	240,000,000
R&D Expense						
Operating Income						
Operating Margin %						
SGA Expense						
Net Income						
Operating Cash Flow						
Capital Expenditure						
EBITDA						
Return on Assets %						
Return on Equity %						
Debt to Equity						

CONTACT INFORMATION:

Phone: 415-835-0300   Fax:
Toll-Free:
Address: 530 Bush Street, Ste 501, San Francisco, CA 94108 United States

STOCK TICKER/OTHER:

Stock Ticker: Private   Exchange:
Employees: 1,077   Fiscal Year Ends: 12/31
Parent Company:

SALARIES/BONUSES:

Top Exec. Salary: $ Bonus: $
Second Exec. Salary: $ Bonus: $

OTHER THOUGHTS:

Estimated Female Officers or Directors: 3
Hot Spot for Advancement for Women/Minorities: Y

Sales, profits and employees may be estimates. Financial information, benefits and other data can change quickly and may vary from those stated here.

Concesionaria Vuela Compania de Aviacion SA de CV (Volaris)

NAIC Code: 481111

www.volaris.mx

TYPES OF BUSINESS:

Airline

BRANDS/DIVISIONS/AFFILIATES:

Controladora Vuela Compania de Aviacion SA de CV
Volaris
Vclub

CONTACTS: Note: Officers with more than one job title may be intentionally listed here more than once.

Enrique Beltranena, CEO
James Nides, COO
Fernando Suarez, CFO
Holger Blankenstein, Chief Commercial Officer
Eduardo Garay Mendoza, Dir.-Human Resources
Luis Fernando Avila, Dir.-IT
Jaime Pous, General Counsel
Manuel Ambriz Lopez, Dir.-Strategy & Planning
Andres Pliego, Head-Investor Rel.
Carlos Alberto Gonzalez Lopez, Dir.-Corp. Controller
Gustavo Acevedo Leon, Dir.-Maintenance
Mario Enrique Geyne Pliego, Dir.-Financial Planning & Fleet
Jimmy Zadigue, Dir.-Internal Audit
Jose Luis Suarez Duran, Dir.-Retail & Customer Svcs.
Gilberto Perezalonso Cifuentes, Chmn.

GROWTH PLANS/SPECIAL FEATURES:

Concesionaria Vuela Compania de Aviacion SA de CV is an airline company offering flights between Mexico and the U.S. The company is a subsidiary of Controladora Vuela Compania de Aviacion SA de CV and operates as Volaris. Its fleet consists of 55 aircraft including the Airbus A319, A320 and A321 families. Volaris is a relatively young airline, launched in 2003, and therefore has a relatively new fleet. It is also an affordable airline designed to open more opportunities for Mexicans to travel by air. The company allows for online check in and allows customers to carry extra luggage for a nominal additional fee. The company's loyalty program, VClub, connects customers with the lowest fares, special promotions and last minute fares at affordable prices. Annually, membership for an individual is $49, while group membership runs at $149. The company is owned by a diverse group of investors, including independent parties, and domestic and international corporations. Additionally, Volaris has a partnership with the National Transplant Center, shipping organs and tissues for transplantation.

FINANCIAL DATA: Note: Data for latest year may not have been available at press time.

In U.S. $	2015	2014	2013	2012	2011	2010
Revenue	996,290,200	769,246,100	712,565,700	640,442,800	486,568,800	371,416,800
R&D Expense						
Operating Income	137,572,100	11,185,320	17,393,000	20,728,430	-20,440,450	28,012,650
Operating Margin %	13.80%	1.45%	2.44%	3.23%	-4.20%	7.54%
SGA Expense	198,726,400	156,349,100	124,258,000	130,683,500	102,526,000	93,374,130
Net Income	135,025,800	33,165,490	14,724,180	11,795,600	-16,086,680	31,359,750
Operating Cash Flow	168,221,900	18,292,090	2,123,974	27,261,310	-8,094,578	29,538,510
Capital Expenditure	79,797,180	87,825,890	63,625,500	46,922,030	66,579,290	17,617,960
EBITDA	216,958,900	54,058,060	34,151,110	27,813,880	-8,980,732	28,406,290
Return on Assets %	19.58%	6.62%	3.81%	3.99%	-5.79%	
Return on Equity %	43.62%	14.35%	10.71%	23.87%	-39.10%	
Debt to Equity	0.03	0.09	0.07	0.60	0.96	

CONTACT INFORMATION:

Phone: 52-55-5261-6400   Fax:
Toll-Free:
Address: Ave. Antonio Dovali Jaime, Tower B, Fl. 13, No. 70, Colonia Zedec Santa Fe, 01210 Mexico

STOCK TICKER/OTHER:

Stock Ticker: VLRS   Exchange: NYS
Employees: 2,805   Fiscal Year Ends:
Parent Company: Controladora Vuela Compania de Aviacion SA de CV

SALARIES/BONUSES:

Top Exec. Salary: $ Bonus: $
Second Exec. Salary: $ Bonus: $

OTHER THOUGHTS:

Estimated Female Officers or Directors:
Hot Spot for Advancement for Women/Minorities:

Concur Technologies Inc

www.concur.com

NAIC Code: 0

TYPES OF BUSINESS:

Software Manufacturer-Expense Reporting
Corporate Expense Management Solutions
Professional Services
Travel and Entertainment Expense Reporting Software
Meeting Expense Reporting Software

BRANDS/DIVISIONS/AFFILIATES:

Concur Travel & Expense
SAP SE

CONTACTS: *Note: Officers with more than one job title may be intentionally listed here more than once.*

Steve Singh, CEO
Elena Donio, Pres.
Frank Pelzer, CFO
Jessica Shapiro, VP-CMO
Mark Nelson, Chief Technology Officer
John Torrey, Executive VP, Divisional
Robert Cavanaugh, Executive VP
Elena Donio, Executive VP

GROWTH PLANS/SPECIAL FEATURES:

Concur Technologies, Inc. provides business automation process services and software products for the management of travel- and meeting-related corporate expenses. The firm's product solutions cover three primary aspects of corporate travel management: travel procurement, expense management and itinerary management. Travel procurement software automates corporate travel booking and processing functions and can be tailored to a company's specific travel policies and preferred vendors. Employees using Concur's travel procurement solutions are able to set their own travel preferences while organizations set policy through technology filters to retain control. Expense management solutions simplify the expense reporting process, while reducing costs and improving internal controls. Its software automatically imports corporate or personal credit card charges to create expense reports and reconciles transaction data from itinerary data captured at the time of booking, corporate card charges incurred during travel and electronic receipts captured directly from the supplier. Concur's itinerary management solutions enable individual business travelers and their organizations to manage and share travel itinerary information and can be imported into other Concur solutions to provide greater insight and control over travel and expense spend for organizations. Its flagship product, Concur Travel & Expense, integrates online travel booking with automated expense reporting to provide unified end-to-end corporate travel procurement and expense reporting. The firm also offers value-added services and software that integrate with the company's primary products. Additionally, Concur offers professional services including consulting, customer support and training. The company has more than 20,000 customers worldwide. Concur is owned by German software giant SAP SE, and operates as a business unit within SAP.

The firm offers employees life, disability, medical, dental and vision insurance; flexible spending accounts; and a 401(k).

FINANCIAL DATA: *Note: Data for latest year may not have been available at press time.*

In U.S. $	2015	2014	2013	2012	2011	2010
Revenue	7,724,603,419	702,588,032	545,800,000	439,825,984	349,488,000	292,936,000
R&D Expense						
Operating Income						
Operating Margin %						
SGA Expense						
Net Income	-20,571,530	-118,295,000	-24,394,000	-7,006,000	-10,743,000	20,581,000
Operating Cash Flow						
Capital Expenditure						
EBITDA						
Return on Assets %						
Return on Equity %						
Debt to Equity						

CONTACT INFORMATION:

Phone: 425 590-5000   Fax: 425 702-8828
Toll-Free: 800-401-8412
Address: 601 108th Avenue NE, Suite 1000, Bellevue, WA 98004 United States

STOCK TICKER/OTHER:

Stock Ticker: Subsidiary
Employees: 2,741
Parent Company: SAP SE

Exchange:
Fiscal Year Ends: 12/31

SALARIES/BONUSES:

Top Exec. Salary: $ Bonus: $
Second Exec. Salary: $ Bonus: $

OTHER THOUGHTS:

Estimated Female Officers or Directors: 2
Hot Spot for Advancement for Women/Minorities:

Condor Hospitality Trust Inc

www.supertelinc.com

NAIC Code: 0

TYPES OF BUSINESS:

Real Estate Investment Trust
Hotels & Motels

BRANDS/DIVISIONS/AFFILIATES:

Supertel Hospitality REIT Trust
E&P REIT Trust
Supertel Limited Partnership
E&P Financing Limited Partnership
Supertel Hospitality Management Inc
TRS Leasing Inc
Supertel Hospitality Inc

CONTACTS: Note: Officers with more than one job title may be intentionally listed here more than once.

J. Blackham, CEO
Arinn Cavey, Chief Accounting Officer
Jeffrey Dougan, COO
James Friend, Director
Jonathan Gantt, Senior VP

GROWTH PLANS/SPECIAL FEATURES:

Condor Hospitality Trust, Inc., formerly Supertel Hospitality, Inc., is a self-administered REIT (real estate investment trust) primarily engaged in acquiring and owning hotels. Through its subsidiaries, Condor's portfolio includes 42 limited-service hotels in 20 states under the following franchise brands: Comfort Inn/Comfort Suites, Days Inn, Super 8, Savannah Suites, Quality Inn, Clarion, Hilton Garden Inn, Key West Inn, Hotel Indigo, Springhill Suites and Supertel Inn. Standard guestroom amenities include high-speed wireless Internet; free local calls; cable TV, including movie channels; an iron and ironing board; and a coffee maker and hairdryer. Select properties also have complimentary continental breakfast, pools, suites, conference centers and meeting facilities. Through its two wholly-owned subsidiaries, Supertel Hospitality REIT Trust and E&P REIT Trust, the firm owns a 99% interest in Supertel Limited Partnership and 100% of E&P Financing Limited Partnership. Together, these four firms, along with other subsidiaries and partnerships, own Condor's properties. The subsidiaries and partnerships include Supertel Hospitality Management, Inc.; SPPR-BMI Holdings, Inc.; and Solomon's Beacon Inn Limited Partnership. To enter into management agreements with independent contractors, in compliance with the REIT Modernization Act of 1999, TRS Leasing, Inc. was created, along with its subsidiaries TRS Subsidiary LLC and SPPR TRS Subsidiary LLC. All hotels are leased to TRS Leasing. In 2015, Supertel Hospitality, Inc. changed its name to Condor Hospitality Trust, Inc. in order to extend the company's brand from economy- and mid-scale hotels to encompass high-end hotels as well.

FINANCIAL DATA: Note: Data for latest year may not have been available at press time.

In U.S. $	2015	2014	2013	2012	2011	2010
Revenue	57,341,000	57,409,000	56,163,000	70,573,000	75,827,000	84,114,000
R&D Expense						
Operating Income	3,332,000	3,524,000	-196,000	6,799,000	4,955,000	5,419,000
Operating Margin %	5.81%	6.13%	-.34%	9.63%	6.53%	6.44%
SGA Expense	5,493,000	4,192,000	3,923,000	3,908,000	4,008,000	3,443,000
Net Income	13,125,000	-16,236,000	-1,351,000	-10,210,000	-17,445,000	-10,585,000
Operating Cash Flow	4,970,000	5,387,000	2,017,000	3,789,000	2,865,000	7,672,000
Capital Expenditure	47,908,000	3,374,000	5,133,000	17,168,000	4,964,000	4,344,000
EBITDA	21,185,000	-5,743,000	15,104,000	12,244,000	7,571,000	15,523,000
Return on Assets %	6.53%	-12.36%	-2.51%	-6.32%	-7.91%	-4.54%
Return on Equity %	36.83%	-76.40%	-13.60%	-36.55%	-41.08%	-19.87%
Debt to Equity	2.15	3.91	2.88	3.07	3.57	2.61

CONTACT INFORMATION:

Phone: 402 371-2520   Fax: 402 371-4229
Toll-Free:
Address: 1800 W. Pasewalk Ave., Norfolk, NE 68701 United States

STOCK TICKER/OTHER:

Stock Ticker: CDOR
Employees: 15
Parent Company:

Exchange: NAS
Fiscal Year Ends: 12/31

SALARIES/BONUSES:

Top Exec. Salary: $321,465   Bonus: $
Second Exec. Salary: Bonus: $30,750
$209,609

OTHER THOUGHTS:

Estimated Female Officers or Directors: 3
Hot Spot for Advancement for Women/Minorities: Y

Sales, profits and employees may be estimates. Financial information, benefits and other data can change quickly and may vary from those stated here.

CorpTrav Management Group

www.corptrav.com

NAIC Code: 561510

TYPES OF BUSINESS:

Travel Agency
Corporate Travel Management

BRANDS/DIVISIONS/AFFILIATES:

HighTouch
E-Track
GetThere
Concur Travel
Virtually There
WebTech
Sabre Traveler Security
Travel Analytics

CONTACTS: Note: Officers with more than one job title may be intentionally listed here more than once.

Bonnie M. Lorefice, CEO
Jane Batio, Pres.
Gerry Lazar, CFO
Lisa Donovan Berry, Sr. VP
Barb Lea-Maijala, VP
Gina Maylath, Managing Dir.

GROWTH PLANS/SPECIAL FEATURES:

CorpTrav Management Group is one of the world's leading travel management firms. The company offers services to business travel and corporate clients through its HighTouch service platform. The firm provides a 24-hour-a-day customer service hotline staffed by its own employees to help customers make decisions regarding their trips. CorpTrav also provides reservation services via the Internet as well as a 24-hour-a-day, 365-days-a-year call-in reservation service. The company's web site provides links and information on airports, flight status, strikes, weather, hotels, travel warnings, visa/passport information and other travel needs. The firm uses various other technologies to improve customer service, such as E-Track for management of unused refundable tickets; a traveler security and data suite for global traveler locating; GetThere and Concur Travel for easy-to-use convenient and flexible on-line booking; Virtually There, to allow travelers to obtain their itinerary, invoice and receipt via the Internet; WebTech for data gathering and reporting from the travel manager's desktop; Sabre Traveler Security, providing risk management for employees while traveling; and Travel Analytics, a report card that measures key performance indicators against a benchmark of more than 40,000 corporations. In addition to corporate services, the company owns and operates Oakbrook Travel/Emerald Cruises, located in Lombard, Illinois. Oakbrook is a full-service leisure travel agency available to the company's corporate clients as well as independent travelers. The firm offers its services worldwide through its online service and offices in Illinois, Texas and California. Its global presence extends throughout such places as Argentina, Bolivia, China, France, Germany, India and the U.K.

FINANCIAL DATA: Note: Data for latest year may not have been available at press time.

In U.S. $	2015	2014	2013	2012	2011	2010
Revenue						
R&D Expense						
Operating Income						
Operating Margin %						
SGA Expense						
Net Income						
Operating Cash Flow						
Capital Expenditure						
EBITDA						
Return on Assets %						
Return on Equity %						
Debt to Equity						

CONTACT INFORMATION:

Phone: 630-691-9100   Fax:
Toll-Free: 800-770-7015
Address: 450 E. 22nd St., Lombard, IL 60148 United States

STOCK TICKER/OTHER:

Stock Ticker: Private   Exchange:
Employees: 150   Fiscal Year Ends: 12/31
Parent Company:

SALARIES/BONUSES:

Top Exec. Salary: $ Bonus: $
Second Exec. Salary: $ Bonus: $

OTHER THOUGHTS:

Estimated Female Officers or Directors: 6
Hot Spot for Advancement for Women/Minorities: Y

Sales, profits and employees may be estimates. Financial information, benefits and other data can change quickly and may vary from those stated here.

Costco Travel Inc

NAIC Code: 561510

www.costcotravel.com

TYPES OF BUSINESS:

Travel Agency

BRANDS/DIVISIONS/AFFILIATES:

Costco Wholesale Corp

CONTACTS: Note: Officers with more than one job title may be intentionally listed here more than once.

Kathy Robinson, Dir.-Operations
Jeffrey H. Brotman, Chmn.-Costco Wholesale Corp.
James D. Sinegal, CEO

GROWTH PLANS/SPECIAL FEATURES:

Costco Travel, Inc., a wholly-owned subsidiary of Costco Wholesale Corp., offers full-service discount vacation planning and booking to Costco's membership of over 70 million cardholders. Packages are featured in quarterly magazine-style publications and stand-alone brochures available in retail warehouse locations, and can also be reviewed in detail on the firm's web site. Costco Travel negotiates and coordinates all travel arrangements on an in-house basis, allowing customers to create custom vacations, choosing accommodations, transportation, sight-seeing tours and length of stay. In addition to hotel, airline and car rental arrangements, the firm is a leading agent for cruise ship bookings. A central toll-free phone number connects Costco members to dedicated travel sales agents who provide personalized booking details and price quotes. Specialty vacations offered by the company include Disney-themed vacations, escorted vacations and houseboat vacations. Through a partnership with Citibank, Costco Travel offers customers an earning credit card that provides members with cash back rewards when used to pay hotel, restaurant, gas and travel bills. The company's 16-year partnership with American Express dissolved mid-2016.

Costco Travel offers employees health, dental and vision coverage; a 401(k); dependent care assistance; long-term car, life and disability insurance; a health care reimbursement account; and an employee stock purchase plan.

FINANCIAL DATA: Note: Data for latest year may not have been available at press time.

In U.S. $	2015	2014	2013	2012	2011	2010
Revenue						
R&D Expense						
Operating Income						
Operating Margin %						
SGA Expense						
Net Income						
Operating Cash Flow						
Capital Expenditure						
EBITDA						
Return on Assets %						
Return on Equity %						
Debt to Equity						

CONTACT INFORMATION:

Phone: 425-313-8100 Fax:
Toll-Free: 877-849-2730
Address: 1605 NW Sammamish Rd., Issaquah, WA 98027 United States

STOCK TICKER/OTHER:

Stock Ticker: Subsidiary Exchange:
Employees: Fiscal Year Ends: 08/31
Parent Company: Costco Wholesale Corp

SALARIES/BONUSES:

Top Exec. Salary: $ Bonus: $
Second Exec. Salary: $ Bonus: $

OTHER THOUGHTS:

Estimated Female Officers or Directors:
Hot Spot for Advancement for Women/Minorities:

Sales, profits and employees may be estimates. Financial information, benefits and other data can change quickly and may vary from those stated here.

Crested Butte Mountain Resort Inc

www.skicb.com

NAIC Code: 713920

TYPES OF BUSINESS:

Ski Resort
Real Estate

BRANDS/DIVISIONS/AFFILIATES:

Evolution Bike Park
Plaza (The)
Lodge at Mountaineer Square (The)
Grand Lodge Crested Butte Hotel & Suites
CNL Lifestyle Properties Inc

CONTACTS: *Note: Officers with more than one job title may be intentionally listed here more than once.*

Tim Mueller, CEO
Ken Stone, COO
Tim Mueller, Pres.

GROWTH PLANS/SPECIAL FEATURES:

Crested Butte Mountain Resort, Inc. (CBMR) is a ski resort located at Mount Crested Butte in Gunnison County, Colorado. The resort is open year-round with amenities and terrain for activities such as skiing, snowboarding, mountain biking and hiking. During winter, CBMR offers runs for every type of skier. During summer, downhill and cross country mountain bikers enjoy Evolution Bike Park, a network of lift-served riding for all levels of mountain bikers. The company also offers lift-served hiking. Lodging establishments include The Plaza, a condominium just 100 yards from the main Silver Queen quad lift, with elevators, restaurant, bar, daily housekeeping, covered parking and two hot tubs; The Lodge at Mountaineer Square, located in the base area and steps away from the ski lifts, hiking and biking as well as shopping and restaurants; and The Grand Lodge Crested Butte Hotel & Suites, featuring 226 oversized hotel rooms and suites to accommodate all types of travelers. CBMR offers bike lessons, providing customized beginner, intermediate and advanced lessons so that riders can either improve riding skills or improve time on the hill.

CBMR offers its employees skiing privileges at 14 Colorado resorts, a 401(k), discount daycare, accident protection plans and discounts at its food and beverage operations and rental shops.

FINANCIAL DATA: *Note: Data for latest year may not have been available at press time.*

In U.S. $	2015	2014	2013	2012	2011	2010
Revenue						
R&D Expense						
Operating Income						
Operating Margin %						
SGA Expense						
Net Income						
Operating Cash Flow						
Capital Expenditure						
EBITDA						
Return on Assets %						
Return on Equity %						
Debt to Equity						

CONTACT INFORMATION:

Phone: 877-547-5143   Fax: 970-349-2250
Toll-Free: 800-810-7669
Address: 12 Snowmass Rd., Mt. Crested Butte, CO 81225 United States

STOCK TICKER/OTHER:

Stock Ticker: Private   Exchange:
Employees: 191   Fiscal Year Ends:
Parent Company: CNL Lifestyle Properties Inc

SALARIES/BONUSES:

Top Exec. Salary: $ Bonus: $
Second Exec. Salary: $ Bonus: $

OTHER THOUGHTS:

Estimated Female Officers or Directors:
Hot Spot for Advancement for Women/Minorities:

Sales, profits and employees may be estimates. Financial information, benefits and other data can change quickly and may vary from those stated here.

Crystal Cruises LLC

www.crystalcruises.com

NAIC Code: 483112

TYPES OF BUSINESS:

Deep Sea Passenger Transportation

BRANDS/DIVISIONS/AFFILIATES:

Genting Hong Kong Limited
Crystal Symphony
Crystal Serenity
Crystal Esprit
Crystal River Cruises
Crystal Luxury Air

CONTACTS: *Note: Officers with more than one job title may be intentionally listed here more than once.*

Edie Rodriguez, CEO
Thomas Mazloum, COO
Tan Sri Lim Kok Thay, Chmn.

GROWTH PLANS/SPECIAL FEATURES:

Crystal Cruises, LLC is a Los Angeles based luxury cruise line. The cruise line has consistently been ranked as one of the world's best cruise lines by industry periodicals such as Conde Nast Traveler and Travel + Leisure for the last 20 years. Crystal Cruises current fleet consists of two cruise ships, the Crystal Symphony and Crystal Serenity, and a yacht, the Crystal Esprit, which will make its inaugural run in the Seychelles Islands in December 2015. Additionally, the firm has commissioned the construction of three new vessels scheduled for delivery beginning in 2018. The Crystal Symphony is the smaller of the two current cruise ships holding 940 passengers, in comparison to the 1,050 passengers and 650 crew capacity of the Crystal Serenity. Each ship, in addition to its dining room, features the complimentary specialty restaurants Prego, featuring Italian cuisine, and Silk Road, featuring Japanese cuisine. Furthermore, the onboard amenities aboard each ship include such items as pools, movies theatres, musical lessons and language instruction. The cruise ships of Crystal Cruises currently sail to all seven continents on itineraries ranging from five to 128 days. The yacht Crystal Esprit has a more intimate setting with a capacity of only 62 guests. The yacht offers various watersports such as snorkeling and skiing as well as underwater exploration in a deep-sea submersible. Each vessel also features gaming in its onboard casino. In May 2015, Genting Honk Kong Limited acquired Crystal Cruises from its founding parent company, Nippon Yusen Kabushiki Kaisha. The following July, the firm announced that in 2017 it would launch Crystal River Cruises and Crystal Luxury Air, offering a 28-day itinerary with visits to 10-12 locales aboard a Boeing 787 Dreamliner.

FINANCIAL DATA: *Note: Data for latest year may not have been available at press time.*

In U.S. $	2015	2014	2013	2012	2011	2010
Revenue	300,000,000	290,000,000	276,000,000			
R&D Expense						
Operating Income						
Operating Margin %						
SGA Expense						
Net Income						
Operating Cash Flow						
Capital Expenditure						
EBITDA						
Return on Assets %						
Return on Equity %						
Debt to Equity						

CONTACT INFORMATION:

Phone: 310-785-9300 Fax:
Toll-Free: 888-722-0021
Address: 11755 Wilshire Blvd., Ste. 900, Los Angeles, CA 90025 United States

STOCK TICKER/OTHER:

Stock Ticker: Subsidiary Exchange:
Employees: Fiscal Year Ends:
Parent Company: Genting Hong Kong Limited

SALARIES/BONUSES:

Top Exec. Salary: $ Bonus: $
Second Exec. Salary: $ Bonus: $

OTHER THOUGHTS:

Estimated Female Officers or Directors:
Hot Spot for Advancement for Women/Minorities:

Sales, profits and employees may be estimates. Financial information, benefits and other data can change quickly and may vary from those stated here.

Ctrip.com International Ltd

NAIC Code: 519130

www.ctrip.com

TYPES OF BUSINESS:

Online Hotel & Flight Booking
Travel Agencies

BRANDS/DIVISIONS/AFFILIATES:

Ctrip.com
C-Travel International Limited
Ctrip.com (Hong Kong) Limited
Ctrip Computer Technology (Shanghai) Co Ltd
Ctrip Travel Information Technology (Shanghai) Co
Ctrip Travel Network Technology (Shanghai) Co Ltd
Ctrip Information Technology (Nantong) Co Ltd
TravelFusion

CONTACTS: Note: Officers with more than one job title may be intentionally listed here more than once.

Jianzhang Liang, CEO
Jane Jie Sun, COO
Xiaofan Wang, CFO
Jianzhang Liang, Chmn.

GROWTH PLANS/SPECIAL FEATURES:

Ctrip.com International, Ltd., based in Shanghai, is a leading travel service provider for hotel accommodations, airline tickets and packaged tours. Customers can access the company's aggregated information and make bookings online in Chinese at Ctrip.com or in local languages at sites for English, German, French, Spanish, Russian, Korean and Japanese speaking customers. Ctrip.com is designed more for independent travel than for group excursions, although services are offered for these as well. The company sells air tickets as an agent for all major domestic Chinese airlines and has supply relationships with 221,000 hotels in China and 522,000 hotels abroad. Ctrip.com engages in various marketing campaigns, including onsite promotions; cross marketing with Chinese domestic airlines, telecommunications service providers and banks; online marketing; traditional advertising; and customer awards programs. In addition to its branch offices in nine major cities in China, the firm maintains a network of ticketing and third-party agency offices in more than 70 cities in China. The firm is a holding company incorporated in the Cayman Islands and conducts all business through its subsidiaries and affiliates, some of which include C-Travel International Limited; Ctrip.com (Hong Kong) Limited; Ctrip Computer Technology (Shanghai) Co., Ltd.; Ctrip Travel Information Technology (Shanghai) Co., Ltd.; Ctrip Travel Network Technology (Shanghai) Co., Ltd.; Ctrip Information Technology (Nantong) Co., Ltd; and China Software Hotel Information System Co. In 2015, the firm purchased a majority stake in TravelFusion, a UK-based leading online low cost carrier.

FINANCIAL DATA: Note: Data for latest year may not have been available at press time.

In U.S. $	2015	2014	2013	2012	2011	2010
Revenue	1,642,585,000	1,107,398,000	811,941,600	626,852,700	527,264,700	434,287,000
R&D Expense	496,909,000	349,895,800	187,766,700	137,451,000	90,661,620	68,409,050
Operating Income	57,434,430	-22,729,580	126,377,900	98,668,430	160,676,800	158,887,800
Operating Margin %	3.49%	-2.05%	15.56%	15.74%	30.47%	36.58%
SGA Expense	629,505,700	463,607,900	288,770,300	234,307,500	154,569,400	112,744,800
Net Income	377,977,800	36,588,060	150,476,300	107,682,100	162,247,500	157,975,100
Operating Cash Flow	459,545,700	295,219,500	369,713,500	249,362,100	279,047,800	233,663,600
Capital Expenditure	99,200,150	723,151,600	98,240,270	81,864,730	32,888,300	25,015,380
EBITDA	546,244,400	72,337,190	199,366,000	113,590,800	174,223,900	160,356,300
Return on Assets %	3.34%	.93%	6.14%	6.66%	12.04%	17.07%
Return on Equity %	9.27%	2.68%	13.29%	10.55%	16.37%	23.21%
Debt to Equity	0.41	0.84	0.66	0.17		

CONTACT INFORMATION:

Phone: 86 2134064880   Fax: 86 2152510000
Toll-Free:
Address: 99 Fu Quan Rd., Shanghai, 200335 China

STOCK TICKER/OTHER:

Stock Ticker: CTRP   Exchange: NAS
Employees: 31,000   Fiscal Year Ends: 12/31
Parent Company:

SALARIES/BONUSES:

Top Exec. Salary: $ Bonus: $
Second Exec. Salary: $ Bonus: $

OTHER THOUGHTS:

Estimated Female Officers or Directors:
Hot Spot for Advancement for Women/Minorities: Y

Sales, profits and employees may be estimates. Financial information, benefits and other data can change quickly and may vary from those stated here.

Dalian Wanda Group Co Ltd

www.wanda-group.com

NAIC Code: 512131

TYPES OF BUSINESS:

Motion Picture Theaters (except Drive-Ins)
Motion Picture and Video Production
Motion Picture and Video Distribution
Performing Arts Companies
Amusement and Theme Parks
Hotels (except Casino Hotels) and Motels
Department Stores
Internet Publishing and Broadcasting and Web Search Portals

BRANDS/DIVISIONS/AFFILIATES:

Wanda Plazas
Qingdao Oriental Movie Metropolis
Continental Film Distribution
China Times
Popular Cinema
Wanda E-commerce
O2O e-commerce
99bill

CONTACTS: Note: Officers with more than one job title may be intentionally listed here more than once.

Wang Jianlin, Chmn.

GROWTH PLANS/SPECIAL FEATURES:

Dalian Wanda Group Co. Ltd. is a private property developer with registered capital totaling $7 billion. The company operates in four major industries: commercial property, culture & tourism, e-commerce and department stores. Dalian Wanda's commercial property division is the largest commercial real estate company in the world, comprising 125 Wanda Plazas and 81 hotels with a total gross floor area of 70 million square feet (21.57 million square meters). Properties under construction include 70 Wanda Plazas and 69 hotels, with a combined gross floor area of 57 million square feet (17.47 million square meters). The culture & tourism division comprises cinemas, film production, film industry parks, performing arts, film technology entertainment, theme parks, entertainment franchises, print media, art investment and travel. This segment operates 187 theatres, with a total 1,657 screens (including 117 IMAX screens); the Qingdao Oriental Movie Metropolis film and television industrial park, which plans to open itself to the public in 2017; film technology entertainment includes Continental Film Distribution, a film distribution, marketing and planning company that plays a key role in Wanda's film industry operations; and print media operates weekly magazines China Times and Popular Cinema. The e-commerce division comprises Wanda E-commerce, a joint venture with Tencent and Baidu, which is developing its O2O e-commerce platform, spanning the areas of film, parenting, dining, shopping, entertainment, leisure, tourism, lifestyle and finance; and 99bill, an independent third-party payment platform. The department store division operates 99 department stores in major cities such as Beijing, Shanghai, Chengdu and Wuhan. In July 2016, the firm, through AMC Entertainment Holdings, Inc., acquired Odeon & UCI Cinema Group, Europes largest cinema chain, for $650 million.

FINANCIAL DATA: Note: Data for latest year may not have been available at press time.

In U.S. $	2015	2014	2013	2012	2011	2010
Revenue	27,337,000,000	22,197,644,000	16,803,616,508			
R&D Expense						
Operating Income						
Operating Margin %						
SGA Expense						
Net Income	2,431,000,000	2,235,113,672	2,203,732,677			
Operating Cash Flow						
Capital Expenditure						
EBITDA						
Return on Assets %						
Return on Equity %						
Debt to Equity						

CONTACT INFORMATION:

Phone: 86-10-85853888   Fax: 86-10-85853222
Toll-Free:
Address: Tower B, Wanda Plaza, No. 93, Jianguo Rd., Chaoyang District, Beijing, 100022 China

STOCK TICKER/OTHER:

Stock Ticker: Private
Employees: 128,518
Parent Company:

Exchange:
Fiscal Year Ends: 12/31

SALARIES/BONUSES:

Top Exec. Salary: $ Bonus: $
Second Exec. Salary: $ Bonus: $

OTHER THOUGHTS:

Estimated Female Officers or Directors:
Hot Spot for Advancement for Women/Minorities:

Dassault Aviation SA

www.dassault-aviation.com

NAIC Code: 336411

TYPES OF BUSINESS:

Aircraft Manufacturing
Business Jets
Military Aircraft
Unmanned Combat Aircraft
Aerospace Technology

BRANDS/DIVISIONS/AFFILIATES:

Dassault Group
Dassault Falcon
Rafale
Maritime Falcon
nEUROn
Dassault Falcon Jet Corp
Dassault Procurement Services Inc
Dassault Falcon Jet Wilmington Corp

CONTACTS: Note: Officers with more than one job title may be intentionally listed here more than once.

Eric Trappier, CEO
Loik Segalen, COO
Claude Defawe, VP-National & Cooperative Military Sales
Jean-Jacques Cara, Sr. VP-Human Resources & Social Rel.
Jean Sass, Exec. VP-Info. Systems Div.
Didier Gondoin, Sr. VP-Eng.
Benoit Berger, Exec. VP-Industrial Oper.
Stephane Fort, Sr. VP-Corp. Comm. & Institutional Rel.
Alain Bonny, Sr. VP-Military Customer Support
Olivier Villa, Sr. VP-Civil Aircraft
Gerald Maria, Sr. VP-Total Quality
Eric Trappier, Chmn.
Benoit Dussaugey, Exec. VP-Intl
Benoit Berger, Exec. VP-Procurement & Purchasing

GROWTH PLANS/SPECIAL FEATURES:

Dassault Aviation SA designs, engineers and produces civil and military aircraft and is one of the largest producers of business jets in the world. It is part of the Dassault Group and operates in three divisions: Dassault Falcon, defense and space. The Dassault Falcon family of luxury business jets includes the Falcon 7X, a mid-size craft with three engines; the Falcon 8X, a large-cabin, long range tri-jet; the Falcon 2000LXS, a large business jet with two engines; and the Falcon 900LX, a large business jet with three engines. The firm's defense operations include the production of the Rafale and Maritime Falcon lines of aircraft as well as acting as the primary contractor for the European nEUROn Uninhabited Combat Aircraft Vehicle (UCAV) project. Dassault's space division develops pyrotechnics equipment for space and military aircraft, aerospace telemetry systems and manned and unmanned vehicles for space travel. The firm operates through a number of subsidiaries, including Dassault Falcon Jet Corp., which is responsible for customizing Falcon interiors in the U.S.; Dassault Procurement Services, Inc.; Dassault Falcon Jet Wilmington Corp., which offers aviation maintenance and services in U.S.; DFS Le Bourget; and Sogitec Industries, which offers simulation training and documentation systems. Dassault's subsidiaries have operations across France as well as in the U.S., the U.K., South America, the Middle East and Asia. In December 2015, Qatar ordered 24 Rafale aircraft. In January 2016, the French and Indian governments signed an intergovernmental agreement for a contract of 36 Rafale fighters to India. The Rafale is a twin-jet fighter aircraft able to operate both from an aircraft carrier and a shore base.

FINANCIAL DATA: Note: Data for latest year may not have been available at press time.

In U.S. $	2015	2014	2013	2012	2011	2010
Revenue	4,717,891,000	4,158,153,000	5,189,206,000	4,452,869,000	3,734,428,000	4,730,657,000
R&D Expense						
Operating Income	408,078,200	398,540,300	563,212,000	617,993,400	425,376,800	668,022,800
Operating Margin %	8.64%	9.58%	10.85%	13.87%	11.39%	14.12%
SGA Expense						1,842,210,000
Net Income	159,820,400	319,552,600	519,061,100	576,018,500	364,552,000	302,216,700
Operating Cash Flow	1,463,014,000	-313,201,900	125,955,300	687,734,700	441,469,900	1,330,595,000
Capital Expenditure	172,039,300	103,259,500	71,751,220	68,310,920	58,008,130	65,845,660
EBITDA	192,911,500	498,098,500	934,061,600	731,299,300	607,269,200	869,994,300
Return on Assets %	1.27%	2.82%	4.49%	4.95%	3.05%	2.43%
Return on Equity %	3.59%	6.14%	9.32%	11.07%	7.27%	6.07%
Debt to Equity	0.30	0.17	0.04	0.05	0.06	0.05

CONTACT INFORMATION:

Phone: 33 153769300   Fax: 33 153769320
Toll-Free:
Address: 9 Rond-Point des Champs-Elysees, Marcel Dassault, Paris, 75008 France

STOCK TICKER/OTHER:

Stock Ticker: DUAVF
Employees: 12,152
Parent Company: Dassault Group

Exchange: GREY
Fiscal Year Ends: 12/31

SALARIES/BONUSES:

Top Exec. Salary: $ Bonus: $
Second Exec. Salary: $ Bonus: $

OTHER THOUGHTS:

Estimated Female Officers or Directors:
Hot Spot for Advancement for Women/Minorities:

Sales, profits and employees may be estimates. Financial information, benefits and other data can change quickly and may vary from those stated here.

Days Inn Worldwide Inc

www.daysinn.com

NAIC Code: 721110

TYPES OF BUSINESS:

Motels

BRANDS/DIVISIONS/AFFILIATES:

Wyndham Worldwide
Days Hotel
Days Inn & Suites
Days Inn Business Place
Days Inn
Wyndham Rewards Card

CONTACTS: *Note: Officers with more than one job title may be intentionally listed here more than once.*

Stephen P. Holmes, CEO
Clyde Guinn, Pres.
Stephen P. Holmes, Chmn.

GROWTH PLANS/SPECIAL FEATURES:

Days Inn Worldwide, Inc., a subsidiary of Wyndham Worldwide, operates one of the world's largest franchised hotel networks. Its operations span over 1,800 low-cost hotels located throughout the U.S. and around the world, including Canada, China, India, Jordan, Bahrain, Azerbaijan, Germany, Guam, Latvia, Philippines, Saudi Arabia, Singapore and the U.K. The franchised hotels come in four varieties: Days Inn, a standard roadside motel; Days Hotel, a slightly larger property, usually in an urban center or near an airport, that features restaurants, lounges and meeting and banquet rooms in addition to guest rooms; Days Inn & Suites, similar to Days Inn but providing larger rooms, often for guests who plan to stay for a longer duration; and Days Inn Business Place, inns offering specialized services catering to the needs of business travelers. Some universal amenities that the chain offers its guests include free high-speed internet, complimentary Daybreak breakfast, hairdryers, alarm clocks and complimentary copies of USA Today. On the company's web site, customers can make reservations online and access special promotions and other information. Additionally, Wyndham's hotel group offers a best-available-rate guarantee, providing its online customers with the lowest rates available for all its hotel brands, including Days Inn. It also offers the Wyndham Rewards Card, which allows customers to earn points at any of Wyndham's hotel chains, a total of more than 7,800 hotels.

FINANCIAL DATA: *Note: Data for latest year may not have been available at press time.*

In U.S. $	2015	2014	2013	2012	2011	2010
Revenue						
R&D Expense						
Operating Income						
Operating Margin %						
SGA Expense						
Net Income						
Operating Cash Flow						
Capital Expenditure						
EBITDA						
Return on Assets %						
Return on Equity %						
Debt to Equity						

CONTACT INFORMATION:

Phone: 973-428-9700   Fax: 973-496-7658
Toll-Free: 800-329-7466
Address: 1 Sylvan Way, Parsippany, NJ 07054 United States

STOCK TICKER/OTHER:

Stock Ticker: Subsidiary   Exchange:
Employees: Fiscal Year Ends: 12/31
Parent Company: Wyndham Worldwide

SALARIES/BONUSES:

Top Exec. Salary: $ Bonus: $
Second Exec. Salary: $ Bonus: $

OTHER THOUGHTS:

Estimated Female Officers or Directors:
Hot Spot for Advancement for Women/Minorities:

Sales, profits and employees may be estimates. Financial information, benefits and other data can change quickly and may vary from those stated here.

Delaware North Companies Inc

www.delawarenorth.com

NAIC Code: 722310

TYPES OF BUSINESS:

Food Service Contractors
Catering & Food Services
Park & Resort Visitor Services
Professional Hockey Team
Event Centers
Casinos

BRANDS/DIVISIONS/AFFILIATES:

Ruby Seven Studios

CONTACTS: Note: Officers with more than one job title may be intentionally listed here more than once.

Jerry Jacobs, Co-CEO
Lou Jacobs, Co-CEO
Charles E. Moran, Pres.
Christopher J. Feeney, CFO
Todd Merry, CMO
Eileen Morgan, Chief Human Resources Officer
Kevin Quinlivan, CIO
Rajat Shah, General Counsel
Nate Brunner, VP-Financial Planning & Analysis
Wendy A. Watkins, VP-Corp. Comm.
Scott Socha, Treas.
John Wentzell, Pres., DNC Sportservice
Paula Halligan, VP-Retail
Simon Dobson, Managing Dir.-U.K.
William J. Bissett, Pres., DNC Gaming & Entertainment
Jeremy M. Jacobs, Chmn.
Gary Brown, Managing Dir.-Australia & New Zealand
Michael Reinert, VP-Supply Mgmt. Svcs.

GROWTH PLANS/SPECIAL FEATURES:

Delaware North Companies, Inc. (DNC) is a worldwide provider of food services and hospitality management at 300 locations serving 500 million guests a year. The firm manages and provides food & beverage concessions, premium dining, entertainment, lodging and retail at many large venues (sports stadiums, entertainment complexes, national & state parks, airports and casinos). Delaware North is a major player in several sectors of sports, including stadiums, arenas and ballparks, with more than 60 venues worldwide at which it operates premium dining, restaurants and food/beverage concession stands. The company is a world-leading airport food service and retail company, operating at more than 30 airports and travel centers in the U.S., Great Britain and Australia. It manages more than 300 restaurants & retail stores, serving more than 350 million travelers each year. Serving the national & state parks, the firm delivers lodging, retail, food service, recreational & transportation services across the U.S. Delaware North also has a portfolio of distinct luxury resorts in Australia and the U.S., including resorts on Australia's Great Barrier Reef: Lizard Island, Wilson Island and Heron Island, as well as the U.S.' Tenaya Lodge at Yosemite and Gideon Putnam Resort in New York. The company operates gaming casinos in the U.S., including video gaming machines, table games, poker rooms, racing simulcast centers, restaurants, lounges, nightclubs, sports bars, event centers, retail shops and hotels. The firm's restaurants are located at venues such as the Rockefeller Center, Lincoln Center, Walt Disney World, Disneyland, Walt Disney Concert Hall, The Empire State Building and more. In March 2016, the firm acquired social casino developer Ruby Seven Studios.

FINANCIAL DATA: Note: Data for latest year may not have been available at press time.

In U.S. $	2015	2014	2013	2012	2011	2010
Revenue	3,210,000,000	2,940,000,000	3,000,000,000	2,620,000,000	2,600,000,000	2,200,000,000
R&D Expense						
Operating Income						
Operating Margin %						
SGA Expense						
Net Income						
Operating Cash Flow						
Capital Expenditure						
EBITDA						
Return on Assets %						
Return on Equity %						
Debt to Equity						

CONTACT INFORMATION:

Phone: 716-858-5000   Fax: 716-858-5479
Toll-Free:
Address: 40 Fountain Plz., Buffalo, NY 14202 United States

STOCK TICKER/OTHER:

Stock Ticker: Private   Exchange:
Employees: 60,000   Fiscal Year Ends: 12/31
Parent Company:

SALARIES/BONUSES:

Top Exec. Salary: $ Bonus: $
Second Exec. Salary: $ Bonus: $

OTHER THOUGHTS:

Estimated Female Officers or Directors: 5
Hot Spot for Advancement for Women/Minorities: Y

Delta Air Lines Inc

www.delta.com

NAIC Code: 481111

TYPES OF BUSINESS:

Airline
Air Freight

BRANDS/DIVISIONS/AFFILIATES:

Virgin Atlantic Airways Ltd

CONTACTS: Note: Officers with more than one job title may be intentionally listed here more than once.

Paul Jacobson, CFO
Craig Meynard, Chief Accounting Officer
Edward Bastian, Director
Steven Sear, Executive VP, Divisional
Joanne Smith, Executive VP
Peter Carter, Executive VP
Glen Hauenstein, President
Wayne West, Senior Executive VP

GROWTH PLANS/SPECIAL FEATURES:

Delta Air Lines, Inc. is a major air carrier that provides scheduled air transportation domestically and internationally for freight and more than 180 million passengers annually. From its multiple hubs (Atlanta, Cincinnati, Detroit, Los Angeles, Boston, Minneapolis/St. Paul, New York-JFK, New York-LaGuardia, Salt Lake City, Seattle, Amsterdam, Paris-Charles de Gaulle and Tokyo-Narita), the company serves 337 destinations in 62 countries. The firm has a total 809 aircraft in fleet, with 618 being company owned and 191 being leased. Delta is a founding member of the SkyTeam international alliance, a global airline alliance that provides customers with 1,000 worldwide destinations, flights and services. Delta also has trans-Atlantic joint ventures with both Air France KLM Group and Alitalia in addition to a trans-Pacific joint venture with Virgin Australia. The company also holds a 49% interest in Virgin Atlantic Airways Ltd., giving Delta a more competitive stance in the vital New York City to London Heathrow route.

Delta offers its employees medical, dental, vision and life insurance; flexible spending accounts; a 401(k) plan; profit sharing; credit union membership; employee assistance programs; adoption assistance, paid holiday and vacation; and free and reduced r

FINANCIAL DATA: Note: Data for latest year may not have been available at press time.

In U.S. $	2015	2014	2013	2012	2011	2010
Revenue	40,704,000,000	40,362,000,000	37,773,000,000	36,670,000,000	35,115,000,000	31,755,000,000
R&D Expense						
Operating Income	7,802,000,000	2,206,000,000	3,400,000,000	2,175,000,000	1,975,000,000	2,217,000,000
Operating Margin %	19.16%	5.46%	9.00%	5.93%	5.62%	6.98%
SGA Expense	11,938,000,000	10,905,000,000	9,829,000,000	9,228,000,000	8,839,999,000	10,122,000,000
Net Income	4,526,000,000	659,000,000	10,540,000,000	1,009,000,000	854,000,000	593,000,000
Operating Cash Flow	7,927,000,000	4,947,000,000	4,504,000,000	2,476,000,000	2,834,000,000	2,832,000,000
Capital Expenditure	2,945,000,000	2,249,000,000	2,568,000,000	1,968,000,000	1,254,000,000	1,342,000,000
EBITDA	9,637,000,000	3,977,000,000	5,058,000,000	3,402,000,000	3,193,000,000	3,123,000,000
Return on Assets %	8.43%	1.23%	21.77%	2.29%	1.97%	1.36%
Return on Equity %	46.03%	6.44%	221.61%			103.85%
Debt to Equity	0.62	0.97	0.84			14.00

CONTACT INFORMATION:

Phone: 404 715-2600   Fax: 404 715-1400
Toll-Free: 866-715-2170
Address: 1030 Delta Blvd., Atlanta, GA 30320 United States

STOCK TICKER/OTHER:

Stock Ticker: DAL
Employees: 83,000
Parent Company:

Exchange: NYS
Fiscal Year Ends: 12/31

SALARIES/BONUSES:

Top Exec. Salary: $800,000   Bonus: $
Second Exec. Salary: Bonus: $
$625,000

OTHER THOUGHTS:

Estimated Female Officers or Directors: 2
Hot Spot for Advancement for Women/Minorities: Y

Sales, profits and employees may be estimates. Financial information, benefits and other data can change quickly and may vary from those stated here.

Deutsche Bahn AG

www.deutschebahn.com

NAIC Code: 482111

TYPES OF BUSINESS:

Line-Haul Railroads
Intermodal Transport
Rail Freight & Passenger Services
Warehousing
Rail Maintenance & Services
Freight Forwarding
Energy Procurement
Urban Subway Transport

BRANDS/DIVISIONS/AFFILIATES:

DB Bahn Long Distance
DB Arriva
DB Schenker Rail
DB Bahn Regional
DB Schenker Logistics
DB Netze Track
DB Netze Stations
Redhead Holdings Ltd

CONTACTS: Note: Officers with more than one job title may be intentionally listed here more than once.

Rudiger Grube, CEO
Richard Lutz, CFO
Ulrich Weber, Human Resources
Volker Kefer, Dir.-Rail Tech. Svcs. & Infrastructure
Gerd Becht, Dir.-Compliance, Privacy & Legal Affairs
Oliver Schumacher, Head-Comm.
Robert Strehl, Head-Investor Rel.
Richard Lutz, Head-Finance
Antje Lussenhop, Head-Public Rel. & Internal Comm.

GROWTH PLANS/SPECIAL FEATURES:

Deutsche Bahn AG (DB), a government-owned German railway company, is one of Europe's largest transportation providers. The company's core business is the railway with more than 4.3 million customers daily. DB carries approximately 2.2 billion train and 2 million bus passengers annually in Germany and neighboring countries. It operates through DB Bahn Long Distance, which provides national and cross-border long-distance rail services; DB Arriva, which provides all regional transport activities outside Germany; DB Schenker Rail, which transports freight in Europe; DB Bahn Regional, which provides a fully comprehensive regional transport network that links conurbation and rural areas; DB Schenker Logistics, a provider of transportation and logistics services; DB Netze Track, a service provider for approximately 340 railway undertakings along a 20,711-mile German rail network; DB Netze Stations, which are the gateways to Deutsche Bahn and surrounding cities and regions; DB Services, which covers six sectors: DB Fahrzeuginstandhaltung (vehicle maintenance), DB Systel (information and communications technology), DB Services, DB Fuhrpark (motor vehicle fleet), DB Kommunikationstechnik (communications) and DB Sicherheit (security); and DB Netze Energy, which manages mixed energy portfolios in Germany, with a unique infrastructure for the supply of power and diesel fuel to mobile and stationary consumers. The company operates through roughly 2,000 locations in over 130 countries. In February 2016, the firm acquired a 75% interest in Redhead Holdings Ltd.

FINANCIAL DATA: Note: Data for latest year may not have been available at press time.

In U.S. $	2015	2014	2013	2012	2011	2010
Revenue	21,684,544,000	42,728,260,000	65,758,380,000	51,934,200,000	49,073,400,000	49,075,871,000
R&D Expense						
Operating Income						
Operating Margin %						
SGA Expense						
Net Income	424,841,050	1,110,056,986	689,668,362	1,550,421,744	1,721,100,000	1,508,725,000
Operating Cash Flow						
Capital Expenditure						
EBITDA						
Return on Assets %						
Return on Equity %						
Debt to Equity						

CONTACT INFORMATION:

Phone: 49-30-297-61131   Fax: 49-30-297-61919
Toll-Free:
Address: Potsdamer Platz 2, Berlin, 10785 Germany

STOCK TICKER/OTHER:

Stock Ticker: Government-Owned
Employees: 307,873
Parent Company:

Exchange:
Fiscal Year Ends: 12/31

SALARIES/BONUSES:

Top Exec. Salary: $ Bonus: $
Second Exec. Salary: $ Bonus: $

OTHER THOUGHTS:

Estimated Female Officers or Directors: 2
Hot Spot for Advancement for Women/Minorities: Y

Deutsche Lufthansa AG

NAIC Code: 481111

www.lufthansa.com

TYPES OF BUSINESS:

Airline
IT Services
Maintenance & Repair
Logistics
Catering
Cargo Airline

BRANDS/DIVISIONS/AFFILIATES:

Lufthansa Passenger Airlines
SWISS International Air Lines
Austrian Airlines
Lufthansa Technik AG
LSG Lufthansa Cargo AG
LSG Service Holding AG
LSG Sky Chefs
Lufthansa Systems AG

CONTACTS: Note: Officers with more than one job title may be intentionally listed here more than once.

Carsten Spohr, CEO
Simone Menne, CFO
Bettina Volkens, Chief Officer-Corp. Human Resources
Harry Hohmeister, IT
Bettina Volkens, Chief Officer-Legal Affairs
Carsten Spohr, Chief Officer-Lufthansa German Airlines
Harry Hohmeister, CEO-Group Airlines & Logistics
Carsten Spohr, Chmn.

GROWTH PLANS/SPECIAL FEATURES:

Deutsche Lufthansa AG is a transportation conglomerate operating one of Europe's largest passenger airlines. The company has over 540 subsidiaries, and it operates in five segments: the passenger airline group, maintenance repair overhaul (MRO), logistics, catering and IT services. The passenger airline group, servicing over 107 million passengers per year, consists of Lufthansa Passenger Airlines, SWISS International Air Lines and Austrian Airlines. It also consists of equity investments in JetBlue, Brussels Airlines, Germanwings, Eurowings and SunExpress. Deutsche Lufthansa flies out of hubs in Zurich, Frankfurt, Munich, Vienna and Brussels. The company is also a member of the Star Alliance network. The MRO segment primarily includes Lufthansa Technik AG, an engineering service provider for civil aircraft. The logistics segment consists of LSG Lufthansa Cargo AG, which transports roughly 1.86 million tons of freight (including mail) and serves approximately 300 destinations. The catering segment is comprised of LSG Service Holding AG, which operates under the LSG Sky Chefs brand. Through 159 subsidiaries, LSG supplies in-flight services from roughly 210 catering facilities at airports in 51 countries. Last, IT services is comprised of Lufthansa Systems AG, which offers customized IT solutions development and IT infrastructure services to over 300 airlines and aviation companies. Other activities include Lufthansa Flight Training Berlin GmbH and Lufthansa AirPlus, a business travel payment and analysis service provider.

Deutsche Lufthansa offers employees job tickets for public transportation; discounted flight tickets; company and private pension schemes; Lufthansa Family Time, which allows employees to take vacation time off for family matters; and the Lufthansa Sports

FINANCIAL DATA: Note: Data for latest year may not have been available at press time.

In U.S. $	2015	2014	2013	2012	2011	2010
Revenue	36,217,380,000	33,906,900,000	33,926,110,000	34,047,000,000	32,464,130,000	30,871,090,000
R&D Expense						
Operating Income	1,756,864,000	866,568,700	959,213,600	1,481,189,000	873,347,600	-1,598,689,000
Operating Margin %	4.85%	2.55%	2.82%	4.35%	2.69%	-5.17%
SGA Expense						7,523,443,000
Net Income	1,918,427,000	62,139,870	353,632,400	1,118,518,000	-14,687,610	1,277,822,000
Operating Cash Flow	3,833,465,000	2,233,646,000	3,717,094,000	3,210,936,000	2,661,846,000	3,474,184,000
Capital Expenditure	2,772,568,000	3,049,373,000	2,761,270,000	2,665,236,000	2,860,694,000	2,596,317,000
EBITDA	4,496,667,000	2,574,850,000	3,184,951,000	3,897,864,000	3,055,022,000	3,639,137,000
Return on Assets %	5.39%	.18%	1.08%	3.50%	-.04%	4.06%
Return on Equity %	34.88%	1.09%	4.37%	12.23%	-.16%	15.77%
Debt to Equity	0.87	1.35	0.79	0.72	0.73	0.76

CONTACT INFORMATION:

Phone: 49-69-696-0   Fax:
Toll-Free:
Address: Von-Gablenz-Strasse 2-6, Koeln, 50679 Germany

STOCK TICKER/OTHER:

Stock Ticker: DLAKF   Exchange: PINX
Employees: 120,652   Fiscal Year Ends: 12/31
Parent Company:

SALARIES/BONUSES:

Top Exec. Salary: $ Bonus: $
Second Exec. Salary: $ Bonus: $

OTHER THOUGHTS:

Estimated Female Officers or Directors: 2
Hot Spot for Advancement for Women/Minorities:

Sales, profits and employees may be estimates. Financial information, benefits and other data can change quickly and may vary from those stated here.

Diamond Resorts Holdings LLC

www.diamondresorts.com

NAIC Code: 561599

TYPES OF BUSINESS:
Time-Share Resorts

BRANDS/DIVISIONS/AFFILIATES:
DiamondResorts.com
THE Club
Diamond Resorts Corporation

CONTACTS: *Note: Officers with more than one job title may be intentionally listed here more than once.*
David Palmer, CEO
C. Bentley, CFO
Stephen Cloobeck, Chairman of the Board
Lisa Gann, Chief Accounting Officer
Howard Lanznar, Chief Administrative Officer
Lowell Kraff, Director
Ronan OGorman, Executive VP, Divisional
Steven Bell, Executive VP, Divisional
Brian Garavuso, Executive VP
Michael Flaskey, Executive VP
Jared Finkelstein, Secretary

GROWTH PLANS/SPECIAL FEATURES:
Diamond Resorts Holdings LLC, operating through Diamond Resorts Corporation (DRC), is a hospitality and vacation ownership firm. It has a worldwide network of 379 vacation destinations located in 35 countries throughout the U.S., Hawaii, Canada, Mexico, the Caribbean, Central America, South America, Europe, Asia, Australia, New Zealand and Africa. This network consists of 109 resort properties with approximately 12,000 units managed by DRC; and 250 affiliated resorts and hotels, as well as 20 cruise itineraries which are not managed by the firm, nor do they carry its brand, but are part of the DRC network through THE Club. THE Club, a points-based vacation system with over 490,000 member-owners. Points, which are renewed annually, may be spent as currency on resort vacations, cruises, airline tickets and other travel purchases. Members may search for a resort by an activity or interest they wish to pursue, or by geographical area. Amenities vary by resort, but may include a full bath, kitchen, dishwasher, washer/dryer, satellite TV, fireplace, deck, pool, sauna, spa, beauty salon, fitness center, movie rentals, high-speed Internet, childcare, 24-hour reception and safe deposit boxes. Besides resort reservations, DRC directly offers flight, cruise and car rental reservations on its DiamondResorts.com site. In October 2015, the firm acquired vacation ownership business of Gold Key Resorts; and in January 2016, it acquired the vacation ownership business of Intrawest resort Club Group.

FINANCIAL DATA: *Note: Data for latest year may not have been available at press time.*

In U.S. $	2015	2014	2013	2012	2011	2010
Revenue	954,040,000	844,566,000	729,788,000	523,668,000	391,021,000	370,825,000
R&D Expense						
Operating Income	300,128,000	213,416,000	105,208,000	-667,000	69,331,000	-20,433,000
Operating Margin %	31.45%	25.26%	14.41%	-.12%	17.73%	-5.51%
SGA Expense	462,912,000	400,088,000	404,376,000	277,380,000	209,129,000	181,934,000
Net Income	149,478,000	59,457,000	-2,525,000	13,643,000	10,303,000	-19,159,000
Operating Cash Flow	175,894,000	118,058,000	-5,409,000	24,600,000	9,292,000	66,001,000
Capital Expenditure	35,318,000	17,950,000	15,204,000	14,335,000	6,276,000	5,553,000
EBITDA	334,645,000	199,163,000	120,063,000	114,347,000	96,762,000	58,668,000
Return on Assets %	8.37%	4.13%	-.22%	1.49%	1.23%	
Return on Equity %	55.53%	25.02%	-4.62%			
Debt to Equity	4.49	3.57	3.76			

CONTACT INFORMATION:
Phone: 702-804-8600   Fax: 702-304-7066
Toll-Free:
Address: 10600 W. Charleston Blvd., Las Vegas, NV 89135 United States

STOCK TICKER/OTHER:
Stock Ticker: DRII   Exchange: NYS
Employees: 7,100   Fiscal Year Ends: 09/30
Parent Company:

SALARIES/BONUSES:
Top Exec. Salary: Bonus: $
$2,000,000
Second Exec. Salary: Bonus: $
$750,000

OTHER THOUGHTS:
Estimated Female Officers or Directors:

Hot Spot for Advancement for Women/Minorities:

Disney Cruise Line

disneycruise.disney.go.com

NAIC Code: 483112

TYPES OF BUSINESS:

Cruise Lines

BRANDS/DIVISIONS/AFFILIATES:

Walt Disney Company (The)
Disney Magic
Disney Wonder
Disney Dream
Disney Fantasy

GROWTH PLANS/SPECIAL FEATURES:

Disney Cruise Line, a wholly-owned subsidiary of The Walt Disney Company., is a vacation cruise line and part of Disney's Parks and Resorts division. The firm operates out of ports in North America and Europe and owns a fleet of four ships: the Disney Magic, the Disney Wonder, the Disney Dream and the Disney Fantasy. Disney Cruise Line caters to children, families and adults, with distinctly-themed areas and activities for each group. The Disney Magic and the Disney Wonder are 84,000-ton and 83,000-ton ships with 877 staterooms, while the Disney Dream and the Disney Fantasy are 130,000 ton ships with 1,250 staterooms. Many of its cruise vacations include a visit to Disney's Castaway Cay, a 1,000-acre private Bahamian island. In 2015, Disney Cruise Line dominated the 2015 Cruise Critic Cruiser's Choice Awards by winning 12 categories, including the best overall cruise line award for the third year in a row. In 2016, the company began sailing the British Isles, as well as to Geiranger, Norway for the first time.

CONTACTS: Note: Officers with more than one job title may be intentionally listed here more than once.

Karl Holz, Pres.
Thomas O. Staggs, Chmn.-Disney Parks & Resorts

FINANCIAL DATA: Note: Data for latest year may not have been available at press time.

In U.S. $	2015	2014	2013	2012	2011	2010
Revenue	1,210,000,000	1,150,000,000	1,080,000,000	950,000,000	942,526,000	509,443,000
R&D Expense						
Operating Income						
Operating Margin %						
SGA Expense						
Net Income						
Operating Cash Flow						
Capital Expenditure						
EBITDA						
Return on Assets %						
Return on Equity %						
Debt to Equity						

CONTACT INFORMATION:

Phone: 407-566-6397   Fax:
Toll-Free: 800-951-3532
Address: 1375 N. Buena Vista Dr., Lake Buena Vista, FL 32830 United States

SALARIES/BONUSES:

Top Exec. Salary: $ Bonus: $
Second Exec. Salary: $ Bonus: $

STOCK TICKER/OTHER:

Stock Ticker: Subsidiary   Exchange:
Employees: Fiscal Year Ends: 09/30
Parent Company: Walt Disney Company (The)

OTHER THOUGHTS:

Estimated Female Officers or Directors:
Hot Spot for Advancement for Women/Minorities:

Sales, profits and employees may be estimates. Financial information, benefits and other data can change quickly and may vary from those stated here.

DLF Limited

www.dlf.in

NAIC Code: 531100

TYPES OF BUSINESS:

Real Estate Development
Commercial Real Estate Management & Leasing
Hotels
Luxury Resorts

BRANDS/DIVISIONS/AFFILIATES:

DLF Utilities Limited

CONTACTS: *Note: Officers with more than one job title may be intentionally listed here more than once.*

T.C. Goyal, Managing Dir.
Ashok Kumar Tyagi, CFO
Kushal P. Singh, Chmn.
Pua Seck Guan, CEO-Int'l

GROWTH PLANS/SPECIAL FEATURES:

DLF Limited is an India-based real estate development and construction company. The firm has over 294 msf (million square feet) of planned projects and 47 msf of projects under construction. DLF is primarily engaged in the development of residential, commercial and retail properties. It is divided into two business units: development and annuity. The development unit develops commercial complexes and mid-income, luxury and super luxury residential communities. Products offered include condominiums, duplexes, row houses and apartments. The annuity business is engaged in the rental of office and retail properties. The firm's business model allows it to earn revenues from both development activities and the leasing of completed properties. The company hopes to continue to grow its business through projects in India's special economic zones (SEZs), which are specially legislated areas designed to encourage foreign investment and exports from the country. DLF is also one of the largest owners of wind power plants in India, managing plants with a combined installed capacity of 228.7 megawatts. The firm's clients have included GE, IBM, Microsoft, Canon, Citibank, Vertex, Hewitt, Fidelity Investments, WNS, Bank of America, Cognizant, Infosys, CSC, Symantec and Sapient. In 2015, the company, through its subsidiary, DLF Utilities Limited, agreed to sell its cinema exhibition business operated under the brand name of DT Cinemas to PVR Limited.

FINANCIAL DATA: *Note: Data for latest year may not have been available at press time.*

In U.S. $	2015	2014	2013	2012	2011	2010
Revenue	1,139,432,000	1,236,162,000	1,354,995,000	1,434,490,000	1,511,220,000	1,169,550,000
R&D Expense						
Operating Income	93,351,940	77,575,380	120,049,900	496,056,300	297,970,800	373,114,800
Operating Margin %	8.19%	6.27%	8.85%	34.58%	19.71%	31.90%
SGA Expense				199,584,900	224,641,900	69,535,500
Net Income	80,478,660	96,265,420	106,054,800	178,886,400	229,532,200	268,500,500
Operating Cash Flow	303,425,200	218,623,400	299,255,400	375,367,800	410,707,300	1,285,288,000
Capital Expenditure	129,481,200	141,420,900	196,540,100	85,781,910	164,057,300	2,071,814,000
EBITDA	473,423,300	179,062,700	243,506,500	667,805,300	399,436,700	421,520,100
Return on Assets %	.82%	1.00%	1.11%	1.88%	2.45%	3.27%
Return on Equity %	2.50%	2.99%	2.60%	4.64%	5.61%	6.64%
Debt to Equity	0.64	0.86	0.56	0.61	0.97	0.71

CONTACT INFORMATION:

Phone: 91-11-4210-2030   Fax:
Toll-Free:
Address: DLF Centre, Sansad Marg, New Delhi, 110 001 India

STOCK TICKER/OTHER:

Stock Ticker: DSFQY
Employees: 2,180
Parent Company:

Exchange: GREY
Fiscal Year Ends: 03/31

SALARIES/BONUSES:

Top Exec. Salary: $ Bonus: $
Second Exec. Salary: $ Bonus: $

OTHER THOUGHTS:

Estimated Female Officers or Directors:
Hot Spot for Advancement for Women/Minorities:

Dollar Thrifty Automotive Group Inc

www.thrifty.com/AboutUs/content.aspx

NAIC Code: 532111

TYPES OF BUSINESS:

Automobile Rental
Used Car Sales
Financial Services

BRANDS/DIVISIONS/AFFILIATES:

Hertz Global Holdings Inc
Thrifty Rental
Dollar Rent A Car

CONTACTS: Note: Officers with more than one job title may be intentionally listed here more than once.

Scott L. Thompson, Pres.
H. Clofford Buster, CFO
Rick L. Morris, CIO
Scott L. Thompson, Chmn.

GROWTH PLANS/SPECIAL FEATURES:

Dollar Thrifty Automotive Group, Inc. (DTG) is a holding company for rental car agencies Thrifty Car Rental and Dollar Rent A Car. These wholly-owned subsidiaries comprise one of the largest car rental companies in the world. DTG itself is a wholly-owned subsidiary of Hertz Global Holdings, Inc. Through corporately-owned and franchised stores, the Thrifty and Dollar operate more than 1,000 locations in 77 countries throughout North, Central and South America, Africa, the Middle East, the Caribbean, Asia and the Pacific. DTG also sells vehicle rental franchises worldwide, and provides sales & marketing, reservations, data processing systems, insurance and other services to franchisees. DTG provides customers supplemental equipment and optional products, including global positioning system equipment, ski racks, infant & child seats, as well as rent-a-toll products for electronic toll payments.

The company offers employees medical, dental and vision coverage; domestic partner benefits; flexible spending accounts; a wellness program; short- and long-term disability; life and AD&D insurance; an employee assistance program; a 401(k); tuition reimbu

FINANCIAL DATA: Note: Data for latest year may not have been available at press time.

In U.S. $	2015	2014	2013	2012	2011	2010
Revenue	1,900,000,000	1,910,000,000	1,875,000,000	1,700,000,000	1,548,928,000	1,537,160,000
R&D Expense						
Operating Income						
Operating Margin %						
SGA Expense						
Net Income						
Operating Cash Flow						
Capital Expenditure						
EBITDA						
Return on Assets %						
Return on Equity %						
Debt to Equity						

CONTACT INFORMATION:

Phone: 918-660-7700   Fax: 918-669-2934
Toll-Free: 888-700-9803
Address: 5330 E. 31st St., Tulsa, OK 74135 United States

STOCK TICKER/OTHER:

Stock Ticker: Subsidiary   Exchange:
Employees: 5,900   Fiscal Year Ends: 12/31
Parent Company: Hertz Global Holdings Inc

SALARIES/BONUSES:

Top Exec. Salary: $ Bonus: $
Second Exec. Salary: $ Bonus: $

OTHER THOUGHTS:

Estimated Female Officers or Directors: 2
Hot Spot for Advancement for Women/Minorities:

Sales, profits and employees may be estimates. Financial information, benefits and other data can change quickly and may vary from those stated here.

Doyle Collection (The)

NAIC Code: 721110

www.doylecollection.com

TYPES OF BUSINESS:

Hotels
Hotel Management

BRANDS/DIVISIONS/AFFILIATES:

Dupont Circle Hotel (The)
Westbury Hotel (The)
Croke Park Hotel (The)
River Lee Hotel (The)
Marylebone Hotel (The)
Bloomsbury Hotel (The)
Kensington Hotel (The)
Bristol Hotel (The)

CONTACTS: Note: Officers with more than one job title may be intentionally listed here more than once.

Patrick King, CEO
Seamus Daly, Corp. Sec.
Bernadette C. Gallagher, Chmn.

GROWTH PLANS/SPECIAL FEATURES:

The Doyle Collection (TDC) is an international hotel operator headquartered in Dublin, Ireland. It has properties in Ireland, the U.K. and the U.S. The company offers business and leisure travelers a portfolio of eight luxury hotels in five cities. The firm's Irish properties are located in Dublin (The Westbury Hotel and The Croke Park Hotel) and Cork (The River Lee Hotel), its U.K. properties are located in London (The Bloomsbury Hotel, The Kensington Hotel and the Marylebone Hotel) and Bristol (The Bristol Hotel), and its U.S. property is located in Washington, D.C. (The Dupont Circle Hotel). Hotels are generally located centrally in their respective cities, giving corporate clients easy access to local business and financial districts. Additionally, the firm's hotels offer corporate hospitality, conference, event and meeting suites to accommodate meetings and events of various sizes. Several of the group's hotels have professional wedding planners on staff to help coordinate wedding and reception activities.

The Doyle Collection offers its U.S. employees discounted health insurance, employee discounts and educational support.

FINANCIAL DATA: Note: Data for latest year may not have been available at press time.

In U.S. $	2015	2014	2013	2012	2011	2010
Revenue	200,000,000	195,000,000	143,649,507	126,626,366	169,523,000	157,197,000
R&D Expense						
Operating Income						
Operating Margin %						
SGA Expense						
Net Income						
Operating Cash Flow						
Capital Expenditure						
EBITDA						
Return on Assets %						
Return on Equity %						
Debt to Equity						

CONTACT INFORMATION:

Phone: 353-1-607-0070   Fax: 353-1-667-2370
Toll-Free:
Address: 146 Pembroke Rd., Ballsbridge, Dublin, 4 United Kingdom

STOCK TICKER/OTHER:

Stock Ticker: Private   Exchange:
Employees: 1,400   Fiscal Year Ends: 12/31
Parent Company:

SALARIES/BONUSES:

Top Exec. Salary: $ Bonus: $
Second Exec. Salary: $ Bonus: $

OTHER THOUGHTS:

Estimated Female Officers or Directors: 1
Hot Spot for Advancement for Women/Minorities:

East Japan Railway Company

www.jreast.co.jp

NAIC Code: 482111

TYPES OF BUSINESS:

Line-Haul Railroads
Retailing
Travel Agency Services
Advertising
Hotel & Restaurant Management
Information Services
Freight Logistics
Credit Cards

BRANDS/DIVISIONS/AFFILIATES:

JR Bus Kanto Co Ltd
Tokyo Monorail Co Ltd
JR EAST VIEW Travel Service Co Ltd
JR East Logistics Co Ltd
Viewcard Co Ltd
Suica
Metropolitan Hotels
HOTEL METS

CONTACTS: Note: Officers with more than one job title may be intentionally listed here more than once.

Tetsuro Tomita, CEO
Tetsuro Tomita, Pres.
Satoshi Seino, Chmn.

GROWTH PLANS/SPECIAL FEATURES:

East Japan Railway Company, also known as JR East, is an operator of passenger railways in Japan, with a service network covering the eastern half of Honshu (Japan's main island), including the Tokyo metropolitan area. Daily, JR East carries nearly 17 million passengers via 70 rail lines which exceed 4,600 miles. The firm operates in four segments: transportation, station space utilization, shopping centers and office buildings and other services. The transportation segment's three main operations are the Shinkansen network, which links Tokyo with Joetsu, Tohoku, Nagano, Yamagata and Akita; the Kanto area network, which comprises railway lines in central Tokyo and railway lines connecting Tokyo with nearby suburban cities; and intercity and regional networks, which provide non-Shinkansen intercity services and regional services not covered by the Kanto network. This division also includes subsidiaries JR Bus Kanto Co., Ltd., a provider of passenger bus services, and Tokyo Monorail Co., Ltd. The station space utilization segment consists of retail outlets and restaurant operations in the firm's railway stations. The shopping centers and office buildings segment develops, remodels and manages buildings in and near stations that offer direct links to its train stations. Lastly, the other services segment includes a number of diversified subsidiaries, including JR EAST VIEW Travel Service Co., Ltd., a travel agency services company; JR East Logistics Co., Ltd., a freight delivery company; Viewcard Co., Ltd., which developed a next-generation fare collection system called Suica; and Nippon Hotel Co., Ltd., which operates hotels under the Metropolitan Hotels and HOTEL METS brands.

FINANCIAL DATA: Note: Data for latest year may not have been available at press time.

In U.S. $	2015	2014	2013	2012	2011	2010
Revenue	27,409,800,000	26,880,240,000	26,571,020,000	25,182,220,000	25,233,740,000	
R&D Expense						
Operating Income	4,251,656,000	4,045,518,000	3,953,716,000	3,580,405,000	3,431,848,000	
Operating Margin %	15.51%	15.05%	14.87%	14.21%	13.60%	
SGA Expense						
Net Income	1,805,577,000	1,999,135,000	1,756,887,000	1,089,862,000	771,456,100	
Operating Cash Flow	6,193,309,000	5,596,625,000	5,852,866,000	5,555,722,000	5,060,426,000	
Capital Expenditure	5,009,706,000	5,116,932,000	4,918,412,000	4,053,762,000	4,862,243,000	
EDITDA	7,403,761,000	7,587,297,000	7,423,822,000	6,898,533,000	6,163,475,000	
Return on Assets %	2.39%	2.72%	2.45%	1.54%	1.08%	
Return on Equity %	8.07%	9.49%	8.98%	5.90%	4.24%	
Debt to Equity	1.13	1.12	1.14	1.19	1.18	

CONTACT INFORMATION:

Phone: 81-3-5334-1150   Fax: 81-3-5334-1110
Toll-Free:
Address: 2-2-2 Yoyogi, Shibuya-ku, Tokyo, 151-8578 Japan

STOCK TICKER/OTHER:

Stock Ticker: EJPRY
Employees: 73,017
Parent Company:

Exchange: PINX
Fiscal Year Ends: 03/31

SALARIES/BONUSES:

Top Exec. Salary: $ Bonus: $
Second Exec. Salary: $ Bonus: $

OTHER THOUGHTS:

Estimated Female Officers or Directors:
Hot Spot for Advancement for Women/Minorities:

easyGroup

NAIC Code: 481111

TYPES OF BUSINESS:

Discount Airline and Travel Services
Online Reservation Services
Online Music Provider
Online Staffing Services
Online Fast Food
Online Car Rental
Public Web Access
Discount Cruises

BRANDS/DIVISIONS/AFFILIATES:

easyJet
easyPizza
easyMobile
easyCar
easyBus
easyInternetcafe
easyHotel
easyCruise

CONTACTS: *Note: Officers with more than one job title may be intentionally listed here more than once.*

Richard Shackleton, Dir.-Comm.
Carolyn McCall, CEO-easyJet
Stelios Haji-Ioannou, Chmn.

GROWTH PLANS/SPECIAL FEATURES:

easyGroup, owned by the serial entrepreneur Stelios Haji-Ioannou, is a private investment group and licenser of the easy brand name, made familiar through easyJet, an airline in which Stelios maintains an interest. The airline carried nearly 70 million passengers in 2015, and is built on a fleet of over 240 Airbus aircraft. Headquarters for the company are located in London Luton Airport, and 95% of its flight bookings are made over the Internet, keeping the company's overhead low. easyJet flies 735 routes between 136 airports worldwide, including the U.K., France, Spain, Switzerland, the Netherlands, Denmark, Italy, Czech Republic, Greece, Germany and Portugal. easyGroup capitalizes on the power of the Internet to drive the efficiency of its business lines. easyGroup's ventures include easyPizza, an online fast food service; easyMobile, a cellular phone service; easyCar, an online car rental agency; easyBus, an airport transportation broker; easyCruise, a discount cruise broker; easyGym, a chain of fitness centers in the U.K.; easyHotel, a discount lodging service; easyProperty, a property rental site; easyFoodstore, a neighborhood store chain that sells food for cheap; easyCoffee, offering low-cost coffee and tea; easyOffice, a serviced office that can be booked; and easyVan, a van rental agency. The firm's Internet-based business model allows it to compete as a high-value, low-cost alternative to larger competitors in these industries. Other e-commerce businesses include easyInternetcafe, a provider of public web access terminals; easyValue.com, a comparison shopping site; easyMusic.com, a music download service; and easyJobs.com, an online employment agency.

FINANCIAL DATA: *Note: Data for latest year may not have been available at press time.*

In U.S. $	2015	2014	2013	2012	2011	2010
Revenue						
R&D Expense						
Operating Income						
Operating Margin %						
SGA Expense						
Net Income						
Operating Cash Flow						
Capital Expenditure						
EBITDA						
Return on Assets %						
Return on Equity %						
Debt to Equity						

CONTACT INFORMATION:

Phone: 44-020-7241-9000   Fax: 44-020-7482-2857
Toll-Free:
Address: 10 Sydney Place, S. Kensington, London, SW7 3NL United Kingdom

STOCK TICKER/OTHER:

Stock Ticker: Private   Exchange:
Employees: Fiscal Year Ends: 09/30
Parent Company:

SALARIES/BONUSES:

Top Exec. Salary: $ Bonus: $
Second Exec. Salary: $ Bonus: $

OTHER THOUGHTS:

Estimated Female Officers or Directors: 1
Hot Spot for Advancement for Women/Minorities: Y

Sales, profits and employees may be estimates. Financial information, benefits and other data can change quickly and may vary from those stated here.

EasyJet plc

NAIC Code: 481111

www.easyjet.com

TYPES OF BUSINESS:
Airline

BRANDS/DIVISIONS/AFFILIATES:
easyGroup
EasyCar.com
easyJet Airline Company Limited
EasyJet.com
easyJet Sterling Limited
easyJet Leasing Limited
easyJet Switzerland SA
easyHotel.com

CONTACTS: Note: Officers with more than one job title may be intentionally listed here more than once.

Carolyn McCall, CEO
Warwick Brady, COO
Andrew Findlay, CFO
Peter Duffy, Dir.-Mktg.
Jacky Simmonds, Dir.-People
Chris Brocklesby, CIO
Giles Pemberton, General Counsel
Paul Moore, Dir.-Comm.
Cath Lynn, Group Commercial Dir.
John Barton, Chmn.
Mike Campbell, Dir.-Europe

GROWTH PLANS/SPECIAL FEATURES:
EasyJet plc is a leading European low-cost airline. Based at Luton Airport outside of London, the company has grown from two routes to Glasgow and Edinburgh, Scotland to 735 routes serving airports in 31 countries, including the U.K., Italy, France, Germany, Spain and Switzerland. The company serves more than 70 million customers annually. The current easyJet fleet consists of 241 aircraft, primarily Airbus A319 and A320 jets. Unlike other low-fare European carriers, easyJet pursues negotiation for landing/take-off slots at major airports that serve major capital cities, seeking to provide inexpensive travel directly through reduced overhead expenses in flight and management operations. EasyJet.com is owned by EasyGroup and affiliated with easyCar.com, easyValue.com, easyHotel.com, easyVan.com and easyBus.com. The company's subsidiaries include easyJet Airline Company Limited, easyJet Sterling Limited and easyJet Leasing Limited. The company also holds a 49% interest in easyJet Switzerland SA.

FINANCIAL DATA: Note: Data for latest year may not have been available at press time.

In U.S. $	2015	2014	2013	2012	2011	2010
Revenue	6,118,052,000	5,910,462,000	5,559,255,000	5,031,792,000	4,506,939,000	3,881,556,000
R&D Expense						
Operating Income	898,254,400	758,554,900	648,884,400	432,154,400	351,207,000	227,174,800
Operating Margin %	14.68%	12.83%	11.67%	8.58%	7.79%	5.85%
SGA Expense	432,154,400	411,264,700	408,653,500	400,819,900		
Net Income	715,470,100	587,521,000	519,629,700	332,928,600	293,760,500	157,977,900
Operating Cash Flow	795,111,800	514,407,300	804,251,000	340,762,200	548,353,000	470,016,800
Capital Expenditure	699,802,800	586,215,400	549,658,600	511,796,100	725,914,900	630,605,900
EBITDA	1,090,178,000	926,977,700	791,195,000	583,604,200	472,628,000	329,011,800
Return on Assets %	11.77%	10.11%	9.14%	5.81%	5.31%	3.15%
Return on Equity %	24.79%	21.48%	20.88%	14.57%	14.03%	8.61%
Debt to Equity	0.14	0.21	0.29	0.46	0.67	0.72

CONTACT INFORMATION:
Phone: 44 1582443330   Fax: 44 1582443355
Toll-Free:
Address: Hangar 89, London Luton Airport, Luton, Bedfordshire LU2 9PF United Kingdom

STOCK TICKER/OTHER:
Stock Ticker: ESYJY
Employees: 10,388
Parent Company:

Exchange: PINX
Fiscal Year Ends: 09/30

SALARIES/BONUSES:
Top Exec. Salary: $ Bonus: $
Second Exec. Salary: $ Bonus: $

OTHER THOUGHTS:
Estimated Female Officers or Directors: 4
Hot Spot for Advancement for Women/Minorities: Y

Sales, profits and employees may be estimates. Financial information, benefits and other data can change quickly and may vary from those stated here.

El Al Israel Airlines Ltd

NAIC Code: 481111

www.elal.co.il

TYPES OF BUSINESS:

Airline
Cargo
Charter Flights
Kosher Catering

BRANDS/DIVISIONS/AFFILIATES:

Matmid Frequent Flyer Club
King David Club
Sun D'Or International Airlines Ltd
Tamam
Catit
Superstar Holidays
Borenstein Caterers
Airtour

CONTACTS: *Note: Officers with more than one job title may be intentionally listed here more than once.*

David Maimon, CEO
Benjamin Livneh, VP-Oper.
Elyezer Shkedy, Pres.
Dganit Palti, VP-Finance
Hanan Matasaro, Sr. VP-Human Resources
Ofer Tsabary, VP-IT & Organization
Shmuel Kuzi, Sr. VP-Eng. & Maintenance
Omer Shalev, General Counsel
Benjamin Livneh, Sr. VP-Oper.
Moran Mazor, Head-Investor Rel.
David Maimon, VP-Commercial & Industry Affairs
Yehudit Grisaro, VP-Customer Service
Gil Ber, Chief Audit Officer
Amikam Cohen, Chmn.
Shali (Shalom) Zahavi, VP-Cargo

GROWTH PLANS/SPECIAL FEATURES:

El Al Israel Airlines, Ltd., founded in 1948, is an international airline carrier with a network of 77 sales offices. The company provides in-flight movies and special meals on request. El Al has code-share agreements with American Airlines, Qantas, Sun D'or, Czech Airlines, Iberia, South African Airways, Swiss Airlines and AeroMexico. The company's fleet includes 43 Boeing aircraft. El Al currently has flights to about 33 international destinations. The company has launched a number of frequent flyer programs, including its Matmid Frequent Flyer Club and King David Club. The Matmid Cards come in Silver, Gold, Platinum and Top Platinum Circle. The Silver Cards are awarded for accumulating over 800 points during 12 consecutive months and include such benefits as waiting list preference, additional luggage allowances and membership in the King David Club. Gold Cards are awarded for accumulating over 1,500 points during 12 consecutive months, Platinum Cards are awarded for accumulating over 3,000 points, and Top Platinum Circle are awarded for accumulating over 7,000 points. Membership in the King David Club includes such benefits as access to King David Lounges at Ben-Gurion in Tel Aviv, JFK in New York, CDG in Paris and Heathrow in London; luggage retrieval priority; and flight check-in at the King David Club counters. The King David Club Lounge at the Ben-Gurion Airport provides communications services, a selection of various publications and a Matmid Service Center. Subsidiaries of the firm include Sun D'Or International Airlines, Ltd.; Tamam; Catit; Superstar Holidays; ACI; Borenstein Caterers; Airtour; and Holiday Lines. Sun D'Or operates charter flights between Israel and Europe. In 2016, the firm phased out the last Boeing 737-700; and signed for the purchase of nine new 787-800 and 787-900 Dreamliner aircraft, and will lease another six from leasing companies.

FINANCIAL DATA: *Note: Data for latest year may not have been available at press time.*

In U.S. $	2015	2014	2013	2012	2011	2010
Revenue	2,054,041,000	2,081,303,000	2,103,020,000	2,015,642,000	2,043,174,000	1,972,239,000
R&D Expense						
Operating Income	169,767,000	-3,650,000	37,999,000	11,478,000	-43,316,000	88,043,000
Operating Margin %	8.26%	-.17%	1.80%	.56%	-2.11%	4.46%
SGA Expense	288,148,000	305,481,000	310,848,000	304,586,000	313,318,000	235,405,000
Net Income	106,534,000	-28,060,000	25,442,000	-18,831,000	-49,395,000	57,055,000
Operating Cash Flow	271,418,000	158,558,000	185,242,000	78,270,000	61,880,000	203,291,000
Capital Expenditure	136,911,000	176,997,000	172,273,000	88,679,000	109,102,000	49,602,000
EBITDA	321,316,000	118,932,000	188,704,000	130,915,000	114,046,000	205,500,000
Return on Assets %	6.56%	-1.78%	1.65%	-1.21%	-2.98%	3.36%
Return on Equity %	69.58%	-19.26%	15.35%	-12.02%	-24.13%	30.73%
Debt to Equity	2.25	4.47	2.64	3.14	3.44	2.26

CONTACT INFORMATION:

Phone: 03-9771111   Fax: 02-6770255
Toll-Free: 800-223-6700
Address: 2 Hapoel Sports Association, Malha, 4/Fl, Lod, Jerusalem 70100 Israel

STOCK TICKER/OTHER:

Stock Ticker: ELALY   Exchange: GREY
Employees: 3,788   Fiscal Year Ends: 12/31
Parent Company:

SALARIES/BONUSES:

Top Exec. Salary: $ Bonus: $
Second Exec. Salary: $ Bonus: $

OTHER THOUGHTS:

Estimated Female Officers or Directors: 1
Hot Spot for Advancement for Women/Minorities: Y

Embraer SA

NAIC Code: 336411

TYPES OF BUSINESS:

Aircraft Manufacturing
Commuter Aircraft
Business Jets
Aircraft Maintenance
Military Aircraft
Agricultural Aircraft
Aircraft Leasing
After-Sales Service

BRANDS/DIVISIONS/AFFILIATES:

EMB
ERJ
Embraer
Lineage
Phenom
Legacy
Embraer Aircraft Maintenance Services
Industria Aeronautica de Portugal

CONTACTS: Note: Officers with more than one job title may be intentionally listed here more than once.

Frederico P. F. Curado, CEO
Artur A. V. Coutinho, COO
Frederico P. F. Curado, Pres.
Jose Antonio de Almeida Filippo, CFO
Jackson Schneider, Exec. VP-People
Mauro Kern, Jr., Exec. VP-Tech.
Mauro Kern, Jr., Exec. VP-Eng.
Jose Antonio de Almeida Filippo, Investor Rel. Officer
Paulo Cesar de Souza e Silva, Pres., Commercial Aviation
Luiz Carlos Siqueira Aguiar, Pres., Defense & Security
Flavio Rimoli, Exec. VP-Corp. Svcs.
Jackson Schneider, Exec. VP-Institutional Rel. & Sustainability
Alexandre Goncalves Silva, Chmn.

GROWTH PLANS/SPECIAL FEATURES:

Embraer SA manufactures commercial aircraft for the global market. Originally a government-controlled company producing aircraft for the Brazilian Air Force, the firm is now one of the leading global manufacturers of commercial aircraft. Its commercial jets business produces three classes of jets: ERJ, EMB and Embraer. The ERJ family is composed of four regionally designed jets: the ERJ 135, ERJ 140, ERJ 145 and ERJ 145 XR. Each jet is built specifically for use in regional networks and seats between 37-50 passengers. The firm's EMB jet is a pressurized twin wing-mounted turboprop aircraft that accommodates up to 30 passengers. The Embraer line of jets includes four models, 170, 175, 190 and 195, and is designed to provide greater mission range, short ground turnaround time, common crew type rating, high-fuel efficiency and enhanced cabin configuration flexibility. The executive jet segment supplies executive jets to fractional ownership companies, charter companies, air-taxi companies and high net-worth individuals. Its models include the Phenom, Legacy and Lineage lines. The company's defense systems business manufactures transport, training, light attack and surveillance aircraft, which it sells to the Brazilian Air Force and the governments of more than 20 other countries. The segment's current development program is focused on the Super Tucano, a light attack and advanced pilot training aircraft. The aviation services business segment includes after-sales support for its aircraft; spare parts, training and aeronautical systems. These operations are conducted through Embraer Aircraft Maintenance Services (EAMS), which is based in the U.S. and Industria Aeronautica de Portugal, located in the Portugal. Additionally, the firm has fully-owned workshops and parts warehouses in the USA, France, China, Singapore and Brazil.

FINANCIAL DATA: Note: Data for latest year may not have been available at press time.

In U.S. $	2015	2014	2013	2012	2011	2010
Revenue	5,928,100,000	6,288,800,000	6,235,000,000	6,177,900,000	5,803,000,000	5,364,100,000
R&D Expense	41,700,000	47,100,000	74,700,000	77,300,000	85,300,000	72,100,000
Operating Income	331,500,000	543,300,000	713,400,000	612,100,000	318,200,000	391,700,000
Operating Margin %	5.59%	8.63%	11.44%	9.90%	5.48%	7.30%
SGA Expense	543,600,000	627,400,000	664,900,000	762,500,000	681,800,000	571,600,000
Net Income	69,200,000	334,700,000	342,000,000	347,800,000	111,600,000	330,200,000
Operating Cash Flow	862,500,000	482,300,000	564,600,000	694,800,000	480,200,000	873,800,000
Capital Expenditure	769,100,000	699,100,000	754,200,000	580,400,000	551,700,000	328,300,000
EBITDA	830,000,000	923,200,000	1,021,300,000	1,038,800,000	737,600,000	750,100,000
Return on Assets %	.62%	3.25%	3.48%	3.79%	1.29%	3.92%
Return on Equity %	1.84%	9.17%	10.07%	11.10%	3.69%	12.30%
Debt to Equity	0.98	0.74	0.70	0.65	0.51	0.57

CONTACT INFORMATION:

Phone: 55 1239271216   Fax: 55 1239226070
Toll-Free:
Address: Ave. Brigadeiro Faria Lima, 2170, Sao Paulo, SP 12227-901 Brazil

STOCK TICKER/OTHER:

Stock Ticker: ERJ
Employees: 23,050
Parent Company:

Exchange: NYS
Fiscal Year Ends: 12/31

SALARIES/BONUSES:

Top Exec. Salary: $ Bonus: $
Second Exec. Salary: $ Bonus: $

OTHER THOUGHTS:

Estimated Female Officers or Directors:
Hot Spot for Advancement for Women/Minorities:

Emirates Group (The)

NAIC Code: 481111

TYPES OF BUSINESS:

Airline
Air Cargo
Airport Ground Services
Hotels & Resorts
Education-Aviation
Aviation Security
IT Services
Travel Agencies

BRANDS/DIVISIONS/AFFILIATES:

Emirates Airline
dnata
Emirates SkyCargo
Emirates Holidays
Arabian Adventures
Emirates Hotels & Resorts
EmQuest
Mercator

CONTACTS: Note: Officers with more than one job title may be intentionally listed here more than once.

Ahmed bin Saeed Al-Maktoum, CEO
Adel Ahmad Al Redha, COO
Thierry Antinori, Chief Commercial Officer
Abdulaziz Al Ali, Exec. VP-Human Resources
Anna Garcia, Mgr.-Public Rel. (Europe)
Nigel Hopkins, Exec. VP-Service Dept.
Timothy Clark, Pres., Emirates Airline
Gary Chapman, Pres., Group Svcs. & Dnata
Ismail Ali Al Albanna, Exec. VP-Dnata
Ahmed bin Saeed Al-Maktoum, Chmn.

GROWTH PLANS/SPECIAL FEATURES:

The Emirates Group operates Emirates Airline, serving more than 151 destinations in 80 countries on six continents. Since starting with two airplanes in 1985, it has expanded its fleet size to 231. The firm's fleet includes Boeing 777, which typically carry 283-368 passengers; and the superjumbo Airbus A380, which can haul 525-853 people. Operating from its hub in Dubai, Emirates has air service agreements with Niger, Ivory Coast, Benin, Gambia, Mozambique, Rwanda, Burkina Faso, Botswana, Chile, Colombia, Panama, Uruguay, Latvia, Portugal, Slovenia, Bosnia-Herzegovina, Croatia, Macedonia and Tajikistan. Besides the airlines, the other major member of the Group is dnata, one of the largest travel management firms in the UAE and sole provider of ground handling services at Dubai International airport. Its other services include aircraft engineering, IT services and airline ticket sales. The company has more than 50 subsidiaries, making it one of the more comprehensive travel and tourism operations in the Middle East region. Some of the subsidiaries include: shipping company Emirates SkyCargo; travel agency Emirates Holidays; tour direction group Arabian Adventures; Emirates Hotels & Resorts (which operates hotels in Dubai and resorts in the UAE, Australia and the Seychelles); travel-related product distributor EmQuest; security firm Transguard; Emirates Aviation College (a training company for the airline industry); and Mercator, an IT solutions provider for the air travel industry. In 2016, dnata agreed to acquire a stake in Destination Management Company.

The firm offers employees benefits including medical coverage, air travel privileges, annual leave provisions (including annual leave tickets for expatriate employees), utilities and transportation allowances and educational assistance.

FINANCIAL DATA: Note: Data for latest year may not have been available at press time.

In U.S. $	2015	2014	2013	2012	2011	2010
Revenue	22,736,847,877	21,971,141,196	19,373,146,558	16,961,000,000	14,762,700,000	11,828,800,000
R&D Expense						
Operating Income						
Operating Margin %						
SGA Expense						
Net Income	2,267,900,622	1,604,410,580	1,159,815,168	772,937,855	493,602,604	963,072,000
Operating Cash Flow						
Capital Expenditure						
EBITDA						
Return on Assets %						
Return on Equity %						
Debt to Equity						

CONTACT INFORMATION:

Phone: 9714-708-1111   Fax: 9714-286-4066
Toll-Free:
Address: P.O. Box 686, Dubai, United Arab Emirates

STOCK TICKER/OTHER:

Stock Ticker: Government-Owned
Employees: 61,205
Parent Company:

Exchange:
Fiscal Year Ends: 03/31

SALARIES/BONUSES:

Top Exec. Salary: $ Bonus: $
Second Exec. Salary: $ Bonus: $

OTHER THOUGHTS:

Estimated Female Officers or Directors: 1
Hot Spot for Advancement for Women/Minorities: Y

Sales, profits and employees may be estimates. Financial information, benefits and other data can change quickly and may vary from those stated here.

Endeavor Air

www.endeavorair.com

NAIC Code: 481111

TYPES OF BUSINESS:

Regional Airline

BRANDS/DIVISIONS/AFFILIATES:

Delta Air Lines Inc
Delta Connection

GROWTH PLANS/SPECIAL FEATURES:

Endeavor Air is an American regional airline that operates as Delta Connection for Delta Air Lines. Endeavor's headquarters are based at the Minneapolis-Saint Paul International Airport, and it has hubs at Detroit Metropolitan Wayne County Airport, Minneapolis-Saint Paul International Airport, New York's LaGuardia Airport and John F. Kennedy International Airport. Its fleet consists of 134 Bombardier regional jet aircraft, which provides 600 daily flights to more than 100 cities in the U.S and Canada. Endeavor is a wholly-owned subsidiary of Delta Air Lines, Inc.

The company offers its employees medical, dental and life insurance; flexible spending accounts; a 401(k); a vision plan; paid disability and sick leave; and critical illness insurance.

CONTACTS: Note: Officers with more than one job title may be intentionally listed here more than once.

Ryan Gumm, CEO
John Daly, COO
Ryan Gumm, Pres.
Loren Neuenschwander, CFO
Bill Donohue, VP-Maintenance & Technical
Mike Becker, Chief Admin. Officer
L. Russell Elander, VP-Flight Oper.
Keith Glazier, VP-Safety, Security & Compliance
D. Philip Reedm Jr., VP-Resource Planning & Scheduling

FINANCIAL DATA: Note: Data for latest year may not have been available at press time.

In U.S. $	2015	2014	2013	2012	2011	2010
Revenue	110,650,000	533,476,000	585,233,000	781,096,000	665,059,000	1,020,766,976
R&D Expense						
Operating Income						
Operating Margin %						
SGA Expense						
Net Income	-2,031,000	-23,083,000	-20,900,000	-99,006,000	-31,478,000	12,770,000
Operating Cash Flow						
Capital Expenditure						
EBITDA						
Return on Assets %						
Return on Equity %						
Debt to Equity						

CONTACT INFORMATION:

Phone: Fax:
Toll-Free: 800-603-4594
Address: 7500 Airline Drive, Minneapolis, MN 55450-1101 United States

STOCK TICKER/OTHER:

Stock Ticker: Subsidiary
Employees: 2,500
Parent Company: Delta Air Lines Inc
Exchange:
Fiscal Year Ends: 12/31

SALARIES/BONUSES:

Top Exec. Salary: $ Bonus: $
Second Exec. Salary: $ Bonus: $

OTHER THOUGHTS:

Estimated Female Officers or Directors:
Hot Spot for Advancement for Women/Minorities: Y

Sales, profits and employees may be estimates. Financial information, benefits and other data can change quickly and may vary from those stated here.

Enterprise Holdings Inc

NAIC Code: 532111

www.enterpriseholdings.com

TYPES OF BUSINESS:

Car & Truck Rental
Vanpool Services

BRANDS/DIVISIONS/AFFILIATES:

Alamo Rent A Car
National Car Rental
Enterprise Rent-A-Car
Enterprise Car Sales
Enterprise Truck Rental
Enterprise CarShare
Enterprise Rideshare
Zimride

CONTACTS: Note: Officers with more than one job title may be intentionally listed here more than once.

Pamela Nicholson, CEO
Christine Taylor, COO
Pamela Nicholson, Pres.
Rick Short, CFO
Patrick T. Farrell, Chief Mktg. Officer
Edward Adams, Sr. VP-Human Resources
Craig Kennedy, CIO
Lee Kaplan, Chief Admin. Officer
Matthew G. Darrah, Exec. VP-North American Oper.
Greg Stubblefield, Chief Strategy Officer
Patrick T. Farrell, Chief Comm. Officer
Rose Langhorst, Treas.
Steve Bloom, Pres., Enterprise Fleet Mgmt.
Jo Ann Taylor Kindle, Pres., Enterprise Holdings Foundation
Andrew C. Taylor, Chmn.
Greg Stubblefield, Exec. VP-Global Sales & Mktg.

GROWTH PLANS/SPECIAL FEATURES:

Enterprise Holdings, Inc. is the parent company of Alamo Rent A Car, National Car Rental and Enterprise Rent-A-Car car rental agencies. The company also owns Enterprise Car Sales, Enterprise Truck Rental, as well as car/ride sharing programs Enterprise CarShare, Enterprise Rideshare and Zimride by Enterprise. The company's combined rental fleet is the largest in the world, at 1.5 million vehicles. It serves more than 6,000 retail and airport locations in the U.S., and approximately 8,6000 worldwide, including Mexico, the Caribbean, Latin America, Canada, Ireland, the U.K., Germany and Asia. Alamo Rent A Car is a budget rental car company catering to leisure and vacation customers, particularly international travelers visiting North America. It operates self-service kiosks at 63 U.S. locations. National Car Rental is a premium rental brand that serves frequent business travelers and offers the Emerald Club frequent-renter benefits program. Enterprise Rent-A-Car boasts over 5,500 retail and airport offices in the U.S. Enterprise Car Sales is a used-car reseller that provides non-negotiable pricing and after-market warranties on used cars acquired through trade-in or extracted from the rental fleet. Enterprise Truck Rental provides commercial-grade trucks such as Â¾- to 1-ton pickups, cargo vans, straight trucks, as well as stakebed trucks (from 16 to 26 feet long), all equipped for commercial use. Enterprise CarShare is a car sharing program that allows customers to rent a car for flexible periods of time through an online membership portal. Enterprise Rideshare specializes in customized vanpool programs and commuter services for individuals and/or companies. Zimride is a ride-sharing platform for companies and universities. In June 2016, the firm acquired vRide, a vanpooling company that has been serving U.S. commuters for nearly 40 years.

Enterprise Holdings offers its employees medical, dental and vision insurance; prescription drug coverage; flexible spending accounts; life insurance; and long-term disability plans.

FINANCIAL DATA: Note: Data for latest year may not have been available at press time.

In U.S. $	2015	2014	2013	2012	2011	2010
Revenue	19,400,000,000	17,800,000,000	16,400,000,000	15,400,000,000	14,100,000,000	12,600,000,000
R&D Expense						
Operating Income						
Operating Margin %						
SGA Expense						
Net Income			2,600,000,000	2,375,000,000	2,100,000,000	1,880,000,000
Operating Cash Flow						
Capital Expenditure						
EBITDA						
Return on Assets %						
Return on Equity %						
Debt to Equity						

CONTACT INFORMATION:

Phone: 314-512-2880   Fax: 314-512-4706
Toll-Free:
Address: 600 Corporate Park Dr., St. Louis, MO 63105 United States

STOCK TICKER/OTHER:

Stock Ticker: Private   Exchange:
Employees: 93,000   Fiscal Year Ends: 03/31
Parent Company:

SALARIES/BONUSES:

Top Exec. Salary: $ Bonus: $
Second Exec. Salary: $ Bonus: $

OTHER THOUGHTS:

Estimated Female Officers or Directors: 5
Hot Spot for Advancement for Women/Minorities: Y

Etihad Airways

www.etihadairways.com

NAIC Code: 481111

TYPES OF BUSINESS:

Airline-Global
Vacation Packages
Air Freight

BRANDS/DIVISIONS/AFFILIATES:

Etihad Holidays
Etihad Cargo
Etihad Guest
Amadeus Gulf
Hala Abu Dhabi
airberlin
Air Seychelles
Alitalia

CONTACTS: Note: Officers with more than one job title may be intentionally listed here more than once.

James Hogan, CEO
Richard Hill, COO
James Hogan, Pres.
James Rigney, CFO
Ray Gammell, Chief People & Performance Officer
Kevin Knight, Chief Strategy & Planning Officer
Peter Baumgartner, Chief Commercial Officer
Mohamed Mubarak Fadhel Al Mazrouei, Chmn.

GROWTH PLANS/SPECIAL FEATURES:

Etihad Airways is the national airline of the UAE. Its fleet consists of 120 aircraft, including Boeing and Airbus aircraft, offering flights to 580 combined network destinations across Asia, Africa, Europe, Australia, the Middle East and North America. Additionally, it has codeshare agreements with more than 49 international airlines. Specializing in luxury flying, the firm offers Diamond, Pearl and Coral Guest Zones rather than traditional economy, business and first class seats. These Guest Zones range from spacious seats in Coral to personal suites and massaging chairs that fold into beds in Diamond. Etihad's loyalty program, Etihad Guest, has more than 1.3 million members. Additional operations include its leisure division, Etihad Holidays, which offers vacation travel packages, and Etihad Cargo, an air cargo services subsidiary. Etihad Holidays offers vacationers custom holiday packages, including flight, hotel booking and car rental, to worldwide destinations. Etihad Cargo offers cargo freighting to 25 of the airline's passenger destinations and 13 freighter-only destinations. It maintains a fleet of nine Boeing and Airbus cargo aircraft. Customers of Etihad Cargo can track their shipment remotely via mobile phone. The company also owns interest in a joint venture with Amadeus International, Amadeus Gulf, which provides global distribution services. Additionally, the firm owns 29.21% of airberlin, 49% stake in Alitalia, 49% in Air Serbia, 24% in Jet Airways, 25.1% in Virgin Australian Holdings and 40% of Air Seychelles and operates Hala Abu Dhabi, an in-house destination management company that provides business and leisure activities in the UAE.

Etihad offers employees special facilities such as gyms and medical care, health insurance, education allowance, tax-free pay and end of service benefits.

FINANCIAL DATA: Note: Data for latest year may not have been available at press time.

In U.S. $	2015	2014	2013	2012	2011	2010
Revenue	9,000,000,000	7,869,000,000	6,100,000,000	4,400,000,000	4,100,000,000	2,950,000,000
R&D Expense						
Operating Income						
Operating Margin %						
SGA Expense						
Net Income						
Operating Cash Flow						
Capital Expenditure						
EBITDA						
Return on Assets %						
Return on Equity %						
Debt to Equity						

CONTACT INFORMATION:

Phone: 971-2-511-0000   Fax: 971-2-511-1200
Toll-Free:
Address: Khalifa City A, Abu Dhabi,   United Arab Emirates

STOCK TICKER/OTHER:

Stock Ticker: Government-Owned   Exchange:
Employees: 26,566   Fiscal Year Ends: 12/31
Parent Company:

SALARIES/BONUSES:

Top Exec. Salary: $ Bonus: $
Second Exec. Salary: $ Bonus: $

OTHER THOUGHTS:

Estimated Female Officers or Directors:
Hot Spot for Advancement for Women/Minorities:

Euro Disney SCA

corporate.disneylandparis.com

NAIC Code: 713110

TYPES OF BUSINESS:

Theme Park
Resorts
Hotels
Golf
Property Developments

BRANDS/DIVISIONS/AFFILIATES:

Walt Disney Company (The)
Prince Alwaleed
Invesco Limited
Euro Disney Associes SCA
Disneland Park
Walt Disney Studios Park
Golf Disneyland
Disney Village

CONTACTS: Note: Officers with more than one job title may be intentionally listed here more than once.

Tom Wolber, Pres,
Daniel Delcourt, Sr. VP-COO
Mark Stead, CFO
Darlene Papalini, Sr. VP-Mktg. & Sales
Daniel Dreux, VP-Human Resources
Gilles Dobelle, General Counsel
Francois Banon, VP-Comm.
Olivier Lambert, Contact-Investor Rel.
Julien Kauffmann, VP-Revenue Mgmt. & Analytics
Francis Borezee, VP-Resort & Real Estate Dev.

GROWTH PLANS/SPECIAL FEATURES:

Euro Disney SCA operates Disneyland Resort Paris, a top European vacation destination, through subsidiary Euro Disney Associes SCA (EDA). Located east of Paris, Disneyland Resort Paris comprises Disneyland Park, Walt Disney Studios Park, seven themed hotels (with a total of 5,800 rooms), two convention centers (including one of France's largest conference centers), Golf Disneyland and Disney Village, a 322,917-square-foot dining, shopping and entertainment center. Combined, the resort's two theme parks, Disneyland Park and Walt Disney Studios Park, offer 58 attractions, including Space Mountain Mission 2, the Twilight Zone Tower of Terror, Big Thunder Mountain and the Cars Race Rally. Wholly-owned EDA-subsidiary EDL Hotels SCA operates Disney Village as well as six of the Disney themed hotels, including Disney's Newport Bay Club, Sequoia Lodge, Hotel Santa Fe, Hotel New York and Hotel Cheyenne. The other two hotels, Disneyland Hotel and the Davy Crockett Ranch, are operated by EDA itself. Located in Hotel New York and Newport Bay Club, the firm's convention centers, totaling almost 183,000 square feet, handle over 1,000 events per year. EDA also has a large stake in Val d'Europe, a 4,800-acre full-scale town near the park, featuring a shopping center, international business center, offices, apartments, homes and hotels. Euro Disney is 76.71%-owned by The Walt Disney Company, with Prince Alwaleed holding 10%, Invesco Limited holding 6% and other shareholders holding the remainder.

FINANCIAL DATA: Note: Data for latest year may not have been available at press time.

In U.S. $	2015	2014	2013	2012	2011	2010
Revenue	1,551,350,000	1,445,825,000	1,479,381,000	1,496,215,000	1,466,162,000	1,441,532,000
R&D Expense						
Operating Income	-63,721,610	-73,889,950	-31,069,930	3,841,374	12,992,880	38,526,720
Operating Margin %	-4.10%	-5.11%	-2.10%	.25%	.88%	2.67%
SGA Expense	288,780,900	265,280,800	274,658,200	274,997,200	263,699,000	263,247,100
Net Income	-95,130,490	-105,524,800	-72,760,140	-96,712,230	-62,817,760	-51,067,680
Operating Cash Flow	78,070,270	88,351,600	107,332,500	161,224,700	190,599,900	267,427,400
Capital Expenditure	166,421,900	157,948,300	131,284,600	167,325,700	86,995,820	
EBITDA	158,061,200	128,573,000	163,032,400	200,203,400	208,451,000	231,047,300
Return on Assets %	-3.78%	-4.32%	-2.93%	-3.56%	-2.11%	-1.47%
Return on Equity %	-40.50%			-211.88%	-48.15%	-24.33%
Debt to Equity	1.71				19.23	12.82

CONTACT INFORMATION:

Phone: 33 164744000   Fax: 33 164745636
Toll-Free:
Address: Route Nationale 34, Immeubles Administratifs, Paris, 77144 France

STOCK TICKER/OTHER:

Stock Ticker: EUDSF   Exchange: PINX
Employees: 13,674   Fiscal Year Ends: 09/30
Parent Company: Walt Disney Company (The)

SALARIES/BONUSES:

Top Exec. Salary: $ Bonus: $
Second Exec. Salary: $ Bonus: $

OTHER THOUGHTS:

Estimated Female Officers or Directors: 1
Hot Spot for Advancement for Women/Minorities:

Sales, profits and employees may be estimates. Financial information, benefits and other data can change quickly and may vary from those stated here.

Eurotunnel Group

www.eurotunnelgroup.com

NAIC Code: 482111

TYPES OF BUSINESS:

Line-Haul Railroads
Passenger Transport
Freight & Logistics
Security Consulting

BRANDS/DIVISIONS/AFFILIATES:

GB Railfreight
Europorte
ElecLink

CONTACTS: *Note: Officers with more than one job title may be intentionally listed here more than once.*

Jacques Gounon, CEO
Michel Boudoussier, COO
Jo Willacy, Dir.-Commercial
Patrick Etienne, Dir.-Bus. Svcs.
Michel Boudoussier, Deputy CEO-Concession & Channel Tunnel
Pascal Sainson, Chmn.-Europorte SAS
Emmanuel Moulin, Deputy CEO-Corporate
Jacques Gounon, Chmn.

GROWTH PLANS/SPECIAL FEATURES:

Eurotunnel Group manages the infrastructure of the Channel Tunnel between the U.K. and France, the longest undersea tunnel in the world, and also operates truck shuttle and passenger services through the tunnel. The Channel, as it is often called, runs from Folkestone to Calais at a total length of 31 miles (approximately 23 of which are underwater), crossing the Strait of Dover at an average depth of 131 feet below the seabed. The company has been granted a concession by the British and French governments to operate the Channel Tunnel until 2086. Eurotunnel operates a fleet of 74 electric locomotives and 17 diesel locomotives. The shuttles and trains are all electric, thus substantially limiting greenhouse gas emissions to a level well below that of the competing maritime companies. Annually, it brings across over 2.5 million cars and 1.5 million trucks. The diesel locomotives are used for rescue and shunting purposes only. Europorte, the group's rail freight subsidiary, provides freight transport and supply chain logistics services throughout France and in the U.K. through its GB Railfreight subsidiary. The firm also earns toll revenue from independent train operators that use the tunnel. Eurotunnel's primary customer, Eurostar, offers direct, high speed rail services between London, Paris and Brussels, with a total trip time between Paris and London averaging 2 hours and 15 minutes. Additionally, mobile telephone and Internet services are also available within the tunnel. Since its official opening in 1994, it has transported more than 300 million passengers and 250 million tons of freight goods. In May 2016, the firm agreed to acquire STAR Capital's 51% stake in ElecLink, which will cause Eurotunnel Groupe to hold 100% of ElecLink.

FINANCIAL DATA: *Note: Data for latest year may not have been available at press time.*

In U.S. $	2015	2014	2013	2012	2011	2010
Revenue	1,380,649,000	1,363,363,000	1,233,743,000	1,155,969,000	965,044,600	832,202,000
R&D Expense						
Operating Income	437,237,600	377,500,900	321,994,100	333,874,100	307,254,600	214,504,600
Operating Margin %	31.66%	27.68%	26.09%	28.88%	31.83%	25.77%
SGA Expense						
Net Income	113,491,100	64,653,710	114,519,300	38,441,980	12,735,280	-64,173,540
Operating Cash Flow	614,956,500	567,634,200	511,335,500	520,394,300	469,984,200	402,666,400
Capital Expenditure	153,236,900	145,304,500	84,665,010	207,689,500	110,160,400	56,383,460
EBITDA	513,347,600	564,958,700	517,428,500	516,203,800	491,834,800	400,879,000
Return on Assets %	1.36%	.78%	1.39%	.47%	.15%	-.79%
Return on Equity %	5.87%	2.70%	4.34%	1.48%	.43%	-1.92%
Debt to Equity	2.46	2.29	1.56		1.61	1.33

CONTACT INFORMATION:

Phone: 33 140980467   Fax: 33 321006902
Toll-Free:
Address: 3, ru La Boetie, Paris, 75008 France

STOCK TICKER/OTHER:

Stock Ticker: GRPTF   Exchange: GREY
Employees: 2,361   Fiscal Year Ends: 12/31
Parent Company:

SALARIES/BONUSES:

Top Exec. Salary: $ Bonus: $
Second Exec. Salary: $ Bonus: $

OTHER THOUGHTS:

Estimated Female Officers or Directors: 1
Hot Spot for Advancement for Women/Minorities:

Expedia Inc

NAIC Code: 519130

www.expedia.com

TYPES OF BUSINESS:

Online Travel Services
Online Reservations
Corporate Travel Services
Vacation Packages
Retail Travel Services Kiosks
Destination Activities & Tours
Online Travel Information

BRANDS/DIVISIONS/AFFILIATES:

Expedia.com
Hotwire.com
Venere
Expedia CruiseShipCenters
trivago GmbH
Travelocity
HomeAway Inc
Orbtiz Worldwide Inc

CONTACTS: Note: Officers with more than one job title may be intentionally listed here more than once.

Dara Khosrowshahi, CEO
Mark Okerstrom, CFO
Barry Diller, Chairman of the Board
Lance Soliday, Chief Accounting Officer
Victor Kaufman, Director
Robert Dzielak, Executive VP

GROWTH PLANS/SPECIAL FEATURES:

Expedia, Inc. is an online travel service offering travel shopping and reservation services, publishing schedules, pricing and availability information for numerous airlines, lodging properties, car rental companies, cruise lines and multiple-destination service providers, including restaurants, attractions and tours. The company's travel portfolio includes more than 269,000 properties, 1.2 million live vacation rental listings in 200 countries, as well as 400 airlines. The Expedia brand web sites, for both USA (Expedia.com) and international travelers, offer a large variety of travel products and services available directly to travelers. It also operates as a merchant by directly contracting from suppliers and selling discounted products directly to the consumer. The firm owns Hotels.com, which provides a full portfolio of hotel contacts around the world, and Hotwire.com, a web site that offers travelers discount airfare. Other subsidiaries include Venere, a resource for European hotels; Classic Vacations, a premium vacation packaging agency; eLong, an online travel service based in Beijing, China; Egencia, a travel management service for corporate customers; Expedia CruiseShipCenters, a network of cruise vacation retail locations; Expedia Local Expert, which specializes in local tours and attractions; Expedia Affiliate Network, which powers bookings for leading airlines and hotels; trivago GmbH, an online hotel metasearch company; wotif.com Holdings Limited, an operator of travel brands in the Asia Pacific; and CarRentals.com, an online car rental booking company. In 2015, Expedia acquired Travelocity, HomeAway, Inc. and Orbitz Worldwide, Inc.

The company offers employees medical, life, AD&D, disability, dental and vision insurance; flexible spending accounts; onsite flu shots; a 401(k); adoption assistance; an employee assistance program; a group legal program; tuition reimbursement; travel as

FINANCIAL DATA: Note: Data for latest year may not have been available at press time.

In U.S. $	2015	2014	2013	2012	2011	2010
Revenue	6,672,317,000	5,763,485,000	4,771,259,000	4,030,347,000	3,449,009,000	3,348,109,000
R&D Expense	830,244,000	686,154,000		484,898,000	380,999,000	362,447,000
Operating Income	413,566,000	517,764,000	366,060,000	431,724,000	479,609,000	731,915,000
Operating Margin %	6.19%	8.98%	7.67%	10.71%	13.90%	21.86%
SGA Expense	3,850,412,000	3,275,241,000	3,151,043,000	2,183,416,000	1,805,204,000	1,518,250,000
Net Income	764,465,000	398,097,000	232,850,000	280,171,000	472,294,000	421,500,000
Operating Cash Flow	1,368,045,000	1,366,959,000	763,200,000	1,229,575,000	1,030,072,000	777,483,000
Capital Expenditure	787,041,000	328,387,000	308,581,000	235,697,000	207,837,000	155,189,000
EBITDA	1,552,502,000	908,162,000	671,526,000	633,797,000	647,724,000	877,384,000
Return on Assets %	6.23%	4.75%	3.14%	4.12%	7.17%	6.69%
Return on Equity %	22.99%	20.26%	10.52%	12.50%	19.38%	15.74%
Debt to Equity	0.65	0.97	0.58	0.54	0.56	0.61

CONTACT INFORMATION:

Phone: 425 679-7200 Fax: 425 564-7240
Toll-Free: 800-397-3342
Address: 333 108th Ave. NE, Bellevue, WA 98004 United States

STOCK TICKER/OTHER:

Stock Ticker: EXPE
Employees: 18,210
Parent Company:

Exchange: NAS
Fiscal Year Ends: 12/31

SALARIES/BONUSES:

Top Exec. Salary:
$1,000,000
Second Exec. Salary:
$465,000

Bonus: $3,500,000

Bonus: $2,500,000

OTHER THOUGHTS:

Estimated Female Officers or Directors: 1

Hot Spot for Advancement for Women/Minorities:

Sales, profits and employees may be estimates. Financial information, benefits and other data can change quickly and may vary from those stated here.

ExpressJet Airlines Inc

www.expressjet.com

NAIC Code: 481111

TYPES OF BUSINESS:

Regional Airline

BRANDS/DIVISIONS/AFFILIATES:

SkyWest Inc
United Express
United
American Eagle

CONTACTS: *Note: Officers with more than one job title may be intentionally listed here more than once.*

Terry Vais, COO
Brad Holt, Pres.
Kevin Wade, VP-Finance
Charlie Tutt, VP-Flight Oper.
Terry Vais, VP-Customer Care
Brandee Reynolds, VP-In-flight Svcs.
Ken Ashworth, VP-Maintenance

GROWTH PLANS/SPECIAL FEATURES:

ExpressJet Airlines, Inc. is a regional air carrier based in Atlanta, Georgia. The airline, which serves as a Delta Connection and United Express carrier, averages over 1,500 daily departures to more than 180 destinations in the U.S., the Bahamas, Mexico and Canada. Its hubs are located at a number of U.S. airports in Atlanta (ATL), Cleveland (CLE), Chicago (ORD), Dallas (DFW), Detroit (DTW), Houston (IAH) and Newark (EWR). ExpressJet transported more than 26 million people in 2015. The carrier's fleet consists of 301 Bombardier and Embraer jet aircraft. Currently, its fleet includes five ERJ135s, 173 ERJ145s, flown under the United Express, United and American Eagle brand names; 62 CRJ200s, primarily used for Delta and American Eagle flights; 38 CRJ700s, flown exclusively for Delta; and 28 CRJ900s, also flown solely for Delta. SkyWest, Inc., the firm's parent company, views the firm as a mission-critical element of its broader operation, both in terms of the potential for profitable regional service and as a conduit for routing passengers to its long-haul domestic and international flights.

Employees of the firm receive benefits including medical, dental, vision and mental health benefits; a prescription drug plan; domestic partner benefits; long-term disability; life insurance; an employee assistance program; a flexible spending account; an

FINANCIAL DATA: *Note: Data for latest year may not have been available at press time.*

In U.S. $	2015	2014	2013	2012	2011	2010
Revenue	1,169,923,000	1,346,859,000	1,466,341,000	1,593,527,000	1,640,837,000	808,001,000
R&D Expense						
Operating Income						
Operating Margin %						
SGA Expense						
Net Income						
Operating Cash Flow						
Capital Expenditure						
EBITDA						
Return on Assets %						
Return on Equity %						
Debt to Equity						

CONTACT INFORMATION:

Phone: 404-856-1000 Fax: 404-856-1405
Toll-Free:
Address: 100 Hartsfield Center Pkwy., Ste. 700, Atlanta, GA 30354 United States

STOCK TICKER/OTHER:

Stock Ticker: Subsidiary
Employees: 8,500
Parent Company: SkyWest Inc

Exchange:
Fiscal Year Ends: 12/31

SALARIES/BONUSES:

Top Exec. Salary: $ Bonus: $
Second Exec. Salary: $ Bonus: $

OTHER THOUGHTS:

Estimated Female Officers or Directors: 2
Hot Spot for Advancement for Women/Minorities: Y

Sales, profits and employees may be estimates. Financial information, benefits and other data can change quickly and may vary from those stated here.

Extended Stay America Inc

www.extendedstayhotels.com

NAIC Code: 721110

TYPES OF BUSINESS:
Hotels, Extended Stay

BRANDS/DIVISIONS/AFFILIATES:
Extended Stay America
Extended Stay Canada

CONTACTS: *Note: Officers with more than one job title may be intentionally listed here more than once.*
Gerardo Lopez, CEO
Jim Donald, Pres.
Jonathan S. Halkyard, CFO
Tom Seddon, CMO
Kevin Alan Henry, Exec. VP-Human Resources
Ames Flynn, Sr. VP-CIO

GROWTH PLANS/SPECIAL FEATURES:
Extended Stay America, Inc. (ESA), is the operator of the Extended Stay Hotels network, which has 629 extended-stay properties with 69,400 rooms in Canada and most of the major metro areas in the U.S. The company owns and manages moderately price extended-stay hotels under two brand names: Extended Stay America (626 locations) and Extended Stay Canada (three locations). ESA targets large corporate customers with multi-location extended-stay needs and has customized its rooms for this purpose with full kitchens, Internet connections and work/study areas. It offers daily, weekly and monthly rates with discounts for extended stays. ESA hotels include kitchen, living and dining areas; laundry facilities; and pet accommodations. Certain locations offer pools, fitness rooms and individual DVD players. The company's properties are typically located near business centers, airports and entertainment areas. All Extended Stay hotels participate in the affiliate program, which allows individuals to insert the company's link on their website and earn commission when individuals use the link to book stays. Other rewards and promotional programs include Kids Stay Free, AAA and Senior discounts, Suite Offer Email Program and a lowest internet price guarantee. In December 2015, the firm sold its portfolio of hotels that formerly operated under the Crossland Economy Studios brand name.

FINANCIAL DATA: *Note: Data for latest year may not have been available at press time.*

In U.S. $	2015	2014	2013	2012	2011	2010
Revenue	1,284,753,000	1,213,475,000	1,132,800,000	1,011,500,000	942,700,000	87,600,000
R&D Expense						
Operating Income						
Operating Margin %						
SGA Expense						
Net Income	113,040,000	39,596,000	86,200,000	20,700,000	45,600,000	1,767,100,000
Operating Cash Flow						
Capital Expenditure						
EBITDA						
Return on Assets %						
Return on Equity %						
Debt to Equity						

CONTACT INFORMATION:
Phone: 980-345-1600   Fax:
Toll-Free: 800-804-3724
Address: 11525 N. Community House Rd., Ste. 100, Charlotte, NC 28277
United States

STOCK TICKER/OTHER:
Stock Ticker: STAY
Employees: 3,700
Parent Company:

Exchange: NYS
Fiscal Year Ends: 12/31

SALARIES/BONUSES:
Top Exec. Salary: $ Bonus: $
Second Exec. Salary: $ Bonus: $

OTHER THOUGHTS:
Estimated Female Officers or Directors:
Hot Spot for Advancement for Women/Minorities:

Fairmont Raffles Hotels International Inc

www.frhi.com

NAIC Code: 721110

TYPES OF BUSINESS:

Hotels, Luxury
Spa Services
Real Estate Holdings

BRANDS/DIVISIONS/AFFILIATES:

Voyager Partners
Swissotel
Raffles
Fairmont Nanjing
Fairmont Chengdu
Fairmont Jakarta
Fairmont Pekin Moscow
Makkah Clock Royal Tower

CONTACTS: Note: Officers with more than one job title may be intentionally listed here more than once.

William R. Fatt, CEO
Chris J. Cahill, COO

GROWTH PLANS/SPECIAL FEATURES:

Fairmont Raffles Hotels International, Inc. is one of the world's largest luxury hotel firms. It operates over 130 hotels worldwide under the Raffles, Fairmont and Swissotel brand names. The firm offers many services to its business travel clients, such as high-speed Internet access; a 24 hour technology help desk; work centers with photocopying services, secretarial services, a private lounge and boardroom; printers for in-room use; a 24-hour fax service; and express checkout. Fairmont offers various types of resort accommodations, including spa resorts, golf resorts, ski resorts, Fairmont Gold and Fairmont Residences. Fairmont Spas feature Willow Stream spa facilities in many of its hotels. Fairmont Golf properties are located in cities around the world such as Acapulco, Mexico; St. Andrews, Scotland; Zimbali, South Africa; and Southampton, Bermuda. Fairmont Ski destinations include the Fairmont Chateau Whistler, Fairmont Le Manoir Richelieu, Fairmont Tremblant and many others. Fairmont Gold is an exclusive, private floor of the hotel with its own private check-in and check-out desk. Fairmont Gold offers a private lounge; a healthy continental breakfast; afternoon canapes and honor bar; complimentary newspapers; computer access in lounge; in-room high-speed Internet access; and a selection of DVDs, CDs, books and games. Fairmont Residences are located worldwide in locations such as Dubai and Vancouver. These properties are designed to be utilized as primary dwelling or as getaway retreats. Recently, Fairmont opened the Fairmont Nanjing and the Fairmont Chengdu in China; the Fairmont Jakarta in Indonesia; the Fairmont Pekin Moscow in Russia; the Makkah Clock Royal Tower in Riyadh, Saudi Arabia; and the Fairmont Jaipur and Fairmont Makati, its first luxury brand hotels in India and the Philippines respectively. The majority owner of the firm is Voyager Partners. In December 2014, Abu Dhabi's first Fairmont Residences became available for purchase. These luxury residences come fully furnished and overlook the Arabian Gulf. In March 2015, Raffles Jakarta was launched, the first Raffles Hotels & Resort property in the Indonesian market. In December of same year, the firm announced its plans to join AccorHotels.

FINANCIAL DATA: Note: Data for latest year may not have been available at press time.

In U.S. $	2015	2014	2013	2012	2011	2010
Revenue	1,000,000,000	950,000,000	925,000,000	858,000,000	800,000,000	750,000,000
R&D Expense						
Operating Income						
Operating Margin %						
SGA Expense						
Net Income						
Operating Cash Flow						
Capital Expenditure						
EBITDA						
Return on Assets %						
Return on Equity %						
Debt to Equity						

CONTACT INFORMATION:

Phone: 416-874-2600   Fax: 416-874-2601
Toll-Free: 800-257-7544
Address: 155 Wellington St. W., Ste. 3300, Toronto, ON M5K 0C3 Canada

STOCK TICKER/OTHER:

Stock Ticker: Subsidiary   Exchange:
Employees: 31,000   Fiscal Year Ends: 12/31
Parent Company: AccorHotels Group

SALARIES/BONUSES:

Top Exec. Salary: $ Bonus: $
Second Exec. Salary: $ Bonus: $

OTHER THOUGHTS:

Estimated Female Officers or Directors:
Hot Spot for Advancement for Women/Minorities:

Sales, profits and employees may be estimates. Financial information, benefits and other data can change quickly and may vary from those stated here.

FelCor Lodging Trust Inc

NAIC Code: 0

www.felcor.com

TYPES OF BUSINESS:
Real Estate Investment Trust
Hotel Ownership

BRANDS/DIVISIONS/AFFILIATES:
FelCor Lodging LP

CONTACTS: Note: Officers with more than one job title may be intentionally listed here more than once.

Richard Smith, CEO
Michael Hughes, CFO
Thomas Corcoran, Chairman of the Board
Jeffrey Symes, Chief Accounting Officer
Troy Pentecost, Executive VP
Jonathan Yellen, Executive VP
Thomas Hendrick, Executive VP

GROWTH PLANS/SPECIAL FEATURES:
FelCor Lodging Trust, Inc. (FelCor) is a hotel real estate investment trust (REIT) that, through its 99.5% partnership interest in FelCor Lodging LP, holds ownership interests in 41 hotels with a total of 12,443 rooms and suites. The company is among the largest U.S. owners of upscale, all-suite style hotel properties. Its hotels are operated under some of the most recognized and respected hotel brands, such as Doubletree, Embassy Suites, Fairmont, Hilton, Holiday Inn, Marriott, Renaissance, Sheraton and Wyndham as well as premium independent brands (Morgans, Knickerbocker and Royalton). FelCor's properties are located in major business and leisure travel markets, including New York, San Francisco, southern Florida, Atlanta, Los Angeles, Orlando, Dallas, San Diego, Boston and Philadelphia. The firm has alliances with the four brand owners that manage most of FelCor's hotels: Hilton Worldwide, whose brands include Embassy Suites Hotels, Hilton and Doubletree; InterContinental Hotels Group, owner of the Holiday Inn brand; Starwood Hotels & Resorts, whose brands include Sheraton and Westin; and Marriott International, Inc., which owns the Marriott and Renaissance hotel brands. In recent years, FelCor disclosed plans to dispose of its interests in several hotels. In early 2015, the firm sold Embassy Suites San Antonio International Airport Hotel, Embassy Suites Hotel (Raleigh) and Westin Hotel in Dallas Park; it also announced the opening of its Knickerbocker Hotel in New York City.

FINANCIAL DATA: Note: Data for latest year may not have been available at press time.

In U.S. $	2015	2014	2013	2012	2011	2010
Revenue	886,254,000	921,587,000	893,436,000	909,525,000	945,992,000	928,311,000
R&D Expense						
Operating Income	79,713,000	67,192,000	15,367,000	8,552,000	27,105,000	-137,540,000
Operating Margin %	8.99%	7.29%	1.72%	.94%	2.86%	-14.81%
SGA Expense	62,855,000	65,652,000	62,731,000	67,943,000	72,235,000	165,634,000
Net Income	-7,428,000	93,318,000	-61,504,000	-128,007,000	-129,854,000	-223,041,000
Operating Cash Flow	144,609,000	104,818,000	68,461,000	47,309,000	45,865,000	58,812,000
Capital Expenditure	81,961,000	170,229,000	161,910,000	146,324,000	346,638,000	136,449,000
EBITDA	194,165,000	234,264,000	144,541,000	66,490,000	165,997,000	71,263,000
Return on Assets %	-2.26%	2.51%	-4.61%	-7.23%	-7.07%	-10.50%
Return on Equity %					-195.35%	-193.06%
Debt to Equity					19.28	17.24

CONTACT INFORMATION:
Phone: 972 444-4900   Fax: 972 444-4949
Toll-Free:
Address: 545 E. John Carpenter Freeway, Ste. 1300, Irving, TX 75062
United States

STOCK TICKER/OTHER:
Stock Ticker: FCH   Exchange: NYS
Employees: 63   Fiscal Year Ends: 12/31
Parent Company:

SALARIES/BONUSES:
Top Exec. Salary: $787,856   Bonus: $
Second Exec. Salary: Bonus: $
$455,831

OTHER THOUGHTS:
Estimated Female Officers or Directors: 1
Hot Spot for Advancement for Women/Minorities:

Ferrovial SA

NAIC Code: 488119

www.ferrovial.com/en

TYPES OF BUSINESS:

Airport Operations
Construction
Infrastructure Services
Toll Roads
Civil Engineering

BRANDS/DIVISIONS/AFFILIATES:

Cintra
Amey
Ferroser
Cespa
Cadagua
Ferrovial Agroman
Budimex

CONTACTS: *Note: Officers with more than one job title may be intentionally listed here more than once.*

Inigo Meiras, CEO
Ernesto Lopez Mozo, CFO
Jaime Aguirre de Carcer, Dir.-Human Resources
Federico Florez, CIO
Santiago Ortiz, Sec.
Santiago Olivares, CEO-Ferrovial Svcs.
Enrique Diaz-Rato, CEO-Cintra
Alejandro de la Joya, CEO-Ferrovial Agroman
Jorge Gil, CEO-Ferrovial Airports
Rafael del Pino Calvo, Chmn.

GROWTH PLANS/SPECIAL FEATURES:

Ferrovial SA is a leading infrastructure and industrial group with a presence in over 25 countries worldwide. The company has four business units: airports, toll roads, services and construction. Ferrovial's airports segment is one of the leading private airport operators in the world, conducting business largely through London Heathrow Airports (LHR). LHR manages four airports in the U.K.: Heathrow, Southampton, Glasgow and Aberdeen. Cintra is the firm's toll road and car parks division. It manages a total of 28 toll roads in Spain, Portugal, Ireland, Colombia, Australia, Greece, Canada, the U.K. and the U.S. The company's services segment consists of Amey, a British infrastructure maintenance subsidiary; Ferroser, an infrastructure management company in Spain; Cespa, a municipal and waste-water treatment subsidiary; and various other infrastructure and maintenance companies, chiefly in Spain and Portugal. Construction, the firm's original business, covers all aspects of civil engineering and building, including roads, railways, hydraulic works, maritime works, hydroelectric and industrial works. This division includes several subsidiaries: Cadagua, a water and waste treatment plant engineering and construction company; Ferrovial Agroman, the group's flagship construction company, engaged in civil engineering; Budimex, one of Poland's largest construction companies; and Webber, a construction group in Texas. In December 2015, the firm offered to acquire Australian services provider Broadspectrum Ltd. for $494 million (U.S.), but Broadspectrum rejected the offer in January 2016.

FINANCIAL DATA: *Note: Data for latest year may not have been available at press time.*

In U.S. $	2015	2014	2013	2012	2011	2010
Revenue	10,960,340,000	9,944,638,000	9,226,076,000	8,683,765,000	8,412,609,000	13,748,730,000
R&D Expense						
Operating Income	1,017,964,000	839,453,100	934,357,700	858,660,000	868,828,400	3,833,465,000
Operating Margin %	9.28%	8.44%	10.12%	9.88%	10.32%	27.88%
SGA Expense						
Net Income	813,467,400	454,186,000	821,376,100	802,169,200	1,432,606,000	2,050,616,000
Operating Cash Flow	1,276,692,000	1,614,507,000	1,464,241,000	1,333,183,000	804,428,900	2,830,189,000
Capital Expenditure	199,977,400	129,928,800	108,462,300	133,318,300	108,462,300	143,486,600
EBITDA	1,307,197,000	1,115,128,000	1,197,605,000	1,106,090,000	1,598,689,000	5,160,998,000
Return on Assets %	2.83%	1.66%	3.22%	3.14%	3.83%	4.94%
Return on Equity %	12.27%	7.05%	12.79%	12.05%	22.39%	52.87%
Debt to Equity	1.10	1.53	1.34	1.27	1.09	4.14

CONTACT INFORMATION:

Phone: 34 915862500   Fax: 34 915862677
Toll-Free:
Address: Principe de Vergara, 135, Madrid, 28002 Spain

STOCK TICKER/OTHER:

Stock Ticker: FRRVY
Employees: 74,032
Parent Company:

Exchange: PINX
Fiscal Year Ends: 12/31

SALARIES/BONUSES:

Top Exec. Salary: $ Bonus: $
Second Exec. Salary: $ Bonus: $

OTHER THOUGHTS:

Estimated Female Officers or Directors:
Hot Spot for Advancement for Women/Minorities:

Sales, profits and employees may be estimates. Financial information, benefits and other data can change quickly and may vary from those stated here.

Finnair Oyj

NAIC Code: 481111

TYPES OF BUSINESS:

Airline
Aircraft Maintenance
Air Freight
Travel Agency Services
Catering
Tour Services
Airport Ground Operations

BRANDS/DIVISIONS/AFFILIATES:

Finnair Group
Finnair Cargo Oy
Finnair Cargo Terminal Operations Oy
Flybe Nordic AB

CONTACTS: Note: Officers with more than one job title may be intentionally listed here more than once.

Pekka Vauramo, CEO
Ville Iho, COO
Pekka Vauramo, Pres.
Pekka Vaehaehyyppae, CFO
Jaakko Schildt, Tech. Svcs.
Petri Schaaf, VP-Sales
Sami Sarelius, General Counsel
Markku Malmipuro, VP-Flight Oper.
Sanna Ahonen, VP-Corp. Dev.
Arja Suominen, Sr. VP-Corp. Comm. & Corp. Responsibility
Hannele Malin, VP-Internal Audit
Gregory Kaldahl, Sr. VP-Resource Mgmt.
Anssi Komulainen, Sr. VP-Customer Service
Kaisa Vikkula, Sr. VP-Travel Svcs.
Juha Jarvinen,, Sr. VP-Cargo

GROWTH PLANS/SPECIAL FEATURES:

Finnair Oyj, part of the Finnair Group, is an airline offering passenger and cargo flights to over 70 cities across the globe in Europe, Asia, Finland, the USA and the Middle East. The firm operates two primary divisions: the airline business, which includes fleet management, flight operations and production management; and travel services, which provides travel agencies and booking services. The company's aircraft includes Airbus and Embraer aircraft, with an average lifespan of eight years. Finnair has expanded its service area from North Atlantic to Asian routes, offering services to destinations in Asia, including Bangkok, Beijing, Chongqing, Hong Kong, Osaka, Shanghai, Seoul and Tokyo. The company also operates subsidiaries Finnair Cargo Oy and Finnair Cargo Terminal Operations Oy, which are both cargo businesses that operate at Helsinki-Vantaa Airport. The company is a member of the oneworld airline alliance, which provides collaborative services with a group of 15 international airlines. Additionally, the company maintains interests in Flybe Nordic AB, a joint venture with the U.K.'s Flybe that offers regional airline services in the Nordic and Baltic countries. The Finnish government controls 55.8% of Finnair Group's outstanding stock. In 2015, Nordic Global Airlines Ltd., 40%-owned by Finnair, ceased operations.

FINANCIAL DATA: Note: Data for latest year may not have been available at press time.

In U.S. $	2015	2014	2013	2012	2011	2010
Revenue	2,625,692,000	2,581,064,000	2,711,897,000	2,767,371,000	2,550,785,000	2,285,956,000
R&D Expense						
Operating Income	137,498,600	-81,911,650	-9,942,379	40,108,460	-99,197,830	-15,026,550
Operating Margin %	5.23%	-3.17%	-.36%	1.44%	-3.88%	-.65%
SGA Expense	83,606,370	73,776,980	82,363,580			
Net Income	101,005,500	-93,435,770	12,202,010	12,992,880	-98,858,880	-25,759,800
Operating Cash Flow	193,198,500	27,341,540	120,890,300	174,782,500	57,394,640	69,031,740
Capital Expenditure	403,118,300	165,405,000	71,517,340	65,642,300	169,811,300	5,875,042
EBITDA	299,514,200	69,822,620	128,008,100	187,775,400	56,151,850	126,539,400
Return on Assets %	3.72%	-4.04%	.10%	.50%	-3.67%	-.94%
Return on Equity %	11.79%	-13.72%	.31%	1.49%	-10.93%	-2.69%
Debt to Equity	0.37	0.65	0.59		0.68	0.79

CONTACT INFORMATION:

Phone: 358 981881   Fax:
Toll-Free: 800-950-5000
Address: Tietotie 11A, Helsinki-Vantaa Airport, 01053 Finland

STOCK TICKER/OTHER:

Stock Ticker: FNNNF   Exchange: GREY
Employees: 5,172   Fiscal Year Ends: 12/31
Parent Company: Finnair Group

SALARIES/BONUSES:

Top Exec. Salary: $ Bonus: $
Second Exec. Salary: $ Bonus: $

OTHER THOUGHTS:

Estimated Female Officers or Directors: 6
Hot Spot for Advancement for Women/Minorities: Y

Sales, profits and employees may be estimates. Financial information, benefits and other data can change quickly and may vary from those stated here.

FirstGroup plc

www.firstgroup.com

NAIC Code: 485113

TYPES OF BUSINESS:

Bus Service
Train Service
School Bus Services
Tram Service
Contract Transit Services
Maintenance Services

BRANDS/DIVISIONS/AFFILIATES:

First Student
First Transit
Greyhound
First Bus
First Rail
Operate Great Western Railway
TransPennine Express
First Hull Trains

CONTACTS: Note: Officers with more than one job title may be intentionally listed here more than once.

Tim OToole, CEO
Matthew Gregory, CFO
Clive Burrows, Dir.-Eng.

GROWTH PLANS/SPECIAL FEATURES:

FirstGroup plc is one of the largest surface transportation companies in the U.K. and North America. The company operates in five divisions: First Student, First Transit, Greyhound, First Bus and First Rail. First Student provides student transportation in North America with its fleet of 47,000 school buses, transporting 6 million students per school day. First Transit is one of the largest private sector providers of public transit management and contracting in North America. This division operates and manages 12,500 vehicles and maintains a further 35,000. Greyhound is the only national operator of scheduled inter-city coach transportation services in the U.S. and Canada. This division provides 3,800 destinations through its fleet of 1,700 vehicles. Point-to-point Greyhound Express serves 1,000 city pairs in more than 135 markets. First Bus is one of the largest bus operators in the U.K., with a fifth of the market outside of London. This division comprises 62,000 buses carrying approximately 1.6 million passengers per day. First Rail is one of the U.K.'s most experienced rail operators, carrying 140 million passengers across its two franchises (Operate Great Western Railway and TransPennine Express) and its open access operation (First Hull Trains). In April 2016, the firm began running the TransPennine Express franchise, with a commitment to introduce new trains, routes and faster journey times.

FINANCIAL DATA: Note: Data for latest year may not have been available at press time.

In U.S. $	2015	2014	2013	2012	2011	2010
Revenue	7,899,808,000	8,770,253,000	9,009,831,000	8,719,727,000	8,377,658,000	
R&D Expense						
Operating Income	320,917,100	303,160,900	268,562,400	584,909,800	402,908,900	
Operating Margin %	4.06%	3.45%	2.98%	6.70%	4.80%	
SGA Expense	2,219,524	3,264,006	1,958,404			
Net Income	98,181,300	70,763,650	45,696,080	256,159,200	134,738,200	
Operating Cash Flow	424,581,900	381,627,600	434,373,900	620,683,300	725,523,100	
Capital Expenditure	559,972,800	361,651,800	278,223,800	223,127,400	274,568,200	
EBITDA	841,852,400	789,889,400	764,560,700	1,041,871,000	880,889,900	
Return on Assets %	1.46%	1.02%	.64%	3.70%	1.90%	
Return on Equity %	5.63%	5.40%	4.23%	21.89%	11.28%	
Debt to Equity	1.23	1.50	2.91	2.62	2.34	

CONTACT INFORMATION:

Phone: 44 1224650100   Fax: 44 1224650140
Toll-Free:
Address: 395 King St., Aberdeen, AB24 5RP United Kingdom

STOCK TICKER/OTHER:

Stock Ticker: FGROF
Employees: 59,500
Parent Company:

Exchange: GREY
Fiscal Year Ends: 03/31

SALARIES/BONUSES:

Top Exec. Salary: $ Bonus: $
Second Exec. Salary: $ Bonus: $

OTHER THOUGHTS:

Estimated Female Officers or Directors:
Hot Spot for Advancement for Women/Minorities:

Flight Centre Limited

www.flightcentre.com.au

NAIC Code: 561510

TYPES OF BUSINESS:

Travel Agencies

BRANDS/DIVISIONS/AFFILIATES:

Liberty Travel
Escape Travel
Cruiseabout
Infinity Holiday
Corporate Traveller
GOGO Vacations
FCm Travel Solutions
Stage and Screen

CONTACTS: *Note: Officers with more than one job title may be intentionally listed here more than once.*

Graham F. Turner, Managing Dir.
Rob Flint, Exec. Gen. Mgr.-Global Corp. Oper.
Dean Smith, Head-U.S.
Graham Turner, Managing Dir.
Chris Galanty, Head-U.K.

GROWTH PLANS/SPECIAL FEATURES:

Flight Centre Limited is Australia's largest traditional high street travel agent. The firm operates on a global scale through its 2,500 stores located in 10 countries. Currently, Flight Centre's various networks extend throughout Australia, New Zealand, the USA, Canada, the U.K., South Africa, Hong Kong, India, China and Singapore. Flight Centre has differentiated its brands into a number of market segments including leisure, wholesale, corporate and other. The brands that make up the leisure segment include Escape Travel, specializing in inclusive holiday packages and tailor-made holidays; Cruiseabout, offering cruise itineraries in Australia and New Zealand; and Liberty Travel, a USA-based travel agency. Wholesale brands include Infinity Holiday, primarily serving Australia; and GOGO Vacations, the firm's more global wholesaler of holiday packages. The corporate brands of Flight Centre include FCm Travel Solutions, an Australian travel management company; Corporate Traveller, handing the business travel of small to medium sized enterprises; and Stage and Screen, specializing solely on travel for those in the entertainment and sports industries. The firm's brands in the other segment include 99 Bikes, a retail brand offering various bikes and bike accessories; Travel Money Oz, a foreign exchange business; Healthwise, offering health and wellness services; and Moneywise, offering various financial services.

FINANCIAL DATA: *Note: Data for latest year may not have been available at press time.*

In U.S. $	2015	2014	2013	2012	2011	2010
Revenue	1,797,847,000	1,679,436,000	1,479,426,000	1,508,581,000	1,382,289,000	1,341,435,000
R&D Expense						
Operating Income	267,981,600	239,288,700	244,020,100	205,183,400	150,989,800	147,466,500
Operating Margin %	14.90%	14.24%	16.49%	13.60%	10.92%	10.99%
SGA Expense	1,194,036,000	1,077,682,000	966,406,000	1,873,618,000	1,096,906,000	1,036,597,000
Net Income	195,186,400	157,423,900	187,220,000	152,210,900	106,367,900	106,412,100
Operating Cash Flow	275,813,300	172,773,100	281,743,000	259,455,300	123,908,200	184,964,300
Capital Expenditure	63,032,570	42,169,050	39,102,260	42,237,520	36,316,190	15,563,760
EBITDA	339,710,200	312,343,300	327,560,100	282,276,400	226,002,700	216,285,800
Return on Assets %	9.87%	8.65%	10.95%	9.68%	7.01%	7.54%
Return on Equity %	21.66%	19.48%	26.13%	25.04%	19.26%	21.17%
Debt to Equity				0.07	0.09	0.11

CONTACT INFORMATION:

Phone: 61-7-3170-7979   Fax: 61-7-3102-5148
Toll-Free:
Address: Level 2, 545 Queen Street, Brisbane, QLD 4000 Australia

STOCK TICKER/OTHER:

Stock Ticker: FGETF   Exchange: GREY
Employees: 7,489   Fiscal Year Ends: 06/30
Parent Company:

SALARIES/BONUSES:

Top Exec. Salary: $ Bonus: $
Second Exec. Salary: $ Bonus: $

OTHER THOUGHTS:

Estimated Female Officers or Directors: 1
Hot Spot for Advancement for Women/Minorities:

Four Seasons Hotels Inc

www.fourseasons.com

NAIC Code: 721110

TYPES OF BUSINESS:

Hotels, Luxury
Luxury Condominiums
Conference Centers
Resort Time Shares

BRANDS/DIVISIONS/AFFILIATES:

Regent Hotels
Four Seasons Hotels
Triples Holdings Limited
Cascade Investment LLC
Four Seasons Hotel Bahrain Bay
Four Seasons Resort Dubai
Four Seasons Hotel Doha
Four Seasons Hotel Riyadh

CONTACTS: *Note: Officers with more than one job title may be intentionally listed here more than once.*

J. Allen Smith, CEO
J. Allen Amith, Pres.
John Davison, CFO
Peter Nowlan, Exec. VP
Chris Hunsberger, Exec. VP-Human Resources
Chris Hunsberger, Exec. VP-Prod. & Innovation
Nick Mutton, Exec. VP-Admin.
Sarah Cohen, Exec. VP
Christopher Norton, Exec. VP-Global Product & Oper.
Scott Woroch, Exec. VP-Worldwide Dev.
John Davison, Exec. VP-Residential
Chris Hart, Pres., Asia Pacific
Chris Hunsberger, Pres., Americas
Isadore Sharp, Chmn.

GROWTH PLANS/SPECIAL FEATURES:

Four Seasons Hotels, Inc. is a leading operator of luxury hotels and resorts. Headquartered in Toronto, the company manages 96 properties in 41 countries, mostly operated under the Four Seasons and Regent brands, owning roughly half of them. The firm offers its guests amenities such as monogrammed terry-cloth bathrobes, concierge service, in-room fax machines, overnight sandal and golf shoe repair and in-room exercise equipment installation, if requested. The No Luggage Required program provides a variety of crucial loan-items to customers who have lost their belongings. Many hotels provide experienced meeting and conference personnel to help guests plan business events such as award galas and multimedia presentations. Moreover, the firm offers a number of branded vacation ownership properties and private residences in Jackson Hole, Wyoming; Scottsdale, Arizona; San Francisco, California; Miami, Florida; Austin, Texas; and Toronto, Canada, among others. The Four Seasons has dozens of new hotels under development, including sites in Tanzania as well as India. The company is privately owned by investment firms controlled by Cascade Investment LLC and Triples Holdings Limited. In recent years, the firm added hotels to its portfolio in China, with plans to open approximately 10 more over the long term. The Four Seasons also recently announced development plans for a new resort property in Cesme, Turkey, scheduled to open in 2016. In March 2015, the firm opened the Four Seasons Hotel Bahrain Bay in Bahrain, along with the recently opened Four Seasons Resort Dubai, Four Seasons Hotel Doha and Four Seasons Hotel Riyadh in the brand's growing portfolio in the Gulf region.

The Four Seasons offers its employees such benefits as medical and dental coverage, disability and life insurance, a retirement pension plan, complimentary stays at Four Seasons properties with discounted meals, education assistance and paid holidays and

FINANCIAL DATA: *Note: Data for latest year may not have been available at press time.*

In U.S. $	2015	2014	2013	2012	2011	2010
Revenue	4,300,000,000	4,025,000,000	4,000,000,000	3,710,000,000	3,520,000,000	3,100,000,000
R&D Expense						
Operating Income						
Operating Margin %						
SGA Expense						
Net Income						
Operating Cash Flow						
Capital Expenditure						
EBITDA						
Return on Assets %						
Return on Equity %						
Debt to Equity						

CONTACT INFORMATION:

Phone: 416-449-1750   Fax: 416-441-4374
Toll-Free:
Address: 1165 Leslie St., Toronto, ON M3C 2K8 Canada

STOCK TICKER/OTHER:

Stock Ticker: Private   Exchange:
Employees: 20,990   Fiscal Year Ends: 12/31
Parent Company: Cascade Investment LLC

SALARIES/BONUSES:

Top Exec. Salary: $ Bonus: $
Second Exec. Salary: $ Bonus: $

OTHER THOUGHTS:

Estimated Female Officers or Directors: 3
Hot Spot for Advancement for Women/Minorities: Y

Frontier Airlines Inc

www.flyfrontier.com

NAIC Code: 481111

TYPES OF BUSINESS:

Airline

BRANDS/DIVISIONS/AFFILIATES:

Indigo Partners LLC
Early Returns
Larry the Linx
Hector the Otter
Sal the Cougar
Jack the Rabbit

CONTACTS: Note: Officers with more than one job title may be intentionally listed here more than once.

Barry Biffle, Pres.
Allen Messick, VP-Eng. & Maintenance
Scott Gould, VP-Flight Oper.
Robert Ashcroft, Sr. VP-Finance
Daniel Shurz, Sr. VP-Commercial
Greg Aretakis, VP-Network & Revenue Mgmt
Jan Fogelberg, VP-Customer Service
Holly Nelson, Chief Accounting Officer
Bill Franke, Chmn.

GROWTH PLANS/SPECIAL FEATURES:

Frontier Airlines, Inc. is a private airline company averaging over 275 flights daily to 59 destinations throughout the U.S., Mexico and Jamaica. The firm has a fleet of 32 Airbus A319-100s, 23 A320-200s and five A321-200s, with 18 A319neo, 2 A320-200, 62 A320neo and 14 A321-200 aircraft on order. The firm distinguishes its fleet from other airlines' by its plain tales, which feature photos of over 50 'spokesanimals' including Larry the Linx, Jack the Rabbit, Sal the Cougar and Hector the Otter. The company's website allows travelers to plan and book flights, check flight status, look up route maps, check in online and manage their frequent flyer accounts. The firm also offers special membership, called Early Returns, which includes special flight discounts and a partnership with MasterCard where members can earn up to 50,000 bonus miles. Early Returns members also have access to special deals from Frontier's partners, including Avis, Budges, e-Mines and Hertz. The firm's site includes a Ways to Save link consisting of low fare options, online deals and email specials. Frontier is owned by Indigo Partners LLC, a private equity and venture capital firm. After a total revamp of the business from 2013-2015, the firm plans to increase its fleet to 114 aircraft between 2016 and 2022.

Employees of the company receive benefits including flight discounts and guest passes for family and friends; medical, dental and vision insurance; and 401(k).

FINANCIAL DATA: Note: Data for latest year may not have been available at press time.

In U.S. $	2015	2014	2013	2012	2011	2010
Revenue	1,604,012,260	1,574,869,290	1,550,000,000	1,433,466,000	1,661,914,000	1,316,949,000
R&D Expense						
Operating Income						
Operating Margin %						
SGA Expense						
Net Income	145,512,190	129,029,050	7,734,000	4,735,000	-72,055,000	-19,379,000
Operating Cash Flow						
Capital Expenditure						
EBITDA						
Return on Assets %						
Return on Equity %						
Debt to Equity						

CONTACT INFORMATION:

Phone: 720-374-4200   Fax:
Toll-Free:
Address: 7001 Tower Rd., Denver, CO 80249 United States

STOCK TICKER/OTHER:

Stock Ticker: Private   Exchange:
Employees: 4,600   Fiscal Year Ends:
Parent Company: Indigo Partners LLC

SALARIES/BONUSES:

Top Exec. Salary: $ Bonus: $
Second Exec. Salary: $ Bonus: $

OTHER THOUGHTS:

Estimated Female Officers or Directors: 2
Hot Spot for Advancement for Women/Minorities:

Galaxy Entertainment Group Ltd

www.galaxyentertainment.com

NAIC Code: 721120

TYPES OF BUSINESS:

Casino Hotels
Construction Materials

BRANDS/DIVISIONS/AFFILIATES:

Galaxy Casino SA
StarWorld
Galaxy Macau
Broadway Macau
City Club Casinos
Waldo Casino
President Casino
Rio Casino

CONTACTS: Note: Officers with more than one job title may be intentionally listed here more than once.

Michael Mecca, COO
Michael Mecca, Pres.
Robert Drake, CFO
Kevin Clayton, CMO
Eileen Lui Wai Ling, Dir.-Human Resources
Ian Farnsworth, Dir.-Info. Systems
Ian Farnsworth, Dir.-Tech.
Eileen Lui Wai Ling, Dir.-Admin.
Raymond Kwok Mun Sang, Dir.-Legal
John Au Chung On, Dir.-Bus. Dev.
Charles So Chak Lum, Deputy COO-Starworld Macau
Baschar Hraki, Dir.-Project Dev
Gabriel Hunterton, COO-Starworld
Gillian Murphy, Sr. VP-Hospitality
Lui Che Woo, Chmn.
Raymond Yap Yin Min, Sr. VP-Intl Premium Market Dev.
Lisa Ng Lai Ming, Sr. VP-Procurement

GROWTH PLANS/SPECIAL FEATURES:

Galaxy Entertainment Group Ltd. is a holding company for Galaxy Casino SA, through which the firm operates hotels, casinos, resorts and entertainment in Macau, China, a territory known for gambling and tourism. Its operations consist of two segments: gaming & entertainment and construction materials. In the gaming & entertainment division, the firm manages three luxury resort hotel and casino properties, StarWorld on the Macau Peninsula, Galaxy Macau and Broadway Macau; as well as four City Club Casinos, with three in the Macau Peninsula (the Waldo, President and Rio Casinos) and one on the Cotai Strip (Grand Waldo Casino). StarWorld is the company's first five-star flagship, a 39-story hotel. Galaxy Macau includes more than 2,200 rooms, suites and villas across three world-class Asian hotels: the Banyan Tree Hotels & Resorts, the Okura Hotels & Resorts and the Galaxy Hotel. Facilities at the Galaxy Macau include more than 50 food & beverage outlets, lush gardens that cover 170,000 square feet (52,000 sm) and a skytop wave pool that features a white sand beach. Broadway Macau is a hawker-style street market entertainment and hotel facility, featuring more than 40 local Macau and Asian food brands, street performances, as well as a 3,000-seat Broadway Theatre. Its hotel comprises 320 rooms and suites, and panoramic views of the Pearl River Delta across to Hengqin Island. Through a number of companies, the construction materials division is involved in the manufacture, sale and distribution of concrete pipes, ready-mix concrete, asphalt and various other building materials. It maintains operations across Hong Kong, Macau and Mainland China. The firm's revenue is typically generated almost entirely from gaming and entertainment operations.

FINANCIAL DATA: Note: Data for latest year may not have been available at press time.

In U.S. $	2015	2014	2013	2012	2011	2010
Revenue	6,575,388,000	9,252,653,000	8,515,049,000	7,317,587,000	5,311,091,000	2,483,898,000
R&D Expense						
Operating Income	562,469,100	1,345,590,000	1,338,853,000	1,009,584,000	445,610,400	167,203,200
Operating Margin %	8.55%	14.54%	15.72%	13.79%	8.39%	6.73%
SGA Expense	1,617,115,000	2,864,554,000	2,631,089,000	2,376,797,000	1,933,512,000	979,267,800
Net Income	536,577,400	1,333,343,000	1,296,199,000	951,390,100	387,361,200	115,857,900
Operating Cash Flow	854,381,400	1,549,957,000	1,717,874,000	1,296,800,000	734,827,600	271,525,300
Capital Expenditure	850,329,900	1,226,910,000	644,202,600	289,574,600	593,381,400	592,243,500
EBITDA	948,457,500	1,609,304,000	1,633,754,000	1,260,348,000	607,201,200	197,158,200
Return on Assets %	7.76%	21.08%	22.17%	18.40%	9.85%	4.07%
Return on Equity %	10.47%	29.20%	37.02%	40.90%	25.65%	10.34%
Debt to Equity	0.01	0.01		0.28	0.74	0.77

CONTACT INFORMATION:

Phone: 852-3150-1111 Fax: 852-3150-1100
Toll-Free:
Address: 1606, 16/F Hutchison House, 10 Harcourt Rd., Hong Kong, Hong Kong

STOCK TICKER/OTHER:

Stock Ticker: GXYEF Exchange: PINX
Employees: 17,000 Fiscal Year Ends: 12/31
Parent Company:

SALARIES/BONUSES:

Top Exec. Salary: $ Bonus: $
Second Exec. Salary: $ Bonus: $

OTHER THOUGHTS:

Estimated Female Officers or Directors: 5
Hot Spot for Advancement for Women/Minorities: Y

Gate Gourmet Inc

NAIC Code: 722310

www.gategourmet.com

TYPES OF BUSINESS:

Airline Catering
Airline Passenger Goods
Rail Line & Ship-Board Catering
Institutional Catering
Pre-Packaged Food Products

BRANDS/DIVISIONS/AFFILIATES:

Gategroup Holding AG

CONTACTS: *Note: Officers with more than one job title may be intentionally listed here more than once.*

Christopher Schmitz, CFO- gategroup
Andrew Gibson, CEO-GateGroup Holding AG
Thomas Bucher, CFO-GateGroup Holding AG
Andreas Schmid, Chmn.-GateGroup Holding AG

GROWTH PLANS/SPECIAL FEATURES:

Gate Gourmet, Inc. produces and markets airline passenger goods, such as premium class passenger meals, beverages, films and blankets. The firm is part of Gategroup Holding AG, a Swiss conglomerate that offers international onboard products and services. Gate Gourmet provides 250 million meals yearly for airline passengers through a network of over 120 flight kitchens in 28 countries across five continents. Gate Gourmet caters approximately 250 airlines, from menu design, meal preparation and delivery. Its premium catering services offers customers customized catering and provisioning service from first and business class cabins or VIP charter flight services to private jet service. Gate Gourmet also provides food and beverages for airport lounges that are managed directly by customers or through a partnership with the company's colleagues at Performa, a Gategroup member that assists leading airlines and hotels in the design, development and delivery of customer experience services. Economy service consists of affordable meals, beverages and snacks for long-haul flights and fresh or shelf-stable food for purchase on short-haul flights. The firm also provides non-airline catering services to rail customers on Amtrak's Acela Express along the U.S. Northeast Corridor as well as with business partnerships such as Starbucks in several Latin American cities and organizations whose requirements are a good match for Gate Gourmet's size, scope and culinary expertise. The firm maintains a catering services agreement with distributor FreshOne, LLC to provide pre-packaged items to grocery, convenience and specialty retailers nationwide.

FINANCIAL DATA: *Note: Data for latest year may not have been available at press time.*

In U.S. $	2015	2014	2013	2012	2011	2010
Revenue	2,650,000,000	2,526,882,804	2,558,254,270	2,712,874,246	2,815,347,515	
R&D Expense						
Operating Income						
Operating Margin %						
SGA Expense						
Net Income						
Operating Cash Flow						
Capital Expenditure						
EBITDA						
Return on Assets %						
Return on Equity %						
Debt to Equity						

CONTACT INFORMATION:

Phone: 703-964-2300   Fax: 703-964-2399
Toll-Free:
Address: 1880 Campus Commons Dr., Ste. 200, Reston, VA 20191 United States

STOCK TICKER/OTHER:

Stock Ticker: Subsidiary   Exchange:
Employees: Fiscal Year Ends: 12/31
Parent Company: Gategroup Holding AG

SALARIES/BONUSES:

Top Exec. Salary: $ Bonus: $
Second Exec. Salary: $ Bonus: $

OTHER THOUGHTS:

Estimated Female Officers or Directors:
Hot Spot for Advancement for Women/Minorities:

Sales, profits and employees may be estimates. Financial information, benefits and other data can change quickly and may vary from those stated here.

GE Aviation

NAIC Code: 336412

www.geaviation.com

TYPES OF BUSINESS:

Aircraft Engine and Engine Parts Manufacturing
Gas Turbine Manufacturing
Marine Engines
Engine Maintenance & Parts
Engine Leasing

BRANDS/DIVISIONS/AFFILIATES:

General Electric Co
GE90
F110
CF34
GE Passport
LM6000
42 MW
LEAP

CONTACTS: Note: Officers with more than one job title may be intentionally listed here more than once.

David L. Joyce, CEO
Anthony Aiello, VP
David Joyce, Pres.
Anne M. Lynch, CFO
Chaker A. Chahrour, VP-Mktg. & Sales
Ernest W. Marshall, Jr., VP-Human Resources
Jim Daily, VP-Systems Global Eng. & Tech.
Mohammad Ehteshami, VP-New Prod. Introduction Oper.
Gary Mercer, Chief Engineer
Michael McAlevey, General Counsel
Bill Fitzgerald, VP
Michael R. McAlevey, VP-Bus. Dev.
Jamie Regg, Sr. Exec.-Global Comm. & GE Advantage
Peter Prowitt, Exec. Dir.-Global Gov't Rel.
Jean Lydon-Rodgers, VP
Paul McElhinney, VP
Jeanne M. Rosario, VP
Chris S. Beaufait, Sr. Exec.-China
Colleen Athans, VP

GROWTH PLANS/SPECIAL FEATURES:

GE Aviation, a subsidiary of General Electric Co., produces jet, turboprop and turbo shaft engines, components and integrated systems. The company manufactures its products for commercial, military, business and general aviation aircraft. GE Aviation has a global service network to support these offerings. Commercial engines by the firm include GE90, GE9X, GEnx, GP7200, CF6, CFM56, LEAP, CF34 and CT7; and its commercial systems include Avionics computing systems, electrical power components, digital systems, structures, Dowty-branded propellers and Unison-branded solid-state ignition systems. Military engines include adaptive cycle, F110, F404, F414, GE3000, GE38, T700, F108 and F103/138; and military systems include Avionics computer systems, electrical power components, structures, Dowty propellers and Unison ignition systems. Business & general aviation (B&GA) engines include advanced turboprop, CF34, GE Passport, CFM56, CF700, CFE738, CJ610, H Series and HF120; and B&GA systems include Avionics computer systems, electrical power components, structures, Dowty propellers and Unison ignition systems. For the marine industry, military gas turbine products include the LM500, LM2500, LM2500+, LM2500+G4 AND LM6000; commercial gas turbine products include the 4.5 MW, 25 MW, 30 MW, 35 MW and 42 MW; and systems for the marine industry include propulsion systems, exhaust energy recovery systems and the firm's optional dry low emissions combustor system. In 2015, the firm launched its all-new turboprop engine, which will power Textron's single engine turboprop. In January 2016, GE Aviation announced plans to build a new turboprop development, test & engine production headquarters in the Czech Republic, scheduled to open in 2020.

FINANCIAL DATA: Note: Data for latest year may not have been available at press time.

In U.S. $	2015	2014	2013	2012	2011	2010
Revenue	24,660,000,000	23,990,000,000	21,911,000,000	19,997,000,000	18,859,000,000	17,619,000,000
R&D Expense						
Operating Income						
Operating Margin %						
SGA Expense						
Net Income	5,507,000,000	4,973,000,000	4,345,000,000	3,747,000,000	3,512,000,000	3,304,000,000
Operating Cash Flow						
Capital Expenditure						
EBITDA						
Return on Assets %						
Return on Equity %						
Debt to Equity						

CONTACT INFORMATION:

Phone: 513-243-2000   Fax:
Toll-Free:
Address: 1 Neumann Way, Cincinnati, OH 45215-6301 United States

STOCK TICKER/OTHER:

Stock Ticker: Subsidiary   Exchange:
Employees: 44,000   Fiscal Year Ends: 12/31
Parent Company: General Electric Co (GE)

SALARIES/BONUSES:

Top Exec. Salary: $ Bonus: $
Second Exec. Salary: $ Bonus: $

OTHER THOUGHTS:

Estimated Female Officers or Directors: 4
Hot Spot for Advancement for Women/Minorities: Y

Genting Hong Kong Limited

NAIC Code: 483112

TYPES OF BUSINESS:

Cruise Lines
Cruise Charters
Leisure and Entertainment Real Estate Development

BRANDS/DIVISIONS/AFFILIATES:

Star Cruises
Dream Cruises
Crystal Cruises
Lloyd Werft Grpi[
Zouk
Resorts World Manila

CONTACTS: Note: Officers with more than one job title may be intentionally listed here more than once.

Tan Sri Lim Kok Thay, CEO
David Chua Ming Huat, Pres.
Tan Wei Tze, CFO
Lim Keong Hui, CIO
William Ng Ko Seng, COO-Cruise
Tan Sri Lim Kok Thay, Chmn.

GROWTH PLANS/SPECIAL FEATURES:

Genting Hong Kong Limited is a global leisure, entertainment and hospitality enterprise. The company has a presence in more than 20 locations worldwide, with offices in Australia, China, Germany, India, Indonesia, Japan, Malaysia, the Philippines, Singapore, Sweden, Taiwan, the U.K. and the U.S. Genting's businesses include Star Cruises, Dream Cruises, Crystal Cruises, German shipyard Lloyd Werft Group, nightlife brand Zouk and Resorts World Manila. Star Cruises owns six vessels (SuperStar Virgo, SuperStar Gemini, SuperStar Aquarius, SuperStar Libra, Star Pisces and The Taipan), and is a leading cruise line in the Asia Pacific. Dream Cruises is an Asian luxury cruise line, with two new vessels: Genting Dream, which launched in 2016, and World Dream, due to launch in late-2017. Crystal Cruises is a world-leading luxury cruise provider, and provides three classes of cruising: Crystal Yacht Cruises, Crystal River Cruises and Crystal Exclusive Class Ocean Cruises. Crystal Cruises offers extensive itineraries ranging from five days to approximately 100-day world cruises. Lloyd Werft Group builds ships, with shipyards located in Bremerhaven, Wismar, Warnemunde and Stralsund, Germany. Zouk is an iconic music-driven entertainment company that provides electronic dance music, as well as a continual flow of internationally-renowned DJs to play. Last, Resorts World Manila is the Philippine's non-stop vacation sport for top-notch entertainment and world-class entertainment. Resorts World Manila features four hotels, including an all-suite Maxims Hotel with shopping mall, cinemas and performing arts theater. In 2016, the firm acquired Nordic Yards' three shipyards in Wismar, Warnemunde and Stralsund, Germany.

FINANCIAL DATA: Note: Data for latest year may not have been available at press time.

In U.S. $	2015	2014	2013	2012	2011	2010
Revenue	689,954,000	570,810,000	554,729,000	520,381,000	515,535,000	388,879,000
R&D Expense						
Operating Income	-88,753,000	-33,478,000	-34,918,000	62,744,000	67,525,000	
Operating Margin %	-12.86%	-5.86%	-6.29%	12.05%	13.09%	
SGA Expense	155,362,000	114,596,000	122,669,000	102,652,000	87,821,000	65,942,000
Net Income	2,112,687,000	384,475,000	551,951,000	198,361,000	182,204,000	67,859,000
Operating Cash Flow	-186,776,000	31,252,000	-93,075,000	64,973,000	86,232,000	67,086,000
Capital Expenditure	401,191,000	188,194,000	140,661,000	86,573,000	36,109,000	24,547,000
EBITDA	2,224,968,000	508,665,000	684,777,000	297,152,000	296,140,000	165,378,000
Return on Assets %	40.70%	9.93%	15.08%	6.03%	6.26%	2.56%
Return on Equity %	48.82%	12.61%	21.11%	8.88%	8.85%	3.56%
Debt to Equity	0.08	0.07	0.13	0.30	0.32	0.11

CONTACT INFORMATION:

Phone: 852 23782000   Fax: 852 23143809
Toll-Free:
Address: Ocean Ctr., 5 Canton Rd., Ste. 1501, Tsimshatsui, Kowloon, Hong Kong

STOCK TICKER/OTHER:

Stock Ticker: GTHKF   Exchange: PINX
Employees: 6,269   Fiscal Year Ends: 12/31
Parent Company:

SALARIES/BONUSES:

Top Exec. Salary: $ Bonus: $
Second Exec. Salary: $ Bonus: $

OTHER THOUGHTS:

Estimated Female Officers or Directors: 2
Hot Spot for Advancement for Women/Minorities: Y

Sales, profits and employees may be estimates. Financial information, benefits and other data can change quickly and may vary from those stated here.

gl Limited

NAIC Code: 531100

www.gl-grp.com/

TYPES OF BUSINESS:

Hotel & Resort Development
Casino Operations
Real Estate Development

BRANDS/DIVISIONS/AFFILIATES:

Hong Leong Group Malaysia
glh Hotels Group Limited
Clermont
Amba
Thistle Express
Clermont Club
GuocoLeisure Limited

CONTACTS: *Note: Officers with more than one job title may be intentionally listed here more than once.*

Michael Bernard DeNoma, CEO
Ho Kah Meng, CFO
Jeanette Ling, Group Legal Counsel
Clay Rumbaoa, COO-Molokai Properties
Michael Bernard DeNoma, CEO-Guoman Hotels Limited
Andy Hughes, CFO-Guoman & Thistle Hotels & Clermont Leisure
Asem Abdin, VP-Intl Mktg.-Clermont Leisure
Quek Leng Chan, Chmn.

GROWTH PLANS/SPECIAL FEATURES:

gl Limited (GL), formerly GuocoLeisure Ltd., is an investment holding company with principal investments in hotel management, gaming operations, oil & gas and property development. It is a member of conglomerate the Hong Leong Group Malaysia. GL owns, leases and/or manages and operate hotels in U.K. and Malaysia through is wholly-owned subsidiaries Guoman Hotel Management (UK) Limited and Guoman Hotel Management (Malaysia) Sdn Bhd. The UK subsidiary manages and operates two distinct hotel brands: Guoman, a premium collection of five deluxe hotels in central London; and Thistle, a group of 32 full-service hotels in London, as well as regional locations throughout the U.K. The Malaysian subsidiary manages and operates two hotels under the Thistle brand in Malaysia. Gaming operations are owned and operated by wholly-owned subsidiary Clermont Leisure (UK) Limited. Its gaming operations are located throughout the U.K., including The Clermont Club, an exclusive members-only casino in Mayfair, London. As for the company's oil and gas investments, GL receives royalties from the Bass Strait Oil Trust, a unit trust managed by Bass Strait Oil Management Limited, a wholly-owned subsidiary of the GL Group in Australia. BHP Billiton Limited and Esso Australia Resources Pty Ltd. currently produce hydrocarbons from designated areas in the Bass Strait, Australia. GL's property development division is operated through two wholly-owned subsidiaries: Molokai Properties Limited and Tabua Investments Limited. Molokai Properties owns a 54,677-acre property on the island of Molokai, Hawaii, and maintains a small staff that performs routine maintenance of buildings and other assets. Tabua Investments is GL's property investment arm in Denarau, Fiji. The company announced that it intends to divest its property investments and eventually exit from Fiji.

FINANCIAL DATA: *Note: Data for latest year may not have been available at press time.*

In U.S. $	2015	2014	2013	2012	2011	2010
Revenue	423,200,000	448,800,000	424,900,000	423,500,000	391,100,000	369,700,000
R&D Expense						
Operating Income	76,200,000	79,700,000	82,600,000	99,500,000	116,200,000	66,400,000
Operating Margin %	18.00%	17.75%	19.43%	23.49%	29.71%	17.96%
SGA Expense	168,400,000	22,500,000	26,000,000			17,900,000
Net Income	47,900,000	39,000,000	44,000,000	77,000,000	80,600,000	49,500,000
Operating Cash Flow	99,900,000	108,700,000	75,600,000	128,900,000	95,700,000	100,700,000
Capital Expenditure	55,400,000	39,200,000	12,800,000	46,600,000	44,600,000	8,200,000
EBITDA	107,200,000	114,100,000	120,200,000	144,000,000	149,500,000	108,600,000
Return on Assets %	2.86%	2.37%	2.73%	4.69%	5.00%	3.06%
Return on Equity %	4.04%	3.35%	3.95%	6.99%	7.77%	5.01%
Debt to Equity	0.26	0.08	0.27	0.28	0.34	0.38

CONTACT INFORMATION:

Phone: 65-6438-0002 Fax: 65-6435-0040
Toll-Free:
Address: 20 Collyer Quay, #18-05, Singapore, 049319 Singapore

STOCK TICKER/OTHER:

Stock Ticker: GUORY Exchange: PINX
Employees: Fiscal Year Ends: 06/30
Parent Company: Hong Leong Group Malaysia

SALARIES/BONUSES:

Top Exec. Salary: $ Bonus: $
Second Exec. Salary: $ Bonus: $

OTHER THOUGHTS:

Estimated Female Officers or Directors: 2
Hot Spot for Advancement for Women/Minorities:

Sales, profits and employees may be estimates. Financial information, benefits and other data can change quickly and may vary from those stated here.

Go-Ahead Group plc (The)

NAIC Code: 485113

www.go-ahead.com

TYPES OF BUSINESS:

Bus Services
Train Service

BRANDS/DIVISIONS/AFFILIATES:

Brighton & Hove
Go North East
Go-Ahead London
Metrobus
Plymouth Citybus
GTR
London Midland
Govia

CONTACTS: *Note: Officers with more than one job title may be intentionally listed here more than once.*

David Brown, Group CEO
Patrick Butcher, CFO
Carolyn Sephton, Group Company Sec.
Samantha Hodder, Group Dir.-Corp. Affairs
Holly Birch, Mgr.-Investor Rel.
Keith Down, Group Dir.-Finance
Chris Burchell, Managing Dir.-Southern
Kevin Carr, Managing Dir.-Go North East
Martin Dean, Managing Dir.-Bus Dev.
Alex Hynes, Managing Dir.-Rail Dev.
Andrew Allner, Chmn.

GROWTH PLANS/SPECIAL FEATURES:

The Go-Ahead Group plc is one of the U.K.'s largest public transport providers serving the bus and rail services sectors. The company operates more than 4,600 buses, utilizing a host of operating subsidiaries such as Brighton & Hove, Go North East, Go-Ahead London, Go South Coast, Metrobus, Plymouth Citybus, Go East Anglia and Oxford Bus Company. These companies cover four main regional areas: London, the Southcoast, the Southeast and the Northeast. The group's rail division includes a fleet of over 700 trains, which operate in the areas of London, Surrey, Sussex, Hampshire, Kent, Milton Keynes, Northampton, Birmingham and Liverpool. Its three main operating companies are GTR (an integration of Great Northern and Thameslink routes with Southern and Gatwick Express routes), Southeastern and London Midland, which are operated by joint venture Govia, in which Go-Ahead owns 65% and the remainder is owned by Keolis. Bus operations account for approximately 30% of group revenue and train operations account for 70%.

FINANCIAL DATA: *Note: Data for latest year may not have been available at press time.*

In U.S. $	2015	2014	2013	2012	2011	2010
Revenue	4,197,773,000	3,528,260,000	3,357,748,000	3,164,519,000	2,998,968,000	2,829,632,000
R&D Expense						
Operating Income	126,382,300	142,963,500	120,376,500	131,213,000	133,563,100	103,273,100
Operating Margin %	3.01%	4.05%	3.58%	4.14%	4.45%	3.64%
SGA Expense		913,922	1,044,482			
Net Income	68,152,440	91,783,840	70,110,850	72,460,930	87,997,590	22,456,360
Operating Cash Flow	536,733,100	224,433,000	150,013,700	198,582,100	129,776,900	169,075,500
Capital Expenditure	63,191,150	92,958,890	77,813,900	106,145,500	73,635,970	78,858,380
EBITDA	222,083,000	227,697,000	210,985,300	217,382,800	213,466,000	186,570,600
Return on Assets %	4.00%	6.22%	4.88%	5.20%	6.67%	1.72%
Return on Equity %	89.99%	164.83%	145.52%	197.15%		
Debt to Equity	4.75	6.31	9.73	8.64	16.81	

CONTACT INFORMATION:

Phone: 44-191-232-3123   Fax:
Toll-Free:
Address: 41-51 Grey St., Fl. 3, London, SW1H 9NP United Kingdom

STOCK TICKER/OTHER:

Stock Ticker: GHGUY   Exchange: PINX
Employees: 13,600   Fiscal Year Ends: 06/30
Parent Company:

SALARIES/BONUSES:

Top Exec. Salary: $ Bonus: $
Second Exec. Salary: $ Bonus: $

OTHER THOUGHTS:

Estimated Female Officers or Directors: 5
Hot Spot for Advancement for Women/Minorities: Y

GoJet Airlines LLC

NAIC Code: 481111

www.gojetairlines.com

TYPES OF BUSINESS:

Regional Airlines

GROWTH PLANS/SPECIAL FEATURES:

GoJet Airlines LLC, a subsidiary of Trans States Holdings, Inc., is a regional carrier primarily serving United Express flights. The firm has been in operation since 2005. The company provides about 220 daily flights to destinations in more than 60 cities across the U.S. and Canada, with more than 4 million passengers annually. Its main airport hubs include Chicago's O'Hare International Airport and Denver's Denver International Airport under the United Express brand and Cincinnati/Northern Kentucky International Airport, Detroit Metropolitan Wayne County Airport and New York's LaGuardia Airport under the Delta Connection brand. The firm's fleet consists of 47 70-seat Bombardier CRJ700 and seven 76-seat CRJ900 aircraft. The company is a member of the Star Alliance.

GoJet offers its employees medical and dental insurance, paid training, 401(k), long-term disability coverage, performance-based bonuses, paid vacation and holidays, flight benefits and travel discounts.

BRANDS/DIVISIONS/AFFILIATES:

Trans States Holdings Inc
Unites Express
Delta Connection

CONTACTS: Note: Officers with more than one job title may be intentionally listed here more than once.

Richard A. Leach, CEO
Richard A. Leach, Pres.

FINANCIAL DATA: Note: Data for latest year may not have been available at press time.

In U.S. $	2015	2014	2013	2012	2011	2010
Revenue	190,000,000	194,300,000	202,400,000	197,859,000	192,583,000	189,065,000
R&D Expense						
Operating Income						
Operating Margin %						
SGA Expense						
Net Income		200,000	8,800,000	-952,000	5,043,000	11,749,000
Operating Cash Flow						
Capital Expenditure						
EBITDA						
Return on Assets %						
Return on Equity %						
Debt to Equity						

CONTACT INFORMATION:

Phone: 314-222-4300   Fax: 314-222-4314
Toll-Free:
Address: 11495 Navaid Rd., Bridgeton, MO 63044 United States

STOCK TICKER/OTHER:

Stock Ticker: Subsidiary   Exchange:
Employees: 570   Fiscal Year Ends:
Parent Company: Trans States Holdings Inc

SALARIES/BONUSES:

Top Exec. Salary: $ Bonus: $
Second Exec. Salary: $ Bonus: $

OTHER THOUGHTS:

Estimated Female Officers or Directors:
Hot Spot for Advancement for Women/Minorities:

Sales, profits and employees may be estimates. Financial information, benefits and other data can change quickly and may vary from those stated here.

GOL Linhas Aereas Inteligentes SA

www.voegol.com.br

NAIC Code: 481111

TYPES OF BUSINESS:

Airline-Regional
Air Freight
Aircraft Maintenance

BRANDS/DIVISIONS/AFFILIATES:

GOL Intelligent Airlines Inc
VRG Linhas Aereas SA
GOL
Varig
Gollog
Voe Facil
Smiles

CONTACTS: *Note: Officers with more than one job title may be intentionally listed here more than once.*

Paulo Sergio Kakinoff, CEO
Edmar Prado Lopes Neto, CFO
Adalberto Bogsan, VP-Tech.
Constantino de Oliveira, Jr., Chmn.

GROWTH PLANS/SPECIAL FEATURES:

GOL Linhas Aereas Inteligentes SA (also known as GOL Intelligent Airlines, Inc.) is a leading South American discount airline. The company's fleet consists of 144 Boeing 737-700/800 aircraft. It operates its passenger air transportation business through VRG Linhas Aereas SA, which offers flights under the GOL and Varig brands. GOL, offering roughly 910 daily flights to 71 destinations, operates based on a low-cost, low-fare business model, with a single class of service in the Brazilian domestic market as well as South America and the Caribbean. It is among the largest low-cost airlines in the world, in terms of passengers transported, and the only low-fare, low-cost airline providing frequent service on routes connecting all of Brazil's major cities and other major South American destinations. The airline's growth strategy has been to focus on underserved markets and markets that do not offer lower-fare alternatives. Varig offers flights with single and dual class services both within Brazil and to other South American destinations. Varig's services focus on business travelers and emphasize business-oriented schedules and destinations, with differentiated onboard services and VIP lounges at principal airports. The company maintains a loyalty rewards program, Smiles, which has over 10.3 million members. Through its Voe Facil program, the firm allows customers without a credit card to purchase airline tickets on a 36 month installment plan. Additional revenues are derived from air cargo services offered through its Gollog division.

FINANCIAL DATA: *Note: Data for latest year may not have been available at press time.*

In U.S. $	2015	2014	2013	2012	2011	2010
Revenue	3,051,336,000	3,141,274,000	2,794,886,000	2,528,806,000	2,352,725,000	2,178,014,000
R&D Expense						
Operating Income	-56,119,830	158,349,800	83,004,830	-282,606,700	-76,300,200	217,754,700
Operating Margin %	-1.83%	5.04%	2.96%	-11.17%	-3.24%	9.99%
SGA Expense	685,889,900	987,881,400	753,960,100	976,654,400	612,577,300	616,104,500
Net Income	-1,392,068,000	-388,880,900	-248,571,400	-472,122,000	-234,525,800	66,842,560
Operating Cash Flow	-187,070,400	302,288,000	126,035,600	41,595,570	-188,023,100	225,900,100
Capital Expenditure	135,604,000	76,606,020	90,190,980	148,233,400	112,557,000	90,179,740
EBITDA	-668,267,100	32,160,710	153,951,600	-179,059,100	71,752,220	301,250,100
Return on Assets %	-43.85%	-12.08%	-8.10%	-15.37%	-7.62%	2.40%
Return on Equity %		-1880.45%	-115.12%	-102.96%	-29.27%	7.73%
Debt to Equity			7.90	4.73	1.55	1.15

CONTACT INFORMATION:

Phone: 55 1121284700   Fax: 55 1150987888
Toll-Free:
Address: Praca Comte Linneu Gomes, S/N Portaria 3, Sao Paulo, 04626-020 Brazil

STOCK TICKER/OTHER:

Stock Ticker: GOL   Exchange: NYS
Employees: 16,875   Fiscal Year Ends: 12/31
Parent Company:

SALARIES/BONUSES:

Top Exec. Salary: $ Bonus: $
Second Exec. Salary: $ Bonus: $

OTHER THOUGHTS:

Estimated Female Officers or Directors:
Hot Spot for Advancement for Women/Minorities:

Golden Tulip Hospitality Group

www.goldentulip.com

NAIC Code: 721110

TYPES OF BUSINESS:

Hotels & Resorts

BRANDS/DIVISIONS/AFFILIATES:

Golden Tulip
Tulip Inns
Royal Tulip
Branche Restaurant, Bar & Lounge
Campanile
Tulip Residences
Louvre Hotels
Kyriad

CONTACTS: *Note: Officers with more than one job title may be intentionally listed here more than once.*

Pierre Frederic Roulot, CEO
Pierre Frederic Roulot, Pres.
Victoire Boissier, CFO
Emmanuelle Greth, Chief Human Resources Officer
Haike Blaauw, Sr. VP-Franchise Oper.

GROWTH PLANS/SPECIAL FEATURES:

Golden Tulip Hospitality Group is a hospitality company with over 240 Tulip Inn, Golden Tulip and Royal Tulip branded hotels in more than 46 countries. Golden Tulip also maintains hotels that operate under the brand names Louvre Hotels, Kyriad, Campanile and Premiere Classe. The company's original brands include Royal Tulip, reserved for five-star hotels located in prime areas near city centers and business districts; Golden Tulip Hotels, which are four-star hotels situated in key locations near city centers, airports, conference venues and business districts; and Tulip Inns, which are three-star budget hotels with fewer amenities than the company's other brands. Golden Tulip also owns and operates the Branche Restaurant, Bar & Lounge chain; and The State Room, exclusively in Royal Tulip Hotels. In addition to its facilities, the company offers several services to business customers including group rates and the Golden Tulip Central Meeting Line, a reservation and planning service for businesses or large groups. The Ambassador Club is the company's frequent stay program through which guests have access to special events and discounts. Golden Tulip franchises and manages hotels in Europe, the Middle East and Africa, the Asia-Pacific Region and the Americas. In recent years, the company has added a new brand concept, Tulip Residences, which provides travelers with extended-stay studios and one-bedroom suites. The accommodations are four-star rated and offer amenities such as high-definition televisions, free Wi-Fi connections, en suite bathrooms and fully equipped kitchen facilities.

FINANCIAL DATA: *Note: Data for latest year may not have been available at press time.*

In U.S. $	2015	2014	2013	2012	2011	2010
Revenue						
R&D Expense						
Operating Income						
Operating Margin %						
SGA Expense						
Net Income						
Operating Cash Flow						
Capital Expenditure						
EBITDA						
Return on Assets %						
Return on Equity %						
Debt to Equity						

CONTACT INFORMATION:

Phone: 33-01-4291-4600   Fax: 33-01-4291-4601
Toll-Free:
Address: 50 Place de L'Ellipse, Village 5, Paris, CS 70050 France

STOCK TICKER/OTHER:

Stock Ticker: Private
Employees: 1,053
Parent Company: Shanghai Jin Jiang International Hotels

Exchange:
Fiscal Year Ends:

SALARIES/BONUSES:

Top Exec. Salary: $ Bonus: $
Second Exec. Salary: $ Bonus: $

OTHER THOUGHTS:

Estimated Female Officers or Directors:
Hot Spot for Advancement for Women/Minorities:

Sales, profits and employees may be estimates. Financial information, benefits and other data can change quickly and may vary from those stated here.

Great Lakes Aviation Ltd

NAIC Code: 481111

www.greatlakesav.com

TYPES OF BUSINESS:

Regional Airline
Charter Services
Cargo Services

BRANDS/DIVISIONS/AFFILIATES:

CONTACTS: *Note: Officers with more than one job title may be intentionally listed here more than once.*

Charles Howell, CEO
Michael Matthews, CFO
Douglas Voss, Chairman of the Board
Michael Tuinstra, Treasurer

GROWTH PLANS/SPECIAL FEATURES:

Great Lakes Aviation, Ltd. is a regional airline that offers service both independently and under code-share agreements with United Airlines. In addition, the company has electronic ticketing interline agreements with American Airlines, Delta Airlines, United Airlines and U.S. Airways. The company serves 28 airports in nine states with a fleet of six Embraer EMB-120 Brasilias and 22 Beechcraft 1900D regional airliners from its hubs in Denver, Los Angeles, Minneapolis and Phoenix. Great Lakes derives approximately 51% of its revenue from the Essential Air Service (EAS) program, which is administered by the U.S. Department of Transportation. This program gives airlines subsidies for serving areas that are unprofitable or minimally profitable. Great Lakes serves 19 EAS communities on a subsidized basis. The firm also offers charter service to private individuals, corporations and athletic teams and carries freight and small packages on most of its scheduled flights. In 2016, the firm entered into a codeshare agreement named Great Lakes Jet Express where they would sell tickets for Elite Airways to and from Denver and Houston to Branson Airport, as well as for Aerodynamics, Inc. on a route from Youngstown to Chicago O'Hare. This practice is controversial, but allows the new carriers to take advantage of Great Lakes' existing distribution and interline agreements with Global Distribution Systems and other airlines.

The firm offers employees medical, dental and vision coverage; life insurance; long-term disability; employee discounts; and employee assistance programs.

FINANCIAL DATA: *Note: Data for latest year may not have been available at press time.*

In U.S. $	2015	2014	2013	2012	2011	2010
Revenue		59,154,520	117,196,400	137,778,900	124,365,500	125,400,300
R&D Expense						
Operating Income		-5,856,457	3,764,594	9,413,037	6,324,686	10,642,770
Operating Margin %		-9.90%	3.21%	6.83%	5.08%	8.48%
SGA Expense		20,458,060	32,345,670	34,175,700	32,117,730	54,006,250
Net Income		-7,370,862	-442,671	2,902,136	10,688,270	5,053,278
Operating Cash Flow		-1,988,869	7,303,414	9,085,267	7,981,283	10,601,180
Capital Expenditure		1,614,469	1,593,121	6,512,188	3,859,011	2,765,732
EBITDA		-586,881	10,164,540	15,243,040	25,261,530	15,949,090
Return on Assets %		-10.37%	-.54%	3.45%	12.71%	5.98%
Return on Equity %		-21.10%	-1.13%	7.71%	32.84%	19.13%
Debt to Equity		0.80		0.58	0.73	0.19

CONTACT INFORMATION:

Phone: 307 432-7000   Fax: 307 432-7001
Toll-Free:
Address: 1022 Airport Pkwy., Cheyenne, WY 82001 United States

STOCK TICKER/OTHER:

Stock Ticker: GLUX   Exchange: PINX
Employees: 657   Fiscal Year Ends: 12/31
Parent Company:

SALARIES/BONUSES:

Top Exec. Salary: $ Bonus: $
Second Exec. Salary: $ Bonus: $

OTHER THOUGHTS:

Estimated Female Officers or Directors:
Hot Spot for Advancement for Women/Minorities:

Greyhound Lines Inc

www.greyhound.com

NAIC Code: 485210

TYPES OF BUSINESS:

Bus Services
Package Delivery Service

BRANDS/DIVISIONS/AFFILIATES:

FirstGroup plc
Greyhound Canada
Valley Transit Company
Crucero USA
Americanos USA
Greyhound PackageXpress
Lucky Streak
Road Rewards

CONTACTS: Note: Officers with more than one job title may be intentionally listed here more than once.

Dave Leach, CEO
Bill Blankenship, COO
Dave Leach, Pres.
Bill Gieseker, CFO
Kimberly Plaskett, VP-Mktg.
Rhonda P. MacAndrew, Sr. VP-Human Resources
Chris Boult, CIO
Myron Watkins, VP-Oper.
Ted F. Burk, Sr. VP-Corp. Dev.

GROWTH PLANS/SPECIAL FEATURES:

Greyhound Lines, Inc., a subsidiary of FirstGroup plc, is the only nationwide provider of scheduled intercity bus service in the U.S., serving more than 3,800 destinations in North America. The company offers seamless service between the U.S. and Canada and operates a fleet of about 1,200 buses. Besides its U.S. network, Greyhound serves riders in Canadian provinces through Greyhound Canada, while subsidiary Greyhound de Mexico allows customers to purchase tickets within Mexico at over 100 agencies and travel across the border. Additionally, Greyhound has three operating subsidiaries that facilitate U.S.-Mexico transborder travel: Valley Transit Company, which serves the Texas-Mexico border; Crucero USA, operating from southern California and Arizona into Mexico; and Americanos USA, traveling to destinations in Mexico from Texas and New Mexico. Through its Greyhound Express service, it offers non-stop service between more than 600 city pairs. The firm also runs Greyhound PackageXpress (GPX), a package delivery service that ships oversized, heavy weight, same day and overnight freight at low rates; Lucky Streak buses, which provide door-to-door service to many casinos and resorts in the country; Greyhound Travel Services, which offers charter packages for organizations, schools and conventions; and the QuickLink service, an alternative to the daily commuter service. The company offers a Road Rewards service, in which passengers can accrue points when traveling and use these points for discounted or free tickets. Charter service is available for special events, conventions, meetings, group travel and tour packages. The company also offers the Discovery Pass, a pass that allows unlimited travel in the U.S. and Canada from 7-60 days of travel. Greyhound generally serves a diverse customer base, consisting primarily of low- to middle-income passengers.

FINANCIAL DATA: Note: Data for latest year may not have been available at press time.

In U.S. $	2015	2014	2013	2012	2011	2010
Revenue	986,000,000	990,600,000	1,100,000,000	1,050,000,000	1,017,360,000	909,052,000
R&D Expense						
Operating Income						
Operating Margin %						
SGA Expense						
Net Income	68,500,000	73,200,000	68,273,037			
Operating Cash Flow						
Capital Expenditure						
EBITDA						
Return on Assets %						
Return on Equity %						
Debt to Equity						

CONTACT INFORMATION:

Phone: 972-789-7000 Fax:
Toll-Free:
Address: One Dallas Center, Dallas, TX 75201 United States

STOCK TICKER/OTHER:

Stock Ticker: Subsidiary
Employees: 7,900
Parent Company: Firstgroup plc

Exchange:
Fiscal Year Ends:

SALARIES/BONUSES:

Top Exec. Salary: $ Bonus: $
Second Exec. Salary: $ Bonus: $

OTHER THOUGHTS:

Estimated Female Officers or Directors: 2
Hot Spot for Advancement for Women/Minorities:

Sales, profits and employees may be estimates. Financial information, benefits and other data can change quickly and may vary from those stated here.

Groupe du Louvre

NAIC Code: 721110

www.groupedulouvre.com

TYPES OF BUSINESS:

Hotels
Luxury Goods
Perfume House

BRANDS/DIVISIONS/AFFILIATES:

Shanghai Jin Jiang International Hotels
Crillon
Concorde Hotel & Resorts
Kyriad Prestige
Campanile
Premiere Classe
Annick Goutal
Baccarat

CONTACTS: Note: Officers with more than one job title may be intentionally listed here more than once.

Steven Goldman, CEO
Jean-Yves Schapiro, Finance Dir.
Pascal Malbequi, General Counsel
Jean-Yves Schapiro, Dir.-Finance
Brigitte Taitttinger, Pres., Annick Goutal
Bernard Granier, COO-Concorde Hotels & Resorts
Pierre Frederic Roulot, Pres., Louvre Hotels
Herve Martin, Pres., Baccarat

GROWTH PLANS/SPECIAL FEATURES:

Groupe du Louvre (Louvre) is a French hotel and luxury goods company. The Louvre chain of hotels includes 97,000 rooms in 1,100 properties. The company operates in four segments: luxury hotel, budget hotel, crystal manufacturer and perfume house. The luxury hotel division encompasses the Crillon and Concorde hotels and resorts. The segment comprises more than 27 prestigious hotels in locations such as Amsterdam, Barcelona, Cannes, Nice, Paris, Prague and Tokyo. The budget hotel division includes more than 800 hotels with a total of roughly 52,000 rooms in nine European countries under four brands: Kyriad, Kyriad Prestige, Campanile and Premiere Classe. The crystal manufacturer division operates through subsidiary Societe du Louvre, which is the majority shareholder of Baccarat, one of the most prestigious crystal manufacturers in the world. Products, which include jewelry, accessories and wristwatches, are sold through a network of 47 owned stores and points of sales worldwide. The perfume house division operates through Annick Goutal, a unique luxury perfume house created in 1980 that distributes products in more than 20 countries. Annick Goutal offers more than 25 fragrances composed mainly of natural elements as well as a skin care line with active rose serum. The perfumery has 11 boutiques and 1,000 points of sale such as Saks Fifth Avenue, Isetan, Bergdorf Goodman, Harrods and Harvey Nichols. In March 2015, the firm was acquired by Shanghai Jin Jiang International Hotels Development Co. Ltd., owner and operator of economy and mid-scale hotels in Asia.

FINANCIAL DATA: Note: Data for latest year may not have been available at press time.

In U.S. $	2015	2014	2013	2012	2011	2010
Revenue	392,605,224	1,811,215,485				
R&D Expense						
Operating Income						
Operating Margin %						
SGA Expense						
Net Income	23,105,898					
Operating Cash Flow						
Capital Expenditure						
EBITDA						
Return on Assets %						
Return on Equity %						
Debt to Equity						

CONTACT INFORMATION:

Phone: 33-1-42-91-4500   Fax:
Toll-Free:
Address: Village 5, 50 Place de l'Ellipse, Paris, 92081 France

STOCK TICKER/OTHER:

Stock Ticker: Subsidiary   Exchange:
Employees: 19,000   Fiscal Year Ends: 12/31
Parent Company: Shanghai Jin Jiang International Hotels

SALARIES/BONUSES:

Top Exec. Salary: $ Bonus: $
Second Exec. Salary: $ Bonus: $

OTHER THOUGHTS:

Estimated Female Officers or Directors: 1
Hot Spot for Advancement for Women/Minorities:

Guangshen Railway Co Ltd   www.gsrc.com

NAIC Code: 482111

TYPES OF BUSINESS:

Line-Haul Railroads
Passenger Transportation
Freight Transportation
Property Leasing
Food & Beverage Sales

BRANDS/DIVISIONS/AFFILIATES:

Guangshen Railway
Hong Kong Through Trains

CONTACTS: *Note: Officers with more than one job title may be intentionally listed here more than once.*

Hu Lingling, Gen. Mgr.
Guo Xiangdong, Deputy Gen. Mgr.
Tang Xiangdong, Chief Accountant
Mu Anyun, Deputy Gen. Mgr.
Wu Yong, Chmn.

GROWTH PLANS/SPECIAL FEATURES:

Guangshen Railway Company, Ltd. operates a segment of the rail transportation system in southern China, running services between Guangzhou and Shenzhen, as well as providing freight transportation and railway network usage and services. The Shenzhen-Guangzhou-Pingshi Railway (Guangshen Railway), operated exclusively by the company, incorporates 300 miles of tracks across the Pearl River Delta in Guangdong Province. The Guangshen Railway links with major railway networks in China, including the Beijing-Guangzhou, Beijing-Kowloon, Sanshui-Maoming, Pinghu-Nantou and Pinghu-Yantian lines, as well as to the Kowloon-Canton Railway in Hong Kong. The network boasts high-speed passenger trains with speeds of up to 200 miles per hour and features four parallel tracks, allowing high-speed passenger trains, regular-speed trains and freight trains to run on separate tracks. Within Hong Kong, the company cooperates with MTR Corp., Ltd. in operating the Hong Kong Through Trains passenger and freight services. In addition to passenger transportation, the firm provides freight transportation and runs various small business ventures that relate to its railway business, such as train maintenance and repair, on-board catering, labor services and the operation of restaurants, hotels and warehouses. Its freight business consists of express container trains for the transport of various cargo types, including full- and single-load cargo, containers, bulk cargo, hazardous cargo and fresh and live cargo. Guangshen's freight segment also maintains business partnerships with local ports, logistic bases, building materials markets, large factories and mines.

FINANCIAL DATA: *Note: Data for latest year may not have been available at press time.*

In U.S. $	2015	2014	2013	2012	2011	2010
Revenue	2,370,268,000	2,230,915,000	2,381,629,000	2,274,793,000	2,214,343,000	2,032,505,000
R&D Expense						
Operating Income	219,152,800	159,164,100	284,609,200	291,556,600	386,477,800	318,057,100
Operating Margin %	9.24%	7.13%	11.95%	12.81%	17.45%	15.64%
SGA Expense	35,448,720	42,103,580	44,680,600	129,430,400	502,112,400	69,297,750
Net Income	161,404,500	99,786,120	192,005,500	198,802,900	271,932,200	223,993,400
Operating Cash Flow	340,602,200	293,255,800	283,885,700	328,239,600	501,787,400	502,149,100
Capital Expenditure	194,783,700	150,674,200	196,152,000		142,196,700	174,604,900
EBITDA	436,603,300	378,690,500	498,139,700	501,051,800	600,077,600	524,037,900
Return on Assets %	3.42%	2.07%	3.85%	4.05%	5.74%	5.01%
Return on Equity %	3.95%	2.47%	4.84%	5.14%	7.28%	6.35%
Debt to Equity				0.13	0.13	0.14

CONTACT INFORMATION:

Phone: 86 7555598693   Fax: 86 75525591480
Toll-Free:
Address: 1052 Heping Rd., Shenzhen, Guangdong 518010 China

STOCK TICKER/OTHER:

Stock Ticker: GSH   Exchange: NYS
Employees: 37,301   Fiscal Year Ends: 12/31
Parent Company:

SALARIES/BONUSES:

Top Exec. Salary: $331,000   Bonus: $
Second Exec. Salary: Bonus: $
$328,000

OTHER THOUGHTS:

Estimated Female Officers or Directors:
Hot Spot for Advancement for Women/Minorities:

Sales, profits and employees may be estimates. Financial information, benefits and other data can change quickly and may vary from those stated here.

Gulfstream Aerospace Corp

www.gulfstream.com

NAIC Code: 336411

TYPES OF BUSINESS:

Aircraft Manufacturing
Business Jets
Support Services
Leasing & Financing

BRANDS/DIVISIONS/AFFILIATES:

General Dynamics Corp
G650ER
G150
G280
G450
G550
G600
G650

CONTACTS: *Note: Officers with more than one job title may be intentionally listed here more than once.*

Larry Flynn, Pres.
Daniel G. Clare, CFO
Sheryl Bunton, VP
Dan Nale, Sr. VP-Programs, Eng. & Test
Ira Berman, Sr. VP-Admin.
Ira Berman, General Counsel
Dennis Stuligross, Sr. VP-Oper.
Joe Lombardo, Exec. VP-Aerospace Group, General Dynamics
Mark Burns, Pres., Product Support
Scott Neal, Sr. VP-Worldwide Sales & Mktg.
Buddy Sams, Sr. VP-Gov't Programs & Sales

GROWTH PLANS/SPECIAL FEATURES:

Gulfstream Aerospace Corp., a subsidiary of General Dynamics Corp., develops, manufactures, markets and provides maintenance and support services for technologically-advanced business jet aircraft. Gulfstream has produced more than 2,200 aircraft for customers around the world since 1958. The company is also a leading provider of aircraft for government special-mission applications, including executive transportation, aerial reconnaissance, maritime surveillance, weather research and astronaut training. Gulfstream's product line includes seven aircraft: the mid-size G150 and G280, the long-range G450; the ultra-long-range G550, G600 and G650; and the extended reach G650ER, extending the nonstop reach of the industry's highest performance long-range business aircraft to 7,500 nautical miles at Mach 0.85. The maximum operating speed for G650ER is 0.925. Gulfstream also routinely accepts aircraft trade-ins for the sale of new Gulfstream models and resells the used planes on the pre-owned market. The group offers several product enhancements for its planes, including the ultra-high-speed broadband multi-link (BBML) system, which allows customers to access the Internet at altitudes up to 51,000 feet; and the Enhanced Vision System (EVS), a forward-looking infrared (FLIR) camera that projects an infrared real-world image on the pilot's heads-up display, which allows the flight crew to see in conditions of low light and reduced visibility. In December 2015, the firm delivered a Gulfstream G650ER to Qatar Airways, the first of up to 30 Gulfstream aircraft Qatar Airways has agreed to purchase.

Employees of the firm receive tuition reimbursement; relocation assistance; a performance-based incentive plan; a wellness program; flexible spending accounts; and medical, dental, vision, disability and life insurance.

FINANCIAL DATA: *Note: Data for latest year may not have been available at press time.*

In U.S. $	2015	2014	2013	2012	2011	2010
Revenue	8,851,000,000	8,649,000,000	8,118,000,000	6,912,000,000	5,998,000,000	
R&D Expense						
Operating Income						
Operating Margin %						
SGA Expense						
Net Income	1,706,000,000	1,611,000,000	1,416,000,000	858,000,000	729,000,000	
Operating Cash Flow						
Capital Expenditure						
EBITDA						
Return on Assets %						
Return on Equity %						
Debt to Equity						

CONTACT INFORMATION:

Phone: 912-965-3000   Fax: 912-965-3084
Toll-Free:
Address: 500 Gulfstream Rd., Savannah, GA 31407 United States

STOCK TICKER/OTHER:

Stock Ticker: Subsidiary   Exchange:
Employees: 16,000   Fiscal Year Ends: 12/31
Parent Company: General Dynamics Corp

SALARIES/BONUSES:

Top Exec. Salary: $ Bonus: $
Second Exec. Salary: $ Bonus: $

OTHER THOUGHTS:

Estimated Female Officers or Directors:
Hot Spot for Advancement for Women/Minorities:

Hawaiian Airlines Inc

www.hawaiianair.com

NAIC Code: 481111

TYPES OF BUSINESS:

Airline
Charter Flights
Air Cargo

BRANDS/DIVISIONS/AFFILIATES:

Hawaiian Holdings Inc
Ohana by Hawaiian

CONTACTS: Note: Officers with more than one job title may be intentionally listed here more than once.

Mark Dunkerley, CEO
Shannon Okinaka, CFO
Lawrence Hershfield, Chairman of the Board
Jonathan Snook, COO, Subsidiary
Peter Ingram, Executive VP, Subsidiary
Ronald Anderson-Lehman, Executive VP, Subsidiary
Aaron Alter, Executive VP
Hoyt Zia, General Counsel, Subsidiary
Barbara Falvey, Senior VP, Subsidiary
Theodoros Panagiotoulias, Senior VP, Subsidiary

GROWTH PLANS/SPECIAL FEATURES:

Hawaiian Airlines, Inc., the sole operating unit of Hawaiian Holdings, Inc., is engaged in the transportation of passengers, cargo and mail to 28 domestic and international destinations in the Pacific region. With approximately 52 aircraft, it is one of the largest airlines headquartered in Hawaii. It operates approximately 208 scheduled flights per day, including flights within the Hawaiian Islands as well as trans-Pacific flights to cities such as Oakland, Los Angeles, San Diego, San Jose, San Francisco, Sacramento, Portland, Las Vegas, Seattle, Phoenix and New York City. The firm has inter-island routes among the four major islands of Hawaii and also provides service to South Pacific routes, functioning as the sole direct provider of air transportation from Hawaii to American Samoa, Japan, South Korea, New Zealand, Australia, the Philippines, Tahiti and Taiwan. The firm also provides charter service to Anchorage, Alaska and Honolulu. Hawaiian Airlines maintains code-sharing alliances with American Airlines, All Nippon Airways, China Airlines, Delta Air Lines, JetBlue, Virgin America, Virgin Atlantic Airways, Virgin Australia, Korean Air and United, which provide reciprocal frequent-flyer mileage accrual, redemption privileges and code-sharing on certain flights. Ohana by Hawaiian is a Hawaiian Airlines subsidiary for interisland travel with flights to and from Molokai and Lanai. In December 2015, the firm set a new record carrying 10.67 million passengers that year. The firm has an Airbus purchase agreement for the delivery of six new A330-800neo aircraft between 2017 and 2020; and announced that its Airbus A330-200 aircraft will be retrofitted with the new Premium Business class seats from mid-2016 to 2017.

Hawaiian Airlines offers its employees benefits including medical and dental plans, domestic partner coverage, an employee assistance program, flexible spending programs, a 401(k) and travel benefits.

FINANCIAL DATA: Note: Data for latest year may not have been available at press time.

In U.S. $	2015	2014	2013	2012	2011	2010
Revenue	2,317,467,000	2,314,879,000	2,155,865,000	1,962,353,000	1,650,459,000	1,310,093,000
R&D Expense						
Operating Income	426,103,000	245,132,000	133,747,000	129,398,000	20,283,000	91,278,000
Operating Margin %	18.38%	10.58%	6.20%	6.59%	1.22%	6.96%
SGA Expense	701,090,000	657,866,000	634,655,000	675,307,000	602,833,000	375,764,000
Net Income	182,646,000	68,926,000	51,854,000	53,237,000	-2,649,000	110,255,000
Operating Cash Flow	476,028,000	300,430,000	243,270,000	311,017,000	178,764,000	150,297,000
Capital Expenditure	118,828,000	442,229,000	342,228,000	290,699,000	281,903,000	140,460,000
EBITDA	454,921,000	267,272,000	208,523,000	207,093,000	87,895,000	162,635,000
Return on Assets %	7.14%	2.89%	2.57%	3.17%	-.20%	10.27%
Return on Equity %	44.91%	18.04%	15.58%	21.66%	-1.05%	48.57%
Debt to Equity	1.55	2.53	1.87	2.05	1.90	0.61

CONTACT INFORMATION:

Phone: 808 835-3700 Fax:
Toll-Free:
Address: 3375 Koapaka St., Ste. G-350, Honolulu, HI 96819 United States

STOCK TICKER/OTHER:

Stock Ticker: HA
Employees: 5,548
Parent Company: Hawaiian Holdings Inc

Exchange: NAS
Fiscal Year Ends: 12/31

SALARIES/BONUSES:

Top Exec. Salary: $695,000 Bonus: $
Second Exec. Salary: $453,750 Bonus: $

OTHER THOUGHTS:

Estimated Female Officers or Directors: 3
Hot Spot for Advancement for Women/Minorities: Y

Sales, profits and employees may be estimates. Financial information, benefits and other data can change quickly and may vary from those stated here.

Heathrow Airport Holdings Ltd   www.heathrowairport.com
NAIC Code: 488119

TYPES OF BUSINESS:
Aircraft Hangar Rental
In-Terminal Retail Concessions
Commuter Rail Service
Commercial Real Estate

BRANDS/DIVISIONS/AFFILIATES:
FGP Topco Limited
Heathrow Airport
Heathrow Express
BAA Lynton

CONTACTS: *Note: Officers with more than one job title may be intentionally listed here more than once.*

John Holland-Kaye, CEO
Normand Boivin, COO
Michael Robin Uzielli, CFO
Carol Hui, General Counsel
John Holland-Kaye, Dir.-Dev.
Clare Harbord, Dir.-Corp. Affairs
Emma Gilthorpe, Dir.-Regulation
Jim O'Sullivan, Managing Dir.-Airports Div.
Ian Ballentine, Dir.-Procurement

GROWTH PLANS/SPECIAL FEATURES:

Heathrow Airport Holdings Ltd., a subsidiary of the Spanish construction company FGP Topco Limited, is a leading airport operator based in the U.K. Heathrow Airport serves 185 destinations and 80 airlines in 84 countries, with its most popular destinations being New York, Dubai, Dublin, Hong Kong and Frankfurt. Heathrow consists of two runways and five terminals. The firm provides all security services at its airport and offers commercial accommodation, including warehouses, hotels, hangars and check-in desks. The firm's Heathrow Express is a non-stop rail service connecting Paddington Station in London to Heathrow Airport. BAA Lynton is the firm's real estate property manager, which acquires, develops and invests in areas surrounding the firm's airports. In December 2014, the firm sold its Aberdeen, Glasgow and Southampton airports in order to improve and expand Heathrow. In January 2016, it announced plans to invest approximately $150 million in public green spaces and community buildings in parkland that surrounds the airport.

FINANCIAL DATA: *Note: Data for latest year may not have been available at press time.*

In U.S. $	2015	2014	2013	2012	2011	2010
Revenue	3,615,714,620	3,959,886,374	4,325,000,000	3,980,170,000	3,523,310,000	3,208,510,000
R&D Expense						
Operating Income						
Operating Margin %						
SGA Expense						
Net Income	917,084,452	1,234,108,825	1,372,416,929	-52,983,000	-395,290,000	-489,714,000
Operating Cash Flow						
Capital Expenditure						
EBITDA						
Return on Assets %						
Return on Equity %						
Debt to Equity						

CONTACT INFORMATION:
Phone: 0844-335-1801   Fax:
Toll-Free:
Address: Nelson Rd., The Compass Centre, Hounslow, Middlesex, TW6 2GW United Kingdom

STOCK TICKER/OTHER:
Stock Ticker: Subsidiary   Exchange:
Employees: Fiscal Year Ends: 12/31
Parent Company: FGP Topco Limited

SALARIES/BONUSES:
Top Exec. Salary: $ Bonus: $
Second Exec. Salary: $ Bonus: $

OTHER THOUGHTS:
Estimated Female Officers or Directors: 5
Hot Spot for Advancement for Women/Minorities: Y

Hertz Global Holdings Inc

www.hertz.com

NAIC Code: 532111

TYPES OF BUSINESS:

Automobile Rental
Truck Rental
Claims Management
Heavy Equipment Rental
Used Automobile Sales
Leasing
Actuarial Services
Franchising

BRANDS/DIVISIONS/AFFILIATES:

Hertz Claims Management
Hertz
Dollar
Thrifty
Firefly
Donlen
Donlen Corporation

CONTACTS: *Note: Officers with more than one job title may be intentionally listed here more than once.*

Lawrence Silber, CEO, Subsidiary
John Tague, CEO
Thomas Kennedy, CFO
Robin Kramer, Chief Accounting Officer
Tyler Best, Chief Information Officer
Linda Levinson, Director
Robert Stuart, Executive VP, Divisional
Richard Frecker, Other Corporate Officer
Jeffrey Foland, Other Executive Officer
Michel Taride, President, Divisional

GROWTH PLANS/SPECIAL FEATURES:

Hertz Global Holdings, Inc. owns one of the largest worldwide airport general-use car rental brands and one of the largest equipment rental businesses in the U.S. and Canada. Hertz is the number one airport car rental brand in the U.S. and at 125 major airports in Europe. The company operates in four segments: U.S. car rental, international car rental, worldwide equipment rental and other operations. U.S. car rental rents cars, crossovers and light trucks, and also provides ancillary products and services. This segment has franchises and associates that operate rental locations under the Hertz, Dollar, Thrifty, Firefly and Donlen brands throughout the USA. International car rental rents the same vehicles and provides the same products and services as the U.S. division, only internationally. This segment maintains a network of company-operated car rental locations, a majority of which are in Europe. Its franchisees and associates also operate rental locations in approximately 150 countries and jurisdictions. Worldwide equipment rental rents industrial, construction, material handling and other equipment. It rents a broad range of earthmoving, material handling, aerial and electrical equipment, air compressors, power generators, pumps, small tools, compaction equipment, construction-related trucks and other types of commercial vehicles. This division's Hertz Entertainment Services unit rents studio and production equipment products used primarily in the U.S. entertainment industry. Other operations comprise the firm's Donlen Corporation, which provides fleet leasing and management services; and subsidiary Hertz Claims Management, which provides claim management services. U.S. car rental derives 60% of company revenues, international car rental derives 20%, worldwide equipment derives 14% and other operations derives 6%. In June 2016, the firm reached an agreement with Lyft to supply rental car rates for drivers who can either use the cars for Lyft business or for personal driving. Lyft provides ridesharing in more than 200 U.S. cities.

FINANCIAL DATA: *Note: Data for latest year may not have been available at press time.*

In U.S. $	2015	2014	2013	2012	2011	2010
Revenue	10,535,000,000	11,046,000,000	10,771,900,000	9,020,807,000	8,298,380,000	7,562,534,000
R&D Expense						
Operating Income	832,000,000	610,000,000	1,472,200,000	450,545,000	1,080,985,000	747,524,000
Operating Margin %	7.89%	5.52%	13.66%	4.99%	13.02%	9.88%
SGA Expense	1,045,000,000	1,088,000,000	1,022,200,000	945,784,000	745,278,000	664,512,000
Net Income	273,000,000	-82,000,000	346,200,000	243,079,000	176,170,000	-48,044,000
Operating Cash Flow	3,332,000,000	3,452,000,000	3,589,600,000	2,717,983,000	2,233,339,000	2,208,679,000
Capital Expenditure	12,985,000,000	11,663,000,000	10,612,200,000	312,786,000	9,736,006,000	8,620,081,000
EBITDA	3,874,000,000	3,930,000,000	4,150,900,000	3,425,493,000	3,061,645,000	2,768,481,000
Return on Assets %	1.15%	-.33%	1.44%	1.18%	1.00%	-.28%
Return on Equity %	12.17%	-3.13%	13.11%	10.25%	8.10%	-2.29%
Debt to Equity	7.87	6.49	5.88	6.16	5.06	5.34

CONTACT INFORMATION:

Phone: 239-301-7000   Fax:
Toll-Free: 800-654-3131
Address: 8501 Williams Road, Estero, FL 33928 United States

STOCK TICKER/OTHER:

Stock Ticker: HTZ
Employees: 30,400
Parent Company:

Exchange: NYS
Fiscal Year Ends: 12/31

SALARIES/BONUSES:

Top Exec. Salary: $800,962   Bonus: $2,647,500
Second Exec. Salary: $553,846   Bonus: $2,780,000

OTHER THOUGHTS:

Estimated Female Officers or Directors: 6
Hot Spot for Advancement for Women/Minorities: Y

Sales, profits and employees may be estimates. Financial information, benefits and other data can change quickly and may vary from those stated here.

Hf Eimskipafelag Islands

NAIC Code: 481212

www.eimskip.is

TYPES OF BUSINESS:

Freight Forwarding
Logistics Services
Travel Tours
Sea Transportation-Freight Services
Ferry Operations

BRANDS/DIVISIONS/AFFILIATES:

Eimskip Norway
Faroe Ship
Eimskip Flytjandi
TVG-Zimsen
Herjolfur
Jac Meisner International Expeditiebedrifj BV
Seatours

CONTACTS: Note: Officers with more than one job title may be intentionally listed here more than once.

Gylfi Sigfusson, CEO
Asbjorn Skulason, VP-Ship Management
Gylfi Sigfusson, Pres.
Hilmar Petur Valgarosson, CFO
Matthias Matthiasson, VP-Transportation Services
Hilmar Valgarsson, Head-Admin.
Asbjorn Skulason, Head-Oper.
Hilmar Valgarsson, Head-Finance
Guomundur Nikulasson, VP-Eimskip Domestic Oper.
Richard Winston Mark dÂ´Abo, Chmn.
Bragi Marinosson, Head-Int'l

GROWTH PLANS/SPECIAL FEATURES:

Hf. Eimskipafelag Islands (Eimskip) is an investment group focused on transportation and logistics services. It specializes in shipping, logistics and supply chain management, with a focus on temperature-controlled cargo. The firm has three main business units: domestic, import and export. The domestic unit consists of domestic transport, warehouse hotel and ferry operations between the Western Islands and mainland Iceland. Services in this unit include transportation services, such as passenger services, airfreight, inland transportation, general forwarding, global reefer logistics, ocean freight, customs documentation, cargo insurance, cold storage and agency services. The import, as well as export business units offer harbor services, bulk transport, sea or air freight, customs documentation, land transport, warehousing and pre-carriage services. The firm's airfreight services include collecting goods at factory warehouses, marking and preparing shipments for transport, transporting shipments to airline carriers, providing freight insurance, handling customs clearance and transporting shipments to the warehouse of destination. The firm provides price quotations for various modes of inland transportation (which can include transport by truck, train or river barge) and also organizes the transportation. Eimskip's general forwarding services include customizing transportation for various logistic requirements. The company can handle both frozen and chilled cargo temperature requirements and provides reefer services covering the entire logistics chain, including discharge of fishing vessels, transportation, warehousing, distribution, inventory control and customs formalities. The firm has five primary subsidiaries: Eimskip Norway, Eimskip Flytjandi, Faroe Ship, TVG-Zimsen and Herjolfur. In 2015, the firm acquired Seatours (SÃ¦ferdir ehf) in StykkishÃ³lmur, Iceland; cold storage operation of St. Anthony Cold Storage Ltd. in Newfoundland and Labrador, Canada; and Jac. Meisner Internationaal Expeditiebedrijf B.V., a forwarding company in the Netherlands.

FINANCIAL DATA: Note: Data for latest year may not have been available at press time.

In U.S. $	2015	2014	2013	2012	2011	2010
Revenue	549,938,768	489,661,378	555,000,000	551,461,940	548,733,000	535,689,000
R&D Expense						
Operating Income						
Operating Margin %						
SGA Expense						
Net Income	195,943,053	41,744,825	40,118,403	16,945,384	16,625,900	16,215,900
Operating Cash Flow						
Capital Expenditure						
EBITDA						
Return on Assets %						
Return on Equity %						
Debt to Equity						

CONTACT INFORMATION:

Phone: 354-525-7000   Fax: 354-525-7009
Toll-Free:
Address: Korngardar 2, Reykjavik, 104 Iceland

STOCK TICKER/OTHER:

Stock Ticker: EIM   Exchange: Iceland
Employees: 1,576   Fiscal Year Ends: 10/31
Parent Company:

SALARIES/BONUSES:

Top Exec. Salary: $ Bonus: $
Second Exec. Salary: $ Bonus: $

OTHER THOUGHTS:

Estimated Female Officers or Directors:
Hot Spot for Advancement for Women/Minorities:

Sales, profits and employees may be estimates. Financial information, benefits and other data can change quickly and may vary from those stated here.

Hilton Worldwide Inc

www.hiltonworldwide.com

NAIC Code: 721110

TYPES OF BUSINESS:

Hotels & Resorts
Timeshare Properties
Conference Centers
Franchising
Management Services
Online Reservations

BRANDS/DIVISIONS/AFFILIATES:

Blackstone Group LP (The)
Hilton Grand Vacations Co LLC
Hilton
Hhonors
DoubleTree
Embassy Suites
Homewood Suites
Hampton Inn

CONTACTS: Note: Officers with more than one job title may be intentionally listed here more than once.

Christopher Nassetta, CEO
Kevin Jacobs, CFO
Jonathan Gray, Chairman of the Board
Michael Duffy, Chief Accounting Officer
James Holthouser, Executive VP, Divisional
Mark Wang, Executive VP, Divisional
Kristin Campbell, Executive VP
Matthew Schuyler, Executive VP
Christopher Silcock, Executive VP
Ian Carter, Executive VP

GROWTH PLANS/SPECIAL FEATURES:

Hilton Worldwide, Inc. owns, manages and develops hotels, resorts and timeshare properties and franchises lodging properties worldwide. Hilton Worldwide consists of 12 hotel brands and more than 4,610 hotels in 100 countries, ranging from affordable focus-service hotels to luxury extended stay suites. Hotel brands include Hilton, Hilton Garden Inn, DoubleTree, Embassy Suites, Homewood Suites, Home2 Suites, Hampton Inn, Conrad Hotels, Curio A Collection by Hilton, tru by Hilton, Canopy by Hilton and The Waldorf Astoria Collection. Additionally, Hilton Grand Vacations Co., LLC is the firm's timeshare brand in which ownership of a deeded real estate interest with club membership points provides members with a lifetime of vacation advantages. Hhonors, the firm's loyalty enrollment program for returning customers, has over 44 million members and includes partner benefits with several airlines. In addition, Hilton Worldwide offers architecture and construction and management services to individuals interested in developing their own properties. The Blackstone Group LP owns 45.9% of the firm's stock. In 2015, Hilton sold Waldorf Astoria New York, and signed agreements to redeploy the proceeds to add five landmark properties: Hilton Orlando Bonnet Creek, Waldorf Astoria Orlando, The Reach in Key West, Casa Marina in Key West (all in Florida) and Parc 55 in San Francisco, California. In February 2016, the firm announced plans to split into three companies by years' end, spinning off its real estate and vacation/timeshare businesses, while retaining its present hotel business.

FINANCIAL DATA: Note: Data for latest year may not have been available at press time.

In U.S. $	2015	2014	2013	2012	2011	2010
Revenue	11,272,000,000	10,502,000,000	9,735,000,000	9,276,000,000	8,783,000,000	8,068,000,000
R&D Expense						
Operating Income	2,071,000,000	1,673,000,000	1,102,000,000	1,100,000,000	975,000,000	553,000,000
Operating Margin %	18.37%	15.93%	11.32%	11.85%	11.10%	6.85%
SGA Expense	547,000,000	491,000,000	748,000,000	460,000,000	416,000,000	637,000,000
Net Income	1,404,000,000	673,000,000	415,000,000	352,000,000	253,000,000	128,000,000
Operating Cash Flow	1,394,000,000	1,366,000,000	2,101,000,000	1,110,000,000	1,167,000,000	833,000,000
Capital Expenditure	372,000,000	337,000,000	332,000,000	536,000,000	482,000,000	168,000,000
EBITDA	2,763,000,000	2,393,000,000	1,921,000,000	1,692,000,000	1,403,000,000	1,939,000,000
Return on Assets %	5.41%	2.55%	1.54%	1.29%	.92%	
Return on Equity %	26.15%	14.76%	12.45%	16.88%	13.54%	
Debt to Equity	1.72	2.43	2.90	6.77	8.78	

CONTACT INFORMATION:

Phone: 703-883-1000   Fax:
Toll-Free: 800-445-8667
Address: 7930 Jones Branch Dr., Ste. 1100, McLean, VA 22102 United States

STOCK TICKER/OTHER:

Stock Ticker: HLT
Employees: 157,000
Parent Company:

Exchange: NYS
Fiscal Year Ends: 12/31

SALARIES/BONUSES:

Top Exec. Salary: $1,246,154   Bonus: $
Second Exec. Salary: $748,077   Bonus: $

OTHER THOUGHTS:

Estimated Female Officers or Directors: 2

Hot Spot for Advancement for Women/Minorities:

HMSHost Corporation

www.hmshost.com

NAIC Code: 722310

TYPES OF BUSINESS:

Food Service Contractors
Food, Beverage & Retail Concessions
Travel Plazas
Food Courts

BRANDS/DIVISIONS/AFFILIATES:

Autogrill SpA
Ciao Gourmet Market
La Tapenade Mediterranean
Z Market
Wicker Park Seafood & Sushi Bar
Beaudevin
Jose Cuervo Tequileria

CONTACTS: Note: Officers with more than one job title may be intentionally listed here more than once.

Steve Johnson, CEO
Silvano Delnegro, COO
Tom Fricke, Pres.
Mark Ratych, CFO
Laura E. FitzRandolph, Exec. VP-Human Resources
Sarah Naqvi, Exec. VP-CIO

GROWTH PLANS/SPECIAL FEATURES:

HMSHost Corporation, a wholly-owned subsidiary of Italy-based Autogrill SpA, is a leading provider of food and beverage concessions for travelers. The firm operates facilities in over 120 airports worldwide as well as 99 roadside travel plazas along major U.S. and Canada toll roads and turnpikes in the Northeast and Midwest. HMSHost also serves tourist destinations such as Space Center Houston and the Empire State Building. The company's international airport operations include food service outlets at major and regional airports in Canada, Australia, Singapore, Ireland, India, Denmark, Sweden, the Netherlands, the U.K., Malaysia, France, Finland, Russia, the Middle East, Vietnam, Indonesia and New Zealand. HMSHost is engaged in a range of national and local brand licensing and franchising relationships, providing its food service with well-known brands ranging from Wolfgang Puck, Quiznos Sub to Starbucks, Pizza Hut and the Chili's Too. The company also develops proprietary branded concepts including Ciao Gourmet Market, La Tapenade Mediterranean, Z Market, Wicker Park Seafood & Sushi Bar, Beaudevin and Jose Cuervo Tequileria. In June 2016, the firm agreed to acquire Concession Management Services, Inc.'s airport restaurants, which would transform the operations of 16 dining locations at Los Angeles International Airport and McCarran International Airport (Las Vegas).

FINANCIAL DATA: Note: Data for latest year may not have been available at press time.

In U.S. $	2015	2014	2013	2012	2011	2010
Revenue	2,800,000,000	2,704,700,000	2,759,400,000	2,700,000,000	2,679,000,000	2,546,400,000
R&D Expense						
Operating Income						
Operating Margin %						
SGA Expense						
Net Income		86,500,000	76,900,000			
Operating Cash Flow						
Capital Expenditure						
EBITDA						
Return on Assets %						
Return on Equity %						
Debt to Equity						

CONTACT INFORMATION:

Phone: 240-694-4100   Fax: 240-694-4790
Toll-Free:
Address: 6905 Rockledge Dr., Bethesda, MD 20817 United States

STOCK TICKER/OTHER:

Stock Ticker: Subsidiary
Employees: 37,000
Parent Company: Autogrill SpA

Exchange:
Fiscal Year Ends: 12/31

SALARIES/BONUSES:

Top Exec. Salary: $ Bonus: $
Second Exec. Salary: $ Bonus: $

OTHER THOUGHTS:

Estimated Female Officers or Directors: 1
Hot Spot for Advancement for Women/Minorities:

Sales, profits and employees may be estimates. Financial information, benefits and other data can change quickly and may vary from those stated here.

HNA Tourism Holding (Group) Co Ltd

www.hnagroup.com/en/business/hna-tourism/tourism-introduction/index.html

NAIC Code: 721110

TYPES OF BUSINESS:

Hotels

BRANDS/DIVISIONS/AFFILIATES:

Easy Life Tourism
Xinhua Travel Network Service Co Ltd
Hong Thai Travel Service Co Ltd
Grand China MICE Co Ltd
Aberdeen Tours Inc
Beijing Capital Airlines Co Ltd
Dee Jet Co Ltd
Capital Helicopter Co Ltd

CONTACTS: Note: Officers with more than one job title may be intentionally listed here more than once.

Xian Hua Li, CEO
Cheng Feng, Chmn.

GROWTH PLANS/SPECIAL FEATURES:

HNA Tourism Holding (Group) Co. Ltd. was founded in Beijing, China, and provides tourism services. The company owns and operates more than 20 subsidiary companies across tourism sectors, including aviation, hospitality management, tourism, online services, finance and investment. HNA Tourism member brands includes Easy Life Tourism, Easy Life Holding Co. Ltd., Xinhua Travel Network Service Co. Ltd., Transforex Currency Exchange Co. Ltd., Beijing Caissa International Travel Service, Co. Ltd., Hong Thai Travel Service Co. Ltd., Grand China MICE Co. Ltd., HNA SAFE Car Rental Co. Ltd., Aberdeen Tours Inc., Beijing Capital Airlines Co. Ltd., HNA Hospitality Group, Deer Jet Co. Ltd., Hainan eKing Technology Co. Ltd., Capital Helicopter Co. Ltd., Beijing Oriental Face Technology Co. Ltd., Hainan Island Card Payment Network Co. Ltd. and Hainan Treasure Island Technology Co. Ltd. Every year, HNA Tourism provides its services to more than 1.6 million tourists worldwide. The firm's assets include 150 aircraft, 200 travel stores, 450 hotels, 1,100 rental cars and more. In April 2016, the firm agreed to acquire Carlson Companies, Inc.

FINANCIAL DATA: Note: Data for latest year may not have been available at press time.

In U.S. $	2015	2014	2013	2012	2011	2010
Revenue						
R&D Expense						
Operating Income						
Operating Margin %						
SGA Expense						
Net Income						
Operating Cash Flow						
Capital Expenditure						
EBITDA						
Return on Assets %						
Return on Equity %						
Debt to Equity						

CONTACT INFORMATION:

Phone: 86-10-59156800   Fax: 86-10-59156800
Toll-Free:
Address: HNA Plaza, 2 Yi, Dongsanhuan N. Rd., Chaoyang District, Beijing, 100027 China

STOCK TICKER/OTHER:

Stock Ticker: Private
Employees:
Parent Company: HNA Group Co Ltd

Exchange:
Fiscal Year Ends:

SALARIES/BONUSES:

Top Exec. Salary: $ Bonus: $
Second Exec. Salary: $ Bonus: $

OTHER THOUGHTS:

Estimated Female Officers or Directors:
Hot Spot for Advancement for Women/Minorities:

Sales, profits and employees may be estimates. Financial information, benefits and other data can change quickly and may vary from those stated here.

Hogg Robinson Group North America

http://www2.hrgworldwide.com/en-noam/Pages/default.aspx

NAIC Code: 561510

TYPES OF BUSINESS:

Travel Agency
Corporate Travel Management
Employee Benefits Consulting
Corporate Event Management
Pensions Software

BRANDS/DIVISIONS/AFFILIATES:

Hogg Robinson Group plc
HRG Universal Super Platform

CONTACTS: Note: Officers with more than one job title may be intentionally listed here more than once.

David Radcliffe, CEO
Kevin Ruffles, COO
Greg Treasure, Pres.
Michele Maher, CFO
Bill Brindle, CIO
David Radcliffe, CEO-Hogg Robinson Group plc
Philip Harrison, Group Finance Dir.-Hogg Robinson Group plc
Kevin Ruffles, COO- Hogg Robinson Group plc
Stewart Harvey, Group Comm. Dir.-Hogg Robinson Group plc

GROWTH PLANS/SPECIAL FEATURES:

Hogg Robinson Group North America (HRG North America), a wholly-owned subsidiary of Hogg Robinson Group plc (HRG), provides corporate travel management services in Canada and the U.S. The company's services are divided into five groups: corporate travel, meetings/groups/events, consulting, government and energy & marine. The corporate travel division provides corporate travel solutions such as booking and pricing for airline and/or rail travel, as well as for hotel stays. Its technology solutions provides speed, control, security, savings and flexibility relating to corporate travel. The meetings, groups & events division books venues for related corporate events. The consulting division provides advice on travel management, implementing improved policies and prepares for upstream trends & developments in order to obtain the best value out of airlines and other suppliers. The government division provides money-saving options for governmental and inter-governmental organizations, and serves its more than 500 government clients. The energy & marine division makes sure ships' crews and energy workers are transported to and from the world's most remote and challenging environments. HRG's clients depend on its 24/7 support when operations need to be ramped up when major events or disasters occur. The company's proprietary technology underpins all of its corporate travel products, services and solutions. Its HRG Universal Super Platform enables flexible service delivery, along with client choices in terms of fares and rates.

FINANCIAL DATA: Note: Data for latest year may not have been available at press time.

In U.S. $	2015	2014	2013	2012	2011	2010
Revenue	115,346,000	100,053,064	99,134,371	125,000,000	119,552,000	107,193,000
R&D Expense						
Operating Income						
Operating Margin %						
SGA Expense						
Net Income	12,282,071	8,623,757				
Operating Cash Flow						
Capital Expenditure						
EBITDA						
Return on Assets %						
Return on Equity %						
Debt to Equity						

CONTACT INFORMATION:

Phone: 212-404-8800   Fax:
Toll-Free:
Address: 16 E. 34th St., 3/F, New York, NY 10016 United States

STOCK TICKER/OTHER:

Stock Ticker: Subsidiary   Exchange:
Employees: Fiscal Year Ends: 03/31
Parent Company: Hogg Robinson Group PLC

SALARIES/BONUSES:

Top Exec. Salary: $ Bonus: $
Second Exec. Salary: $ Bonus: $

OTHER THOUGHTS:

Estimated Female Officers or Directors: 1
Hot Spot for Advancement for Women/Minorities:

Sales, profits and employees may be estimates. Financial information, benefits and other data can change quickly and may vary from those stated here.

Hogg Robinson Group plc

www.hrgworldwide.com

NAIC Code: 561510

TYPES OF BUSINESS:

Corporate Services
Corporate Travel Management
Expense Management
Travel Consulting
Events & Meetings Management

BRANDS/DIVISIONS/AFFILIATES:

HRG Universal Super Platform

CONTACTS: Note: Officers with more than one job title may be intentionally listed here more than once.

David J. Radcliffe, CEO
Kevin Ruffles, COO
Michele Maher, CFO
John Harvey, Group Mktg. Dir.
Bill Brindle, CIO
Keith J. Burgess, General Counsel
Stewart Harvey, Dir.-Commercial
John D. Coombe, Chmn.
Bill Brindle, Dir.-Dist.

GROWTH PLANS/SPECIAL FEATURES:

Hogg Robinson Group plc (HRG) is an international corporate services company that specializes in travel, expense and data management via proprietary technology. The company's services are divided into five groups: corporate travel, meetings/groups/events, consulting, government and energy & marine. The corporate travel division provides corporate travel solutions such as booking and pricing for airline and/or rail travel, as well as for hotel stays. Its technology solutions provides speed, control, security, savings and flexibility relating to corporate travel. The meetings, groups & events division books venues for related corporate events. The consulting division provides advice on travel management, implementing improved policies and prepares for upstream trends & developments in order to obtain the best value out of airlines and other suppliers. The government division provides money-saving options for governmental and inter-governmental organizations, and serves its more than 500 government clients. The energy & marine division makes sure ships' crews and energy workers are transported to and from the world's most remote and challenging environments. HRG's clients depend on its 24/7 support when operations need to be ramped up when major events or disasters occur. The company's proprietary technology underpins all of its corporate travel products, services and solutions. Its HRG Universal Super Platform enables flexible service delivery, along with client choices in terms of fares and rates.

HRG offers its employees a flexible benefits package, allowing the employee to choose fewer benefits in one area for greater benefits elsewhere.

FINANCIAL DATA: Note: Data for latest year may not have been available at press time.

In U.S. $	2015	2014	2013	2012	2011	2010
Revenue	430,979,300	444,949,300	448,082,700	488,556,400	467,405,600	
R&D Expense						
Operating Income	45,957,200	50,657,370	58,490,980	56,271,460	49,482,330	
Operating Margin %	10.66%	11.38%	13.05%	11.51%	10.58%	
SGA Expense			1,175,042			
Net Income	19,192,350	21,934,120	31,334,460	29,114,930	24,937,000	
Operating Cash Flow	40,212,550	54,182,500	783,361	38,776,390	44,390,480	
Capital Expenditure	14,883,870	18,670,110	12,664,340	12,533,780	11,358,740	
EBITDA	51,571,290	59,013,220	72,852,010	71,547,010	60,841,070	
Return on Assets %	3.29%	3.76%	5.18%	4.60%	3.86%	
Return on Equity %				273.61%	259.86%	
Debt to Equity					7.35	

CONTACT INFORMATION:

Phone: 44 1256312600   Fax: 44 1256346999
Toll-Free:
Address: Victoria St., Global House, Hampshire, RG21 3BT United Kingdom

STOCK TICKER/OTHER:

Stock Ticker: HOGGF   Exchange: GREY
Employees: 6,053   Fiscal Year Ends: 03/31
Parent Company:

SALARIES/BONUSES:

Top Exec. Salary: $ Bonus: $
Second Exec. Salary: $ Bonus: $

OTHER THOUGHTS:

Estimated Female Officers or Directors: 1
Hot Spot for Advancement for Women/Minorities: Y

Holidaybreak PLC

www.holidaybreak.co.uk

NAIC Code: 561520

TYPES OF BUSINESS:

Packaged Vacations
Camping Tours
Scuba Diving
Adventure Tours
Reservations
Educational Tours

BRANDS/DIVISIONS/AFFILIATES:

Cox & Kings Limited
Bookit
PGL Travel Ltd
NST Travel Group
EST Travel Group
Meininger
TravelPlus

GROWTH PLANS/SPECIAL FEATURES:

Holidaybreak plc, a subsidiary of Cox & King Limited, is a leading European provider of specialty vacations, such as outfitted camping vacations, city getaways and activity-based small group tours and treks. The company operates in segments: hotel breaks, education and MEININGER. The hotel breaks segment provides domestic short break trips through market-leading Bookit (the Netherlands). The education segment provides residential outdoor education and adventure trips for school children through the PGL Travel Ltd brand. It also provides education travel tours for secondary schools and further education students through NST Travel Group and EST Travel Group. The Meininger segment is a German school trip accommodation provider, which also offers language travel and gap year trips through TravelPlus (Germany).

CONTACTS: Note: Officers with more than one job title may be intentionally listed here more than once.

Peter Kerker, Group CEO
Alex Williamson, Comp. Sec.
Navneet Bali, Head-Corp. Dev.
Navneet Bali, Group Dir.-Finance
Martin Davies, Managing Dir.-Education Div.
Steve Whitfield, Managing Dir.-Camping Div.
Karel Vos, Managing Dir.-Hotel Break Div.
Patrick Richards, COO-Holidaybreak Combined Buying Group

FINANCIAL DATA: Note: Data for latest year may not have been available at press time.

In U.S. $	2015	2014	2013	2012	2011	2010
Revenue	359,011,507	650,000,000	640,000,000	623,820,000		
R&D Expense						
Operating Income						
Operating Margin %						
SGA Expense						
Net Income	-4,753,459					
Operating Cash Flow						
Capital Expenditure						
EBITDA						
Return on Assets %						
Return on Equity %						
Debt to Equity						

CONTACT INFORMATION:

Phone: 44-844-346-1470   Fax:
Toll-Free:
Address: Hartford Manor, Greenbank Ln., Northwich, Cheshire CW8 1HW United Kingdom

STOCK TICKER/OTHER:

Stock Ticker: Subsidiary   Exchange:
Employees: Fiscal Year Ends: 10/31
Parent Company: Cox & Kings Limited

SALARIES/BONUSES:

Top Exec. Salary: $ Bonus: $
Second Exec. Salary: $ Bonus: $

OTHER THOUGHTS:

Estimated Female Officers or Directors: 3
Hot Spot for Advancement for Women/Minorities: Y

HomeAway Inc

www.homeaway.com

NAIC Code: 519130

TYPES OF BUSINESS:

Online Vacation Property Rental Services

BRANDS/DIVISIONS/AFFILIATES:

VacationRentals.com
OwnersDirect.co.uk
HomeAway.co.uk
VRBO.com
HomeAway.de
Abritel.fr
Homelidays.com
Glad to Have You Inc

CONTACTS: *Note: Officers with more than one job title may be intentionally listed here more than once.*

Brian Sharples, CEO
Lynn Atchison, CFO
Mariano Dima, Chief Marketing Officer
Ross Buhrdorf, Chief Technology Officer
Thomas Hale, COO
Carl Shepherd, Director
Melissa Fruge, Senior VP

GROWTH PLANS/SPECIAL FEATURES:

HomeAway, Inc. is involved in vacation rental properties. Through its web site, HomeAway.com, the firm connects homeowners and property managers with travelers who prefer vacation rental homes instead of hotels. The site includes photos, detailed descriptions and lists of amenities and nearby attractions for properties located in 190 countries. HomeAway owns and operates several other online vacation rental web sites, including HomeAway.com, VRBO.com and VacationRentals.com in the U.S.; HomeAway.co.uk and OwnersDirect.co.uk in the U.K.; HomeAway.de in Germany; Abritel.fr and Homelidays.com in France; HomeAway.es and Toprural.com in Spain; AlugueTemporada.com.br in Brazil; Stayz.com.au and HomeAway.com.au in Australia; and Bookabach.co.nz in New Zealand. The company also owns and operates BedandBreakfast.com, an international site featuring bed-and-breakfast properties as well as the Asia Pacific short-term rental site, travelmob.com. In total, the firm lists over 1 million paid listings and vacation rentals. The firm's customers can purchase the HomeAway Carefree Rental Guarantee, which offers property insurance coverage. The company has received funding from Institutional Venture Partners, Redpoint Ventures, Google Ventures, Austin Ventures, Technology Crossover Ventures and Trident Capital. HomeAway has offices in the U.S., France, the U.K., Germany, Brazil, Switzerland, Spain and Australia. In 2014, the firm acquired Glad to Have You, Inc., a vacation rental mobile guest management solution company. In November 2015, the firm agreed to be acquired by Expedia, Inc. for $3.9 billion.

The firm offers employees benefits including life, disability, medical, dental and vision insurance; a 401(k); vacation time; stock options; and flexible spending accounts.

FINANCIAL DATA: *Note: Data for latest year may not have been available at press time.*

In U.S. $	2015	2014	2013	2012	2011	2010
Revenue	522,800,000	446,761,984	346,488,992	280,404,000	230,223,008	167,884,000
R&D Expense						
Operating Income						
Operating Margin %						
SGA Expense						
Net Income		13,384,000	17,686,000	14,961,000	6,178,000	16,934,000
Operating Cash Flow						
Capital Expenditure						
EBITDA						
Return on Assets %						
Return on Equity %						
Debt to Equity						

CONTACT INFORMATION:

Phone: 512 684-1100   Fax:
Toll-Free: 877-228-3145
Address: 1011 W. 5th St., Ste. 300, Austin, TX 78703 United States

STOCK TICKER/OTHER:

Stock Ticker: Subsidiary   Exchange:
Employees: 1,780   Fiscal Year Ends: 12/31
Parent Company: Expedia Inc

SALARIES/BONUSES:

Top Exec. Salary: $ Bonus: $
Second Exec. Salary: $ Bonus: $

OTHER THOUGHTS:

Estimated Female Officers or Directors: 2
Hot Spot for Advancement for Women/Minorities: Y

Sales, profits and employees may be estimates. Financial information, benefits and other data can change quickly and may vary from those stated here.

Homeinns Hotel Group

NAIC Code: 721110

www.homeinns.com

TYPES OF BUSINESS:

Economy Hotels
Midscale Hotels

BRANDS/DIVISIONS/AFFILIATES:

Yitel
Motel 168
Home Inns

CONTACTS: *Note: Officers with more than one job title may be intentionally listed here more than once.*

David Jian Sun, CEO
Jason Xiangxin Zong, COO
Jason Zong, Pres.
Huiping Yan, CFO
May Wu, Chief Strategy Officer
Neil Shen, Co-Chmn.
Yi Liu, Co-Chmn.

GROWTH PLANS/SPECIAL FEATURES:

Homeinns Hotel Group is an economy hotel chain in China, with more than 2,500 locations in 335 cities. Home Inns leases real estate properties on which it develops and operates hotels, franchises its brand to hotel owners and manages these hotel properties. For the leased-and-operated hotels, the company is responsible for hotel development and customization to conform to the standards of Home Inns as well as repairs, maintenance and operating expenses. For the franchised and managed hotels, the firm is responsible for managing the hotel, while the franchisee is responsible for cost of development and customization. A typical Homeinns hotel has 80-160 guest rooms. Each hotel has a standardized design, appearance, decor, color scheme, lighting scheme and set of guest amenities in each room, including free in-room broadband Internet access, a work space, air conditioning and a supply of cold and hot drinking water. The firm's hotels are strategically located to provide guests with convenient access to major business districts, ground transportation hubs, major highways, shopping centers, industrial development zones, colleges and universities and large residential neighborhoods. In addition, the company operates under the Yitel brand, which is aimed at China's midscale hotel market, and the Motel 168 brand.

FINANCIAL DATA: *Note: Data for latest year may not have been available at press time.*

In U.S. $	2015	2014	2013	2012	2011	2010
Revenue	1,029,000,000	969,205,184	921,224,256	837,026,816	573,405,824	459,908,992
R&D Expense						
Operating Income						
Operating Margin %						
SGA Expense						
Net Income	25,800,000	79,295,768	30,323,756	-4,137,910	54,324,900	55,556,260
Operating Cash Flow						
Capital Expenditure						
EBITDA						
Return on Assets %						
Return on Equity %						
Debt to Equity						

CONTACT INFORMATION:

Phone: 86 2133373333   Fax: 86 2164835661
Toll-Free:
Address: Caobao Rd., No. 124, Xuhui District, Shanghai, 200235 China

STOCK TICKER/OTHER:

Stock Ticker: Subsidiary   Exchange:
Employees: 25,176   Fiscal Year Ends: 12/31
Parent Company: BTG Hotels Group Holdings Co

SALARIES/BONUSES:

Top Exec. Salary: $ Bonus: $
Second Exec. Salary: $ Bonus: $

OTHER THOUGHTS:

Estimated Female Officers or Directors: 1
Hot Spot for Advancement for Women/Minorities:

Hongkong and Shanghai Hotels Ltd

www.hshgroup.com

NAIC Code: 721110

TYPES OF BUSINESS:

Hotels
Commercial Properties
Resorts & Luxury Clubs
Apartments
Golf Courses
Property Management
Laundry Services
Park Attractions & Tramways

BRANDS/DIVISIONS/AFFILIATES:

Peninsula Group (The)
Landmark (The)
Peninsula Merchandising Ltd
Peak Tramways
Peninsula Office Tower
Peninsula Hong Kong
Peninsula Clubs and Consultancy Services Ltd
Tai Pan Laundry & Dry Cleaning Services Ltd

CONTACTS: Note: Officers with more than one job title may be intentionally listed here more than once.

Clement King Man Kwok, CEO
Peter Camille Borer, COO
Ingvar Herland, Gen. Mgr.-R&D
Ingvar Herland, Gen. Mgr.-Tech.
Christobelle Liao, Corp. Counsel
Paul Tchen, Gen. Mgr.-Oper. Planning & Support
Ming Chen, Sr. Mgr.-Bus. Dev.
Sian Griffiths, Dir.-Comm.-The Peninsula Hotels
Ming Chen, Sr. Mgr.-Investor Rel.
Martin Lew, Gen. Mgr.-Oper., Financial Control
Martyn Sawyer, Gen Mgr.-Properties & Clubs
Jonathan Crook, Gen. Mgr.-Peninsula Shanghai
Rainy Chan, VP-Hong Kong & Bangkok
Nicolas Beliard, Gen. Mgr.-Peninsula Bangkok
Michael Kadoorie, Chmn.
Maria Razumich-Zec, Regional VP-U.S. East Coast

GROWTH PLANS/SPECIAL FEATURES:

Hongkong and Shanghai Hotels, Ltd. (HSH), celebrating its 150th Anniversary in 2016, owns and operates luxury hotels, resorts and other commercial properties. The Peninsula Group, HSH's hotel management division, owns hotels located in Hong Kong, Beijing, Shanghai, Chicago, New York, Bangkok, Manila, Beverly Hills, Tokyo and Paris. The company also owns Repulse Bay, a self-contained residential, retail and commercial complex. The firm's Landmark property in Ho Chi Minh City features 65 fully furnished apartments on the upper floors, a restaurant and bar, rooftop swimming pool with a poolside bar, deck, gymnasium, sauna, squash court and office space on the lower levels. HSH owns the Peninsula Office Tower, part of the extension of the Peninsula Hong Kong. The building includes nine floors of high-end office space with office units ranging from 6,200 to 11,200 square feet. Another office property owned by HSH is the St. John's Building in Hong Kong, with 21 floors of office space. Subsidiary Peninsula Clubs and Consultancy Services, Ltd. manages high-end clubs such as The Hong Kong Club, The Hong Kong Bankers Club and Butterfield's. The firm has a 75% ownership stake in the Thai Country Club, a 72-hole golf course in Thailand. The firm's other operations include Peak Tramways, one of the oldest operating funicular railways in the world, operating out of Hong Kong; Peninsula Merchandising, Ltd., a subsidiary that owns and operates boutiques selling Peninsula-brand products; and Tai Pan Laundry & Dry Cleaning Services, Ltd., a commercial laundry service for major hotels, clubs and restaurants. The company recently entered the European market with the opening of its new hotel, The Peninsula Paris, housed in the 100 year old Beaux Arts building. In December 2015, the firm announced plans to construct a 190-room hotel in central London, The Peninsula London, due to open in 2021.

FINANCIAL DATA: Note: Data for latest year may not have been available at press time.

In U.S. $	2015	2014	2013	2012	2011	2010
Revenue	740,315,800	752,824,100	710,269,800	667,715,500	645,922,600	606,978,900
R&D Expense						
Operating Income	130,757,700	142,492,400	117,475,600	105,354,100	107,546,300	102,388,200
Operating Margin %	17.66%	18.92%	16.53%	15.77%	16.65%	16.86%
SGA Expense						
Net Income	128,952,400	147,779,500	220,766,500	200,521,000	291,303,500	387,888,800
Operating Cash Flow	157,321,900	184,659,800	168,669,700	124,310,100	128,823,400	131,402,500
Capital Expenditure	179,501,700	52,741,530	415,355,700	112,833,400	40,233,150	35,590,860
EBITDA	210,708,200	241,398,900	311,420,100	290,271,900	386,341,400	482,410,900
Return on Assets %	2.24%	2.63%	4.12%	3.98%	6.03%	8.66%
Return on Equity %	2.76%	3.22%	5.01%	4.81%	7.46%	11.53%
Debt to Equity	0.16	0.12	0.14	0.09	0.10	0.11

CONTACT INFORMATION:

Phone: 852-2840-7788   Fax: 852-2840-7567
Toll-Free:
Address: 2 Ice House St., St. George's Bldg., 8th Fl., Central, Hong Kong

STOCK TICKER/OTHER:

Stock Ticker: HKSHY
Employees: 5,772
Parent Company:

Exchange: PINX
Fiscal Year Ends: 12/31

SALARIES/BONUSES:

Top Exec. Salary: $ Bonus: $
Second Exec. Salary: $ Bonus: $

OTHER THOUGHTS:

Estimated Female Officers or Directors: 13
Hot Spot for Advancement for Women/Minorities: Y

Sales, profits and employees may be estimates. Financial information, benefits and other data can change quickly and may vary from those stated here.

Hospitality Properties Trust

NAIC Code: 0

TYPES OF BUSINESS:

Real Estate Investment Trust
Hotels
Travel Centers

BRANDS/DIVISIONS/AFFILIATES:

InterContinental Hotels & Resorts
Courtyard by Marriott
Candlewood Suites
Staybridge Suites
Residence Inn by Marriott
Crowne Plaza Hotels & Resorts
Hyatt Place
SpringHill Suites by Marriott

CONTACTS: Note: Officers with more than one job title may be intentionally listed here more than once.

John Murray, Assistant Secretary
Mark Kleifges, CFO
Jennifer Clark, Executive VP
Ethan Bornstein, Senior VP
Barry Portnoy, Trustee
John Harrington, Trustee
William Lamkin, Trustee
Adam Portnoy, Trustee
Donna Fraiche, Trustee

GROWTH PLANS/SPECIAL FEATURES:

Hospitality Properties Trust (HPT) is a real estate investment trust (REIT) that owns 302 hotels as well as 193 travel centers, located in 45 U.S. states, Puerto Rico and Canada. HPT's hotel properties currently include the following brands: Courtyard by Marriott, Candlewood Suites, Staybridge Suites, Residence Inn by Marriott, Crowne Plaza Hotels & Resorts, Hyatt Place, InterContinental Hotels & Resorts, Marriott Hotels and Resorts, Radisson Hotels & Resorts, TownePlace Suites by Marriott, Country Inns & Suites by Carlson, Holiday Inn Hotels & Resorts, SpringHill Suites by Marriott, Wyndham Hotels & Resorts and Park Plaza Hotels & Resorts. The company's 193 travel centers include 147 operated under the TravelCenters of America brand and 46 operated under the Petro Stopping Centers or Petro brand name. All of HPT's management agreements or leases share nine points: first, managers are required to pay a fixed minimum rent; second, operators must pay percentage returns on gross hotel revenues exceeding a certain threshold; third, all agreements are long-term (15 years or more); fourth, each hotel is part of a combination of hotels and is subject to cross-default obligations with respect to all other hotels in the same combination; fifth, each combination of hotels is geographically diverse; sixth, contract renewals may only be pursued for a combination of hotels, not for each hotel individually; seventh, the firm's agreements require the deposit of 5% to 6% of gross hotel revenues into escrows to fund periodic renovations; eighth, the properties are located near major demand generators, such as urban centers, airports or educational facilities; and finally, each management agreement or lease includes security terms to ensure payments to HPT. In June 2015, the firm acquired combined economic ownership of approximately half of Reit Management & Research LLC.

FINANCIAL DATA: Note: Data for latest year may not have been available at press time.

In U.S. $	2015	2014	2013	2012	2011	2010
Revenue	1,921,904,000	1,736,322,000	1,563,855,000	1,296,982,000	1,210,333,000	1,085,488,000
R&D Expense						
Operating Income	335,935,000	339,170,000	273,583,000	278,460,000	325,843,000	330,843,000
Operating Margin %	17.47%	19.53%	17.49%	21.46%	26.92%	30.47%
SGA Expense	109,837,000	45,897,000	50,087,000	44,032,000	40,963,000	38,961,000
Net Income	166,418,000	197,185,000	133,178,000	151,923,000	190,440,000	21,351,000
Operating Cash Flow	530,893,000	461,745,000	391,089,000	363,908,000	355,102,000	341,444,000
Capital Expenditure	630,585,000	284,621,000	515,872,000	630,940,000	69,345,000	7,091,000
EBITDA	642,637,000	654,494,000	573,027,000	550,477,000	554,394,000	398,790,000
Return on Assets %	2.35%	2.95%	1.74%	1.92%	3.10%	-.15%
Return on Equity %	5.56%	6.39%	3.96%	4.41%	6.58%	-.32%
Debt to Equity	1.29	1.04	0.96	1.18	0.87	0.85

CONTACT INFORMATION:

Phone: 617 964-8389   Fax: 617 969-5730
Toll-Free:
Address: 255 Washington St., 2 Newton Pl., Ste. 300, Newton, MA 02458-1634 United States

STOCK TICKER/OTHER:

Stock Ticker: HPT
Employees: 500
Parent Company:

Exchange: NAS
Fiscal Year Ends: 12/31

SALARIES/BONUSES:

Top Exec. Salary: $ Bonus: $
Second Exec. Salary: $ Bonus: $

OTHER THOUGHTS:

Estimated Female Officers or Directors: 1
Hot Spot for Advancement for Women/Minorities:

Host Hotels & Resorts LP

www.hosthotels.com

NAIC Code: 0

TYPES OF BUSINESS:

Real Estate Investment Trust
Hotels

BRANDS/DIVISIONS/AFFILIATES:

CONTACTS: *Note: Officers with more than one job title may be intentionally listed here more than once.*

C. Edward Walter, CEO

GROWTH PLANS/SPECIAL FEATURES:

Host Hotels & Resorts, LP (HHR) is a leading hotel real estate investment trust (REIT). HHR operates a portfolio of 105 primarily luxury and upper-upscale hotels containing approximately 57,000 rooms, with the majority located in the U.S., and 12 properties located outside of the U.S. in Australia, Brazil, Canada, Chile, Mexico and New Zealand. Its brands include Marriott, Westin, Ritz-Carlton, Sheraton, W, Hyatt, Hilton/Embassy Suites, Novotel, ibis, St. Regis, The Luxury Collection, Fairmont and Swissotel. Additionally, the firm owns an interest in five international joint ventures that own 10 luxury and upper upscale hotels located in Italy, Spain, Belgium, the U.K., Poland, France and the Netherlands, and a 25% stake in an Asian joint venture which owns one hotel in Australia, minority interests in two operating hotels in India and five additional hotels in India currently under development. Its properties typically include meeting and banquet facilities, a variety of restaurants and lounges, swimming pools, exercise facilities and/or spas, gift shops and parking facilities. During 2015, the firm acquired 643-room Phoenician, a Luxury Collection resort; and completed the sale of the Sheraton Needham.

HHR offers its employees medical, dental, prescription, vision and hearing coverage; free onsite fitness centers; associate assistance programs; long- and short-term disability and life insurance; a 401(k); company paid parking; hotel discounts; health an

FINANCIAL DATA: *Note: Data for latest year may not have been available at press time.*

In U.S. $	2015	2014	2013	2012	2011	2010
Revenue	5,387,000,000	5,354,000,000	5,166,000,000	5,286,000,000	4,998,000,000	4,437,000,000
R&D Expense						
Operating Income	650,000,000	710,000,000	512,000,000	383,000,000	324,000,000	223,000,000
Operating Margin %	12.06%	13.26%	9.91%	7.24%	6.48%	5.02%
SGA Expense	716,000,000	656,000,000	719,000,000	901,000,000	869,000,000	768,000,000
Net Income	558,000,000	732,000,000	317,000,000	61,000,000	-15,000,000	-130,000,000
Operating Cash Flow	1,171,000,000	1,150,000,000	1,019,000,000	782,000,000	661,000,000	520,000,000
Capital Expenditure	663,000,000	436,000,000	436,000,000	638,000,000	542,000,000	326,000,000
EBITDA	1,530,000,000	1,676,000,000	1,242,000,000	1,171,000,000	1,013,000,000	818,000,000
Return on Assets %	4.65%	5.85%	2.45%	.46%	-.11%	-1.10%
Return on Equity %	7.75%	10.05%	4.51%	.90%	-.23%	-2.22%
Debt to Equity	0.38	0.54	0.65	0.79	0.86	0.86

CONTACT INFORMATION:

Phone: 240 744-1000   Fax: 240 380-6338
Toll-Free:
Address: 6903 Rockledge Dr., Ste. 1500, Bethesda, MD 20817 United States

STOCK TICKER/OTHER:

Stock Ticker: HST
Employees: 240
Parent Company:

Exchange: NYS
Fiscal Year Ends: 12/31

SALARIES/BONUSES:

Top Exec. Salary: $952,750   Bonus: $
Second Exec. Salary: $551,580   Bonus: $

OTHER THOUGHTS:

Estimated Female Officers or Directors: 2
Hot Spot for Advancement for Women/Minorities: Y

Hotel Properties Ltd

NAIC Code: 721110

www.hotelprop.com

TYPES OF BUSINESS:

Hotels
Condominiums
Restaurants
Retail Properties & Operations
Food Distribution

BRANDS/DIVISIONS/AFFILIATES:

HPL Hotels & Resorts Pte Ltd
Concorde Hotels & Resorts (Malaysia) Sdn Bhd

CONTACTS: *Note: Officers with more than one job title may be intentionally listed here more than once.*

Ong Beng Seng, Managing Dir.
Chuang Sheue Ling, Corp. Sec.
Buong Lik Lau, Head-Hotel Div.
Arthur Tan Keng Hock, Chmn.

GROWTH PLANS/SPECIAL FEATURES:

Hotel Properties Ltd. (HPL) is a diversified hotel holding company headquartered in Singapore. It invests in premium commercial and residential properties mainly throughout the Asia Pacific region, including hotels, condominiums, shopping centers, restaurants, a food distribution chain and retail operations. It owns or has interests in 27 hotels in 11 countries including Bhutan, Czech Republic, Indonesia, Maldives, Malaysia, Seychelles, Singapore, South Africa, Thailand, Tanzania and Vanuatu. These include three Four Seasons properties and a Hard Rock Hotel in Indonesia; two Four Seasons Resorts, one Holiday Inn Resort, a Gili Lankanfushi and a Six Senses Laamu in the Maldives; two Concorde Hotels, a Casa Del Mar, a Hard Rock Hotel and The Lakehouse Cameron Highlands in Malaysia; a Four Seasons Hotel, a Hilton and a Concorde Hotel in Singapore; a Hard Rock Hotel, a Point Yamu and a Metropolitan in Thailand; a Four Seasons Resort in Seychelles; and a Holiday Inn in Vanuatu. Furthermore, through its subsidiaries HPL Hotels & Resorts Pte. Ltd. and Concorde Hotels & Resorts (Malaysia) Sdn. Bhd., HPL provides hotel management services. The company owns three shopping centers and a residential tower in Singapore as well as a residential property in Thailand. In its lifestyle division, the company owns Hard Rock Cafes in Indonesia, Malaysia, the Philippines, Singapore and Thailand.

FINANCIAL DATA: *Note: Data for latest year may not have been available at press time.*

In U.S. $	2015	2014	2013	2012	2011	2010
Revenue	429,044,861	461,300,113	552,954,370	428,473,032	391,200,000	357,860,000
R&D Expense						
Operating Income						
Operating Margin %						
SGA Expense						
Net Income	60,658,066	101,261,000	141,962,460	109,796,027	55,800,000	113,570,000
Operating Cash Flow						
Capital Expenditure						
EBITDA						
Return on Assets %						
Return on Equity %						
Debt to Equity						

CONTACT INFORMATION:

Phone: 65-734-5250   Fax: 65-732-0347
Toll-Free:
Address: 50 Cuscaden Rd., 08-01 HPL House, Singapore, 249724 Singapore

STOCK TICKER/OTHER:

Stock Ticker: H15
Employees: 4,400
Parent Company:

Exchange: Singapore
Fiscal Year Ends: 12/31

SALARIES/BONUSES:

Top Exec. Salary: $ Bonus: $
Second Exec. Salary: $ Bonus: $

OTHER THOUGHTS:

Estimated Female Officers or Directors: 1
Hot Spot for Advancement for Women/Minorities:

Hotels.com LP

www.hotels.com

NAIC Code: 519130

TYPES OF BUSINESS:

Online Hotel Reservations System
Online Travel Information
Lodging Options

BRANDS/DIVISIONS/AFFILIATES:

Expedia Inc
800-2-Hotels
Welcome Rewards

CONTACTS: *Note: Officers with more than one job title may be intentionally listed here more than once.*

Scott Booker, Pres.
Matthew Walls, VP-Mktg.
Stuart Silberg, Chief Technology Officer
Taylor Cole, Dir.-Public Rel.
Dara Khoosrowshahi, CEO-Expedia, Inc.

GROWTH PLANS/SPECIAL FEATURES:

Hotels.com, LP, a subsidiary of Expedia, Inc., is a leading specialized provider of discount lodging reservation services for destinations around the world. Hotels.com's room supply relationships include a wide range of independent hotel operators and lodging properties as well as hotels associated with several national chains, such as Hilton, Sheraton, Radisson and Best Western. Through its web site, customers have access to some 240,000 properties worldwide, with accommodations ranging from standard hotels to condos and all-inclusive resorts. The firm's booking engine allows users to quickly compare price, quality, amenities, location and availability of hotel rooms in seconds. The site also provides users with extensive virtual tours of rooms being offered as well as user reviews. Hotels.com offers various perks to its customers, including a Welcome Rewards program that provides customers with a one night free stay after every ten bookings at a partner hotel. In addition, the company's Price Match Guarantee offers customers a rebate if a booked room is found at a lower price on another site. In addition to its web portal, it operates a toll-free call center service, 800-2-Hotels, which allows customers to book accommodations over the phone as well as receive travel advice from one of the company's agents.

FINANCIAL DATA: *Note: Data for latest year may not have been available at press time.*

In U.S. $	2015	2014	2013	2012	2011	2010
Revenue						
R&D Expense						
Operating Income						
Operating Margin %						
SGA Expense						
Net Income						
Operating Cash Flow						
Capital Expenditure						
EBITDA						
Return on Assets %						
Return on Equity %						
Debt to Equity						

CONTACT INFORMATION:

Phone: 214-361-7311   Fax: 214-361-7299
Toll-Free: 800-246-8357
Address: 5400 LBJ Freeway, Suite 500, Dallas, TX 75240 United States

SALARIES/BONUSES:

Top Exec. Salary: $ Bonus: $
Second Exec. Salary: $ Bonus: $

STOCK TICKER/OTHER:

Stock Ticker: Subsidiary   Exchange:
Employees: 864   Fiscal Year Ends: 12/31
Parent Company: EXPEDIA INC

OTHER THOUGHTS:

Estimated Female Officers or Directors: 2
Hot Spot for Advancement for Women/Minorities:

Sales, profits and employees may be estimates. Financial information, benefits and other data can change quickly and may vary from those stated here.

Hotwire Inc

NAIC Code: 519130

TYPES OF BUSINESS:

Travel Reservations
Hotel Reservations
Car Rental Reservations
Discount Airfare
Cruise Reservations
Vacation Packages

BRANDS/DIVISIONS/AFFILIATES:

Expedia Inc
TripStarter
Trip Watcher
Hotwire.com

CONTACTS: *Note: Officers with more than one job title may be intentionally listed here more than once.*

Pierre-Etienne Chartier, VP-Oper.
Henrik Kjellberg, Pres.
Jai Vijan, CTO
Pierre-Etienne Chartier, VP-Oper.

GROWTH PLANS/SPECIAL FEATURES:

Hotwire, Inc., a wholly-owned subsidiary of Expedia, Inc., offers discount prices on airfare, hotel accommodations, rental cars, cruises and vacation packages through its web site, Hotwire.com. The company offers discounts to its customers by helping travel suppliers book unsold airline seats, hotel rooms and rental cars. It also features the opaque purchase service, allowing customers to book travel arrangements based on hotel price, star rating and neighborhood preferences, without knowing the name of the hotel until after purchase. The company offers airline tickets from domestic and international airlines. It partners with several U.S. carriers, including United, Delta and U.S. Airways, as well as international airlines, such as British Airways and Lufthansa. Additionally, the firm partners with a variety of hotels, such as Embassy Suites and the Hilton; car rental companies, such as Hertz; and technology suppliers, such as Sabre, DHISCO, Sita and Ita Software. Travel planning tools available through Hotwire's site include TripStarter, which helps customers plan ideal travel times to destination cities by aggregating historic airfare and hotel pricing data as well as compiling historic weather information; and Trip Watcher, which allows users to flag certain travel options and sends out price status alerts. Hotwire also offers Groupon Getaways with Expedia, which offer discount rates for weekend getaway package trips.

Hotwire offers employees health benefits; a 401(k); disability, life, medical and dental insurance; flexible spending accounts; an employee assistance program; a fitness subsidy; and discounted travel opportunities.

FINANCIAL DATA: *Note: Data for latest year may not have been available at press time.*

In U.S. $	2015	2014	2013	2012	2011	2010
Revenue						
R&D Expense						
Operating Income						
Operating Margin %						
SGA Expense						
Net Income						
Operating Cash Flow						
Capital Expenditure						
EBITDA						
Return on Assets %						
Return on Equity %						
Debt to Equity						

CONTACT INFORMATION:

Phone: 415-343-8400   Fax: 415-343-8401
Toll-Free: 866-468-9473
Address: 655 Montgomery Street, Ste 600, San Francisco, CA 94111
United States

STOCK TICKER/OTHER:

Stock Ticker: Subsidiary   Exchange:
Employees: 351   Fiscal Year Ends: 12/31
Parent Company: EXPEDIA INC

SALARIES/BONUSES:

Top Exec. Salary: $ Bonus: $
Second Exec. Salary: $ Bonus: $

OTHER THOUGHTS:

Estimated Female Officers or Directors:
Hot Spot for Advancement for Women/Minorities: Y

Howard Johnson International Inc

www.hojo.com

NAIC Code: 721110

TYPES OF BUSINESS:

Hotels
Restaurants
Vacation Specials
Travel Packages

BRANDS/DIVISIONS/AFFILIATES:

Wyndham Worldwide
HoJo.com Booking Advantage
Rise & Dine
HoJo
TripFinder Vacation Packages

CONTACTS: *Note: Officers with more than one job title may be intentionally listed here more than once.*

Mary K. Mahoney, CEO
Mary K. Mahoney, Pres.

GROWTH PLANS/SPECIAL FEATURES:

Howard Johnson International, Inc., a subsidiary of Wyndham Worldwide, owns and franchises mid-priced hotels. Its portfolio currently includes over 500 hotels and locations in 14 countries. Howard Johnson's hotels feature a variety of amenities, including an airport shuttle, business centers, free high-speed Internet access, free Rise & Dine breakfast, gym/fitness centers, meeting/banquet facilities, pet friendly rooms, pools and restaurants. Customers can search for a hotel on the firm's web site using any or all of these amenities as search criteria. The firm's Hotel Package Deals feature several destinations for a given week, offering various packages viewable on the firm's web site. These packaged specials often include discounted hotel fees and location-specific promotions. TripFinder Vacation Packages offer a travel package program through which customers can rent cars or purchase air fares in addition to securing hotel reservations. The company participates in the Wyndham Rewards program, which is a free program that offers customers redeemable points or airline miles for staying at any one of Wyndham's hotel locations. Additionally, Howard Johnson features the HoJo.com Booking Advantage program, which guarantees customers a 10% lower price than any competitor. The company also has two HoJo restaurants in the U.S., one in Lake George, New York, and one in Bangor, Maine.

FINANCIAL DATA: *Note: Data for latest year may not have been available at press time.*

In U.S. $	2015	2014	2013	2012	2011	2010
Revenue						
R&D Expense						
Operating Income						
Operating Margin %						
SGA Expense						
Net Income						
Operating Cash Flow						
Capital Expenditure						
EBITDA						
Return on Assets %						
Return on Equity %						
Debt to Equity						

CONTACT INFORMATION:

Phone: 973-428-9700   Fax: 973-496-7658
Toll-Free: 800-544-9881
Address: 1 Sylvan Way, Parsippany, NJ 07054 United States

STOCK TICKER/OTHER:

Stock Ticker: Subsidiary   Exchange:
Employees: 10,000   Fiscal Year Ends: 12/31
Parent Company: Wyndham Worldwide

SALARIES/BONUSES:

Top Exec. Salary: $ Bonus: $
Second Exec. Salary: $ Bonus: $

OTHER THOUGHTS:

Estimated Female Officers or Directors: 1
Hot Spot for Advancement for Women/Minorities:

Sales, profits and employees may be estimates. Financial information, benefits and other data can change quickly and may vary from those stated here.

Hutchison Whampoa Properties Ltd

www.hutchison-
whampoa.com/en/businesses/property.php
NAIC Code: 531100

TYPES OF BUSINESS:

Real Estate Operations & Development
Hotels
Office & Industrial Properties
Residential Properties
Marine Docks & Repair Yards

BRANDS/DIVISIONS/AFFILIATES:

Hutchison Whampoa Limited
Hongkong & Whampoa Dock Company Limited
Hutchison Properties Limited
Cavendish International Holdings Limited
Harbour Plaza Hotels & Resorts
Hutchison Premium Services
Pacific Property Net

CONTACTS: Note: Officers with more than one job title may be intentionally listed here more than once.

Kin Ning Fok, Managing Dir.
Frank John Sixt, CFO
Ka-shing Li, Chmn.

GROWTH PLANS/SPECIAL FEATURES:

Hutchison Whampoa Properties Ltd. (Hutchison) is the property development and investment subsidiary of Hutchison Whampoa Limited (HWL). Hutchison was established by HWL to hold the property interests of Hongkong & Whampoa Dock Company Limited (HWD), Hutchison Properties Limited (HPL) and Cavendish International Holdings Limited (CIHL). The company operates within HWL's property & hotels group. HWL's other property & hotels group company is joint-venture Harbour Plaza Hotels & Resorts. Hutchison's properties are organized by location into China, Hong Kong and the U.K. Its Chinese properties make up the majority of its portfolio and are divided by city into Beijing, Changchun, Changsha, Changzhou, Chengdu, Chongqing, Dalian, Dongguan, Foshan, Guangzhou, Huizhou, Jianmen, Nanjing, Qingdao, Shanghai, Shenzhen, Tianjin, Wuhan, Xian, Zhongshan and Zhuhai. The firm's Hong Kong properties consist of assets of 28 Barker Road. Finally its U.K. assets include a Lots Toad Power Station; the Albion Riverside, Chelsea Waterfront and Convoys Wharf. The firm's services include property management, project management, marketing and e-business. Property management services offered by Hutchison include the deployment of security guards, caretakers and maintenance workers. The company's project management team supervises and coordinates the design and construction of its developments through external consultants and contractors. Hutchison's in-house marketing team is responsible for the leasing and sale of its properties, and provides property-related services to other HWL subsidiaries, including tenancy negotiations, valuations, feasibility studies and general real estate guidance. The company's e-business operations comprise subsidiaries Hutchison Premium Services and Pacific Property Net, both of which operate real estate web sites.

FINANCIAL DATA: Note: Data for latest year may not have been available at press time.

In U.S. $	2015	2014	2013	2012	2011	2010
Revenue	4,385,000,000	3,303,000,000	2,221,520,000	2,066,013,600	2,211,680,000	2,081,080,000
R&D Expense						
Operating Income						
Operating Margin %						
SGA Expense						
Net Income						
Operating Cash Flow						
Capital Expenditure						
EBITDA						
Return on Assets %						
Return on Equity %						
Debt to Equity						

CONTACT INFORMATION:

Phone: 852-2128-7500   Fax: 852-2128-7888
Toll-Free:
Address: 18 Tak Fung St., Hunghom, Fl. 3, One Harbourfront, Hong Kong, Hong Kong

STOCK TICKER/OTHER:

Stock Ticker: Subsidiary   Exchange:
Employees: 260,000   Fiscal Year Ends: 12/31
Parent Company: Hutchison Whampoa Limited

SALARIES/BONUSES:

Top Exec. Salary: $ Bonus: $
Second Exec. Salary: $ Bonus: $

OTHER THOUGHTS:

Estimated Female Officers or Directors:
Hot Spot for Advancement for Women/Minorities:

Sales, profits and employees may be estimates. Financial information, benefits and other data can change quickly and may vary from those stated here.

Hyatt Hotels Corporation

www.hyatt.com

NAIC Code: 721110

TYPES OF BUSINESS:

Hotel Ownership & Management
Timeshares
Golf Courses
Gaming
Retirement Communities
Motels & Inns
Hotel Franchising

BRANDS/DIVISIONS/AFFILIATES:

Hyatt Regency
Grand Hyatt
Hyatt Place
Hyatt Gold Passport
Andaz
Hyatt House
Hyatt Residence Club
Park Hyatt

CONTACTS: *Note: Officers with more than one job title may be intentionally listed here more than once.*

Mark Hoplamazian, CEO
Thomas Pritzker, Chairman of the Board
Bradley OBryan, Chief Accounting Officer
Patrick Grismer, Executive VP
Maryam Banikarim, Executive VP
Rena Reiss, Executive VP
H. Floyd, Executive VP
Peter Sears, Executive VP
David Udell, Executive VP
Peter Fulton, Executive VP
Stephen Haggerty, Other Corporate Officer
Robert Webb, Other Executive Officer

GROWTH PLANS/SPECIAL FEATURES:

Hyatt Hotels Corporation (Hyatt) owns, operates, manages and franchises full-service luxury hotels in 52 countries across the globe. The company owns, manages or franchises approximately 599 hotels with approximately 156,336 rooms. Hyatt's operations consist of several brands. Hyatt and Hyatt Regency host business and leisure travelers, although Hyatt Regency caters mainly to larger groups. Grand Hyatt hotels cater to leisure and business travelers and include accommodations for banquets and conferences. Park Hyatt hotels are smaller, full-service luxury hotels featuring world class art and restaurants in a few of the world's most visited cities. The Andaz branded hotels are boutique-style hotels that feature restaurants and bars aimed at local clientele as well as single travelers. The two select service brands, Hyatt House and Hyatt Place, are extended-stay brands designed to feel more like home. Hyatt Residence Club provides vacation ownership and vacation rental opportunities, offering members timeshare or points-based resort vacation opportunities. Hyatt Ziva and Hyatt Zilara are the company's all-inclusive resort brands which are developed, sold and managed as part of the Hyatt Residence club. Hyatt's guest loyalty program, Hyatt Gold Passport, has over 20 million members.

The firm offers employees complementary hotel rooms; medical, dental, vision and prescription drug coverage; and tuition assistance.

FINANCIAL DATA: *Note: Data for latest year may not have been available at press time.*

In U.S. $	2015	2014	2013	2012	2011	2010
Revenue	4,328,000,000	4,415,000,000	4,184,000,000	3,949,000,000	3,698,000,000	3,527,000,000
R&D Expense						
Operating Income	323,000,000	279,000,000	233,000,000	159,000,000	153,000,000	108,000,000
Operating Margin %	7.46%	6.31%	5.56%	4.02%	4.13%	3.06%
SGA Expense	308,000,000	349,000,000	323,000,000	316,000,000	283,000,000	276,000,000
Net Income	124,000,000	344,000,000	207,000,000	88,000,000	113,000,000	66,000,000
Operating Cash Flow	538,000,000	473,000,000	456,000,000	499,000,000	393,000,000	450,000,000
Capital Expenditure	269,000,000	253,000,000	232,000,000	301,000,000	331,000,000	520,000,000
EBITDA	582,000,000	950,000,000	731,000,000	518,000,000	445,000,000	421,000,000
Return on Assets %	1.57%	4.21%	2.61%	1.16%	1.53%	.91%
Return on Equity %	2.87%	7.32%	4.31%	1.82%	2.27%	1.30%
Debt to Equity	0.26	0.29	0.27	0.25	0.25	0.29

CONTACT INFORMATION:

Phone: 312 750-1234   Fax:
Toll-Free: 800-323-7249
Address: 71 S. Wacker Dr., 12th Fl., Chicago, IL 60606 United States

STOCK TICKER/OTHER:

Stock Ticker: H
Employees: 45,000
Parent Company:

Exchange: NYS
Fiscal Year Ends: 12/31

SALARIES/BONUSES:

Top Exec. Salary: $1,060,833   Bonus: $
Second Exec. Salary: $727,083   Bonus: $

OTHER THOUGHTS:

Estimated Female Officers or Directors: 3

Hot Spot for Advancement for Women/Minorities: Y

Sales, profits and employees may be estimates. Financial information, benefits and other data can change quickly and may vary from those stated here.

Iberia Lineas Aereas de Espana SA

www.iberia.com

NAIC Code: 481111

TYPES OF BUSINESS:

Airline
Air Freight
Aircraft Maintenance
Express Delivery Services

BRANDS/DIVISIONS/AFFILIATES:

International Consolidated Airlines Group SA
Iberia Regional
Ibera Express
Iberia Cargo
IAG Cargo

CONTACTS: *Note: Officers with more than one job title may be intentionally listed here more than once.*

Luis Gallego Martin, CEO

GROWTH PLANS/SPECIAL FEATURES:

Iberia Lineas Aereas de Espana SA (Iberia), a subsidiary of International Consolidated Airlines Group SA (IAG), is a Spanish airline and cargo transport company that operates in three core markets: Spain, Europe and the Americas. The airline offers hundreds of daily flights and employs a fleet of 79 all-Airbus aircraft, including A319s, A320s, A321s, A330s and A340s, with additional A320neo, A321neo and A330s on order. It operates flights to 109 destinations. The company extends its service to other destinations using a number of codesharing agreements with other airlines, including British Airways, Finnair, Mexicana, El Al, Royal Jordania and Comair. Iberia's subsidiaries include Iberia Regional, Iberia Express and Iberia Cargo. Iberia Regional is based in Valencia, Spain, and operates a network of 91 domestic and international routes to 51 destinations. The regional airline also charters flights. Iberia Express is a low-cost airline operating short- and medium-haul routes from Iberia's Madrid hub, providing feeder flights onto Iberia's long-haul network. Iberia Cargo (also referred to as IAG Cargo) is the cargo handling division of the company, and maintains two global hubs at London's Heathrow and Madrid's Barajas airports.

FINANCIAL DATA: *Note: Data for latest year may not have been available at press time.*

In U.S. $	2015	2014	2013	2012	2011	2010
Revenue	5,171,439,818	5,436,267,269	5,363,659,084	6,121,548,616	5,793,133,249	6,426,450,000
R&D Expense						
Operating Income						
Operating Margin %						
SGA Expense						
Net Income						
Operating Cash Flow						
Capital Expenditure						
EBITDA						
Return on Assets %						
Return on Equity %						
Debt to Equity						

CONTACT INFORMATION:

Phone: 34-91-587-74-62   Fax: 34-91-587-74-69
Toll-Free:
Address: Velazquez 130, Madrid, 28006 Spain

STOCK TICKER/OTHER:

Stock Ticker: Subsidiary   Exchange:
Employees: 18,667   Fiscal Year Ends: 12/31
Parent Company: International Consolidated Airlines Group SA (IAG)

SALARIES/BONUSES:

Top Exec. Salary: $ Bonus: $
Second Exec. Salary: $ Bonus: $

OTHER THOUGHTS:

Estimated Female Officers or Directors: 1
Hot Spot for Advancement for Women/Minorities:

Sales, profits and employees may be estimates. Financial information, benefits and other data can change quickly and may vary from those stated here.

Indian Hotels Company Limited (The)   www.tajhotels.com

NAIC Code: 721110

TYPES OF BUSINESS:

Hotels
Spas
Apartments
Private Jet Rental
Air Catering
Travel Agency

BRANDS/DIVISIONS/AFFILIATES:

Taj Wellington Mews
Tata Group
Taj Hotels, Resorts and Places
TajAir Ltd
TajSATS Air Catering Ltd
IndiTravel Private Limited
Roots Corporation Ltd
Jiva Spas

CONTACTS: Note: Officers with more than one job title may be intentionally listed here more than once.

Rakesh Sarna, Managing Dir.
Prabhat Verm, Sr.VP-Operations
Anil P. Goel, CFO
Beejal Desai, VP-Legal
Abhijit Mukerji, Exec. Dir.-Hotel Oper.
Rajiv Gujral, Sr. VP-Mergers, Acquisitions & Dev.
Anil P. Goel, Exec. Dir.-Finance
Veer Vijay Singh, COO-Upper Upscale Hotels
Prabhat Verma, COO-The Gateway Hotels & Resorts
Jyoti Narang, COO-Luxury Div.

GROWTH PLANS/SPECIAL FEATURES:

The Indian Hotels Company Limited (IHCL), which, together with its subsidiaries, does business as Taj Hotels, Resorts and Palaces (Taj), is one of the world's premier operators of luxury hotels. Part of Indian conglomerate Tata Group, IHCL owns more than 93 hotels in 55 locations across India and 16 additional hotels in Sri Lanka, the Maldives, Malaysia, Australia, the U.S., the U.K. Bhutan, Africa and the Middle East. The company operates hotels in the value, mid-market, premium and luxury segments. The firm's hotel brands include Taj, a chain of luxury full-service resorts, hotels and palaces including historic properties, modern business-oriented hotels, beach resorts and safari lodges; Taj Exotica, a resort and spa brand; Taj Safaris, ecotourism lodges in the Indian jungle; The Gateway Hotel, a mid to upscale full-service hotel and resort brand; Ginger, a line of economy hotels operated by wholly-owned subsidiary Roots Corporation Ltd.; and The Gateway Hotel, a pan-India network of hotels and resorts that offers business and leisure travelers a hotel with a nomadic design theme. Taj Wellington Mews provides 80 furnished apartments for short-term and extended-stay travelers, and includes butler service, 24-hour concierge services, baby-sitting services and recreation options. Taj offers a variety of services through Jiva Spas, including yoga, meditation, Indian healing ceremonies and other treatments. Besides hotels, IHCL offers chartered private luxury jets through subsidiary TajAir Ltd. and catering services for domestic and international airlines through TajSATS Air Catering Ltd. Subsidiary Taj Luxury Residences offers apartments in three locations, staffed with personal butlers, a round-the-clock concierge and 24-hour-a-day babysitting service. Finally, IndiTravel Private Limited offers travel services from ticketing to car rentals and passport assistance.

FINANCIAL DATA: Note: Data for latest year may not have been available at press time.

In U.S. $	2015	2014	2013	2012	2011	2010
Revenue	623,982,700	605,741,300	557,649,200	511,371,600	434,233,300	375,556,900
R&D Expense						
Operating Income	-34,632,600	-61,399,570	-43,468,020	43,983,460	41,242,410	
Operating Margin %	-5.55%	-10.13%	-7.79%	8.60%	9.49%	
SGA Expense			107,584,800	102,189,100	86,781,120	79,964,240
Net Income	-56,325,640	-82,507,170	-64,092,950	455,849	-12,999,140	-17,638,080
Operating Cash Flow	73,706,010	80,283,040	74,748,790	79,690,140	76,396,410	67,131,940
Capital Expenditure	46,944,990	50,973,150	63,325,760	47,704,740	61,472,570	41,227,510
EBITDA	39,475,620	9,605,601	-502,030	91,792,480	75,064,620	73,142,890
Return on Assets %	-3.89%	-5.88%	-4.64%	.03%	-.99%	-1.53%
Return on Equity %	-15.54%	-19.72%	-14.19%	.10%	-3.19%	-4.80%
Debt to Equity	2.06	1.14	1.15	0.99	1.45	1.75

CONTACT INFORMATION:

Phone: 91 22 - 61371637   Fax: 91 22 - 61371710
Toll-Free:
Address: 9/Fl, Express Towers, Barrister Rajni Patel Marg, Mumbai, 400021 India

STOCK TICKER/OTHER:

Stock Ticker: IDHCF   Exchange: GREY
Employees: 10,020   Fiscal Year Ends: 03/31
Parent Company: TATA Group

SALARIES/BONUSES:

Top Exec. Salary: $ Bonus: $
Second Exec. Salary: $ Bonus: $

OTHER THOUGHTS:

Estimated Female Officers or Directors: 2
Hot Spot for Advancement for Women/Minorities:

Sales, profits and employees may be estimates. Financial information, benefits and other data can change quickly and may vary from those stated here.

IndiGo (InterGlobe Aviation)
NAIC Code: 481111

TYPES OF BUSINESS:
Airline
Travel Insurance

BRANDS/DIVISIONS/AFFILIATES:
InterGlobe Enterprises Limited
IndiGo
Book.GoIndigo.in

GROWTH PLANS/SPECIAL FEATURES:
InterGlobe Aviation, operating as IndiGo, is a low-cost, domestic passenger airline operating in India. With a fleet of 101 Airbus-A320-200s, IndiGo offers 671 daily flights across 39 cities throughout the country and five international destinations. The firm offers online booking and check-in services through its e-commerce site, Book.GoIndigo.in. The company is a subsidiary of Indian travel corporation InterGlobe Enterprises Limited, which in addition to offering domestic air transport, manages hotels (through a joint venture with Accor) and provides airline management services, business process and IT outsourcing and aircraft sales and maintenance services. In August 2015, IndiGo placed a massive order for 250 new Airbus A320neo aircraft worth $27 billion.

CONTACTS: Note: Officers with more than one job title may be intentionally listed here more than once.
Aditya Ghosh, Pres.
Pankaj Madan, CFO

FINANCIAL DATA: Note: Data for latest year may not have been available at press time.

In U.S. $	2015	2014	2013	2012	2011	2010
Revenue						
R&D Expense						
Operating Income						
Operating Margin %						
SGA Expense						
Net Income						
Operating Cash Flow						
Capital Expenditure						
EBITDA						
Return on Assets %						
Return on Equity %						
Debt to Equity						

CONTACT INFORMATION:
Phone: 91-124-435-2500   Fax: 91-124-406-8536
Toll-Free:
Address: Level 1, Tower C, Mehrauli-Gurgaon Rd., Gurgaon, Haryana 122 002 India

STOCK TICKER/OTHER:
Stock Ticker: Subsidiary   Exchange:
Employees: 20,000   Fiscal Year Ends:
Parent Company: Interglobe Enterprises Limited

SALARIES/BONUSES:
Top Exec. Salary: $ Bonus: $
Second Exec. Salary: $ Bonus: $

OTHER THOUGHTS:
Estimated Female Officers or Directors:
Hot Spot for Advancement for Women/Minorities: Y

Innkeepers USA Trust

www.innkeepersusa.com

NAIC Code: 0

TYPES OF BUSINESS:

Real Estate Investment Trust
Hotels
Hotel Development

BRANDS/DIVISIONS/AFFILIATES:

Island Hospitality Management
Apollo Investment Corporation

CONTACTS: *Note: Officers with more than one job title may be intentionally listed here more than once.*

Mark A. Murphy, Sec.
Richard A. Mielbye, Sr. VP-Dev.
Roger Pollak, VP-Acct., Innkeepers Hospitality
Marc A. Beilinson, Chief Restructuring Officer
John J. Hannan, Chmn.-Apollo

GROWTH PLANS/SPECIAL FEATURES:

Innkeepers USA Trust, owned by Apollo Investment Corp., is a real estate investment trust (REIT) that specializes in the ownership of multi-brand, upscale, extended-stay hotels in the U.S. The firm seeks to acquire hotel properties in markets with high barriers to entry and with strong underlying demand growth. Innkeepers USA owns interests in 64 hotels with an aggregate of 8,300 rooms/suites in 18 states and Washington, D.C. Sixty-three of these hotels are managed by Island Hospitality Management. The firm's hotels operate under the following brands: Residence Inn, TownePlace Suites and Courtyard by Marriott; Sheraton; Double Tree; Embassy Suites; Hyatt Summerfield Suites; Westin; Best Western; Bulfinch Hotel; Hampton Inn; and Hilton. In addition to its acquisitions of existing hotels in the upscale and extended-stay market, Innkeepers USA also acquires under-performing mid-priced and full service hotels that have the potential for strategic repositioning or re-flagging to a premium franchise brand in the upscale segment. During 2010, burdened with a large debt load, the firm filed for bankruptcy. It is currently in the restructuring process.

FINANCIAL DATA: *Note: Data for latest year may not have been available at press time.*

In U.S. $	2015	2014	2013	2012	2011	2010
Revenue						
R&D Expense						
Operating Income						
Operating Margin %						
SGA Expense						
Net Income						
Operating Cash Flow						
Capital Expenditure						
EBITDA						
Return on Assets %						
Return on Equity %						
Debt to Equity						

CONTACT INFORMATION:

Phone: 561-835-1800   Fax: 561-835-0457
Toll-Free:
Address: 340 Royal Poinciana Way, Ste. 306, Palm Beach, FL 33480
United States

STOCK TICKER/OTHER:

Stock Ticker: Private   Exchange:
Employees: 33   Fiscal Year Ends: 12/31
Parent Company: Apollo Investment Corporation

SALARIES/BONUSES:

Top Exec. Salary: $ Bonus: $
Second Exec. Salary: $ Bonus: $

OTHER THOUGHTS:

Estimated Female Officers or Directors:
Hot Spot for Advancement for Women/Minorities:

Sales, profits and employees may be estimates. Financial information, benefits and other data can change quickly and may vary from those stated here.

InterContinental Hotels Group plc

NAIC Code: 721110

www.ihgplc.com

TYPES OF BUSINESS:

Hotel & Motel Development & Management
Hotels

BRANDS/DIVISIONS/AFFILIATES:

InterContinental Hotels Group Europe
InterContinental Hotels Group The Americas
InterContinental Hotels Group AMEA
InterContinental Hotels Group Greater China
InterContinental Hotels & Resorts
Hualuxe Hotels and Resorts
Holiday Inn
Kimpton Hotels & Restaurants

CONTACTS: Note: Officers with more than one job title may be intentionally listed here more than once.

Richard Solomons, CEO
Paul Edgecliffe-Johnson, CFO
Tracy Robbins, Exec. VP-Global Human Resources & Oper. Support
George Turner, General Counsel
Kirk Kinsell, Pres., Americas
Kenneth Macpherson, CEO-Greater China
Angela Brav, CEO-Europe
Patrick Cescau, Chmn.
Jan Smits, CEO-Asia, Middle East & Africa

GROWTH PLANS/SPECIAL FEATURES:

InterContinental Hotels Group plc (IHG) is an international hotel and hospitality firm. The company operates under the following 12 brands: InterContinental Hotels & Resorts, Kimpton Hotels & Restaurants, Hualuxe Hotels and Resorts, Hotel Indigo, Even Hotels, Crowne Plaza Hotels & Resorts, Holiday Inn, Holiday Inn Express, Holiday Inn Club Vacations, Staybridge Suites and Candlewood Suites. Hotel use is more prevalent within the U.S., Canada, Latin America and the Caribbean (64%), with the remaining percentage nearly equally-divided between Europe, Asia/Middle East/Africa and Greater China. IHG's hotels are located in nearly 100 countries, with more than 5,000 hotels and 744,000 guest rooms. The company's hotels are primarily franchised (4,219 hotels), 806 hotels are managed by IHG and seven are IHG-owned and -leased. Subsidiaries include InterContinental Hotels Group Europe, with headquarters in Denham, U.K.; InterContinental Hotels Group The Americas, with headquarters in Atlanta, USA; InterContinental Hotels Group Asia, Middle East and Africa with headquarters in Singapore; and InterContinental Hotels Group Greater China, with headquarters in Shanghai. In 2015, the firm acquired Kimpton Hotels & Restaurants, an independent boutique hotel operator; and sold its ownership stake in InterContinental Hong Kong to Supreme Key Limited for $938 million. IHG will retain its 37-year management contract on the Hong Kong hotel, with three 10-year extension rights.

The firm typically offers employees benefits including life, disability, medical and dental insurance; paid time off; employee discounts; a pension or 401(k); incentive programs; and educational assistance.

FINANCIAL DATA: Note: Data for latest year may not have been available at press time.

In U.S. $	2015	2014	2013	2012	2011	2010
Revenue	1,803,000,000	1,858,000,000	1,903,000,000	1,835,000,000	1,768,000,000	1,628,000,000
R&D Expense						
Operating Income	1,499,000,000	680,000,000	673,000,000	610,000,000	616,000,000	437,000,000
Operating Margin %	83.13%	36.59%	35.36%	33.24%	34.84%	26.84%
SGA Expense	420,000,000	483,000,000	541,000,000	379,000,000	359,000,000	366,000,000
Net Income	1,222,000,000	391,000,000	372,000,000	544,000,000	473,000,000	280,000,000
Operating Cash Flow	628,000,000	543,000,000	624,000,000	472,000,000	479,000,000	462,000,000
Capital Expenditure	203,000,000	248,000,000	245,000,000	128,000,000	103,000,000	91,000,000
EBITDA	1,580,000,000	760,000,000	744,000,000	707,000,000	717,000,000	547,000,000
Return on Assets %	37.10%	13.55%	11.96%	17.46%	16.44%	9.86%
Return on Equity %			329.20%	127.25%	115.64%	133.33%
Debt to Equity	4.00			4.03	1.22	2.86

CONTACT INFORMATION:

Phone: 44-1895-512000   Fax: 44-1895-512101
Toll-Free: 800-621-0555
Address: Broadwater Park, Denham, Buckinghamshire UB9 5HR United Kingdom

STOCK TICKER/OTHER:

Stock Ticker: IHG   Exchange: NYS
Employees: 7,311   Fiscal Year Ends: 12/31
Parent Company:

SALARIES/BONUSES:

Top Exec. Salary: $785,000   Bonus: $
Second Exec. Salary: $450,000   Bonus: $

OTHER THOUGHTS:

Estimated Female Officers or Directors: 4
Hot Spot for Advancement for Women/Minorities: Y

Sales, profits and employees may be estimates. Financial information, benefits and other data can change quickly and may vary from those stated here.

International Airlines Group (IAG)

www.iairgroup.com

NAIC Code: 481111

TYPES OF BUSINESS:

Airlines

BRANDS/DIVISIONS/AFFILIATES:

British Airways
Iberia
Vueling
Aer Lingus
Qatar Airways

CONTACTS: *Note: Officers with more than one job title may be intentionally listed here more than once.*

Willie Walsh, CEO
Enrique Dupuy De Lome Chavarri, CFO
Luis Gallego Martin, Chmn.

GROWTH PLANS/SPECIAL FEATURES:

International Airlines Group (IAG) is one of the world's largest airline groups. IAG is the parent company of British Airways, Iberia airlines, Vueling airlines and Aer Lingus. British Airways and Iberia are both founding members of the oneworld alliance. The oneworld alliance serves some 1,000 destinations in 155 countries. In total, IAG has a fleet of 533 aircraft carrying over 95 million passengers each year to 274 destinations. British Airways is the largest airline in the U.K., with a presence at Heathrow (the airline's main home), Gatwick and London City airports. In service with its group companies, the airline has a fleet of 280 aircraft flying to more than 70 different countries. Iberia is a Spanish airline with its hub located at Madrid-Barajas Airport, the main airport serving Madrid. The airline has a fleet of 135 aircraft serving 120 destinations in 43 countries. Vueling Airlines SA is a leading airline at Barcelona-El Prat Airport in Spain, and operates more than 285 routes to more than 131 cities in Europe, the Middle East and Africa. The airline has 21 operational bases and 90 aircraft. Aer Lingus is the national airline of Ireland whose primary mission is to connect Ireland with the world through its fleet of 50 aircraft from central airport locations in the U.K., continental Europe and North America on over 100 routes. In 2016, it was announced that Qatar Airways increased its shareholding of IAG to a total 15.01%, with plans to increase it to 20%.

FINANCIAL DATA: *Note: Data for latest year may not have been available at press time.*

In U.S. $	2015	2014	2013	2012	2011	2010
Revenue	25,825,330,000	22,788,380,000	20,979,550,000	20,468,870,000	18,193,420,000	8,913,116,000
R&D Expense					423,681,100	67,788,320
Operating Income	2,618,913,000	1,162,580,000	595,412,900	-692,577,100	589,763,300	472,263,400
Operating Margin %	10.14%	5.10%	2.83%	-3.38%	3.24%	5.29%
SGA Expense	2,606,485,000	2,412,157,000	2,301,435,000	2,397,469,000	836,063,800	312,958,400
Net Income	1,689,075,000	1,109,479,000	137,837,500	-1,065,416,000	634,956,900	222,574,400
Operating Cash Flow	2,223,478,000	2,103,717,000	1,376,116,000	383,007,600	869,959,000	1,057,508,000
Capital Expenditure	2,304,824,000	2,962,377,000	2,481,075,000	1,399,842,000	1,210,032,000	724,212,500
EBITDA	3,844,763,000	2,433,623,000	1,665,348,000	721,952,300	1,928,596,000	1,134,334,000
Return on Assets %	5.76%	4.42%	.60%	-4.76%	3.44%	1.52%
Return on Equity %	34.32%	26.56%	2.81%	-18.59%	14.20%	7.80%
Debt to Equity	1.43	1.69	1.16	0.86	0.79	1.62

CONTACT INFORMATION:

Phone: 44 20 0564 2000   Fax:
Toll-Free:
Address: Newall Rd., 2 Wolrd Business Ctr., Heathrow, Hounslow, 28006 United Kingdom

STOCK TICKER/OTHER:

Stock Ticker: BABWF
Employees: 59,484
Parent Company:

Exchange: PINX
Fiscal Year Ends:

SALARIES/BONUSES:

Top Exec. Salary: $ Bonus: $
Second Exec. Salary: $ Bonus: $

OTHER THOUGHTS:

Estimated Female Officers or Directors: 5
Hot Spot for Advancement for Women/Minorities: Y

Sales, profits and employees may be estimates. Financial information, benefits and other data can change quickly and may vary from those stated here.

Interstate Hotels & Resorts Inc

www.interstatehotels.com

NAIC Code: 721110

TYPES OF BUSINESS:
Hotel Management
Corporate Hotel Management
Engineering & Design Consulting
Construction Management
Procurement Services

BRANDS/DIVISIONS/AFFILIATES:
Thayer Lodging Group
Shanghai Jin Jiang International Hotels
Colony Hotels & Resorts

CONTACTS: Note: Officers with more than one job title may be intentionally listed here more than once.
James R. Abrahamson, CEO
Samuel E. Knighton, COO
Samuel E. Knighton, Pres.
Carrie McIntyre, CFO
George J. Brennan, Exec. VP-Mktg. & Sales
Laura E. FitzRandolph, Exec. VP-Human Resources
Leslie Ng, CIO
Christopher L. Bennett, Chief Admin. Officer
Christopher L. Bennett, General Counsel
Thomas J. Bardenett, Exec. VP-Oper.
Edward J. Blum, Exec. VP-Dev. & Acquisitions
Joseph A. Klam, Exec. VP-Finance
Leslie Ng, Chief Investment Officer
James Rowe, Sr. VP-Investment Strategy & Capital Markets
Jim Biggar, Exec. VP-Hotel Oper., Full Service
Greg Juceam, Exec. VP-Hotel Oper., Full Service
Kenneth W. McLaren, Exec. VP-Int'l Oper.

GROWTH PLANS/SPECIAL FEATURES:
Interstate Hotels & Resorts, Inc. is an independent hotel management companies. The company is wholly-owned subsidiary of a joint venture between Thayer Lodging Group and Shanghai Jin Jiang International Hotels. The firm divides its operations into three primary categories: hotel management services, hotel development services and design and construction services. Interstate manages luxury, full-service, select-service and extended-stay hospitality properties, consisting of more than 430 properties with over 76,000 rooms. These properties are located in 39 U.S. states, Washington, D.C., Canada, the U.K., Ireland, The Netherlands, Belgium, Hungary, Russia, China and India. The company's brand portfolio includes Best Western, Comfort Inn, Courtyard by Marriott, Crowne Plaza, Days Inn, Doubletree, Embassy Suites, Fairfield Inn, Hampton Inn, Hilton, Holiday Inn, Homewood Suites, Hyatt Place, Marriott, Radisson, Renaissance, Sheraton and Westin. The firm offers management services to unbranded hotels through its Colony Hotels & Resorts division. The company's development services comprise hotel brand and site validation, owner and brand relations, joint venture partnerships, financing, acquisitions and conversions and renovations. Finally, its design and construction services consist of pre-design budgeting, construction and design consulting, purchase order placement and reporting, shipment monitoring and technical services.

The firm offers employees medical, dental and vision coverage; health care flexible spending accounts; an employee assistance program; life insurance; short- and long-term disability; a 401(k) plan; discounted hotel rooms; and a corporate discount program

FINANCIAL DATA: Note: Data for latest year may not have been available at press time.

In U.S. $	2015	2014	2013	2012	2011	2010
Revenue						
R&D Expense						
Operating Income						
Operating Margin %						
SGA Expense						
Net Income						
Operating Cash Flow						
Capital Expenditure						
EBITDA						
Return on Assets %						
Return on Equity %						
Debt to Equity						

CONTACT INFORMATION:
Phone: 703-387-3100 Fax:
Toll-Free:
Address: 4501 N. Fairfax Dr., Ste 500, Arlington, VA 22203 United States

STOCK TICKER/OTHER:
Stock Ticker: Subsidiary Exchange:
Employees: 19,000 Fiscal Year Ends: 12/31
Parent Company: Thayer Lodging Group

SALARIES/BONUSES:
Top Exec. Salary: $ Bonus: $
Second Exec. Salary: $ Bonus: $

OTHER THOUGHTS:
Estimated Female Officers or Directors: 1
Hot Spot for Advancement for Women/Minorities:

Sales, profits and employees may be estimates. Financial information, benefits and other data can change quickly and may vary from those stated here.

Interval Leisure Group Inc

NAIC Code: 561599

www.iilg.com

TYPES OF BUSINESS:

Timeshare Exchange Broker

BRANDS/DIVISIONS/AFFILIATES:

Interval Network
Hyatt Residential Group
Hyatt Residence Club

CONTACTS: Note: Officers with more than one job title may be intentionally listed here more than once.

William Harvey, CFO
Craig Nash, Chairman of the Board
John Galea, Chief Accounting Officer
Jeanette Marbert, COO
Victoria Kincke, General Counsel
David Gilbert, President, Divisional
John Burlingame, President, Divisional
Kelvin Bloom, President, Subsidiary

GROWTH PLANS/SPECIAL FEATURES:

Interval Leisure Group, Inc. is a membership-based travel and vacation management company. The firm operates in two primary segments: exchange & rental and vacation ownership. Exchange & rental offers access to vacation accommodations and other travel-related transactions and services to leisure travelers. The segment works with resort developers, and operates vacation rental properties, providing owners of vacation interests with flexibility and choice by delivering access to alternate accommodations through exchange networks encompassing a variety of resorts. Its principal exchange network is the Interval Network, in which more than 3,000 resorts located in over 80 nation participated through 2015. Hyatt Residence Club encompasses 16 resorts within the network exchange program. Exchange & rental comprised 73.8% of consolidated revenue for fiscal 2015. Vacation ownership engages in the management of vacation ownership resorts; sales, marketing and financing of vacation ownership interests; and related services to owners and associations. This segment provides services to nearly 200 vacation ownership properties as well as sales and marketing of vacation ownership interests in the Hyatt Residence Club resorts. Vacation ownership comprised 28.1% of consolidated 2015 revenue. In October 2015, Interval Leisure Group announced the acquisition of the vacation ownership business of Starwood Hotels & Resorts Worldwide, Inc., and an additional five hotels that are expected to be converted to vacation ownership properties.

FINANCIAL DATA: Note: Data for latest year may not have been available at press time.

In U.S. $	2015	2014	2013	2012	2011	2010
Revenue	697,436,000	614,373,000	501,215,000	473,339,000	428,794,000	409,440,000
R&D Expense						
Operating Income	128,144,000	127,094,000	132,745,000	109,781,000	98,784,000	104,477,000
Operating Margin %	18.37%	20.68%	26.48%	23.19%	23.03%	25.51%
SGA Expense	221,128,000	194,785,000	166,296,000	158,829,000	148,012,000	139,735,000
Net Income	73,315,000	78,930,000	81,217,000	40,702,000	41,126,000	42,418,000
Operating Cash Flow	142,722,000	110,658,000	109,864,000	80,438,000	95,907,000	91,403,000
Capital Expenditure	20,297,000	19,087,000	14,700,000	15,040,000	13,038,000	16,443,000
EBITDA	169,139,000	162,161,000	156,030,000	127,060,000	142,205,000	141,578,000
Return on Assets %	5.62%	6.71%	8.40%	4.32%	4.19%	4.36%
Return on Equity %	17.96%	21.68%	26.37%	16.63%	17.37%	21.15%
Debt to Equity	0.96	1.27	0.73	0.95	1.36	1.59

CONTACT INFORMATION:

Phone: 305 666-1861   Fax: 305 667-0653
Toll-Free: 888-784-3447
Address: 6262 Sunset Dr., Miami, FL 33143 United States

STOCK TICKER/OTHER:

Stock Ticker: IILG
Employees: 6,100
Parent Company:

Exchange: NAS
Fiscal Year Ends: 12/31

SALARIES/BONUSES:

Top Exec. Salary: $750,000   Bonus: $
Second Exec. Salary: $435,000   Bonus: $

OTHER THOUGHTS:

Estimated Female Officers or Directors: 3
Hot Spot for Advancement for Women/Minorities: Y

Sales, profits and employees may be estimates. Financial information, benefits and other data can change quickly and may vary from those stated here.

InTown Suites Management Inc

www.intownsuites.com

NAIC Code: 721110

TYPES OF BUSINESS:

Hotels
Extended-Stay Hotels

BRANDS/DIVISIONS/AFFILIATES:

Westmont Hospitality Group
Intown Suites

CONTACTS: *Note: Officers with more than one job title may be intentionally listed here more than once.*

Jonathan Pertchik, CEO
Dennis Cassel, Pres.
Collier Daily, Dir-Mktg. & Communications

GROWTH PLANS/SPECIAL FEATURES:

InTown Suites Management, Inc. is a private corporation that develops, owns and operates budget extended-stay properties. The company does not offer reservations for less than seven days and prefers long-term commitments or apartment leases. A seven-day stay at InTown Suites is generally cheaper than renting a nightly room at a traditional hotel for a few days. Most facilities are located in predominately retail-oriented locations near shops, restaurants and movie theaters, with proximity to major metropolitan areas, spanning more than 180 locations across 21 states. The firm's properties feature studio suites with full amenities, including complete kitchens, high-speed Internet, a dining area, cable TV, a full size bath, voicemail service, laundry facilities, pool areas and weekly housekeeping. The company also offers specialized services for corporate customers. The firm is currently focused on accelerating the growth of its operations, and it will convert all newly acquired properties to the InTown Suites brand. Certain locations are also undergoing renovation and development, which is in some cases significantly increasing the number of rooms. Westmont Hospitality Group operates InTown Suites' properties. In late 2015, the firm acquired four new locations in Hampton Roads, Virginia: Chesapeake/Battlefield, Hampton, Norfolk and Newport News City Center, which will obtain an InTown Suites makeover before opening.

FINANCIAL DATA: *Note: Data for latest year may not have been available at press time.*

In U.S. $	2015	2014	2013	2012	2011	2010
Revenue						
R&D Expense						
Operating Income						
Operating Margin %						
SGA Expense						
Net Income						
Operating Cash Flow						
Capital Expenditure						
EBITDA						
Return on Assets %						
Return on Equity %						
Debt to Equity						

CONTACT INFORMATION:

Phone: 770-799-5000   Fax: 770-437-8190
Toll-Free: 800-553-9338
Address: 2727 Paces Ferry Rd., Ste. 2-1200, Atlanta, GA 30339 United States

STOCK TICKER/OTHER:

Stock Ticker: Private   Exchange:
Employees: 1,100   Fiscal Year Ends: 12/31
Parent Company:

SALARIES/BONUSES:

Top Exec. Salary: $ Bonus: $
Second Exec. Salary: $ Bonus: $

OTHER THOUGHTS:

Estimated Female Officers or Directors:
Hot Spot for Advancement for Women/Minorities:

Sales, profits and employees may be estimates. Financial information, benefits and other data can change quickly and may vary from those stated here.

Intrawest Resorts Holding Inc

www.intrawest.com

NAIC Code: 713920

TYPES OF BUSINESS:

Ski Resorts
Golf Courses
Beach Resorts
Meeting & Conference Planning
Vacation Ownership Club
Luxury Adventure Travel
Helicopter Skiing & Hiking

BRANDS/DIVISIONS/AFFILIATES:

Steamboat Ski & Resort
Winter Park Resort
Stratton Mountain Resort
Snowshe Mountain Resort
Mont Tremblant Resort
Blue Mountain Ski Resort

CONTACTS: Note: Officers with more than one job title may be intentionally listed here more than once.

Lindsay Goszulak, Chief Accounting Officer
Sky Foulkes, COO
Thomas Marano, Director
Wesley Edens, Director
Travis Mayer, Executive VP
Karen Sanford, General Counsel

GROWTH PLANS/SPECIAL FEATURES:

Intrawest Resorts Holdings, Inc. is one of North America's largest developers and operators of destination resorts and real estate. The firm operates the following mountain resorts and lodging operations: Steamboat Ski & Resort, Winter Park Resort, Stratton Mountain Resort, Snowshoe Mountain Resort, Mont Tremblant Resort and Blue Mountain Ski Resort. These resorts comprise the company's mountain division, comprising the majority of its annual revenue. Steamboat features 2,965 skiable acres and a maximum vertical drop of 3,668 feet; Winter Park is comprised of seven territories, including Winter Park Mountain, Mary Jane Mountain, Vasquez Cirque and Vasquez Ridge, with more than 3,000 skiable acres; Stratton features a vertical drop of 2,003 feet and snowmaking on 93% of its trails; Snowshoe has the biggest vertical drop in the region and 100% snowmaking coverage; Mont Tremblant is ranked as one of the top ski resorts in Eastern North America with 2,116 feet of vertical drop and snowmaking on 77% of its trails; and Blue Mountain consists of 360 skiable acres and snowmaking on 93% of its trails. Intrawest's hospitality division focuses on providing management services to properties owned by third parties, including Honua Kai Resort and Spa in Maui, Hawaii and the Westin Monache Resort at Mammoth Lakes, California. The company maintains Canadian Mountain Holidays, one of the largest heli-skiing operations in the world. In early 2016, the firm sold Intrawest Resort Club Group, its timeshare business, to Diamond Resorts International, Inc. for about $85 million.

FINANCIAL DATA: Note: Data for latest year may not have been available at press time.

In U.S. $	2015	2014	2013	2012	2011	2010
Revenue	587,589,000	527,106,000	524,407,000	513,447,000	559,523,000	
R&D Expense						
Operating Income	36,422,000	17,319,000	3,478,000	-19,332,000	-196,516,000	
Operating Margin %	6.19%	3.28%	.66%	-3.76%	-35.12%	
SGA Expense						
Net Income	-6,920,000	-188,572,000	-295,957,000	-336,063,000	-498,867,000	
Operating Cash Flow	79,137,000	44,089,000	41,765,000	43,390,000	21,140,000	
Capital Expenditure	41,873,000	50,707,000	29,679,000	30,061,000	27,567,000	
EBITDA	93,966,000	42,040,000	73,047,000	47,527,000	-104,609,000	
Return on Assets %	-.62%	-16.88%	-24.01%	-25.02%		
Return on Equity %	2.24%					
Debt to Equity	2.17	1.65				

CONTACT INFORMATION:

Phone: 303-749-8200   Fax: 403-749-8340
Toll-Free:
Address: 1621 18th St., Ste. 300, Denver, CO 80202 United States

STOCK TICKER/OTHER:

Stock Ticker: SNOW   Exchange: NYS
Employees: 4,000   Fiscal Year Ends: 06/30
Parent Company:

SALARIES/BONUSES:

Top Exec. Salary: $438,394   Bonus: $
Second Exec. Salary: $385,995   Bonus: $

OTHER THOUGHTS:

Estimated Female Officers or Directors: 1
Hot Spot for Advancement for Women/Minorities:

Sales, profits and employees may be estimates. Financial information, benefits and other data can change quickly and may vary from those stated here.

ITC Limited
NAIC Code: 312230

TYPES OF BUSINESS:
Tobacco Manufacturing
Specialty Papers
Hotels & Tourism
Agriculture
Information Technology
Apparel Manufacturing & Retail
Commodities Trading
Real Estate Development

BRANDS/DIVISIONS/AFFILIATES:
Russell Credit Limited
Landbase India Limited
ITC Infotech India Limited
Surya Nepal Private Limited
Fortune Park Hotels Limited
e-Choupal
Wills Lifestyle
Sunfeast

CONTACTS: Note: Officers with more than one job title may be intentionally listed here more than once.
Yogesh C. Deveshwar, CEO
Rajiv Tandon, CFO
Anand Nayak, Head-Human Resources
T.V. Ramaswamy, Head-R&D
Kannadiputhur S. Suresh, General Counsel
S. Sivakumar, CEO-Agri Bus. & IT Bus.
Biswa B. Chatterjee, Exec. VP
Yogesh C. Deveshwar, Chmn.

GROWTH PLANS/SPECIAL FEATURES:
ITC Limited is an India-based consumer goods and services company. It is active in six business sectors: fast moving consumer goods (FMCG), hotels, paperboards, packaging, agri-business and information technology (IT). FMCG produces cigarettes such as its India Kings brand; packaged foods, including ready-to-eat foods, snack foods and confectionery products, marketed under the Kitchens of India and Sunfeast brands; and personal care products such as perfumes, shampoos and soaps. Other products include education and stationery products (notebooks and classroom materials), safety matches (under the Mangaldeep brand) and incense sticks (sourced from small-scale providers around India). It is also active in the lifestyle retail market, operating Wills Lifestyle retail stores and youth-focused clothing stores under the John Players name. The hotels segment, operating as ITC Hotels, manages over 100 hotels in 70 locations throughout India. Its subsidiaries include Bay Islands Hotels Limited, Srinivasa Resorts Limited and Fortune Park Hotels Limited. The paperboards segment produces paperboards and specialty papers. The packaging segment produces consumer packaging. Paperboard and packaging products are produced through its four mills in India. Agri-business sells such products as feed ingredients, rice, wheat, nuts, marine products, cigarette leaf tobacco, fruits, coffee and spices, both in India and abroad. This segment also includes operations of e-Choupal, a service for rural Indian farmers that establishes village Internet kiosks for farmers to access information on the web. The IT segment, operating through ITC Infotech India Limited, provides services and consulting to industries including banking, consumer packaged goods, manufacturing, travel, transportation and media. Subsidiaries of the company include Russell Credit Limited, an investment company; Landbase India Limited, a hospitality real estate development firm; and Surya Nepal Private Limited, focused on the manufacture and sale of cigarettes and garments.

FINANCIAL DATA: Note: Data for latest year may not have been available at press time.

In U.S. $	2015	2014	2013	2012	2011	2010
Revenue	5,785,230,000	5,261,193,000	4,666,262,000	3,899,969,000	3,318,112,000	
R&D Expense						
Operating Income	2,134,937,000	1,939,181,000	1,651,396,000	1,390,314,000	1,107,574,000	
Operating Margin %	36.90%	36.85%	35.39%	35.64%	33.37%	
SGA Expense				557,291,600	1,012,676,000	
Net Income	1,439,525,000	1,324,551,000	1,133,376,000	943,528,300	755,192,700	
Operating Cash Flow	1,466,344,000	1,093,975,000	1,057,961,000	890,414,500	812,419,600	
Capital Expenditure	491,610,700	430,100,900	393,916,000	367,634,700	212,951,500	
EBITDA	2,288,072,000	2,082,926,000	1,779,378,000	1,488,844,000	1,211,733,000	
Return on Assets %	22.24%	23.32%	23.25%	22.17%	20.00%	
Return on Equity %	32.77%	35.28%	35.70%	34.84%	32.45%	
Debt to Equity						

CONTACT INFORMATION:
Phone: 91 3322889371   Fax: 91 3322889371
Toll-Free:
Address: 37 Jawaharlal Nehru Rd., Kolkata, West Bengal 700 071 India

STOCK TICKER/OTHER:
Stock Ticker: ITCTY   Exchange: GREY
Employees: 25,917   Fiscal Year Ends: 03/31
Parent Company:

SALARIES/BONUSES:
Top Exec. Salary: $ Bonus: $
Second Exec. Salary: $ Bonus: $

OTHER THOUGHTS:
Estimated Female Officers or Directors: 1
Hot Spot for Advancement for Women/Minorities:

Jameson Inn Inc

www.jamesoninns.com

NAIC Code: 721110

TYPES OF BUSINESS:

Hotels

BRANDS/DIVISIONS/AFFILIATES:

Jameson Inn
America's Best Franchising Inc

GROWTH PLANS/SPECIAL FEATURES:

Jameson Inn, Inc., a subsidiary of Vantage Hospitality Group, Inc., operates hotels in nine states in the southeastern and Midwestern U.S. Jameson owns 27 hotels under the Jameson Inn brand. Most of the Jameson Inn hotels are designed with a southern colonial style, although some newer locations are designed in a more contemporary style. All hotels owned by the firm typically offer amenities such as swimming pools, fitness centers, deluxe continental breakfast, free premium channels and wake up service. In addition, the hotel also allows small and medium sized pets for a small fee. In order to attract more business travelers, Jameson offers workstations equipped with data ports, meeting spaces and fax and photocopy machines.

CONTACTS: Note: Officers with more than one job title may be intentionally listed here more than once.

Thomas W. Kitchen, CEO
Sterling F. Stoudenmire, IV, CEO

FINANCIAL DATA: Note: Data for latest year may not have been available at press time.

In U.S. $	2015	2014	2013	2012	2011	2010
Revenue						
R&D Expense						
Operating Income						
Operating Margin %						
SGA Expense						
Net Income						
Operating Cash Flow						
Capital Expenditure						
EBITDA						
Return on Assets %						
Return on Equity %						
Debt to Equity						

CONTACT INFORMATION:

Phone: 404-350-9990 Fax: 404-601-6106
Toll-Free: 800-526-3766
Address: 4770 S. Atlanta Rd., Smyrna, GA 30080 United States

STOCK TICKER/OTHER:

Stock Ticker: Subsidiary Exchange:
Employees: 1,750 Fiscal Year Ends: 12/31
Parent Company: Vantage Hospitality Group Inc

SALARIES/BONUSES:

Top Exec. Salary: $ Bonus: $
Second Exec. Salary: $ Bonus: $

OTHER THOUGHTS:

Estimated Female Officers or Directors:
Hot Spot for Advancement for Women/Minorities:

Sales, profits and employees may be estimates. Financial information, benefits and other data can change quickly and may vary from those stated here.

Janus Hotels and Resorts Inc

www.janushotels.com

NAIC Code: 721110

TYPES OF BUSINESS:

Hotel Management
Management, Financial & Legal Consulting
Food & Beverage Services
Staffing Services

BRANDS/DIVISIONS/AFFILIATES:

CONTACTS: *Note: Officers with more than one job title may be intentionally listed here more than once.*

Michael Nanosky, CEO
Michael Nanosky, Pres.
Rick Tonges, CFO
Greg Cappel, VP-Mktg. & Sales
Laura Flannery, Human Resources
Eric Glazer, General Counsel
Scott Wielkiewicz, Corp. Controller
Harry Yeaggy, Vice Chmn.
Barb Soete, Controller
Louis Beck, Chmn.

GROWTH PLANS/SPECIAL FEATURES:

Janus Hotels and Resorts, Inc. is an independently-owned full-service hotel management company. It owns or manages 30 hotels with approximately 8,000 guest rooms, concentrated in Florida. Its locations include nationally recognized brands such as Days Inn, Holiday Inn, Radisson and Best Western. Janus operates each hotel according to a business plan specifically tailored to the characteristics of the hotel and its market, employing centralized management, accounting and purchasing systems to reduce cost and increase operating margins. The firm focuses primarily on continuing sales and marketing to increase revenue. Janus also provides food and beverage services, including lounges, coffee shops and locally and nationally branded restaurants. The company offers support services in the areas of administration, legal issues, brand relationships, maintenance of property, staffing, cash controls, liquor license issues, financial review and management, property development and customer service strategies. The firm also provides receivership services that involve quickly securing the asset, management services designed to stabilize the property and services aimed at restoring staff and customer confidence.

FINANCIAL DATA: *Note: Data for latest year may not have been available at press time.*

In U.S. $	2015	2014	2013	2012	2011	2010
Revenue						
R&D Expense						
Operating Income						
Operating Margin %						
SGA Expense						
Net Income						
Operating Cash Flow						
Capital Expenditure						
EBITDA						
Return on Assets %						
Return on Equity %						
Debt to Equity						

CONTACT INFORMATION:

Phone: 561-997-2325   Fax: 561-997-5331
Toll-Free:
Address: 2300 Corporate Blvd. NW, Ste. 232, Boca Raton, FL 33431-8596 United States

STOCK TICKER/OTHER:

Stock Ticker: Private   Exchange:
Employees: 30   Fiscal Year Ends: 12/31
Parent Company:

SALARIES/BONUSES:

Top Exec. Salary: $ Bonus: $
Second Exec. Salary: $ Bonus: $

OTHER THOUGHTS:

Estimated Female Officers or Directors: 7
Hot Spot for Advancement for Women/Minorities: Y

Japan Airlines Co Ltd

www.jal.com

NAIC Code: 481111

TYPES OF BUSINESS:

International Airline
Domestic Airline
Aircraft Maintenance
Air Cargo
Ground Support Services
Hotels

BRANDS/DIVISIONS/AFFILIATES:

J-Air Co Ltd
Japan Air Commuter Co Ltd
Japan Transocean Air Co Ltd
JAL Mileage Bank

CONTACTS: *Note: Officers with more than one job title may be intentionally listed here more than once.*

Yoshiharu Ueki, Pres.
Nobuhiro Sato, Gen. Mgr.-Eng. & Maintenance Div.
Nobuyoshi Gondo, Corp. Sec.
Toshinori Shin, Exec. Officer-Flight Oper.
Toshiaki Norita, Exec. Officer-Corp. Planning
Norikazu Saito, Exec. Officer-Finance & Accounting
Makoto Yoneyama, Exec. Officer-Corp. Control
Ryuzo Toyoshima, Pres., JAL EXPRESS
Tsuyoshi Yamamura, Exec. Officer-Cargo & Mail
Tetsuya Onuki, Pres., J-Air
Masaru Onishi, Chmn.
Tadashi Fujita, Exec. Officer-Int'l Passenger Sales
Toshiki Oka, Exec. Officer-Purchasing

GROWTH PLANS/SPECIAL FEATURES:

Japan Airlines Co. Ltd. (JAL) is the flag carrier airline of Japan and the second largest in the country. The company's main hubs are Tokyo's Narita International Airport and Tokyo International Airport (Haneda), as well as Osaka's Kansai International Airport and Osaka International Airport. JAL group companies include J-Air Co. Ltd., a regional commuter airline; 60%-owned Japan Air Commuter Co. Ltd., providing feeder services to Japan Airlines from its main base at Kagoshima Airport; and Japan Transocean Air Co. Ltd., which provides domestic services from its main base at Naha Airport. Together, JAL's group destinations include 54 international routes and 117 domestic routes. Destinations including codesharing are 395 for international routes and 132 for domestic routes. JAL's fleet currently comprises an all-Boeing aircraft featuring 737s, 767s, 777s and 787s; with 30 Airbus A350s, 14 Boeing 737-800s, four Boeing 777-200ERs, 21 Boeing 787-9s and 35 Mitsubishi Regional Jet MRJ90s on order. The company is a member of the oneworld alliance, which reaches more than 305 airports in 51 countries and regions. JAL Mileage Bank (JMB) is the company's loyalty program, with more than 29 million members worldwide.

FINANCIAL DATA: *Note: Data for latest year may not have been available at press time.*

In U.S. $	2015	2014	2013	2012	2011	2010
Revenue	13,373,020,000	13,021,290,000	12,320,140,000	11,981,750,000		
R&D Expense						
Operating Income	1,786,990,000	1,658,731,000	1,941,663,000	2,037,930,000		
Operating Margin %	13.36%	12.73%	15.76%	17.00%		
SGA Expense	254,758,700		215,197,800			
Net Income	1,530,770,000	1,694,473,000	1,755,743,000	1,855,879,000		
Operating Cash Flow	2,597,003,000	2,465,750,000	2,633,938,000	2,552,589,000		
Capital Expenditure						
EBITDA	2,560,445,000	2,434,940,000	2,731,497,000	2,904,171,000		
Return on Assets %	10.59%	13.00%	14.90%	17.15%		
Return on Equity %	20.32%	26.48%	36.00%	48.03%		
Debt to Equity	0.08	0.13	0.19	0.41		

CONTACT INFORMATION:

Phone: 81-3-5460-6600   Fax:
Toll-Free:
Address: 2-4-11 Higashi-shinagawa, Shinagawa-ku, Tokyo, 1408637 Japan

STOCK TICKER/OTHER:

Stock Ticker: JAPSY   Exchange: PINX
Employees: 31,534   Fiscal Year Ends: 03/31
Parent Company:

SALARIES/BONUSES:

Top Exec. Salary: $ Bonus: $
Second Exec. Salary: $ Bonus: $

OTHER THOUGHTS:

Estimated Female Officers or Directors:
Hot Spot for Advancement for Women/Minorities:

Sales, profits and employees may be estimates. Financial information, benefits and other data can change quickly and may vary from those stated here.

Jet Airways India Ltd

NAIC Code: 481111

TYPES OF BUSINESS:

Airline-Global
Airline-Domestic

BRANDS/DIVISIONS/AFFILIATES:

Jet Airways Konnect
JetXtras
JetPrivilege

CONTACTS: *Note: Officers with more than one job title may be intentionally listed here more than once.*

Cramer Ball, CEO
K.M. Unni, COO
Amit Agarwal, CFO
Bram Steller, VP-Sales
Samar B. Srivastava, VP-Human Resources
Dato K. Jeyakanthan, Sr. VP-Prod.& Aircraft projects
Chhattar Singh Tomar, VP-Eng. & Maintenance
Ashok Barimar, General Counsel
Abdulrahman Albusaidy, Chief Strategy & Planning Officer
Belson Coutinho, VP-e-commerce & Innovations
Ragini Chopra, VP-Corp. Comm. & Public Rel.
Mahalingam Shivkumar, Sr. VP-Finance
Gaurang Shetty, Sr. VP-Commercial
Anita Goyal, Exec. VP-Network Planning & Revenue Mgmt.
Mohammad Ali El Ariss, VP-Cargo
Sonu Kripalani, VP-Sales (India)
Naresh Goyal, Chmn.
Gerry Oh, VP-Asia Pacific
Raj Sivakumar, Sr. VP-Alliances & Planning

GROWTH PLANS/SPECIAL FEATURES:

Jet Airways India, Ltd. is one of India's most popular airlines. With hubs in Mumbai, Delhi, Chennai, Kolkata, Pune and Bengaluru, the company offers flights to 73 destinations, including both domestic and international flights to locations such as Muscat, Dubai, Dhaka, Bangkok, London, Newark, Toronto, Singapore, Hong Kong, Colombo, Kathmandu and Kuwait. Jet Airways maintains a total fleet of 116 aircraft, including 10 Airbus A330-200, four Airbus 330-300, 10 Boeing 777-300ER, two Boeing 737-900ER, 57 Boeing 737-700/800/900, two ATR 72-600 and 15 ATR 72-500. The airline's in-flight services are typical of an international airline, with a variety of menu choices, entertainment options, seat preferences and programs for children. Jet Airways Konnect, the company's all-economy service on select domestic routes, operates about 430 flights daily. Through JetXtras, the firm offers packaged vacations, including hotels, car rentals and meal planning. JetPrivilege, the firm's frequent flyer program, offers various benefits on five membership levels. Depending on the membership level, JetPrivilege offers several benefits, including tele check-in, bonus mile incentives, an additional baggage allowance, priority tagging of luggage, lounge access, check-in at premiere counters, upgrade vouchers, priority stand-by at airports and waiver of cancellation fees on published fares. The JetPrivilege program maintains redemption and discount partnerships with airline, rental car, entertainment, hotel, lifestyle, publishing, retail and telecommunication companies. JetPrivilege has alliances with various airlines, including Air France, Delta Airlines, American Airlines, Virgin Atlantic, United Airlines, South African Airways and Austrian Airlines.

FINANCIAL DATA: *Note: Data for latest year may not have been available at press time.*

In U.S. $	2015	2014	2013	2012	2011	2010
Revenue	3,131,183,008	3,053,570,926	3,048,400,000	2,702,600,000	2,344,200,000	1,946,100,000
R&D Expense						
Operating Income						
Operating Margin %						
SGA Expense						
Net Income	-313,168,876	-662,469,515	-126,200,000	-229,800,000	-13,900,000	-68,000,000
Operating Cash Flow						
Capital Expenditure						
EBITDA						
Return on Assets %						
Return on Equity %						
Debt to Equity						

CONTACT INFORMATION:

Phone: 91-22-4019-1000   Fax:
Toll-Free: 877-835-9538
Address: Sahar Airport Rd., Siroya Centre, Andheri E., Mumbai, 400099 India

STOCK TICKER/OTHER:

Stock Ticker: 532617   Exchange: Bombay
Employees: 13,256   Fiscal Year Ends: 03/31
Parent Company:

SALARIES/BONUSES:

Top Exec. Salary: $ Bonus: $
Second Exec. Salary: $ Bonus: $

OTHER THOUGHTS:

Estimated Female Officers or Directors: 3
Hot Spot for Advancement for Women/Minorities: Y

Sales, profits and employees may be estimates. Financial information, benefits and other data can change quickly and may vary from those stated here.

Jet Aviation Management AG

www.jetaviation.com

NAIC Code: 481211

TYPES OF BUSINESS:

Charter Aircraft
Aircraft Maintenance & Repair
Aircraft Management Services
Engineering Services
Private Aircraft Handling
Fixed Base Operations
Aircraft Sales & Brokerage

BRANDS/DIVISIONS/AFFILIATES:

General Dynamics Corp
Jet Aviation St. Louis
Paragon Aviation Network
Avject Corporation

CONTACTS: Note: Officers with more than one job title may be intentionally listed here more than once.

Robert Smith, Pres.
Wim Buesink, CFO
Nancy Groesch, Sr. VP-Human Resources
Laurie Phelan, General Counsel
David Paddock, Sr. VP-Bus. Dev. & Strategic Planning
Heinz Aebi, Sr. VP-Corp. Comm.
Gary Dempsey, Pres., Aircraft Svcs., Americas
Neil Boyle, VP
Charles F. Krugh, Sr. VP
Jurg Reuthinger, Sr. VP-Aircraft Mgmt. & Charter EMEA & Asia

GROWTH PLANS/SPECIAL FEATURES:

Jet Aviation Management AG, a wholly-owned subsidiary of General Dynamics Corp., is a leading business aviation service company. With headquarters in the Switzerland and the U.S., it provides services at over 25 airport facilities and stations around the world, operates a fleet of nearly 300 managed aircraft and supplies charter services. Its fleet includes both corporate and private jets, with managed aircraft ranging from Sikorsky S76 helicopters to Boeing jets. The company provides services including aircraft management, such as planning, accounting, maintenance and provision of flight crews; executive charter services; business aircraft sales and acquisition; maintenance, repair and overhaul (MRO); fixed base operations (FBO); completion services such as outfitting and refurbishing; engineering and avionics retrofit; aviation personnel-placement services; and aircraft exterior painting. The firm offers these services through a number of subsidiaries, including Jet Aviation St. Louis, a U.S. subsidiary that provides avionics, component overhaul, complex structural repair, completions, interior refurbishment, paint and FBO services. The company is a part of the Paragon Aviation Network, a group of FBO firms that provide first-class experience for aviation travelers across North America. In 2016, the firm acquired Los Angeles-based Avjet Corporation, a global jet charter and management company. That same year, Jet Aviation announced plans to establish an FBO facility at Los Angeles/Van Nuys Airport.

FINANCIAL DATA: Note: Data for latest year may not have been available at press time.

In U.S. $	2015	2014	2013	2012	2011	2010
Revenue	1,050,000,000	1,100,000,000	1,025,000,000	1,000,000,000		
R&D Expense						
Operating Income						
Operating Margin %						
SGA Expense						
Net Income						
Operating Cash Flow						
Capital Expenditure						
EBITDA						
Return on Assets %						
Return on Equity %						
Debt to Equity						

CONTACT INFORMATION:

Phone: 41-58-158-4111   Fax: 41-58-158-7079
Toll-Free:
Address: Aeschengraben 6, Basel, 4051 Switzerland

STOCK TICKER/OTHER:

Stock Ticker: Subsidiary   Exchange:
Employees: 4,500   Fiscal Year Ends: 12/31
Parent Company: General Dynamics Corp

SALARIES/BONUSES:

Top Exec. Salary: $ Bonus: $
Second Exec. Salary: $ Bonus: $

OTHER THOUGHTS:

Estimated Female Officers or Directors: 2
Hot Spot for Advancement for Women/Minorities:

Sales, profits and employees may be estimates. Financial information, benefits and other data can change quickly and may vary from those stated here.

JetBlue Airways Corporation

www.jetblue.com

NAIC Code: 481111

TYPES OF BUSINESS:

Airline
In-Flight Entertainment

BRANDS/DIVISIONS/AFFILIATES:

JetBlue Getaways
TrueBlue
Mint
Blue
Blue Plus
Blue Flex

CONTACTS: *Note: Officers with more than one job title may be intentionally listed here more than once.*

Mark Powers, CFO
Joel Peterson, Chairman of the Board
Alexander Chatkewitz, Chief Accounting Officer
Frank Sica, Director
Martin St George, Executive VP, Divisional
James Hnat, Executive VP, Divisional
Robin Hayes, President

GROWTH PLANS/SPECIAL FEATURES:

JetBlue Airways Corporation is a low-fare, low-cost passenger airline. It primarily operates on point-to-point routes with its fleet of Airbus A321, Airbus A320 and EMBRAER 190 aircraft types. It serves 87 cities in the U.S., Caribbean and Latin America. The majority of its average 900 daily flights have as an origin or destination one of the company's six focus cities: Boston, Fort Lauderdale, Los Angeles/Long Beach, New York, Orlando and San Juan, Puerto Rico. The company's flights are single-class, but feature leather seats and seat-back televisions with 36 channels of free DirecTV programming, 100 stations of free SiriusXM satellite radio and movie channel offerings from JetBlue Features. JetBlue sells vacation packages through JetBlue Getaways, a one-stop website designed to meet customers' demand for packaged travel planning. The firm also participates in three major global distribution systems: Sabre, Galileo and Amadeus; and four major online travel agents (OTAs): Expedia, Travelocity, Orbitz and Priceline. JetBlue also offers customers a choice to purchase tickets from three branded fares: Blue, Blue Plus and Blue Flex. Each fare includes different offerings such as free checked bags, reduced change fees and additional TrueBlue rewards points. The company's premium transcontinental product, Mint, includes 16 fully lie-flat seats in select Airbus aircraft, four of which are in suites with a privacy door.

JetBlue offers employees medical, dental, vision and life insurance; short- and long-term disability insurance; a group legal plan; flexible spending accounts; pilot loss of license; health risk assessments; disease management programs; an airline credit

FINANCIAL DATA: *Note: Data for latest year may not have been available at press time.*

In U.S. $	2015	2014	2013	2012	2011	2010
Revenue	6,416,000,000	5,817,000,000	5,441,000,000	4,982,000,000	4,504,000,000	3,779,000,000
R&D Expense						
Operating Income	1,216,000,000	515,000,000	428,000,000	376,000,000	322,000,000	333,000,000
Operating Margin %	18.95%	8.85%	7.86%	7.54%	7.14%	8.81%
SGA Expense	1,804,000,000	1,525,000,000	1,358,000,000	1,248,000,000	1,146,000,000	1,070,000,000
Net Income	677,000,000	401,000,000	168,000,000	128,000,000	86,000,000	97,000,000
Operating Cash Flow	1,598,000,000	912,000,000	758,000,000	698,000,000	614,000,000	523,000,000
Capital Expenditure	941,000,000	857,000,000	637,000,000	828,000,000	528,000,000	299,000,000
EBITDA	1,562,000,000	1,082,000,000	733,000,000	646,000,000	566,000,000	567,000,000
Return on Assets %	8.20%	5.28%	2.33%	1.81%	1.25%	1.47%
Return on Equity %	23.59%	17.19%	8.35%	7.02%	5.04%	6.07%
Debt to Equity	0.43	0.77	0.99	1.30	1.62	1.72

CONTACT INFORMATION:

Phone: 718 286-7900   Fax: 718 709-3621
Toll-Free: 800-538-2583
Address: 27-01 Queens Plaza North, Long Island City, NY 11101 United States

STOCK TICKER/OTHER:

Stock Ticker: JBLU
Employees: 16,862
Parent Company:

Exchange: NAS
Fiscal Year Ends: 12/31

SALARIES/BONUSES:

Top Exec. Salary: $542,500   Bonus: $
Second Exec. Salary: $424,917   Bonus: $

OTHER THOUGHTS:

Estimated Female Officers or Directors: 5
Hot Spot for Advancement for Women/Minorities: Y

John Q Hammons Hotels & Resorts LLC   www.jqhhotels.com

NAIC Code: 721110

TYPES OF BUSINESS:

Hotels

BRANDS/DIVISIONS/AFFILIATES:

CONTACTS: *Note: Officers with more than one job title may be intentionally listed here more than once.*

Jacqueline Dowdy, CEO
Joe Morrissey, COO
Phill Burgess, VP-Sales & Revenue Mgmt.
Kent Foster, VP-Human Resources
Christopher Smith, Sr. VP-Admin. & Control
Greggory Groves, General Counsel
Joe Morrissey, Sr. VP-Oper.
Rod Dornbusch, VP-Capital Planning & Asset Mgmt.
Kent Foster, VP-Human Resources
Rick Beran, VP-Food & Beverage

GROWTH PLANS/SPECIAL FEATURES:

John Q. Hammons Hotels & Resorts LLC is a leading independent owner, manager and developer of low-cost upscale hotels in the U.S. The company owns and operates 35 hotels with nearly 8,500 rooms in 16 states. These properties operate under the Embassy Suites by Hilton, IHG (Holiday Inn Express & Suites), JQH Hotels & Resorts, Marriott, Renaissance and Sheraton trade names and are marketed to a range of customers, including frequent business travelers, groups and conventions and leisure travelers. John Q. Hammons Hotels Management LLC manages all of the firm's hotels, which are generally located near a state capitol, university, airport, corporate headquarters or other major facility. Most of the hotels contain a multi-storied atrium, extensive meeting space and large rooms or suites, and some hotels feature signature full-service spas. U.S. locations include Alabama, Arizona, Arkansas, Colorado, Illinois, Kansas, Missouri, Nebraska, New Mexico, North Carolina, Oklahoma, South Carolina, South Dakota, Tennessee, Texas and Virginia.

FINANCIAL DATA: *Note: Data for latest year may not have been available at press time.*

In U.S. $	2015	2014	2013	2012	2011	2010
Revenue	461,000,000	456,000,000	445,000,000	430,900,000		
R&D Expense						
Operating Income						
Operating Margin %						
SGA Expense						
Net Income						
Operating Cash Flow						
Capital Expenditure						
EBITDA						
Return on Assets %						
Return on Equity %						
Debt to Equity						

CONTACT INFORMATION:

Phone: 417-864-4300   Fax:
Toll-Free: 800-641-4026
Address: 300 John Q. Hammons Pkwy., Ste. 900, Springfield, MO 65806
United States

STOCK TICKER/OTHER:

Stock Ticker: Private   Exchange:
Employees: 5,800   Fiscal Year Ends: 12/31
Parent Company:

SALARIES/BONUSES:

Top Exec. Salary: $ Bonus: $
Second Exec. Salary: $ Bonus: $

OTHER THOUGHTS:

Estimated Female Officers or Directors: 1
Hot Spot for Advancement for Women/Minorities:

Sales, profits and employees may be estimates. Financial information, benefits and other data can change quickly and may vary from those stated here.

JTB Global Marketing & Travel Inc   www.jtbgmt.com

NAIC Code: 561510

TYPES OF BUSINESS:

Travel Agency
Tours
Travel-Related Services
Online Reservations
Corporate Travel Planning

BRANDS/DIVISIONS/AFFILIATES:

JTB Corp

GROWTH PLANS/SPECIAL FEATURES:

JTB Global Marketing & Travel, Inc., a subsidiary of JTB Corp., is a premier travel destination company for travelers visiting Japan. Its destinations include Mt. Fuji/Hakone, Tokyo, Hiroshima, Hokkaido, Nara, Nikko, Okinawa, Osaka and Takayama. Ways to travel and explore the country include cruising, dinner plans, festivals, hot springs, ski & snowboarding, train packages, hotel packages and seasonal packages. JTB Global's offerings can be arranged for individuals, groups and companies. Headquartered in Tokyo, the firm has additional offices in Hokkaido, Tohoku, Aichi, Kyoto, Fukuoka and Okinawa.

CONTACTS: Note: Officers with more than one job title may be intentionally listed here more than once.

Hisanori Zama, CEO
Hisanori Zama, Pres.
Yuriko Endo, Dir.-Luxury Mktg.
Haruhiko Sakano, Gen. Sales Mgr.-Europe & Latin America Team
Keiji Osaki, Gen. Sales Mgr.-North America & Pan Pacific Team
Ikuko Sekine, Oper. Mgr.-North America & Pan Pacific Team

FINANCIAL DATA: Note: Data for latest year may not have been available at press time.

In U.S. $	2015	2014	2013	2012	2011	2010
Revenue	430,000,000	448,916,714				
R&D Expense						
Operating Income						
Operating Margin %						
SGA Expense						
Net Income						
Operating Cash Flow						
Capital Expenditure						
EBITDA						
Return on Assets %						
Return on Equity %						
Debt to Equity						

CONTACT INFORMATION:

Phone: 81-3-5796-5400   Fax: 81-3-5495-0688
Toll-Free:
Address: JTB Bldg. 2-3-11, Higashi-Shinagawa, Shinagawa-ku, Tokyo, 140-8604 Japan

STOCK TICKER/OTHER:

Stock Ticker: Subsidiary   Exchange:
Employees: 26,646   Fiscal Year Ends: 03/31
Parent Company: JTB Corp

SALARIES/BONUSES:

Top Exec. Salary: $ Bonus: $
Second Exec. Salary: $ Bonus: $

OTHER THOUGHTS:

Estimated Female Officers or Directors: 2
Hot Spot for Advancement for Women/Minorities: Y

Sales, profits and employees may be estimates. Financial information, benefits and other data can change quickly and may vary from those stated here.

Kampgrounds of America Inc

www.koa.com

NAIC Code: 721211

TYPES OF BUSINESS:

Campgrounds
RV Camping Services
Rental Cabins

BRANDS/DIVISIONS/AFFILIATES:

KOA
Kamping Kabins
Kamping Kottages
Kamping Lodges
Care Camps

CONTACTS: Note: Officers with more than one job title may be intentionally listed here more than once.

Patrick Hittmeier, CEO
John J. Burke, CFO
Whitney Hepp, Dir.-Mktg.
Nicole Kreiger, Dir.-Human Resources
John Adams, CIO
Mike Zimmerman, General Counsel
Jef Sutherland, VP-Franchise Oper.
Mike Gast, VP-Comm.

GROWTH PLANS/SPECIAL FEATURES:

Kampgrounds of America, Inc. (KOA), founded in 1962, operates and franchises one of the largest networks of commercial campsites in North America, with approximately 500 established KOA campgrounds. These campgrounds offer toll-free reservations, restrooms, showers, laundry facilities, playgrounds and pools as well as RV sites and cabins, which come in three basic varieties: Kamping Kabins, Kamping Kottages and Kamping Lodges. Kottages and Lodges offer full bathrooms with showers. The company also offers tent camping, which features a kamp store, kamping kitchens and tent sites with electricity. Additionally, the firm offers free high-speed wireless Internet access, bike rentals, cable TV and swimming pools. KOA has a scout program that is open to Boy Scouts, Girl Scouts and Girl Guides throughout the U.S., which gives special discounts to troops interested in using KOA facilities for camping and earning badges. The firm also runs Care Camps, specifically for children with cancer, and hosts annual fundraising events to sponsor them.

KOA employees who have completed one season in the Work Kamper program receive benefits including entrance into various cash drawings, discounted camping and free camping for two to five days while traveling to their next assignment.

FINANCIAL DATA: Note: Data for latest year may not have been available at press time.

In U.S. $	2015	2014	2013	2012	2011	2010
Revenue						
R&D Expense						
Operating Income						
Operating Margin %						
SGA Expense						
Net Income						
Operating Cash Flow						
Capital Expenditure						
EBITDA						
Return on Assets %						
Return on Equity %						
Debt to Equity						

CONTACT INFORMATION:

Phone: 406-248-7444   Fax: 406-255-7402
Toll-Free: 888-562-0000
Address: 550 N. 31st St., Billings, MT 59101 United States

STOCK TICKER/OTHER:

Stock Ticker: Private
Employees:
Parent Company:

Exchange:
Fiscal Year Ends: 12/31

SALARIES/BONUSES:

Top Exec. Salary: $ Bonus: $
Second Exec. Salary: $ Bonus: $

OTHER THOUGHTS:

Estimated Female Officers or Directors: 1
Hot Spot for Advancement for Women/Minorities:

Sales, profits and employees may be estimates. Financial information, benefits and other data can change quickly and may vary from those stated here.

KAYAK Software Corporation

www.kayak.com

NAIC Code: 519130

TYPES OF BUSINESS:

Online Travel Services

BRANDS/DIVISIONS/AFFILIATES:

KAYAK.com
KAYAK Trips
Explore
Price Forecast
Priceline Group Inc (The)

CONTACTS: *Note: Officers with more than one job title may be intentionally listed here more than once.*

Daniel Stephen Hafner, CEO
Paul M. English, Pres.
Paul D. Schwenk, Sr. VP-Eng.
Keith D. Melnick, Chief Comm. Officer

GROWTH PLANS/SPECIAL FEATURES:

KAYAK Software Corporation operates travel planning search and aggregation sites that allow users to compile and compare data gathered from hundreds of travel sites. The company offers users comparison rates for hotels, airfare, rental cars and vacation packages. KAYAK.com's tools and features include KAYAK Trips, Explore and Price Forecast, along with its mobile application. KAYAK Trips allows users to create, manage and share trips, and includes the capability of receiving flight status alerts in real-time. Explore is an Internet feature that displays the prices to various places around the world, on a map, derived from the user's existing location. Price Forecast analyzes upcoming airline ticket prices using a machine-learning algorithm and presents recommendations based on user queries. Prices vary depending on when flights are chosen and purchased by the consumer. KAYAK is available in over 30 countries and 18 languages. Each year the company processes over 1 billion queries for travel information, and its free mobile app has been downloaded more than 40 million times. The firm is owned by The Priceline Group Inc.

FINANCIAL DATA: *Note: Data for latest year may not have been available at press time.*

In U.S. $	2015	2014	2013	2012	2011	2010
Revenue	375,000,000	360,000,000	335,000,000	292,723,008	224,534,000	170,698,000
R&D Expense						
Operating Income						
Operating Margin %						
SGA Expense						
Net Income	8,591,807	7,584,130		4,145,000		
Operating Cash Flow						
Capital Expenditure						
EBITDA						
Return on Assets %						
Return on Equity %						
Debt to Equity						

CONTACT INFORMATION:

Phone: 203 899-3100   Fax: 203-899-3125
Toll-Free:
Address: 7 Market Street, Stamford, CT 06902 United States

STOCK TICKER/OTHER:

Stock Ticker: Subsidiary   Exchange:
Employees: 205   Fiscal Year Ends: 12/31
Parent Company: The Priceline Group Inc

SALARIES/BONUSES:

Top Exec. Salary: $ Bonus: $
Second Exec. Salary: $ Bonus: $

OTHER THOUGHTS:

Estimated Female Officers or Directors: 1
Hot Spot for Advancement for Women/Minorities: Y

Keikyu Corporation

www.keikyu.co.jp

NAIC Code: 482111

TYPES OF BUSINESS:

Line-Haul Railroads
Bus & Taxi Services
Department Store
Real Estate Development & Brokerage
Hotels & Resorts
Restaurants
Maintenance & Repair-Trains & Other Vehicles
Construction & Civil Engineering

BRANDS/DIVISIONS/AFFILIATES:

CONTACTS: *Note: Officers with more than one job title may be intentionally listed here more than once.*

Kazuyuki Harada, Pres.
Mamoru Imai, Sr. Exec. Dir.
Kazuyuki Harada, Sr. Exec. Dir.
Kazunori Miyazawa, Exec. Dir.
Toshiyuki Ogura, Exec. Dir.
Tsuneo Ishiwata, Chmn.

GROWTH PLANS/SPECIAL FEATURES:

Keikyu Corporation is one of Japan's largest private railway operators, carrying 2.47 million passengers per day. The firm provides railway service in Tokyo and the Chiba prefecture, including service between the Tokyo International Airport (Haneda Airport) and downtown Tokyo. The group is comprised of 69 operating companies divided into five primary divisions, of which the largest is transportation, followed by retail, leisure services, real estate and other businesses. The transportation division's primary subsidiaries are its railway companies. Other Keikyu transportation subsidiaries include taxi and bus companies. The retail segment comprises companies that operate a department store, supermarkets and shopping centers located primarily along Keikyu railway lines. Activities in the leisure services division include hotel operations, travel agencies and leisure facilities such as restaurants, coffee shops and golf courses. The real estate segment consists of firms that develop and market housing lots; build and sell built-for-sale housing; sell condominiums; develop and lease office buildings and research facilities; and broker real estate. Other subsidiaries operate in various industries, including construction; the maintenance, repair and upgrading of trains and automobiles; civil engineering; electrical equipment; nursing and child care services; building management; driving schools; and information processing.

FINANCIAL DATA: *Note: Data for latest year may not have been available at press time.*

In U.S. $	2015	2014	2013	2012	2011	2010
Revenue	3,159,596,000	3,123,148,000	3,052,857,000	2,937,775,000	2,981,890,000	
R&D Expense						
Operating Income	266,354,400	254,480,200	189,719,000	188,843,800	194,114,600	
Operating Margin %	8.42%	8.14%	6.21%	6.42%	6.50%	
SGA Expense						
Net Income	107,613,800	92,318,560	84,730,590	41,241,520	70,409,930	
Operating Cash Flow	584,084,200	409,322,400	380,392,600	411,669,300	435,388,000	
Capital Expenditure	489,050,700	423,324,800	572,766,900	440,181,400	766,712,400	
EBITDA	555,880,400	551,653,900	548,730,000	529,387,200	493,177,800	
Return on Assets %	1.03%	.91%	.86%	.42%	.71%	
Return on Equity %	4.69%	4.60%	4.44%	2.21%	3.83%	
Debt to Equity	1.29	1.69	1.85	1.96	1.98	

CONTACT INFORMATION:

Phone: 81 357898888   Fax:
Toll-Free:
Address: 2-20-20 Takanawa, Minato-ku, Tokyo, 108-8625 Japan

STOCK TICKER/OTHER:

Stock Ticker: KHEXF   Exchange: GREY
Employees: 1,490   Fiscal Year Ends: 03/31
Parent Company:

SALARIES/BONUSES:

Top Exec. Salary: $ Bonus: $
Second Exec. Salary: $ Bonus: $

OTHER THOUGHTS:

Estimated Female Officers or Directors:
Hot Spot for Advancement for Women/Minorities:

Keio Corporation

NAIC Code: 482112

TYPES OF BUSINESS:

Short Line Railroads
Real Estate Development
Retail Sales
Hotels
Construction
Transportation Services

BRANDS/DIVISIONS/AFFILIATES:

CONTACTS: Note: Officers with more than one job title may be intentionally listed here more than once.

Taizo Takahashi, Managing Dir.
Tadashi Nagata, Pres.
Tadashi Nagata, Chmn.

GROWTH PLANS/SPECIAL FEATURES:

Keio Corporation provides rail and bus services in metropolitan Tokyo. It leads the Keio Group, which brings together several companies divided into transportation, merchandise sales, real estate, leisure services, construction and other groups. The non-transportation operations originated from efforts to develop land along its service routes, most notably along the Keio Line, which extends from Shinjuku to Tokyo's southwestern suburbs of Keio-hachioji. The transportation group operates 52.6 miles of train networks with 69 stations, carrying about 1.69 million passengers daily. The main lines are the Keio Line and the Sagamihara Line, which, along with four smaller lines, service Tokyo and the northern Kanagawa Prefecture. Rail services include reserved women-only cars on express trains with morning, late afternoon and late evening schedules. The transportation segment also operates certain bus and taxi services. The merchandise segment is dominated by department stores, but also includes retail stores, book sellers and others. The real estate division has sale and leasing operations. The leisure group is made up of travel services, hotels, restaurants and advertising services. The firm's remaining businesses include building maintenance, accounting services, railcar maintenance and construction.

FINANCIAL DATA: Note: Data for latest year may not have been available at press time.

In U.S. $	2015	2014	2013	2012	2011	2010
Revenue	4,154,254,708	3,377,037,782	3,821,800,000	3,760,200,000	3,767,000,000	3,883,300,000
R&D Expense						
Operating Income						
Operating Margin %						
SGA Expense						
Net Income	150,587,647	134,399,457	142,000,000	119,700,000	89,300,000	115,300,000
Operating Cash Flow						
Capital Expenditure						
EBITDA						
Return on Assets %						
Return on Equity %						
Debt to Equity						

CONTACT INFORMATION:

Phone: 81-42-337-3106   Fax:
Toll-Free:
Address: 1-9-1 Sekido, Tama-shi, Tokyo, 206-8502 Japan

STOCK TICKER/OTHER:

Stock Ticker: 9008   Exchange: Tokyo
Employees: 12,500   Fiscal Year Ends: 03/31
Parent Company:

SALARIES/BONUSES:

Top Exec. Salary: $ Bonus: $
Second Exec. Salary: $ Bonus: $

OTHER THOUGHTS:

Estimated Female Officers or Directors:
Hot Spot for Advancement for Women/Minorities:

Keisei Electric Railway Co Ltd

www.keisei.co.jp

NAIC Code: 482112

TYPES OF BUSINESS:

Short Line Railroads
Taxi & Limousine Service
Buses
Real Estate Development
Department Stores
Construction Services
Driving Schools

BRANDS/DIVISIONS/AFFILIATES:

Keisei Skyliner
Keisei Transit Ltd
Oriental Land Co Ltd
Kyousei Building Services Inc
Keisei Bus Ltd
Taxi Narashino Inc
Kashima Railroad Ltd
Tokyo Disneyland

CONTACTS: *Note: Officers with more than one job title may be intentionally listed here more than once.*

Saegusa Norio, Pres.
Hikaru Kaneko, Manager-Bus. Planning Office
Hideki Iida, Sr. Managing Dir.
Satoshi Okagishi, Sr. Managing Dir.
Norio Saito, Managing Dir.
Takashi Murase, Dir.-Dev. Promotion

GROWTH PLANS/SPECIAL FEATURES:

Keisei Electric Railway Co. Ltd. is a transportation and real estate development company that provides railway service in Tokyo and the Chiba prefecture, including service between the Tokyo Narita International Airport and downtown Tokyo. The group has 129 subsidiaries operating primarily through two divisions: transportation and real estate. The transportation division's primary subsidiaries are its railway companies. In all, this division operates 69 stations and 598 railcars, carrying passengers over 94 miles of track. In addition to commuter routes, it also operates the Keisei Skyliner high speed train, offering a 41-minute trip between Narita Airport and downtown Tokyo. Its other high speed train is the Access Express, which also operates on the Narita Sky Access line. The transportation segment also includes the group's bus and taxi companies, including Keisei Bus, Ltd.; Keisei Transit, Ltd.; Chiba City Bus, Ltd.; Taxi Narashino, Inc.; Train Taxi Kominato, Inc.; and Keisei Bus Town, Ltd. The real estate segment sells, leases, develops and manages real estate in the Tokyo and Chiba areas, and comprises Kyousei Building Services, Inc., a facilities management firm; Keisei New Estate, Inc., a real estate management company; and Kashima Railroad, Ltd., a real estate leasing firm. The company also holds a minority stake in Oriental Land Co., Ltd., which operates Tokyo Disneyland.

FINANCIAL DATA: *Note: Data for latest year may not have been available at press time.*

In U.S. $	2015	2014	2013	2012	2011	2010
Revenue	2,196,296,218	2,027,911,250	2,350,300,000	2,217,600,000	2,290,900,000	2,335,500,000
R&D Expense						
Operating Income						
Operating Margin %						
SGA Expense						
Net Income	226,493,497	238,785,214	211,600,000	129,700,000	115,800,000	127,700,000
Operating Cash Flow						
Capital Expenditure						
EBITDA						
Return on Assets %						
Return on Equity %						
Debt to Equity						

CONTACT INFORMATION:

Phone: 81-3-3621-2270   Fax:
Toll-Free:
Address: Chiba Prefecture Yawata 3, chome-1, Yubinbango, Ichikawa, 272-8510 Japan

STOCK TICKER/OTHER:

Stock Ticker: 9009
Employees: 8,664
Parent Company:

Exchange: Tokyo
Fiscal Year Ends: 03/31

SALARIES/BONUSES:

Top Exec. Salary: $ Bonus: $
Second Exec. Salary: $ Bonus: $

OTHER THOUGHTS:

Estimated Female Officers or Directors:
Hot Spot for Advancement for Women/Minorities:

Sales, profits and employees may be estimates. Financial information, benefits and other data can change quickly and may vary from those stated here.

Kerzner International Limited   www.kerzner.com

NAIC Code: 721120

TYPES OF BUSINESS:

Casino Hotels
Luxury Resort Hotels
Resort Development

BRANDS/DIVISIONS/AFFILIATES:

Atlantis
One & Only
Mazagan Beach & Golf Resourt

CONTACTS: *Note: Officers with more than one job title may be intentionally listed here more than once.*

Ali Tabbal, COO
Bonnie S. Biumi, Pres.
Saif Al Yaarubi, CFO
Helen McCabe-Young, Exec. VP-Sales & Mktg.
Stuart Thomson, Exec. VP-Human Resources
Monica Digilio, Exec. VP-Admin.
Tim Brown, Sr. VP-Project Planning & Dev.
George Markantonis, Pres., Kerzner Int'l Bahamas
Serge Zaalof, Pres., Atlantis & The Palm
H. E. Mohammed Al Shaibani, Chmn.

GROWTH PLANS/SPECIAL FEATURES:

Kerzner International Limited is a resort and gaming company that develops, operates and manages premier resorts, casinos and luxury hotels. The company's flagship property is Atlantis Paradise Island in the Bahamas. The over 2,300-room ocean themed resort features three interconnected hotel towers built around 100 acres of pools and marine environments, home to over 50,000 marine animals. Atlantis, The Palm, located in Dubai, is an ocean-themed hotel and resort, featuring restaurants, water park, spa & fitness centers, night life entertainment, as well as rooms for meetings and events. Currently under construction is the Atlantis Sanya, located in China, is an artifacts-themed resort encompassing more than 62 acres, restaurants, bars & lounges, spas, water park, fresh & saltwater pools, marine exhibits, dolphin interaction center alongside a beach. Kerzner's One & Only brand of resort properties are located in Mexico, the Bahamas, South Africa, Dubai, Mauritius, Maldives, the Great Barrier Reef and Australia, with others currently under construction in Mexico, China, Bahrain and Montenegro. One & Only resorts are designed to reflect the uniqueness of their surroundings, each ultra-luxurious, with an authentic sense of place. The company's Mazagan Beach & Golf Resort in Morocco, features an 18-hole Gary Player golf course, the largest casino in Morocco, five-star hotel accommodations and a wide range of family activities. Mazagan is a year-round destination for the entire family.

FINANCIAL DATA: *Note: Data for latest year may not have been available at press time.*

In U.S. $	2015	2014	2013	2012	2011	2010
Revenue	400,000,000	380,000,000	395,000,000	375,000,000		
R&D Expense						
Operating Income						
Operating Margin %						
SGA Expense						
Net Income						
Operating Cash Flow						
Capital Expenditure						
EBITDA						
Return on Assets %						
Return on Equity %						
Debt to Equity						

CONTACT INFORMATION:

Phone: 242-363-6000   Fax: 954-809-2337
Toll-Free:
Address: Coral Towers, Paradise Island, C5 Bahamas

STOCK TICKER/OTHER:

Stock Ticker: Private
Employees: 8,574
Parent Company:

Exchange:
Fiscal Year Ends: 12/31

SALARIES/BONUSES:

Top Exec. Salary: $ Bonus: $
Second Exec. Salary: $ Bonus: $

OTHER THOUGHTS:

Estimated Female Officers or Directors: 2
Hot Spot for Advancement for Women/Minorities:

Sales, profits and employees may be estimates. Financial information, benefits and other data can change quickly and may vary from those stated here.

Kimpton Hotel & Restaurant Group LLC   www.kimptonhotels.com

NAIC Code: 721110

TYPES OF BUSINESS:

Hotels
Restaurants
Hotel Management Services

BRANDS/DIVISIONS/AFFILIATES:

InterContinental Hotels Group PLC
Area 31
Hotel Vintage Plaza
Hotel Burnham
Cafe Pescatore
Sazerac
Silverleaf Tavern
Scala's Bistro

CONTACTS: Note: Officers with more than one job title may be intentionally listed here more than once.

Mike DeFrino, CEO
Judy Miles, General Counsel
Joe Long, Exec. VP-Dev.
Lisa Demoney, Sr. Dir.-Digital Mktg. & Media
Stephanie Moustirats, Dir.-Hotel Public Rel.
James Alderman, Sr. VP-Acquisitions & Dev.
James Lin, Sr. VP-Restaurant Oper.
Barry Pollard, Sr. VP-Hotel Oper.
Christine Lawson, Sr. VP-Hotel Sales & Catering

GROWTH PLANS/SPECIAL FEATURES:

Kimpton Hotel & Restaurant Group LLC, based in San Francisco, owns 59 lifestyle boutique hotels in 30 U.S. cities. Its holdings also consist of more than 60 restaurants and bars next to or within its hotels. The firm specializes in renovating old, disused buildings to transform them into unique hotels as well as small, European-style restaurants. Its themed hotels include Hotel Vintage Plaza in Portland, Oregon, which has an Italian romance theme; Hotel Vintage in Seattle, highlighting local Washington wines; and Hotel Burnham in Chicago, which focuses on its significance in Chicago's history. Some notable restaurants run by Kimpton include San Francisco bistros Cafe Pescatore, Scala's Bistro and Puccini & Pinetti; Sazerac in Seattle; Atwood Cafe in Chicago; Area 31 in Miami; Firefly in Washington, D.C.; Ruby Room in Boston; and Silverleaf Tavern in New York City. The company also offers full service spas at some of its locations. Special services offered by its hotels include the Mind, Body, Spa Program, which offers in-room massage, yoga, Pilates and meditation; pet packages, which include pet-friendly amenities and services; and Hosted Evening Wine Hour. The company is also engaged in comprehensive management services for other companies, offering everything from financial management to facilities renovation. The company is owned by hotel giant InterContinental Hotels Group PLC. Kimpton plans to open eight additional hotels, located in California, Colorado, Illinois, North Carolina, Ohio, Wisconsin, as well as in the Cayman Islands. It plans to open another in Nashville, Tennessee in 2017. In January 2016, Kimpton announced the signing of its first Kimpton Hotels & Restaurants hotel outside the Americas, debuting in Amsterdam. After a complete renovation, the 270-room hotel will open in 2017.

The firm offers employees medical, dental, vision and life insurance; long- and short-term disability; paid vacation time; tuition reimbursement; and employee discounts.

FINANCIAL DATA: Note: Data for latest year may not have been available at press time.

In U.S. $	2015	2014	2013	2012	2011	2010
Revenue	1,200,000,000	1,049,880,000	1,000,000,000	945,000,000	905,000,000	780,000,000
R&D Expense						
Operating Income						
Operating Margin %						
SGA Expense						
Net Income						
Operating Cash Flow						
Capital Expenditure						
EBITDA						
Return on Assets %						
Return on Equity %						
Debt to Equity						

CONTACT INFORMATION:

Phone: 415-397-5572   Fax: 415-296-8031
Toll-Free: 800-546-7866
Address: 222 Kearny St., Ste. 200, San Francisco, CA 94108 United States

STOCK TICKER/OTHER:

Stock Ticker: Subsidiary   Exchange:
Employees: 7,754   Fiscal Year Ends: 12/31
Parent Company: InterContinental Hotels Group PLC

SALARIES/BONUSES:

Top Exec. Salary: $ Bonus: $
Second Exec. Salary: $ Bonus: $

OTHER THOUGHTS:

Estimated Female Officers or Directors: 9
Hot Spot for Advancement for Women/Minorities: Y

Sales, profits and employees may be estimates. Financial information, benefits and other data can change quickly and may vary from those stated here.

Kintetsu Corporation

NAIC Code: 482111

TYPES OF BUSINESS:

Line-Haul Railroads
Retail Operations
Real Estate Development
Hotels & Leisure Facilities
Car Rental
Buses & Taxies
Train Car Manufacturing
Television Broadcasting

BRANDS/DIVISIONS/AFFILIATES:

Kintetsu Group Holdings Co Ltd
Kintetsu Preparatory Corporation
Kintetsu Real Estate Co Ltd
Kintetsu Hotel Systems Inc
Kintetsu Retail Service Corporation

CONTACTS: Note: Officers with more than one job title may be intentionally listed here more than once.

Yoshinori Yoshida, Pres.
Yoshinori Yoshida, Sr. Exec. VP
Michiyoshi Wadabayashi, Sr. Exec. VP
Kazuyasu Ueda, Sr. Managing Exec. Officer
Takashi Miwa, Sr. Managing Exec. Officer
Tetsuya Yamaguchi, Chmn.

GROWTH PLANS/SPECIAL FEATURES:

Kintetsu Corporation (also known as Kintetsu Preparatory Corporation) operates the company's railway business, offering passenger rail, bus, taxi and freight truck transportation services in the Kansai region. This area includes the Osaka, Kyoto, Ise-Shima, Nagoya and Nara prefectures. Major Kintetsu stations include the Osaka-Namba Station, Osaka-Uehommachi Station, Tsuruhashi Station, Kyoto Station, Yamato-Saidaiji Station, Kintetsu-Nara Station, Oasaka-Abenobashi Station, Kashiharajingu-mae Station, Yoshino Station, Yamato-Yagi Station, Kashikojima Station, Toba Station, Ujiyamada Station, Ise-Nakagawa Station, Shiroko Station and Kintetsu-Nagoya Station. Sister companies under the Kintetsu umbrella include Kintetsu Real Estate Co. Ltd., which operates the company's real estate business; Kintetsu Hotel Systems, Inc., which operates the hotel business; and Kintetsu Retail Service Corporation, which operates the retail business. All of the companies are subsidiaries of holding company, Kintetsu Group Holdings Co. Ltd.

FINANCIAL DATA: Note: Data for latest year may not have been available at press time.

In U.S. $	2015	2014	2013	2012	2011	2010
Revenue	12,270,010,000	12,394,930,000	9,270,203,000	9,375,958,000	9,547,169,000	
R&D Expense						
Operating Income	561,141,300	543,220,500	471,905,700	399,874,700	396,990,700	
Operating Margin %	4.57%	4.38%	5.09%	4.26%	4.15%	
SGA Expense						
Net Income	276,518,100	259,989,700	198,908,000	86,182,550	142,749,200	
Operating Cash Flow	872,605,800	919,227,500	783,588,900	808,650,000	557,909,200	
Capital Expenditure	537,283,500	578,594,600	632,943,500	618,523,400	856,156,900	
EBITDA	1,085,844,000	1,057,203,000	967,002,800	802,812,400	922,429,800	
Return on Assets %	1.42%	1.26%	1.06%	.46%	.77%	
Return on Equity %	9.24%	10.17%	10.56%	4.96%	8.60%	
Debt to Equity	2.64	2.85	4.62	5.12	5.75	

CONTACT INFORMATION:

Phone: 81-6-6775-3355   Fax:
Toll-Free:
Address: 6-1-55 Uehommachi, Tennoji-ku, Osaka, 543-8585 Japan

STOCK TICKER/OTHER:

Stock Ticker: KINUF   Exchange: GREY
Employees: 8,218   Fiscal Year Ends:
Parent Company: Kintetsu Group Holdings Co Ltd

SALARIES/BONUSES:

Top Exec. Salary: $ Bonus: $
Second Exec. Salary: $ Bonus: $

OTHER THOUGHTS:

Estimated Female Officers or Directors:
Hot Spot for Advancement for Women/Minorities:

Sales, profits and employees may be estimates. Financial information, benefits and other data can change quickly and may vary from those stated here.

KLM Royal Dutch Airlines

www.klm.com

NAIC Code: 481111

TYPES OF BUSINESS:

Airline
Maintenance Services
Charter Services
Cargo

BRANDS/DIVISIONS/AFFILIATES:

Air France-KLM SA
KLM Cityhopper
Martinair
Transavia.com
Flying Blue

CONTACTS: *Note: Officers with more than one job title may be intentionally listed here more than once.*

Pieter Elbers, CEO
Rene de Groot, COO
Camiel Eurlings, Pres.
Erik Swelheim, CFO
Erik Varwijk, Managing Dir.
Pieter Elbers, Managing Dir.

GROWTH PLANS/SPECIAL FEATURES:

KLM Royal Dutch Airlines, a subsidiary of Air France-KLM SA, is an international airline operating worldwide through its Amsterdam Airport Schiphol hub. The firm's fleet includes Boeing 787s, 777s, 747s and 737s, as well as Airbus A330s. KLM has seven Airbus A350s on order, expected to be delivered in 2020. The airline forms the core of the KLM Group, which also includes KLM Cityhopper, the service for short flights around Europe; Martinair, which operates mostly cargo and passenger holiday destination flights; and Transavia.com, which is the firm's charter, regional and low-cost airline. KLM operates scheduled passenger and cargo services to more than 135 destinations. Passenger aircraft are configured in a three-class layout, including business, economy comfort and economy. Its frequent-flyer program is called Flying Blue, and has codeshare agreements with other airlines. SkyTeam, the global airline alliance network of which KLM is a part, also extends the company's flying scope. Moreover, KLM provides aircraft and engine maintenance services.

FINANCIAL DATA: *Note: Data for latest year may not have been available at press time.*

In U.S. $	2015	2014	2013	2012	2011	2010
Revenue		10,721,900,000	9,629,580,288	12,633,767,183	12,196,100,000	10,048,000,000
R&D Expense						
Operating Income						
Operating Margin %						
SGA Expense						
Net Income		378,000,000	369,082,656	-58,678,757	197,759,000	-515,250,000
Operating Cash Flow						
Capital Expenditure						
EBITDA						
Return on Assets %						
Return on Equity %						
Debt to Equity						

CONTACT INFORMATION:

Phone: 31 206499123   Fax:
Toll-Free:
Address: Amsterdamseweg 55, Amstelveen, 1182 GP Netherlands

STOCK TICKER/OTHER:

Stock Ticker: KLMR   Exchange: GREY
Employees: 31,778   Fiscal Year Ends: 03/31
Parent Company: Air France-KLM SA

SALARIES/BONUSES:

Top Exec. Salary: $ Bonus: $
Second Exec. Salary: $ Bonus: $

OTHER THOUGHTS:

Estimated Female Officers or Directors:
Hot Spot for Advancement for Women/Minorities:

Sales, profits and employees may be estimates. Financial information, benefits and other data can change quickly and may vary from those stated here.

Korean Air Lines Co Ltd

NAIC Code: 481111

TYPES OF BUSINESS:

Airline
Air Cargo
Aerospace-Aircraft & Helicopter Manufacturing
Aircraft Maintenance & Engineering Services
Catering
Hotels

BRANDS/DIVISIONS/AFFILIATES:

Hanjin Group
Jin Air
Korean Air Cargo

CONTACTS: Note: Officers with more than one job title may be intentionally listed here more than once.

Yang Ho Cho, CEO
Chang Hoon Chi, COO
Chang Hun Chi, Co-CEO
Yeong Sik Kang, VP
Sang Gyun Lee, VP
Won Tae Cho, Managing Dir.
Hyeon Ah Cho, Managing Dir.
Choong Hoon Cho, Chmn.

GROWTH PLANS/SPECIAL FEATURES:

Korean Air Lines Co. Ltd., part of the Hanjin Group, is an air carrier and a leading cargo carrier in Korea. The airline flies to 129 cities in 46 countries and has a fleet of 158 aircraft. Destinations include Tokyo, Bangkok, Sydney, Los Angeles, Dallas, Toronto, Paris, London and Moscow. Korean Air has codeshare agreements with more than 40 airlines, including Air France, Aeromexico, China Southern Airlines, Kenya Airways, Air Europa, Czech Airlines, Delta, Garuda Indonesia, Saudia and Vietnam Airlines. It is also a member of SkyTeam, a global airline partnership. Korean Air Cargo, the firm's cargo division, focuses on transporting specialized items such as precious works of art, dangerous goods, temperature-sensitive perishables, live animals and pharmaceuticals. The firm's maintenance and engineering division has maintenance capabilities including avionics and electronics, engine repair and overhaul and aircraft modifications. The firm's aircraft manufacturing division produces military aircraft including helicopters and fighter jets and supplies parts for industry leaders such as Boeing and Airbus. The company also offers hotel, tour and limousine services through Hanjin Travel, one of its business partners. In addition, Korean Air operates an aerospace division. Jin Air, one of the company's subsidiaries, is a short-haul carrier that offers low-cost flights.

FINANCIAL DATA: Note: Data for latest year may not have been available at press time.

In U.S. $	2015	2014	2013	2012	2011	2010
Revenue	9,850,539,000	10,773,318,055	10,539,326,914	11,443,400,000	10,907,096,000	11,216,397,000
R&D Expense						
Operating Income						
Operating Margin %						
SGA Expense						
Net Income	-480,348,000	189,520,003	261,369,567	230,453,000	-212,200,000	437,966,000
Operating Cash Flow						
Capital Expenditure						
EBITDA						
Return on Assets %						
Return on Equity %						
Debt to Equity						

CONTACT INFORMATION:

Phone: 82-2-2656-7114   Fax: 82-2-2656-7169
Toll-Free: 800-438-5000
Address: 260 Hanuel-gil, Gangseo-gu, Seoul, 157-712 South Korea

STOCK TICKER/OTHER:

Stock Ticker: 3490   Exchange: Seoul
Employees: 16,056   Fiscal Year Ends: 12/31
Parent Company:

SALARIES/BONUSES:

Top Exec. Salary: $ Bonus: $
Second Exec. Salary: $ Bonus: $

OTHER THOUGHTS:

Estimated Female Officers or Directors:
Hot Spot for Advancement for Women/Minorities:

Sales, profits and employees may be estimates. Financial information, benefits and other data can change quickly and may vary from those stated here.

Kuoni Reisen Holding AG

NAIC Code: 561520

TYPES OF BUSINESS:

Tour Operators

BRANDS/DIVISIONS/AFFILIATES:

Kiwi Holding IV Sarl

CONTACTS: Note: Officers with more than one job title may be intentionally listed here more than once.

Zubin Karkaria, CEO
Prisca Havranek-Kosicek, CFO
Rolf Schafroth, CEO-Global Travel Services Div.
Stefan Leser, CEO-Outbound & Specialists Div.
Zubin Karkaria, CEO-VFS Global

GROWTH PLANS/SPECIAL FEATURES:

Kuoni Reisen Holding AG (Kuoni) is engaged in leisure travel and destination management businesses. Kuoni is a business-to-business (B2B) service which provides travel services to agencies and tour operators who in turn pass on the service to consumers. The company operates through three business divisions: global travel distribution, global travel services and VFS global. Global travel distribution provides companies with easy access to hotel accommodation and destination services. It sells approximately 40,000 rooms per day online, with 40% of its turnover being sourced from Asia, the Middle East and Africa. Global travel services (GTS) sources and coordinates destination services such as accommodation, transportation, tours, activities, venues and events. GTS is a world leader in the growing group travel market, handling 50,000 leisure tours per year, with 60% of its turnover being sourced from the Asia-Pacific markets. VFS global is an outsourcing and technology services specialist for governments and diplomatic missions. VFS works for 50 client governments, operates 2,151 application centers in 124 countries and holds an estimated 48% market share of the global outsourced applications market. This division generates more than 70% of its turnover from applicants from the Asia-Pacific region. In May 2016, the firm was acquired by Kiwi Holding IV Sarl, which holds a 98.02% share of the voting rights and 97.52% of the share capital of Kuoni.

FINANCIAL DATA: Note: Data for latest year may not have been available at press time.

In U.S. $	2015	2014	2013	2012	2011	2010
Revenue	3,481,520,000	5,726,944,000	5,893,783,000	6,077,344,000	5,314,057,000	4,141,649,000
R&D Expense						
Operating Income	84,420,650	93,751,630	106,188,100	55,391,180	77,128,460	60,677,860
Operating Margin %	2.42%	1.63%	1.80%	.91%	1.45%	1.46%
SGA Expense	9,564,901	62,159,380	66,924,160	76,931,960	85,834,590	95,428,610
Net Income	-306,804,600	69,070,020	70,812,500	-15,369,340	34,667,570	24,097,310
Operating Cash Flow	117,378,000	66,566,520	166,748,500	110,669,000	105,135,900	121,648,900
Capital Expenditure	39,715,140	68,569,940	47,877,530	60,736,080	59,460,420	45,063,160
EBITDA	148,775,800	190,026,500	195,216,500	149,271,700	180,554,100	122,496,200
Return on Assets %	-14.57%	2.76%	2.83%	-.60%	1.47%	1.16%
Return on Equity %	-45.28%	8.57%	9.03%	-1.97%	4.81%	3.75%
Debt to Equity	0.41	0.28	0.28	0.04	0.38	0.44

CONTACT INFORMATION:

Phone: 41 442774444   Fax:
Toll-Free:
Address: Neue Hard 7, Zurich, CH-8010 Switzerland

STOCK TICKER/OTHER:

Stock Ticker: KUIRY
Employees: 7,968
Parent Company:

Exchange: PINX
Fiscal Year Ends: 12/31

SALARIES/BONUSES:

Top Exec. Salary: $ Bonus: $
Second Exec. Salary: $ Bonus: $

OTHER THOUGHTS:

Estimated Female Officers or Directors:
Hot Spot for Advancement for Women/Minorities:

Sales, profits and employees may be estimates. Financial information, benefits and other data can change quickly and may vary from those stated here.

La Quinta Holdings Inc

NAIC Code: 721110

www.lq.com

TYPES OF BUSINESS:

Hotels, Motels & Suites
Hotel Management
Franchising

BRANDS/DIVISIONS/AFFILIATES:

La Quinta Properties
La Quinta Inns
La Quinta Inns and Suites
Blackstone Group LP

CONTACTS: Note: Officers with more than one job title may be intentionally listed here more than once.

James Forson, CFO
Mitesh Shah, Chairman of the Board
Julie Cary, Chief Marketing Officer
John Cantele, COO
Mark Chloupek, Executive VP
Rajiv Trivedi, Executive VP
Keith Cline, President

GROWTH PLANS/SPECIAL FEATURES:

La Quinta Holdings, Inc., owned by the Blackstone Group LP, is the operator of the La Quinta motels and suites properties. La Quinta is a leading limited-service lodging brand that provides comfortable guest rooms in convenient locations at affordable prices. The firm is one of the largest owners and operators of limited-service hotels in the U.S. It maintains 886 hotels and 87,500 rooms in 48 states, as well as Canada, Mexico and Honduras, under the brands La Quinta Inns and La Quinta Inns and Suites. The firm also licenses its brand name to franchisees for royalties and other fees. The company markets its services to both leisure guests and business travelers. All of the firm's hotels are owned through La Quinta Properties, a real estate investment trust (REIT). A typical La Quinta Inn features approximately 130 guest rooms with amenities including movies-on-demand, interactive video games, free high-speed Internet, complimentary continental breakfast, a swimming pool, fax services and 24-hour front desk message services. La Quinta Inn and Suites properties also feature deluxe two-room suites with microwaves and refrigerators as well as fitness centers, courtyards and expanded food offerings. The Blackstone Group LP holds a 28.3% interest in the company and can currently appoint 20% of the company's directors. Currently, La Quinta has a pipeline of 228 franchised hotels to be located in the U.S., Mexico, Columbia, Nicaragua, Guatemala and Chile. In May 2015, the firm expanded into the Latin American market with a franchise agreement for an LQ Hotel by La Quinta in Chile. In September of the same year, the firm sold 24 geographically dispersed hotels

The firm offers employees medical, dental and vision coverage; life insurance; long-term disability; an employee assistance program; flexible spending accounts; a 401(k) plan; tuition reimbursement; an internal referral bonus program; and room rate discou

FINANCIAL DATA: Note: Data for latest year may not have been available at press time.

In U.S. $	2015	2014	2013	2012	2011	2010
Revenue	1,029,974,000	976,938,000	873,893,000	818,012,000	751,541,000	705,853,000
R&D Expense						
Operating Income	128,071,000	136,669,000	156,181,000	129,595,000	101,849,000	89,084,000
Operating Margin %	12.43%	13.98%	17.87%	15.84%	13.55%	12.62%
SGA Expense	250,677,000	261,781,000	190,055,000	180,987,000	154,949,000	155,967,000
Net Income	26,365,000	-337,297,000	3,976,000	-30,954,000	63,513,000	68,828,000
Operating Cash Flow	290,495,000	286,082,000	232,858,000	248,187,000	220,429,000	200,777,000
Capital Expenditure	100,776,000	78,630,000	115,632,000	102,899,000	96,152,000	69,640,000
EBITDA	311,489,000	311,690,000	321,570,000	292,328,000	267,571,000	282,284,000
Return on Assets %	.84%	-10.48%	.12%	-.90%	1.82%	
Return on Equity %	3.40%	-59.99%	1.25%	-12.26%	33.50%	
Debt to Equity	2.27	2.31		9.00	15.17	

CONTACT INFORMATION:

Phone: 214-492-6600   Fax: 214-492-6616
Toll-Free:
Address: 909 Hidden Ridge, Ste. 600, Irving, TX 75038 United States

STOCK TICKER/OTHER:

Stock Ticker: LQ   Exchange: NYS
Employees: 7,719   Fiscal Year Ends: 12/31
Parent Company: Blackstone Group LP

SALARIES/BONUSES:

Top Exec. Salary: $832,403   Bonus: $
Second Exec. Salary: $479,912   Bonus: $

OTHER THOUGHTS:

Estimated Female Officers or Directors: 2
Hot Spot for Advancement for Women/Minorities:

Lagardere SCA

www.lagardere.com

NAIC Code: 511110

TYPES OF BUSINESS:
Newspaper, Periodical, Book, and Directory Publishers
Duty Free Retail

BRANDS/DIVISIONS/AFFILIATES:
Lagardere Publishing
Lagardere Travel Retail
Lagardere Active
Lagadere Sports & Entertainment
Relay
Aelia Duty Free

CONTACTS: *Note: Officers with more than one job title may be intentionally listed here more than once.*
Arnauld Legardere, CEO
Pierre Leroy, Co-Managing Partner
Gerard Adsuar, CFO
Ramzi Khiroun, Chief External Relations Officer
Thierry Funck-Brentano, Co-Managing Partner

GROWTH PLANS/SPECIAL FEATURES:
Lagardere SCA is a diversified media group operating in 30 countries. The firm is structured around four divisions: Lagardere Publishing, Lagardere Travel Retail, Lagardere Active and Lagardere Sports & Entertainment. Lagardere Publishing is a trade book publisher for the general public and education markets. This division is a federation of publishing companies with a large degree of editorial independence, united by common management rules and expands its books into the digital marketshare. Lagardere Travel Retail is a leading travel retail company, present in more than 30 countries, primarily located in travel retail locations such as travel essentials, duty-free, fashion and foodservice stores. This division's international brands include Relay and Aelia Duty Free, and has numerous restaurant and distribution brands either under license or directly operated. Lagardere Active is engaged in providing French media under brands such as Elle, Paris Match, Europe 1, Gulli and Doctissimo. It is one of France's premier mainstream magazine publishers, with 15 press titles on the domestic market, and an additional 81 under license worldwide. This division is also a major player in television and radio, with 16 TV channels and 24 radio stations worldwide. Lagardere Sports & Entertainment is an agency with a global network of local experts dedicated to delivering innovative sports & entertainment media and solutions to clients.

FINANCIAL DATA: *Note: Data for latest year may not have been available at press time.*

In U.S. $	2015	2014	2013	2012	2011	2010
Revenue	8,126,765,000	8,100,779,000	8,152,751,000	8,724,438,000	9,092,758,000	9,421,534,000
R&D Expense						
Operating Income	122,020,100	153,654,900	1,725,229,000	257,598,000	-552,479,900	387,526,800
Operating Margin %	1.50%	1.89%	21.16%	2.95%	-6.07%	4.11%
SGA Expense	2,649,418,000	2,520,619,000	2,399,729,000	2,408,767,000	2,487,854,000	2,716,077,000
Net Income	83,606,370	46,322,450	1,476,669,000	100,553,600	-798,779,800	184,160,000
Operating Cash Flow	592,023,500	237,261,300	378,488,300	441,758,000	290,362,700	599,932,200
Capital Expenditure	292,622,300	281,324,100	334,425,500	298,271,400	285,843,400	257,598,000
EBITDA	508,417,100	413,512,600	1,969,269,000	545,701,100	-204,496,700	658,682,600
Return on Assets %	.93%	.51%	14.77%	.97%	-7.13%	1.48%
Return on Equity %	3.72%	1.69%	45.39%	3.03%	-20.68%	4.09%
Debt to Equity	0.74	0.51	0.21	0.74	0.62	0.50

CONTACT INFORMATION:
Phone: 33-1-40-69-16-00   Fax:
Toll-Free:
Address: 4 rue de Presbourg, Paris, 75016 France

STOCK TICKER/OTHER:
Stock Ticker: LGDDF
Employees: 29,531
Parent Company:

Exchange: PINX
Fiscal Year Ends:

SALARIES/BONUSES:
Top Exec. Salary: $ Bonus: $
Second Exec. Salary: $ Bonus: $

OTHER THOUGHTS:
Estimated Female Officers or Directors:
Hot Spot for Advancement for Women/Minorities:

Sales, profits and employees may be estimates. Financial information, benefits and other data can change quickly and may vary from those stated here.

Las Vegas Sands Corp (The Venetian)   www.lasvegassands.com

NAIC Code: 721120

TYPES OF BUSINESS:

Hotel Casinos
Convention & Conference Centers
Shopping Center Development
Casino Property Development

BRANDS/DIVISIONS/AFFILIATES:

Venetian Resort Hotel Casino (The)
Sands Expo and Convention Center (The)
Sands China Ltd
Sands Macao Casino (The)
Palazzo Resort Hotel Casino (The)
Venetian Macao Resort Hotel (The)
Marina Bay Sands Pte Ltd
Cotai Strip

CONTACTS: Note: Officers with more than one job title may be intentionally listed here more than once.

George Tanasijevich, CEO, Subsidiary
Sheldon Adelson, CEO
Patrick Dumont, CFO
Randy Hyzak, Chief Accounting Officer
George Markantonis, COO, Subsidiary
Robert Goldstein, COO
Ira Raphaelson, Executive VP
Stephanie Marz, Vice President, Divisional

GROWTH PLANS/SPECIAL FEATURES:

Las Vegas Sands Corp. (LVSC) is an international hotel, resort and casino firm. Its flagship property is The Venetian Resort Hotel Casino, which is connected to The Palazzo Resort Hotel Casino. Together, The Venetian and The Palazzo offer 225,000 square feet of gaming space, with 240 table games and 2,350 slot machines, as well as 7,092 hotel suites. LVSC also runs the 1.2 million square foot convention and trade show facility, The Sands Expo and Convention Center, and a supplemental event and conference center. Additionally, the firm operates the Sands Casino Resort Bethlehem in eastern Pennsylvania, which features 145,000 square feet of gaming space, a 300-room hotel, 150,000 square feet of retail space and other amenities. Outside the U.S., LVSC has operations in Macao, through majority-owned subsidiary Sands China Ltd., and Singapore, through Marina Bay Sands Pte. Ltd. The company's largest development project, the multi-billion dollar Cotai Strip, is a collection of hotel properties, casinos and entertainment venues in Macao. Sands China runs The Sands Macao and The Venetian Macao Resort Hotel, the anchor property on the Cotai Strip. Other properties on the Cotai Strip include the Four Seasons Macao and the Plaza Casino. Its Singapore property, Marina Bay Sands features three 55-story hotel towers, gaming space, convention space, two state-of-the-art theaters and The Shoppes at Marina Bay Sands.

FINANCIAL DATA: Note: Data for latest year may not have been available at press time.

In U.S. $	2015	2014	2013	2012	2011	2010
Revenue	11,688,460,000	14,583,850,000	13,769,880,000	11,131,130,000	9,410,745,000	6,853,182,000
R&D Expense	10,372,000	14,325,000	15,809,000	19,958,000	11,309,000	1,783,000
Operating Income	2,841,475,000	4,099,226,000	3,408,243,000	2,311,382,000	2,389,887,000	1,180,586,000
Operating Margin %	24.31%	28.10%	24.75%	20.76%	25.39%	17.22%
SGA Expense	1,491,093,000	1,459,113,000	1,532,614,000	1,412,760,000	1,131,809,000	948,281,000
Net Income	1,966,236,000	2,840,629,000	2,305,997,000	1,524,093,000	1,560,123,000	599,394,000
Operating Cash Flow	3,449,971,000	4,832,844,000	4,439,412,000	3,057,757,000	2,662,496,000	1,870,151,000
Capital Expenditure	1,528,642,000	1,178,656,000	943,982,000	1,449,234,000	1,508,593,000	2,023,981,000
EBITDA	3,924,666,000	5,138,481,000	4,422,191,000	3,213,186,000	3,172,176,000	1,857,689,000
Return on Assets %	9.07%	12.60%	10.27%	6.86%	5.86%	1.95%
Return on Equity %	28.02%	38.18%	31.31%	20.44%	18.39%	6.66%
Debt to Equity	1.37	1.37	1.22	1.43	1.21	1.57

CONTACT INFORMATION:

Phone: 702 414-1000   Fax: 702 414-4884
Toll-Free:
Address: 3355 Las Vegas Blvd. S., Las Vegas, NV 89109 United States

STOCK TICKER/OTHER:

Stock Ticker: LVS   Exchange: NYS
Employees: 48,500   Fiscal Year Ends: 12/31
Parent Company:

SALARIES/BONUSES:

Top Exec. Salary: Bonus: $
$3,250,000
Second Exec. Salary: Bonus: $
$1,538,462

OTHER THOUGHTS:

Estimated Female Officers or Directors:

Hot Spot for Advancement for Women/Minorities:

Sales, profits and employees may be estimates. Financial information, benefits and other data can change quickly and may vary from those stated here.

LaSalle Hotel Properties

www.lasallehotels.com

NAIC Code: 0

TYPES OF BUSINESS:
Real Estate Investment Trust
Luxury Hotels
Property Investment

BRANDS/DIVISIONS/AFFILIATES:
Le Montrose Suite Hotel
Indianapolis Marriott Downtown
Westin Copley Place
Liaison Capitol Hill (The)
Hotel Solamar
Westin Michigan Avenue
Westin Market Street (The)

CONTACTS: *Note: Officers with more than one job title may be intentionally listed here more than once.*
Michael Barnello, CEO
Kenneth Fuller, CFO
Stuart Scott, Chairman of the Board
Alfred Young, COO
Donald Washburn, Trustee
Jeffrey Foland, Trustee
Denise Coll, Trustee
Darryl Hartley-Leonard, Trustee

GROWTH PLANS/SPECIAL FEATURES:
LaSalle Hotel Properties is a self-managed and self-administered real estate investment trust (REIT) that owns and invests in luxury hotels. The firm primarily works with hotels located in convention, resort or major urban business markets. It currently owns interests in 47 upscale and luxury full-service hotels with over 12,000 rooms/suites located in 10 states and Washington, D.C. The firm is comprised of hotel investors, asset managers and financial experts rather than hotel operators, and its hotels are operated and managed by unrelated hotel operating companies such as Westin Hotels and Resorts, Noble House Hotels & Resorts, Hilton Hotels Corporation, Hyatt Hotels Corporation, Kimpton Hotel & Restaurant Group LLC and others. The firm seeks to improve revenue growth through renovations, redevelopment and/or expansions; brand or franchise conversion; acquisitions of appropriate full-service hotels in the U.S. and abroad; and selective development of hotel properties in favorable upscale markets. It is currently focused on acquiring hotels in eight primary urban markets: Boston, Chicago, Los Angeles, New York, San Diego, San Francisco, Seattle and Washington, D.C. Properties owned by the company include the Le Montrose Suite Hotel, located in West Hollywood; Indianapolis Marriott Downtown; The Liaison Capitol Hill in Washington D.C.; Westin Copley Place in Boston; Westin Michigan Avenue in Chicago; and Hotel Solamar located in San Diego. In January 2015, it acquired The Westin Market Street in San Francisco, California and renamed it Park Central San Francisco.

FINANCIAL DATA: *Note: Data for latest year may not have been available at press time.*

In U.S. $	2015	2014	2013	2012	2011	2010
Revenue	1,164,358,000	1,052,475,000	929,456,000	818,662,000	679,351,000	563,983,000
R&D Expense						
Operating Income	134,537,000	215,803,000	90,725,000	80,639,000	49,868,000	7,696,000
Operating Margin %	11.55%	20.50%	9.76%	9.85%	7.34%	1.36%
SGA Expense	831,242,000	765,094,000	86,492,000	72,908,000	60,265,000	55,524,000
Net Income	135,552,000	212,845,000	89,935,000	71,296,000	43,617,000	1,961,000
Operating Cash Flow	337,519,000	283,236,000	245,565,000	216,364,000	165,495,000	131,572,000
Capital Expenditure	582,228,000	294,019,000	421,921,000	457,818,000	588,677,000	490,039,000
EBITDA						
Return on Assets %	3.17%	5.42%	2.07%	1.48%	.49%	-1.13%
Return on Equity %	5.12%	8.69%	3.58%	2.49%	.80%	-1.81%
Debt to Equity	0.60	0.41	0.59	0.67	0.53	0.56

CONTACT INFORMATION:
Phone: 301 941-1500   Fax: 301 941-1553
Toll-Free:
Address: 7550 Wisconsin Avenue, 10/Fl, Bethesda, MD 20814 United States

STOCK TICKER/OTHER:
Stock Ticker: LHO
Employees: 35
Parent Company:

Exchange: NYS
Fiscal Year Ends: 12/31

SALARIES/BONUSES:
Top Exec. Salary: $815,000   Bonus: $
Second Exec. Salary: $510,167   Bonus: $

OTHER THOUGHTS:
Estimated Female Officers or Directors:
Hot Spot for Advancement for Women/Minorities:

Sales, profits and employees may be estimates. Financial information, benefits and other data can change quickly and may vary from those stated here.

LastMinute.com NV

www.lastminute.com

NAIC Code: 519130

TYPES OF BUSINESS:

Online Travel Agency
Online Reservations & Ticket Sales
Vacation packages
Entertainment packages
Dining discounts/packages

BRANDS/DIVISIONS/AFFILIATES:

lastminute.com group
AllHotels.com
eXhilaration
TravelPrice.com

CONTACTS: *Note: Officers with more than one job title may be intentionally listed here more than once.*

Matthew Crummack, CEO
Matthew Crummack, Pres.

GROWTH PLANS/SPECIAL FEATURES:

LastMinute.com is one of the U.K's top online travel and leisure websites. The company is a wholly-owned subsidiary of lastminute.com, formerly known as Bravofly Rumbo Group. The firm offers customers last-minute opportunities for travel services, including airfare, hotel reservations, car rentals and package vacations, with 80,000 hotels and flights to choose from globally. LastMinute also offers tickets for entertainment events, restaurant reservations, museum admissions and other activity planning services in the U.K., Ireland, France, Belgium, the Netherlands, Germany, Italy, Spain, Sweden, Australia, Japan, New Zealand, South Africa and the U.S. The company is one of the largest retailers of West End theater tickets. The firm's registered subscribers can make purchases by telephone, over the Internet and through an interactive voice recognition service from 14 days to 3 hours before departure. The company has relationships with thousands of individual suppliers for which it serves as a third party in facilitating contracts. LastMinute offers suppliers an alternative way to distribute excess inventory at short notice without threatening their core businesses, providing consumers with a range of products at reduced prices. The concept is based on the idea of matching supply and demand and ensuring that excess inventory is not wasted. LastMinute owns and operates several subsidiaries, including eXhilaration, AllHotels.com and TravelPrice.com. In May 2015, Bravofly Rumbo Group closed its acquisition of LastMinute from Sabre Corporation.

FINANCIAL DATA: *Note: Data for latest year may not have been available at press time.*

In U.S. $	2015	2014	2013	2012	2011	2010
Revenue	282,521,360	161,596,365	135,427,600	82,443,750		
R&D Expense						
Operating Income						
Operating Margin %						
SGA Expense						
Net Income	-20,253,539	7,915,699	13,531,767	7,474,900		
Operating Cash Flow						
Capital Expenditure						
EBITDA						
Return on Assets %						
Return on Equity %						
Debt to Equity						

CONTACT INFORMATION:

Phone: 44-20-7866-4200   Fax: 44-20-7866-4001
Toll-Free: 800-083-4000
Address: 77 Hatton Garden, Amsterdam, 1075 United Kingdom

STOCK TICKER/OTHER:

Stock Ticker: Subsidiary   Exchange:
Employees: Fiscal Year Ends: 09/30
Parent Company: lastminute.com group

SALARIES/BONUSES:

Top Exec. Salary: $ Bonus: $
Second Exec. Salary: $ Bonus: $

OTHER THOUGHTS:

Estimated Female Officers or Directors:
Hot Spot for Advancement for Women/Minorities:

Sales, profits and employees may be estimates. Financial information, benefits and other data can change quickly and may vary from those stated here.

LATAM Airlines Group SA

www.latamairlinesgroup.net

NAIC Code: 481111

TYPES OF BUSINESS:

Airline
Air Cargo
Domestic Service
International Service

BRANDS/DIVISIONS/AFFILIATES:

LAN Airlines SA
Transporte Aereo SA
LAN Peru SA
LAN Argentina SA
TAM SA
LAN Cargo SA
Aerolinhas Brasileiras SA
Aerea Carguera de Colombia SA

CONTACTS: *Note: Officers with more than one job title may be intentionally listed here more than once.*

Enrique Cueto Plaza, CEO
Hernan Pasman, COO
Andres Osorio Hermansen, CFO
Jerome Cadier, CMO
Emilio del Real Sota, Exec. VP-Human Resources
Roberto Alvo Milosawlewitsch, Exec. VP-Corp. Functions
Marco Antonio Bologna, CEO-TAM SA
Ignacio Cueto Plaza, CEO-LAN Airlines
Cristian Ureta Larrain, Exec. VP-Cargo
Armando Valdivieso Montes, Exec. VP-Spanish Speaking Countries
Mauricio Rolim Amaro, Chmn.
Damian Scokin, Exec. VP-Intl Bus.

GROWTH PLANS/SPECIAL FEATURES:

LATAM Airlines Group SA is one of Latin America's leading passenger airlines and a main air cargo operator in the region. Through the combination with Brazil's cargo network, the company's passenger route network extends to 144 destinations worldwide, with an additional 90 destinations via codesharing. LATAM's fleet consists of 328 aircraft with an average age of 6.9 years, comprising Airbus 319/320/321 narrowbody aircraft; Airbus 330/350 and Boeing 767/777/787 aircraft; and Boeing 767/777 freighter aircraft. LATAM's passenger business is operated through several subsidiaries, including LAN Airlines SA; TAM Linhas Aereas SA; Transporte Aereo SA, which does business as LAN Express; LAN Peru SA; Aerolane Lineas Aereas Nacionales del Ecuador SA (LAN Ecuador); and LAN Argentina SA. The company serves domestic passengers in Argentina, Brazil, Chile, Colombia, Ecuador and Peru and international passenger services to the U.S., Europe and the Asia Pacific. The firm provides cargo services to all of its passenger destinations and to 20 additional destinations served only by freighter aircraft. Its cargo operations are carried out by various companies, including TAM SA and LAN Cargo SA, and are complemented by the operations of companies such as Aero Transportes Mas de Carga SA de CV (MasAir) in Mexico, Aerolinhas Brasileiras SA (ABSA) in Brazil and Linea Aerea Carguera de Colombia SA (LANCO) in Colombia.

FINANCIAL DATA: *Note: Data for latest year may not have been available at press time.*

In U.S. $	2015	2014	2013	2012	2011	2010
Revenue	9,740,045,000	12,093,500,000	12,924,540,000	9,722,189,000	5,585,440,000	4,390,502,000
R&D Expense						
Operating Income	448,540,000	541,416,000	585,814,000	276,076,000	506,651,000	490,028,000
Operating Margin %	4.60%	4.47%	4.53%	2.83%	9.07%	11.16%
SGA Expense	1,661,310,000	1,937,732,000	2,162,011,000	1,673,123,000	885,545,000	331,831,000
Net Income	-219,274,000	-259,985,000	-281,114,000	10,956,000	320,197,000	419,702,000
Operating Cash Flow	1,715,475,000	1,331,439,000	1,408,698,000	1,203,812,000	762,574,000	1,125,337,000
Capital Expenditure	1,622,198,000	1,496,204,000	1,425,270,000	2,448,530,000	1,394,640,000	1,048,394,000
EBITDA	-25,604,000	495,267,000	178,636,000	421,200,000	521,437,000	657,311,000
Return on Assets %	-1.13%	-1.20%	-1.30%	.07%	4.43%	6.68%
Return on Equity %	-6.04%	-5.39%	-5.41%	.33%	23.35%	35.03%
Debt to Equity		1.67		1.47	2.06	2.21

CONTACT INFORMATION:

Phone: 56-2-565-3944   Fax: 56-2-565-8764
Toll-Free: 866-435-9526
Address: Presidente Riesco 5711, 20/Fl, Las Condes, Santiago,   Chile

STOCK TICKER/OTHER:

Stock Ticker: LFL   Exchange: NYS
Employees: 52,997   Fiscal Year Ends: 12/31
Parent Company:

SALARIES/BONUSES:

Top Exec. Salary: $36,377   Bonus: $
Second Exec. Salary: $ Bonus: $

OTHER THOUGHTS:

Estimated Female Officers or Directors: 1
Hot Spot for Advancement for Women/Minorities:

Sales, profits and employees may be estimates. Financial information, benefits and other data can change quickly and may vary from those stated here.

Leading Hotels of the World Ltd (The)

www.lhw.com

NAIC Code: 561599

TYPES OF BUSINESS:

Hotel Marketing & Travel Agency
Brand Support
Loyalty Programs
Reservation Services
Spa Marketing
Hospitality Training
Architectural & Project Management Services

BRANDS/DIVISIONS/AFFILIATES:

Hotel Representatives AG
LHW Services GmbH
Leading Hotels of Europe & Egypt (The)
Leaders Club
Leading Spas of the World
Linx Technlogies
Leading Hotel Schools of the World
Private Label Company (The)

CONTACTS: Note: Officers with more than one job title may be intentionally listed here more than once.

Ted Teng, CEO
Ted Teng, Pres.
Daniel Neumann, CFO
Shannon Knapp, Sr. VP-Mktg.
Patricia Smith, Sr. VP-Human Resources
Phil Koserowski, VP-Interactive Mktg.
Philip Ho, VP-Asia Pacific
Deniz Omurgonulsen, VP-Membership
Andrea Kracht, Chmn.
Claudia Roth, VP-EMEA
Jon Londeen, Sr. VP-Dist. & Reservations Mgmt.

GROWTH PLANS/SPECIAL FEATURES:

The Leading Hotels of the World Ltd. (LHW) is a hospitality organization representing luxury hotels. Founded in 1928 as The Leading Hotels of Europe & Egypt, today LHW represents more than 375 hotels, resorts and spas in 75 countries. The company serves these businesses through a network of 25 regional offices around the world. Each year, LHW publishes a directory of its member hotels as one of its marketing endeavors. Additional marketing service include extensive sales and promotional activities, advertising and public relations support and an array of special programs for member hotels and their guests. For example, it offers travelers a hotel loyalty program called the Leaders Club, which allow customers to accrue benefits such as welcome gifts, advance hotel preferences, priority reservations and access to an online newsletter. LHW's brand extensions comprise Leading Spas of the World, a global evaluation and certification program for the spa industry. LHWSpas.com offers information and images from participants in the Leading Spas program. Additionally, LHW operates several joint ventures and ancillary businesses, including Linx Technologies, offering online leisure activities management platforms; Leading Hotel Schools of the World, providing hospitality training; The Private Label Company, which offers hotels brand support; Leading Quality Assurance, offering quality assessment audits and training to luxury hospitality and travel businesses; and Leading Interactive Reservations, which provides e-commerce solutions for online marketing and reservations to the hospitality industry. LHW is owned by Hotel Representative AG and LHW Services GmbH.

FINANCIAL DATA: Note: Data for latest year may not have been available at press time.

In U.S. $	2015	2014	2013	2012	2011	2010
Revenue						
R&D Expense						
Operating Income						
Operating Margin %						
SGA Expense						
Net Income						
Operating Cash Flow						
Capital Expenditure						
EBITDA						
Return on Assets %						
Return on Equity %						
Debt to Equity						

CONTACT INFORMATION:

Phone: 212-515-5600   Fax: 212-515-5829
Toll-Free: 800-745-8883
Address: 485 Lexington Ave, Ste 401, New York, NY 10017 United States

STOCK TICKER/OTHER:

Stock Ticker: Joint Venture   Exchange:
Employees: Fiscal Year Ends:
Parent Company: Hotel Representative AG

SALARIES/BONUSES:

Top Exec. Salary: $ Bonus: $
Second Exec. Salary: $ Bonus: $

OTHER THOUGHTS:

Estimated Female Officers or Directors: 2
Hot Spot for Advancement for Women/Minorities: Y

Learjet Inc

www.learjet.bombardier.com

NAIC Code: 336411

TYPES OF BUSINESS:

Aircraft Manufacturing
Business Jet Manufacturing

BRANDS/DIVISIONS/AFFILIATES:

Bombardier Inc
Learjet 70
Learjet 75

GROWTH PLANS/SPECIAL FEATURES:

Learjet, Inc., a subsidiary in the aerospace division of Bombardier, Inc., is one of the top manufacturers of high-performance business jets. A pioneer in the industry, the firm has built over 2,000 aircraft since producing its first jet in 1964. Currently, it produces two models: Learjet 70 and Learjet 75. The Learjet 70 offers quick-climbing cruise power with a climbing capacity of up to 45,000 feet, powerful engines, new winglet design and exceptional hot and high capabilities and high definition cabin management system among other features. The Learjet 75 combines comfort with cutting-edge technology. It is certified for operations up to 51,000 feet with superior brakes for shorter runways. It includes features such as six or eight passenger seating, personal touch-screen monitors, integrated speaker systems and high-definition bulkhead monitors among others. The learjet aircrafts can be customized to suit the functional requirements and personal aesthetics of the clients.

CONTACTS:
Note: Officers with more than one job title may be intentionally listed here more than once.

Ralph Acs, Gen. Mgr.
Guy C. Hachey, Pres.

FINANCIAL DATA:
Note: Data for latest year may not have been available at press time.

In U.S. $	2015	2014	2013	2012	2011	2010
Revenue						
R&D Expense						
Operating Income						
Operating Margin %						
SGA Expense						
Net Income						
Operating Cash Flow						
Capital Expenditure						
EBITDA						
Return on Assets %						
Return on Equity %						
Debt to Equity						

CONTACT INFORMATION:

Phone: 316-946-2000   Fax: 316-946-2220
Toll-Free:
Address: 1 Learjet Way, Wichita, KS 67209 United States

STOCK TICKER/OTHER:

Stock Ticker: Subsidiary   Exchange:
Employees: Fiscal Year Ends: 12/31
Parent Company: Bombardier Inc

SALARIES/BONUSES:

Top Exec. Salary: $ Bonus: $
Second Exec. Salary: $ Bonus: $

OTHER THOUGHTS:

Estimated Female Officers or Directors:
Hot Spot for Advancement for Women/Minorities: Y

Sales, profits and employees may be estimates. Financial information, benefits and other data can change quickly and may vary from those stated here.

Liberty Travel Inc

www.libertytravel.com

NAIC Code: 561510

TYPES OF BUSINESS:

Travel Agency
Vacation Packages

BRANDS/DIVISIONS/AFFILIATES:

Flight Centre Limited
Flight Centre
Student Flights
Escape Travel
Travel Associates
GOGO Vacations
Worldwide Traveler

CONTACTS: *Note: Officers with more than one job title may be intentionally listed here more than once.*

Emma Jup, CEO
Emma Jupp, Pres.
Christina Pedroni, Sr. VP-Sales

GROWTH PLANS/SPECIAL FEATURES:

Liberty Travel, Inc., a subsidiary of Flight Centre Limited, is a provider of leisure travel services, selling directly to holiday travelers through approximately 160 locations in 14 states. The company's web site accepts reservation bookings and features helpful tips and tools, such as a currency converter, weather updates, passport information and packing advice. Through the years, the firm has offered travelers touring packages to over 200 destinations in Europe, Asia, Central America and Canada. These packages include cruises, skiing, beach trips, adventures and golf vacations. A travel protection program offers customers a broad spectrum of insurance benefits in the case of an accident overseas. Liberty also offers a management program for small to mid-size businesses as well as special rates for group and incentive travel. The Flight Centre brand offers flights/airfare, holiday/vacation packages, hotel & resort accommodations, car rental & car hire services, cruises, tours, European rail passes, travel insurance, visa/travel advice and consultation on foreign currency requirements. The Student Flights brand provides low-cost travel deals for students, as well as for anyone/everyone. The Escape Travel brand offers affordable airfares, accommodations, all-inclusive cruise packages, tours and more. The Travel Associates brand uniquely tailors travel destinations and holidays for individual clients or groups. GOGO Vacations provides wholesale travel, offering customized land and air travel packages. Worldwide Traveler provides exclusive, hand-selected hotels & resorts in the world's most desirable destinations renowned for outstanding services, amenities and locations.

Liberty offers its employees health, dental and life insurance; a 401(k) savings plan; membership in the International Airlines Travel Agent Network (IATAN); discounted travel opportunities; and personal health and wellness consultations by its in-house h

FINANCIAL DATA: *Note: Data for latest year may not have been available at press time.*

In U.S. $	2015	2014	2013	2012	2011	2010
Revenue						
R&D Expense						
Operating Income						
Operating Margin %						
SGA Expense						
Net Income						
Operating Cash Flow						
Capital Expenditure						
EBITDA						
Return on Assets %						
Return on Equity %						
Debt to Equity						

CONTACT INFORMATION:

Phone: 201-934-3500   Fax: 201-934-3651
Toll-Free: 888-271-1584
Address: 69 Spring St., Ramsey, NJ 07446 United States

STOCK TICKER/OTHER:

Stock Ticker: Subsidiary   Exchange:
Employees: Fiscal Year Ends:
Parent Company: Flight Centre Limited

SALARIES/BONUSES:

Top Exec. Salary: $ Bonus: $
Second Exec. Salary: $ Bonus: $

OTHER THOUGHTS:

Estimated Female Officers or Directors: 1
Hot Spot for Advancement for Women/Minorities:

Sales, profits and employees may be estimates. Financial information, benefits and other data can change quickly and may vary from those stated here.

Loews Hotels Holding Corporation

www.loewshotels.com

NAIC Code: 721110

TYPES OF BUSINESS:

Hotels, Luxury
Hotel Management Services

BRANDS/DIVISIONS/AFFILIATES:

Loews Corporation
Loews Miami Beach Hotel
Loews Santa Monica Beach Hotel
Loews Royal Pacific Resort at Universal Orlando
Loews Portofino Bay Hotel at Universal Orlando
Loews Don CeSar Beach Resort & Spa
Loews Boston Hotel
Loews Chicago Hotel

CONTACTS: Note: Officers with more than one job title may be intentionally listed here more than once.

Kirk Kinsell, CEO
Jack Adler, Pres.
Shawn Hauver, VP-Oper.
Lark-Marie Anton, Sr. VP-Public Rel. & Mktg. Comm.

GROWTH PLANS/SPECIAL FEATURES:

Loews Hotels Holding Corporation, a subsidiary of the Loews Corporation, currently has a portfolio of 26 owned and/or operated luxury hotels and resorts. Located in 21 cities throughout the U.S. and Canada, the firm's properties include the 790-room Loews Miami Beach Hotel in Florida, the 581-room Loews Philadelphia Hotel, the 347-room Loews Santa Monica Beach Hotel in Southern California and the 142-room Loews Hotel Vogue in Montreal. Loews Hotels operates three joint venture hotels with Universal Studios in Orlando, Florida: Loews Royal Pacific Resort at Universal Orlando, its largest hotel with 1,000 rooms; the 750-room Loews Portofino Bay Hotel at Universal Orlando; the 650-room Hard Rock Hotel at Universal Orlando; and the 277-room Loews Don CeSar Beach Resort in St. Pete Beach, Florida. Loews Hotels' business amenities include high-speed Internet access, a power breakfast with notable business leaders, notarization services, private dining rooms, boardrooms and concierge services. The YouFirst Loyalty Program rewards guests based on number of stays and offers free Internet access, late checkout, guaranteed rooms and upgrades for guests who visit at least twice a year. Loews Hotels offers facilities for weddings, meetings and special events; and special programs and services designed for people traveling with pets, children and teenagers. Recently, the company completed renovations on its Boston-based hotel, located in the city's Back Bay area. Following its reopening, the hotel was renamed the Loews Boston Hotel. In early 2015, the firm agreed to purchase the 158-room Mandarin Oriental San Francisco Hotel, and the new Loews Chicago Hotel opened for business.

FINANCIAL DATA: Note: Data for latest year may not have been available at press time.

In U.S. $	2015	2014	2013	2012	2011	2010
Revenue	604,000,000	472,659,000	380,000,000	397,938,000	337,000,000	308,000,000
R&D Expense						
Operating Income						
Operating Margin %						
SGA Expense						
Net Income	12,000,000	11,000,000	141,000,000	61,000,000	13,000,000	1,000,000
Operating Cash Flow						
Capital Expenditure						
EBITDA						
Return on Assets %						
Return on Equity %						
Debt to Equity						

CONTACT INFORMATION:

Phone: 212-521-2000   Fax: 212-521-2525
Toll-Free: 800-235-6397
Address: 667 Madison Ave., New York, NY 10021 United States

STOCK TICKER/OTHER:

Stock Ticker: Subsidiary   Exchange:
Employees: 2,169   Fiscal Year Ends: 12/31
Parent Company: Loews Corporation

SALARIES/BONUSES:

Top Exec. Salary: $ Bonus: $
Second Exec. Salary: $ Bonus: $

OTHER THOUGHTS:

Estimated Female Officers or Directors: 2
Hot Spot for Advancement for Women/Minorities: Y

Sales, profits and employees may be estimates. Financial information, benefits and other data can change quickly and may vary from those stated here.

LOT Polish Airlines (Polskie Linie Lotnicze)   www.lot.com

NAIC Code: 481111

TYPES OF BUSINESS:

Airline
Air Cargo
Airport Services
Mechanical Services
Catering
Automobile Sales-Cars & Parts
Charter Flights

BRANDS/DIVISIONS/AFFILIATES:

TFS Silesia
LOT Polish Airlines
LOT Charters
LOT Cargo
Central European Engine Services
WRO-LOT
LOT Travel

CONTACTS: Note: Officers with more than one job title may be intentionally listed here more than once.

Rafal Milczarski, CEO
Borys Buta, COO
Tomasz Balcerzak, Mgmt. Board-Oper. Affairs
Marek Klucinski, Dir.-Corp. Comm.
Krzysztof Zbroja, Mgmt. Board
Andrzej Relidzynski, Chmn.

GROWTH PLANS/SPECIAL FEATURES:

LOT Polish Airlines (Polskie Linie Lotnicze) (PLL LOT), founded in 1920, is a major air carrier in Poland. The company is 99.82% owned by the Polish government, 0.144% by TFS Silesia and 0.036% owned by its employees. Also known as LOT Polish Airlines, PLL LOT's business activities includes international and national passenger air transport, luggage, airmail and goods transport as well as air transport-related services, air tourism, air training and aircraft rental. PLL LOT, whose hub is Warsaw Chopin Airport, flies to 60 destinations throughout North America, Europe, Africa, Tokyo and the Middle East. The company's fleet consists of 44 aircraft, which include Boeing 787 Dreamliners, Boeing 737-400s, Embraer 195s, Embraer 175s, Embraer 170s and Bombardier DHC-8Q400s. Subsidiaries include LOT Charters and LOT Cargo, which handle passengers, cargo, mail, goods, baggage loading/unloading, package insurance and freight service; Central European Engine Services (CEES), an engine services provider; WRO-LOT, which provides airport services; and LOT Travel, a travel agency. In 2015, the firm began accepting bitcoin through a Polish payments platform called PSP, which comprises a number of Polish banks. Bitcoin is a type of digital currency in which encryption techniques are used to regulate the generation of units of currency and verifies the transfer of funds independently of a central bank.

FINANCIAL DATA: Note: Data for latest year may not have been available at press time.

In U.S. $	2015	2014	2013	2012	2011	2010
Revenue	9,354,000,000	9,257,000,000	9,230,000,000	9,150,000,000	9,000,000,000	8,720,726,000
R&D Expense						
Operating Income						
Operating Margin %						
SGA Expense						
Net Income		26,000,000	-18,000,000			
Operating Cash Flow						
Capital Expenditure						
EBITDA						
Return on Assets %						
Return on Equity %						
Debt to Equity						

CONTACT INFORMATION:

Phone: 48-22-577-99-52   Fax:
Toll-Free:
Address: ul.17 Stycznia 43, Warsaw, 02-146 Poland

STOCK TICKER/OTHER:

Stock Ticker: Government-Owned
Employees:
Parent Company:

Exchange:
Fiscal Year Ends: 12/31

SALARIES/BONUSES:

Top Exec. Salary: $ Bonus: $
Second Exec. Salary: $ Bonus: $

OTHER THOUGHTS:

Estimated Female Officers or Directors:
Hot Spot for Advancement for Women/Minorities:

Mahindra & Mahindra Limited

www.mahindra.com

NAIC Code: 336111

TYPES OF BUSINESS:

Automotive & Farm Equipment Manufacturing & Distribution
Software Engineering
Real Estate Development
Hotels
Financial Services
Automobile Finance
Housing Finance
Information Technology

BRANDS/DIVISIONS/AFFILIATES:

Mahindra Special Group Services
Mahindra & Mahindra-Automotive Design
Zest
Mahindra Lifescapes Developers
Tech Mahindra Limited
Mahindra First Choice Services
Mahindra First Choice Wheels
Mahindra Ocean Blue Marine

CONTACTS: *Note: Officers with more than one job title may be intentionally listed here more than once.*

Anand G. Mahindra, Managing Dir.
V.S. Parthasarathy, Group CFO
Ruzbeh Irani, Chief Brand Officer
Rajeev Dubey, Pres., Group Human Resources
Ulhas Yargop, CTO
Rajan Wadhera, Chief Exec.-Prod. Dev.
S.P. Shukla, Pres., Group Strategy
Anita Arjundas, CEO-Real Estate Sector
Anoop Mathur, Pres., Two Wheeler Sector
S. Durgassankar, Exec. VP-Mergers & Acquisitions
Pravin Shah, CEO-Automotive Div.
Keshub Mahindra, Chmn.
Ruzbeh Irani, Chief Exec.-Intl Oper.

GROWTH PLANS/SPECIAL FEATURES:

Mahindra & Mahindra Limited is one of the largest industrial companies in India and a leading producer of multi-utility vehicles. Mahindra & Mahindra is the flagship company of the Mahindra Group. The company operates in ten sectors: systech, automotive & farm equipment, defense systems, financial services, hospitality, information technology, real estate, two wheelers, aftermarket and Mahindra Partners. The systech sector conducts the group's aerospace, components, steel and consulting business through subsidiaries such as Mahindra Aerospace, Mahindra Special Group Services and Mahindra Consulting Engineers. The automotive & farm equipment sector carries out the automotive, farm equipment, agri-business, energy and construction equipment businesses through subsidiaries including Mahindra & Mahindra-Automotive Design and Mahindra Shubhlabh Services. The defense systems sector produces various assault vehicles for the Indian army and sea mines and torpedo decoy launchers for the Indian navy through Mahindra & Mahindra-Defense Division and Defense Land Systems. The financial services sector operates the financial services, insurance broking and rural housing finance businesses through subsidiaries such as Mahindra & Mahindra Financial Services Ltd. and Mahindra Rural Housing Finance Ltd. The hospitality sector owns resorts and holiday destinations through firms such as Zest and Club Mahindra Fundays. The information technology sector, through subsidiaries such as Tech Mahindra Limited, provides software engineering and related services. The real estate sector conducts the infrastructure and real estate businesses via Mahindra Logistics and Mahindra Lifescapes Developers. The two wheeler sector manufactures scooters through Mahindra Two Wheelers and Mahindra Racing. The aftermarket sector handles the pre-owned car business through Mahindra First Choice Services and Mahindra First Choice Wheels. Finally, Mahindra Partners oversees the steel, retail, industrial equipment, logistics, leisure boat and solar energy businesses through companies such as Mahindra Ocean Blue Marine and Mahindra Solar One.

FINANCIAL DATA: *Note: Data for latest year may not have been available at press time.*

In U.S. $	2015	2014	2013	2012	2011	2010
Revenue	10,718,200,000	11,023,940,000	10,239,570,000	8,851,458,000	5,488,415,000	
R&D Expense						
Operating Income	626,814,600	852,982,700	751,498,200	960,195,100	642,186,900	
Operating Margin %	5.84%	7.73%	7.33%	10.84%	11.70%	
SGA Expense				851,484,100		
Net Income	467,389,600	695,233,700	610,658,800	455,837,000	472,944,700	
Operating Cash Flow	157,142,700	-36,310,000	-137,301,400	9,133,365	-346,519,600	
Capital Expenditure	708,938,900	546,017,700	490,319,100	497,116,600	120,330,700	
EBITDA	1,408,916,000	1,176,985,000	1,062,034,000	1,180,401,000	792,567,800	
Return on Assets %	3.42%	5.66%	5.84%	5.48%	7.17%	
Return on Equity %	12.76%	21.57%	22.32%	20.13%	25.16%	
Debt to Equity	0.86	1.09	0.99	0.95	1.19	

CONTACT INFORMATION:

Phone: 91 2224901441   Fax:
Toll-Free:
Address: Mahindra Towers, G.M. Bhosale Marg, Mumbai, Maharashtra 400 018 India

STOCK TICKER/OTHER:

Stock Ticker: MAHDY
Employees: 19,427
Parent Company:

Exchange: GREY
Fiscal Year Ends: 03/31

SALARIES/BONUSES:

Top Exec. Salary: $ Bonus: $
Second Exec. Salary: $ Bonus: $

OTHER THOUGHTS:

Estimated Female Officers or Directors: 1
Hot Spot for Advancement for Women/Minorities:

Sales, profits and employees may be estimates. Financial information, benefits and other data can change quickly and may vary from those stated here.

MakeMyTrip Limited

www.makemytrip.com

NAIC Code: 519130

TYPES OF BUSINESS:

Online Travel Services

BRANDS/DIVISIONS/AFFILIATES:

MakeMyTrip (India) Private Limited
MakeMyTrip.com Inc
MakeMyTrip.com
hoteltravel.com
MakeMyTrip.ae
easytobook.com

CONTACTS: *Note: Officers with more than one job title may be intentionally listed here more than once.*

Deep Kalra, CEO
Mohit Gupta, COO
Mohit Kabra, CFO
Saujanya Shrivastava, CMO
Yuvaraj Srivastava, Chief Human Resources Officer
Sanket Atal, CTO
Amit Somani, Chief Prod. Officer
Keyur Joshi, Chief Commercial Officer
Mohit Gupta, Chief Bus. Officer-Holidays
Deep Kalra, Chmn.
Amit Saberwal, Chief Bus. Officer-Intl Markets

GROWTH PLANS/SPECIAL FEATURES:

MakeMyTrip Limited is the leading online travel site in India. The company is the parent company of both MakeMyTrip (India) Private Limited and MakeMyTrip.com, Inc. Founded in 2000 to serve the market for U.S. citizens traveling to India, it has since expanded into the domestic Indian market, offering domestic and international travel arrangements to residents of India. Through its web site, MakeMyTrip.com, users can research, plan and book travel accommodations in India and overseas. Products available for booking through its portal include airfare, hotels, rail and bus tickets, car hire services and full vacation packages. In addition to its web sites, MakeMyTrip operates 20 travel stores in major metros of India and has two international offices in New York and San Francisco. The company provides access to all major domestic full-service and low-cost airlines operating in India and all major airlines operating to and from India. MakeMyTrip offers access to over 20,000 hotels and guesthouses in India, more than 190,000 hotels and properties outside of India, Indian Railways ticketing and several major Indian bus operators. It generates revenue through commissions and incentive payments from airlines, service fees charged to customers and fees from its GDS (Global Distribution System) service provider. MakeMyTrip.com, Inc. is the company's U.S. subsidiary, operating its U.S. offices. Additionally, the company operates the website MakemyTrip.ae in the UAE, hoteltravel.com and easytobook.com. In April 2015, the firm acquired certain assets of Mygola.com.

FINANCIAL DATA: *Note: Data for latest year may not have been available at press time.*

In U.S. $	2015	2014	2013	2012	2011	2010
Revenue	299,662,000	255,374,600	228,822,000	196,599,300	124,721,400	
R&D Expense						
Operating Income	-14,540,000	-15,321,590	-18,062,000	4,005,360	4,061,905	
Operating Margin %	-4.85%	-5.99%	-7.89%	2.03%	3.25%	
SGA Expense	124,406,000	102,325,100	100,736,600	81,317,950	54,212,150	
Net Income	-18,252,000	-20,934,330	-27,592,520	7,183,935	4,827,471	
Operating Cash Flow	10,827,000	-3,957,596	13,595,900	10,878,930	-6,332,157	
Capital Expenditure	6,968,000	5,568,734	6,984,526	9,007,092	2,846,381	
EBITDA	-10,026,000	-7,359,168	-14,730,540	4,679,815	7,574,292	
Return on Assets %	-6.63%	-9.01%	-15.12%	5.07%	5.90%	
Return on Equity %	-11.44%	-15.92%	-25.08%	7.36%	18.81%	
Debt to Equity						

CONTACT INFORMATION:

Phone: 91 1244395000   Fax:
Toll-Free: 800-102-8747
Address: 103 Udyog Vihar, Phase 1, Gurgaon, Haryana 122016 India

STOCK TICKER/OTHER:

Stock Ticker: MMYT   Exchange: NAS
Employees: 1,774   Fiscal Year Ends: 03/31
Parent Company:

SALARIES/BONUSES:

Top Exec. Salary: $ Bonus: $
Second Exec. Salary: $ Bonus: $

OTHER THOUGHTS:

Estimated Female Officers or Directors:
Hot Spot for Advancement for Women/Minorities:

Sales, profits and employees may be estimates. Financial information, benefits and other data can change quickly and may vary from those stated here.

Malaysian Aviation Group Bhd

www.malaysiaairlines.com

NAIC Code: 481111

TYPES OF BUSINESS:

Airline
Air Cargo
Engineering Services
Ground Handling

BRANDS/DIVISIONS/AFFILIATES:

MASwings
MAB Kargo
MAS Academy
AeroDarat Services
MAB Pesawat
Firefly
Malaysian Airline System Berhad

CONTACTS: *Note: Officers with more than one job title may be intentionally listed here more than once.*

Christoph R. Mueller, Group CEO
Izham Ismail, COO
Mohd Dukrl Husin, Dir.-Finance
Claudia Cadena, Interim Human Resource Officer
Tan Kok Meng, CIO
Izham Ismail, Dir.-Oper.
Mohd Sukri Husin, Dir.-Corp. Svcs.
Mohd Salleh Ahmad Tabran, Dir.-Customer Svc.
Azhari Mohd Dahlan, CEO-MAS Aerospace & Eng.
Ignatius Ong Ming Choy, CEO-Firefly
Tan Sri Md Nor Md Yusof, Chmn.

GROWTH PLANS/SPECIAL FEATURES:

Malaysian Aviation Group Bhd, the owner of Malaysian Airline System Berhad (MAS) is a major international airline operating out of Kuala Lumpur, Malaysia. The company's fleet connects customers to 53 destinations to, from and around Malaysia. Its fleet consists of aircraft from manufacturers Boeing 737s and Airbus 330s and 380s. The company also operates two passenger airline subsidiaries: Firefly, a community airline that flies to 15 domestic and regional destinations from Penang International Airport and the Sultan Abdul Aziz Shah Airport; and MASwings, Malaysia's first commuter airline, offering services within the Malaysian Borneo states of Sarawak and Sabah as well as the federal territory of Labuan. The firm also operates MAB Kargo, a freight line, out of the Kuala Lumpur International Airport. In addition to air passengers and cargo, MAS operates an engineering division that offers maintenance, repair, calibration and engineering and maintenance training services. MAS also operates a ground handling division and MAS Academy, which trains employees of the company and other organizations in airline technology, business, finance, operations management and related sectors. MAB Leasing/MAB Pesawat are aircraft leasing firms that provide customized aviation leasing solutions and asset management to the group's airlines. MAS has code-sharing and joint service agreements with a number of airlines, including Singapore Airlines, South African Airways, British Midlands International, Alitalia, KLM Royal Dutch Airlines, Dragon Air, Korean Air, Swiss International Airlines and Sri Lankan Airlines. It also maintains interline agreements with Lufthansa, United and AeroMex. The firm underwent a significant reorganization during 2015-2016 after a 2015 bankruptcy.

FINANCIAL DATA: *Note: Data for latest year may not have been available at press time.*

In U.S. $	2015	2014	2013	2012	2011	2010
Revenue		3,900,000,000	3,627,428,352	3,312,873,984	3,404,451,840	3,236,535,040
R&D Expense						
Operating Income						
Operating Margin %						
SGA Expense						
Net Income			-292,646,240	-107,860,920	-629,329,280	59,179,676
Operating Cash Flow						
Capital Expenditure						
EBITDA						
Return on Assets %						
Return on Equity %						
Debt to Equity						

CONTACT INFORMATION:

Phone: 60 378404523   Fax: 60 378465505
Toll-Free:
Address: Sultan Abdul Airport, MAS Complex A, Admin 1 Bldg., 3/Fl, Subang, 47200 Malaysia

STOCK TICKER/OTHER:

Stock Ticker: Private
Employees: 19,577
Parent Company:

Exchange:
Fiscal Year Ends: 12/31

SALARIES/BONUSES:

Top Exec. Salary: $ Bonus: $
Second Exec. Salary: $ Bonus: $

OTHER THOUGHTS:

Estimated Female Officers or Directors: 5
Hot Spot for Advancement for Women/Minorities: Y

Sales, profits and employees may be estimates. Financial information, benefits and other data can change quickly and may vary from those stated here.

Mandarin Oriental International Ltd

www.mandarinoriental.com

NAIC Code: 721110

TYPES OF BUSINESS:

Hotels, Luxury
Condominiums

BRANDS/DIVISIONS/AFFILIATES:

Mandarin Oriental Hotel Group Intl Ltd
Residences at Mandarin Oriental
Spa at Mandarin Oriental

CONTACTS: *Note: Officers with more than one job title may be intentionally listed here more than once.*

Edouard Ettedgui, CEO
Stuart Dickie, CFO
Michael Hobson, Chief Mktg. Officer
Paul Clark, Group Dir.-Human Resources
Monika Nerger, CIO
Vincent Marot, Group Dir.-Tech. Services
Kieren Barry, Group Counsel
Terry L. Stinson, Dir.-Dev.
Jill Kluge, Group Dir.-Brand Comm.
Christoph Mares, Dir.-Oper., EMEA
Andrew Hirst, Dir.-Oper., Asia
Richard Baker, Exec. VP-Americas Oper.
David Nicholls, Group Dir.-Food & Beverage
Simon L. Keswick, Chmn.
Terry L. Stinson, Pres., The Americas

GROWTH PLANS/SPECIAL FEATURES:

Mandarin Oriental International, Ltd. (MOI) is an international hotel investment and management group. MOI operates in two business segments, hotel ownership & hotel management, and four geographical regions: Hong Kong & Macau, Other Asia, Europe and the Americas. Through subsidiary Mandarin Oriental Hotel Group International Ltd., the company either currently operates or is in the process of developing 47 luxury and first class hotels with over 11,000 rooms and a presence in 25 countries worldwide. MOI has 21 hotel properties in Asia, 10 in the Americas and 16 in Europe, the Middle East and North Africa. These include the original flagship properties of the Mandarin Oriental in Hong Kong and in Bangkok as well as locations in Singapore, Jakarta, Kuala Lumpur, Macau, Manila, London, Geneva, Tokyo, Munich, Prague and Bermuda. The company has U.S. hotels in New York City, Boston, Miami, Las Vegas, Atlanta and Washington, D.C. In addition to hotel rooms, the Mandarin Oriental New York offers the Residences at Mandarin Oriental, 65 luxury condominiums located above the hotel. Another 14 of the firm's properties also feature the Residences at Mandarin Oriental condominiums. The Spa at Mandarin Oriental can also be found in many of the firm's hotels worldwide, including in London, Miami, Boston and New York City. Each spa is unique and offers specialized treatments to clients. In 2015, the firm sold its San Francisco hotel, and acquired the Ritz Hotel in Madrid.

FINANCIAL DATA: *Note: Data for latest year may not have been available at press time.*

In U.S. $	2015	2014	2013	2012	2011	2010
Revenue	607,300,000	679,900,000	668,600,000	648,300,000	614,200,000	513,200,000
R&D Expense						
Operating Income	107,300,000	120,800,000	111,800,000	85,900,000	89,100,000	64,900,000
Operating Margin %	17.66%	17.76%	16.72%	13.24%	14.50%	12.64%
SGA Expense	137,900,000	149,100,000	148,400,000	147,200,000	147,800,000	121,700,000
Net Income	89,300,000	97,000,000	96,300,000	72,300,000	67,500,000	44,400,000
Operating Cash Flow	140,200,000	159,500,000	156,900,000	126,000,000	146,300,000	114,200,000
Capital Expenditure	51,500,000	32,300,000	38,800,000	55,000,000	66,200,000	74,700,000
EBITDA	169,900,000	198,800,000	192,700,000	158,500,000	151,200,000	114,700,000
Return on Assets %	4.71%	4.94%	5.08%	4.14%	3.97%	2.48%
Return on Equity %	8.18%	9.97%	9.95%	7.78%	7.45%	4.60%
Debt to Equity	0.35	0.53	0.24	0.61	0.63	0.63

CONTACT INFORMATION:

Phone: 852 28959288   Fax: 852 28373500
Toll-Free: 852 28811288
Address: 281 Gloucester Rd., 7th Fl., Hong Kong,   Hong Kong

STOCK TICKER/OTHER:

Stock Ticker: MNOIY   Exchange: PINX
Employees: Fiscal Year Ends: 12/31
Parent Company:

SALARIES/BONUSES:

Top Exec. Salary: $ Bonus: $
Second Exec. Salary: $ Bonus: $

OTHER THOUGHTS:

Estimated Female Officers or Directors: 2
Hot Spot for Advancement for Women/Minorities:

Marcus Corporation (The)

www.marcuscorp.com

NAIC Code: 721110

TYPES OF BUSINESS:

Hotels & Motels
Movie & IMAX Theaters
Hotels/Resorts

BRANDS/DIVISIONS/AFFILIATES:

Marcus Theatres Corp
MCS Capital LLC
Funset Boulevard

CONTACTS: *Note: Officers with more than one job title may be intentionally listed here more than once.*

Rolando Rodriguez, CEO, Subsidiary
Gregory Marcus, CEO
Douglas Neis, CFO
Stephen Marcus, Chairman of the Board
Thomas Kissinger, General Counsel

GROWTH PLANS/SPECIAL FEATURES:

The Marcus Corporation is an owner and operator of movie theaters, hotels and resorts. Through its Marcus Theatres Corp. subsidiary, the company owns or operates 55 movie theaters, with 681 screens in Wisconsin, Ohio, Illinois, Minnesota, North Dakota, Nebraska and Iowa. Marcus also operates a family entertainment center, Funset Boulevard, adjacent to its theater in Appleton, Wisconsin. In addition, Marcus Corporation owns or manages approximately 5,211 hotel and resort rooms, and also manages hotels and other properties for third parties. Owned hotels and resorts include the Pfister Hotel, the InterContinental Milwaukee and The Hilton Milwaukee City Center in Milwaukee, Wisconsin; the Hilton Madison at Monona Terrace in Madison, Wisconsin; The Grand Geneva Resort & Spa in Lake Geneva, Wisconsin; the Hotel Phillips in Kansas City, Missouri; the Four Points by Sheraton Chicago Downtown/Magnificent Mile in Chicago, Illinois; and the Skirvin Hilton in Oklahoma City, Oklahoma. Subsidiary MCS Capital LLC acquires and develops new hotel investments. In 2015, the firm began a partnership with Fandango, allowing its moviegoers to purchase tickets through Fandango's online web site. That same year, Marcus Corporation sold Hotel Phillips in Kansas City, Missouri.

FINANCIAL DATA: *Note: Data for latest year may not have been available at press time.*

In U.S. $	2015	2014	2013	2012	2011	2010
Revenue	488,067,000	447,939,000	412,836,000	413,898,000	377,004,000	
R&D Expense						
Operating Income	50,194,000	48,382,000	38,204,000	46,515,000	33,497,000	
Operating Margin %	10.28%	10.80%	9.25%	11.23%	8.88%	
SGA Expense	87,103,000	80,324,000	77,255,000	74,623,000	67,675,000	
Net Income	23,995,000	25,001,000	17,506,000	22,734,000	13,558,000	
Operating Cash Flow	80,452,000	66,440,000	63,202,000	69,028,000	61,502,000	
Capital Expenditure	74,988,000	56,673,000	23,491,000	38,017,000	25,186,000	
EBITDA	87,941,000	81,948,000	78,151,000	81,570,000	65,698,000	
Return on Assets %	3.04%	3.29%	2.36%	3.18%	1.93%	
Return on Equity %	7.16%	7.90%	5.38%	6.65%	4.01%	
Debt to Equity	0.72	0.78	0.84	0.40	0.58	

CONTACT INFORMATION:

Phone: 414 905-1000   Fax: 414 905-2879
Toll-Free:
Address: 100 E. Wisconsin Ave., Ste. 1900, Milwaukee, WI 53202-4125
United States

STOCK TICKER/OTHER:

Stock Ticker: MCS
Employees: 7,100
Parent Company:

Exchange: NYS
Fiscal Year Ends: 05/31

SALARIES/BONUSES:

Top Exec. Salary:
$1,002,442
Second Exec. Salary:
$759,327

Bonus: $

Bonus: $

OTHER THOUGHTS:

Estimated Female Officers or Directors: 2

Hot Spot for Advancement for Women/Minorities: Y

Sales, profits and employees may be estimates. Financial information, benefits and other data can change quickly and may vary from those stated here.

Marriott International Inc

NAIC Code: 721110

www.marriott.com

TYPES OF BUSINESS:

Hotels & Resorts
Suites Hotels
Corporate Apartments
Extended Stay Lodging
Luxury Hotels
Business Hotels

BRANDS/DIVISIONS/AFFILIATES:

Marriott Hotels
Ritz-Carlton Hotel Company LLC (The)
BVLGARI Hotels and Resorts
Renaissance Hotels
Courtyard by Marriott
Fairfield Inn & Suites by Marriott
TownePlace Suites by Marriott
JW Marriott

CONTACTS: Note: Officers with more than one job title may be intentionally listed here more than once.

Bancroft Gordon, Assistant General Counsel
David Grissen, President, Divisional
Arne Sorenson, CEO
Kathleen Oberg, CFO
J. Marriott, Chairman of the Board
Stephanie Linnartz, Chief Marketing Officer
Bao Giang Val Bauduin, Controller
Sterling Colton, Director Emeritus
William Shaw, Director Emeritus
Edward Ryan, Executive VP
Anthony Capuano, Executive VP
David Rodriguez, Executive VP
Amy McPherson, Managing Director, Geographical
Argiris Kyriakidis, Managing Director, Geographical
Craig Smith, Managing Director, Geographical

GROWTH PLANS/SPECIAL FEATURES:

Marriott International, Inc. operates 4,424 hotels and related lodging facilities in 79 countries and territories, totaling nearly 760,000 rooms. The company operates through three segments: North American full-service lodging, North American limited-service lodging and international. Marriott develops, operates and franchises hotels under various brand names, including Marriott Hotels, JW Marriott, The Ritz-Carlton, BuVLGARI Hotels and Resorts, Renaissance Hotels, Courtyard by Marriott, Residence Inn by Marriott, Fairfield Inn & Suites, SpringHill Suites by Marriott, EDITION, Autograph Collection Hotels, Marriott Executive Apartments, Marriott Vacation Club, Gaylor Hotels, AC Hotels by Marriott, Protea Hotels, Moxy Hotels and TownePlace Suites by Marriott. The firm also operates 41 home and condominium projects and 28 Marriott Executive Apartments located in 15 countries. Additionally, Marriott Golf manages 35 golf resorts worldwide. The company operates 15 system-wide hotel reservation centers: six in the U.S. and Canada and nine in other countries and territories. In 2015, Marriott debuted its first property in Italy, on a private island called JW Marriott Venice Resort & Spa. In February 2016, it expanded its footprint in Chhattisgarh, India with Courtyard by Marriott Raipur; signed for five hotels to open in Japan by 2018 with Mori Trust Group, which will be under the Marriott Hotels brand; and announced plans to open two new hotels in Cartagena, Colombia by 2018. As of March 2016, Marriott is in a competition with the Anbang Insurance Group for the right to acquire Starwood Hotels & Resorts Worldwide Inc.

FINANCIAL DATA: Note: Data for latest year may not have been available at press time.

In U.S. $	2015	2014	2013	2012	2011	2010
Revenue	14,486,000,000	13,796,000,000	12,784,000,000	11,814,000,000	12,317,000,000	11,691,000,000
R&D Expense						
Operating Income	1,350,000,000	1,159,000,000	988,000,000	940,000,000	526,000,000	695,000,000
Operating Margin %	9.31%	8.40%	7.72%	7.95%	4.27%	5.94%
SGA Expense	634,000,000	659,000,000	726,000,000	645,000,000	752,000,000	780,000,000
Net Income	859,000,000	753,000,000	626,000,000	571,000,000	198,000,000	458,000,000
Operating Cash Flow	1,430,000,000	1,224,000,000	1,140,000,000	989,000,000	1,089,000,000	1,151,000,000
Capital Expenditure	426,000,000	476,000,000	465,000,000	690,000,000	257,000,000	363,000,000
EBITDA	1,561,000,000	1,351,000,000	1,144,000,000	1,131,000,000	688,000,000	909,000,000
Return on Assets %	13.26%	11.02%	9.53%	9.32%	2.65%	5.41%
Return on Equity %					49.25%	33.59%
Debt to Equity						1.69

CONTACT INFORMATION:

Phone: 301 380-3000   Fax: 301 380-3967
Toll-Free: 800-721-7033
Address: 10400 Fernwood Rd., Bethesda, MD 20817 United States

STOCK TICKER/OTHER:

Stock Ticker: MAR
Employees: 123,500
Parent Company:

Exchange: NAS
Fiscal Year Ends: 12/31

SALARIES/BONUSES:

Top Exec. Salary: $3,000,000   Bonus: $

Second Exec. Salary: $1,236,000   Bonus: $

OTHER THOUGHTS:

Estimated Female Officers or Directors: 7

Hot Spot for Advancement for Women/Minorities: Y

Martinair Holland NV

www.martinair.com

NAIC Code: 481111

TYPES OF BUSINESS:

Airline
Air Cargo
Charter Services
Flight & Aviation Training
Aircraft Leasing

BRANDS/DIVISIONS/AFFILIATES:

Air France-KLM SA
Martinair Cargo
Martinair Flight Academy
Regional Jet Center Martinair

GROWTH PLANS/SPECIAL FEATURES:

Martinair Holland NV, a subsidiary of Air France-KLM SA, provides scheduled and charter air service for cargo. It operates through three core businesses and subsidiaries: Martinair Cargo, a specialized full freighter airline; Martinair Flight Academy, which trains pilots; and Regional Jet Center Martinair, which provides technical maintenance of Embraer aircraft. The company's fleet consists of one Boeing 747-400BCF. In 2015, parent Air France-KLM announced it would be reducing its cargo operations by 2016, phasing out all of Martinair's McDonnell Douglas MD-11Fs without replacement, and cutting more than 300 jobs.

CONTACTS: *Note: Officers with more than one job title may be intentionally listed here more than once.*

Marcel de Nooijer, CEO

FINANCIAL DATA: *Note: Data for latest year may not have been available at press time.*

In U.S. $	2015	2014	2013	2012	2011	2010
Revenue						
R&D Expense						
Operating Income						
Operating Margin %						
SGA Expense						
Net Income						
Operating Cash Flow						
Capital Expenditure						
EBITDA						
Return on Assets %						
Return on Equity %						
Debt to Equity						

CONTACT INFORMATION:

Phone: 31-20-60-11-222   Fax:
Toll-Free:
Address: Piet Guilonardweg 17, Schiphol, 1117 EE Netherlands

STOCK TICKER/OTHER:

Stock Ticker: Subsidiary   Exchange:
Employees: 2,474   Fiscal Year Ends:
Parent Company: Air France-KLM SA

SALARIES/BONUSES:

Top Exec. Salary: $ Bonus: $
Second Exec. Salary: $ Bonus: $

OTHER THOUGHTS:

Estimated Female Officers or Directors:
Hot Spot for Advancement for Women/Minorities:

Mediterranean Shipping Company SA

www.mscgva.ch

NAIC Code: 483111

TYPES OF BUSINESS:

Container Cargo Shipping
Cruise Ships

BRANDS/DIVISIONS/AFFILIATES:

MSC Cruises

CONTACTS: *Note: Officers with more than one job title may be intentionally listed here more than once.*

Diego Aponte, CEO
Fabio Santucci, Pres.
Luca Catassi, CFO
Diego Aponte, VP
Gianluigi Aponte, Chmn.

GROWTH PLANS/SPECIAL FEATURES:

Mediterranean Shipping Company SA (MSC) provides worldwide cargo shipping through its fleet of container vessels. Its offers coverage with one bill of lading, allowing its cargo ships to rapidly provide 200 direct and combined weekly liner services to 315 ports on six continents. The firm's total cargo intake capacity is 2.6 million TEUs (twenty-foot equivalent units), provided through its 480 container vessels. The firm serves its customers through a network of approximately 480 offices in 150 countries around the globe, with major operations in Australia, Chile, India, Lebanon, New Zealand and the U.K. MSC also works in the cruise ship business through its subsidiary MSC Cruises, which possesses 15 luxury cruise liners with capacities ranging from about 500 to more than 4,000 passengers. MSC Cruises' fleet operates in the Mediterranean, the Caribbean, the Atlantic Ocean, the Indian Ocean, North America, South America, West Africa and South Africa. These cruise ships feature Italian cuisine and classical music.

FINANCIAL DATA: *Note: Data for latest year may not have been available at press time.*

In U.S. $	2015	2014	2013	2012	2011	2010
Revenue	28,190,000,000					
R&D Expense						
Operating Income						
Operating Margin %						
SGA Expense						
Net Income						
Operating Cash Flow						
Capital Expenditure						
EBITDA						
Return on Assets %						
Return on Equity %						
Debt to Equity						

CONTACT INFORMATION:

Phone: 41-22-703-8888   Fax: 41-22-703-8787
Toll-Free:
Address: 12-14, Chemin Rieu, Geneva, CH-1208 Switzerland

SALARIES/BONUSES:

Top Exec. Salary: $ Bonus: $
Second Exec. Salary: $ Bonus: $

STOCK TICKER/OTHER:

Stock Ticker: Private   Exchange:
Employees: 24,000   Fiscal Year Ends:
Parent Company:

OTHER THOUGHTS:

Estimated Female Officers or Directors:
Hot Spot for Advancement for Women/Minorities:

Sales, profits and employees may be estimates. Financial information, benefits and other data can change quickly and may vary from those stated here.

Melia Hotels International SA

www.solmelia.com

NAIC Code: 721110

TYPES OF BUSINESS:

Hotel & Resort Management
Real Estate Development

BRANDS/DIVISIONS/AFFILIATES:

Melia Hotels
TRYP by Wyndham
Sol Hotels
Paradisus Resorts
Gran Melia
ME by Melia
Innside
Club Melia

CONTACTS: *Note: Officers with more than one job title may be intentionally listed here more than once.*

Gabriel Escarrer Jaume, CEO
Luis Del Olmo Pinero, Exec. VP-Mktg.
Gabriel Canaves, Exec. VP-Human Resources
Pilar Dols, Exec. VP-Admin.
Juan Ignacio Pardo, Exec. VP-Legal & Compliance
Pilar Dols, Exec. VP-Finance
Andre Gerondeau, Exec. VP-Hotels
Mark Hoddinott, Exec. VP-Real Estate
Onofre Servera, Exec. VP-Club Melia
Gabriel Escarrer Julia, Chmn.

GROWTH PLANS/SPECIAL FEATURES:

Melia Hotels International SA is a leading Spanish hotel chain in the city and resort markets. It manages and operates more than 350 hotels and resorts under management or franchise agreements in 35 countries. The company has locations throughout Europe, the Americas, the Mediterranean, the Middle East and Asia Pacific. In the hotels segment, the firm's brands include Sol Hotels, TRYP by Wyndham, Melia Hotels, Gran Melia, Paradisus Resorts, ME by Melia and Innside. Sol Hotels are located in major tourist destinations in the Mediterranean and the Caribbean. The TRYP by Wyndham brand is designed to appeal to upscale business travelers by providing the latest in technology services and conference facilities within the setting of a scenic resort. Melia Hotels are usually in the four- to five-star range, offering luxury accommodations and amenities. Gran Melia operates in the premium luxury market of the hotel sector. Paradisus Resorts cater to destination-driven resort vacations. The ME by Melia brand of luxury hotels, located in urban and resort destinations, integrates contemporary cuisine, design and music. Innside is an upscale German hotel chain featuring modern, minimalist architecture and the latest in communications technology for business travelers. In addition, the company developed the YHI Spa brand to offer spa services at select locations. Club Melia is a chain of membership resorts offering family villas and condominiums. The firm also offers MeliaRewards, a four tier rewards program where cardholders can earn points to trade in with over 35 Melia partners. The company's Asia-Pacific division is focused on expanding the firm's brands into China and also attracting Chinese travelers to its international properties. In February 2016, it announced plans to open 25 new hotels that year, with two already opened (Sol Costa Atlantis in Spain and Melia Braco Village in Jamaica).

FINANCIAL DATA: *Note: Data for latest year may not have been available at press time.*

In U.S. $	2015	2014	2013	2012	2011	2010
Revenue	1,963,854,000	1,654,371,000	1,527,493,000	1,539,257,000	1,508,668,000	1,413,107,000
R&D Expense						
Operating Income	185,231,000	149,595,500	-31,212,290	180,039,500	168,457,800	160,261,000
Operating Margin %	9.43%	9.04%	-2.04%	11.69%	11.16%	11.34%
SGA Expense	165,767,700					
Net Income	40,645,120	34,353,180	-82,723,980	42,172,640	47,431,930	58,745,900
Operating Cash Flow						
Capital Expenditure	72,540,950	45,762,060	39,361,650	45,504,460	152,298,000	186,002,700
EBITDA	331,124,200	257,975,400	71,752,340	295,396,000	248,949,300	268,770,800
Return on Assets %	1.12%	.92%	-2.13%	1.09%	1.18%	1.53%
Return on Equity %	2.90%	2.62%	-6.66%	3.47%	3.83%	5.05%
Debt to Equity	0.56	0.79	0.98	0.91	1.13	1.07

CONTACT INFORMATION:

Phone: 34 971224554   Fax: 34-971-22-44-08
Toll-Free:
Address: Calle Gremio Toneleros 24, Palma de Mallorca, 07009 Spain

STOCK TICKER/OTHER:

Stock Ticker: SMIZF   Exchange: PINX
Employees: 19,514   Fiscal Year Ends: 12/31
Parent Company:

SALARIES/BONUSES:

Top Exec. Salary: $ Bonus: $
Second Exec. Salary: $ Bonus: $

OTHER THOUGHTS:

Estimated Female Officers or Directors: 1
Hot Spot for Advancement for Women/Minorities:

Meritus Hotels & Resorts Inc

www.meritushotels.com

NAIC Code: 721110

TYPES OF BUSINESS:

Hotels & Resorts

BRANDS/DIVISIONS/AFFILIATES:

Overseas Union Enterprise Ltd
Mandarin Orchard Singapore
Marina Mandarin Singapore
Meritus Pelangi Beach Resort & Spa, Langkawi

CONTACTS: Note: Officers with more than one job title may be intentionally listed here more than once.

Michael Ow Kum Fei, Pres.
Tan Choon Kwang, COO
Kim Seng Tan, Pres.

GROWTH PLANS/SPECIAL FEATURES:

Meritus Hotels & Resorts, Inc. is a hotel management firm based in Singapore. Meritus is a subsidiary of Overseas Union Enterprise Ltd., operating under the real estate developer's hospitality division. Meritus operates two hotels in Singapore, the Mandarin Orchard Singapore and the Marina Madarin Singapore; and one resort in Malaysia, the Meritus Pelangi Beach Resort & Spa, Langkawi. Mandarin Orchard is the firm's flagship five-star hotel, featuring two buildings, with 36 stories and 40 stories respectively. Together, they offer more than 1,000 rooms and suites, club lounges, free Wi-Fi, restaurants and walking distance to shopping and transportation. Marina Mandarin Singapore is a 575-room hotel that features free Wi-Fi, Halal-certified kitchens, covered walkways to city destinations and MRT stations, a swimming pool and views of Marina Bay. Meritus Pelangi is a 355-room hotel designed in the style of a traditional Malay Village. Meritus Pelangi features Wi-Fi, nearby restaurants and shops and a view of the ocean.

FINANCIAL DATA: Note: Data for latest year may not have been available at press time.

In U.S. $	2015	2014	2013	2012	2011	2010
Revenue						
R&D Expense						
Operating Income						
Operating Margin %						
SGA Expense						
Net Income						
Operating Cash Flow						
Capital Expenditure						
EBITDA						
Return on Assets %						
Return on Equity %						
Debt to Equity						

CONTACT INFORMATION:

Phone: 65-6235-7788   Fax: 65-6235 6688
Toll-Free:
Address: 333 Orchard Rd., 37th Fl., Main Tower, Singapore, 238867 Singapore

STOCK TICKER/OTHER:

Stock Ticker: Subsidiary   Exchange:
Employees: Fiscal Year Ends: 12/31
Parent Company: Overseas Union Enterprise Ltd

SALARIES/BONUSES:

Top Exec. Salary: $ Bonus: $
Second Exec. Salary: $ Bonus: $

OTHER THOUGHTS:

Estimated Female Officers or Directors: 3
Hot Spot for Advancement for Women/Minorities: Y

Merlin Entertainments Group Plc

www.merlinentertainments.biz

NAIC Code: 713110

TYPES OF BUSINESS:
Location-Based Visitor Attractions
Theme Parks & Hotels

BRANDS/DIVISIONS/AFFILIATES:
Blackstone Group LP (The)
Warwick Castle
Gardaland Resort
Heide Park
LEGOLAND
Madame Tussauds
SEA LIFE
Shrek's Adventure

CONTACTS: Note: Officers with more than one job title may be intentionally listed here more than once.
Nick Varney, CEO
Andrew Carr, CFO
Natalie Bickford, Dir.-Human Resources
Mark Allsop, CIO
Grant Stenhouse, Dir.-Project Dev.

GROWTH PLANS/SPECIAL FEATURES:
Merlin Entertainments Group Plc., majority-owned by The Blackstone Group LP, operates 124 location-based visitor attractions in 25 countries. Merlin maintains three operating groups: resort theme parks, midway attractions and LEGOLAND parks. Resort theme parks include six resorts, mostly located in the U.K. Warwick Castle recreates Medieval England for visitors, including jousting shows and hawking demonstrations. Gardaland Resort in Italy offers over 32 rides, a 247-room hotel and approximately 10 shows. Heide Park, an 8.5-million-square-foot resort in North Germany, offers 40 rides and various hotel accommodations. Chessington World of Adventures & Zoo offers various rides and animal attractions. Family-themed Alton Towers Resort offers two hotels with their own water park and other rides and events. Thorpe Park features 25 rides and attractions, including Stealth, one of Europe's fastest rollercoasters. Midway attractions consist of 12 brands. Madame Tussauds worldwide attractions, The Eye Brand 360-degree views, Sea Life aquariums, The Dungeons horror attractions, LEGOLAND Discovery Center for small children, The Sanctuaries marine life, The Blackpool Tower ballroom, Wildlife park in Australia, Australian Treetop Adventures rainforest experience, Hotham Alpine Resort for skiing in the Australian Alps National Park, Falls Creek ski resort in Victoria, Australia and Shrek's Adventure in London, England. Last, the firm operates six LEGOLAND parks and resorts located in Billund (Denmark), Windsor (U.K.), California (U.S.), Deutschland (Germany), Florida (U.S.) and Malaysia. Merlin offers a Merlin Annual Pass in the U.K., Germany, the U.S and Australia, which provides access to more than 90 top attractions within a 12-month time period.

FINANCIAL DATA: Note: Data for latest year may not have been available at press time.

In U.S. $	2015	2014	2013	2012	2011	2010
Revenue	1,668,560,000	1,630,697,000	1,556,278,000	1,402,217,000	1,235,100,000	1,045,787,000
R&D Expense						
Operating Income	379,930,300	406,042,300	339,456,600	259,814,900	300,288,500	206,285,200
Operating Margin %	22.76%	24.89%	21.81%	18.52%	24.31%	19.72%
SGA Expense	88,780,960	80,947,340				
Net Income	221,952,400	211,507,600	189,312,300	99,225,780	87,475,350	-5,222,409
Operating Cash Flow	424,320,700	466,100,000	476,544,800	454,349,600	381,235,900	238,925,200
Capital Expenditure	280,704,500	250,675,600	198,451,600	212,813,200	227,174,800	134,477,000
EBITDA	514,407,300	509,184,900	489,600,900	473,933,600	389,069,500	308,122,100
Return on Assets %	6.15%	5.90%	5.56%	3.20%	3.14%	- .19%
Return on Equity %	15.42%	16.20%	18.67%	13.06%	12.76%	-2.09%
Debt to Equity	0.94	1.14	1.34	2.31	2.29	2.29

CONTACT INFORMATION:
Phone: 44-1202-666900   Fax: 44-1202-661303
Toll-Free:
Address: 3 Market Close, Poole, BH15 1NQ United Kingdom

STOCK TICKER/OTHER:
Stock Ticker: MIINF   Exchange: PINX
Employees: 18,821   Fiscal Year Ends: 12/31
Parent Company:

SALARIES/BONUSES:
Top Exec. Salary: $ Bonus: $
Second Exec. Salary: $ Bonus: $

OTHER THOUGHTS:
Estimated Female Officers or Directors:
Hot Spot for Advancement for Women/Minorities:

Mesa Air Group Inc

www.mesa-air.com

NAIC Code: 481111

TYPES OF BUSINESS:

Regional Airline
Air Freight
Repair & Overhaul Services
Financial Services
Training Services
Hotel Management

BRANDS/DIVISIONS/AFFILIATES:

Mesa Airlines Inc
American Eagle
United Express

CONTACTS: *Note: Officers with more than one job title may be intentionally listed here more than once.*

Jonathan G. Ornstein, CEO
John N. Selvaggio, COO
Michael J. Lotz, Pres.
Michael J. Lotz, CFO
Robert Hornberg, CIO
Gary Appling, Sr. VP-Eng. & Tech. Svcs.
David Butler, Sr. VP-Admin.
Christopher Pappaioanou, General Counsel
Todd Bourg, Dir.-Planning
Darren Zapfe, Sr. VP-Finance
Kenley Brown, VP-Inflight Svcs.
Tyler Campbell, Dir.-Safety
Don Wade, Dir.-Maintenance
Alvin Isaacs, Chief Pilot
Jonathan G. Ornstein, Chmn.

GROWTH PLANS/SPECIAL FEATURES:

Mesa Air Group, Inc. is a holding company whose principal subsidiaries operate as regional air carriers providing scheduled passenger and airfreight service. The firm operates more than 125 aircraft with 565 daily departures to 99 cities in 36 states as well as Canada and Mexico. The firm provides regional air service for American Airlines under the American Eagle brands and for United Airlines under the United Express banner. Mesa's fleet consists of the Bombardier line, including 85 Canadair regional jets, 64 CRJ900s and 1 CRJ200 for American and 20 CRJ700s for United; and the Embraer line, including 41 E175 E-Jets for United (with seven more scheduled for 2016 delivery). The company has eight maintenance bases at airports in Phoenix (PHX), Dallas (DFW), Washington Dulles (IAD), Louisville (SDF), Tucson (TUS), El Paso (ELP), Midland (MAF) and Houston (IAH). Mesa Air employs approximately 1,200 pilots, 900 flight attendants and 400 maintenance personnel. Subsidiary Mesa Airlines, Inc. is an American regional airline based in Phoenix, Arizona, and operates as American Eagle and United Express.

The company offers employees health, dental and vision coverage; 401(k) plan; long-term disability; life insurance; flexible spending accounts; travel benefits; and attendance incentive.

FINANCIAL DATA: *Note: Data for latest year may not have been available at press time.*

In U.S. $	2015	2014	2013	2012	2011	2010
Revenue	1,287,000,000	1,200,000,000	1,150,000,000	1,000,000,000	531,000,000	787,831,000
R&D Expense						
Operating Income						
Operating Margin %						
SGA Expense						
Net Income						
Operating Cash Flow						
Capital Expenditure						
EBITDA						
Return on Assets %						
Return on Equity %						
Debt to Equity						

CONTACT INFORMATION:

Phone: 602-685-4000   Fax: 602-685-4350
Toll-Free:
Address: 410 N. 44th St., Ste. 700, Phoenix, AZ 85008 United States

STOCK TICKER/OTHER:

Stock Ticker: Private   Exchange:
Employees: 2,800   Fiscal Year Ends: 09/30
Parent Company:

SALARIES/BONUSES:

Top Exec. Salary: $ Bonus: $
Second Exec. Salary: $ Bonus: $

OTHER THOUGHTS:

Estimated Female Officers or Directors:
Hot Spot for Advancement for Women/Minorities:

MGM Growth Properties LLC

www.mgmgrowthproperties.com

NAIC Code: 721120

TYPES OF BUSINESS:

Casino Hotels
Full Service Restaurants

BRANDS/DIVISIONS/AFFILIATES:

The Park in Las Vegas
Mandalay Bay
The Mirage
Monte Carlo
New York-New York
MGM Grand Detroit
Beau Rivage
Gold Strike Tunica

CONTACTS: Note: Officers with more than one job title may be intentionally listed here more than once.

James Stewart, CEO
Andy Chien, CFO
James Murren, Chairman of the Board

GROWTH PLANS/SPECIAL FEATURES:

MGM Growth Properties LLC is a real estate investment trust engaged in the acquisition, ownership and leasing of large-scale destination entertainment and leisure resorts, whose diverse amenities include casino gaming, hotel, convention, dining, entertainment and retail offerings. The portfolio of the firm consists of nine premier destination resorts operated by MGM Resorts International, including properties that are among the world's finest casino resorts, and The Park in Las Vegas. The Park in Las Vegas is a dining and entertainment complex located between New York-New York and Monte Carlo. Of MGM Growth's nine premier destination resorts, six are large-scale entertainment and gaming-related properties located on the Las Vegas Strip including Mandalay Bay, The Mirage, Monte Carlo, New York-New York, Luxor and Excalibur. Outside of Las Vegas, the firm owns three market leading casino resort properties including MGM Grand Detroit in Detroit, Michigan and Beau Rivage and Gold Strike Tunica, both of which are located in Mississippi. Combined, these properties comprise 24,466 hotel rooms, approximately 2.5 million convention square footage, over 100 retail outlets, over 200 food and beverage outlets and approximately 20 entertainment venues. In April 2016, MGM Growth announced both the pricing of an initial public offering (IPO) and the completion and closing of that same IPO.

FINANCIAL DATA: Note: Data for latest year may not have been available at press time.

In U.S. $	2015	2014	2013	2012	2011	2010
Revenue						
R&D Expense						
Operating Income	-261,954,000	-246,242,000				
Operating Margin %						
SGA Expense	10,351,000	11,634,000				
Net Income	-261,954,000	-246,242,000				
Operating Cash Flow	-58,473,000	-59,980,000				
Capital Expenditure	129,308,000	90,504,000				
EBITDA	-65,138,000	-59,980,000				
Return on Assets %	.58%	-3.12%				
Return on Equity %	1.26%	-4.01%				
Debt to Equity	2.73					

CONTACT INFORMATION:

Phone: 702-632-7777   Fax:
Toll-Free:
Address: 3950 Las Vegas Blvd. S., Las Vegas, NV 89109 United States

STOCK TICKER/OTHER:

Stock Ticker: MGP
Employees:
Parent Company:

Exchange: NYS
Fiscal Year Ends:

SALARIES/BONUSES:

Top Exec. Salary: $ Bonus: $
Second Exec. Salary: $ Bonus: $

OTHER THOUGHTS:

Estimated Female Officers or Directors:
Hot Spot for Advancement for Women/Minorities:

Sales, profits and employees may be estimates. Financial information, benefits and other data can change quickly and may vary from those stated here.

MGM Resorts International

NAIC Code: 721120

TYPES OF BUSINESS:

Casino Hotels & Resorts
Casino & Resort Management

BRANDS/DIVISIONS/AFFILIATES:

MGM China Holdings Ltd
MGM Hospitality
MGM Growth Properties LLC
Bellagio
MGM Grand Las Vegas
Mandalay Bay
Luxor
Circus Circus Las Vegas

CONTACTS: Note: Officers with more than one job title may be intentionally listed here more than once.

Andrew Hagopian III, Assistant General Counsel
James Murren, CEO
Daniel DArrigo, CFO
Robert Selwood, Chief Accounting Officer
Corey Sanders, COO
Willie Davis, Director Emeritus
Robert Baldwin, Director
Phyllis James, Executive VP, Divisional
John McManus, Executive VP
William Hornbuckle, President

GROWTH PLANS/SPECIAL FEATURES:

MGM Resorts International (MGM) is a leading international developer and operator of integrated hotels, resorts and casinos. MGM's wholly-owned domestic resorts include 16 properties located in Las Vegas, as well as eight within Michigan and Mississippi. These resorts include the following brand lines: Bellagio, MGM Grand Las Vegas, Mandalay Bay, The Mirage, Luxor, Excalibur, New York-New York, Monte Carlo, Circus Circus Las Vegas, MGM Grand Detroit, Beau Rivage and Gold Strike. In China, MGM has a 51% stake in MGM Macau (with Macau SAR) via MGM China Holdings Ltd. Other properties include 50%-owned CityCenter, located in Las Vegas, Nevada; 50%-owned Borgata, located in Atlantic City, New Jersey; and 50%-owned Grand Victoria, located in Elgin, Illinois. These properties total more than 47,500 guest rooms and suites, 1.9 million square feet of casino gaming space, nearly 30,000 slot machines and over 1,700 gaming tables. Wholly-owned subsidiary MGM Hospitality designs, develops and manages luxury non-gaming hotels, resorts and residences in China, including the MGM Grand Sanya. MGM Growth Properties LLC is a real estate investment trust which contributes to the real estate development and management of the company's properties. Scheduled to open in late-2016, MGM National Harbor is a casino resort located in Prince George's County, Maryland, and is expected to comprise 3,600 slots, 160 gaming tables, a 300-room hotel, luxury spa, rooftop pool, 93,100 square feet of high-end retail, fine & casual dining restaurants, a 3,000-seat theater venue, as well as 50,000 square feet of meeting/event space. MGM Springfield is a casino-hotel establishment expected to open in late-2018. In 2015, the firm sold Railroad Pass, Gold Strike, Circus Circus Reno and its 50% stake in Silver Legacy.

The firm offers employees health insurance, savings plans, employee assistance & wellness programs, child development center, life & disability insurance, auto/home/renter/pet insurance and adoption assistance.

FINANCIAL DATA: Note: Data for latest year may not have been available at press time.

In U.S. $	2015	2014	2013	2012	2011	2010
Revenue	9,190,068,000	10,081,980,000	9,809,663,000	9,160,844,000	7,849,312,000	6,019,233,000
R&D Expense						
Operating Income	-156,232,000	1,323,538,000	1,111,512,000	126,908,000	-3,025,958,000	-1,080,497,000
Operating Margin %	-1.70%	13.12%	11.33%	1.38%	-38.55%	-17.95%
SGA Expense	3,158,924,000	1,637,819,000	1,633,270,000	2,182,830,000	1,535,758,000	2,708,765,000
Net Income	-447,720,000	-149,873,000	-156,606,000	-1,767,691,000	3,114,637,000	-1,437,397,000
Operating Cash Flow	1,005,079,000	1,130,670,000	1,310,448,000	909,351,000	675,126,000	504,014,000
Capital Expenditure	1,466,819,000	957,041,000	562,124,000	422,763,000	301,244,000	207,491,000
EBITDA	571,219,000	2,043,712,000	1,794,337,000	309,842,000	4,735,609,000	-469,022,000
Return on Assets %	-1.72%	-.56%	-.59%	-6.54%	13.33%	-6.93%
Return on Equity %	-9.72%	-3.60%	-3.64%	-33.82%	68.56%	-41.85%
Debt to Equity	2.41	3.15	3.17	3.15	2.24	4.08

CONTACT INFORMATION:

Phone: 702 693-7120   Fax: 702 693-8626
Toll-Free:
Address: 3600 Las Vegas Blvd. S., Las Vegas, NV 89109 United States

STOCK TICKER/OTHER:

Stock Ticker: MGM   Exchange: NYS
Employees: 62,000   Fiscal Year Ends: 12/31
Parent Company:

SALARIES/BONUSES:

Top Exec. Salary: Bonus: $
$2,000,000
Second Exec. Salary: Bonus: $
$1,650,000

OTHER THOUGHTS:

Estimated Female Officers or Directors: 5

Hot Spot for Advancement for Women/Minorities: Y

Millennium & Copthorne Hotels plc

www.mill-cop.com

NAIC Code: 721110

TYPES OF BUSINESS:

Hotels, Luxury
Restaurants
Property Management
Apartments
Conference & Event Centers
Casino
Theaters
Fitness & Spa Facilities

BRANDS/DIVISIONS/AFFILIATES:

Leng's Collection
Millennium Collection
Copthorn Collection
Hard Days Night Hotel

CONTACTS: Note: Officers with more than one job title may be intentionally listed here more than once.

Wong Hong Ren, CEO
Andrew Cherry, Interim CFO
Kwek Leng Beng, Chmn.

GROWTH PLANS/SPECIAL FEATURES:

Millennium & Copthorne Hotels plc (MCH) is a global hotel company that owns, manages and/or operates 120 hotels worldwide. MCH hotels are individually tailored to their location, yet seamlessly blend Asian hospitality with Western comfort. The company's hotels and resorts are grouped into three collections: Leng's Collection, Millennium Collection and Copthorne Collection. The Leng's Collection of hotels comprise unique historic properties as well as trendy urban properties under the following brands: The Bailey's Hotel, The Chelsea Harbour Hotel, Grand Hotel Palace Rome, M Hotels, Studio M Hotels and M Social. The Millennium Collection of hotels are created with timeless elegance, and are famous for their conference and banquet offerings. Brands include Grand Millennium Hotels and Millennium Hotels. The Copthorne Collection of hotels are reasonably-priced accommodations for both the business and leisure traveler. Brands include Copthorne Hotels and Kingsgate Hotels. Headquartered in London, England, the firm has offices in the U.S., Asia, Australia and the United Arab Emirates. In 2015, the firm acquired Beatles-inspired Hard Days Night Hotel, located in the heart of Liverpool.

FINANCIAL DATA: Note: Data for latest year may not have been available at press time.

In U.S. $	2015	2014	2013	2012	2011	2010
Revenue	1,105,845,000	1,078,428,000	1,354,562,000	1,003,094,000	1,071,247,000	970,976,400
R&D Expense						
Operating Income	146,227,500	254,592,400	300,810,800	216,468,900	234,355,600	155,236,100
Operating Margin %	13.22%	23.60%	22.20%	21.58%	21.87%	15.98%
SGA Expense	446,516,000	424,320,700	453,174,600	438,421,200		
Net Income	84,864,150	143,616,300	298,330,100	176,256,300	210,071,400	125,598,900
Operating Cash Flow	231,091,600	366,874,200	138,785,500	207,982,400	213,204,900	215,293,800
Capital Expenditure	110,976,200	560,103,400	104,839,900	72,852,610	140,613,400	24,675,880
EBITDA	248,064,400	342,067,800	406,303,400	284,751,900	311,908,400	221,691,300
Return on Assets %	1.59%	2.93%	6.76%	4.01%	4.94%	3.23%
Return on Equity %	2.86%	4.83%	10.23%	6.36%	8.01%	5.20%
Debt to Equity	0.29	0.22	0.10	0.07	0.15	0.16

CONTACT INFORMATION:

Phone: 44 2078722444   Fax: 44 2078722460
Toll-Free: 866-866-8086
Address: Scarsdale Place, Kensington, London, W8 5SR United Kingdom

STOCK TICKER/OTHER:

Stock Ticker: MLCTF
Employees: 10,870
Parent Company:

Exchange: GREY
Fiscal Year Ends: 12/31

SALARIES/BONUSES:

Top Exec. Salary: $ Bonus: $
Second Exec. Salary: $ Bonus: $

OTHER THOUGHTS:

Estimated Female Officers or Directors:
Hot Spot for Advancement for Women/Minorities:

Sales, profits and employees may be estimates. Financial information, benefits and other data can change quickly and may vary from those stated here.

Morgans Hotel Group Co

NAIC Code: 721110

TYPES OF BUSINESS:

Boutique Luxury Hotels & Resorts
Boutique Hotels
Property Management

BRANDS/DIVISIONS/AFFILIATES:

Mondrian
Hudson
Delano
Clift
Shore Club
SBE Entertainment Group

CONTACTS: *Note: Officers with more than one job title may be intentionally listed here more than once.*

Richard Szymanski, CEO
Howard Lorber, Chairman of the Board
Meredith Deutsch, Executive VP
Chadi Farhat, Former COO

GROWTH PLANS/SPECIAL FEATURES:

Morgans Hotel Group Co. (MHG) operates, owns, develops and redevelops luxury hotels. The firm, which is known for its establishment of the boutique hotel sector, primarily maintains hotels in gateway cities and select resort markets in the U.S. and Europe that feature avant-garde modern design. MHG owns or partially owns and operates 13 hotel properties in New York, Florida, California, London, Nevada and Istanbul. The firm's fully-owned and managed hotels include the Hudson, Delano South Beach and Clift. The company also owns and manages two hotels through long-term joint venture agreements. MHG has a 50% interest in Mondrian South Beach in Miami Beach and a small interest in the Shore Club in Miami Beach. Significant media attention has been devoted to MHG's hotels, which it attributes to its public spaces, modern design, celebrity guests and high-profile events for which its hotels are known. Designers of its hotels have included Phillippe Starck, Benjamin Noriega-Ortiz, Andree Putman and David Chipperfield. The firm also operates three restaurants at Mandalay Bay in Las Vegas. Upcoming hotels include the Mondrian in Doha, the Delano in Dubai, the Delano in Cartagena and the Delano in Cesme. In 2015, the firm sold its 90% interest in The Light Group and sold its 20% interest in Mondrian SoHo. In May 2016, MHG agreed to be acquired by the privately held SBE Entertainment Group.

FINANCIAL DATA: *Note: Data for latest year may not have been available at press time.*

In U.S. $	2015	2014	2013	2012	2011	2010
Revenue	219,982,000	234,961,000	236,486,000	189,919,000	207,332,000	236,370,000
R&D Expense	663,000	4,709,000	2,987,000	5,783,000		
Operating Income	11,870,000	1,452,000	-1,910,000	-14,362,000	-21,006,000	-10,391,000
Operating Margin %	5.39%	.61%	-.80%	-7.56%	-10.13%	-4.39%
SGA Expense	20,904,000	26,030,000	29,765,000	32,217,000	34,563,000	34,538,000
Net Income	22,097,000	-50,724,000	-44,155,000	-55,687,000	-85,403,000	-81,409,000
Operating Cash Flow	5,691,000	-3,864,000	-3,147,000	-39,464,000	9,750,000	-7,252,000
Capital Expenditure	7,127,000	5,334,000	9,467,000	32,571,000	17,842,000	13,055,000
EBITDA	34,316,000	30,327,000	25,464,000	7,260,000	1,213,000	-27,512,000
Return on Assets %	.95%	-11.85%	-10.06%	-11.63%	-14.98%	-11.58%
Return on Equity %						
Debt to Equity						

CONTACT INFORMATION:

Phone: 212 277-4100   Fax: 212 277-4260
Toll-Free:
Address: 475 Tenth Ave., New York, NY 10018 United States

SALARIES/BONUSES:

Top Exec. Salary: $506,389   Bonus: $108,352
Second Exec. Salary: $400,000   Bonus: $80,800

STOCK TICKER/OTHER:

Stock Ticker: MHGC   Exchange: NAS
Employees: 2,600   Fiscal Year Ends: 12/31
Parent Company: SBE Entertainment Group

OTHER THOUGHTS:

Estimated Female Officers or Directors: 1
Hot Spot for Advancement for Women/Minorities:

Movenpick Hotels & Resorts Management AG www.moevenpick-hotels.com

NAIC Code: 721110

TYPES OF BUSINESS:
Hotels, Resort, Without Casinos

BRANDS/DIVISIONS/AFFILIATES:
Movenpick Holding
Kingdom Group

GROWTH PLANS/SPECIAL FEATURES:
Movenpick Hotels & Resorts Management AG is an international upscale hotel management company with 83 hotels, resorts or cruises operating in 24 countries. With a focus on expansion in its core markets of Europe, Africa, the Middle East and Asia, the firm has approximately 20 properties planned or under construction. Movenpick Hotels & Resorts specializes in business and conference hotels, as well as holiday resorts, all reflecting a sense of place and respect for their local communities. Additionally, the firm offers cruises down the Nile and on Lake Nasser in Egypt. The company has more than 55 properties that are Green Globe certified. Movenpick Hotels & Resorts is owned by the Movenpick Holding (66.7%) and Kingdom Group (33.3%).

CONTACTS: Note: Officers with more than one job title may be intentionally listed here more than once.
Jean Gabriel Peres, CEO
Ola Ivarsson, COO-Europe
Pascal Voyame, CFO
Andreas Mattmuller, COO-Middle East & Africa
Craig Cochrane, Sr. VP-Human Resources
Floor Bleeker, CIO
Jurgen Fischer, Chmn.

FINANCIAL DATA: Note: Data for latest year may not have been available at press time.

In U.S. $	2015	2014	2013	2012	2011	2010
Revenue	1,045,000,000	1,010,000,000	948,946,171	872,743,548		
R&D Expense						
Operating Income						
Operating Margin %						
SGA Expense						
Net Income						
Operating Cash Flow						
Capital Expenditure						
EBITDA						
Return on Assets %						
Return on Equity %						
Debt to Equity						

CONTACT INFORMATION:
Phone: 41-44-828-40-00 Fax: 41-44-828-40-10
Toll-Free:
Address: Oberneuhofstrasse 12, Baar, 6340 Switzerland

STOCK TICKER/OTHER:
Stock Ticker: Private Exchange:
Employees: 16,000 Fiscal Year Ends:
Parent Company: Movenpick Holding

SALARIES/BONUSES:
Top Exec. Salary: $ Bonus: $
Second Exec. Salary: $ Bonus: $

OTHER THOUGHTS:
Estimated Female Officers or Directors:
Hot Spot for Advancement for Women/Minorities:

Sales, profits and employees may be estimates. Financial information, benefits and other data can change quickly and may vary from those stated here.

MSC Cruises SA

www.msccruises.com

NAIC Code: 483112

TYPES OF BUSINESS:

Deep Sea Passenger Transportation

BRANDS/DIVISIONS/AFFILIATES:

Mediterranean Shipping Company SA
MSC Armonia
MSC Divina
MSC Fantasia
MSC Magnifica
MSC Opera
MSC Preziosa
MSC Splendida

CONTACTS: *Note: Officers with more than one job title may be intentionally listed here more than once.*

Pierfrancesco Vago, Chmn.

GROWTH PLANS/SPECIAL FEATURES:

MSC Cruises SA is a Swiss-based cruise company in the Mediterranean, South African and Brazilian regions, as well as across the globe. The cruise line comprises a fleet of 15 ships: MSC Armonia, MSC Divina, MSC Fantasia, MSC Lirica, MSC Magnifica, MSC Meraviglia, MSC Musica, MSC Opera, MSC Orchestra, MSC Poesia, MSC Preziosa, MSC Seaside, MSC Seavie, MSC Sinfonia and MSC Splendida. The fleet cruises year round in the Mediterranean and Caribbean, as well as seasonally in Northern Europe, the Canary Islands, Morocco, South America, the Indian Ocean, Africa and more. Itineraries cover more than 1,000 routes around the world. MSC ships are elegantly-designed with natural stone and marble predominantly sourced from Italy, as well as with superior-quality fabrics, gold-leaf mosaics and Swarovski crystal staircases. More than 11 million travelers have enjoyed a cruise with MSC. In 2015, the firm ordered four new ships from STX France and Fincantieri, with options for three more. The first two ships are due to be delivered in 2017, and the others are due in 2020. MSC Cruises is a subsidiary of Mediterranean Shipping Company SA.

FINANCIAL DATA: *Note: Data for latest year may not have been available at press time.*

In U.S. $	2015	2014	2013	2012	2011	2010
Revenue	1,710,000,000	1,696,068,750				
R&D Expense						
Operating Income						
Operating Margin %						
SGA Expense						
Net Income						
Operating Cash Flow						
Capital Expenditure						
EBITDA						
Return on Assets %						
Return on Equity %						
Debt to Equity						

CONTACT INFORMATION:

Phone: 41-61-260-01-01   Fax: 41-61-260-01-99
Toll-Free:
Address: Weisse Gasse 6, Basel, 4001 Switzerland

STOCK TICKER/OTHER:

Stock Ticker: Private   Exchange:
Employees: Fiscal Year Ends:
Parent Company: Mediterranean Shipping Company SA

SALARIES/BONUSES:

Top Exec. Salary: $ Bonus: $
Second Exec. Salary: $ Bonus: $

OTHER THOUGHTS:

Estimated Female Officers or Directors:
Hot Spot for Advancement for Women/Minorities:

MTR Corp Ltd

www.mtr.com.hk

NAIC Code: 482112

TYPES OF BUSINESS:

Short Line Railroads
Property Management
Advertising Space
Telecommunication Services
Consulting Services
Octopus Cards

BRANDS/DIVISIONS/AFFILIATES:

Next Tran
TraxComm Limited
Octopus Cards Limited
MTR Tourist

CONTACTS: *Note: Officers with more than one job title may be intentionally listed here more than once.*

Lincoln Leong Kwok-kuen, CEO
Jacob Kam Chak-pui, COO
Herbert Hui Leung-wah, Dir.-Finance
Jeny Yeung Mei-chun, Dir- Commercial
Margaret Cheng Wai-ching, Dir.-Human Resources
Gillian Elizabeth Meller, Dir.-Legal
Jacob Kam Chak-pui, Dir.-Oper.
Wong May-kay, Gen. Mgr.-Corp. Rel.
Lincoln Leong Kwok-kuen, Deputy CEO
Chew Tai Chong, Dir.-Projects
David Tang Chi-fai, Dir.-Property
Ma Si-Hang, Chmn.

GROWTH PLANS/SPECIAL FEATURES:

MTR Corp. Ltd. is the sole operator of the mass transit railways in Hong Kong, transporting more than 5.5 million passengers every week. The MTR railway network covers approximately 137 miles serving 87 stations. It also owns 68 light rail stops connecting Hong Kong Island and Kowloon in addition to several newer districts. The company's commuter network is made up of the Urban Lines, Tseung Kwan O Line, LOHAS Park, West Rail Line, East Rail Line, Ma On Shan Line, Light Rail and Kowloon Southern Link. It also operates the Hangzhou line 1 through a joint venture with Hangzhou Metro Group Company, the first metro line to serve Hangzhou. Additionally, it is involved in the Beijing Metro Line 4 and Shenzhen Metro Longhua Line operations. In addition to its railway operations, MTR also develops residential and commercial properties above and adjacent to existing railway stations as well as along new line extensions, and engages in related commercial activities, including rental of retail and advertising space and provision of ATM banking facilities and personal telecommunication services through subsidiary TraxComm Limited. The company also provides overseas consulting services. MTR subsidiary Octopus Cards Limited operates a smart card network that is used for a variety of purposes, including as a form of payment at retailers and to pay transit fares; as an entrance card to offices, warehouses and car parks; as an elevator floor access card for work or home; and as a time clock punch card. MTR also offers the Smartphone apps Next Tran and MTR Tourist to provide commuters and visitors real time information about train schedules and navigational assistance.

FINANCIAL DATA: *Note: Data for latest year may not have been available at press time.*

In U.S. $	2015	2014	2013	2012	2011	2010
Revenue	5,377,444,000	5,178,212,000	4,991,361,000	4,608,630,000	4,309,976,000	3,806,417,000
R&D Expense				41,651,620	15,861,150	27,853,720
Operating Income	1,623,382,000	1,579,925,000	1,453,809,000	1,159,540,000	1,702,817,000	1,519,833,000
Operating Margin %	30.18%	30.51%	29.12%	25.16%	39.50%	39.92%
SGA Expense	380,796,400	392,402,100	362,098,300	421,416,400	393,691,700	358,358,700
Net Income	1,675,607,000	2,012,431,000	1,679,605,000	1,744,984,000	1,897,663,000	1,555,037,000
Operating Cash Flow	1,905,014,000	2,068,912,000	1,903,853,000	1,745,887,000	1,421,571,000	1,406,484,000
Capital Expenditure	2,891,113,000	1,690,437,000	1,722,288,000	1,434,595,000	1,295,069,000	251,844,000
EBITDA	2,596,456,000	2,875,380,000	2,506,964,000	2,534,044,000	2,810,647,000	2,465,441,000
Return on Assets %	5.55%	7.04%	6.16%	6.68%	7.75%	6.73%
Return on Equity %	7.79%	9.88%	8.77%	9.90%	11.96%	10.78%
Debt to Equity	0.02	0.12	0.16	0.16	0.18	0.27

CONTACT INFORMATION:

Phone: 852 28818888   Fax:
Toll-Free:
Address: 33 Wai Yip St., Kowloon Bay, Telford Plz., Kowloon, Hong Kong

STOCK TICKER/OTHER:

Stock Ticker: MTRJY
Employees: 16,624
Parent Company:

Exchange: PINX
Fiscal Year Ends: 12/31

SALARIES/BONUSES:

Top Exec. Salary: $ Bonus: $
Second Exec. Salary: $ Bonus: $

OTHER THOUGHTS:

Estimated Female Officers or Directors: 5
Hot Spot for Advancement for Women/Minorities: Y

Sales, profits and employees may be estimates. Financial information, benefits and other data can change quickly and may vary from those stated here.

National Express Group plc

www.nationalexpressgroup.com

NAIC Code: 485210

TYPES OF BUSINESS:

Interurban and Rural Bus Transportation
Bus Service
Airport Shuttles
Coach Service
School Bus Operations

BRANDS/DIVISIONS/AFFILIATES:

National Express Coach
Eurolines
Airlink
King's Ferry
Stock Transportation
Durham School Services
Asla
Bahrain Public Transport Company

CONTACTS: Note: Officers with more than one job title may be intentionally listed here more than once.

Dean Finch, CEO
Matthew Ashley, Group Dir.-Finance
Michal Hampson, General Counsel
Jorge Cosmen, Deputy Chmn.
Andrew Chivers, Managing Dir.-U.K. Rail
Peter Coates, Managing Dir.-U.K. Bus
David Duke, Managing Dir.-North America
John Armitt, Chmn.
Javier Carbajo, CEO-Spain

GROWTH PLANS/SPECIAL FEATURES:

National Express Group plc is a transportation provider delivering public transport services to the general public in the U.K., North America, Morocco, Continental Europe and Spain. The company serves passengers throughout the world using over 27,000 vehicles. In the U.K., the firm's services include buses, trains, light rail, coach service and airport transfers. The U.K. Bus division operates high frequency urban bus services in the West Midlands, London and Dundee, among other locations. The U.K. Rail division operates a range of inter-city, commuter and rural passenger train services including National Express East Coast, National Express East Anglia, Stansted Express and the London commuter service c2c. The firm is the only national scheduled coach service provider in the U.K., providing coach services to nearly 1,000 destinations under the National Express Coach brand. The company's other coach brands include Eurolines, with coach services from the U.K. to destinations in Europe; Airlink, a coach/bus service for airlines; and King's Ferry, a coach service in London and south England. The company's North American division includes Stock Transportation, a Canadian company, and Durham School Services, located in the U.S. Together, these firms serve school districts in 32 states and four Canadian provinces. In Spain, National Express is the leading operator of coach and bus services through the Alsa and Continental Auto brands. The Alsa brand offers both long-distance coaching from Spain to other European destinations as well as regional urban bus operations. In addition, the Bahrain Public Transport Company, a bus company in which National Express holds a 50% share, began operating a 10-year concession in Bahrain. Approximately 66% of the company's operating profit comes from business outside of the U.K., primarily from North America, Spain and Morocco.

FINANCIAL DATA: Note: Data for latest year may not have been available at press time.

In U.S. $	2015	2014	2013	2012	2011	2010
Revenue	2,506,495,000	2,438,082,000	2,469,286,000	2,390,819,000	2,921,938,000	2,775,580,000
R&D Expense						
Operating Income	219,080,100	149,099,800	153,930,500	153,538,800	227,697,000	112,151,200
Operating Margin %	8.74%	6.11%	6.23%	6.42%	7.79%	4.04%
SGA Expense						
Net Income	139,699,400	77,161,100	74,158,210	78,336,140	132,127,000	80,163,980
Operating Cash Flow	330,186,800	303,160,900	365,699,200	203,935,100	245,975,500	221,952,400
Capital Expenditure	161,764,100	82,514,060	122,596,100	139,307,800	141,527,300	67,760,760
EBITDA	396,903,100	329,272,900	358,779,500	2,341,075,000	438,160,100	317,391,900
Return on Assets %	4.44%	2.56%	2.42%	2.48%	4.18%	2.52%
Return on Equity %	13.05%	6.91%	6.38%	6.48%	10.70%	6.93%
Debt to Equity	0.92	0.90	0.84	0.88	0.75	0.72

CONTACT INFORMATION:

Phone: 44 8450130130   Fax: 44 1216666498
Toll-Free:
Address: National Express House, Mill Ln., Birmingham, B5 6DD United Kingdom

STOCK TICKER/OTHER:

Stock Ticker: NXPGF   Exchange: GREY
Employees: 42,622   Fiscal Year Ends: 12/31
Parent Company:

SALARIES/BONUSES:

Top Exec. Salary: $ Bonus: $
Second Exec. Salary: $ Bonus: $

OTHER THOUGHTS:

Estimated Female Officers or Directors: 1
Hot Spot for Advancement for Women/Minorities:

Sales, profits and employees may be estimates. Financial information, benefits and other data can change quickly and may vary from those stated here.

NAV Canada

www.navcanada.ca

NAIC Code: 488111

TYPES OF BUSINESS:
Air Traffic Control Service
Navigation Technology Solutions

BRANDS/DIVISIONS/AFFILIATES:
NAVCANatm

CONTACTS: *Note: Officers with more than one job title may be intentionally listed here more than once.*

Neil R. Wilson, CEO
Rob Thurgur, VP-Oper.
John W. Crichton, Pres.
Brian K. Aitken, CFO
Raymond G. Bohn, Exec. VP-Human Resources
Claudio Silvestri, CIO
Sidney Koslow, CTO
Kim Troutman, VP-Eng.
Neil R. Wilson, General Counsel
Larry Lachance, VP-Oper.
John Morris, Dir.-Communications
Brian K. Aitken, VP-Finance
Charles Lapointe, VP-Tech. Oper.
John F. David, VP-Safety & Quality
Rudy Kellar, Exec. VP-Service Delivery

GROWTH PLANS/SPECIAL FEATURES:

NAV Canada owns and operates Canada's civil air navigation service (ANS), directing the air traffic throughout Canada and oceanic airspace assigned to the country under international agreements. The company, a non-share capital private firm, was created by the nation's airlines, air controllers and business jet operators. The firm collects fees from airlines and other aircraft owners for its services, which include air traffic control, flight information, weather briefings, aeronautical information, airport advisory services and electronic aids to navigation. Annually, the company manages 12 million aircraft movements through its infrastructure of seven control centers. Additionally, the company provides other ANS enterprises with its proprietary NAVCANatm air traffic management technology solutions. In the place of shareholders, the company is managed by four members: the government of Canada, the Air Transport Association of Canada (representing air carriers), the Canadian Business Aviation Association (representing business and general aviation) and the NAV Canada Bargaining Agents Association (representing employees). The company also has Flight Information Centres (FIC) in Halifax, Quebec City, London, North Bay, Winnipeg, Edmonton, Whitehorse and Kamloops.

FINANCIAL DATA: *Note: Data for latest year may not have been available at press time.*

In U.S. $	2015	2014	2013	2012	2011	2010
Revenue	999,767,332	957,207,577	965,300,658	952,193,374	923,550,159	1,220,000,000
R&D Expense						
Operating Income						
Operating Margin %						
SGA Expense						
Net Income						
Operating Cash Flow						
Capital Expenditure						
EBITDA						
Return on Assets %						
Return on Equity %						
Debt to Equity						

CONTACT INFORMATION:
Phone: 613-563-7835   Fax: 613-563-3411
Toll-Free: 800-876-4693
Address: 77 Metcalfe St., Ottawa, ON K1P 5L6 Canada

STOCK TICKER/OTHER:
Stock Ticker: Nonprofit
Employees: 4,600
Parent Company:

Exchange:
Fiscal Year Ends: 08/31

SALARIES/BONUSES:
Top Exec. Salary: $ Bonus: $
Second Exec. Salary: $ Bonus: $

OTHER THOUGHTS:
Estimated Female Officers or Directors: 1
Hot Spot for Advancement for Women/Minorities:

NBCUniversal LLC

www.nbcuni.com

NAIC Code: 515120

TYPES OF BUSINESS:

Television Broadcasting
Online News & Information
TV & Movie Production
Radio Broadcasting
Interactive Online Content
Cable Television Programming
Theme Parks
Film, TV & Home Video Distribution

BRANDS/DIVISIONS/AFFILIATES:

Universal Studios Japan
Comcast Corp
Hulu LLC
Universal Pictures
Universal Orlando Resort
NBC Sports Network
CNBC International
Bravo Media

CONTACTS: *Note: Officers with more than one job title may be intentionally listed here more than once.*

Stephen B. Burke, CEO
Anand Kini, CFO
Linda Yaccarino, Chairman- Advertising, Sales & Client Partnerships
Craig Robinson, Chief Diversity Officer
Jeff Shell, Chmn.-Universal Filmed Entertainment
Kimberley D. Harris, General Counsel
Maggie McLean Suniewick, Sr. VP-Strategic Integration
Cameron Blanchard, Exec. VP-Comm.
Patricia Fili-Krushel, Chmn.-NBCUniversal News Group
Robert Greenblatt, Chmn., NBC Entertainment
Bonnie Hammer, Chmn., NBCUniversal Cable Entertainment Group
Ted Harbert, Chmn., NBC Broadcasting
Kevin MacLellan, Chmn., NBCUniversal Int'l
Matt Bond, Exec. VP-Content Dist.

GROWTH PLANS/SPECIAL FEATURES:

NBCUniversal LLC is one of the world's largest entertainment and media companies in the development, production and marketing of news, entertainment and information to a global audience. The company is a product of a 2004 merger of Vivendi Universal Entertainment and NBC (National Broadcasting Company). The firm is a wholly owned subsidiary of Comcast Corp. The firm operates in eight divisions: cable, broadcast, digital, film, parks, local media, TV studios production and international. The cable division includes Bravo Media, Golf Channel, NBC Sports Network, Sprout, Universal HD, Chiller, E!, MSNBC, NBCUniversal International Television, SYFY, USA Network, CLOO, Esquire Network, CNBC, The Weather Channel Company and Oxygen Media. The broadcast division includes NBC Entertainment, NBC News, NBC Sports, Telemundo, NBC Entertainment and NBC Olympics. The digital division consists of Fandango, GolfNow, Hulu LLC and Seeso. The film division includes Focus Features, Universal Pictures, Universal Pictures International and Universal Pictures Home Entertainment. The parks division includes Universal Orlando Resort, Universal Studios Japan, Universal Studios Singapore and Universal Studios Hollywood. The local media division consists of Cozi TV, NBC Sports Regional Networks, TeleXitos and NBCUniversal owned television stations. The international division includes CNBC International, NBCUniversal International Television. The TV studios production division consists of Universal Cable Productions, Telemundo Studios and Universal Television.

NBC Universal offers its employees medical, dental, vision and prescription drug coverage; a 401(k) plan; health club discounts; same-sex domestic partner benefits; life insurance; and flexible spending accounts.

FINANCIAL DATA: *Note: Data for latest year may not have been available at press time.*

In U.S. $	2015	2014	2013	2012	2011	2010
Revenue	26,000,000,000	25,400,000,000	23,740,000,000	22,349,100,000	21,124,000,000	20,374,000,000
R&D Expense						
Operating Income						
Operating Margin %						
SGA Expense						
Net Income	5,591,000,000	5,588,000,000	4,732,000,000	3,989,076,000	3,769,000,000	3,684,000,000
Operating Cash Flow						
Capital Expenditure						
EBITDA						
Return on Assets %						
Return on Equity %						
Debt to Equity						

CONTACT INFORMATION:

Phone: 212-664-4444   Fax: 212-664-4085
Toll-Free:
Address: 30 Rockefeller Plz., New York, NY 10112 United States

STOCK TICKER/OTHER:

Stock Ticker: Subsidiary   Exchange:
Employees: 40,000   Fiscal Year Ends: 12/31
Parent Company: Comcast Corp

SALARIES/BONUSES:

Top Exec. Salary: $ Bonus: $
Second Exec. Salary: $ Bonus: $

OTHER THOUGHTS:

Estimated Female Officers or Directors: 12
Hot Spot for Advancement for Women/Minorities: Y

NetJets Inc

NAIC Code: 481211

www.netjets.com

TYPES OF BUSINESS:
Charter Aircraft
Fractional Aircraft Ownership

BRANDS/DIVISIONS/AFFILIATES:
Berkshire Hathaway Inc
NetJets Aviation Inc
Marquis Jet Partners Inc
NetJets Executive Jet Management
NetJets Europe
NetJets China
NetJets Share

CONTACTS: *Note: Officers with more than one job title may be intentionally listed here more than once.*
Adam Johnson, CEO
Bill Noe, Pres.
Peter S. Richards, CFO
Chuck Suma, Sr. VP-Aircraft Mgmt.
Adam Johnson, Chmn.

GROWTH PLANS/SPECIAL FEATURES:
NetJets, Inc., owned by Berkshire Hathaway, Inc., is a leading provider of fractional aircraft ownership. NetJets manages over 700 aircraft, of which individuals and businesses can buy a portion based on the number of actual flight hours they need. Owners are guaranteed use of an aircraft, within as little as four hours' notice, 24-hours-a-day, every day of the year. The company provides light, midsize and large cabin aircraft; flight crew management; ground support; and service in the U.S., Europe and China. The firm's NetJets Share interest ownership plan is for people who fly 50 or more hours per year and want the advantages of owning an asset. Share sizes start at 50 annual flight hours and increase in 25-hour increments, and there are additional fees involved such as a one-time acquisition fee, monthly management fees and occupied hourly fee. For clients who want to buy fewer hours, NetJets offers the Marquis Jet Card, a pre-pay card for 25 hours of flight time. The company operates 14 different kinds of planes, including the Cessna Citation, Hawker, Gulfstream, Dassault Falcon, Bombardier and Embraer Phenom models. NetJets operates through several subsidiaries: NetJets Aviation, Inc., which operates most the firm's U.S. aircraft; NetJets Europe; NetJets China; Marquis Jet Partners, Inc., a private jet card provider; and NetJets Executive Jet Management, which operates aircraft charter services out of Cincinnati.

NetJets offers pilots medical, dental and vision benefits; a 401(k) plan; meal allowances; and paid hotel and travel expenses.

FINANCIAL DATA: *Note: Data for latest year may not have been available at press time.*

In U.S. $	2015	2014	2013	2012	2011	2010
Revenue	4,398,750,000	4,416,000,000	4,128,000,000	2,818,000,000	3,475,000,000	3,210,000,000
R&D Expense						
Operating Income						
Operating Margin %						
SGA Expense						
Net Income	286,021,000	332,021,000	310,300,000	259,000,000	227,000,000	205,000,000
Operating Cash Flow						
Capital Expenditure						
EBITDA						
Return on Assets %						
Return on Equity %						
Debt to Equity						

CONTACT INFORMATION:
Phone: 614-239-5500 Fax:
Toll-Free: 877-356-5823
Address: 4111 Bridgeway Ave., Columbus, OH 43219 United States

STOCK TICKER/OTHER:
Stock Ticker: Subsidiary   Exchange:
Employees: 6,200   Fiscal Year Ends: 12/31
Parent Company: Berkshire Hathaway Inc

SALARIES/BONUSES:
Top Exec. Salary: $ Bonus: $
Second Exec. Salary: $ Bonus: $

OTHER THOUGHTS:
Estimated Female Officers or Directors:
Hot Spot for Advancement for Women/Minorities:

NH Hotel Group SA

NAIC Code: 721110

TYPES OF BUSINESS:

Hotels
Golf Courses
Restaurants

BRANDS/DIVISIONS/AFFILIATES:

NH Hotels
Hesperia
nhow
NH Collection

CONTACTS: Note: Officers with more than one job title may be intentionally listed here more than once.

Frederico Gonzalez Tejera, CEO
Ramon Aragones Marin, COO
Roberto Chollet Ibarra, CFO
Isidoro Martinez de la Escalera, CMO
Fernando Cordova, Head-Human Resources
Inigo Capell Arrieta, Chief Resources Officer

GROWTH PLANS/SPECIAL FEATURES:

NH Hotel Group SA, based in Spain, is a hotel operator with nearly 400 hotels with 60,000 rooms in 29 countries across Europe, the Americas and Africa, ranging from budget hotels to four-star resorts. In Europe, NH has hotels in Spain, Andorra, Germany, Italy, Luxembourg, Switzerland, Belgium, Austria, the U.K., France, Portugal, Poland, the Czech Republic, Romania and Hungary. In the Americas, the firm has hotels in Mexico, the U.S., Argentina, Colombia, Venezuela, Chile, Uruguay and the Dominican Republic. In South Africa, the company has two hotels, one in Plettenberg Bay and the other in Cape Town. The firm's hotel brands include NH Hotels, a three to four star urban chain; Hesperia, a chain of resorts located in privileged surroundings; nhow, unconventional and cosmopolitan hotels, each with a unique personality in major international cities; and NH Collection, premium hotels located in major capitals across Europe and America. In November 2015, the firm signed with AXA Investment Mangers-Real Assets operate a new hotel development under its nhow brand, to be located in the Shoreditch district of London and operational in 2019.

FINANCIAL DATA: Note: Data for latest year may not have been available at press time.

In U.S. $	2015	2014	2013	2012	2011	2010
Revenue	1,555,343,000	1,408,828,000	1,424,124,000	1,452,980,000	1,503,769,000	1,448,356,000
R&D Expense						
Operating Income	11,659,700	-29,757,090	-37,099,760	-442,431,400	27,349,450	10,343,460
Operating Margin %	.74%	-2.11%	-2.60%	-30.44%	1.81%	.71%
SGA Expense						
Net Income	1,059,767	-10,789,740	-44,987,010	-330,030,500	11,864,200	-53,602,980
Operating Cash Flow	102,020,100	36,281,780	52,290,140	108,752,700	149,829,400	113,060,700
Capital Expenditure	198,941,400	124,157,700	44,741,840	59,924,300	76,325,840	79,831,660
EBITDA	192,527,400	141,979,400	83,066,320	-316,625,200	226,192,500	150,301,700
Return on Assets %	.03%	-.35%	-1.44%	-9.90%	.19%	-1.20%
Return on Equity %	.08%	-.90%	-4.31%	-29.50%	.54%	-3.51%
Debt to Equity	0.74	0.66	0.77	0.21	0.19	0.57

CONTACT INFORMATION:

Phone: 34 914519718   Fax:
Toll-Free: 800-232-9860
Address: Santa Engracia 120, Edifico Central, Madrid, 28003 Spain

STOCK TICKER/OTHER:

Stock Ticker: NHHEY   Exchange: PINX
Employees: 13,795   Fiscal Year Ends: 12/31
Parent Company:

SALARIES/BONUSES:

Top Exec. Salary: $ Bonus: $
Second Exec. Salary: $ Bonus: $

OTHER THOUGHTS:

Estimated Female Officers or Directors:
Hot Spot for Advancement for Women/Minorities: Y

Sales, profits and employees may be estimates. Financial information, benefits and other data can change quickly and may vary from those stated here.

Nippon Yusen Kabushiki Kaisha (NYK)

www.nyk.com

NAIC Code: 483111

TYPES OF BUSINESS:

Deep Sea Shipping
Inland Shipping
Cruise Ships
Logistics Services
Research & Development
Maritime Security Systems
Wind Power Technology
Real Estate

BRANDS/DIVISIONS/AFFILIATES:

NYK Cruises
Yusen Real Estate Corporation
Monohakobi Technology Institute Co Ltd
NYK Line (Vietnam) Co Ltd
Nippon Cargo Airlines

CONTACTS: Note: Officers with more than one job title may be intentionally listed here more than once.

Yasumi Kudo, Pres.
Kenji Mizushima, CFO
Alexander Larin, CEO-Rolf Logistics Bus.
Koichi Chikaraishi, CEO-Automobile Transportation Headquarters
Koji Miyahara, Chmn.

GROWTH PLANS/SPECIAL FEATURES:

Nippon Yusen Kabushiki Kaisha (NYK), which means the Mail Shipping Corporation of Japan, is one of the world's premier ocean freight companies. In conjunction with several partners, the NYK Line runs one of the world's largest cargo fleets, with 832 vessels. These vessels include bulk carrier ships, wood chip carries car carriers, container ships, tankers, liquefied natural gas (LNG) carriers and other ships, as well as three cruise ships. The company operates through five primary business units: global logistics, bulk shipping, cruise, real estate and others. The global logistics segment is comprised of three divisions: liner trade, air cargo transportation and logistics. The liner trade business consists of container transport services linking Asia, Europe, the Americas, Australia and Africa, and conventional cargo transport, moving heavy-lift cargo and steel between Asia, the Middle East, Europe and the South Pacific. Its air cargo transportation business, operated by Nippon Cargo Airlines, provides air cargo services between Japan and North America, Europe and Asia using a fleet of Boeing 747s. NYK's logistics business provides overland transport, warehousing, delivery and ocean freight forwarding and includes over 447 logistics centers and warehouses in 38 countries. The bulk shipping division transports dry bulk such as iron ore, coal, grain, steel, wood and cement; and cars. Its tanker fleet specializes in the overseas transport of crude oil, LNG, liquefied petroleum gas (LPG) and various other chemicals. The cruise segment through subsidiary, NYK Cruises operates luxury cruise ship Asuka II. The real estate segment manages commercial and residential buildings through Yusen Real Estate Corporation. The others segment consists of firm's technology development business Monohakobi Technology Institute Co., Ltd. In September 2015, the firm acquired NYK Line (Vietnam) Co. Ltd.

FINANCIAL DATA: Note: Data for latest year may not have been available at press time.

In U.S. $	2015	2014	2013	2012	2011	2010
Revenue	23,885,870,000	22,249,130,000	18,866,490,000	17,978,590,000	19,185,400,000	
R&D Expense						
Operating Income	658,273,200	447,471,000	173,379,500	-239,910,900	1,216,719,000	
Operating Margin %	2.75%	2.01%	.91%	-1.33%	6.34%	
SGA Expense						
Net Income	519,919,700	371,482,000	216,162,500	-697,237,400	815,860,200	
Operating Cash Flow	1,356,962,000	1,357,698,000	934,333,800	296,726,100	1,736,231,000	
Capital Expenditure	1,889,343,000	2,326,959,000	3,053,583,000	3,075,840,000	2,770,352,000	
EBITDA	2,038,268,000	1,770,660,000	1,467,599,000	856,435,400	2,289,427,000	
Return on Assets %	1.85%	1.32%	.83%	-3.42%	3.62%	
Return on Equity %	6.21%	4.82%	3.07%	-11.52%	11.67%	
Debt to Equity	1.21	1.54	1.77	1.58	1.28	

CONTACT INFORMATION:

Phone: 81 332845151   Fax:
Toll-Free:
Address: 3-2, Marunouchi 2-Chome, Chiyoda-ku, Tokyo, 100-0005 Japan

STOCK TICKER/OTHER:

Stock Ticker: NYUKF
Employees: 1,619
Parent Company:

Exchange: PINX
Fiscal Year Ends: 03/31

SALARIES/BONUSES:

Top Exec. Salary: $ Bonus: $
Second Exec. Salary: $ Bonus: $

OTHER THOUGHTS:

Estimated Female Officers or Directors:
Hot Spot for Advancement for Women/Minorities:

Norwegian Air Shuttle ASA
NAIC Code: 481111

www.norwegian.com

TYPES OF BUSINESS:
Airline

BRANDS/DIVISIONS/AFFILIATES:
Norwegian Group (The)
Norwegian Long Haul ASA
Norwegian Air Shuttle Sweden AB
Call Norwegian AS
Norwegian Finans Holding ASA
NAS Asset Management Norway AS
Norwegian Reward
Bank Norwegian AS

CONTACTS: Note: Officers with more than one job title may be intentionally listed here more than once.
Bjorn Kjos, CEO
Frode E. Foss, CFO
Gunnar Martinsen, Chief Human Resources Officer
Dag Skage, CIO
Frode Berg, Chief Legal Officer
Anne-Sissel Skanvik, Chief Comm. Officer
Asgeir Nyseth, CEO-Norwegian Longhaul
Bjorn H. Kise, Chmn.

GROWTH PLANS/SPECIAL FEATURES:
Norwegian Air Shuttle ASA (Norwegian) is a low-cost airline serving passengers across Europe, North Africa, the Middle East, Southeast Asia and the U.S. As a low-cost airline, the airline is able to offer lower fares by providing fewer comforts. The airline currently operates 424 routes to 130 destinations. Norwegian's fleet consists of more than 100 jet aircraft and has 250 undelivered aircraft on firm order. Of these currently operated aircraft, 96 are Boeing 737-800s with a capacity of 186/189 passengers, for short-haul operations; and eight Boeing 787-8 Dreamliners with a capacity of 291 passengers for long-haul operations. The firm has one of the younger, more modern fleets in commercial operation with an average fleet age of just 3.6 years. The airline has 30 more Boeing 787-9 Dreamliners on order. It also has orders placed for advanced, high-efficiency aircraft including 100 Boeing 737 MAX and 100 Airbus A320 NEO. The firm has a number of directly or indirectly wholly-owned subsidiaries, which together comprise The Norwegian Group. Norwegian Long Haul ASA operates the long haul operations of the group. Norwegian Air Shuttle Sweden AB provides technical services as well as supplying crew in Finland and Sweden. Call Norwegian AS provides airport Wi-Fi, mobile broadband and mobile and content services. Norwegian Finans Holding ASA holds a 20% interest in Bank Norwegian AS, the operator of the airline's loyalty program Norwegian Reward. NAS Asset Management Norway AS is a Special Purpose Vehicle established to oversee aircraft financing. The company's strategy includes a focus on nonstop flights from Europe to the U.S., and by the end of 2016 it hoped to have as many as 37 nonstop routes into the U.S. Long term,k it will increase service into such areas as India, Africa and Latin America.

FINANCIAL DATA: Note: Data for latest year may not have been available at press time.

In U.S. $	2015	2014	2013	2012	2011	2010
Revenue	2,728,287,000	2,371,105,000	1,882,224,000	1,558,227,000	1,277,618,000	1,020,075,000
R&D Expense						
Operating Income	42,201,100	-171,163,100	117,664,100	48,957,270	50,471,920	25,503,160
Operating Margin %	1.54%	-7.21%	6.25%	3.14%	3.95%	2.50%
SGA Expense	74,298,440	56,924,730	41,181,910			
Net Income	29,869,550	-129,811,400	39,020,500	55,412,150	14,819,380	20,736,080
Operating Cash Flow	285,976,900	34,838,910	288,664,400	245,323,000	81,783,660	97,638,360
Capital Expenditure	631,897,300	608,455,400	248,262,300	335,442,600	265,686,600	223,217,500
EBITDA	202,850,800	-80,379,570	181,956,200	95,705,080	86,141,570	48,159,300
Return on Assets %	.90%	-5.71%	2.41%	4.36%	1.56%	2.93%
Return on Equity %	9.70%	-44.04%	12.43%	20.91%	6.52%	10.05%
Debt to Equity	5.57	4.72	2.08	1.72	1.38	1.09

CONTACT INFORMATION:
Phone: 47-67-59-30-00   Fax: 47-67-59-30-01
Toll-Free: 800-357-4159
Address: Oksenoyveien 3, Lysaker, 1366 Norway

STOCK TICKER/OTHER:
Stock Ticker: NWARF   Exchange: PINX
Employees: 4,314   Fiscal Year Ends:
Parent Company:

SALARIES/BONUSES:
Top Exec. Salary: $ Bonus: $
Second Exec. Salary: $ Bonus: $

OTHER THOUGHTS:
Estimated Female Officers or Directors: 4
Hot Spot for Advancement for Women/Minorities: Y

Norwegian Cruise Line Holdings Ltd (NCL)

www.ncl.com

NAIC Code: 483112

TYPES OF BUSINESS:

Cruise Lines
Luxury Cruise Lines

BRANDS/DIVISIONS/AFFILIATES:

Regent Seven Seas
Oceania Cruises
Prestige Cruises International

CONTACTS: Note: Officers with more than one job title may be intentionally listed here more than once.

Daniel Farkas, Assistant Secretary
Frank Del Rio, CEO
Wendy Beck, CFO
Faye Ashby, Chief Accounting Officer
Jason Montague, COO, Divisional
Walter Revell, Director
Harry Sommer, Executive VP,Divisional
T. Lindsay, Executive VP,Divisional
Andrew Stuart, President, Divisional
Robert Binder, Vice Chairman, Divisional

GROWTH PLANS/SPECIAL FEATURES:

Norwegian Cruise Line Holdings Ltd. (NCLH) is one of the largest cruise line operators in the world. It offers a wide variety of cruises ranging in length from one day to three weeks and itineraries originating from 19 ports (of which 13 are in North America). In addition to the traditional cruise markets in the Caribbean and Mexico, Norwegian sails to destinations in Europe, including the Mediterranean and the Baltic, Bermuda, Alaska and Hawaii. The firm owns Prestige Cruises International, which in turn owns Oceania Cruises and Regent Seven Seas Cruises. These two brands operate a total of eight ships with over 6,400 berths. Oceania operates a fleet of five mid-size ships, providing customers with an upscale and sophisticated experience including personalized service and elegant accommodations. Oceania offers destination-oriented cruises to approximately 330 ports around the globe. Regent offers a luxury all-inclusive cruise vacation experience, including free air transportation, a pre-cruise hotel night stay, premium wines and top shelf liquors, gratuities and unlimited shore excursions. The brand operates three all-suite ships, with itineraries to approximately 300 ports worldwide. Overall, the company has a combined fleet of 22 ships, which offer itineraries to more than 520 destinations worldwide. By 2019, the firm's fleet of major ships will total 27. In January 2015, NCLH expanded its sales presence in Sao Paulo, Brazil, with the establishment of a sales, marketing and reservations center. In October of same year, NCLH announced that it will introduce its first purpose-built ship customized for the China market by 2017.

FINANCIAL DATA: Note: Data for latest year may not have been available at press time.

In U.S. $	2015	2014	2013	2012	2011	2010
Revenue	4,345,048,000	3,125,881,000	2,570,294,000	2,276,246,000	2,219,324,000	2,012,128,000
R&D Expense						
Operating Income	702,486,000	502,941,000	395,887,000	357,093,000	316,112,000	230,241,000
Operating Margin %	16.16%	16.08%	15.40%	15.68%	14.24%	11.44%
SGA Expense	554,999,000	403,169,000	301,155,000	251,183,000	251,351,000	264,398,000
Net Income	427,137,000	338,352,000	101,714,000	168,556,000	126,859,000	22,617,000
Operating Cash Flow	1,041,178,000	635,601,000	475,281,000	398,594,000	356,990,000	418,946,000
Capital Expenditure	1,122,734,000	1,051,974,000	894,851,000	303,840,000	184,797,000	977,466,000
EBITDA	1,152,821,000	807,818,000	640,998,000	574,623,000	527,161,000	422,154,000
Return on Assets %	3.58%	3.71%	1.61%	2.93%	2.28%	.43%
Return on Equity %	11.70%	11.04%	4.39%	8.72%	7.09%	1.31%
Debt to Equity	1.52	1.59	1.08	1.36	1.53	1.80

CONTACT INFORMATION:

Phone: 305-436-4000   Fax: 305-436-4140
Toll-Free:
Address: 7665 Corporate Center Dr., Miami, FL 33126 United States

STOCK TICKER/OTHER:

Stock Ticker: NCLH   Exchange: NAS
Employees: 2,700   Fiscal Year Ends: 12/31
Parent Company:

SALARIES/BONUSES:

Top Exec. Salary: Bonus: $
$1,837,500
Second Exec. Salary: Bonus: $757,500
$891,027

OTHER THOUGHTS:

Estimated Female Officers or Directors: 4

Hot Spot for Advancement for Women/Minorities: Y

Sales, profits and employees may be estimates. Financial information, benefits and other data can change quickly and may vary from those stated here.

Oakwood Worldwide

www.oakwood.com

NAIC Code: 721110

TYPES OF BUSINESS:

Rental Housing
Temporary Housing
Corporate Apartments

BRANDS/DIVISIONS/AFFILIATES:

Oakwood Corporate Housing
Oakwood Premier
Oakwood Residence
Oakwood Apartment
ExecuStay
Oakwood Asia Pacific Pte Ltd
Personal Property Protection
Insurance Housing Solutions

CONTACTS: Note: Officers with more than one job title may be intentionally listed here more than once.

Howard Ruby, CEO
Ric Villarreal, Pres.
Chris Brenk, CFO
Patricia Hintze, VP-Global Sales
Marina Lubinsky, CIO
Howard Ruby, Chmn.

GROWTH PLANS/SPECIAL FEATURES:

Oakwood Worldwide offers temporary housing, corporate housing and multifamily property management. The firm provides approximately 25,000 furnished and unfurnished accommodations throughout the U.S., the U.K. and the Asia Pacific region through its Oakwood Corporate Housing, Oakwood Premier, Oakwood Residence and Oakwood Apartment brands. Each apartment is equipped with fine furnishings, housewares, telephone service and cable television service. Oakwood services for temporary housing include weekly housekeeping, an on-call concierge and maintenance services. These services are available in most areas nationwide on a day-by-day pay schedule, and are often used by production crews for the footage of television shows or movies. The company also manages traditional long-term apartment residences through its apartment communities in the U.S., with both furnished and unfurnished apartments. Oakwood has apartments of all styles, residing in differing natural environments, and will custom fit its models to its clients. The company's ExecuStay subsidiary offer temporary housing for a stay of at least a month in over 300 cities across the U.S., including both urban and suburban locations. Its Insurance Housing Solutions subsidiary is a resource for insurance professionals and displaced policyholders seeking emergency housing assistance. In 2014, the firm launched Personal Property Protection, a new travel insurance service tailored to meet the needs of extended stay business travelers by protecting their personal belongings and reducing their financial responsibility for accidental damage to their accommodations; it also formed a corporate and serviced apartment joint venture with Mapletree Group, with Mapletree acquiring a 40% stake in Oakwood Asia Pacific Pte. Ltd. Oakwood Asia will focus on acquiring and developing within Asia, Europe and North America.

Oakwood offers its employees medical, dental, vision, prescription, life, disability and AD&D insurance; a 401(k) plan; educational reimbursement; an employee assistance program; corporate discounts and bonus opportunities; flexible spending accounts; and

FINANCIAL DATA: Note: Data for latest year may not have been available at press time.

In U.S. $	2015	2014	2013	2012	2011	2010
Revenue	860,000,000	840,000,000	821,000,000	750,000,000		
R&D Expense						
Operating Income						
Operating Margin %						
SGA Expense						
Net Income						
Operating Cash Flow						
Capital Expenditure						
EBITDA						
Return on Assets %						
Return on Equity %						
Debt to Equity						

CONTACT INFORMATION:

Phone: 310-478-1021   Fax: 310-444-2210
Toll-Free: 877-902-0832
Address: 2222 Corinth Ave., Los Angeles, CA 90064 United States

STOCK TICKER/OTHER:

Stock Ticker: Private   Exchange:
Employees: 1,064   Fiscal Year Ends:
Parent Company:

SALARIES/BONUSES:

Top Exec. Salary: $ Bonus: $
Second Exec. Salary: $ Bonus: $

OTHER THOUGHTS:

Estimated Female Officers or Directors: 3
Hot Spot for Advancement for Women/Minorities: Y

Sales, profits and employees may be estimates. Financial information, benefits and other data can change quickly and may vary from those stated here.

Oberoi Group (EIH Ltd)

www.oberoihotels.com

NAIC Code: 721110

TYPES OF BUSINESS:

Luxury Hotels
Commercial Hotels
Cruise Ships
Travel Agency
Charter Aircraft
Tour Services
In-flight Catering
Car Rental

BRANDS/DIVISIONS/AFFILIATES:

EIH Ltd
Oberoi
Trident
Oberoi Philae (The)
Oberoi Zahra (The)
Maidens Hotel
Clarke's Hotel
Connections

CONTACTS: *Note: Officers with more than one job title may be intentionally listed here more than once.*

Kapil Chopra, Pres.
Rai Bahadur Mohan Singh Oberoi, Chmn.

GROWTH PLANS/SPECIAL FEATURES:

Oberoi Group, also known as EIH, Ltd., owns or manages 30 Oberoi and Trident brand luxury hotels and two small cruise ships in six countries. Additionally, the group operates airport restaurants, travel and tour services, in-flight catering, car rentals, project management and corporate air charters. Oberoi has eleven hotels in India, two hotels in Indonesia, two hotels and a Nile river boat in Egypt (The Oberoi Philae and The Oberoi Zahra), one hotel in Mauritius, one hotel in Saudi Arabia and one hotel in the UAE. The company also operates two heritage hotels, the Maidens Hotel and the Clarke's Hotel, which are located in historic colonial areas. The firm offers a member program called Connections, which rewards points for staying at the hotels. These points can be redeemed for a variety of things, including additional stay at the group's hotels. Many of the hotels feature spas, which can also be used by non-guests. Upcoming hotels include The Oberoi Sukhvilas in Chandigarh, India; The Oberoi in Marrakech, Morocco; and The Oberoi in Al Zorah, United Arab Emirates. The Oberoi aviation segment of the group offers an aircraft for charter, a Hawker 850 XP. The planes can be booked with as little as 48 hours notice and fly between locations within India along with a limited international service. The company has a long term agreement with Lufthansa Airlines to integrate its hotels with Lufthansa's frequent flyer program.

Oberoi maintains The Oberoi Centre of Learning and Development (OCLD), which offers a specialized two year course in hospitality management.

FINANCIAL DATA: *Note: Data for latest year may not have been available at press time.*

In U.S. $	2015	2014	2013	2012	2011	2010
Revenue	250,608,522	241,972,062	201,797,000	215,129,000	202,036,000	258,585,000
R&D Expense						
Operating Income						
Operating Margin %						
SGA Expense						
Net Income	9,487,804	16,838,324	6,571,853	23,412,000	12,482,000	11,929,000
Operating Cash Flow						
Capital Expenditure						
EBITDA						
Return on Assets %						
Return on Equity %						
Debt to Equity						

CONTACT INFORMATION:

Phone: 91-11-2389-0505   Fax: 91-11-2389-0582
Toll-Free: 800-562-3764
Address: 7 Sham Nath Marg, Delhi, 110 054 India

STOCK TICKER/OTHER:

Stock Ticker: EIHOTEL   Exchange: India
Employees: 9,851   Fiscal Year Ends: 03/31
Parent Company:

SALARIES/BONUSES:

Top Exec. Salary: $ Bonus: $
Second Exec. Salary: $ Bonus: $

OTHER THOUGHTS:

Estimated Female Officers or Directors:
Hot Spot for Advancement for Women/Minorities: Y

Sales, profits and employees may be estimates. Financial information, benefits and other data can change quickly and may vary from those stated here.

Oceania Cruises

NAIC Code: 483112

www.oceaniacruises.com

TYPES OF BUSINESS:
Cruise Line

BRANDS/DIVISIONS/AFFILIATES:
Norwegian Cruise Lines Holdings Ltd (NCL)
Regatta
Insignia
Nautica
Sirena
Marina
Riviera

GROWTH PLANS/SPECIAL FEATURES:
Oceania Cruises, owned by Norwegian Cruise Line Holdings Ltd., is a leading global upper-premium cruise line. The finest cuisine at sea, destination specialists, as well as intimate and luxurious offerings are the pillars that define Oceania's five-star rating. The company offers diverse voyages, which call on more than 330 ports across Europe, Asia, Africa, Australia, New Zealand, the South Pacific and the Americas. Oceania's 684-guest Regatta, Insignia, Nautica and Sirena all have a gross tonnage of 30,277 and 343 cabins; the Marina and Riviera are designed for 1,260 guests, 626 cabins and a gross tonnage of 66,084. Destinations include 180-day world cruises, grand voyages, transoceanic voyages, Africa, Alaska, Asia, Australia & New Zealand, Baltic & Scandinavia, Canada & New England, Caribbean, Panama Canal, Mexico, Mediterranean, South America, South Pacific and Tahiti.

CONTACTS: Note: Officers with more than one job title may be intentionally listed here more than once.
Frank J. Del Rio, CEO
Jason M. Montague, COO
James A. Rodriguez, Sr. VP-Mktg. & Sales
Robin Lindsay, Exec. VP-Vessel Oper.
Victor Gonzalez, Exec. VP-Passenger Svcs.
Frank Del Rio, CEO
Kunal S. Kamlani, Pres.
Robert J. Binder, Vice Chmn.

FINANCIAL DATA: Note: Data for latest year may not have been available at press time.

In U.S. $	2015	2014	2013	2012	2011	2010
Revenue	835,000,000	820,000,000	805,000,000	765,000,000	706,500,000	615,000,000
R&D Expense						
Operating Income						
Operating Margin %						
SGA Expense						
Net Income	51,886,687	41,617,633	12,499,733	20,478,054	15,412,239	
Operating Cash Flow						
Capital Expenditure						
EBITDA						
Return on Assets %						
Return on Equity %						
Debt to Equity						

CONTACT INFORMATION:
Phone: 305-514-2300　　Fax:
Toll-Free: 855-623-2642
Address: 7665 Corporate Center Drive, Miami, FL 33126 United States

STOCK TICKER/OTHER:
Stock Ticker: Subsidiary　　　　　　Exchange:
Employees:　　　　　　　　　　Fiscal Year Ends: 12/31
Parent Company: Norwegian Cruise Line Holdings Ltd (NCL)

SALARIES/BONUSES:
Top Exec. Salary: $　　　　Bonus: $
Second Exec. Salary: $　　　Bonus: $

OTHER THOUGHTS:
Estimated Female Officers or Directors: 1
Hot Spot for Advancement for Women/Minorities:

Omega World Travel

NAIC Code: 561510

www.owt.net

TYPES OF BUSINESS:

Travel Agencies
Corporate & Government Travel Arrangements
Program Management Services
Online Services
Training Services

BRANDS/DIVISIONS/AFFILIATES:

Cruise.com
TravTech Inc
Omega Meetings and Incentives

CONTACTS: *Note: Officers with more than one job title may be intentionally listed here more than once.*

Gloria Bohan, CEO
Goran Gligorovic, Exec. VP-Managing Dir.
Gloria Bohan, Pres.
George Fant, CIO

GROWTH PLANS/SPECIAL FEATURES:

Omega World Travel is a U.S. travel management company. It provides technology-based travel services and personalized services through locations worldwide. Omega's focus is corporate travel arrangements, but it also manages government contracts, group travel and leisure travel. The majority of the firm's revenues come from airline reservations. Omega also provides services through its web site, with features including online booking and flight tracking, airline strike updates, links to travel and security sites and other information. Omega Meetings & Incentives provides complete program and logistics management services for groups of 20-45,000. Additionally, through its Cruise.com site, the company offers discounts on travel with major cruise lines. The firm also owns TravTech, Inc., a web-based travel application developer. TavTech is also the principle technology innovator supplying Cruise.com with the latest in cruise information. Omega operates its own 24-hour-a-day service centers and myriad online services, such as comprehensive account management, benchmarking and trends analysis; travel technology solutions; global delivery systems (GDS) options; risk management services; travel management reporting; real-time quality assurance and point-of-sale through fulfillment; and an international rate specialist. The company has locations in 13 states as well as in Europe and the Middle East.

FINANCIAL DATA: *Note: Data for latest year may not have been available at press time.*

In U.S. $	2015	2014	2013	2012	2011	2010
Revenue	1,300,000,000					
R&D Expense						
Operating Income						
Operating Margin %						
SGA Expense						
Net Income						
Operating Cash Flow						
Capital Expenditure						
EBITDA						
Return on Assets %						
Return on Equity %						
Debt to Equity						

CONTACT INFORMATION:

Phone: 703-359-0200   Fax: 703-359-8880
Toll-Free: 800-283-3238
Address: 3102 Omega Office Park, Fairfax, VA 22031 United States

STOCK TICKER/OTHER:

Stock Ticker: Private
Employees: 1,100
Parent Company:

Exchange:
Fiscal Year Ends: 12/31

SALARIES/BONUSES:

Top Exec. Salary: $ Bonus: $
Second Exec. Salary: $ Bonus: $

OTHER THOUGHTS:

Estimated Female Officers or Directors: 1
Hot Spot for Advancement for Women/Minorities:

Sales, profits and employees may be estimates. Financial information, benefits and other data can change quickly and may vary from those stated here.

Orbitz Worldwide Inc

NAIC Code: 519130

www.orbitz.com

TYPES OF BUSINESS:

Online Reservation Systems
Discount Air Fares

BRANDS/DIVISIONS/AFFILIATES:

Orbitz.com
eBookers
RatesToGo
HotelClub
Orbitz for Business
Orbitz Partner Network
CheapTickets
Expedia Inc

CONTACTS: Note: Officers with more than one job title may be intentionally listed here more than once.

Michael Randolfi, CFO
Scott Forbes, Director
James Rogers, General Counsel
Guillaume Cussac, Managing Director, Divisional
Chris Brown, Other Executive Officer
Samuel Fulton, Senior VP, Divisional
Barry Diller, Chmn.

GROWTH PLANS/SPECIAL FEATURES:

Orbitz Worldwide, Inc. is a global online travel company that uses technology to enable leisure and business travelers to search for, plan and book a broad range of travel products and services. Travel products include air travel, hotels, vacation packages, car rentals, cruises and travel insurance as well as destination services, such as ground transportation, event tickets and tours, through a portfolio of web sites. For customers, the firm offers access to travel inventory from a broad base of suppliers. For suppliers, the company represents a distribution channel that reaches millions of potential customers. The firm's consumer brands include Orbitz, a full-service travel company that offers products and services from various suppliers; CheapTickets, a U.S. travel site designed for value-conscious customers; Orbitz for Business, which offers corporate travel solutions, including online booking and call center support; eBookers, which offers customers the ability to book travel products and services throughout Europe; and HotelClub and RatesToGo, which enable customers to book hotel reservations in over 140 countries. With Orbitz.com membership, customers also have access to Orbitz weekly Insider Steals and Mobile Steals (through the Orbitz mobile app), which offer members discounts of 50% or more from hotels and destinations around the world. Orbitz Partner Network (www.orbitz.com/OPN) delivers private label travel solutions to a broad range of partners including many of the world's largest airlines. In September 2015, Orbitz was acquired by Expedia, Inc.

The company offers its employees medical, dental and vision coverage; travel discounts; a 401(k) plan; flexible spending accounts; short- and long-term disability coverage; tuition reimbursement; legal plan; fitness club discounts; and beverage services.

FINANCIAL DATA: Note: Data for latest year may not have been available at press time.

In U.S. $	2015	2014	2013	2012	2011	2010
Revenue	919,604,000	932,006,976	847,003,008	778,796,032	766,819,008	757,486,976
R&D Expense						
Operating Income						
Operating Margin %						
SGA Expense						
Net Income	50,400,000	17,280,000	165,084,992	-301,737,984	-37,277,000	-58,237,000
Operating Cash Flow						
Capital Expenditure						
EBITDA						
Return on Assets %						
Return on Equity %						
Debt to Equity						

CONTACT INFORMATION:

Phone: 312 894-5000   Fax: 312 894-5001
Toll-Free: 888-656-4546
Address: 500 W. Madison St., Ste. 1000, Chicago, IL 60661 United States

STOCK TICKER/OTHER:

Stock Ticker: Subsidiary
Employees: 1,530
Parent Company: Expedia Inc

Exchange:
Fiscal Year Ends: 12/31

SALARIES/BONUSES:

Top Exec. Salary: $ Bonus: $
Second Exec. Salary: $ Bonus: $

OTHER THOUGHTS:

Estimated Female Officers or Directors: 3
Hot Spot for Advancement for Women/Minorities: Y

Palace Entertainment Holdings Llc   www.palaceentertainment.com

NAIC Code: 713110

TYPES OF BUSINESS:

Amusement Parks
Auto Racetracks
Water Parks

BRANDS/DIVISIONS/AFFILIATES:

Parques Reunidos SA
Castle Park
Lake Compounce
SeaLife Park
Noah's Ark
Raging Waters
Waterworld
Boomers!

CONTACTS: Note: Officers with more than one job title may be intentionally listed here more than once.

Rolf Paegert, COO
Fernando Eiroa, Pres.
Meghan Gardner, Dir.-Mktg.
Sam Sutton, Exec. VP-Human Resources
Dan Vogt, Exec. Dir.-IT

GROWTH PLANS/SPECIAL FEATURES:

Palace Entertainment Holdings Llc, a wholly-owned subsidiary of Parques Reunidos SA, owns and operates multiple-attraction entertainment and amusement parks designed for families. The company comprises 22 locations across the U.S., including eight theme parks, nine water parks and five family entertainment centers. Through these locations, Palace Entertainment hosts over 13 million visitors every year. Theme parks include Castle Park in Riverside, California; Dutch Wonderland in Lancaster, Idlewild & SoakZone in Ligonier, as well as Kennywood in Pittsburgh, Pennsylvania; Lake Compounce in Bristol, Connecticut; Miami Seaquarium in Miami, Florida; SeaLife Park in Oahu, Hawaii; and Story Land in Glen, New Hampshire. Theme parks consist of features such as rides, miniature golf courses, arcades, shows, water attractions and sea life attractions. Water parks include Noah's Ark in Wisconsin; three Raging Waters sites and a Waterworld California site, all in California; Sandcastle in Pennsylvania; Splish Splash in New York; Water Country in New Hampshire; and Wet'n Wild Emerald Point in North Carolina. Family entertainment centers comprise Boomers!, located in New York and California; and Malibu Grand Prix and Mountasia, both in Georgia. These entertainment centers can include reserved areas for celebrating parties, go kart racing, miniature golf, arcades and batting cages.

FINANCIAL DATA: Note: Data for latest year may not have been available at press time.

In U.S. $	2015	2014	2013	2012	2011	2010
Revenue						
R&D Expense						
Operating Income						
Operating Margin %						
SGA Expense						
Net Income						
Operating Cash Flow						
Capital Expenditure						
EBITDA						
Return on Assets %						
Return on Equity %						
Debt to Equity						

CONTACT INFORMATION:

Phone: 949-261-0404   Fax: 949-261-1414
Toll-Free:
Address: 4590 MacArthur Blvd., Ste. 400, Newport Beach, CA 92660 United States

STOCK TICKER/OTHER:

Stock Ticker: Subsidiary   Exchange:
Employees: 740   Fiscal Year Ends: 12/31
Parent Company: Parques Reunidos SA

SALARIES/BONUSES:

Top Exec. Salary: $ Bonus: $
Second Exec. Salary: $ Bonus: $

OTHER THOUGHTS:

Estimated Female Officers or Directors:
Hot Spot for Advancement for Women/Minorities:

Sales, profits and employees may be estimates. Financial information, benefits and other data can change quickly and may vary from those stated here.

Parques Reunidos SA

NAIC Code: 713110

TYPES OF BUSINESS:

Amusement Parks
Water Parks
Nature Parks
Family Entertainment Centers
Cable Cars

BRANDS/DIVISIONS/AFFILIATES:

Candover Investments Inc
Bobbejaanland
BonBon-Land
Mirabilandia
Movie Park Germany
Raging Waters
L'Oceanografic
Miami Seaquarium

GROWTH PLANS/SPECIAL FEATURES:

Parques Reunidos SA, owned by Candover Investments, Inc., operates 55 amusement, marine, water and zoo parks located throughout Europe, the U.S. and Argentina. Its portfolio consists of 23 amusement, marine & water theme parks, including Bobbejaanland in Belgium, BonBon-Land in Denmark, Mirabilandia in Italy, Movie Park Germany in Germany and Raging Waters in the U.S. Zoo and nature parks include L'Oceanografic and Zoo Aquarium, both located in Spain; Marineland in France; Lakes Aquarium and Blackpool Zoo, both in England; and Sea Life Park and Miami Seaquarium; both in the U.S. Parques Reunidos also owns and operates two cable cars in Spain, the Madrid and the Benalmadena.

CONTACTS:
Note: Officers with more than one job title may be intentionally listed here more than once.

Fernando Eiroa, CEO
James Cleary, Sr. VP-Palace Entertainment

FINANCIAL DATA:
Note: Data for latest year may not have been available at press time.

In U.S. $	2015	2014	2013	2012	2011	2010
Revenue	736,197,066	614,784,911	585,315,046			
R&D Expense						
Operating Income						
Operating Margin %						
SGA Expense						
Net Income	22,432,459	9,414,703	8,868,651			
Operating Cash Flow						
Capital Expenditure						
EBITDA						
Return on Assets %						
Return on Equity %						
Debt to Equity						

CONTACT INFORMATION:

Phone: 902-345-012   Fax:
Toll-Free:
Address: Casa de Campo, S/N, Madrid, N 28 011 Spain

STOCK TICKER/OTHER:

Stock Ticker: Subsidiary   Exchange:
Employees: Fiscal Year Ends: 09/30
Parent Company: Candover Investments Inc

SALARIES/BONUSES:

Top Exec. Salary: $ Bonus: $
Second Exec. Salary: $ Bonus: $

OTHER THOUGHTS:

Estimated Female Officers or Directors:
Hot Spot for Advancement for Women/Minorities:

Piedmont Airlines Inc

www.piedmont-airlines.com

NAIC Code: 481111

TYPES OF BUSINESS:

Regional Airline

BRANDS/DIVISIONS/AFFILIATES:

American Airlines Group Inc
American Eagle
Allegheny Airlines
US Airways Group Inc
AMR Corporation

CONTACTS: *Note: Officers with more than one job title may be intentionally listed here more than once.*

Lyle Hogg, CEO
Stephen Keefer, VP-Operations
Stephen R. Farrow, Pres.
Tim McMasters, VP-Finance
Michelle Foose, VP-Human Resources
William W. Arndt, VP-Eng. & Maintenance
Michael J. Scrobola, VP-Flight Oper.
Eric H. Morgan, VP-Customer Service

GROWTH PLANS/SPECIAL FEATURES:

Piedmont Airlines, Inc., as a wholly-owned subsidiary of American Airlines Group, Inc., operates a regional airline under the American Eagle brand. Based in Salisbury, Maryland, Piedmont operates nearly 400 daily departures to 55 destinations throughout the eastern U.S. The firm's hubs include Charlotte Douglas International Airport in North Carolina, and Philadelphia International Airport in Pennsylvania. It also offers several flights to cities on the west coast and in the Southwest U.S. The company began in 1931 and in 1967 became a pioneer in code sharing, when Piedmont (then Henson Aviation) contracted with what was formerly Allegheny Airlines (then became US Airways) to provide turbo-prop service along routes to Washington, D.C., Philadelphia and Baltimore. Eventually, US Airways Group Inc. merged with AMR Corporation and began trading under the American Airlines Group. Service to Washington, D.C. and Philadelphia remain key components of Piedmont's network today. The firm's fleet is composed of 43 deHavilland DHC-8 turboprop aircraft, which feature a passenger capacity of up to 48. Beginning in February 2016, Piedmont expanded its fleet to include Embraer 145 regional jets, with plans to receive a minimum of 20 E145s by mid 2017.

FINANCIAL DATA: *Note: Data for latest year may not have been available at press time.*

In U.S. $	2015	2014	2013	2012	2011	2010
Revenue						
R&D Expense						
Operating Income						
Operating Margin %						
SGA Expense						
Net Income						
Operating Cash Flow						
Capital Expenditure						
EBITDA						
Return on Assets %						
Return on Equity %						
Debt to Equity						

CONTACT INFORMATION:

Phone: 410-742-2996   Fax: 410-742-4092
Toll-Free:
Address: 5443 Airport Terminal Rd., Salisbury, MD 21804 United States

STOCK TICKER/OTHER:

Stock Ticker: Subsidiary   Exchange:
Employees: 5,800   Fiscal Year Ends: 12/31
Parent Company: American Airlines Group Inc

SALARIES/BONUSES:

Top Exec. Salary: $ Bonus: $
Second Exec. Salary: $ Bonus: $

OTHER THOUGHTS:

Estimated Female Officers or Directors:
Hot Spot for Advancement for Women/Minorities:

Sales, profits and employees may be estimates. Financial information, benefits and other data can change quickly and may vary from those stated here.

Pinnacle Entertainment Inc

www.pnkinc.com

NAIC Code: 721120

TYPES OF BUSINESS:

Casinos
Hospitality & Entertainment Facilities
Racetrack Facilities

BRANDS/DIVISIONS/AFFILIATES:

Gaming and Leisure Properties Inc
L'Auberge Casino Resort
L'Auberge Baton Rouge
River City Casino & Hotel
Belterra Casino Resort
Boomtown Casino Hotel
Cactus Petes and The Horseshu Jackpot
Heartland Poker Tour

CONTACTS: *Note: Officers with more than one job title may be intentionally listed here more than once.*

Anthony Sanfilippo, CEO
Carlos Ruisanchez, CFO
James Martineau, Chairman of the Board
Virginia Shanks, Chief Administrative Officer
Neil Walkoff, Executive VP, Divisional
Troy Stremming, Executive VP, Divisional
John Godfrey, Executive VP

GROWTH PLANS/SPECIAL FEATURES:

Pinnacle Entertainment, Inc. is a developer, owner and operator of casinos and other hospitality facilities. The company owns and operates 15 gaming entertainment properties, located in Colorado, Indiana, Iowa, Louisiana, Mississippi, Missouri, Nevada and Texas. The company's largest casino resort, L'Auberge Casino Resort located in Lake Charles, Louisiana, offers 995 guestrooms, suites and villas, as well as 1,616 slot machines, 75 table games, a golf course and a full-service spa. L'Auberge Casino Hotel in Baton Rouge, Louisiana, features 1,480 slot machines, 56 table games, a hotel with 205 guestrooms and a rooftop pool, three dining outlets, an amphitheater style event lawn feature and a multi-purpose event center. The River City Casino & Hotel in St. Louis, Missouri includes 200 hotel rooms, 2,018 slot machines and 62 table games. Other properties include Belterra Casino Resort located near Vevay, Indiana; six Ameristar Casino Hotels in Iowa, Indiana, Missouri, Mississippi and Colorado; two Boomtown Casino Hotels featuring dockside riverboat casinos in New Orleans and Bossier City, Louisiana; and Cactus Petes and The Horseshu Jackpot, featuring a hotel, gaming, dining, golf course and showroom entertainment. The company also owns the Heartland Poker Tour, a live and televised poker tournament series; and owns a majority interest in Retama Park Racetrack outside of San Antonio, Texas. In April 2016, the firm was acquired by Gaming and Leisure Properties, Inc. in an all-stock transaction, operating as GLP's wholly-owned subsidiary. Prior to the acquisition, Pinnacle spun off Belterra Park Gaming & Entertainment, located in Cincinnati, Ohio, into a stand-alone publicly-traded company.

FINANCIAL DATA: *Note: Data for latest year may not have been available at press time.*

In U.S. $	2015	2014	2013	2012	2011	2010
Revenue	2,291,848,000	2,210,543,000	1,487,836,000	1,002,836,000		
R&D Expense	14,247,000	12,962,000	89,009,000	21,508,000		
Operating Income	301,166,000	310,473,000	104,387,000	136,695,000		
Operating Margin %	13.14%	14.04%	7.01%	13.63%		
SGA Expense	426,064,000	421,399,000	287,381,000	181,175,000		
Net Income	48,887,000	43,843,000	-255,870,000	-31,805,000		
Operating Cash Flow	408,226,000	328,486,000	161,067,000	186,906,000		
Capital Expenditure	109,032,000	255,815,000	292,623,000	300,521,000		
EBITDA	543,933,000	543,536,000	142,773,000	201,831,000		
Return on Assets %	-1.74%	.87%	-4.95%			
Return on Equity %	-33.65%	17.83%	-119.73%			
Debt to Equity	4.78	14.30	20.42			

CONTACT INFORMATION:

Phone: 702 541-7777   Fax:
Toll-Free:
Address: 3980 Howard Hughes Pkwy, Las Vegas, NV 89169 United States

STOCK TICKER/OTHER:

Stock Ticker: PNK   Exchange: NAS
Employees: 14,738   Fiscal Year Ends: 12/31
Parent Company: Gaming and Leisure Properties Inc

SALARIES/BONUSES:

Top Exec. Salary: Bonus: $
$1,200,000
Second Exec. Salary: Bonus: $
$800,000

OTHER THOUGHTS:

Estimated Female Officers or Directors: 3

Hot Spot for Advancement for Women/Minorities: Y

Sales, profits and employees may be estimates. Financial information, benefits and other data can change quickly and may vary from those stated here.

Pleasant Holidays LLC

www.pleasantholidays.com

NAIC Code: 561520

TYPES OF BUSINESS:

Packaged Vacations
Hotels
Cruises
Tours

BRANDS/DIVISIONS/AFFILIATES:

Automobile Club of Southern California
Pleasant Holidays
Journese
Air By Pleasant
Pleasant Activities

CONTACTS: Note: Officers with more than one job title may be intentionally listed here more than once.

Jack E. Richards, CEO
Jack E. Richards, Pres.
Duke Ah Moo, VP-Prod. Dev.
Amy Frank, Mgr.-Destination Mktg.

GROWTH PLANS/SPECIAL FEATURES:

Pleasant Holidays, LLC, a subsidiary of the Automobile Club of Southern California, is a travel company specializing in vacation packages to Hawaii, Las Vegas, Mexico, the Caribbean, Europe, Australia, New Zealand, Central America, Orlando, New York, Canada, Fiji, Cook Islands, Tahiti, Bora Bora and French Polynesia. The company is headquartered near Los Angeles and has regional offices in Honolulu, Hawaii and San Diego, California. The company manages a portfolio of four distinct brands: Pleasant Holidays, Journese, Air by Pleasant and Pleasant Activities. Pleasant Holidays has been named Best Tour Operator-Hawaii for nine consecutive years by Travel Weekly Magazine. The firm's Journese brand specializes in premium and luxury vacation travel to Australia, New Zealand, Hawaii, Mexico, Tahiti, Costa Rica, Europe and the Caribbean. Journese offers over 100 boutique and luxury resorts as well as Avis car rentals. Its Air By Pleasant brand is one of the largest international air consolidators, serving 180 countries and over 1000 destinations worldwide via partnership agreements with 80 airlines. The Pleasant Activities brand provides over 1,000 sightseeing tours, attractions and luaus in Hawaii and operates 40 activity and concierge desks in major hotels throughout Hawaii. Since its inception, the company has sold over 14 million vacation packages through its various brands. Pleasant Holidays has a partnership with Norwegian Cruise Line to provide cruises to Hawaii, Tahiti or Fiji. The firm's Caribbean portfolio includes hotels and resorts located in Bonaire, Grenada, Harbour Island in the Bahamas, St. Croix and the U.S. Virgin Islands.

FINANCIAL DATA: Note: Data for latest year may not have been available at press time.

In U.S. $	2015	2014	2013	2012	2011	2010
Revenue						
R&D Expense						
Operating Income						
Operating Margin %						
SGA Expense						
Net Income						
Operating Cash Flow						
Capital Expenditure						
EBITDA						
Return on Assets %						
Return on Equity %						
Debt to Equity						

CONTACT INFORMATION:

Phone: 818-991-3390   Fax: 805-744-6223
Toll-Free: 800-742-9244
Address: 2404 Townsgate Rd., Westlake Village, CA 91361 United States

STOCK TICKER/OTHER:

Stock Ticker: Subsidiary   Exchange:
Employees: 400   Fiscal Year Ends: 12/31
Parent Company: Automobile Club of Southern California

SALARIES/BONUSES:

Top Exec. Salary: $ Bonus: $
Second Exec. Salary: $ Bonus: $

OTHER THOUGHTS:

Estimated Female Officers or Directors: 1
Hot Spot for Advancement for Women/Minorities:

Sales, profits and employees may be estimates. Financial information, benefits and other data can change quickly and may vary from those stated here.

Priceline Group Inc (The)

NAIC Code: 519130

www.priceline.com

TYPES OF BUSINESS:

Online Retail-Travel Services
Auction-Based Travel Sales
Online Financial Services

BRANDS/DIVISIONS/AFFILIATES:

Name Your Own Price
Booking.com
Agoda.com
RentalCars.com
Priceline.com
Kayak Software Corporation
OpenTable Inc
PriceMatch

CONTACTS: Note: Officers with more than one job title may be intentionally listed here more than once.

Gillian Tans, CEO, Subsidiary
Jeffery Boyd, CEO
Daniel Finnegan, CFO
Maelle Gavet, Executive VP, Divisional
Glenn Fogel, Executive VP, Divisional
Peter Millones, Executive VP

GROWTH PLANS/SPECIAL FEATURES:

The Priceline Group, Inc. is a leading online travel company that offers its customers a broad range of travel services, including airline tickets, hotel rooms, car rentals, vacation packages, cruises and destination services primarily through its proprietary Priceline.com website. Within the U.S., the firm offers customers the ability to purchase travel services in a traditional, price-disclosed manner or the opportunity to use the Name Your Own Price service, which allows customers to make offers on travel goods and services at discounted prices. To make an offer, a customer specifies the origin and destination of the trip, the dates on which the customer wishes to depart and return, the price the customer is willing to pay and the customer's valid credit card to guarantee the offer. In total, Priceline is affiliated with eight domestic airlines and 13 international airlines. The company enables customers to make hotel reservations on a worldwide basis, primarily under the Booking.com and Agoda.com brands internationally, and primarily under the Priceline.com brand in the U.S. Through these operations, Priceline works with more than 600,000 chain-owned and independently owned hotels, offering hotel reservations on various web sites and in 42 different languages. Through subsidiary RentalCars.com, the company offers retail price-disclosed rental car reservations through over 28,000 locations. The firm's international business represents approximately 87% of the company's gross bookings and contributes more than 94% of Priceline's consolidated operating income. Subsidiary KAYAK Software Corporation provides a price comparison service allowing consumers to search and compare prices for travel services. In 2014, Priceline acquired OpenTable, Inc., a restaurant booking service. In May 2015, the firm acquired PriceMatch, a cloud-based data and analytics solution for hotels.

Employee benefits include annual bonuses; medical, life, AD&D, disability and dental coverage; a 401(k) savings and investment plan with company match; tuition reimbursement; an employee assistance plan; flexible spending accounts; and travel agent discou

FINANCIAL DATA: Note: Data for latest year may not have been available at press time.

In U.S. $	2015	2014	2013	2012	2011	2010
Revenue	9,223,987,000	8,441,971,000	6,793,306,000	5,260,956,000	4,355,610,000	3,084,905,000
R&D Expense	113,617,000	97,498,000	71,890,000	43,685,000	33,813,000	20,998,000
Operating Income	3,258,907,000	3,073,312,000	2,412,414,000	1,829,793,000	1,398,922,000	786,797,000
Operating Margin %	35.33%	36.40%	35.51%	34.78%	32.11%	25.50%
SGA Expense	4,946,789,000	4,205,500,000	3,113,607,000	2,145,062,000	1,593,321,000	1,055,413,000
Net Income	2,551,360,000	2,421,753,000	1,892,663,000	1,419,566,000	1,056,371,000	527,541,000
Operating Cash Flow	3,102,231,000	2,914,397,000	2,301,436,000	1,785,750,000	1,341,812,000	777,297,000
Capital Expenditure	173,915,000	131,504,000	84,445,000	55,158,000	46,833,000	22,593,000
EBITDA	3,561,043,000	3,285,621,000	2,497,801,000	1,889,074,000	1,453,339,000	826,691,000
Return on Assets %	15.76%	19.08%	22.24%	26.93%	30.72%	22.25%
Return on Equity %	29.38%	31.29%	35.02%	43.87%	48.15%	33.65%
Debt to Equity	0.70	0.44	0.25	0.22	0.03	0.26

CONTACT INFORMATION:

Phone: 203-2998000   Fax:
Toll-Free:
Address: 800 Connecticut Ave., Norwalk, CT 06854 United States

STOCK TICKER/OTHER:

Stock Ticker: PCLN   Exchange: NAS
Employees: 12,700   Fiscal Year Ends:
Parent Company:

SALARIES/BONUSES:

Top Exec. Salary: $865,000   Bonus: $
Second Exec. Salary: $360,335   Bonus: $

OTHER THOUGHTS:

Estimated Female Officers or Directors: 1
Hot Spot for Advancement for Women/Minorities: Y

Princess Cruise Lines Ltd

www.princess.com

NAIC Code: 483112

TYPES OF BUSINESS:

Cruise Lines

BRANDS/DIVISIONS/AFFILIATES:

Carnival Corporation & plc
Royal Princess
Princess Live!
Princess Luxury Bed
Majestic Princess

CONTACTS: *Note: Officers with more than one job title may be intentionally listed here more than once.*

Jan Swartz, CEO
Jan Swartz, Pres.
Jim Baer, VP-Sales

GROWTH PLANS/SPECIAL FEATURES:

Princess Cruise Lines Ltd., a subsidiary of Carnival Corporation & plc, is a leading cruise line. The company's fleet includes 18 ships, carrying 1.7 million guests each year. Princess offers more than 150 itineraries to more than 300 destinations, with cruises generally from three to 14 days. It also sails two world cruises over 100 days. The firm sources the majority of its passengers from North America, with other markets including Australia and the U.K. The firm's Royal Princess features a 50% larger atrium, the social hub of the ship, as well as an over-water SeaWalk, a top-deck glass-bottomed walkway extending more than 28 feet beyond the edge of the vessel, plush private poolside cabanas that appear to be floating on the water, water and light shows, a Princess Live! television studio, a pastry shop and balconies on all outside staterooms. In December 2015, the firm unveiled its new Princess Luxury Bed, designed to deliver the ultimate night of sleep at sea. The bed features a plush, 2-inch mattress top, 8 Â½-inch medium-firm mattress, individually wrapped coils, a European-inspired duvet and 100% Jacquard-woven cotton linens. Princess plans to roll out more than 44,000 beds to every stateroom across its fleet by the end of 2018. Also in 2015, the cruise line announced that its third Royal Class ship, the Majestic Princess, will debut in 2017.

FINANCIAL DATA: *Note: Data for latest year may not have been available at press time.*

In U.S. $	2015	2014	2013	2012	2011	2010
Revenue	2,985,660,000	3,017,960,000	2,936,640,000	2,922,580,000	3,000,670,000	1,942,314,000
R&D Expense						
Operating Income						
Operating Margin %						
SGA Expense						
Net Income						
Operating Cash Flow						
Capital Expenditure						
EBITDA						
Return on Assets %						
Return on Equity %						
Debt to Equity						

CONTACT INFORMATION:

Phone: 661-753-0000   Fax: 661-284-4747
Toll-Free: 000-774-0207
Address: 24305 Town Center Dr., Santa Clarita, CA 91355 United States

STOCK TICKER/OTHER:

Stock Ticker: Subsidiary   Exchange:
Employees: Fiscal Year Ends: 11/30
Parent Company: Carnival Corporation & plc

SALARIES/BONUSES:

Top Exec. Salary: $ Bonus: $
Second Exec. Salary: $ Bonus: $

OTHER THOUGHTS:

Estimated Female Officers or Directors: 1
Hot Spot for Advancement for Women/Minorities:

Sales, profits and employees may be estimates. Financial information, benefits and other data can change quickly and may vary from those stated here.

PT Garuda Indonesia Tbk

www.garuda-indonesia.com

NAIC Code: 481111

TYPES OF BUSINESS:

Airline
Aircraft Maintenance
Air Freight
Ground Handling
Hotel
Airline Catering
Computer Reservation System
Airlines IT

BRANDS/DIVISIONS/AFFILIATES:

Citilink
GMF AeroAsia
PT Aerowisata
PT Abacus Distribution Systems
PT Gapura Angkasa
PT Aero Systems Indonesia
Cargo Garuda
Garuda Sentra Medika

CONTACTS: Note: Officers with more than one job title may be intentionally listed here more than once.

Arif Wibowo, CEO
I Gusti Danadiputra, Dir.-Finance

GROWTH PLANS/SPECIAL FEATURES:

PT Garuda Indonesia, 100%-owned by the Indonesian government, is the national airline of the Republic of Indonesia. The company and its subsidiaries carry over 25 million passengers per year with a fleet of 143 aircraft offering service to 60 domestic and 73 international destinations. Departure hubs include Jakarta, Denpasar, Medan and Makassar. Destinations include Singapore, Tokyo and Amsterdam and London. Flights to India were cancelled in 2016. PT Garuda's fleet includes 13 ATR 72-600s, eight Airbus A330-200s, 15 A330-300s, 76 Boeing 737-800s, two 747-400s, 10 777-300ERs and 18 Bombardier CRJ1000 Next Gens, for a total of 142, in-service aircraft. The firm has 83 additional aircraft on order. The airline has codesharing agreements, and is a member of the SkyTeam alliance. PT Garuda subsidiaries include Citilink, a low-cost airline; GMF AeroAsia, which provides aircraft maintenance; PT Aerowisata, which provides travel, hotel, transportation and catering services; PT Abacus Distribution Systems Indonesia, a computer reservation provider; PT Gapura Angkasa, a provider of ground handling services; PT Aero Systems Indonesia, which provides IT solutions; Cargo Garuda Indonesia, providing cargo services; and Garuda Sentra Medika, an aircrew health services company.

FINANCIAL DATA: Note: Data for latest year may not have been available at press time.

In U.S. $	2015	2014	2013	2012	2011	2010
Revenue	3,470,369,000	3,588,158,000	3,386,052,000	3,156,342,000	2,738,527,000	1,967,376,000
R&D Expense						
Operating Income	168,745,400	-399,313,000	56,448,280	168,072,100	111,694,700	-7,367,381
Operating Margin %	4.86%	-11.12%	1.66%	5.32%	4.07%	- .37%
SGA Expense	534,515,400	1,021,778,000	842,828,200	820,035,500	449,192,400	342,672,100
Net Income	76,480,240	-373,041,300	11,038,840	110,598,400	88,930,500	56,552,750
Operating Cash Flow						
Capital Expenditure	142,061,200	250,334,600	567,103,700	29,335,990	48,879,000	59,766,990
EBITDA	171,048,000	-399,313,000	56,448,280	168,072,100	111,694,700	207,228,200
Return on Assets %	2.38%	-12.32%	.40%	4.90%	5.09%	3.68%
Return on Equity %	8.32%	-36.94%	.99%	11.37%	14.68%	15.70%
Debt to Equity	0.93	0.61	0.41	0.39	0.38	0.97

CONTACT INFORMATION:

Phone: 62 212311355   Fax: 62 212311223
Toll-Free:
Address: Jl Kebon Sirih No. 44, Jakarta, 10110 Indonesia

STOCK TICKER/OTHER:

Stock Ticker: PSEOY   Exchange: PINX
Employees: 7,008   Fiscal Year Ends:
Parent Company:

SALARIES/BONUSES:

Top Exec. Salary: $ Bonus: $
Second Exec. Salary: $ Bonus: $

OTHER THOUGHTS:

Estimated Female Officers or Directors: 3
Hot Spot for Advancement for Women/Minorities: Y

Qantas Airways Ltd

www.qantas.com

NAIC Code: 481111

TYPES OF BUSINESS:

Airline
Air Freight
Low-Cost Regional Airline
Catering
Travel Services
Ground Handling Services
Defense Forces Maintenance & Support

BRANDS/DIVISIONS/AFFILIATES:

QantasLink
Jetstar
Qantas Freight

CONTACTS: Note: Officers with more than one job title may be intentionally listed here more than once.

Alan Joyce, CEO
Tino La Spina, CFO
Olivia Wirth, Dir-Mktg.
Jon Scriven, Human Resources
Andrew Fitch, General Counsel
Olivia Wirth, Group Exec.-Corp. Affairs
Jayne Hrdlicka, CEO-Jetstar Group
Lyell Strambi, CEO-Qantas Domestic
Lesley Grant, CEO-Quantas Loyalty
Leigh Clifford, Chmn.
Simon Hickey, CEO-Qantas International

GROWTH PLANS/SPECIAL FEATURES:

Qantas Airways Ltd., founded in 1920, is one of the world's oldest airlines and a long-distance travel provider, with services from Australia to North America and Europe. The company has operations worldwide that span 85 domestic and international destinations. Qantas operates 131 aircraft that carry more than 49.2 million passengers to destinations in Australia and around the world. The company operates aircraft models such as B717s, B737-800, B747-400, A380 and A330, with eight Boeing 787-9s on order for delivery in 2017. In addition to Qantas' mainline operation, the company operates a number of subsidiaries, including QantasLink and Jetstar. Additionally, Qantas has subsidiaries that operate in specialist markets, such as in-flight catering, ground handling, freight, holiday and travel operations and defense contracting. Qantas also operates Qantas Freight, a specialized airfreight division, which provides cargo, mail and express services internationally and domestically in partnership with Australia Post. Quantas is a member of oneworld alliance, a global airline affiliation connecting 1,000 destinations in 150 countries.

FINANCIAL DATA: Note: Data for latest year may not have been available at press time.

In U.S. $	2015	2014	2013	2012	2011	2010
Revenue	11,816,800,000	11,529,980,000	12,098,300,000	11,345,860,000	10,930,460,000	
R&D Expense						
Operating Income	581,253,800	-3,019,629,000	155,203,900	-748,630,600	-69,233,110	
Operating Margin %	4.91%	-26.18%	1.28%	-6.59%	-.63%	
SGA Expense	3,635,880,000	3,750,000,000	3,968,351,000	3,883,141,000	3,922,702,000	
Net Income	423,767,500	-2,162,964,000	3,804,017	-186,396,800	190,200,900	
Operating Cash Flow	1,558,125,000	813,298,900	1,078,058,000	1,377,054,000	1,355,752,000	
Capital Expenditure	1,033,932,000	883,292,800	948,722,000	1,689,744,000	1,831,254,000	
EBITDA	1,699,635,000	-1,725,502,000	1,341,297,000	1,059,038,000	1,428,028,000	
Return on Assets %	3.19%	-15.15%	.02%	-1.16%	1.22%	
Return on Equity %	17.67%	-64.53%	.08%	-4.07%	4.13%	
Debt to Equity	1.39	1.84	0.88	0.92	0.88	

CONTACT INFORMATION:

Phone: 61 296913636   Fax: 61 296913339
Toll-Free: 800-227-4500
Address: 10 Bourke Road, Mascot, NSW 2020 Australia

STOCK TICKER/OTHER:

Stock Ticker: QUBSF   Exchange: PINX
Employees: 25,665   Fiscal Year Ends: 06/30
Parent Company:

SALARIES/BONUSES:

Top Exec. Salary: $ Bonus: $
Second Exec. Salary: $ Bonus: $

OTHER THOUGHTS:

Estimated Female Officers or Directors: 6
Hot Spot for Advancement for Women/Minorities: Y

Qatar Airways

www.qatarairways.com

NAIC Code: 481111

TYPES OF BUSINESS:

Air Transportation-Regional & Commuter Airline Services
Airport Operation
Duty Free Shops

BRANDS/DIVISIONS/AFFILIATES:

Privilege Club
Qatar Executive
Qatar Duty Free
International Consolidated Airlines Group SA

CONTACTS: *Note: Officers with more than one job title may be intentionally listed here more than once.*

Akbar Al Baker, CEO
Marwan Koleilat, Chief Comm. Officer
Bart Vos, Exec. VP-Comm.

GROWTH PLANS/SPECIAL FEATURES:

Qatar Airways, the national airline of the State of Qatar, is 100% government-owned after a 2014 buyout of private investors who had owned one-half of the firm. The firm's fleet consists of more than 340 aircraft on order, including various models of Airbus and Boeing planes. Some of the luxury accommodations found on Qatar's planes include in-flight entertainment systems offering every passenger a choice of more than 1,000 audio and video options; menus developed by professional chefs; spacious seating that can also be adapted into an office space; and duty-free shopping (through its Qatar Duty Free division). Some of Qatar's destinations include Europe, Middle East and Africa (EMEA); Asia; India; Islands in the Indian Ocean; and Chicago, Washington and New York in the U.S. Additionally, the firm has codeshare partnerships with several airlines, including Asiana Airlines, Malaysia Airlines, MEA (Middle East Airlines), Philippine Airlines, US Airways, Azerbaijan Airlines, Oman Air, the SNCF and ANA (All Nippon Airways). The firm's loyalty program, Privilege Club, has reciprocal agreements with many international airlines. The Privilege Club operates on a three-tier membership level (Gold, Silver and Burgundy), with benefits that include flexible last minute awards, free date changes on award tickets, free add-ons, infant award tickets, priority waitlist, priority standby and extra baggage allowance. Additionally, the firm operates Qatar Executive, which features two Bombardier aircraft and corporate jet service. The company is a member of the oneworld alliance, one of the world's three largest airline alliances. In December 2014, Qatar Airways commenced service of the world's first Airbus A350 XWB (extra wide body) aircraft. In 2015, the firm acquired a 9.99% stake in International Consolidated Airlines Group SA (IAG) and announced it will be adding an all-premium class Airbus A319 to its corporate jet fleet, Qatar Executive.

FINANCIAL DATA: *Note: Data for latest year may not have been available at press time.*

In U.S. $	2015	2014	2013	2012	2011	2010
Revenue	9,789,067,023	9,390,003,928	8,408,599,856	7,632,121,357	6,752,368,786	
R&D Expense						
Operating Income						
Operating Margin %						
SGA Expense						
Net Income	445,232,671	102,450,207	27,191,876	98,604,909	823,996	
Operating Cash Flow						
Capital Expenditure						
EBITDA						
Return on Assets %						
Return on Equity %						
Debt to Equity						

CONTACT INFORMATION:

Phone: 974-449-6666   Fax: 974-462-1762
Toll-Free:
Address: Airport Rd., Qatar Airways Tower,, Doha,   Qatar

STOCK TICKER/OTHER:

Stock Ticker: Government-Owned   Exchange:
Employees: 36,549   Fiscal Year Ends: 03/31
Parent Company:

SALARIES/BONUSES:

Top Exec. Salary: $ Bonus: $
Second Exec. Salary: $ Bonus: $

OTHER THOUGHTS:

Estimated Female Officers or Directors:
Hot Spot for Advancement for Women/Minorities:

Ramada Worldwide Inc

www.ramada.com

NAIC Code: 721110

TYPES OF BUSINESS:

Hotels & Motels

BRANDS/DIVISIONS/AFFILIATES:

Wyndham Worldwide
Ramada
Ramada Limited Hotel
Ramada Hotel
Ramada Plaza Hotel
Ramada Resort
Ramada Hotel & Resorts
Ramada Resort Akiriki

CONTACTS: Note: Officers with more than one job title may be intentionally listed here more than once.

Keith J. Pierce, Pres.
Stephen P. Holmes, CEO

GROWTH PLANS/SPECIAL FEATURES:

Ramada Worldwide, Inc., a subsidiary of Wyndham Worldwide, is a leading franchisor of hotel and motel properties. The company owns nearly 900 properties throughout the U.S. and in more than 50 other countries, and offers discounts for seniors, groups, government employees and AAA and AARP members. The franchise also participates in the Wyndham Rewards program, in which guests can earn rewards points, gift cards or resort vacations by staying in participating hotels. The company's core brand, Ramada, offers room service, bell service, onsite restaurants and cocktail lounges and full-service meeting facilities. Ramada Limited Hotel properties offer less expensive rates and limited amenities. These properties provide accommodations for the mid-market traveler and include swimming pools, on-site restaurants or a-la-carte food service, plus business services, meeting rooms and fitness facilities. Ramada Plaza Hotel properties are full-service hotels, offering on-site restaurants and lounges, conference and banquet facilities, as well as business center and fitness facilities. Ramada Resort properties are designed for leisure travelers on extended stays and offer playgrounds, pools, spas, fitness centers, dining room services and car rental facilities. The franchise's resort properties, principally located outside the U.S. and Canada, include Ramada Hotel & Resorts, which feature oversized rooms, pools, saunas, golf and tennis facilities, restaurants and lounges; and Ramada Hotel & Suites, offering luxury suites, restaurants and meeting and banquet facilities. In 2015, Ramada expanded its brand in the South Pacific with waterfront, 80-room Ramada Resort Akiriki, located in Vanautu's capital Port Vila.

Wyndham Worldwide and its subsidiaries offer employees a choice of medical, dental and vision plans; flexible spending accounts; adoption reimbursement; business travel accident insurance; an educational assistance program; and a 401(k) plan.

FINANCIAL DATA: Note: Data for latest year may not have been available at press time.

In U.S. $	2015	2014	2013	2012	2011	2010
Revenue						
R&D Expense						
Operating Income						
Operating Margin %						
SGA Expense						
Net Income						
Operating Cash Flow						
Capital Expenditure						
EBITDA						
Return on Assets %						
Return on Equity %						
Debt to Equity						

CONTACT INFORMATION:

Phone: 973-428-9700   Fax: 605-496-7658
Toll-Free: 800-854-9517
Address: 1 Sylvan Way, Parsippany, NJ 07054 United States

SALARIES/BONUSES:

Top Exec. Salary: $ Bonus: $
Second Exec. Salary: $ Bonus: $

STOCK TICKER/OTHER:

Stock Ticker: Subsidiary   Exchange:
Employees: 30,000   Fiscal Year Ends: 12/31
Parent Company: Wyndham Worldwide

OTHER THOUGHTS:

Estimated Female Officers or Directors:
Hot Spot for Advancement for Women/Minorities:

Red Lion Hotels Corporation

www.redlion.com

NAIC Code: 721110

TYPES OF BUSINESS:

Hotels
Event Ticketing Services
Property Management Services
Entertainment Productions
Guest Loyalty Programs

BRANDS/DIVISIONS/AFFILIATES:

Red Lion Hotels
WestCoast Entertainment
Leo Hotel Collection
TicketsWest
GuestHouse International
Settle Inn
Red Lion Inn & Suites
Hotel RL

CONTACTS: Note: Officers with more than one job title may be intentionally listed here more than once.

Gregory Mount, CEO
David Wright, CFO
Robert Wolfe, Chairman of the Board
William Linehan, Chief Marketing Officer
Harry Sladich, Executive VP, Divisional
Thomas Mckeirnan, Executive VP

GROWTH PLANS/SPECIAL FEATURES:

Red Lion Hotels Corporation owns, operates and franchises midscale, full, select and limited service hotels in the western U.S. Its hotel brands include Red Lion Hotels, Red Lion Inn & Suites, Hotel RL, GuestHouse and Settle Inn. The firm currently holds interests in approximately 55 hotels across nine states and one Canadian province, offering a total of 11,820 rooms and over 662,322 square feet of meeting space. Red Lion operates in three segments: hotels, franchise and entertainment. The hotels segment, deriving 81.5% revenue, consists of the operations of its 19 company-operated hotels, of which 14 are wholly-owned and 5 are leased. The franchise segment (6.6%) licenses the firm's 36 franchised hotels. To support its hotels, Red Lion provides services in marketing, sales, advertising, guest loyalty programs, revenue management, reservation systems, quality assurance and brand standards. This segment's Leo Hotel Collection is a unique, historic and boutique style of hotels. The entertainment segment (11.8%), operating through TicketsWest and WestCoast Entertainment, offers ticketing services, ticketing inventory management systems, call center services, promotion services and outlet/electronic channel distribution for event locations. TicketsWest offers tickets for live music, sporting events, family events (such as circuses, expos and fairs) and theater events. The company has also developed an electronic ticketing platform that integrates with its electronic hotel distribution system. In 2015, the firm sold its Bellevue and Wenatchee hotels in Washington; formed a joint venture to accelerate its national growth strategy, which includes selling a 45% stake in 12 wholly-owned hotels to the joint venture and concurrently refinancing all of the company's secured debt; and acquired GuestHouse International, as well as Settle Inn.

The firm offers employees life, medical, dental and vision insurance; a flexible spending plan; an associate travel program; and an employee assistance program.

FINANCIAL DATA: Note: Data for latest year may not have been available at press time.

In U.S. $	2015	2014	2013	2012	2011	2010
Revenue	142,920,000	145,426,000	120,055,000	150,707,000	156,080,000	163,494,000
R&D Expense						
Operating Income	13,880,000	6,759,000	-4,428,000	-9,870,000	7,480,000	-4,302,000
Operating Margin %	9.71%	4.64%	-3.68%	-6.54%	4.79%	-2.63%
SGA Expense	16,388,000	13,563,000	12,409,000	10,881,000	12,755,000	12,144,000
Net Income	2,719,000	2,303,000	-17,047,000	-14,674,000	-7,148,000	-8,609,000
Operating Cash Flow	9,680,000	10,578,000	7,087,000	13,470,000	1,881,000	19,491,000
Capital Expenditure	16,542,000	24,891,000	13,193,000	8,442,000	46,278,000	10,615,000
EBITDA	24,395,000	19,984,000	10,193,000	6,174,000	26,937,000	17,026,000
Return on Assets %	1.06%	1.00%	-6.87%	-5.18%	-2.24%	-2.52%
Return on Equity %	1.97%	1.65%	-11.75%	-9.20%	-4.24%	-4.96%
Debt to Equity	0.65	0.43	0.51	0.20	0.58	0.48

CONTACT INFORMATION:

Phone: 509 459-6100 Fax: 509 325-7324
Toll-Free: 800-733-5466
Address: 201 W. North River Dr., Ste. 100, Spokane, WA 99201 United States

STOCK TICKER/OTHER:

Stock Ticker: RLH
Employees: 1,783
Parent Company:

Exchange: NYS
Fiscal Year Ends: 12/31

SALARIES/BONUSES:

Top Exec. Salary: $407,173 Bonus: $260,200
Second Exec. Salary: $298,360 Bonus: $170,589

OTHER THOUGHTS:

Estimated Female Officers or Directors: 2
Hot Spot for Advancement for Women/Minorities: Y

Sales, profits and employees may be estimates. Financial information, benefits and other data can change quickly and may vary from those stated here.

Red Rock Resorts Inc

redrock.sclv.com/Home/Corporate/Corporate

NAIC Code: 721120

TYPES OF BUSINESS:

Casino Hotels

BRANDS/DIVISIONS/AFFILIATES:

Red Rock Casino, Resort & Spa
Green Valley Ranch, Resort, Casino & Spa
Boulder Station
Sunset Station
Texas Station
Wildfire Casino & Lanes
Wild Wild West
Gun Lake Casino

CONTACTS: Note: Officers with more than one job title may be intentionally listed here more than once.

Frank Fertitta, CEO
Marc Falcone, CFO
Daniel Roy, COO
Richard Haskins, President
Stephen Cavallaro, Vice Chairman

GROWTH PLANS/SPECIAL FEATURES:

Red Rock Resorts, Inc., formerly Station Casinos Corp., is a leading gaming, development and management company operating 21 strategically-located casino and entertainment properties. In total, the firm has developed over $5 billion of regional gaming and entertainment destinations in multiple jurisdictions. Additionally, Red Rock is an established leader in the Native American gaming, managing facilities in northern California and western Michigan. The Las Vegas portfolio of the firm consists of nine major gaming and entertainment facilities as well as 10 smaller casinos. Combined, the Las Vegas portfolio of casinos offers approximately 19,300 slot machines, 300 table games and 4,000 hotel rooms. Properties of the firm include: Red Rock Casino, Resort & Spa; Green Valley Ranch, Resort, Casino & Spa; Boulder Station; Palace Station; Santa Fe Station; Sunset Station; Texas Station; Fiesta Henderson; Fiesta Ranch; Barley's; Wildfire Sunset; Wildfire Boulder; Wildfire Casino & Lanes; Wild Wild West; Gun Lake Casino; and Graton Resort & Casino. Moreover, Red Rock also controls seven gaming-entitled development sites consisting of approximately 398 acres in Las Vegas and Reno, Nevada.

FINANCIAL DATA: Note: Data for latest year may not have been available at press time.

In U.S. $	2015	2014	2013	2012	2011	2010
Revenue	1,352,135,000	1,291,616,000	1,256,137,000	1,230,221,000		
R&D Expense						
Operating Income	287,189,000	237,061,000	214,976,000	170,421,000		
Operating Margin %	21.23%	18.35%	17.11%	13.85%		
SGA Expense	329,022,000	320,760,000	328,042,000	324,050,000		
Net Income	137,658,000	100,542,000	-94,998,000	21,115,000		
Operating Cash Flow	349,440,000	269,791,000	250,690,000	217,836,000		
Capital Expenditure	129,925,000	102,748,000	86,728,000	62,048,000		
EBITDA	425,054,000	414,880,000	349,029,000	354,591,000		
Return on Assets %	1.03%	3.29%	-3.06%			
Return on Equity %	5.23%	15.79%	-14.49%			
Debt to Equity	3.73	3.37	3.27			

CONTACT INFORMATION:

Phone: 702-495-3000   Fax:
Toll-Free: 866-767-7773
Address: 1505 S. Pavilion Ctr. Dr., Las Vegas, NV 89135 United States

STOCK TICKER/OTHER:

Stock Ticker: RRR
Employees: 11,800
Parent Company:

Exchange: NAS
Fiscal Year Ends:

SALARIES/BONUSES:

Top Exec. Salary:
$1,000,108
Second Exec. Salary:
$1,000,000

Bonus: $1,239,961

Bonus: $1,000,000

OTHER THOUGHTS:

Estimated Female Officers or Directors:

Hot Spot for Advancement for Women/Minorities:

Sales, profits and employees may be estimates. Financial information, benefits and other data can change quickly and may vary from those stated here.

Republic Airways Holdings Inc
NAIC Code: 481111

TYPES OF BUSINESS:
Regional Airline

GROWTH PLANS/SPECIAL FEATURES:
Republic Airways Holdings, Inc. is a holding company that offers scheduled commercial passenger services through two wholly-owned regional airlines: Republic Airlines and Shuttle America. Republic Airlines operates a fleet of Embraer E-Jet 170, 175 and 190 aircraft; and Shuttle America operates the Embraer ERJ 145, E-Jet 170 and 175. Republic Airlines operates under the U.S. Airways Express, United Express and American Eagle brands; and Shuttle America operates under the Delta Connection and United Express brands. The airlines offer approximately 1,000 flights daily to 105 cities in 38 U.S. states, Canada, the Caribbean and the Bahamas through Republic's fixed-fee codeshare agreements. In February 2016, the firm filed for U.S. bankruptcy protection due to plunging profits and a pilot shortage. That June, the bankruptcy court approved the company's amendment with United Airlines, which provided interrelated operational and economic benefits, as well as uninterrupted flying on all of Republic Airway's aircraft.

Employee benefits include medical, dental, vision, life, accidental death and disability insurance; a 401(k); a flexible benefit program; and reduced and free travel rates for employees and immediate families.

BRANDS/DIVISIONS/AFFILIATES:
Republic Airlines
Shuttle America
U.S. Airways Express
United Express
American Eagle
Delta Connection

CONTACTS: Note: Officers with more than one job title may be intentionally listed here more than once.
Bryan Bedford, CEO
Paul Kinstedt, COO
Lars Arnell, Senior VP, Divisional
Joe Allman, Senior VP
Matthew Koscal, Vice President, Divisional
Scott Hornback, Vice President, Divisional
Ethan Blank, Vice President

FINANCIAL DATA: Note: Data for latest year may not have been available at press time.

In U.S. $	2015	2014	2013	2012	2011	2010
Revenue	1,344,000,000	1,375,400,000	1,346,500,000	2,810,900,000	2,864,500,000	2,653,651,000
R&D Expense						
Operating Income	84,800,000	185,500,000	191,000,000	212,900,000	-105,600,000	133,354,000
Operating Margin %	6.30%	13.48%	14.18%	7.57%	-3.68%	5.02%
SGA Expense	418,700,000	387,900,000	518,100,000	1,417,400,000	999,200,000	974,799,000
Net Income	-27,100,000	64,300,000	26,700,000	51,300,000	-151,800,000	-13,846,000
Operating Cash Flow	196,700,000	320,500,000	240,600,000	252,400,000	131,500,000	256,418,000
Capital Expenditure	474,800,000	569,200,000	476,000,000	36,800,000	105,900,000	87,425,000
EBITDA	277,500,000	377,900,000	344,200,000	403,800,000	95,100,000	334,641,000
Return on Assets %	-.76%	1.90%	.77%	1.35%	-3.67%	-.31%
Return on Equity %	-4.44%	10.98%	5.01%	10.53%	-28.36%	-2.45%
Debt to Equity		3.27	3.43	3.58	4.50	3.78

CONTACT INFORMATION:
Phone: 317 484-6000   Fax:
Toll-Free:
Address: 8909 Purdue Rd., Ste. 300, Indianapolis, IN 46268 United States

STOCK TICKER/OTHER:
Stock Ticker: RJETQ
Employees: 5,935
Parent Company:

Exchange: PINX
Fiscal Year Ends: 12/31

SALARIES/BONUSES:
Top Exec. Salary: $463,462   Bonus: $415,000
Second Exec. Salary: $338,462   Bonus: $130,000

OTHER THOUGHTS:
Estimated Female Officers or Directors:
Hot Spot for Advancement for Women/Minorities:

Sales, profits and employees may be estimates. Financial information, benefits and other data can change quickly and may vary from those stated here.

ResortQuest International Inc

www.wyndhamvacationrentals.com/resortquest/index.htm

NAIC Code: 561599

TYPES OF BUSINESS:

Timeshare Rentals
Property Management Services
Real Estate Sales

BRANDS/DIVISIONS/AFFILIATES:

Wyndham Worldwide
Wyndham Exchange & Rentals

CONTACTS: Note: Officers with more than one job title may be intentionally listed here more than once.

Jennifer Rogers, Operations Manager
John W McConmy, Sr. VP
Geoff Ballotti, CEO-Pres., Wyndham Exchange & Rentals

GROWTH PLANS/SPECIAL FEATURES:

ResortQuest International, Inc. provides vacation condominium and home rental property management services. The firm is a subsidiary of Wyndham Exchange & Rentals, itself a division of travel services giant Wyndham Worldwide. The company markets and provides management services for nearly 10,000 premier beach, golf, ski and tennis destination resort locations. In conjunction with Partner Affiliates in North America and Europe, ResortQuest provides management services to approximately 50,000 vacation rental properties. ResortQuest conducts its business through two divisions: vacation rentals and real estate sales. Vacation rental properties are generally second homes or investment properties owned by individuals who assign ResortQuest the responsibility of managing, marketing and renting their properties. Vacation properties include hotels, lodges, condominiums, town homes, cottages, villas and vacation homes. Properties are located in over 100 locations across the U.S., Canada, Mexico, the Caribbean and Europe. The company offers real estate brokerage services throughout its U.S. resort locations, primarily in Delaware and Florida. This division allows customers to list a home as a ResortQuest property or to buy a vacation home.

The company offers its employees benefits that include health coverage, paid time off and a 401(k) plan.

FINANCIAL DATA: Note: Data for latest year may not have been available at press time.

In U.S. $	2015	2014	2013	2012	2011	2010
Revenue	505,000,000	500,000,000	475,000,000	450,000,000	435,000,000	
R&D Expense						
Operating Income						
Operating Margin %						
SGA Expense						
Net Income						
Operating Cash Flow						
Capital Expenditure						
EBITDA						
Return on Assets %						
Return on Equity %						
Debt to Equity						

CONTACT INFORMATION:

Phone: 850-837-4774   Fax: 850-837-5390
Toll-Free: 800-467-3529
Address: 546 Mary Esther Cut-Off NW, Ste. 3, Fort Walton Beach, FL 32548 United States

STOCK TICKER/OTHER:

Stock Ticker: Subsidiary   Exchange:
Employees: 5,000   Fiscal Year Ends: 12/31
Parent Company: Wyndham Worldwide

SALARIES/BONUSES:

Top Exec. Salary: $ Bonus: $
Second Exec. Salary: $ Bonus: $

OTHER THOUGHTS:

Estimated Female Officers or Directors:
Hot Spot for Advancement for Women/Minorities:

Sales, profits and employees may be estimates. Financial information, benefits and other data can change quickly and may vary from those stated here.

Rezidor Hotel Group AB

NAIC Code: 721110

www.rezidor.com

TYPES OF BUSINESS:

Hotel Management

BRANDS/DIVISIONS/AFFILIATES:

Radisson Blu
Park Inn by Radisson
Quorvus Collection
Filini
RBG Bar & Grill
Verres en Vers
Sure Bar

CONTACTS: Note: Officers with more than one job title may be intentionally listed here more than once.

Wolfgang Neumann, CEO
Olivier Harnisch, COO
Wolfgang Neumann, Pres.
Knut Kleiven, CFO
Eric De Neef, Sr. VP
Michael Farrell, Sr. VP-Human Resources
Eugene Staal, Sr. VP-Tech. Dev.
Marianne Ruhngard, General Counsel
Elie Younes, Head-Group Dev.
Trudy Rautio, Chmn.

GROWTH PLANS/SPECIAL FEATURES:

Rezidor Hotel Group AB is a hospitality management company that franchises, leases and manages hotel properties in 80 countries across the Europe, Middle East, the Nordics and Africa (EMEA) regions. The company currently has over 446 available hotels, with more than 100,000 rooms in operation and/or under development. The firm's brands include Radisson Blu and Park Inn by Radisson, which are operated under a franchise agreement with Carlson Hotels Worldwide and Quorvus Collection. Radisson Blu is a first-class full-service hotel brand that currently operates over 228 hotels in EMEA. Park Inn by Radisson is an up and coming mid-market hotel brand primarily located in EMEA. Its operations currently oversee more than 150 locations. The Quorvus Collection is a new generation of luxury hotels for contemporary global travelers. The Quorvus Collection brand expects a portfolio growth to 20 hotels in operation and development by 2020. Rezidor's hotels are located in countries such as Azerbaijan, Bulgaria, Croatia, Czech Republic, Estonia, Georgia, Hungary, Kazakhstan, Latvia, Lithuania, Poland, Romania, Russia, Slovakia, Turkey, Ukraine and Uzbekistan. The firm also operates four bar and restaurant brands: Filini, an Italian restaurant chain; RBG Bar & Grill, a trendy casual restaurant; Verres En Vers, a brasserie-style French restaurant; and Sure Bar, a style-focused casual bar. In April 2016, Carlson Hotels agreed to be acquired by HNA Tourism Group, along with Carlson's 51.3% stake in Rezidor. The transaction is subject to regulatory approvals.

FINANCIAL DATA: Note: Data for latest year may not have been available at press time.

In U.S. $	2015	2014	2013	2012	2011	2010
Revenue		1,058,977,000	1,038,841,000	1,043,575,000	976,401,500	887,713,200
R&D Expense						
Operating Income		34,683,080	49,891,540	-1,046,209	-8,662,298	4,418,710
Operating Margin %		3.27%	4.80%	-.10%	-.88%	.49%
SGA Expense		16,198,170	16,871,540	17,574,290		
Net Income		16,004,970	26,176,700	-19,035,140	-13,450,460	-2,998,531
Operating Cash Flow		46,558,580	61,667,610	18,649,870	15,916,850	53,805,220
Capital Expenditure		60,794,260	35,576,770	30,918,540	15,750,760	17,234,210
EBITDA		80,576,210	89,001,240	46,815,050	41,727,490	40,955,820
Return on Assets %		3.50%	6.11%	-4.49%	-3.16%	-.67%
Return on Equity %		7.56%	15.20%	-10.71%	-7.00%	-1.45%
Debt to Equity		0.02	0.11	0.11	0.06	0.04

CONTACT INFORMATION:

Phone: 33-2-702-9200   Fax: 32-2-702-9300
Toll-Free:
Address: Ave. du Bourget 44, Brussels, B-1130 Belgium

STOCK TICKER/OTHER:

Stock Ticker: REZIF   Exchange: GREY
Employees: 5,518   Fiscal Year Ends: 12/31
Parent Company:

SALARIES/BONUSES:

Top Exec. Salary: $ Bonus: $
Second Exec. Salary: $ Bonus: $

OTHER THOUGHTS:

Estimated Female Officers or Directors: 3
Hot Spot for Advancement for Women/Minorities: Y

Sales, profits and employees may be estimates. Financial information, benefits and other data can change quickly and may vary from those stated here.

Ritz-Carlton Hotel Company LLC (The)

www.ritzcarlton.com

NAIC Code: 721110

TYPES OF BUSINESS:

Hotels, Luxury
Condominiums
Golf Courses
Spas
Time Share Units

BRANDS/DIVISIONS/AFFILIATES:

Marriott International Inc
Six Senses
La Prairie
ESPA
Ritz-Carlton Destination Club (The)
Residencies at the Ritz-Carlton (The)
Ritz-Carlton Koh Samui
Ritz-Carlton Reserve

CONTACTS: Note: Officers with more than one job title may be intentionally listed here more than once.

Herve Humler, COO
Herve Humler, Pres.

GROWTH PLANS/SPECIAL FEATURES:

The Ritz-Carlton Hotel Company, LLC, a subsidiary of Marriott International, Inc., is one of the world's best-known luxury hotel chains, operating 91 hotels in 30 countries and territories. The firm maintains international sales offices in locations such as Chicago, New York, Los Angeles, Dubai, Shanghai, Tokyo and London. In an attempt to cater to an upscale client base, full-service luxury spas are offered at most of the company's resorts. Some spas at Ritz-Carlton hotels operate under the brand names Six Senses, La Prairie and ESPA. Besides its hotels, the firm provides vacation properties and residential suites under The Ritz-Carlton Destination Club and The Residencies at the Ritz-Carlton. The Ritz-Carlton Destination Club is the firm's time-share ownership unit, offering a flexible alternative to a second home. Membership is currently available in locations such as Aspen Highlands, Bachelor Gulch and Vail, Colorado; St. Thomas, U.S. Virgin Islands; San Francisco and North Lake Tahoe, California; Jupiter, Florida; Abaco, Bahamas; and Kauai Lagoons and Maui, Hawaii. The Residencies at the Ritz-Carlton offer luxury condominiums and estate homes throughout the U.S. and in Canada, Thailand, Israel, the Bahamas and Malaysia. Ritz-Carlton also markets its 12 luxury golf courses (many designed by leading names in the golf world such as Greg Norman and Jack Nicklaus) and fitness facilities to both local residents and visitors and hosts many PGA and Senior PGA tournaments. In November 2015, the firm signed with YTL Hotels for the development of two new hotels in Asia Pacific, the Ritz-Carlton, Koh Samui, in Thailand, and Ritz-Carlton Reserve in Niseko Village, Japan.

The firm offers employees health care & dependent care spending accounts; tuition reimbursement; dental & vision insurance; short- and long-term disability coverage; credit union membership; and employee assistance programs.

FINANCIAL DATA: Note: Data for latest year may not have been available at press time.

In U.S. $	2015	2014	2013	2012	2011	2010
Revenue	2,400,000,000	2,355,320,000	2,222,213,400	2,126,520,000	2,217,060,000	2,104,380,000
R&D Expense						
Operating Income						
Operating Margin %						
SGA Expense						
Net Income						
Operating Cash Flow						
Capital Expenditure						
EBITDA						
Return on Assets %						
Return on Equity %						
Debt to Equity						

CONTACT INFORMATION:

Phone: 301-547-4700   Fax:
Toll-Free: 888-241-3333
Address: 4445 Willard Ave., Ste. 800, Chevy Chase, MD 20815 United States

STOCK TICKER/OTHER:

Stock Ticker: Subsidiary   Exchange:
Employees: 40,000   Fiscal Year Ends: 12/31
Parent Company: Marriott International Inc

SALARIES/BONUSES:

Top Exec. Salary: $ Bonus: $
Second Exec. Salary: $ Bonus: $

OTHER THOUGHTS:

Estimated Female Officers or Directors: 1
Hot Spot for Advancement for Women/Minorities:

Sales, profits and employees may be estimates. Financial information, benefits and other data can change quickly and may vary from those stated here.

Rolls-Royce plc

NAIC Code: 336412

www.rolls-royce.com

TYPES OF BUSINESS:

Aircraft Engine and Engine Parts Manufacturing
Power Generation Solutions
Marine Propulsion Systems
Aftermarket & Support Services

BRANDS/DIVISIONS/AFFILIATES:

Rolls-Royce Leasing Limited
Rolls-Royce Fuel Cell Systems Limited
Rolls-Royce Power Engineering plc
Alpha Partners Leasing Limited
Composite Technology & Applications Limited
Xian XR Aero Components Co Limited
Techjet Aerofoils Limited

CONTACTS: Note: Officers with more than one job title may be intentionally listed here more than once.

John Rishton, CEO
David Smith, CFO
Mary Humiston, Dir.-Human Resources
Colin P. Smith, Dir.-Tech.
Rob Webb, General Counsel
Alain Michaelis, Dir.-Oper.
Miles Cowdry, Dir.-Corp. Dev.
Lawrie Haynes, Pres., Nuclear & Marine
Andrew Heath, Pres., Energy
John Paterson, Pres., Marine & Industrial Power Systems
Ian Davis, Chmn.
James M. Guyette, CEO
Tony Wood, Pres., Aerospace

GROWTH PLANS/SPECIAL FEATURES:

Rolls-Royce plc designs and produces engines and power systems for civilian aerospace, defense aerospace, marine and energy markets worldwide. In civilian aerospace, its customers include roughly 380 airlines and 13,000 gas turbine engines currently in service. Defense aerospace operations serve 160 armed forces customers in 103 countries, with offerings including military transport aircraft, helicopters and combat aircraft. In the marine sector, the company serves more than 4,000 customers, including 70 navies, with equipment installed on over 30,000 vessels operating around the world. The firm's energy solutions include power generation and distribution equipment sold worldwide. Additionally, the firm has begun to increase its involvement in nuclear energy capabilities and applications. Rolls-Royce also offers support services for its engines through a global network of maintenance centers. Services include operation management, repairs and overhauls and customer training. Rolls-Royce has subsidiaries and joint ventures in the U.K., Brazil, France, China, Italy, Norway and various other places. These include Rolls-Royce Leasing Limited, Rolls-Royce Fuel Cell Systems Limited, Rolls-Royce Power Engineering plc, Alpha Partners Leasing Limited, Composite Technology & Applications Limited, Xian XR Aero Components Co. Limited and Techjet Aerofoils Limited. In January 2015, the firm obtained a major order from Chinese locomotive manufacturer CNR Dalian for the delivery of 232 MTU (maximum transmission unit) Series 4000 engines that will be installed in new freight locomotives for South African operator Transnet Freight Rail. That April, it received an order to supply engines for 50 Emirates A380 planes. In January 2016, Rolls-Royce announced plans to invest more than $400 million in a new Washington, U.K. fleet support plant which will manufacture a range of aerospace discs for in-service engines.

FINANCIAL DATA: Note: Data for latest year may not have been available at press time.

In U.S. $	2015	2014	2013	2012	2011	2010
Revenue	17,919,390,000	17,933,750,000	20,253,810,000	15,877,430,000	14,523,520,000	14,472,600,000
R&D Expense	1,067,983,000	1,035,343,000	891,726,400	768,999,700	604,493,900	550,964,200
Operating Income	1,957,098,000	1,692,061,000	2,004,100,000	1,792,592,000	1,548,444,000	1,475,331,000
Operating Margin %	10.92%	9.43%	9.89%	11.29%	10.66%	10.19%
SGA Expense	1,382,633,000	1,467,497,000	1,727,312,000	1,291,241,000		
Net Income	108,365,000	90,086,560	1,784,758,000	2,978,079,000	1,109,762,000	703,719,600
Operating Cash Flow	1,428,329,000	1,698,589,000	2,663,429,000	1,638,531,000	1,639,837,000	1,698,589,000
Capital Expenditure	1,168,514,000	1,468,803,000	1,530,166,000	894,337,600	1,011,842,000	881,281,500
EBITDA	1,359,132,000	1,138,485,000	3,416,761,000	4,234,068,000	2,044,573,000	1,477,942,000
Return on Assets %	.37%	.30%	6.63%	13.20%	5.20%	3.40%
Return on Equity %	1.45%	1.15%	23.38%	43.01%	20.01%	13.89%
Debt to Equity	0.57	0.34	0.38	0.20	0.26	0.28

CONTACT INFORMATION:

Phone: 44 2072229020　　Fax: 44 2072279170
Toll-Free:
Address: 62 Buckingham Gate, London, SW1E 6AT United Kingdom

STOCK TICKER/OTHER:

Stock Ticker: RYCEF　　　　　　　Exchange: PINX
Employees: 54,100　　　　　　　　Fiscal Year Ends: 12/31
Parent Company:

SALARIES/BONUSES:

Top Exec. Salary: $　　　　Bonus: $
Second Exec. Salary: $　　　Bonus: $

OTHER THOUGHTS:

Estimated Female Officers or Directors: 4
Hot Spot for Advancement for Women/Minorities: Y

Rosewood Hotels & Resorts LLC www.rosewoodhotels.com

NAIC Code: 721110

TYPES OF BUSINESS:

Hotel & Resort Management
Spas
Private Residences

BRANDS/DIVISIONS/AFFILIATES:

Rosewood Hotel Group
Rosewood Inn of the Anasazi
Rosewood Siem Reap
Rosewood Phnom Penh
Rosewood Luang Prabang

CONTACTS: *Note: Officers with more than one job title may be intentionally listed here more than once.*

Sonia Cheng, CEO
Radha Arora, Pres.
Sheri Line, Corp. Dir.-Human Resources
George Fong, Sr. VP-Architecture & Design
Susan Aldridge, General Counsel
Elias Assaly, VP-Oper.
Stephen Miano, Sr. VP-Finance
Katherine Blaisdell, VP-Construction Dev.
Erin Green, VP-Dev., Americas
James Simmonds, VP-Dev., Asia Pacific
Paul Arnold, VP-Dev., EMEA

GROWTH PLANS/SPECIAL FEATURES:

Rosewood Hotels & Resorts, LLC, a subsidiary of Rosewood Hotel Group, operates ultra-luxury boutique hotels and resorts worldwide. It has 18 hotels and resorts in the U.S., Canada, Mexico, the Caribbean, France, the UAE, Saudi Arabia, Thailand, Cambodia, Indonesia and China. Several facilities are currently under construction including Rosewood Beijing, Rosewood Phuket and Rosewood Dubai. Besides constructing its own facilities, Rosewood has acquired existing properties and management contracts, including the Rosewood Inn of the Anasazi in Santa Fe, New Mexico. Its facilities are generally small, featuring less than 200 accommodations. The company uses architecture and decor to attempt to capture the unique history, geography and culture of each hotel or resort location. Amenities offered at Rosewood's facilities might include tennis courts, a courtesy car with 5-mile radius, unpacking and packing services, babysitting services, twice-daily housekeeping with nightly turndown service, pools and fitness centers as well as shops and various dining facilities. Some locations also offer business centers stocked with computers, printers, faxes and copiers. In addition, several hotels and resorts also feature private residences, which offer owners the same services and amenities as resort guests. The private residences often come fully furnished and feature floor plan inclusions such as full kitchens, fireplaces, private pools and terraces. Rosewood plans to expand to 50 properties by 2020. In October 2015, the firm was appointed to manage Rosewood Siem Reap, scheduled to open in 2019, which will be the company's second property in Cambodia, following Rosewood Phnom Penh, which opened in 2016. Also, Rosewood Luang Prabang in Laos is scheduled to open in 2017.

FINANCIAL DATA: *Note: Data for latest year may not have been available at press time.*

In U.S. $	2015	2014	2013	2012	2011	2010
Revenue	575,000,000	563,000,000	546,000,000	500,000,000	471,000,000	
R&D Expense						
Operating Income						
Operating Margin %						
SGA Expense						
Net Income						
Operating Cash Flow						
Capital Expenditure						
EBITDA						
Return on Assets %						
Return on Equity %						
Debt to Equity						

CONTACT INFORMATION:

Phone: 214-880-4231   Fax:
Toll-Free: 888-767-3966
Address: 500 Crescent Court, Ste. 300, Dallas, TX 75201 United States

STOCK TICKER/OTHER:

Stock Ticker: Subsidiary   Exchange:
Employees: 6,000   Fiscal Year Ends:
Parent Company: Rosewood Hotel Group

SALARIES/BONUSES:

Top Exec. Salary: $ Bonus: $
Second Exec. Salary: $ Bonus: $

OTHER THOUGHTS:

Estimated Female Officers or Directors: 4
Hot Spot for Advancement for Women/Minorities: Y

Royal Caribbean Cruises Ltd

www.royalcaribbean.com

NAIC Code: 483112

TYPES OF BUSINESS:

Cruise Line
Rail Tours
Online Travel Services
Academic Tours

BRANDS/DIVISIONS/AFFILIATES:

Royal Caribbean International
Celebrity Cruises
Azamara Club Cruises
Pullmantur
CDF Croisieres de France
TUI Cruises
Celebrity Xpedition
SkySea Cruises

CONTACTS: *Note: Officers with more than one job title may be intentionally listed here more than once.*

Lawrence Pimentel, CEO, Subsidiary
Michael Bayley, CEO, Subsidiary
Lisa Lutoff-Perlo, CEO, Subsidiary
Jorge Vilches, CEO, Subsidiary
Richard Fain, CEO
Jason Liberty, CFO
Henry Pujol, Chief Accounting Officer
Adam Goldstein, COO
Harri Kulovaara, Executive VP, Divisional
Bradley Stein, General Counsel

GROWTH PLANS/SPECIAL FEATURES:

Royal Caribbean Cruises, Ltd. is a global cruise vacation firm, serving the contemporary, premium and deluxe cruise markets, including the budget and luxury segments. With 44 ships offering 110,900 berths, the firm operates five brand names: Royal Caribbean International, Celebrity Cruises, Azamara Club Cruises, Pullmantur and CDF Croisieres de France. It also has a 50% joint venture investment in TUI Cruises with TUI AG. Royal Caribbean's ships have itineraries that call on approximately 490 destinations worldwide. Royal Caribbean International operates 23 ships with 68,600 berths, offering cruise itineraries that range from 2-24 nights. Its destinations include Alaska, Asia, Australia, Bahamas, Bermuda, Canada, the Caribbean, Europe, the Panama Canal, South America and New Zealand. The Celebrity Cruises brand operates 10 ships with 23,100 berths targeted toward higher-end clientele. It also operates Celebrity Xpedition, a ship that travels to the Galapagos Islands and offers pre-cruise tours of Ecuador. Azamara Club Cruises consists of two smaller ships, of about 1,400 passengers each, that focus on cruises to unique destinations, with an emphasis on on-board lectures and fine dining. Its ships sail in Asia, the Mediterranean, South America and less traveled Caribbean Islands. Pullmantur serves the Spanish, Portuguese and Latin American cruise markets, and it operates three ships with 6,200 berths. CDF Croisieres de France serves the French market and operates two ships with an aggregate capacity of 2,800 births. TUI Cruises operates four ships, Mein Schiff 1, 2, 3 and 4, with a capacity of 8,800 berths. Mein Schiff 5 and 6 are on order for a late-2016/mid-2017 delivery, and will bring aggregate capacity to 5,000 berths. Moreover, 35%-owned SkySea Cruises, which offers a custom-tailored product for Chinese cruise guests. In June 2016, the firm signed an agreement with Miami-Dade Country to build and operate a new cruise terminal at PortMiami.

FINANCIAL DATA: *Note: Data for latest year may not have been available at press time.*

In U.S. $	2015	2014	2013	2012	2011	2010
Revenue	8,299,074,000	8,073,855,000	7,959,894,000	7,688,024,000	7,537,263,000	6,752,504,000
R&D Expense						
Operating Income	874,902,000	941,859,000	798,148,000	403,110,000	931,628,000	802,633,000
Operating Margin %	10.54%	11.66%	10.02%	5.24%	12.36%	11.88%
SGA Expense	1,086,504,000	1,048,952,000	1,044,819,000	1,011,543,000	960,602,000	848,079,000
Net Income	665,783,000	764,146,000	473,692,000	18,287,000	607,421,000	547,467,000
Operating Cash Flow	1,946,366,000	1,743,759,000	1,412,068,000	1,381,734,000	1,455,739,000	1,663,019,000
Capital Expenditure	1,613,340,000	1,811,398,000	763,777,000	1,291,499,000	1,173,626,000	2,187,189,000
EBITDA	1,770,516,000	1,794,890,000	1,560,825,000	1,104,565,000	1,634,054,000	1,446,349,000
Return on Assets %	3.19%	3.74%	2.37%	.09%	3.07%	2.88%
Return on Equity %	8.14%	8.94%	5.53%	.21%	7.43%	7.09%
Debt to Equity	0.96	0.92	0.73	0.83	0.93	1.00

CONTACT INFORMATION:

Phone: 305 539-6000   Fax: 305 539-0562
Toll-Free:
Address: 1050 Caribbean Way, Miami, FL 33132 United States

STOCK TICKER/OTHER:

Stock Ticker: RCL   Exchange: NYS
Employees: 66,000   Fiscal Year Ends: 12/31
Parent Company:

SALARIES/BONUSES:

Top Exec. Salary: $1,038,462   Bonus: $
Second Exec. Salary: $568,939   Bonus: $300,000

OTHER THOUGHTS:

Estimated Female Officers or Directors: 3

Hot Spot for Advancement for Women/Minorities: Y

Ryanair Holdings plc

www.ryanair.com

NAIC Code: 481111

TYPES OF BUSINESS:

Airline

BRANDS/DIVISIONS/AFFILIATES:

Ryanair Ltd
Aviation Insurance Limited
Aviation Finance and Leasing Sarl
Ryanair.com Ltd

CONTACTS: *Note: Officers with more than one job title may be intentionally listed here more than once.*

Michael OLeary, CEO
Michael Hickey, COO
Neil Sorahan, CFO
Kenny Jacobs, Chief Mktg. Officer
Edward Wilson, Chief People Officer
John Hurley, CTO
Michael Hickey, Dir.-Eng.
Juliusz Komorek, Dir.-Legal Affairs
David O'Brien, Dir.-Flight & Ground Oper.
Juliusz Komorek, Dir.-Regulatory Affairs
Ray Conway, Chief Pilot
Edward Wilson, Dir.-Personnel & In-Flight
Caroline Green, Dir.-Customer Service
David Bonderman, Chmn.

GROWTH PLANS/SPECIAL FEATURES:

Ryanair Holdings plc operates a low fares scheduled passenger airline serving short-haul, point-to-point routes between Ireland, the U.K., Continental Europe and Morocco. The firm flies from 84 bases at airports in Dublin, London, Glasgow, Brussels, Frankfurt, Milan, Stockholm, Rome, Barcelona, Nottingham East Midlands, Liverpool, Shannon, Pisa, Cork, Marseille, Madrid, Bremen, Dusseldorf, Bristol, Alicante, Belfast, Bournemouth, Birmingham, Kerry, Edinburgh, Reus, Alghero, Cagliari, Trapani, Bologna and Pescara. The company transports approximately 90 million passengers per year and offers over 1,800 scheduled short-haul flights per day. It serves 200 locations throughout Europe and Morocco, with an operating fleet of 340 Boeing 737-800s aircraft. Ryanair has an additional 330 Boeing 737s on order, with plans to then lower fares and grow traffic to 180 million passengers per year by 2024. The company also has a corporate jet charter service, offering a Boeing 737-700 for corporate or group hire. Booking for the company's flights is done almost exclusively online through its web site, which also offers online booking of car rental, hotels, hostels, tours and travel services, such as travel insurance, gift vouchers, financial deals and airport transfers. Ryanair owns wholly-owned subsidiaries Ryanair Ltd.; Aviation Insurance Limited; Aviation Finance and Leasing Sarl; and Ryanair.com Ltd. The firm is among the top air carriers in the world in terms of total international passengers per year.

FINANCIAL DATA: *Note: Data for latest year may not have been available at press time.*

In U.S. $	2015	2014	2013	2012	2011	2010
Revenue	6,387,979,000	5,690,544,000	5,518,020,000	4,960,117,000	4,100,666,000	
R&D Expense						
Operating Income	1,178,285,000	744,096,700	811,433,700	771,890,200	551,576,100	
Operating Margin %	18.44%	13.07%	14.70%	15.56%	13.45%	
SGA Expense	956,050,200	856,287,400	715,738,400	672,240,400	599,593,300	
Net Income	979,211,400	590,667,700	643,204,100	633,148,800	423,229,000	
Operating Cash Flow	1,908,711,000	1,180,206,000	1,156,366,000	1,152,751,000	888,374,200	
Capital Expenditure	890,859,700	571,460,900	351,033,800	358,829,500	1,013,671,000	
EBITDA	1,620,495,000	1,159,643,000	1,219,975,000	1,187,888,000	895,379,000	
Return on Assets %	8.25%	5.88%	6.34%	6.36%	4.63%	
Return on Equity %	23.67%	15.94%	17.30%	17.90%	12.91%	
Debt to Equity	1.01	0.82	0.98	1.02	1.16	

CONTACT INFORMATION:

Phone: 353 18121212 Fax: 353 18121213
Toll-Free:
Address: Airside Business Park, Swords, County Dublin, Ireland

STOCK TICKER/OTHER:

Stock Ticker: RYAAY Exchange: NAS
Employees: 9,393 Fiscal Year Ends: 03/31
Parent Company:

SALARIES/BONUSES:

Top Exec. Salary: $1,129,816 Bonus: $903,853
Second Exec. Salary: $ Bonus: $

OTHER THOUGHTS:

Estimated Female Officers or Directors: 3

Hot Spot for Advancement for Women/Minorities: Y

Sales, profits and employees may be estimates. Financial information, benefits and other data can change quickly and may vary from those stated here.

Ryman Hospitality Properties Inc

rymanhp.com

NAIC Code: 721110

TYPES OF BUSINESS:

Hotels & Convention Centers
Vacation Property Management
Live Entertainment Venues
Golf Courses
Radio Station Operation

BRANDS/DIVISIONS/AFFILIATES:

Gaylord Opryland Resort & Convention Center
Gaylord Palms Resort & Convention Center
Gaylord Texan Resort & Convention Center
Gaylord National Resort & Convention Center
Grand Ole Opry (The)
General Jackson Showboat
Gaylord Springs Golf Links
AC Hotel

CONTACTS: *Note: Officers with more than one job title may be intentionally listed here more than once.*

Colin Reed, CEO
Mark Fioravanti, CFO
Jennifer Hutcheson, Controller
Scott Lynn, General Counsel
Patrick Chaffin, Senior VP, Divisional
Bennett Westbrook, Senior VP, Divisional
Todd Siefert, Treasurer

GROWTH PLANS/SPECIAL FEATURES:

Ryman Hospitality Properties, Inc. is a real estate investment trust (REIT) that owns hospitality assets focused on the large group meetings and conventions sector of the lodging market. The firm's hospitality assets include four upscale, meetings-focused resorts totaling 7,795 rooms and 1.9 million square feet of meeting and exhibit space that are managed by Marriott International, Inc. under the Gaylord Hotels brand. Its hotels consist of the Gaylord Opryland Resort & Convention Center in Nashville, Tennessee; the Gaylord Palms Resort & Convention Center near Orlando, Florida; the Gaylord Texan Resort & Convention Center near Dallas, Texas; and the Gaylord National Resort & Convention Center near Washington, D.C. Other assets managed by Marriott include the General Jackson Showboat; the Gaylord Springs Golf Links, a championship golf course; the Wildhorse Saloon; and the Inn at Opryland, a 303-room overflow hotel adjacent to Gaylord Opryland. Additionally, the firm owns The Grand Ole Opry, a live country music variety show and one of the longest-running radio shows in the U.S.; the Ryman Auditorium; and the country radio station WSM-AM radio. In December 2014, the firm acquired a 192-room hotel that it rebranded AC Hotel at National Harbor, Washington D.C.

FINANCIAL DATA: *Note: Data for latest year may not have been available at press time.*

In U.S. $	2015	2014	2013	2012	2011	2010
Revenue	1,092,124,000	1,040,991,000	954,562,000	986,594,000	952,144,000	769,961,000
R&D Expense						
Operating Income	162,062,000	153,105,000	76,188,000	-4,754,000	79,531,000	-65,986,000
Operating Margin %	14.83%	14.70%	7.98%	-.48%	8.35%	-8.56%
SGA Expense	96,277,000	87,388,000	82,820,000	186,590,000	179,301,000	200,490,000
Net Income	111,511,000	126,452,000	118,352,000	-26,644,000	10,177,000	-89,128,000
Operating Cash Flow	234,362,000	247,004,000	137,699,000	176,470,000	153,919,000	139,484,000
Capital Expenditure	79,815,000	79,583,000	36,959,000	95,233,000	132,592,000	194,647,000
EBITDA	277,940,000	298,725,000	203,259,000	160,604,000	217,450,000	54,071,000
Return on Assets %	4.70%	5.00%	4.56%	-1.04%	.39%	-3.37%
Return on Equity %	28.55%	20.88%	14.08%	-2.80%	.98%	-8.45%
Debt to Equity	3.77	3.34	1.52	1.05	1.02	1.06

CONTACT INFORMATION:

Phone: 615-316-6000   Fax: 615-316-6555
Toll-Free:
Address: 1 Gaylord Dr., Nashville, TN 37214 United States

STOCK TICKER/OTHER:

Stock Ticker: RHP   Exchange: NYS
Employees: 682   Fiscal Year Ends: 12/31
Parent Company:

SALARIES/BONUSES:

Top Exec. Salary: $782,830   Bonus: $156,544
Second Exec. Salary: $469,407   Bonus: $63,817

OTHER THOUGHTS:

Estimated Female Officers or Directors: 1
Hot Spot for Advancement for Women/Minorities:

Sales, profits and employees may be estimates. Financial information, benefits and other data can change quickly and may vary from those stated here.

Sabre Corporation

www.sabre-holdings.com

NAIC Code: 519130

TYPES OF BUSINESS:

Travel Reservations System for Airlines
Travel Marketing Solutions
Distribution & Technology Solutions
Consulting Services

BRANDS/DIVISIONS/AFFILIATES:

Sabre Travel Network
Sabre Airline Solutions
Sabre Hospitality Solutions
MySabre
GetThere

CONTACTS:
Note: Officers with more than one job title may be intentionally listed here more than once.

Thomas Klein, CEO
Richard Simonson, CFO
Lawrence Kellner, Chairman of the Board
Jami Kindle, Chief Accounting Officer
Deborah Kerr, Chief Technology Officer
Rachel Gonzalez, Executive VP
William Robinson, Executive VP
Hugh Jones, Executive VP
Sean Menke, Executive VP
Alexander Alt, General Manager, Divisional
Steve Milton, Secretary
Gregory Webb, Vice Chairman

GROWTH PLANS/SPECIAL FEATURES:

Sabre Corporation is a provider of travel products and services through its three brands and businesses: Sabre Travel Network, Sabre Airline Solutions and Sabre Hospitality Solutions. Sabre Travel Network markets and distributes travel-related products and services through online and traditional travel agencies and corporate channels. Users of the Sabre system can access information about, book reservations for and purchase a variety of travel offerings, including airline trips, hotel stays, car rentals, cruises and tour packages through brands GetThere, Moneydirect and TRAMS. Sabre tools allow travel agencies to book travel online, automate certain processes and manage reservations. The company's online booking portal for agents, MySabre, offers agents and suppliers merchandising opportunities at the point of sale. Buyers and sellers of travel products may also connect through Sabre GDS (global distribution system), an online portal with over 400 airlines, 100,000 hotels, 25 car rental companies, 14 cruise lines and 50 railroads. The Sabre Airline Solutions segment provides passenger management services, software products and consulting services to airlines. The Sabre Hospitality Solutions segment offers hotel suppliers marketing, distribution and consulting services utilized by over 18,000 international hotels. In 2014, the company went public on NASDAQ under ticker symbol SABR. In 2015, the firm agreed to acquire the Trust Group of Companies; and sold Travelocity.com to Expedia.

FINANCIAL DATA:
Note: Data for latest year may not have been available at press time.

In U.S. $	2015	2014	2013	2012	2011	2010
Revenue	2,960,896,000	2,631,417,000	3,049,525,000	3,039,060,000	2,855,961,000	2,832,393,000
R&D Expense						
Operating Income	459,769,000	421,345,000	176,760,000	-618,785,000	128,245,000	-62,534,000
Operating Margin %	15.52%	16.01%	5.79%	-20.36%	4.49%	-2.20%
SGA Expense	557,077,000	468,152,000	792,929,000	547,928,000	806,435,000	565,342,000
Net Income	545,482,000	69,223,000	-100,494,000	-611,356,000	-66,074,000	-268,852,000
Operating Cash Flow	529,207,000	387,659,000	157,188,000	305,754,000	356,444,000	352,852,000
Capital Expenditure	286,697,000	227,227,000	226,026,000	193,262,000	164,638,000	130,457,000
EBITDA	811,249,000	710,975,000	487,559,000	-274,102,000	424,562,000	222,290,000
Return on Assets %	10.78%	1.21%	-2.89%	-12.96%	-1.87%	
Return on Equity %	192.59%					
Debt to Equity	6.56	36.54				

CONTACT INFORMATION:

Phone: 682-605-1000   Fax:
Toll-Free:
Address: 3150 Sabre Dr., Southlake, TX 76092 United States

STOCK TICKER/OTHER:

Stock Ticker: SABR   Exchange: NAS
Employees: 8,000   Fiscal Year Ends: 12/31
Parent Company:

SALARIES/BONUSES:

Top Exec. Salary: $936,923   Bonus: $
Second Exec. Salary: Bonus: $
$639,231

OTHER THOUGHTS:

Estimated Female Officers or Directors: 1
Hot Spot for Advancement for Women/Minorities:

Sales, profits and employees may be estimates. Financial information, benefits and other data can change quickly and may vary from those stated here.

Sabre Travel Network

www.sabretravelnetwork.com

NAIC Code: 519130

TYPES OF BUSINESS:

Airline Reservation Systems
Travel Application Service Provider
Online Reservation Systems
Business-to-Business Travel Services
Marketing Services

BRANDS/DIVISIONS/AFFILIATES:

Sabre Corporation
Sabre Global Distribution System
TRAMS
GetThere
Trams.com
GetThere.com
Sabre Red

CONTACTS: *Note: Officers with more than one job title may be intentionally listed here more than once.*

Sean Menke, Exec. VP-Oper.
Jan Altemeier, Sr. VP-Global Oper.
Candi Clarke, VP-Acct. Mgmt. & Sales
Jay Jones, Sr. VP-The Americas
Hans Belle, VP
Rajiv Rajian, VP-Global Sales & Account Mgmt.
Harald Eisenacher, Sr. VP-EMEA
David Gross, Sr. VP-Travel Supplier Dist.

GROWTH PLANS/SPECIAL FEATURES:

Sabre Travel Network, a subsidiary of Sabre Corporation, distributes its travel agency customers' travel-related products and services through one of the world's largest distribution systems. The network provides travel agency subscribers with pricing information from airlines, hotels, car rental companies and cruise lines. Approximately 370,000 travel agents in 130 countries subscribe to the firm's Sabre Global Distribution System (GDS), which enables them to make reservations with over 400 airlines, 125,000 hotels, 25 car rental companies and 16 cruise lines. The system allows users to check schedules, availability, pricing and policies. The Sabre GDS also provides information on currency, medical and visa requirements and weather. The Sabre Red platform features a portfolio of capabilities and applications through four benefit suites: Sabre Red Value Suite, providing access to accurate and best-priced travel options in the world; Sabre Red Service Suite, a personalized service for travel agencies; Sabre Red Revenue Suite, which helps lower costs and increase revenue; and Sabre Red Efficiency Suite, a workflow management solutions service. Other brands include TRAMS (Trams.com), which helps over 11,000 agency locations increase revenues, optimize customer management and streamline processes; and GetThere (GetThere.com), a leading web-based corporate travel booking tool which processes more than 12 million transactions annually.

FINANCIAL DATA: *Note: Data for latest year may not have been available at press time.*

In U.S. $	2015	2014	2013	2012	2011	2010
Revenue	2,102,792,000	1,854,785,000	1,821,498,000			
R&D Expense						
Operating Income						
Operating Margin %						
SGA Expense						
Net Income	751,546,000	657,326,000	667,498,000	670,778,000	594,418,000	
Operating Cash Flow						
Capital Expenditure						
EBITDA						
Return on Assets %						
Return on Equity %						
Debt to Equity						

CONTACT INFORMATION:

Phone: 682-605-1000   Fax:
Toll-Free:
Address: 3150 Sabre Dr., Southlake, TX 76092 United States

STOCK TICKER/OTHER:

Stock Ticker: Subsidiary   Exchange:
Employees: Fiscal Year Ends: 12/31
Parent Company: SABRE CORPORATION

SALARIES/BONUSES:

Top Exec. Salary: $ Bonus: $
Second Exec. Salary: $ Bonus: $

OTHER THOUGHTS:

Estimated Female Officers or Directors: 2
Hot Spot for Advancement for Women/Minorities:

Sales, profits and employees may be estimates. Financial information, benefits and other data can change quickly and may vary from those stated here.

Sands China Ltd

NAIC Code: 721110

TYPES OF BUSINESS:

Resorts & Casinos
Ferry & Limo Services
Travel Agency

BRANDS/DIVISIONS/AFFILIATES:

Las Vegas Sands Corp
Venetian Macao
Sands Macao
Plaza Macao
Sands Cotai Central
Cotai Arena (The)
Cotai Expo
Cotai Water Jet

CONTACTS: Note: Officers with more than one job title may be intentionally listed here more than once.

Sheldom Gary Adelson, CEO
Wilfred Wong, COO
Edward Matthew Tracy, Pres.
Toh Hup Hock, CFO
David Alec Andrew Fleming, General Counsel
Sheldon Gary Adelson, Chmn.

GROWTH PLANS/SPECIAL FEATURES:

Sands China Ltd., a subsidiary of Las Vegas Sands Corp., is a developer, owner and operator of resorts in Macao, China's hub of tourism and gaming. Its properties include the Venetian Macao, the Sands Macao, the Plaza Macao and Sands Cotai Central. The Venetian Macao features a 39-floor luxury hotel with over 2,900 suites, 374,000 square feet of gaming and casino space, 1 million square feet of retail and dining space as well as the Malo Clinic and Spa, one of Asia's largest medical and beauty spas, and Macao's largest entertainment venue, The Cotai Arena. The Sands Macao offers approximately 249,000 square feet of gaming space and a 289-suite hotel tower as well as several restaurants, VIP facilities, a theater and other high-end services and amenities. The Plaza Macao features approximately 108,000 square feet of gaming space; Paiza mansions that average 7,000 square feet each; retail space, which is connected to the mall at The Venetian Macao; several food and beverage offerings; and conference, banquet and other facilities. Additionally, the firm owns the Four Seasons Hotel Macao, Cotai Strip, a 360-room facility connected to the Venetian Macao and the Plaza Macao. Four Seasons Hotels, Inc. manages and operates the facility. The Sands Cotai Central, located in the center of the Cotai Strip, consists of nearly 5,800 hotel rooms under the brand names Conrad, Sheraton and Holiday Inn, and nearly 100 boutiques and galleries. In total, its properties cover a combined 9,000 suites and hotel rooms and over 100 different restaurants and food outlets. Sands China also owns Cotai Expo, a convention and exhibition hall in Asia; the 1,800-seat luxury Venetian Theatre; and Cotai Water Jet, a major high-speed ferry companies that operates between Hong Kong and Macao.

The company offers its employees full medical and dental insurance plans, 24-hour staff meals, staff shuttle buses and employee discounts.

FINANCIAL DATA: Note: Data for latest year may not have been available at press time.

In U.S. $	2015	2014	2013	2012	2011	2010
Revenue	6,820,078,000	9,505,230,000	8,907,859,000	6,511,374,000	4,880,787,000	4,142,304,000
R&D Expense						
Operating Income	1,518,772,000	2,624,182,000	2,290,120,000	1,281,163,000	1,202,272,000	785,686,000
Operating Margin %	22.26%	27.60%	25.70%	19.67%	24.63%	18.96%
SGA Expense	787,112,000	961,473,000	1,059,937,000	925,930,000	613,388,000	219,043,000
Net Income	1,459,442,000	2,547,704,000	2,214,882,000	1,235,681,000	1,133,050,000	666,450,000
Operating Cash Flow	1,967,522,000	3,223,849,000	3,078,706,000	1,900,631,000	1,376,058,000	1,362,852,000
Capital Expenditure	1,123,636,000	726,489,000	609,925,000	1,001,351,000	784,504,000	347,452,000
EBITDA	2,065,570,000	3,154,345,000	2,805,867,000	1,653,340,000	1,469,361,000	1,147,932,000
Return on Assets %	13.19%	22.33%	20.27%	12.04%	12.18%	8.43%
Return on Equity %	23.79%	39.56%	36.80%	22.26%	22.94%	16.56%
Debt to Equity	0.57	0.49	0.46	0.57	0.60	0.62

CONTACT INFORMATION:

Phone: 853 8118-2888   Fax: 853 2888-3382
Toll-Free:
Address: Venetian Macao-Hotel, L2 Estr, Baia de N. Snhora da Esparanc, Taipa Macao

STOCK TICKER/OTHER:

Stock Ticker: SCHYY   Exchange: PINX
Employees: 15,339   Fiscal Year Ends: 12/31
Parent Company: LAS VEGAS SANDS CORP

SALARIES/BONUSES:

Top Exec. Salary: $ Bonus: $
Second Exec. Salary: $ Bonus: $

OTHER THOUGHTS:

Estimated Female Officers or Directors:
Hot Spot for Advancement for Women/Minorities:

SAS AB

NAIC Code: 481111

TYPES OF BUSINESS:

Airline
Air Cargo
Travel Services
Aircraft Maintenance

BRANDS/DIVISIONS/AFFILIATES:

Scandinavian Airlines Danmark
Scandinavian Airlines Norge
Scandinavian Airlines Sverige
SAS Technical Services
SAS Ground Services
SAS Cargo
Blue1
Wideroe

CONTACTS: Note: Officers with more than one job title may be intentionally listed here more than once.

Rickard Gustafson, CEO
Lars Sandahl Sorensen, COO
Rickard Gustafson, Pres.
Goran Jansson, CFO
Mats Lonnkvist, General Counsel
Flemming J. Jensen, Exec. VP-Oper.
Henriette Fenger Ellekrog, Exec. VP-Corp. Comm.
Sture Stolen, VP-Investor Rel.
Joakim Landholm, Exec. VP-Commercial
Benny Zakrisson, Exec. VP-Infrastructure
Fritz H. Schur, Chmn.

GROWTH PLANS/SPECIAL FEATURES:

SAS AB (SAS) is Scandinavia's leading airline, transporting more than 28 million passengers annually. The company's 119 destinations include Europe, the U.S. and Asia. With the legal name Scandinavian Airlines Systems, it is the flag carrier of Sweden, Norway and Denmark, and the largest airline in Scandinavia. SAS' fleet include Airbus A319, A320, A321, A330 and A340 aircraft, Boeing 737-600/700/800 aircraft and Bombardier CRJ900 aircraft. The first Airbus A320 neo is scheduled to be delivered late 2016, and will be based in Stockholm. The first seven A320 neos will replace the oldest Boeing 737 aircraft. As part of Star Alliance, the firm flies customers to 1,300 destinations worldwide. The company's SAS Go Light platform aims at competing with low-cost carriers for travelers with hand luggage only. SAS Go offers economy 3-3 seating on intraEuropean flights and 2-4-2 on the A330s and A340s; the program also offers free coffee and tea to GO passengers on short-haul services, except for very short flights. SAS Plus is a premium economy class on intercontinental flights, with wider seats than those in the SAS Go section. For long-haul business class flights, SAS Business features wide sleeper seats. Some seats convert into flat beds with power sockets and a 15-inch screen; others convert into angled beds. In June 2016, the firm sold its minority, 20%, share in Wideroe AS to WF Holding AS. Wideroe will continue to be a regional partner to SAS.

FINANCIAL DATA: Note: Data for latest year may not have been available at press time.

In U.S. $	2015	2014	2013	2012	2011	2010
Revenue	4,717,065,000	4,521,483,000	5,018,291,000		4,926,687,000	4,844,718,000
R&D Expense						
Operating Income	264,702,900	18,202,040	164,294,300		76,853,070	-231,035,100
Operating Margin %	5.61%	.40%	3.27%		1.55%	-4.76%
SGA Expense						215,926,200
Net Income	113,733,000	-87,560,150	21,176,230		-200,698,400	-263,870,100
Operating Cash Flow	361,185,600	130,388,500	122,298,700		-57,342,380	-18,439,980
Capital Expenditure	485,149,900	147,162,900	223,302,200		160,844,200	296,586,200
EBITDA	439,109,400	189,872,300	361,542,600		215,807,200	-15,941,660
Return on Assets %	3.20%	-2.26%	.49%		-4.16%	-5.26%
Return on Equity %	17.04%	-9.21%	1.60%		-12.55%	-21.24%
Debt to Equity	1.38	2.09	0.78		0.80	0.64

CONTACT INFORMATION:

Phone: 46-8-797-0000   Fax:
Toll-Free:
Address: kabinvagen 5, Stockholm, SE-195 87 Sweden

STOCK TICKER/OTHER:

Stock Ticker: SASDY   Exchange: PINX
Employees: 12,329   Fiscal Year Ends: 10/31
Parent Company:

SALARIES/BONUSES:

Top Exec. Salary: $ Bonus: $
Second Exec. Salary: $ Bonus: $

OTHER THOUGHTS:

Estimated Female Officers or Directors: 4
Hot Spot for Advancement for Women/Minorities: Y

SBE Entertainment Group LLC

sbe.com

NAIC Code: 721110

TYPES OF BUSINESS:

Hotels, Resort, Without Casinos

BRANDS/DIVISIONS/AFFILIATES:

SLS Hotels
Raleigh Miami Beach (The)
Redbury (The)
TownHouse Miami
Katsuya
Bazaar by Jose Andres (The)
Cleo
Greystone Manor

CONTACTS: Note: Officers with more than one job title may be intentionally listed here more than once.

Sam Nazarian, CEO

GROWTH PLANS/SPECIAL FEATURES:

SBE Entertainment Group LLC is a hospitality company that develops, manages and operates award-winning hotels, restaurants and night clubs. The company has more than 100 properties operating or in development. Hotel, residence and casino brands include SLS Hotels, The Raleigh Miami Beach, The Redbury and TownHouse Miami. Restaurant brands include Katsuya, The Bazaar by Jose Andres, Cleo, Tres by Jose Andres, 800 Degrees Neapolitan Pizzeria, Umami Burger and K-Ramen Burger & Beer. Nightlife brands include Hyde, Greystone Manor, The Library by The Redbury, The Sayers Club, Create, Double Barrel Roadhouse, XIV Sessions, Foxtail, Doheny Room and Fourteen. SBE construction/real estate development subsidiary, Dakota Development, manages all aspects of design and development for SBE properties. In May 2016, the firm agreed to acquire Morgans Hotel Group Co., owner and operator of 13 boutique hotels at locations such as New York, Los Angles and Miami Beach.

FINANCIAL DATA: Note: Data for latest year may not have been available at press time.

In U.S. $	2015	2014	2013	2012	2011	2010
Revenue						
R&D Expense						
Operating Income						
Operating Margin %						
SGA Expense						
Net Income						
Operating Cash Flow						
Capital Expenditure						
EBITDA						
Return on Assets %						
Return on Equity %						
Debt to Equity						

CONTACT INFORMATION:

Phone: 323-655-8000   Fax:
Toll-Free:
Address: 5900 Wilshire Blvd., Fl. 31, Los Angeles, CA 90036 United States

STOCK TICKER/OTHER:

Stock Ticker: Private
Employees:
Parent Company:

Exchange:
Fiscal Year Ends:

SALARIES/BONUSES:

Top Exec. Salary: $ Bonus: $
Second Exec. Salary: $ Bonus: $

OTHER THOUGHTS:

Estimated Female Officers or Directors:
Hot Spot for Advancement for Women/Minorities:

Sales, profits and employees may be estimates. Financial information, benefits and other data can change quickly and may vary from those stated here.

Scandic Hotels AB

www.scandichotels.com

NAIC Code: 721110

TYPES OF BUSINESS:

Hotels

BRANDS/DIVISIONS/AFFILIATES:

EQT Partners AB
Scandic Antwerpen
Hotel Scandic The Reef
Scandic Palace Hotel Copenhagen
Scandic Hamburg Emporio

CONTACTS:
Note: Officers with more than one job title may be intentionally listed here more than once.

Frank Fiskers, CEO
Martin Creydt, COO
Anders Ehrling, Pres.
Jan Johansson, CFO
Klaus Johansen, VP-Sales
Lena Bjurner, Sr. VP-Human Resources
Thomas Engelhart, Chief Commercial Officer
Pelle Ekman, Sr. VP-Commercial Oper.
Martin Creydt, Chief Dev. Officer
Margareta Thorgren, VP-Group Comm.
Gunilla Rudebjer, Sr. VP-Finance
Joakim Nilsson, VP-Sweden
Ulrika Garbrant, VP-Food & Beverage
Aki Kayhko, VP-Finland
Svein Arild Steen-Mevold, VP-Norway
Jens Mathiesen, VP-Denmark

GROWTH PLANS/SPECIAL FEATURES:

Scandic Hotels AB, which is owned by private equity firm EQT Partners AB, is one of Scandinavia's largest hotel operators. The company has 230 hotels, featuring 44,000 rooms, located in seven countries: Sweden, Norway, Finland, Denmark, Germany, Belgium and Poland. Scandic Hotels also has partnerships with numerous hotel, travel and entertainment companies to provide more options to its customers. Its hotels include Scandic Antwerpen, Scandic Palace Hotel Copenhagen, Hotel Scandic The Reef and Scandic Hamburg Emporio. The firm has a long history of being environmentally conscious, and all of its Swedish hotels carry the Swan eco-label, a certification earned for effort and results toward sustainable practices. In an effort to simplify services for customers, Scandic Hotels' pricing plan offers two price levels: early and flex. Early means a reduced price reservation without the option to cancel or change, while flex is a higher, flexible reservation price.

FINANCIAL DATA:
Note: Data for latest year may not have been available at press time.

In U.S. $	2015	2014	2013	2012	2011	2010
Revenue	1,494,083,703	1,082,590,000	1,385,330,000	1,405,090,000		
R&D Expense						
Operating Income						
Operating Margin %						
SGA Expense						
Net Income	25,843,517	38,261,000	31,866,200	48,709,700		
Operating Cash Flow						
Capital Expenditure						
EBITDA						
Return on Assets %						
Return on Equity %						
Debt to Equity						

CONTACT INFORMATION:

Phone: 46-85-17-350-00　　Fax: 46-85-17-350-11
Toll-Free:
Address: Sveavagen 167, Stockholm, SE-102 33 Sweden

STOCK TICKER/OTHER:

Stock Ticker: Private　　　　　　　　Exchange:
Employees: 9,887　　　　　　　　　　Fiscal Year Ends: 12/31
Parent Company: EQT Partners AB

SALARIES/BONUSES:

Top Exec. Salary: $　　　　Bonus: $
Second Exec. Salary: $　　　Bonus: $

OTHER THOUGHTS:

Estimated Female Officers or Directors: 3
Hot Spot for Advancement for Women/Minorities: Y

Shangri-La Asia Ltd

www.shangri-la.com

NAIC Code: 721110

TYPES OF BUSINESS:

Hotels, Luxury
Property Management
Health Spas
Golf Courses
Commercial Real Estate Leasing
Serviced Apartments

BRANDS/DIVISIONS/AFFILIATES:

Shangri-La Hotels
Shangri-La Resorts
Kerry Hotels
Hotel Jen
Traders Hotels

CONTACTS: *Note: Officers with more than one job title may be intentionally listed here more than once.*

Khoon Chen Kuok, CEO
Kung Wei Liu, COO
Ching Leun Teo, Sec.
Judy Reeves, Dir.-Public Rel., North America

GROWTH PLANS/SPECIAL FEATURES:

Shangri-La Asia, Ltd. is an investment holding company that owns and manages hotels and resorts, primarily under the Shangri-La Hotels, Shangri-La Resorts, Kerry Hotels, Hotel Jen and Traders Hotels brands. Its portfolio consists of 73 luxury hotels and resorts (amounting to a room inventory of over 32,000) located in Hong Kong, mainland China, Singapore, Malaysia, the Philippines, Thailand, Australia, France and Maldives, among other areas. Shangri-La Hotels are five-star luxury hotels located in premier city addresses across Asia Pacific, North America, the Middle East and Europe. Shangri-La Resorts offers travelers and families relaxing environments at some of the world's most exotic destinations. Kerry Hotels are vibrant places, full of life and activity. Each Kerry hotel has a unique style. Hotel Jen features a brand of style and service delivery that appeals to the next generation of travelers: life, travel and discovery. Traders Hotels are a blend of simplicity and warmth of Asian hospitality, designed to complement guests at work, rest or play. Shangri-La Asia also operates a golf course in Bali, Indonesia (53%-owned); and operates a wine trading business in Hong Kong and Mainland China (20%-owned). Rental properties owned and managed by the firm include office, commercial and services apartment spaces, with a total of 3.2 million square feet of gross leasable space. The majority of these properties are located in Mainland China, with the rest in Singapore, Malaysia and other countries.

FINANCIAL DATA: *Note: Data for latest year may not have been available at press time.*

In U.S. $	2015	2014	2013	2012	2011	2010
Revenue	2,122,624,000	2,111,584,000	2,081,081,000	2,057,249,000	1,912,089,000	1,575,095,000
R&D Expense						
Operating Income	153,326,000	224,574,000	217,197,000	302,008,000	239,465,000	220,710,000
Operating Margin %	7.22%	10.63%	10.43%	14.68%	12.52%	14.01%
SGA Expense	292,348,000	288,817,000	279,516,000	263,649,000	252,586,000	199,895,000
Net Income	140,131,000	180,889,000	392,298,000	358,895,000	252,979,000	287,076,000
Operating Cash Flow	338,912,000	348,108,000	383,038,000	292,740,000	454,694,000	326,134,000
Capital Expenditure	785,789,000	198,825,000	689,784,000	998,368,000	289,109,000	586,581,000
EBITDA	740,048,000	749,205,000	983,531,000	868,253,000	700,602,000	644,691,000
Return on Assets %	1.03%	1.35%	3.16%	3.27%	2.73%	3.51%
Return on Equity %	2.10%	2.73%	6.35%	6.17%	4.93%	6.47%
Debt to Equity	0.55	0.63	0.70	0.63	0.42	0.30

CONTACT INFORMATION:

Phone: 852 25993000   Fax: 852 25993131
Toll-Free:
Address: 683 Kings Rd., Kerry Ctr., 28/F, Quarry Bay, Quarry Bay, Hong Kong

STOCK TICKER/OTHER:

Stock Ticker: SHALY   Exchange: PINX
Employees: 28,100   Fiscal Year Ends: 12/31
Parent Company:

SALARIES/BONUSES:

Top Exec. Salary: $ Bonus: $
Second Exec. Salary: $ Bonus: $

OTHER THOUGHTS:

Estimated Female Officers or Directors: 1
Hot Spot for Advancement for Women/Minorities: Y

Sales, profits and employees may be estimates. Financial information, benefits and other data can change quickly and may vary from those stated here.

Shun Tak Holdings Limited

NAIC Code: 721110

www.shuntakgroup.com

TYPES OF BUSINESS:

Investment Holding Company
High-Speed Ferry Services
Real Estate Investment
Hotel Management
Casino Management

BRANDS/DIVISIONS/AFFILIATES:

Shun Tak & CITS Coach (Macao) Limited
Shun Tak-China Travel Ship Management Limited
TuboJET
Shun Tak Real Estate Ltd
Shun Tak Property Management Ltd
Shun Tak Macau Services Ltd
Clean Living (Macau) Ltd
Macau Tower Convention & Entertainment Center

CONTACTS: Note: Officers with more than one job title may be intentionally listed here more than once.

Pansy Ho, Managing Dir.
Daisy Ho, Deputy Managing Dir.
Maisy Ho, Exec. Dir.
David Shum, Exec. Dir.
Rogier Verhoeven, Exec. Dir.
Stanley Ho, Chmn.

GROWTH PLANS/SPECIAL FEATURES:

Shun Tak Holdings Limited is a publicly traded Hong Kong-based conglomerate with core businesses in the transportation, property, hospitality and investment sectors. The transportation segment maintains ferry and air services through the joint venture Shun Tak-China Travel Ship Management Limited, which is known under the brand name TurboJET. The company shares ownership of TurboJET with China Travel International Investment Hong Kong Limited. TurboJET operates one of the largest fleets of high-speed passenger ferries in Asia. It also maintains airport routes that connect Hong Kong International airport with Shenzhen and Macau. The segment additionally maintains bus services in Macau and the Guangdong province through joint venture Shun Tak & CITS Coach (Macao) Limited, operating 144 vehicles. Shun Tak's property division develops and invests in property in Hong Kong and Macau. Its major operations include property development and sales, developing residential, retail and commercial properties; property leasing and asset management through Shun Tak Real Estate Ltd., which markets and leases residential, retail and commercial properties; property management services through Shun Tak Property Management Ltd., which maintains the company's owned properties; cleaning services through Shun Tak Macau Services, Ltd.; and laundry services through Clean Living (Macau), Ltd. Shun Tak's hospitality segment is engaged in hotel and casino management, managing the Macau Tower Convention & Entertainment Center and owning a 70% interest in Hong Kong SkyCity Marriot Hotel. The firm's investments segment holds interests in several hotels in Macau as well as Macau International Airport and Macau Matters Co. Ltd., which specializes in retail facility operations.

FINANCIAL DATA: Note: Data for latest year may not have been available at press time.

In U.S. $	2015	2014	2013	2012	2011	2010
Revenue	568,075,500	1,230,020,000	461,098,500	708,552,100	382,771,700	412,158,900
R&D Expense						
Operating Income	180,864,600	538,017,200	134,314,000	249,747,400	90,239,730	75,380,930
Operating Margin %	31.83%	43.74%	29.12%	35.24%	23.57%	18.28%
SGA Expense						
Net Income	96,026,980	574,213,300	181,364,700	330,478,400	100,659,100	110,040,800
Operating Cash Flow	55,588,410	335,537,200	18,132,770	96,726,540	-38,908,030	34,499,280
Capital Expenditure	8,924,538	109,165,300	3,514,856	4,684,067	12,702,070	3,017,228
EBITDA	209,066,900	768,508,200	278,685,900	469,211,400	171,906,300	170,875,600
Return on Assets %	1.57%	10.37%	3.87%	8.06%	2.76%	3.18%
Return on Equity %	2.82%	18.72%	6.83%	14.27%	5.01%	5.82%
Debt to Equity	0.30	0.35	0.34	0.18	0.35	0.28

CONTACT INFORMATION:

Phone: 852-2859-3111   Fax: 852-2857-7181
Toll-Free:
Address: 200 Connaught Rd., Penthouse, 39 Fl. W. Tower, Hong Kong, Hong Kong

STOCK TICKER/OTHER:

Stock Ticker: SHTGF   Exchange: GREY
Employees: 3,370   Fiscal Year Ends: 12/31
Parent Company:

SALARIES/BONUSES:

Top Exec. Salary: $ Bonus: $
Second Exec. Salary: $ Bonus: $

OTHER THOUGHTS:

Estimated Female Officers or Directors: 4
Hot Spot for Advancement for Women/Minorities: Y

Sales, profits and employees may be estimates. Financial information, benefits and other data can change quickly and may vary from those stated here.

Silvercar Inc

NAIC Code: 532111

www.silvercar.com

TYPES OF BUSINESS:

Passenger Car Rental

BRANDS/DIVISIONS/AFFILIATES:

CONTACTS: Note: Officers with more than one job title may be intentionally listed here more than once.

Luke Schneider, CEO
Kay Stroman, VP-Operations
Christopher Donus, VP-Finance
Russell Lemmer, VP-Mktg. & Business Dev.
Kay Stroman, VP-Human Resources
Allen Darnell, CTO

GROWTH PLANS/SPECIAL FEATURES:

Silvercar, Inc. is a car rental program operating through 13 airport locations throughout the U.S. Located in Austin, Chicago, Dallas, Denver, Ft. Lauderdale, Las Vegas, Los Angeles, Miami, New Jersey, Brooklyn, New York City, Phoenix and San Francisco, the company uses mobile technologies to connect clients to its rental services. Apps are available for download on iPhone and Android smartphones, and allow access to each step of the rental process: making a reservation, accessing the car, receiving the receipt, etc. The App also allows users to unlock their car, assess their car and pair the phone for hands-free calling and music. This method of car rental eliminates the need for concierge services and gate checkpoints, as customers can simply walk off their plane and straight to their vehicle. Silvercar solely offers the Audi A4 for rental, which comes with such complementary services as a navigation system, SiriusXM satellite radio, Wi-fi hot spot, Bluetooth pairing, toll tracking, quattro all-wheel drive, leather seats and road-side assistance. There is no need to fuel up the car before returning it to its location, as the company utilizes fuel sensors that track how much gas the client has used and charges that exact amount, plus an additional $5 flat fee. Silvercar is privately held, funded by some of the world's most influential investors, led by Austin Ventures.

FINANCIAL DATA: Note: Data for latest year may not have been available at press time.

In U.S. $	2015	2014	2013	2012	2011	2010
Revenue						
R&D Expense						
Operating Income						
Operating Margin %						
SGA Expense						
Net Income						
Operating Cash Flow						
Capital Expenditure						
EBITDA						
Return on Assets %						
Return on Equity %						
Debt to Equity						

CONTACT INFORMATION:

Phone: 512-201-4050   Fax:
Toll-Free:
Address: 712 Congress Avenue, Ste 201, Austin, TX 78701 United States

STOCK TICKER/OTHER:

Stock Ticker: Private
Employees:
Parent Company:

Exchange:
Fiscal Year Ends:

SALARIES/BONUSES:

Top Exec. Salary: $ Bonus: $
Second Exec. Salary: $ Bonus: $

OTHER THOUGHTS:

Estimated Female Officers or Directors:
Hot Spot for Advancement for Women/Minorities:

Sales, profits and employees may be estimates. Financial information, benefits and other data can change quickly and may vary from those stated here.

Silversea Cruises

www.silversea.com

NAIC Code: 483112

TYPES OF BUSINESS:

Cruise Line

BRANDS/DIVISIONS/AFFILIATES:

Silver Cloud
Silver Wind
Silver Shadow
Silver Whisper
Silver Spirit
Silver Explorer
Silver Discover
Silver Galapagos

CONTACTS: Note: Officers with more than one job title may be intentionally listed here more than once.

Brad Ball, Dir.-Media Rel.
Ellen Bettridge, Pres., Americas
Kristian C. Anderson, VP-Sales, North America
Keith Spondike, VP-Mktg., Americas
Manfredi Lefebvre d'Ovidio, Chmn.
Steve Odell, Pres., Europe & Asia Pacific

GROWTH PLANS/SPECIAL FEATURES:

Silversea Cruises is a cruise line operating ten ships that cater to the ultra-luxury cruise market. The company offers cruise itineraries in the Mediterranean, Caribbean, Central America, Asia, Galapagos Islands, Alaska, Northern Europe, British Isles, Antarctica, Africa, Indian Ocean, Australia, New Zealand. Micronesia, Melanesia, Polynesia, South America, the Arctic, Canada, New England (U.S.) and Russia. It also markets several transoceanic cruises between the U.K., Spain, Africa and North America. Its ships are sized for visiting smaller ports and out of the way destinations, with accommodations for 100 to 540 passengers per ship. The company's four original ships, Silver Cloud, Silver Wind, Silver Shadow and Silver Whisper, are designed to house fewer guests, while still providing larger cruise ship amenities, such as show lounges featuring nightly entertainment, casinos, spas and fitness facilities. Silver Muse is a new ultra-luxury ship scheduled to be delivered in 2017, and will accommodate 596 guests. Silver Explorer is one of the firm's expedition-focused ships, which carries only 132 guests and features an ice-rated hull that allows the ship to visit the earth's remote Polar Regions. Other expedition ships include Silver Galapagos, Silver Discoverer and Silver Cloud Expedition. Silver Spirit is a 540-guest ultra-luxury vessel. The firm's itineraries feature extensive, multi-day luxury excursion options to on-shore attractions. Silversea also offers specialty cruises and attractions such as extended world traversing voyages up to 115 days, wine tasting cruises, culinary cruises, presentations by famous explorers and authors and golf-oriented instruction and excursions. Voyages often feature lecturers or celebrities, which in the past have included Spa Chef Jacky Oberti, actor John Lithgow and the geologist Jon Vidar Sigurdsson.

FINANCIAL DATA: Note: Data for latest year may not have been available at press time.

In U.S. $	2015	2014	2013	2012	2011	2010
Revenue						
R&D Expense						
Operating Income						
Operating Margin %						
SGA Expense						
Net Income						
Operating Cash Flow						
Capital Expenditure						
EBITDA						
Return on Assets %						
Return on Equity %						
Debt to Equity						

CONTACT INFORMATION:

Phone: 377-9770-2424   Fax: 377-9770-2428
Toll-Free:
Address: 7, Rue du Gabian, Gildo Pastor Ctr., Monte Carlo, 98000 Monaco

STOCK TICKER/OTHER:

Stock Ticker: Private
Employees: 2,000
Parent Company:

Exchange:
Fiscal Year Ends:

SALARIES/BONUSES:

Top Exec. Salary: $ Bonus: $
Second Exec. Salary: $ Bonus: $

OTHER THOUGHTS:

Estimated Female Officers or Directors: 1
Hot Spot for Advancement for Women/Minorities: Y

Singapore Airlines Ltd

www.singaporeair.com

NAIC Code: 481111

TYPES OF BUSINESS:

Airline
Regional Airline
Tour Packages
Engineering Services
Cargo Services

BRANDS/DIVISIONS/AFFILIATES:

Budget Aviation Holdings
SilkAir Private Limited
Singapore Airlines Cargo
Vistara
Temasek Holdings Private Limited

CONTACTS: *Note: Officers with more than one job title may be intentionally listed here more than once.*

Goh Choon Phong, CEO
Stephen Barnes, CFO
Lee Wen Fen, Acting Sr. VP-Mktg & Planning
Tan Pee Teck, Sr. VP-Prod. & Services
Mervyn Sirisena, Sr. VP-Eng.
Ng Chin Hwee, Exec. VP-Oper.
Lee Lik Hsin, Sr. VP-Corp. Planning
Chan Hon Chew, Sr. VP-Finance
Mak Swee Wah, Exec. VP-Commercial
Gerard Yeap Beng Hock, Sr. VP-Flight Oper.
Marvin Tan Meng Hung, Acting Sr. VP-Cabin Crew
Christopher Cheng Kian Hai, Sr. VP-Human Resources
Paul Tan Wah Liang, Regional VP-Europe

GROWTH PLANS/SPECIAL FEATURES:

Singapore Airlines, Ltd. (Singapore Air) is engaged in passenger and air cargo transportation. It is the flag carrier of Singapore and operates from its hub at Changi Airport, with a strong presence in Asia and Oceania. Singapore Air's fleet consists of 107 Airbus A330, A350, A380 and Boeing 777 aircraft, departing from Singapore to 64 international destinations. Among the company's airline-related subsidiaries include Budget Aviation Holdings, a Singapore-based holding company for a group of low-cost carriers operating in the Asia-Pacific region; SilkAir Private Limited, a regional airline headquartered in Singapore that operates scheduled passenger services from Singapore to 51 cities in Southeast Asia, the Indian Subcontinent, China and Australia; Singapore Airlines Cargo, a cargo airline that operates nine freighters and manages the bellyhold (the cargo stowed under the main deck of an aircraft) of all Singapore Airlines aircraft; and Vistara, an Indian airline based in Gurgaon with its hub at Delhi-Indira Gandhi International Airport. Singapore Airlines is majority-owned by the Singapore government investment and holding company Temasek Holdings Private Limited (56%). In June 2016, the firm expanded its U.S. operations with non-stop San Francisco flights and second daily Los Angeles flights.

The company offers its employees profit sharing bonuses and an annual free air-ticket to any Singapore Air destination.

FINANCIAL DATA: *Note: Data for latest year may not have been available at press time.*

In U.S. $	2015	2014	2013	2012	2011	2010
Revenue	11,537,270,000	11,298,890,000	11,190,900,000	11,012,710,000	10,765,890,000	
R&D Expense						
Operating Income	303,450,300	192,195,100	169,884,800	211,911,200	942,297,000	
Operating Margin %	2.63%	1.70%	1.51%	1.92%	8.75%	
SGA Expense	1,002,113,000	566,875,500	536,411,800	513,805,000	561,835,300	
Net Income	272,690,200	266,464,100	280,843,500	294,111,100	851,499,100	
Operating Cash Flow	1,532,224,000	1,555,127,000	1,374,495,000	1,262,128,000	2,435,015,000	
Capital Expenditure	1,950,191,000	1,930,327,000	1,452,025,000	1,258,051,000	921,617,300	
EBITDA	1,524,812,000	1,379,016,000	1,583,590,000	1,581,811,000	2,360,820,000	
Return on Assets %	1.58%	1.59%	1.70%	1.44%	4.64%	
Return on Equity %	2.86%	2.72%	2.91%	2.47%	7.89%	
Debt to Equity			0.07	0.07	0.07	

CONTACT INFORMATION:

Phone: 65 6541-5880 Fax: 65 6545-6083
Toll-Free:
Address: 25 Airline Rd., 07-E Airline House, Singapore, 819829 Singapore

STOCK TICKER/OTHER:

Stock Ticker: SINGF Exchange: PINX
Employees: 23,963 Fiscal Year Ends: 03/31
Parent Company:

SALARIES/BONUSES:

Top Exec. Salary: $ Bonus: $
Second Exec. Salary: $ Bonus: $

OTHER THOUGHTS:

Estimated Female Officers or Directors:
Hot Spot for Advancement for Women/Minorities: Y

Sales, profits and employees may be estimates. Financial information, benefits and other data can change quickly and may vary from those stated here.

Six Flags Entertainment Corporation

NAIC Code: 713110

TYPES OF BUSINESS:

Theme Parks

BRANDS/DIVISIONS/AFFILIATES:

Six Flags Discovery Kingdom
Six Flags Wild Safari
Six Flags Great Adventure
Six Flags America
Six Flags Over Texas

CONTACTS: *Note: Officers with more than one job title may be intentionally listed here more than once.*

Barber Marshall, CFO
James Reid-Anderson, Chairman of the Board
Michael Israel, Chief Information Officer
John Duffey, Director
Lance Balk, Executive VP
Nancy Krejsa, Senior VP, Divisional
David McKillips, Senior VP, Divisional
Walter Hawrylak, Senior VP, Divisional
John Odum, Senior VP, Divisional
Thomas Iven, Senior VP, Divisional
Brett Petit, Senior VP, Divisional
Leonard Russ, Senior VP, Divisional
Mario Centola, Vice President

GROWTH PLANS/SPECIAL FEATURES:

Six Flags Entertainment Corporation (Six Flags) is an operator of regional theme parks, water parks and zoological parks. The company operates 18 parks, including 16 in the U.S., one in Mexico City and one in Montreal. The firm's parks offer state-of-the-art and traditional thrill rides, water attractions, themed areas, concerts and shows, restaurants, game venues and retail outlets. Altogether, its parks contain over 800 rides, including over 130 roller coasters. Six Flags holds exclusive long-term licenses for theme park usage of certain Warner Bros. and DC Comics characters, including Bugs Bunny, Daffy Duck, Tweety Bird, Yosemite Sam, Superman and Batman throughout the U.S. (excluding the Las Vegas metropolitan area), Canada and Mexico. In addition, it has certain rights to use Hanna-Barbera and Cartoon Network characters, including Yogi Bear, Scooby-Doo and The Flintstones. The company's operations include Six Flags Over Texas, the oldest of the parks and the original source of the company name; Six Flags Discovery Kingdom in California, featuring marine and land animal exhibits; Six Flags America in Largo, Maryland, near Washington D.C.; and Six Flags Great Adventure in New Jersey, the firm's largest location, encompassing a theme park, a water park and the adjacent Six Flags Wild Safari, a 350-acre drive-through safari attraction. In 2014, the firm announced that a Six Flags-branded them park will open in Dubai in late 2017, as well as multiple Six Flags-branded theme parts in China over the next decade.

Six Flags offers its employees incentive bonuses, unlimited admission, free and discounted passes, health benefits and flexible scheduling.

FINANCIAL DATA: *Note: Data for latest year may not have been available at press time.*

In U.S. $	2015	2014	2013	2012	2011	2010
Revenue	1,263,938,000	1,175,793,000	1,109,930,000	1,070,332,000	1,013,174,000	
R&D Expense						
Operating Income	355,789,000	228,785,000	288,492,000	204,564,000	153,956,000	
Operating Margin %	28.14%	19.45%	25.99%	19.11%	15.19%	
SGA Expense	234,810,000	310,955,000	606,700,000	637,554,000	612,933,000	
Net Income	154,690,000	76,022,000	118,552,000	354,009,000	-22,660,000	
Operating Cash Flow	473,761,000	392,323,000	368,682,000	371,632,000	274,937,000	
Capital Expenditure	114,399,000	108,709,000	101,928,000	99,989,000	91,680,000	
EBITDA	446,840,000	341,175,000	407,044,000	407,101,000	239,092,000	
Return on Assets %	6.23%	2.95%	4.18%	12.41%	-.84%	
Return on Equity %	124.69%	25.45%	18.73%	42.76%	-2.78%	
Debt to Equity	61.86	6.20	3.73	1.56	1.20	

CONTACT INFORMATION:

Phone: 972 595-5000   Fax:
Toll-Free:
Address: 924 Avenue J East, Grand Prairie, TX 75050 United States

STOCK TICKER/OTHER:

Stock Ticker: SIX   Exchange: NYS
Employees: 1,900   Fiscal Year Ends: 12/31
Parent Company:

SALARIES/BONUSES:

Top Exec. Salary: Bonus: $
$1,546,154
Second Exec. Salary: Bonus: $94,095
$637,500

OTHER THOUGHTS:

Estimated Female Officers or Directors: 1

Hot Spot for Advancement for Women/Minorities:

Sixt AG

NAIC Code: 532111

TYPES OF BUSINESS:

Automobile Rental
e-Commerce
Automobile Leasing
Used Car Sales
Fleet Management
Insurance Services

BRANDS/DIVISIONS/AFFILIATES:

SIXTI GmbH & Co. Autovermietung KG
Sixt Leasing AG
TUV SUD Car Registration & Services GmbH
myDriver

CONTACTS: *Note: Officers with more than one job title may be intentionally listed here more than once.*

Erich Sixt, CEO
Detlev Patsch, COO
Julian zu Putilitz, CFO
Frank Elsner, Head-Press Rel.
Julian zu Pulitz, Controller

GROWTH PLANS/SPECIAL FEATURES:

Sixt AG, along with its subsidiaries, provides automobile rentals, full-service leasing, used car sales and e-commerce services in over 100 countries throughout the world. The company operates through two business units. The vehicle rental unit rents automobiles, including cars, trucks and holiday cars, to corporate and private customers; it also offers a limousine service and used car sales. It possesses one of the largest fleets of BMW and Mercedes Benz vehicles in the world. SIXTI GmbH & Co. Autovermietung KG, a subsidiary of Sixt, offers no-frills car rental with rates as low as about $14 per day. SIXTI provides customers with cars such as the Ford Fiesta, Toyota Camry and Chevrolet Cruz for economy car rentals. The leasing unit is operated through subsidiary Sixt Leasing AG, which provides a broad range of leasing services, including pure-play finance leasing, full-service leasing, fleet management, fleet consulting, billing and reporting. Sixt's online platform offers access to its vehicle rental and leasing offers, the sale of new and used vehicles, travel management and insurance services. The company has partnership collaborations with various airlines and hotel groups worldwide. Recently-established subsidiary, myDriver, is a limousine and chauffeur service. Additionally, the firm's joint venture with TUV SUD, called TUV SUD Car Registration & Services GmbH, provides official vehicle registration services.

FINANCIAL DATA: *Note: Data for latest year may not have been available at press time.*

In U.S. $	2015	2014	2013	2012	2011	2010
Revenue	2,004,479,680	2,016,900,000	2,414,730,000	2,058,400,000	2,017,200,000	1,984,300,000
R&D Expense						
Operating Income						
Operating Margin %						
SGA Expense						
Net Income	122,768,800	123,500,000	122,300,000	102,100,000	126,100,000	91,600,000
Operating Cash Flow						
Capital Expenditure						
EBITDA						
Return on Assets %						
Return on Equity %						
Debt to Equity						

CONTACT INFORMATION:

Phone: 49-89-74444-0   Fax: 49-89-74444-86666
Toll-Free:
Address: Zugspitzstrasse 1, Pullach im Isartal, 82049 Germany

STOCK TICKER/OTHER:

Stock Ticker: SIX2
Employees: 4,308
Parent Company:

Exchange: Frankfurt
Fiscal Year Ends: 12/31

SALARIES/BONUSES:

Top Exec. Salary: $ Bonus: $
Second Exec. Salary: $ Bonus: $

OTHER THOUGHTS:

Estimated Female Officers or Directors:
Hot Spot for Advancement for Women/Minorities:

SkyWest Inc

NAIC Code: 481111

TYPES OF BUSINESS:

Airline-Regional
Air Freight

BRANDS/DIVISIONS/AFFILIATES:

SkyWest Airlines Inc
ExpressJet Airlines Inc

CONTACTS: *Note: Officers with more than one job title may be intentionally listed here more than once.*

Robert Simmons, CFO
Jerry Atkin, Chairman of the Board
Eric Woodward, Chief Accounting Officer
Michael Thompson, COO, Subsidiary
Terry Vais, COO, Subsidiary
Wade Steel, Other Executive Officer
Russell Childs, President
Brad Sheehan, Senior VP, Subsidiary

GROWTH PLANS/SPECIAL FEATURES:

SkyWest, Inc. is a holding company for SkyWest Airlines, Inc. and ExpressJet Airlines, Inc., which provide scheduled passenger air service in the U.S, Canada, Mexico and the Caribbean. SkyWest Airlines provides regional jet and turboprop service primarily in the Western U.S., including service to 205 cities in 40 states, four cities in Mexico and the Bahamas and five Canadian provinces, with more than 1,600 daily departures. ExpressJet offers an average of 2,200 daily departures from major hubs such as Atlanta, Cleveland, Denver, Newark, Houston, Memphis, Minneapolis, Chicago (O'Hare) and Washington, D.C. (Dulles). Substantially all of the company's flights are operated as Delta Connection, United Express, US Airways Express or Alaska under code-share arrangements with Delta, United Airlines, Continental, US Airways Group and Alaska Airlines. The firm generally provides regional flying to partners under long-term, fixed-fee code-share agreements. Among other features of the fixed-fee agreements, partners generally reimburse the companies for specified direct operating expenses, including fuel expense, which is passed through to the partners, and pay them a fee for operating the aircraft. The firm also provides ground handling services for other airlines. The company maintains a fleet of 362 regional aircraft. The remaining aircraft are subleased or assigned to other airlines. The firm operates two types of regional jet aircraft: the Bombardier Aerospace regional jet, comprising the CRJ200, CRJ700 and the CRJ900 aircraft; and the Embraer ERJ-145, ERJ-135 and ERJ-175 aircraft.

Employee benefits include: reduced airfare; medical, dental and vision insurance; domestic partner benefits; flexible spending plans; performance awards; educational savings plans; credit union membership; a 401(k); and an employee assistance program.

FINANCIAL DATA: *Note: Data for latest year may not have been available at press time.*

In U.S. $	2015	2014	2013	2012	2011	2010
Revenue	3,095,563,000	3,237,447,000	3,297,725,000	3,534,372,000	3,654,923,000	2,765,145,000
R&D Expense						
Operating Income	234,515,000	24,848,000	153,111,000	165,987,000	41,105,000	201,826,000
Operating Margin %	7.57%	.76%	4.64%	4.69%	1.12%	7.29%
SGA Expense	1,257,479,000	1,309,179,000	1,325,995,000	1,675,181,000	1,501,577,000	1,250,279,000
Net Income	117,817,000	-24,154,000	58,956,000	51,157,000	-27,335,000	96,350,000
Operating Cash Flow	420,104,000	285,539,000	289,890,000	288,824,000	162,126,000	347,089,000
Capital Expenditure	721,276,000	675,439,000	152,001,000	64,939,000	186,198,000	151,265,000
EBITDA	534,679,000	309,294,000	412,195,000	415,234,000	284,395,000	468,917,000
Return on Assets %	2.55%	-.55%	1.38%	1.19%	-.62%	2.20%
Return on Equity %	8.10%	-1.70%	4.17%	3.75%	-1.98%	6.94%
Debt to Equity	1.11	1.09	0.90	1.06	1.20	1.22

CONTACT INFORMATION:

Phone: 435 634-3000   Fax: 435 634-3105
Toll-Free:
Address: 444 S. River Rd., St. George, UT 84790 United States

STOCK TICKER/OTHER:

Stock Ticker: SKYW   Exchange: NAS
Employees: 18,500   Fiscal Year Ends: 12/31
Parent Company:

SALARIES/BONUSES:

Top Exec. Salary: $430,800   Bonus: $
Second Exec. Salary: Bonus: $
$330,000

OTHER THOUGHTS:

Estimated Female Officers or Directors: 1
Hot Spot for Advancement for Women/Minorities: Y

Smiths Detection

www.smithsdetection.com

NAIC Code: 334511

TYPES OF BUSINESS:

Baggage Inspection Systems
Cargo Inspection Systems
X-Ray Equipment
Explosive Detection Equipment
Biometric Identification
Diagnostic Equipment

BRANDS/DIVISIONS/AFFILIATES:

Smiths Group plc

CONTACTS:
Note: Officers with more than one job title may be intentionally listed here more than once.

Richard Ingram, Pres.
Lily Liu, VP-Finance
Diana Houghton, VP-Strategy & Mktg.
Darren Littleboy, VP-Human Resources
Shaun Hood, VP-Product & Technology
Brian Boso, CTO
Christopher Roberts, General Counsel
David Anning, VP-Global Oper.
Andrew Davis, Dir.-Comm.
Hermann Ries, VP-Tech. Innovation
Terry Gibson, VP-Service

GROWTH PLANS/SPECIAL FEATURES:

Smiths Detection, Inc. is a subsidiary of the Smiths Group plc that develops, manufactures and sells threat detection and screening technologies for military, homeland security and transportation applications. The company's technologies are used to detect and identify constantly evolving chemical, biological, radiological, nuclear and explosive threats. Smiths Detection separates its products into five categories based on intended market sector: transportation, critical infrastructure, ports & borders, emergency responders and military. Transportation products are based largely on trace detection and X-ray screening technologies, and include air cargo, passenger checkpoint, checked baggage, customs screening, perimeter fence and mass transit solutions. Critical infrastructure products include access control checkpoints, mail screening and loading dock and HVAC (heating, ventilation and air conditioning) system monitoring solutions. Ports and borders products include container, mobile cargo and freight screening, passenger terminal, luggage inspection and general security solutions. The emergency responders segment consists of identification, surveillance and communication equipment for emergency responders, HAZMAT teams, law enforcement and federal and local government agencies to use during a toxic threat. Military products include advanced integrated sensing technologies for personal protection, decontamination, chemical and biological detection and protective shelters.

Smiths Detection offers employees medical, dental and prescription drug plans; flexible spending accounts; retirement account plans; tuition reimbursement; an employee assistance program; and credit union membership.

FINANCIAL DATA:
Note: Data for latest year may not have been available at press time.

In U.S. $	2015	2014	2013	2012	2011	2010
Revenue	629,982,641	767,929,977	932,631,707	813,024,704	786,731,000	887,857,000
R&D Expense						
Operating Income						
Operating Margin %						
SGA Expense						
Net Income	55,573,000	225,861,758				
Operating Cash Flow						
Capital Expenditure						
EBITDA						
Return on Assets %						
Return on Equity %						
Debt to Equity						

CONTACT INFORMATION:

Phone: 44-19-2369-6555   Fax: 44-19-2369-6559
Toll-Free:
Address: 459 Park Avenue, Bushey, Watford, WD23 2BW United Kingdom

STOCK TICKER/OTHER:

Stock Ticker: Subsidiary
Employees: 2,150
Parent Company: Smiths Group plc

Exchange:
Fiscal Year Ends: 07/31

SALARIES/BONUSES:

Top Exec. Salary: $ Bonus: $
Second Exec. Salary: $ Bonus: $

OTHER THOUGHTS:

Estimated Female Officers or Directors: 1
Hot Spot for Advancement for Women/Minorities:

Sales, profits and employees may be estimates. Financial information, benefits and other data can change quickly and may vary from those stated here.

Sodexo Inc

NAIC Code: 722310

TYPES OF BUSINESS:

Food Service Outsourcing
Facilities Management
Laundry Services
Sports Arena Management
Plant Management
Grounds Keeping
Asset Management
Outsourced Procurement Services

BRANDS/DIVISIONS/AFFILIATES:

Sodexho Group
Sodexo Foundation
Entegra Procurement Services

CONTACTS: *Note: Officers with more than one job title may be intentionally listed here more than once.*

Michel Landel, CEO
Sian Herbert-Jones, CFO
Elisabeth Carpentier, Group Chief Human Resources Officer
Michel Landel, Pres.
Debbie White, CEO-Sodexo U.K. & Ireland
Pierre Bellon, Chmn.

GROWTH PLANS/SPECIAL FEATURES:

Sodexo, Inc. is the North American subsidiary of French firm Sodexo Group, a global contract foodservice supplier. The company is one of the largest providers of contract food and facilities management services in the U.S., Mexico and Canada, with more than 32,000 sites. In total, it serves 75 million consumers each day. Sodexo offers a wide variety of outsourcing solutions in food service, facilities management, business strategy, wellness, motivation solutions and corporate citizenship. The company provides these services to corporations; health care, long-term care and retirement centers; conference centers; schools; college campuses; military bases; and government and remote sites. Services to college stadiums and arenas involve concession stands, catering, physical plant management and sports field management. The firm also has a contract to manage the food operations for the U.S. Marine Corps, which includes meal preparation, operation of clean dining facilities and bringing national brands to Navy bases, Army bases and international locations. In addition, the company sponsors the Sodexo Foundation, an independent charitable organization that supports initiatives addressing the problems of hunger in children and families. The Entegra Procurement Services unit provides food and supplies purchasing management for 10,000 clients in hospitality and other industries.

The firm offers employees a pension plan; a 401(k) savings plan; health and family care spending accounts; employee assistance plans; tuition reimbursement; and medical, life, disability, dental and vision insurance.

FINANCIAL DATA: *Note: Data for latest year may not have been available at press time.*

In U.S. $	2015	2014	2013	2012	2011	2010
Revenue	9,200,000,000	8,800,000,000	9,350,000,000	9,200,000,000	9,000,000,000	8,000,000,000
R&D Expense						
Operating Income						
Operating Margin %						
SGA Expense						
Net Income						
Operating Cash Flow						
Capital Expenditure						
EBITDA						
Return on Assets %						
Return on Equity %						
Debt to Equity						

CONTACT INFORMATION:

Phone: 301-987-4000   Fax: 301-987-4438
Toll-Free: 800-763-3946
Address: 9801 Washingtonian Blvd., Gaithersburg, MD 20878 United States

STOCK TICKER/OTHER:

Stock Ticker: Subsidiary
Employees: 132,600
Parent Company: Sodexo Group

Exchange:
Fiscal Year Ends: 08/31

SALARIES/BONUSES:

Top Exec. Salary: $ Bonus: $
Second Exec. Salary: $ Bonus: $

OTHER THOUGHTS:

Estimated Female Officers or Directors: 2
Hot Spot for Advancement for Women/Minorities: Y

Sales, profits and employees may be estimates. Financial information, benefits and other data can change quickly and may vary from those stated here.

Sonesta International Hotels Corp

www.sonesta.com

NAIC Code: 721110

TYPES OF BUSINESS:

Hotels
River Cruise Ships
Hotels
Resorts

BRANDS/DIVISIONS/AFFILIATES:

Sonesta Collection
Sonesta Art Collection
Royal Sonesta Hotels
Sonesta Hotels & Resorts
Sonesta ES Suites
Sonest Posadas del Inca
Sonesta Cruise Collection

CONTACTS: Note: Officers with more than one job title may be intentionally listed here more than once.

Carlos Flores, CEO
Scott Weiler, VP-Mktg. & Communications
Lorie Juliano, Dir.-Comm.

GROWTH PLANS/SPECIAL FEATURES:

Sonesta International Hotels Corp., doing business as Sonesta Collection, specializes in providing upscale accommodation. There are currently more than 65 Sonesta hotels and resorts as well as Nile cruise ships, totaling more than 12,000 rooms. The properties are located in the U.S, the Caribbean, Chile, Colombia, Ecuador, Panama, Peru, Africa and Egypt. Locations feature the Sonesta Art Collection, a collection of art that consists of more than 7,000 contemporary paintings, sculptures, original prints and tapestries by world-renowned artists, which are placed in public places and guestrooms inside its hotels. Some of the company's resorts also offer Just Us Kids, a complimentary supervised children's program for ages 5-13. Family packages, children's menus, baby-sitting and discounts on a second room add to the appeal for families. Sonesta's portfolio covers a full range of services such as Royal Sonesta Hotels, which provides all the amenities customers need for an indulgent and culture-filled stay; Sonesta Hotels & Resorts, which are located in urban and resort destinations; Sonesta ES Suites, providing extended stay studio apartment accommodations; Sonesta Posadas del Inca, providing urban and country inns embedded in the culture of Peru, minus the formality; and Sonesta Cruise Collection, a fleet of luxury river ships in Africa and Egypt.

FINANCIAL DATA: Note: Data for latest year may not have been available at press time.

In U.S. $	2015	2014	2013	2012	2011	2010
Revenue						
R&D Expense						
Operating Income						
Operating Margin %						
SGA Expense						
Net Income						
Operating Cash Flow						
Capital Expenditure						
EBITDA						
Return on Assets %						
Return on Equity %						
Debt to Equity						

CONTACT INFORMATION:

Phone: 617-421-5400   Fax: 617-421-5402
Toll-Free: 800-766-3782
Address: 225 Washington Street, Newton, MA 02458 United States

STOCK TICKER/OTHER:

Stock Ticker: Private   Exchange:
Employees: 766   Fiscal Year Ends: 12/31
Parent Company: Hospitality Properties Trust

SALARIES/BONUSES:

Top Exec. Salary: $ Bonus: $
Second Exec. Salary: $ Bonus: $

OTHER THOUGHTS:

Estimated Female Officers or Directors: 2
Hot Spot for Advancement for Women/Minorities: Y

Sales, profits and employees may be estimates. Financial information, benefits and other data can change quickly and may vary from those stated here.

Spirit Aerosystems Holdings Inc

www.spiritaero.com

NAIC Code: 336413

TYPES OF BUSINESS:

Aircraft Fuselage Wing Tail and Similar Assemblies Manufacturing
Aerostructures
Fuselages
Wings & Flight Control Components
Engineering, Design & Materials Testing
Custom Tool Fabrication
Spare Parts & Maintenance Services
Supply Chain Management

BRANDS/DIVISIONS/AFFILIATES:

Onex Corp

CONTACTS: Note: Officers with more than one job title may be intentionally listed here more than once.

Sanjay Kapoor, CFO
Robert Johnson, Chairman of the Board
Mark Suchinski, Chief Accounting Officer
Samantha Marnick, Chief Administrative Officer
John Pilla, Chief Technology Officer
Thomas Gentile, Director
Michelle Lohmeier, General Manager, Divisional
Michelle Lohmeie, General Manager, Divisional
Stacy Cozad, Secretary
Heidi Wood, Senior VP, Divisional
Krisstie Kondrotis, Senior VP, Divisional
Duane Hawkins, Senior VP, Divisional
Philip Anderson, Senior VP, Divisional
Ronald Rabe, Senior VP, Divisional
James Sharp, Vice President, Subsidiary

GROWTH PLANS/SPECIAL FEATURES:

Spirit Aerosystems Holdings, Inc. is an independent designer and manufacturer of aircraft parts and aerostructures for commercial and military aircraft. The firm operates through three principal segments: fuselages, propulsion systems and wing systems. The fuselages segment produces forward, mid and rear fuselage sections and offers services that include numerical control programming, materials testing, onsite planning and global supply chain management. The propulsion systems segment primarily produces nacelles (aerodynamic engine enclosures that enhance propulsion installation efficiency, dampen engine noise and provide thrust reversing capabilities), struts/pylons (structures that attach engines to airplane wings) and engine structural components. The wing systems segment produces wings, wing components and flight control surfaces. Spirit Aerosystems is also engaged in tooling, the fabrication of custom tools and the manufacturing of structural components for military aircraft. The firm's tooling capabilities include tool design, computer numerical control (CNC) programming, machining, composite, aluminum and invar tooling. The company offers spare parts and components for all items of which it is the original production supplier and provides maintenance, repair and overhaul work for nacelles, fuselage doors, structural components and modification kits. Spirit Aerosystems is the largest independent supplier of aerostructures to Boeing and one of the largest to Airbus. The company is majority-controlled by Onex Corp. With its headquarters in Wichita, Kansas, the firm operates throughout the U.S., Europe and Asia.

Employee benefits include a company profit sharing bonus; 401(k); relocation benefits; medical, vision and life insurance; health care spending accounts; disability coverage; and tuition assistance.

FINANCIAL DATA: Note: Data for latest year may not have been available at press time.

In U.S. $	2015	2014	2013	2012	2011	2010
Revenue	6,643,900,000	6,799,200,000	5,961,000,000	5,397,700,000	4,863,800,000	4,172,400,000
R&D Expense	27,800,000	29,300,000	34,700,000	34,100,000	35,700,000	51,500,000
Operating Income	863,000,000	354,000,000	-364,300,000	92,300,000	356,100,000	357,000,000
Operating Margin %	12.98%	5.20%	-6.11%	1.71%	7.32%	8.55%
SGA Expense	220,800,000	233,800,000	200,800,000	172,200,000	159,900,000	156,000,000
Net Income	788,700,000	358,800,000	-621,400,000	34,800,000	192,400,000	218,900,000
Operating Cash Flow	1,289,700,000	361,600,000	260,600,000	544,400,000	-47,300,000	125,100,000
Capital Expenditure	360,100,000	220,200,000	272,600,000	249,000,000	249,700,000	288,100,000
EBITDA	1,041,900,000	526,500,000	-199,400,000	250,500,000	491,900,000	476,900,000
Return on Assets %	14.41%	6.98%	-11.81%	.66%	3.79%	4.57%
Return on Equity %	42.16%	23.13%	-35.74%	1.75%	10.19%	12.93%
Debt to Equity	0.51	0.70	0.77	0.58	0.58	0.65

CONTACT INFORMATION:

Phone: 316 526-9000   Fax:
Toll-Free: 800-501-7597
Address: 3801 S. Oliver St., Wichita, KS 67210 United States

STOCK TICKER/OTHER:

Stock Ticker: SPR   Exchange: NYS
Employees: 13,496   Fiscal Year Ends: 12/31
Parent Company: Onex Corp

SALARIES/BONUSES:

Top Exec. Salary: Bonus: $
$1,255,284
Second Exec. Salary: Bonus: $250,000
$424,840

OTHER THOUGHTS:

Estimated Female Officers or Directors: 2

Hot Spot for Advancement for Women/Minorities: Y

Spirit Airlines Inc

www.spiritair.com

NAIC Code: 481111

TYPES OF BUSINESS:

Airline
Low-Fare Carrier

BRANDS/DIVISIONS/AFFILIATES:

Free Spirit
Big Front Seat
$9 Fare Club

CONTACTS: *Note: Officers with more than one job title may be intentionally listed here more than once.*

Edward Christie, CFO
H. Gardner, Chairman of the Board
Edmundo Miranda, Chief Accounting Officer
Robert Fornaro, Director
Thomas Canfield, General Counsel
Martha Villa, Other Executive Officer
John Bendoraitis, Senior VP

GROWTH PLANS/SPECIAL FEATURES:

Spirit Airlines, Inc. is a leading private low-fare airline in the U.S. The company flies to 56 destinations including the U.S., Mexico, the Caribbean, the Bahamas and Central and Latin America and offers over 400 daily flight departures. Its all-Airbus fleet currently consists of A321s, A320s and A319s, with an average age of 5.1 years. Approximately 45 A320neo and 10 A321neo aircraft are on order, along with 19 A320s and 18 A321s (which are scheduled for delivery through 2018). The firm also offers personalized packages through both scheduled and charter flights to its destinations. Spirit Airlines reduces its costs by offering typically standard services, such as checked baggage, on an optional, pay-for-service basis. The airline operates a fully integrated Spanish-language customer service plan that includes a web site and dedicated reservation line. Some of the other benefits the company offers its customers include the Big Front Seat seating option, with more leg room and side room than the standard six inches, more side room than the standard and fewer adjacent seats. The company's frequent flyer program is called Free Spirit. In addition, the firm offers a $9 Fare Club program if customers pay a membership fee of $59.95 for the first year, and $69.95 per year afterward without written cancellation. Members receive offers on exclusive deals on flights before promotions are offered to the public, and have access to reduced bag fee options. In 2015, the firm launched its first international flight departing from Houston's George Bush Intercontinental Airport to Cancun, Mexico, the first of seven international flights the carrier added that month.

FINANCIAL DATA: *Note: Data for latest year may not have been available at press time.*

In U.S. $	2015	2014	2013	2012	2011	2010
Revenue	2,141,463,000	1,931,580,000	1,654,385,000	1,318,388,000	1,071,186,000	781,265,000
R&D Expense						
Operating Income	509,122,000	355,263,000	282,292,000	173,990,000	144,382,000	68,873,000
Operating Margin %	23.77%	18.39%	17.06%	13.19%	13.47%	8.81%
SGA Expense	464,786,000	388,811,000	329,631,000	275,587,000	233,091,000	197,622,000
Net Income	317,220,000	225,464,000	176,918,000	108,460,000	76,448,000	72,481,000
Operating Cash Flow	472,985,000	260,512,000	195,376,000	113,631,000	171,198,000	27,033,000
Capital Expenditure	558,959,000	186,569,000	19,812,000	23,771,000	14,093,000	5,325,000
EBITDA	585,140,000	399,965,000	314,357,000	189,840,000	152,482,000	74,627,000
Return on Assets %	15.04%	10.19%	10.04%	13.02%	12.51%	10.03%
Return on Equity %	28.47%	25.44%	26.17%	20.67%	42.27%	
Debt to Equity	0.48	0.13				

CONTACT INFORMATION:

Phone: 954 447-7920   Fax: 248-727-2688
Toll-Free: 800-772-7117
Address: 2800 Executive Way, Miramar, FL 33025 United States

STOCK TICKER/OTHER:

Stock Ticker: SAVE
Employees: 4,326
Parent Company:

Exchange: NAS
Fiscal Year Ends: 12/31

SALARIES/BONUSES:

Top Exec. Salary: $496,025   Bonus: $
Second Exec. Salary: $336,900   Bonus: $

OTHER THOUGHTS:

Estimated Female Officers or Directors: 1
Hot Spot for Advancement for Women/Minorities:

Stagecoach Group plc

www.stagecoach.com

NAIC Code: 485113

TYPES OF BUSINESS:

Bus Transit Systems
Commuter Rail Systems
Tram Services
Sightseeing Transportation
Charter Buses
School Bus Transportation

BRANDS/DIVISIONS/AFFILIATES:

megabus.com
South West Trains
Virgin Trains East Coast
Stagecoach Supertram
Twin America LLC
Virgin Rail Group

CONTACTS: Note: Officers with more than one job title may be intentionally listed here more than once.

Martin Griffiths, CEO
Ross Paterson, Dir.-Finance

GROWTH PLANS/SPECIAL FEATURES:

Stagecoach Group plc, based in Scotland, is a public transportation company that operates more than 10,000 vehicles across the U.K., U.S. and Canada. The company operates in three segments: U.K. Bus, U.K. Rail and North America. The U.K. Bus segment connects communities in approximately 100 cities in the U.K. with a fleet of 8,500 buses and coaches. This division operates through several regional companies with major operations in London, Liverpool, Newcastle, Hull, Manchester, Oxford, Sheffield and Cambridge. Approximately 1 billion passengers use its services every year. U.K Bus also runs a budget inter-city coach service, megabus.com, which has a network covering 110 locations in the U.K. and over 120 cities in North America. The U.K. Rail segment operates a passenger rail network in the U.K. This division comprises two subsidiaries: South West Trains, which runs services in southwest England out of the London Waterloo railway station, and operates Island Line services on the Isle of Wight; and Virgin Trains East Coast (90%-owned by Stagecoach, 10%-owned by Virgin Group), which provides inter-city train services between London and a number of locations such as Edinburgh, Newcastle, Leeds and York. Stagecoach is also the U.K.'s biggest tram operator, running the Stagecoach Supertram network in Sheffield and the Manchester Metrolink system. The North America segment provides bus and coach transport services in the U.S. and Canada, including commuter/transit services, inter-city services, tour, charter and sightseeing operations. The North America business operates 2,400 vehicles, and has a joint venture, Twin America LLC, with CitySights NY. In addition, Virgin Rail Group is 49%-owned by Stagecoach, and operates the West Coast Trains via contract through March 2017.

The firm offers employees benefits that include annual and public holiday pay, defined benefit or defined contribution pension schemes and free or discounted bus or rail travel.

FINANCIAL DATA: Note: Data for latest year may not have been available at press time.

In U.S. $	2015	2014	2013	2012	2011	2010
Revenue	4,183,672,000	3,825,415,000	3,661,953,000	3,382,424,000	3,120,128,000	
R&D Expense						
Operating Income	247,803,300	261,773,300	285,143,600	311,386,100	248,847,800	
Operating Margin %	5.92%	6.84%	7.78%	9.20%	7.97%	
SGA Expense	647,839,900	574,073,300	530,205,100			
Net Income	181,870,400	172,992,300	207,329,600	245,844,900	230,308,200	
Operating Cash Flow	411,917,500	324,181,100	408,784,100	297,807,900	257,856,500	
Capital Expenditure	254,461,900	211,638,100	245,192,100	233,311,100	204,587,900	
EBITDA	437,246,200	426,148,600	468,058,400	501,743,000	427,715,300	
Return on Assets %	6.96%	7.33%	9.09%	10.77%	10.23%	
Return on Equity %	160.66%	477.47%		199.36%	136.26%	
Debt to Equity	7.79	8.32			2.40	

CONTACT INFORMATION:

Phone: 44 1738442111   Fax: 44 1738643648
Toll-Free:
Address: 10 Dunkeld Rd., Perth, Scotland PH1 5TW United Kingdom

STOCK TICKER/OTHER:

Stock Ticker: SAGKF   Exchange: GREY
Employees: 40,125   Fiscal Year Ends: 04/30
Parent Company:

SALARIES/BONUSES:

Top Exec. Salary: $ Bonus: $
Second Exec. Salary: $ Bonus: $

OTHER THOUGHTS:

Estimated Female Officers or Directors: 2
Hot Spot for Advancement for Women/Minorities: Y

Sales, profits and employees may be estimates. Financial information, benefits and other data can change quickly and may vary from those stated here.

Starwood Capital Group Global LLC

www.starwoodcapital.com

NAIC Code: 721110

TYPES OF BUSINESS:

Real Estate Investments
Energy Investments
Commercial and Residential Development
Industrial Properties
Recreational Properties
Retail Properties
Office Buildings
Golf Courses

BRANDS/DIVISIONS/AFFILIATES:

Starwood Real Estate Securities
Starwood Energy Group
SH Group
1 Hotels & Resorts
Starwood Property Trust Inc
iStar Financial
Starwood Hotels & Resorts Worldwide
Colony Starwood Homes

CONTACTS: Note: Officers with more than one job title may be intentionally listed here more than once.

Barry S. Sternlicht, CEO
Steven M. Hankin, COO
Jerome C. Silvey, CFO
Ellis F. Rinaldi, Co-General Counsel
Jeffrey G. Dishner, Head-Real Estate Acquisitions & Debt Investments
Madison F. Grose, Co-General Counsel
Christopher D. Graham, Sr. Managing Dir.-Acquisitions
Barry S. Sternlicht, Chmn.

GROWTH PLANS/SPECIAL FEATURES:

Starwood Capital Group Global LLC is a private equity real estate investment firm with approximately $45 billion in assets under management. The company specializes in real estate-related investments on behalf of select private and institutional investor partners. It has invested in a wide range of property types, including multifamily, office, retail, hotel, industrial, residential and commercial land, senior housing, mixed-use and golf property, through equity, preferred equity, mezzanine debt and senior debt capital structures. Starwood operates through a number of subsidiaries and affiliated companies. Subsidiary Starwood Real Estate Securities is a hedge fund designed for global public real estate securities investment. Starwood Energy Group is an energy fund focused on investment in transmission, natural gas, wind and solar power generation facilities in North America. SH Group manages the eco-focused brand 1 Hotels & Resorts and also holds the license for Baccarat-brand hotels. Starwood Property Trust, Inc. is a real estate investment trust (REIT) which originates and invests in commercial mortgage loans and other commercial-related debt investments. iStar Financial is the firm's mezzanine debt centered portfolio. Starwood Hotels & Resorts Worldwide, Inc. encompasses the firm's Starwood and Westin hotel chain operations. Starwood is headquartered in Greenwich, Connecticut, with additional offices in Georgia, California, Washington, D.C., the U.K., Luxembourg, France and Brazil. In January 2016, the firm merged Starwood Waypoint Residential Trust with Colony American Homes, forming Colony Starwood Homes, a publicly-traded company under ticker SFR.

FINANCIAL DATA: Note: Data for latest year may not have been available at press time.

In U.S. $	2015	2014	2013	2012	2011	2010
Revenue						
R&D Expense						
Operating Income						
Operating Margin %						
SGA Expense						
Net Income						
Operating Cash Flow						
Capital Expenditure						
EBITDA						
Return on Assets %						
Return on Equity %						
Debt to Equity						

CONTACT INFORMATION:

Phone: 203-422-7700   Fax: 203-422-7784
Toll-Free:
Address: 591 W. Putnam Ave., Greenwich, CT 06830 United States

STOCK TICKER/OTHER:

Stock Ticker: Private   Exchange:
Employees: 2,200   Fiscal Year Ends:
Parent Company:

SALARIES/BONUSES:

Top Exec. Salary: $ Bonus: $
Second Exec. Salary: $ Bonus: $

OTHER THOUGHTS:

Estimated Female Officers or Directors: 1
Hot Spot for Advancement for Women/Minorities:

Sales, profits and employees may be estimates. Financial information, benefits and other data can change quickly and may vary from those stated here.

Starwood Hotels & Resorts Worldwide Inc www.starwoodhotels.com

NAIC Code: 721110

TYPES OF BUSINESS:

Hotels & Resorts
Financial Services
Hotel Management & Franchising
Spa Services

BRANDS/DIVISIONS/AFFILIATES:

Sheraton
W
Four Points
Westin
Le Meridien
St. Regis
Luxury Collection (The)
Aloft

CONTACTS: *Note: Officers with more than one job title may be intentionally listed here more than once.*

Thomas Mangas, CEO
Bruce Duncan, Chairman of the Board
Alan Schnaid, Chief Accounting Officer
Kenneth Siegel, Chief Administrative Officer
Martha Poulter, Chief Information Officer
Robyn Arnell, Controller
Jeffrey Cava, Executive VP
Kristen Prohl, Other Executive Officer
Simon Turner, President, Divisional
Sergio Rivera, President, Geographical

GROWTH PLANS/SPECIAL FEATURES:

Starwood Hotels & Resorts Worldwide, Inc. is involved in the global operation of hotels and resorts, primarily in the luxury and upscale segments of the industry. It owns, leases, manages or franchises approximately 1,222 properties with approximately 354,200 rooms in nearly 100 countries. The company's hotel brand names include St. Regis, The Luxury Collection, Phoenician, Tremont, Hotel Alfonso, Hotel Imperial, Hotel Maria Cristina, The Gritti Palace, Hotel Goldener Hirsch, W, Westin, Sheraton, Four Points, Le Meridien, Aloft and Element. The firm's earnings are derived mainly from its hotel and leisure operations; the receipt of franchise fees; and the development, ownership and operation of vacation ownership resorts. Additionally, Starwood provides financing to customers who purchase interests in resorts. The firm's frequent guest loyalty program, Starwood Preferred Guest, is unique in the hotel industry for its lack of capacity controls and blackout dates. In November 2015, the firm received an acquisition offer from Marriott. In March 2016, Starwood received a competing acquisition offer from Anbang Insurance Group, a China-based firm that has a history of acquiring hotels for its investment portfolio. The following week, Mariott countered with another offer valuing Starwood at $13.6 billion.

The firm offers employees dental, vision and health insurance; life insurance; wellness programs; dependent care flexible spending accounts; an employee assistance program; and adoption assistance.

FINANCIAL DATA: *Note: Data for latest year may not have been available at press time.*

In U.S. $	2015	2014	2013	2012	2011	2010
Revenue	5,763,000,000	5,983,000,000	6,115,000,000	6,321,000,000	5,624,000,000	5,071,000,000
R&D Expense						
Operating Income	740,000,000	883,000,000	925,000,000	912,000,000	630,000,000	600,000,000
Operating Margin %	12.84%	14.75%	15.12%	14.42%	11.20%	11.83%
SGA Expense	388,000,000	402,000,000	384,000,000	370,000,000	352,000,000	344,000,000
Net Income	489,000,000	633,000,000	635,000,000	562,000,000	489,000,000	477,000,000
Operating Cash Flow	890,000,000	994,000,000	1,151,000,000	1,184,000,000	641,000,000	764,000,000
Capital Expenditure	261,000,000	327,000,000	364,000,000	362,000,000	385,000,000	227,000,000
EBITDA	1,065,000,000	1,162,000,000	1,198,000,000	1,039,000,000	906,000,000	858,000,000
Return on Assets %	5.77%	7.26%	7.20%	6.10%	5.05%	23.53%
Return on Equity %	34.66%	25.91%	19.54%	18.45%	18.02%	101.55%
Debt to Equity	1.75	1.68	0.45	0.52	0.87	1.30

CONTACT INFORMATION:

Phone: 914 640-8100   Fax: 914 640-8310
Toll-Free:
Address: 1 StarPoint, White Plains, NY 06902 United States

STOCK TICKER/OTHER:

Stock Ticker: HOT   Exchange: NYS
Employees: 180,400   Fiscal Year Ends: 12/31
Parent Company:

SALARIES/BONUSES:

Top Exec. Salary: Bonus: $
$1,250,000
Second Exec. Salary: Bonus: $500,000
$365,909

OTHER THOUGHTS:

Estimated Female Officers or Directors: 4

Hot Spot for Advancement for Women/Minorities: Y

Station Casinos LLC

www.stationcasinos.com

NAIC Code: 721120

TYPES OF BUSINESS:

Casino Hotel
Casino Management
Restaurants
Movie Theaters & Entertainment Venues

BRANDS/DIVISIONS/AFFILIATES:

Palace Station Hotel & Casino
Texas Station Gambling Hall & Hotel
Boulder Station Hotel & Casino
Santa Fe Station Hotel & Casino
Barley's Casino & Brewing Company
Sunset Station Hotel & Casino
Fiesta Rancho Casino Hotel
Green Valley Ranch Station Resort

CONTACTS: Note: Officers with more than one job title may be intentionally listed here more than once.

Frank J. Fertitta, III, CEO
Daniel J. Roy, COO
Stephen L. Cavallaro, Pres.
Marc J. Falcone, Exec. VP
Richard J. Haskins, General Counsel
Scott M. Nielson, Chief Dev. Officer
Wes D. Allison, Chief Acct. Officer
Thomas M. Friel, Exec. VP
Frank J. Fertitta, III, Chmn.

GROWTH PLANS/SPECIAL FEATURES:

Station Casinos LLC is a gaming and entertainment company concentrated in the Las Vegas area, mainly targeting locals and repeat customers. Its properties include nine major casinos and hotels and 10 smaller casinos, featuring more than 4,000 hotel rooms, 2,909 slot machines and 131 gaming tables. Other offerings include movie screens, bowling lanes, live entertainment venues, retail outlets, sports betting and convention banquet space. Station Casinos' owned and operated properties in Las Vegas include Palace Station Hotel & Casino; Boulder Station Hotel & Casino; Santa Fe Station Hotel & Casino; Red Rock Casino, Resort & Spa; Wild Wild West Gambling Hall & Hotel; Wildfire Rancho; Texas Station Gambling Hall & Hotel; and Fiesta Rancho Casino Hotel. In Henderson, Nevada, it owns Sunset Station Hotel & Casino; Fiesta Henderson Casino Hotel; Wildfire Boulder; and Green Valley Ranch Station Resort, Spa & Casino. The firm also owns 50% of three properties in Henderson: Barley's Casino & Brewing Company, The Greens Gaming & Dining and Wildfire Casino & Lanes. Additionally, the company manages Graton Resort and Casino in Sonoma County, California and Gun Lake Casino in Allegan County, Michigan. In October 2015, the firm filed a registration statement with the Securities and Exchange Commission relating to the proposed initial public offering of its common stock.

The firm offers employees benefits including onsite childcare, tuition reimbursement, a 401(k) and employee discounts.

FINANCIAL DATA: Note: Data for latest year may not have been available at press time.

In U.S. $	2015	2014	2013	2012	2011	2010
Revenue	1,352,135,000	1,291,616,000	1,261,478,000	1,229,476,000	1,178,148,000	944,955,000
R&D Expense						
Operating Income						
Operating Margin %						
SGA Expense						
Net Income	132,504,000	71,326,000	-113,493,000	13,318,000	-40,816,000	-563,769,000
Operating Cash Flow						
Capital Expenditure						
EBITDA						
Return on Assets %						
Return on Equity %						
Debt to Equity						

CONTACT INFORMATION:

Phone: 702-495-3000   Fax: 702-495-3530
Toll-Free: 800-634-3101
Address: 1505 S. Pavilion Ctr. Dr., Las Vegas, NV 89135 United States

STOCK TICKER/OTHER:

Stock Ticker: Private   Exchange:
Employees: 12,000   Fiscal Year Ends: 12/31
Parent Company:

SALARIES/BONUSES:

Top Exec. Salary: $ Bonus: $
Second Exec. Salary: $ Bonus: $

OTHER THOUGHTS:

Estimated Female Officers or Directors:
Hot Spot for Advancement for Women/Minorities:

Sales, profits and employees may be estimates. Financial information, benefits and other data can change quickly and may vary from those stated here.

Strategic Hotels & Resorts Inc

NAIC Code: 531120

www.strategichotels.com

TYPES OF BUSINESS:

Real Estate Investment Trust
Hotels

BRANDS/DIVISIONS/AFFILIATES:

Strategic Hotel Capital LLC
Blackstone Real Estate Partners VIII LP
Blackstone Group L P

CONTACTS: Note: Officers with more than one job title may be intentionally listed here more than once.

Stephen A. Schwarzman, CEO-Blackstone Real Estate
Diane Morefield, CFO
Jon Stanner, CFO
George Stowers, Sr. VP-Design & Construction
Bryce White, VP-IT
Paula Maggio, Executive VP

GROWTH PLANS/SPECIAL FEATURES:

Strategic Hotels & Resorts, Inc. (SHR) is a portfolio company of The Blackstone Group, which owns and manages upper upscale and luxury hotels in North America and Europe through its investment in the operating partnership Strategic Hotel Capital LLC and its subsidiaries. The company owns or leases 16 hotels; owns 53.5% and 51.0% interests in affiliates that each own one hotel where it asset manages such hotels; owns land held for development including 50.7 acres of oceanfront land in Nayarit, Mexico, 13.8 acres of land in Scottsdale, Arizona and a 20,000 square-foot oceanfront land parcel in Santa Monica, California. In total, the 16 hotels and resorts consists of 7,532 rooms, 807,000 square feet of multi-purpose meeting and banqueting space, world class restaurants, wine and cocktail bars, high-end spas and retail offerings. The firm does not operate any of its hotels directly; instead, it employs internationally known hotel management companies to operate them under management contracts or operating leases. The company's existing hotels are operated under the Fairmont, Four Seasons, Hyatt, InterContinental, Loews, JW Marriot, Marriott, Montage, Renaissance, Ritz-Carlton and Westin brands. In December 2015, the firm was acquired by Blackstone Real Estate Partners VIII L.P., part of The Blackstone Group L.P.

FINANCIAL DATA: Note: Data for latest year may not have been available at press time.

In U.S. $	2015	2014	2013	2012	2011	2010
Revenue	1,381,600,000	1,089,081,984	900,012,992	808,316,992	763,838,016	686,292,992
R&D Expense						
Operating Income						
Operating Margin %						
SGA Expense						
Net Income		344,483,008	10,975,000	-55,306,000	-5,206,000	-231,051,008
Operating Cash Flow						
Capital Expenditure						
EBITDA						
Return on Assets %						
Return on Equity %						
Debt to Equity						

CONTACT INFORMATION:

Phone: 312 658-5000　　Fax: 312 658-5799
Toll-Free:
Address: 200 W. Madison St., Ste. 1700, Chicago, IL 60606 United States

STOCK TICKER/OTHER:

Stock Ticker: Private　　Exchange:
Employees: 35　　Fiscal Year Ends: 12/31
Parent Company: Blackstone Real Estate Partners VIII LP

SALARIES/BONUSES:

Top Exec. Salary: $　　Bonus: $
Second Exec. Salary: $　　Bonus: $

OTHER THOUGHTS:

Estimated Female Officers or Directors: 3
Hot Spot for Advancement for Women/Minorities: Y

Sunburst Hospitality Corporation

www.snbhotels.com

NAIC Code: 721110

TYPES OF BUSINESS:

Hotels
Hotel Management

BRANDS/DIVISIONS/AFFILIATES:

Comfort Inns & Suites
Holiday Inn Express
Crowne Plaza
Quality Inn
Clarion
Sleep Inn
Arlington Court
Best Western

CONTACTS: *Note: Officers with more than one job title may be intentionally listed here more than once.*

Pamela Williams, CEO
Ned Heiss, VP-Oper.
Pam Williams, Pres.
Joe Smith, CFO
Tonio Noonan, VP-Mktg. & Sales
Mark Elbaum, VP-Information Systems
Leon Vainikos, Regional General Counsel
Ned Heiss, VP-Oper.
Chris Milke, VP-Acquisitions & Dev.
Joe Smith, Treas.
Chris Milke, VP-Acquisitions & Dev.

GROWTH PLANS/SPECIAL FEATURES:

Sunburst Hospitality Corporation owns, acquires and manages hotels, a championship golf course and townhomes. The company maintains operations in seven states: Arkansas, Maryland, California, New York, Florida, Ohio and Virginia. The firm's hotels are extended-stay, full-service and limited service. On average, Sunburst Hospitality produces annual revenues of $100 million. Sunburst Hospitality owns and operates hotels under several brand names including Comfort Inns & Suites, Holiday Inn Express, Crowne Plaza, Quality Inn, Clarion, Sleep Inn, Super 8, Clarion, Arlington Court and Best Western. Sunburst constantly seeks to expand its hotel business through acquisitions. The firm seeks to acquire existing 70-300 room extended-stay, limited-service and full-service hotels, with or without food and beverage service. Additionally, the company develops residential real estate and operates The Vista on Courthouse, a 252-unit residential complex in Arlington, Virginia.

FINANCIAL DATA: *Note: Data for latest year may not have been available at press time.*

In U.S. $	2015	2014	2013	2012	2011	2010
Revenue						
R&D Expense						
Operating Income						
Operating Margin %						
SGA Expense						
Net Income						
Operating Cash Flow						
Capital Expenditure						
EBITDA						
Return on Assets %						
Return on Equity %						
Debt to Equity						

CONTACT INFORMATION:

Phone: 301-592-3800   Fax: 301-592-3830
Toll-Free:
Address: 10770 Columbia Pike, Ste. 300, Silver Spring, MD 20901 United States

STOCK TICKER/OTHER:

Stock Ticker: Private
Employees: 3,500
Parent Company:

Exchange:
Fiscal Year Ends: 12/31

SALARIES/BONUSES:

Top Exec. Salary: $ Bonus: $
Second Exec. Salary: $ Bonus: $

OTHER THOUGHTS:

Estimated Female Officers or Directors: 2
Hot Spot for Advancement for Women/Minorities:

Sales, profits and employees may be estimates. Financial information, benefits and other data can change quickly and may vary from those stated here.

Sunstone Hotel Investors Inc

www.sunstonehotels.com

NAIC Code: 0

TYPES OF BUSINESS:

Real Estate Investment Trust
Hotel Ownership
Online Purchasing Systems

BRANDS/DIVISIONS/AFFILIATES:

Sunstone Hotel TRS Lessee Inc
Sunstone Hotel Partnership LLC

CONTACTS: *Note: Officers with more than one job title may be intentionally listed here more than once.*

Bryan Giglia, CFO
Marc Hoffman, COO
Douglas Pasquale, Director
Robert Springer, Executive VP
John Arabia, President

GROWTH PLANS/SPECIAL FEATURES:

Sunstone Hotel Investors, Inc. is a real estate investment trust (REIT) that acquires, owns, manages and renovates luxury, upper upscale and upscale full service hotels. Sunstone maintains interests in 29 hotels, with a total of 13,845 rooms, located in 13 states and Washington, D.C. The company's hotels are marketed under the brand names Hilton, Fairmont, Sheraton, Hyatt and Marriott. Third-party managers operate the company's hotels through agreements with wholly-owned subsidiary Sunstone Hotel TRS Lessee, Inc. At December 2015, the firm's 29 hotels had an average of 477 rooms and generated a comparable RevPAR (revenue per available room) of $162.42. Sunstone specializes in acquiring under-performing properties and developing them into profitable upscale and luxury properties. The firm prefers to acquire major brand properties situated in one of the top 25 U.S. markets, with upscale potential and a location with high barriers to entry. In addition, the company owns Sunstone Hotel Partnership LLC, the entity that directly or indirectly owns Sunstone's hotel properties. In 2015, the firm sold its BuyEfficient LLC subsidiary. In May 2016, it sold its leasehold interest in the 203-room Sheraton Cerritos hotel for $42 million.

FINANCIAL DATA: *Note: Data for latest year may not have been available at press time.*

In U.S. $	2015	2014	2013	2012	2011	2010
Revenue	1,249,180,000	1,141,998,000	923,824,000	829,084,000	834,729,000	643,090,000
R&D Expense						
Operating Income	180,436,000	156,743,000	99,198,000	79,010,000	58,718,000	32,001,000
Operating Margin %	14.44%	13.72%	10.73%	9.52%	7.03%	4.97%
SGA Expense	312,202,000	282,880,000	237,369,000	249,137,000	260,235,000	213,841,000
Net Income	347,355,000	81,231,000	65,956,000	47,765,000	80,957,000	38,542,000
Operating Cash Flow	300,061,000	278,595,000	171,119,000	171,496,000	156,390,000	45,402,000
Capital Expenditure	164,232,000	402,533,000	568,238,000	229,324,000	218,688,000	199,394,000
EBITDA	571,619,000	315,708,000	241,450,000	227,520,000	192,621,000	133,214,000
Return on Assets %	8.68%	1.93%	1.39%	.57%	1.91%	.71%
Return on Equity %	15.77%	3.70%	3.14%	1.65%	5.58%	2.17%
Debt to Equity	0.46	0.62	0.78	1.11	1.55	1.22

CONTACT INFORMATION:

Phone: 949 330-4000   Fax: 949 369-3134
Toll-Free:
Address: 120 Vantis, Ste. 350, Aliso Viejo, CA 92656 United States

STOCK TICKER/OTHER:

Stock Ticker: SHO
Employees: 50
Parent Company:

Exchange: NYS
Fiscal Year Ends: 12/31

SALARIES/BONUSES:

Top Exec. Salary: $691,486   Bonus: $
Second Exec. Salary: $507,018   Bonus: $

OTHER THOUGHTS:

Estimated Female Officers or Directors: 3
Hot Spot for Advancement for Women/Minorities: Y

Super 8 Worldwide Inc

www.super8.com

NAIC Code: 721110

TYPES OF BUSINESS:

Hotel Franchising
Economy Motels
Online Reservations & Services

BRANDS/DIVISIONS/AFFILIATES:

Wyndham Worldwide Corporation
Wyndham Rewards

CONTACTS: *Note: Officers with more than one job title may be intentionally listed here more than once.*

Stephen P. Holmes, CEO-Wyndham Worldwide
John Valletta, Pres.
Jim Darby, VP-Oper.
Stephen P. Holmes, Chmn.-Wyndham Worldwide

GROWTH PLANS/SPECIAL FEATURES:

Super 8 Worldwide, Inc. is a subsidiary of Wyndham Worldwide Corporation and one of the world's largest franchised economy lodging chains, with a portfolio of nearly 1,800 motels. The firm offers lodging for the budget traveler, with many rooms below $50 per night. Super 8 motels are found in every domestic state besides Hawaii and in every Canadian province. Super 8 also operates 400 properties in China, three in Brazil, one in Germany and one in Saudi Arabia. The company offers numerous promotions, such as guaranteed best rates, group and corporate rates and AAA and AARP discounts. Super 8's web site offers customers a wide array of integrated travel resources, including flight tracking, driving directions, street maps, airport maps, destination guides and weather information, in addition to online reservations, location information and special promotional programs. A search feature can automatically find the Super 8 motel and room with the best available rate for a given date in the travel area. The company offers several in-room products and services, including in-room coffee makers, bath amenities and expanded breakfast choices. In addition, the firm is a member of Wyndham Rewards, one of the largest hotel reward programs in the world based on the 7,400 participating hotels. The program allows customers to earn points toward hotel stays as well as airline miles, gifts, meals and other incentives.

FINANCIAL DATA: *Note: Data for latest year may not have been available at press time.*

In U.S. $	2015	2014	2013	2012	2011	2010
Revenue						
R&D Expense						
Operating Income						
Operating Margin %						
SGA Expense						
Net Income						
Operating Cash Flow						
Capital Expenditure						
EBITDA						
Return on Assets %						
Return on Equity %						
Debt to Equity						

CONTACT INFORMATION:

Phone: 973-753-0000   Fax: 973-490-2305
Toll-Free: 800-800-8000
Address: 22 Sylvan Way, Parsippany, NJ 07054 United States

STOCK TICKER/OTHER:

Stock Ticker: Subsidiary   Exchange:
Employees: 1,190   Fiscal Year Ends: 12/31
Parent Company: Wyndham Worldwide Corporation

SALARIES/BONUSES:

Top Exec. Salary: $ Bonus: $
Second Exec. Salary: $ Bonus: $

OTHER THOUGHTS:

Estimated Female Officers or Directors:
Hot Spot for Advancement for Women/Minorities:

Sales, profits and employees may be estimates. Financial information, benefits and other data can change quickly and may vary from those stated here.

SuperShuttle International Inc

www.supershuttle.com

NAIC Code: 485999

TYPES OF BUSINESS:

Airport Shuttle Service
Car & Van Transportation

BRANDS/DIVISIONS/AFFILIATES:

Transdev
1-800-BLUE-VAN
ExecuCar

CONTACTS: Note: Officers with more than one job title may be intentionally listed here more than once.

Brian Wier, CEO
Mike Hogan, CIO

GROWTH PLANS/SPECIAL FEATURES:

SuperShuttle International, Inc. offers shared ride, door-to-door ground transportation. It is a wholly owned subsidiary of Transdev. SuperShuttle offers customers travel accommodations from a home, hotel or office to the airport, charging, on average, less than a taxi or limo because it essentially car pools customers in a single, distinctly colored blue and yellow van. It attempts to speed up the travel process by grouping together passengers traveling to or from the same area using a proprietary dispatch system. Reservations for transportation can be made online via the firm's web site or by phone through 1-800-BLUE-VAN. Additionally, SuperShuttle has partnered with various online travel sites, such as Expedia, Orbitz and Travelocity, allowing customers to make reservations at the same time they make their other travel plans. Each driver owns their own van, effectively making them individual franchise owners. For their affiliation with the company, drivers receive the benefits of the dispatch service and reservation system as well as financing options and marketing partnerships. Since virtually pioneering the shared ride concept in Los Angeles in 1983, the firm has expanded across the country and now serves more than 8 million customers annually. With a fleet of approximately 1,200 vans, the company provides 24-hour service in more than 50 cities surrounding 40 airports, including New York, Houston, Dallas/Ft. Worth, Denver, San Francisco, Miami, Baltimore and Washington, D.C. as well as Paris, Cancun and Stockholm. SuperShuttle offers chartered van services and group and employee ground transportation in all of its cities of operation. Additionally, it offers business class sedan transportation to all the airports the firm serves in the U.S. through subsidiary ExecuCar.

FINANCIAL DATA: Note: Data for latest year may not have been available at press time.

In U.S. $	2015	2014	2013	2012	2011	2010
Revenue						
R&D Expense						
Operating Income						
Operating Margin %						
SGA Expense						
Net Income						
Operating Cash Flow						
Capital Expenditure						
EBITDA						
Return on Assets %						
Return on Equity %						
Debt to Equity						

CONTACT INFORMATION:

Phone: 602-232-4610   Fax: 602-256-6118
Toll-Free:
Address: 4610 South 35th Street, Phoenix, AZ 85040 United States

STOCK TICKER/OTHER:

Stock Ticker: Subsidiary   Exchange:
Employees: 16,000   Fiscal Year Ends: 09/30
Parent Company: Transdev

SALARIES/BONUSES:

Top Exec. Salary: $ Bonus: $
Second Exec. Salary: $ Bonus: $

OTHER THOUGHTS:

Estimated Female Officers or Directors:
Hot Spot for Advancement for Women/Minorities:

Supranational Hotels Ltd

www.supranationalhotels.com/

NAIC Code: 561599

TYPES OF BUSINESS:

Hotel Marketing
Internet Booking

BRANDS/DIVISIONS/AFFILIATES:

GROWTH PLANS/SPECIAL FEATURES:

Supranational Hotels Ltd. is an international hotel representative company. The company focuses on small independent hotels that would not otherwise be able to compete against large chain hotels. Supranational's hotel portfolio, which in total covers more than 800 hotels, includes over 40 well-renowned hotel chains as well as independently-owned hotels in over 70 countries. The firm provides its members with Supranational Internet booking technology, an image library, public relations services, marketing, sales services, a connection to major travel portals, a GDS (global distribution system) marketing advisory center, marketing intelligence reports, booking statistics and international voice reservation centers, among other services. Supranational was started by five hotel companies in 1974 and is owned by a number of the firm's major hotel members.

CONTACTS: *Note: Officers with more than one job title may be intentionally listed here more than once.*

Cho Wong, Managing Dir.
Adriano Albertino, Dir.-Finance
Natalia Hall, Dir.-Sales & Mktg.
Alison Boud, Dir.-Oper. & Reservations
Catt McLeod, Dir.-Bus. Dev.
James FitzRoy, Mgr.-Mktg. Support
Pal Semb-Johansson, Chmn.
Robert Koncz, Mgr.-Int'l Sales

FINANCIAL DATA: *Note: Data for latest year may not have been available at press time.*

In U.S. $	2015	2014	2013	2012	2011	2010
Revenue						
R&D Expense						
Operating Income						
Operating Margin %						
SGA Expense						
Net Income						
Operating Cash Flow						
Capital Expenditure						
EBITDA						
Return on Assets %						
Return on Equity %						
Debt to Equity						

CONTACT INFORMATION:

Phone: 44-20-7357-0770   Fax: 44-20-7407-1715
Toll-Free:
Address: 36 Shad Thames, Butlers Wharf, London, SE1 2YE United Kingdom

STOCK TICKER/OTHER:

Stock Ticker: Cooperative
Employees:
Parent Company:

Exchange:
Fiscal Year Ends: 12/31

SALARIES/BONUSES:

Top Exec. Salary: $ Bonus: $
Second Exec. Salary: $ Bonus: $

OTHER THOUGHTS:

Estimated Female Officers or Directors: 6
Hot Spot for Advancement for Women/Minorities: Y

Sales, profits and employees may be estimates. Financial information, benefits and other data can change quickly and may vary from those stated here.

Swire Pacific Ltd

NAIC Code: 483111

TYPES OF BUSINESS:

Deep Sea Shipping
Airlines and Air Freight
International & Regional Airlines
Apparel Retail
Real Estate, Hotels, Commercial Properties
Aircraft Maintenance
Airline Catering Service
Beverage Manufacturing & Distribution

BRANDS/DIVISIONS/AFFILIATES:

Swire Group
Swire Properties
Swire Properties Inc
Swire Hotels
Cathay Pacific Airways Limited
Hong Kong Aircraft Engineering Company Limited
HUD Group (The)
Swire Beverages Ltd

CONTACTS: Note: Officers with more than one job title may be intentionally listed here more than once.

Martin Cubbon, Dir.-Finance
Martin Cubbon, CEO-Swire Properties Limited
Kenny Tang, CEO-Dragon Airlines
Kin Wing Tang, CEO-Hong Kong Aircraft Engineering Company Limited
John Robert Slosar, Exec. Chmn.

GROWTH PLANS/SPECIAL FEATURES:

Swire Pacific Ltd. is part of the Swire Group and one of Hong Kong's leading listed companies. It operates several core businesses, organized into five divisions: property, aviation, beverages, marine services and trading and industrial. Swire Properties develops and manages retail, office, hotel and residential properties primarily throughout mainland China and Hong Kong. Swire Properties, Inc., its U.S. subsidiary, develops and trades properties in Florida, specifically downtown Miami, including office space, retail space and hotels. The Swire Hotels subsidiary develops and manages urban hotels throughout Mainland China, Hong Kong and the U.K., including The Upper House and EAST in Hong Kong and The Opposite House in Beijing. The company's aviation holdings include international passenger and freight airline Cathay Pacific Airways Limited, with nearly 700 worldwide destinations; Hong Kong Dragon Airlines, with more than 29 destinations and cargo operations in Asia, Europe, the U.S. and the Middle East; and Hong Kong Aircraft Engineering Company Limited, a provider of base and line maintenance at Hong Kong International Airport. Swire Beverages, Ltd., a joint venture between Swire Pacific (owning 87.5%) and The Coca-Cola Company, manufactures and distribute Coca-Cola products in Mainland China and Hong Kong. The firm's marine services holdings include Swire Pacific Offshore Operations (Pte) Ltd.(SPO), one of the largest offshore energy support fleets in the world, with a fleet of 71 vessels; and the HUD Group, which provides ship repair, towage and salvage, mechanical and electrical engineering and steelwork services. Trading and industrial subsidiary Swire Resources Limited acts as the holding company for various retail and wholesale interests in sports and active footwear and apparel, operating more than 180 retail locations in China. In October 2013, the company agreed to acquire TIMCO Aviation Services., Inc., and that December also agreed to acquire DCH Commercial Centre.

FINANCIAL DATA: Note: Data for latest year may not have been available at press time.

In U.S. $	2015	2014	2013	2012	2011	2010
Revenue	7,851,267,000	7,904,911,000	6,632,924,000	5,655,724,000	4,679,167,000	3,765,539,000
R&D Expense						
Operating Income	2,122,685,000	1,766,261,000	2,151,700,000	3,002,914,000	4,052,200,000	4,380,642,000
Operating Margin %	27.03%	22.34%	32.43%	53.09%	86.60%	116.33%
SGA Expense	1,672,771,000	1,408,805,000	1,274,436,000	985,454,200	908,211,700	766,235,200
Net Income	1,731,702,000	1,427,374,000	1,713,906,000	2,254,604,000	4,153,557,000	4,932,687,000
Operating Cash Flow	1,542,658,000	1,866,457,000	1,528,989,000	1,067,855,000	1,231,238,000	928,844,100
Capital Expenditure	554,366,300	802,341,800	829,035,000	928,715,100	1,258,060,000	899,314,000
EBITDA	3,328,133,000	2,562,800,000	2,839,274,000	3,557,023,000	4,840,744,000	5,567,133,000
Return on Assets %	3.73%	3.13%	3.96%	5.69%	11.43%	15.66%
Return on Equity %	6.14%	5.04%	6.18%	7.99%	14.91%	21.43%
Debt to Equity	0.27	0.27	0.23	0.19	0.11	0.14

CONTACT INFORMATION:

Phone: 852 2840808   Fax: 852 25269365
Toll-Free:
Address: 1 Pacific Place, 88 Queensway, 33rd Fl., Hong Kong, Hong Kong

STOCK TICKER/OTHER:

Stock Ticker: SWRAY   Exchange: PINX
Employees: 82,000   Fiscal Year Ends: 12/31
Parent Company:

SALARIES/BONUSES:

Top Exec. Salary: $ Bonus: $
Second Exec. Salary: $ Bonus: $

OTHER THOUGHTS:

Estimated Female Officers or Directors:
Hot Spot for Advancement for Women/Minorities:

Swiss International Air Lines Ltd

www.swiss.com

NAIC Code: 481111

TYPES OF BUSINESS:

Airline
Charter Airline

BRANDS/DIVISIONS/AFFILIATES:

Deutsche Lufthansa AG
Swiss AviationSoftware Ltd
Swiss WorldCargo
Swiss AviationTraining Ltd
Edelweiss Air AG
Swiss Global Air Lines

CONTACTS:
Note: Officers with more than one job title may be intentionally listed here more than once.

Thomas Kluhr, CEO
Roland Busch, CFO
Markus Binkert, Chief Commercial Officer
Christoph Casparis, Head-Legal
Patrick Heiz, Dir.-Corp. Dev.
Daniel Barlocher, Head-Corp. Comm.
Jean-Pierre Tappy, Managing Dir.
Andreas Thurnheer, Head-Swiss European Air Lines Ltd.
Ronald Schauffele, CEO-Swiss Aviation Software
Ignazio Strano, Head-Network, Fleet Dev. & Commercial Rel.
Bruno Gehrig, Chmn.
Oliver Evans, Chief Cargo Officer

GROWTH PLANS/SPECIAL FEATURES:

Swiss International Air Lines Ltd., a subsidiary of Deutsche Lufthansa AG, is Switzerland's national airline. The firm serves over 102 destinations in 46 countries, such as Florence, Tel Aviv, Madrid, Vienna, Hamburg, Prague and Nice. It owns a fleet of 83 aircraft, including Airbus A319, A320, A321, A330, A340, Avro RJ100, Boeing 777 and Bombardier C Series 100 aircraft. The firm also wet-leases 12 aircraft consisting of four Fokker 100s, four Embraer 90s and four Dash 8s. Swiss is a member of the Star Alliance, the world's largest network of airlines, which includes Air China and United. The firm has flight hubs in Basel, Geneva and Zurich, and carries more than 16 million passengers on more than 145,000 flights annually. The company is also involved in the information technology sector. It has designed and developed AMOS, a fully integrated maintenance software solution for engineering and logistic requirements. AMOS is marketed by the firm's subsidiary, Swiss AviationSoftware Ltd.; it is used by over 130 airlines and maintenance, repair and overhaul companies worldwide. Swiss WorldCargo, the company's cargo division, acts as a wholesaler for airport-to-airport freight to over 130 locations in over 80 countries. Subsidiary Swiss AviationTraining Ltd. is an aircraft management and commercial charter specialist. The firm also offers flights to more than 40 destinations through subsidiary Edelweiss Air AG, as well as flights to 36 destinations through subsidiary Swiss Global Air Lines.

FINANCIAL DATA:
Note: Data for latest year may not have been available at press time.

In U.S. $	2015	2014	2013	2012	2011	2010
Revenue	5,208,028,867	4,571,617,760	5,500,000,000	5,451,780,365	5,236,810,000	5,060,960,000
R&D Expense						
Operating Income						
Operating Margin %						
SGA Expense						
Net Income	468,579,046	348,589,611				
Operating Cash Flow						
Capital Expenditure						
EBITDA						
Return on Assets %						
Return on Equity %						
Debt to Equity						

CONTACT INFORMATION:

Phone: 41 61 582 0000   Fax: 41 61 582 3333
Toll-Free:
Address: Malzgasse 15, Basel, 4052 Switzerland

STOCK TICKER/OTHER:

Stock Ticker: Subsidiary   Exchange:
Employees: 8,564   Fiscal Year Ends: 12/31
Parent Company: Deutsche Lufthansa AG

SALARIES/BONUSES:

Top Exec. Salary: $ Bonus: $
Second Exec. Salary: $ Bonus: $

OTHER THOUGHTS:

Estimated Female Officers or Directors:
Hot Spot for Advancement for Women/Minorities:

Sales, profits and employees may be estimates. Financial information, benefits and other data can change quickly and may vary from those stated here.

Textron Inc
NAIC Code: 336411

www.textron.com

TYPES OF BUSINESS:
Helicopters & General Aviation Aircraft Manufacturing
Aerospace
Electrical Test & Measurement Equipment
Fiber Optic Equipment
Off-Road Vehicles
Financing

BRANDS/DIVISIONS/AFFILIATES:
Bell Helicopter
Greenlee
Textron Aviation
Textron Financial Corporation
Jacobsen
Kautex
E-Z-GO
Textron Systems

CONTACTS: *Note: Officers with more than one job title may be intentionally listed here more than once.*
Scott Donnelly, CEO
Frank Connor, CFO
Mark Bamford, Chief Accounting Officer
Cheryl Johnson, Executive VP, Divisional
Robert Lupone, Executive VP

GROWTH PLANS/SPECIAL FEATURES:

Textron, Inc. is a global multi-industry company active in the aircraft, defense, industrial and finance industries. The company divides its operations into five segments: Bell Helicopter, Textron Systems, Textron Aviation, industrial and finance. Bell Helicopter supplies helicopters, tilt rotor aircraft and helicopter-related spare parts and services for military and commercial applications. It also offers commercially-certified helicopters to corporate; offshore petroleum exploration; utility; charter; and police, fire, rescue and emergency medical helicopter operators. Textron Systems manufactures weapons systems and surveillance and intelligence products for the defense, aerospace, homeland security and general aviation markets. It sells most of its products to U.S. government customers, but also to customers outside the U.S. through foreign military sales sponsored by the U.S. government and directly through commercial sales channels. Textron Aviation is home to the Beechcraft, Cessna and Hawker brands, which account for more than half of all general aviation aircraft flying. Its product portfolio includes five business lines: business jets, general aviation and special mission turboprop aircraft, high performance piston aircraft, military trainer and defense aircraft and a customer service organization. The industrial segment includes the business of E-Z-GO, Jacobsen, Kautex and Greenlee. These companies design, manufacture and sell diverse products such as golf carts, off-road utility vehicles, turf maintenance equipment, blow-molded fuel systems, electrical test and measurement instruments and fiber optic connectors. The finance segment consists of Textron Financial Corporation and its subsidiaries, which mostly support the company's other segments. In 2014, the firm acquired Beech Holdings LLC, and merged it with its Cessna business to form business segment, Textron Aviation.

Textron offers its employees medical, prescription, dental and vision coverage; flexible spending accounts; life, AD&D, business travel and disability insurance; adoption assistance; discounts on products and auto and home insurance; and educational assis

FINANCIAL DATA: *Note: Data for latest year may not have been available at press time.*

In U.S. $	2015	2014	2013	2012	2011	2010
Revenue	13,423,000,000	13,878,000,000	12,104,000,000	12,237,000,000	11,275,000,000	10,525,000,000
R&D Expense						
Operating Income	1,140,000,000	1,096,000,000	847,000,000	1,053,000,000	337,000,000	86,000,000
Operating Margin %	8.49%	7.89%	6.99%	8.60%	2.98%	.81%
SGA Expense	1,304,000,000	1,361,000,000	1,126,000,000	1,168,000,000	1,183,000,000	1,231,000,000
Net Income	697,000,000	600,000,000	498,000,000	589,000,000	242,000,000	86,000,000
Operating Cash Flow	1,090,000,000	1,208,000,000	810,000,000	927,000,000	1,063,000,000	984,000,000
Capital Expenditure	420,000,000	429,000,000	444,000,000	480,000,000	423,000,000	270,000,000
EBITDA	1,601,000,000	1,503,000,000	1,236,000,000	1,436,000,000	986,000,000	749,000,000
Return on Assets %	4.75%	4.35%	3.83%	4.42%	1.67%	.50%
Return on Equity %	15.09%	13.86%	13.50%	20.53%	8.46%	2.96%
Debt to Equity	0.67	0.90	0.72	1.15	1.56	1.99

CONTACT INFORMATION:
Phone: 401 421-2800   Fax: 401 421-2878
Toll-Free:
Address: 40 Westminster St., Providence, RI 02903 United States

STOCK TICKER/OTHER:
Stock Ticker: TXT   Exchange: NYS
Employees: 34,000   Fiscal Year Ends: 12/31
Parent Company:

SALARIES/BONUSES:
Top Exec. Salary: $1,151,154   Bonus: $
Second Exec. Salary: $925,000   Bonus: $

OTHER THOUGHTS:
Estimated Female Officers or Directors: 10

Hot Spot for Advancement for Women/Minorities: Y

Sales, profits and employees may be estimates. Financial information, benefits and other data can change quickly and may vary from those stated here.

Thai Airways International PCL   www.thaiairways.com

NAIC Code: 481111

TYPES OF BUSINESS:

Airline
Cargo Services
Catering Services
Aircraft Maintenance & Repair
Travel Agency
Ground Support

BRANDS/DIVISIONS/AFFILIATES:

Thai Ministry of Finance

CONTACTS: Note: Officers with more than one job title may be intentionally listed here more than once.

Charamporn Jotikasthira, Pres.
Narongchai Wongthanavimok, CFO
Montree Jumrieng, Exec. VP-Tech. Dept.
Teerapol Chotichanapibal, Exec. VP-Strategy & Bus. Dev.
Asdavut Watanangura, Exec. VP-Oper. Support
Wasukarn Visansawatdi, Exec. VP-Finance & Acct. Dept.
Danuj Bunnag, Exec. VP-Prod. & Customer Services
Chokchai Panyayong, Sr. Exec. VP-Commercial
Pandit Chanapai, Managing Dir.-Ground Services Bus. Unit
Kanit Sangsubhan, Chmn.

GROWTH PLANS/SPECIAL FEATURES:

Thai Airways International PCL is an international airline based in Thailand. The airline is a member of the Star Alliance. The firm's operations include ground services, ground support and equipment services, technical and maintenance services, cargo and mail services and catering services. The ground services segment provides station management and administration and passenger services such as check-in, transfer and lounge services. The ground support segment provides passenger and cargo technical services, ramp and ground support equipment and flight operation support. The technical and maintenance department handles aircraft repair. The cargo and mail services segment provides air cargo and mail services across multiple domestic and international destinations. The catering services segment offers two lines of business: preparation and delivery of food for aircraft uplift and food preparation for ground distribution. Thai Airway flies to 78 destinations in 35 countries. Its fleet consists of 79 aircraft including Airbus A320s, A330s, A350s, A380s and Boeing 737s, 747s, 777s and 787s. Thai Airways is 51%-owned by the Thai Ministry of Finance.

FINANCIAL DATA: Note: Data for latest year may not have been available at press time.

In U.S. $	2015	2014	2013	2012	2011	2010
Revenue	5,270,475,000	5,433,159,000	5,951,435,000	6,158,920,000	5,509,005,000	5,314,981,000
R&D Expense						
Operating Income	-407,161,900	-482,763,000	-372,926,200	362,749,400	-96,920,470	646,983,100
Operating Margin %	-7.72%	-8.88%	-6.26%	5.88%	-1.75%	12.17%
SGA Expense	1,274,100,000	1,173,558,000	1,246,992,000	1,122,583,000	1,085,296,000	1,311,540,000
Net Income	-376,317,500	-450,291,900	-347,487,000	179,664,600	-294,115,200	442,737,100
Operating Cash Flow	535,524,600	173,596,700	742,254,700	898,837,600	264,398,600	815,334,000
Capital Expenditure	112,932,600	247,057,900	841,179,100	536,393,200	364,235,400	279,313,200
EBITDA	314,802,900	109,522,200	204,681,700	955,043,500	511,323,300	1,238,111,000
Return on Assets %	-4.27%	-5.08%	-3.94%	2.15%	-3.58%	5.42%
Return on Equity %	-35.22%	-31.84%	-19.16%	9.43%	-13.98%	22.64%
Debt to Equity	4.72	3.56	2.66	1.48	1.95	1.49

CONTACT INFORMATION:

Phone: 0-2545-1000   Fax: 0-2513-0203
Toll-Free:
Address: 89 Vibhavadi Rangsit Rd., Bangkok, 10900 Thailand

STOCK TICKER/OTHER:

Stock Ticker: TAWNF   Exchange: PINX
Employees: 25,323   Fiscal Year Ends: 12/31
Parent Company:

SALARIES/BONUSES:

Top Exec. Salary: $ Bonus: $
Second Exec. Salary: $ Bonus: $

OTHER THOUGHTS:

Estimated Female Officers or Directors: 1
Hot Spot for Advancement for Women/Minorities:

Sales, profits and employees may be estimates. Financial information, benefits and other data can change quickly and may vary from those stated here.

Thomas Cook Group plc

www.thomascookgroup.com

NAIC Code: 561520

TYPES OF BUSINESS:

Vacations Packages
Hotels
Resorts
Airlines
Tours

BRANDS/DIVISIONS/AFFILIATES:

Ving
Club 18.30
Sunprime Hotels
Neckerman
clubjumbo.fr
Tjareborg
Direct Holidays
Pegase

CONTACTS: Note: Officers with more than one job title may be intentionally listed here more than once.

Peter Frankhauser, CEO
Michael Healy, CFO
Frank Meysman, Chmn.

GROWTH PLANS/SPECIAL FEATURES:

Thomas Cook Group plc is an international leisure travel group that owns a fleet of 97 aircraft, a network of owned or franchised travel stores and a number of hotels and resort properties. It splits its business into three geographic divisions: the U.K. and Ireland, Continental Europe and Northern Europe. The U.K. and Ireland division transports over 6 million passengers annually, maintains 830 retail outlets and has a fleet of 32 aircraft. Continental Europe transports over 7 million passengers annually, maintains 2,274 retail outlets and has a fleet of six aircraft. Northern Europe transports 1.7 million passengers annually, maintains six retail outlets and has a fleet of 11 aircraft. Thomas Cook Group utilizes the brand names Thomas Cook, Airtours, Hotels4u, Club18.30, flexibletrips, Cresta, Escapades, The co-operative travel Neckermann, Sentido, Smartline, Oger Tours, Sunwing Family Resorts, Sunprime Hotels, Suncooncet Resorts, Bucher Last Minute, Air Marin, TourVital, DeLuxe Hotel, Jet tours, Club Eldorado, clubjumbo.fr, Pegase, Intourist, happy events, Voel je, Ving, Spies, Tjareborg and Direct Holidays. The firm sells its travel packages on the Internet, by phone, through television and in a network of shops. The company's specialty vacations include basic retail travel, package holidays, winter getaways, foreign exchange programs and cruises. In 2015, the firm (49%) established a joint venture with Fosun International Limited (51%) to develop domestic, inbound and outbound tourism activities for the Chinese market under the Thomas Cook brands.

FINANCIAL DATA: Note: Data for latest year may not have been available at press time.

In U.S. $	2015	2014	2013	2012	2011	2010
Revenue	10,228,090,000	11,212,510,000	12,161,030,000	12,391,730,000	12,806,520,000	11,606,930,000
R&D Expense						
Operating Income	275,482,100	70,502,530	16,972,830	-416,878,800	-348,073,600	218,035,600
Operating Margin %	2.69%	.62%	.13%	-3.36%	-2.71%	1.87%
SGA Expense	462,183,200	315,955,700	346,115,200	471,975,200	371,835,600	354,471,000
Net Income	30,028,850	-154,061,100	-259,814,900	-764,952,400	-679,827,100	-3,394,566
Operating Cash Flow	618,855,500	437,376,800	445,341,000	198,321,000	241,144,800	298,069,000
Capital Expenditure	261,120,500	203,674,000	196,232,000	180,564,800	243,494,800	357,604,500
EBITDA	472,628,000	343,373,400	321,961,500	-202,107,200	-121,290,500	416,487,100
Return on Assets %	.39%	-1.95%	-3.26%	-9.30%	-7.66%	-.03%
Return on Equity %	7.83%	-31.20%	-43.45%	-75.43%	-36.34%	-.15%
Debt to Equity	3.48	3.48	2.54	2.89	0.89	0.59

CONTACT INFORMATION:

Phone: 44 2075576400   Fax: 44 2075576401
Toll-Free:
Address: 200 Aldersgate, 3/F, South Bldg, London, EC1A 4HD United Kingdom

STOCK TICKER/OTHER:

Stock Ticker: TCKGF   Exchange: GREY
Employees: 21,813   Fiscal Year Ends: 09/30
Parent Company:

SALARIES/BONUSES:

Top Exec. Salary: $ Bonus: $
Second Exec. Salary: $ Bonus: $

OTHER THOUGHTS:

Estimated Female Officers or Directors: 5
Hot Spot for Advancement for Women/Minorities: Y

Sales, profits and employees may be estimates. Financial information, benefits and other data can change quickly and may vary from those stated here.

Thousand Trails LP

www.1000trails.com

NAIC Code: 721211

TYPES OF BUSINESS:

RV Parks & Campsites
Campground Management
Park Concession Services
Construction & Engineering Services

BRANDS/DIVISIONS/AFFILIATES:

Equity LifeStyle Properties Inc

CONTACTS: *Note: Officers with more than one job title may be intentionally listed here more than once.*

Samuel Zell, Chmn.

GROWTH PLANS/SPECIAL FEATURES:

Thousand Trails LP, a subsidiary of Equity LifeStyle Properties, Inc., is one of the nation's largest owners and operators of private campgrounds. Members have access to campsites in more than 80 membership-based preserves across 22 U.S. states and British Columbia, Canada. The preserves are gated and guarded 24-hours-a-day by park rangers. Members may bring their own tent or travel trailer, or reserve one of Thousand Trails' cabins, cottages, yurts or other accommodations, such as covered wagons. The cabins usually feature two or more beds that sleep 4-6 people as well as a dinette, kitchen, TV and full bathroom. Larger and deluxe cabins sometimes feature a deck and microwave. Cottages, typically larger than cabins, feature two bedrooms plus a sofa bed, sleeping six or more adults; a kitchen with a dishwasher, microwave, gas oven, pots, pans, utensils and dishes; full baths; and satellite TV. Cottages are often grouped into a small community separate from the rest of the preserve. Thousand Trails' yurts are large, permanent dome-shaped tents that typically feature two queen-size futons that sleep 4-6 people; a full bathroom; a kitchen with a dining table, stove, toaster, utensils, pots and pans; and a TV. Campsite amenities generally include hiking trails, miniature golf, lodges, pools, spas, lakes, boating and fishing; campgrounds also usually include barbeque pits, electricity, water, sewer connections for RVs and restroom and shower facilities. The company's web site allows members to make reservations online and offers details on all its preserves, including local attractions and a map listing amenities offered at each preserve.

FINANCIAL DATA: *Note: Data for latest year may not have been available at press time.*

In U.S. $	2015	2014	2013	2012	2011	2010
Revenue						
R&D Expense						
Operating Income						
Operating Margin %						
SGA Expense						
Net Income						
Operating Cash Flow						
Capital Expenditure						
EBITDA						
Return on Assets %						
Return on Equity %						
Debt to Equity						

CONTACT INFORMATION:

Phone: 228-497-8722   Fax: 228-497-8722
Toll-Free: 800-205-0606
Address: 3801 Parkwood Blvd, Ste 100, Frisco, TX 75034 United States

STOCK TICKER/OTHER:

Stock Ticker: Subsidiary   Exchange:
Employees: Fiscal Year Ends: 06/30
Parent Company: Equity LifeStyle Properties Inc

SALARIES/BONUSES:

Top Exec. Salary: $ Bonus: $
Second Exec. Salary: $ Bonus: $

OTHER THOUGHTS:

Estimated Female Officers or Directors:
Hot Spot for Advancement for Women/Minorities:

Sales, profits and employees may be estimates. Financial information, benefits and other data can change quickly and may vary from those stated here.

Tix Corporation
NAIC Code: 561599

www.tixcorp.com

TYPES OF BUSINESS:
Theatrical Ticket Offices

BRANDS/DIVISIONS/AFFILIATES:
Tix4Tonight LLC

CONTACTS: *Note: Officers with more than one job title may be intentionally listed here more than once.*
Joseph Marsh, CEO, Subsidiary
Mitchell Francis, CEO
Steve Handy, CFO
Richard Bradley, CFO
Kimberly Simon, COO
Lee Marshall, Other Executive Officer
John Ballard, President, Divisional
Steve Boulay, Vice President, Divisional

GROWTH PLANS/SPECIAL FEATURES:

Tix Corporation is an entertainment company providing ticketing services, event merchandising and the production and promotion of live entertainment. The company operates through its wholly-owned subsidiary, Tix4Tonight LLC, a premier ticket broker in Las Vegas, having sold more than 13 million discount tickets. Tix4Tonight has 11 discount ticket booths, offering discounts for non-sold-out shows as well as discount dinner reservations to 50 restaurants and buffets on a daily basis. The company has offered its same-day, last-minute discounts to Las Vegas shows since 2002. Same-day shows, concerts, sporting events, attractions and dinner reservations offer up to 50% savings. In May 2016, the company announced that Tix4Tonight would be partnering with Expedia LX Partner Business, Inc., which does business as Expedia Local Expert under Expedia, Inc. Tix4Tonight will serve as the Las Vegas Guest Services Partner for Expedia's brands, catering to Las Vegas visitors who book their travel through Expedia. The service will provide both pre-arrival concierge services, in-market concierge-type desk services and related customer service support at physical locations in Las Vegas. Tix4Tonight will operate all new co-branded locations and convert three of its existing locations to Expedia Local Expert. Tix4Tonight's remaining eight locations will continue to be operated separately.

FINANCIAL DATA: *Note: Data for latest year may not have been available at press time.*

In U.S. $	2015	2014	2013	2012	2011	2010
Revenue	23,421,000	22,696,000	22,154,000	24,325,000	34,542,000	30,882,000
R&D Expense						
Operating Income	5,531,000	4,457,000	1,687,000	2,022,000	347,000	2,120,000
Operating Margin %	23.61%	19.63%	7.61%	8.31%	1.00%	6.86%
SGA Expense	7,899,000	7,943,000	9,790,000	10,773,000	14,078,000	12,749,000
Net Income	16,792,000	4,148,000	1,574,000	1,375,000	29,000	-3,020,000
Operating Cash Flow	6,563,000	6,119,000	2,243,000	4,669,000	7,211,000	2,826,000
Capital Expenditure	121,000	544,000	641,000	281,000	166,000	698,000
EBITDA	6,136,000	5,316,000	2,775,000	3,198,000	2,234,000	3,850,000
Return on Assets %	102.60%	47.65%	13.73%	8.82%	.16%	-12.47%
Return on Equity %	127.47%	107.79%	27.58%	15.87%	.31%	-18.73%
Debt to Equity	0.01	0.09	0.45	0.08	0.11	

CONTACT INFORMATION:
Phone: 818 761-1002   Fax: 818 761-1072
Toll-Free:
Address: 12001 Ventura Place, Ste. 340, Studio City, CA 91604 United States

STOCK TICKER/OTHER:
Stock Ticker: TIXC
Employees: 134
Parent Company:

Exchange: PINX
Fiscal Year Ends: 12/31

SALARIES/BONUSES:
Top Exec. Salary: $425,000   Bonus: $50,000
Second Exec. Salary: $321,000   Bonus: $25,000

OTHER THOUGHTS:
Estimated Female Officers or Directors: 1
Hot Spot for Advancement for Women/Minorities:

Sales, profits and employees may be estimates. Financial information, benefits and other data can change quickly and may vary from those stated here.

TMI Hospitality Inc

www.tmihospitality.com

NAIC Code: 721110

TYPES OF BUSINESS:

Hotels
Construction Services
Communications Services
Property Management

BRANDS/DIVISIONS/AFFILIATES:

Starwood Capital Group
TMI Communications Inc
Room In The Inn Program
Marriott
Hilton Worldwide
IHG InterContinental Hotels Group
Choice Hotels
Hyatt

CONTACTS: Note: Officers with more than one job title may be intentionally listed here more than once.

Lauris Molbert, CEO
Doug Dobmeier, Exec. VP-Oper.
Lisa Helbling, CFO
Ann Christenson, Chief People Officer
Tracy Koenig, CIO
Robert McConn, Jr., General Counsel
Douglas Dobmeier, Sr. VP-Oper.
Charles A. Krumwiede, Sr. VP-Property Support & Quality
Robert McConn, Jr., General Counsel

GROWTH PLANS/SPECIAL FEATURES:

TMI Hospitality, Inc. builds and operates select-service and extended-stay hotels across the U.S. It is a leading hotel property-management company, operating 186 hotels in 25 states. TMI Hospitality operates properties under brand names such as Marriott's Courtyard, Residence Inn, Fairfield Inn & Suites, Springhill Suites and TownePlace Suitest; Hilton Worldwide's Homewood Suites, Home2 Suites and Hampton Inn; IHG InterContinental Hotels Group's Staybridge Suites, Holiday Inn Express & Suites and Holiday Inn Express; Choice Hotels International's Comfort Suites, Comfort Inn and Cambria Suites; Hyatt's Hyatt Place; Carlson's Country Inn & Suites; and Best Western's Best Western Plus. The company's properties offer many amenities, including cable television, indoor and outdoor pools, complimentary breakfast, free local phone calls and 24-hour coffee service. In addition, children under 18 stay free. The firm also provides its Room In The Inn Program, offering free rooms to guests visiting friends or family members in a hospital, nursing home or treatment facility during the Christmas and Thanksgiving seasons. Through subsidiary TMI Communications, Inc., the company provides nationwide telecommunications services to the hospitality industry. In 2015, the firm was acquired by Starwood Capital Group, a leading global private investment firm.

TMI Hospitality offers its employees medical, dental and vision coverage; an employee stock ownership program; lodging discounts; a flexible spending account; training; and an education assistance program.

FINANCIAL DATA: Note: Data for latest year may not have been available at press time.

In U.S. $	2015	2014	2013	2012	2011	2010
Revenue						
R&D Expense						
Operating Income						
Operating Margin %						
SGA Expense						
Net Income						
Operating Cash Flow						
Capital Expenditure						
EBITDA						
Return on Assets %						
Return on Equity %						
Debt to Equity						

CONTACT INFORMATION:

Phone: 701-235-1060   Fax: 701-235-0948
Toll-Free:
Address: 4850 32nd Avenue South, Fargo, ND 58104 United States

STOCK TICKER/OTHER:

Stock Ticker: Private
Employees: 4,000
Parent Company: Starwood Capital Group

Exchange:
Fiscal Year Ends: 12/31

SALARIES/BONUSES:

Top Exec. Salary: $ Bonus: $
Second Exec. Salary: $ Bonus: $

OTHER THOUGHTS:

Estimated Female Officers or Directors: 2
Hot Spot for Advancement for Women/Minorities:

Sales, profits and employees may be estimates. Financial information, benefits and other data can change quickly and may vary from those stated here.

Tobu Railway Co Ltd

NAIC Code: 482111

TYPES OF BUSINESS:

Line-Haul Railroads
Railway Management & Services
Real Estate
Buses
Hotels
Retail
Construction

BRANDS/DIVISIONS/AFFILIATES:

Tobu Group
Tobu World Square
Tobu Hotel Levant Tokyo
Tobu Zoological Park
Tokyo Skytree

CONTACTS: Note: Officers with more than one job title may be intentionally listed here more than once.

Yoshizumi Nezu, Pres.
Kenichi Tsunoda, Sr. Managing Dir.
Takao Suzuki, Sr. Managing Dir.
Naoyuki Hosaka, Sr. Managing Dir.
Zengo Takeda, Sr. Managing Dir.

GROWTH PLANS/SPECIAL FEATURES:

Tobu Railway Co., Ltd. owns and operates the second-largest private rail network in Japan, with a service area that spans portions of the Tokyo metropolitan region, extending from eastern Tokyo to Chiba, Saitama, Tochigi and Gunma. The company owns and operates 287 miles of rail lines, serving students, commuters and international travelers. In total, the firm operates 203 stations with a daily average of over 2.3 million passengers. The firm is part of the Tobu Group of companies, which, excepting Tobu Railway, includes 92 subsidiaries and 14 affiliates divided into transportation, leisure, real estate, retail distribution and other segments. Other businesses primarily consist of the company's construction subsidiaries. Tobu Group's leisure business operates health clubs, golf courses, theme parks and hotels, primarily along the Tobu Railway network. Its properties include Tobu Hotel Levant Tokyo, operated in partnership with Marriott; Tobu Zoological Park; and Tobu World Square, a tourist destination that has miniature renderings of historical sites all over the world. The real estate segment develops and manages condominiums, housing developments and department stores along its railways and in Tokyo. The retail segment operates four department stores, a chain of supermarkets and various other retail enterprises. Tokyo Skytree, a tower situated in Eastern Tokyo that stands twice as high as the Eifel Tower, is a recent development which includes about 300 shops and restaurants as well as an aquarium and a planetarium.

FINANCIAL DATA: Note: Data for latest year may not have been available at press time.

In U.S. $	2015	2014	2013	2012	2011	2010
Revenue	4,860,575,000	4,913,845,122	5,541,300,000	6,604,110,000	7,159,300,000	7,064,350,000
R&D Expense						
Operating Income						
Operating Margin %						
SGA Expense						
Net Income	255,450,000	274,377,853	275,000,000	194,694,000	168,100,000	170,530,000
Operating Cash Flow						
Capital Expenditure						
EBITDA						
Return on Assets %						
Return on Equity %						
Debt to Equity						

CONTACT INFORMATION:

Phone: 81-3-5962-2067   Fax:
Toll-Free:
Address: 2-18-12 Oshiage, Sumida-ku, Tokyo, 131-8522 Japan

STOCK TICKER/OTHER:

Stock Ticker: 9001   Exchange: Tokyo
Employees: 19,559   Fiscal Year Ends: 03/31
Parent Company:

SALARIES/BONUSES:

Top Exec. Salary: $ Bonus: $
Second Exec. Salary: $ Bonus: $

OTHER THOUGHTS:

Estimated Female Officers or Directors:
Hot Spot for Advancement for Women/Minorities:

Sales, profits and employees may be estimates. Financial information, benefits and other data can change quickly and may vary from those stated here.

Trailways Transportation System Inc   www.trailways.com

NAIC Code: 485210

TYPES OF BUSINESS:

Bus Transportation
Sightseeing Packages
Tour Services
Intermodal Shipping Services

BRANDS/DIVISIONS/AFFILIATES:

CONTACTS: Note: Officers with more than one job title may be intentionally listed here more than once.

Sheila Ryba, CEO
Gale Ellsworth, Pres.
Thomas Bazow, Corp. Sec.
Curtis A. Riggs, Treas.

GROWTH PLANS/SPECIAL FEATURES:

Trailways Transportation System, Inc. is a franchise organization that comprises 70 independently owned and operated transportation, tour and travel companies. The company provides services such as charter and tour busing; scheduled route transportation; sightseeing and travel planning; shuttle service; and transit and supplementary intermodal delivery via ground, air, rail and sea. The Trailways network extends across more than 1,000 destinations across North America, the Netherlands and Germany. Trailways' transportation system also includes a network of industry suppliers, professional organizations and other trade-related entities. In addition, most of the firm's scheduled route companies provide long-haul service for passengers through agreements with Greyhound Lines. Trailways offers its franchisees a well-known brand identity; uniform operating standards; nationwide business networking; industry-wide coalitions and legislative support; driver and vehicle pools; employee search and referrals; rebates and discounts on industry vehicles, equipment, replacement parts and service; and discounts on fuel.

FINANCIAL DATA: Note: Data for latest year may not have been available at press time.

In U.S. $	2015	2014	2013	2012	2011	2010
Revenue						
R&D Expense						
Operating Income						
Operating Margin %						
SGA Expense						
Net Income						
Operating Cash Flow						
Capital Expenditure						
EBITDA						
Return on Assets %						
Return on Equity %						
Debt to Equity						

CONTACT INFORMATION:

Phone: 703-691-3052   Fax: 703-691-9047
Toll-Free: 800-992-4618
Address: 3554 Chain Bridge Rd., Ste. 202, Fairfax, VA 22030 United States

STOCK TICKER/OTHER:

Stock Ticker: Private   Exchange:
Employees: Fiscal Year Ends:
Parent Company:

SALARIES/BONUSES:

Top Exec. Salary: $ Bonus: $
Second Exec. Salary: $ Bonus: $

OTHER THOUGHTS:

Estimated Female Officers or Directors: 2
Hot Spot for Advancement for Women/Minorities: Y

Trans States Airlines Inc

NAIC Code: 481111

TYPES OF BUSINESS:

Regional Airlines

BRANDS/DIVISIONS/AFFILIATES:

Trans States Holdings Inc
Trans States Airlines Aviators Program

CONTACTS: *Note: Officers with more than one job title may be intentionally listed here more than once.*

Richard A. Leach, CEO
Fred Oxley, COO
Richard A. Leach, Pres.
Jeff Holmstedt, Dir.-Maintenance
David Hayes, General Counsel
Keith Stamper, Dir.-Flight Oper.
Aaron Armstrong, Dir.-Quality Assurance
Al Blosse, VP-Maintenance
Matt Conrad, Dir.-Safety
Shonn Clark, Dir.-Inflight Svcs.

GROWTH PLANS/SPECIAL FEATURES:

Trans States Airlines, Inc., a subsidiary of Trans States Holdings, Inc., is one of the largest U.S.-based independent regional airlines, operating primarily in midwestern and northeastern states. The company is affiliated with the Express services of United Airlines and American Eagle of American Airlines. It operates an all-jet fleet of Embraer E145 regional aircraft, offering more than 237 flights per day to more than 70 cities. Annually, the firm carries nearly 3 million passengers aboard its flights. Trans State maintains hubs at LaGuardia Airport and Pittsburgh International Airport under the American Eagle brand and Cleveland Hopkins International Airport, O'Hare International Airport, Washington Dulles International Airport and Denver International Airport under the United Express brand. The company maintains its corporate headquarters, as well as training and maintenance facilities, in Bridgeton, Missouri. In June 2016, the firm launched a new pipeline program for aspiring commercial pilots. The Trans States Airlines Aviators Program is a long-term internship for student pilots enrolled in a professional pilot training program. The program identifies promising pilots early on in their flight training and begins preparing them for the Trans States Airlines flight deck while they are still in school. Any student with a private pilot's license and currently enrolled in a pilot training program is eligible to apply.

Trans States offers its employees medical, dental and prescription drug benefits; life and long-term disability insurance; a 401(k) program; and discounts on hotels, cruises and car rentals.

FINANCIAL DATA: *Note: Data for latest year may not have been available at press time.*

In U.S. $	2015	2014	2013	2012	2011	2010
Revenue						
R&D Expense						
Operating Income						
Operating Margin %						
SGA Expense						
Net Income						
Operating Cash Flow						
Capital Expenditure						
EBITDA						
Return on Assets %						
Return on Equity %						
Debt to Equity						

CONTACT INFORMATION:

Phone: 314-222-4300   Fax: 314-222-4314
Toll-Free:
Address: 11495 Navaid Rd., Ste. 340, Bridgeton, MO 63044 United States

STOCK TICKER/OTHER:

Stock Ticker: Subsidiary
Employees:
Parent Company: Trans States Holdings Inc

Exchange:
Fiscal Year Ends: 09/30

SALARIES/BONUSES:

Top Exec. Salary: $ Bonus: $
Second Exec. Salary: $ Bonus: $

OTHER THOUGHTS:

Estimated Female Officers or Directors: 1
Hot Spot for Advancement for Women/Minorities:

Sales, profits and employees may be estimates. Financial information, benefits and other data can change quickly and may vary from those stated here.

Transat AT Inc

NAIC Code: 481211

www.transat.com

TYPES OF BUSINESS:

Chartered Air Transportation and Tours
Air Transportation

BRANDS/DIVISIONS/AFFILIATES:

Air Transat
Transat Discoveries
Transat Holidays
Turissimo Caribe Excursiones
Transat Holidays USA Inc
Jonview Canada
Tourgreece
Ocean Hotels

CONTACTS: *Note: Officers with more than one job title may be intentionally listed here more than once.*

Jean-Marc Eustache, CEO
Denis Petrin, CFO
Michel Bellefeuille, Chief Information Officer
Bernard Bussieres, General Counsel
Annick Guerard, General Manager, Subsidiary
Joseph Adamo, General Manager, Subsidiary
Jean-François Lemay, General Manager, Subsidiary
Patrice Caradec, General Manager, Subsidiary
Michel Lemay, Other Executive Officer
Andre de Montigny, President, Subsidiary
Daniel Godbout, Senior VP, Divisional
Christophe Hennebelle, Vice President, Divisional

GROWTH PLANS/SPECIAL FEATURES:

Transat A.T., Inc. is an integrated tour operator based in Canada that focuses on holiday travel. The company's business includes developing and marketing vacation travel services in the Americas and Europe, focusing on package and air-travel format. Currently, Transat offers trips to more than 60 destination countries and distributes products in roughly 25 countries. It divides its operations into five segments: air transportation, outgoing tour operators, incoming tour operators & destination services, retail distribution and hotels. The air transportation segment consists of Air Transat, one of the largest international charter airlines focusing on holiday travel in Canada. It carries approximately 3 million passengers annually aboard its fleet of Boeing narrow-body and Airbus wide-body jets. In the outgoing tour operators segment, Transat has six main tour operators in Canada (Transat Holidays, Nolitours by Transat, Air Transat, TMR Holidays, Canadian Affair and Transat Discoveries). It also has outgoing travel operators in France and Europe through Vacances Transat and Look Voyages, respectively. The company's incoming tour operators & destination services include subsidiaries in Florida, Canada, Mexico, the Dominican Republic and Greece, such as Transat Holidays USA, Inc.; Jonview Canada; Tourgreece; Trafic Tours; and Turissimo Caribe Excursiones. Its retail distribution segment, through Transat Distribution Canada, operates a distribution network consisting of several travel agency brands, such as Club Voyages, Marlin Travel, TravelPlus, tripcentral.ca, exitnow.ca, Look Voyages and Voyages en Liberte. The hotels segment includes the firm's 35% ownership in Caribbean Investments BV, operating as Ocean Hotels, a joint venture with H10 Hotels that operates six properties in Mexico, the Dominican Republic and Cuba.

FINANCIAL DATA: *Note: Data for latest year may not have been available at press time.*

In U.S. $	2015	2014	2013	2012	2011	2010
Revenue		2,842,574,080	2,763,756,032	2,813,802,240	2,771,336,192	2,650,664,192
R&D Expense						
Operating Income						
Operating Margin %						
SGA Expense						
Net Income		17,329,546	43,905,304	-12,628,030	-9,252,273	49,702,272
Operating Cash Flow						
Capital Expenditure						
EBITDA						
Return on Assets %						
Return on Equity %						
Debt to Equity						

CONTACT INFORMATION:

Phone: 514 987-1616   Fax: 514 987-9546
Toll-Free:
Address: Place du Parc, 300 Leo-Pariseau St., Ste. 600, Montreal, QC H2X 4C2 Canada

STOCK TICKER/OTHER:

Stock Ticker: TRZ.A
Employees: 5,091
Parent Company:

Exchange: TSE
Fiscal Year Ends: 10/31

SALARIES/BONUSES:

Top Exec. Salary: $ Bonus: $
Second Exec. Salary: $ Bonus: $

OTHER THOUGHTS:

Estimated Female Officers or Directors: 2
Hot Spot for Advancement for Women/Minorities: Y

Travel Leaders Group LLC

www.travelleaders.com

NAIC Code: 561510

TYPES OF BUSINESS:

Travel Agencies
Franchising
Business Travel

BRANDS/DIVISIONS/AFFILIATES:

Travel Leaders
www.TravelLeadersHosts.com
Independent Contractor Center of Excellence

CONTACTS: *Note: Officers with more than one job title may be intentionally listed here more than once.*

Ninan Chacko, CEO
Dave Zitur, COO
Roger E. Block, Pres., Franchise Group
William Lynch, CFO
Robert Brill, General Counsel
J. D. O'Hara, Sr. VP-Corp. Dev.
Michael Batt, Chmn.

GROWTH PLANS/SPECIAL FEATURES:

Travel Leaders Franchise Group LLC is the largest travel agency franchisor in North America and is comprised of the Travel Leaders brand. Over 1,000 system-wide full-service and client-dedicated franchised locations produce annual sales of approximately $5 billion. With nearly 4,000 travel agents across the U.S., the travel agency's resources offer great discounts, value-added amenities and enhanced vacation experiences. Travel Leader's agents are located across 41 states and 291 cities. Travel Leaders Franchise Group has been named the top travel business franchisor by Entrepreneur Magazine for the past 19 consecutive years. The firm recently launched an independent contractor (IC) recruitment campaign and website, www.TravelLeadersHosts.com, as part of its Independent Contractor Center of Excellence program. The recruitment campaign aims to make it easier for ICs to be matched with a Travel Leaders franchise agency as one's host, so it can leverage the national Travel Leaders brand to maximize customer service to local clients.

FINANCIAL DATA: *Note: Data for latest year may not have been available at press time.*

In U.S. $	2015	2014	2013	2012	2011	2010
Revenue	290,000,000	282,500,000	271,000,000	260,000,000	250,000,000	
R&D Expense						
Operating Income						
Operating Margin %						
SGA Expense						
Net Income						
Operating Cash Flow						
Capital Expenditure						
EBITDA						
Return on Assets %						
Return on Equity %						
Debt to Equity						

CONTACT INFORMATION:

Phone: 800-335-8747   Fax:
Toll-Free: 800-335-8747
Address: 3033 Campus Drive, Suite W320, Plymouth, MN 55441 United States

STOCK TICKER/OTHER:

Stock Ticker: Private
Employees: 1,000
Parent Company:

Exchange:
Fiscal Year Ends:

SALARIES/BONUSES:

Top Exec. Salary: $ Bonus: $
Second Exec. Salary: $ Bonus: $

OTHER THOUGHTS:

Estimated Female Officers or Directors:
Hot Spot for Advancement for Women/Minorities:

TravelCenters of America LLC

www.tatravelcenters.com

NAIC Code: 447190

TYPES OF BUSINESS:

Travel Centers, Retail
Restaurants
Gas Stations
Convenience Stores
Motels
Truck Maintenance
Wireless Internet Access

BRANDS/DIVISIONS/AFFILIATES:

TravelCenters of America
Petro
Minit Mart
Country Pride
Iron Skillet
RoadKing
Reserve-It!

CONTACTS: Note: Officers with more than one job title may be intentionally listed here more than once.

Thomas OBrien, CEO
Andrew Rebholz, CFO
William Myers, Chief Accounting Officer
Barry Richards, Executive VP
Michael Lombardi, Executive VP
Mark Young, Executive VP
Barry Portnoy, Managing Director
Jennifer Clark, Secretary

GROWTH PLANS/SPECIAL FEATURES:

TravelCenters of America LLC (TA) is a full-service national travel center chain in the U.S. Originally a subsidiary of Hospitality Properties Trust (HPT), TA became a publicly-owned company after a spin-off from HPT, though the majority of its properties are still leased from HPT. The company has 252 locations under the TravelCenters of America or TA (176) and Petro (76) brands in 43 states and Canada, which serve virtually all major trucking fleets and a variety of other highway travelers. In addition, TA's business also includes 204 convenience stores not located on a travel center property in 11 U.S. states (primarily Midwestern). These gasoline/convenience locations operate under the Minit Mart brand name. The company offers a variety of services to travelers, including diesel and gasoline sales, truck repair and maintenance, full-service dining and fast-food courts, travel and convenience stores, showers, business services, laundry facilities, weigh scales and video arcades. TA operates full-service restaurants under such brand names as Country Pride and Iron Skillet. Many locations offer customers a variety of fast-food choices such as Burger King, Dunkin' Donuts and Popeye's Chicken & Biscuits. TA publishes a magazine called RoadKing, which includes articles and advertising of interest to professional truck drivers; and its Reserve-It! parking program allows drivers to reserve for a fee a parking space in advance of arriving at a travel center.

TA offers its employees medical, dental, vision, disability, AD&D, business travel and life insurance; vacation and bereavement leave; mortgage counseling; various incentive programs; flexible spending accounts; credit union membership; jury duty, educati

FINANCIAL DATA: Note: Data for latest year may not have been available at press time.

In U.S. $	2015	2014	2013	2012	2011	2010
Revenue	5,850,633,000	7,778,633,000	7,944,731,000	7,995,724,000	7,888,857,000	5,962,481,000
R&D Expense						
Operating Income	78,297,000	113,640,000	21,190,000	41,470,000	32,400,000	-41,537,000
Operating Margin %	1.33%	1.46%	.26%	.51%	.41%	- .69%
SGA Expense	1,239,004,000	1,139,589,000	1,072,709,000	992,996,000	958,952,000	940,769,000
Net Income	27,719,000	60,969,000	31,623,000	32,198,000	23,574,000	-65,571,000
Operating Cash Flow	136,888,000	161,125,000	71,513,000	83,072,000	30,141,000	28,305,000
Capital Expenditure	295,437,000	169,825,000	164,242,000	188,694,000	124,851,000	59,485,000
EBITDA	150,680,000	179,224,000	78,242,000	95,581,000	81,424,000	3,966,000
Return on Assets %	1.72%	4.32%	2.77%	3.16%	2.46%	-7.36%
Return on Equity %	4.93%	11.92%	7.83%	9.58%	8.27%	-23.16%
Debt to Equity	1.30	1.08	1.00	0.99	1.14	0.39

CONTACT INFORMATION:

Phone: 440 808-9100   Fax: 440 808-3306
Toll-Free: 888-982-5528
Address: 24601 Center Ridge Rd., Ste. 200, Westlake, OH 44145-5639
United States

STOCK TICKER/OTHER:

Stock Ticker: TA
Employees: 21,730
Parent Company:

Exchange: NAS
Fiscal Year Ends: 12/31

SALARIES/BONUSES:

Top Exec. Salary: $300,000   Bonus: $2,564,500
Second Exec. Salary: Bonus: $957,250
$300,000

OTHER THOUGHTS:

Estimated Female Officers or Directors: 1
Hot Spot for Advancement for Women/Minorities:

Sales, profits and employees may be estimates. Financial information, benefits and other data can change quickly and may vary from those stated here.

Travelocity.com LP

NAIC Code: 519130

TYPES OF BUSINESS:

Online Travel Services
Online Reservations
Retail Travel Service Kiosks
Corporate Travel Agency

BRANDS/DIVISIONS/AFFILIATES:

Expedia Inc

GROWTH PLANS/SPECIAL FEATURES:

Travelocity.com LP, a wholly-owned subsidiary of Expedia, Inc., is a leading provider of online travel services for business and leisure travelers. Travelocity provides access to vacation packages, domestic and international flights, hotel accommodations, rental car companies and cruises as well as last minute packages at discounted prices. Additionally, Travelocity has a customer care unit staffed by representatives who are able to answer questions, change travel arrangements and handle travel-related emergencies 24-hours-a-day. In 2015, the firm was acquired by Expedia for $280 million.

CONTACTS: Note: Officers with more than one job title may be intentionally listed here more than once.

Jonathan Perkel, Sr. VP
Carl Sparks, Pres.
Bradley E. Wilson, CMO
Scott Miskimens, CTO
Jonathan Perkel, General Counsel
Stephen Dumaine, Sr. VP-Global Strategy & Prod. Innovation
Yannis Karnis, Pres., Travelocity Business
Noreen Henry, Sr. VP-Global Partner Svcs.
Roshan Mendis, Pres., Travelocity North America & Zuji
Scott Quigley, VP-Sales & Customer Care

FINANCIAL DATA: Note: Data for latest year may not have been available at press time.

In U.S. $	2015	2014	2013	2012	2011	2010
Revenue						
R&D Expense						
Operating Income						
Operating Margin %						
SGA Expense						
Net Income						
Operating Cash Flow						
Capital Expenditure						
EBITDA						
Return on Assets %						
Return on Equity %						
Debt to Equity						

CONTACT INFORMATION:

Phone: 682-605-1000   Fax: 972-582-2346
Toll-Free: 888-872-8356
Address: 5400 LBJ Fwy., Ste. 500, Dallas, TX 75240 United States

STOCK TICKER/OTHER:

Stock Ticker: Subsidiary   Exchange:
Employees: 1,554   Fiscal Year Ends: 12/31
Parent Company: Expedia Inc

SALARIES/BONUSES:

Top Exec. Salary: $ Bonus: $
Second Exec. Salary: $ Bonus: $

OTHER THOUGHTS:

Estimated Female Officers or Directors: 2
Hot Spot for Advancement for Women/Minorities:

Travelport Worldwide Limited

www.travelport.com

NAIC Code: 519130

TYPES OF BUSINESS:
Online Travel Reservation Systems
Travel Distribution Services & Solutions
Consumer Travel Reservation Sites

BRANDS/DIVISIONS/AFFILIATES:
Blackstone Group LP (The)
One Equity Parnters
Technology Crossover Ventures
eNett International (Jersey) Limited
Travel Commerce Platform
Mobile Travel Technologies Ltd

CONTACTS: Note: Officers with more than one job title may be intentionally listed here more than once.
Gordon Wilson, CEO
Douglas Steenland, Chairman of the Board
Bernard Bot, CFO
Bryan Conway, CMO
Matthew Minetola, CIO
Terence Conley, Executive VP, Divisional
Philip Emery, Executive VP
Thomas Murphy, Executive VP
Matthew Minetola, Executive VP
Kurt Ekert, Executive VP
Gordon Wilson, President
Rochelle Boas, Secretary
Bryan Conway, Senior VP
Christopher Roberts, Vice President, Divisional
Kate Aldridge, Vice President, Divisional

GROWTH PLANS/SPECIAL FEATURES:
Travelport Worldwide Limited, one of the largest travel companies in the world, offers a wide variety of travel-related services to travel professionals and travel suppliers. Products and services include distribution technology, travel packaging, consultation and retail sales for both the business and consumer markets. The firm offers these services in more than 180 countries, with sales and support offices in 40 countries. Travelport facilitates travel commerce by connecting travel providers such as airlines and hotel chains with online and offline travel agencies and other travel buyers via its Travel Commerce Platform (TCP). In 2015, the TCP system processed up to 3 billion travel-related messages per day and over 11 billion application programming interface (API) calls every month. That same year it created over 340 million individual travel itineraries, issued 117 million airline tickets, sold over 65 million hotel room nights and sold 91 million car rentals. Travelport provides air distribution services to approximately 400 airlines globally, as well as hotel reservation services for 330 hotel chains that represent more than 650,000 hotel properties and serve over 36,000 rental car locations, 60 cruise-lines and tour operators and 13 major rail networks worldwide. Additionally, Travelport is a majority-owner and joint venture partner in eNett International (Jersey) Limited, a provider of payment solutions to the travel industry. Priceline, Orbitz Worldwide and Expedia are the company's largest OTA (online travel agency) customers, accounting for approximately 15% of net revenue. The company is owned by The Blackstone Group, One Equity Partners, Technology Crossover Ventures and members of the Travelport management team. In 2015, the firm acquired Mobile Travel Technologies Ltd., a mobile travel provider.

FINANCIAL DATA: Note: Data for latest year may not have been available at press time.

In U.S. $	2015	2014	2013	2012	2011	2010
Revenue	2,221,000,000	2,148,000,000	2,076,000,000	2,002,000,000	2,035,000,000	
R&D Expense						
Operating Income	191,000,000	161,000,000	208,000,000	138,000,000	200,000,000	
Operating Margin %	8.59%	7.49%	10.01%	6.89%	9.82%	
SGA Expense	456,000,000	430,000,000	396,000,000	446,000,000	397,000,000	
Net Income	16,000,000	86,000,000	-206,000,000	-292,000,000	98,000,000	
Operating Cash Flow	262,000,000	58,000,000	100,000,000	181,000,000	112,000,000	
Capital Expenditure	106,000,000	112,000,000	107,000,000	92,000,000	77,000,000	
EBITDA	425,000,000	394,000,000	414,000,000	365,000,000	427,000,000	
Return on Assets %	.54%	2.87%	-6.59%	-9.25%		
Return on Equity %						
Debt to Equity						

CONTACT INFORMATION:
Phone: 770-563-7400   Fax:
Toll-Free:
Address: Axis One, Axis Park 10 Hurricane Way Langley, Berkshire, SL3 8AG United Kingdom

STOCK TICKER/OTHER:
Stock Ticker: TVPT
Employees: 3,400
Parent Company:

Exchange: NYS
Fiscal Year Ends: 12/31

SALARIES/BONUSES:
Top Exec. Salary: $810,755   Bonus: $
Second Exec. Salary: $550,000   Bonus: $

OTHER THOUGHTS:
Estimated Female Officers or Directors:
Hot Spot for Advancement for Women/Minorities:

Travelzoo Inc

NAIC Code: 519130

www.travelzoo.com

TYPES OF BUSINESS:

Travel Services-Online

BRANDS/DIVISIONS/AFFILIATES:

Azzurro Capital Inc
Travelzoo Top 20
Travelzoo Network
SuperSearch
Fly.com
Local Deals
Getaway

CONTACTS: Note: Officers with more than one job title may be intentionally listed here more than once.

Holger Bartel, CEO, Geographical
Glen Ceremony, CFO
Ralph Bartel, Director
Mike Stitt, President, Geographical
Vivian Hong, President, Geographical
Richard Singer, President, Geographical

GROWTH PLANS/SPECIAL FEATURES:

Travelzoo, Inc. is a global Internet media company that publishes travel and entertainment offers from travel and entertainment firms. Its publications and products, which serve over 28 million subscribers, include the Travelzoo web sites, the Travelzoo e-mail newsletters, the Travelzoo smartphone app and the Newsflash e-mail alert services. Travelzoo websites have a 24/7 publication schedule that reaches 8.4 million unique visitors each month. Travelzoo Top 20 is a weekly publication that has 28 million members. Newsflash is a regionally-targeted email alert services that provides a single, time-sensitive news offer within two hours of an offer being identified. Local Deals and Getaway are locally-targeted email alert systems with a twice-per-week publication schedule. Travelzoo Network is a network of third-party websites that list outstanding deals published by Travelzoo. SuperSearch is a travel search tool that uses a proprietary algorithm to recommend sites and enable one-click searching. Fly.com is a travel search engine that enables users to find and compare the best flight, hotel and rental care options from multiple sources. Revenues are generally primarily from advertising fees, with Travelzoo's advertising base including more than 2,000 travel, entertainment and local businesses. Advertising businesses include airlines, hotels, cruise lines, vacation packagers, tour operators, destinations, car rental companies, travel agents, theater and performing arts groups, restaurants, spas and activity companies. Travelzoo operates in three geographical segments: Asia Pacific (Australia, China, Hong Kong, Japan, Taiwan and Southeast Asia), North America (U.S. and Canada) and Europe (France, Germany, Spain and the U.K.). The North American segment generates approximately 62% of the firm's revenue, with Europe generating 30% and Asia Pacific 8%. Azzurro Capital, Inc. holds a 51.2% stake in Travelzoo, Inc.

FINANCIAL DATA: Note: Data for latest year may not have been available at press time.

In U.S. $	2015	2014	2013	2012	2011	2010
Revenue	141,716,000	142,076,000	158,234,000	151,168,000	148,342,000	112,784,000
R&D Expense	12,528,000					
Operating Income	7,146,000	21,050,000	2,278,000	25,489,000	15,022,000	23,512,000
Operating Margin %	5.04%	14.81%	1.43%	16.86%	10.12%	20.84%
SGA Expense	103,218,000	110,703,000	116,554,000	106,934,000	120,037,000	82,019,000
Net Income	10,864,000	16,352,000	-5,011,000	18,198,000	3,319,000	13,157,000
Operating Cash Flow	4,192,000	1,530,000	16,852,000	36,700,000	15,631,000	23,925,000
Capital Expenditure	1,282,000	3,260,000	5,461,000	3,421,000	2,460,000	1,279,000
EBITDA	9,934,000	23,874,000	5,258,000	28,028,000	17,747,000	25,901,000
Return on Assets %	13.65%	15.93%	-4.71%	21.90%	4.94%	23.46%
Return on Equity %	35.50%	45.96%	-13.42%	46.60%	8.23%	34.32%
Debt to Equity						

CONTACT INFORMATION:

Phone: 212 484-4900   Fax: 212 521-4230
Toll-Free:
Address: 590 Madison Ave., 37th Fl., New York, NY 10022 United States

STOCK TICKER/OTHER:

Stock Ticker: TZOO   Exchange: NAS
Employees: 473   Fiscal Year Ends: 12/31
Parent Company: Azzurro Capital Inc

SALARIES/BONUSES:

Top Exec. Salary: $600,000   Bonus: $
Second Exec. Salary: Bonus: $
$470,000

OTHER THOUGHTS:

Estimated Female Officers or Directors: 2
Hot Spot for Advancement for Women/Minorities: Y

Sales, profits and employees may be estimates. Financial information, benefits and other data can change quickly and may vary from those stated here.

TripAdvisor Inc

www.TripAdvisor.com

NAIC Code: 519130

TYPES OF BUSINESS:

Online Travel Information

BRANDS/DIVISIONS/AFFILIATES:

tripadvisor.com
airfarewatchdog.com
bookingbuddy.com
cruisecritic.com
everytrail.com
familyvacationcritic.com
independenttraveler.com
jetsetter.com

CONTACTS: Note: Officers with more than one job title may be intentionally listed here more than once.

Barrie Seidenberg, CEO, Divisional
Stephen Kaufer, CEO
Gregory Maffei, Chairman of the Board
Noel Watson, Chief Accounting Officer
Seth Kalvert, General Counsel
Dermot Halpin, President, Divisional
Ernst Teunisssen, Senior VP

GROWTH PLANS/SPECIAL FEATURES:

TripAdvisor, Inc. operates a major web-based travel network through its primary web site, tripadvisor.com, offering traveling advice, reviews, flight searches and planning services such as TripAdvisor mobile. TripAdvisor's sites offer over 320 million reviews/opinions and receive more than 350 million unique monthly visitors. It features information about over 6.2 million accommodations, restaurants and attractions. The sites operate in 46 countries worldwide. In addition, it features over 625,000 traveler attraction photos and videos. The company also operates 23 sites that are available in several countries and languages, such as airfarewatchdog.com, bookingbuddy.com, cruisecritic.com, everytrail.com, familyvacationcritic.com, flipkey.com, gateguru.com, holidaylettings.co.uk, holidaywatchdog.com, independenttraveler.com, jetsetter.com, thefork.com, niumba.com and onetime.com. The company's TripAdvisor for Business division offers access to TripAdvisor's monthly visitors to the tourism industry. TripAdvisor for Business provides services such as vacation rental listings, helping property managers and individual home owners list their properties and showcase hotel alternatives; and business listings, allowing hoteliers to connect directly to millions of researching travelers.

The firm offers employees benefits including medical, dental, discounted vision, life and disability insurance; flexible spending accounts; paid vacation; tuition assistance; fitness subsidies; sick and parental leave; adoption assistance; product discoun

FINANCIAL DATA: Note: Data for latest year may not have been available at press time.

In U.S. $	2015	2014	2013	2012	2011	2010
Revenue	1,492,000,000	1,246,000,000	944,661,000	762,966,000	637,063,000	484,635,000
R&D Expense	207,000,000	171,000,000	130,673,000	86,640,000	57,448,000	53,667,000
Operating Income	232,000,000	340,000,000	294,574,000	296,296,000	272,757,000	226,300,000
Operating Margin %	15.54%	27.28%	31.18%	38.83%	42.81%	46.69%
SGA Expense	902,000,000	630,000,000	466,474,000	341,880,000	253,946,000	174,814,000
Net Income	198,000,000	226,000,000	205,443,000	194,069,000	177,677,000	138,776,000
Operating Cash Flow	382,000,000	387,000,000	349,523,000	239,066,000	217,882,000	196,915,000
Capital Expenditure	109,000,000	81,000,000	55,455,000	29,282,000	21,323,000	18,813,000
EBITDA	342,000,000	396,000,000	330,002,000	318,922,000	297,932,000	253,780,000
Return on Assets %	9.68%	13.17%	14.82%	18.17%	22.79%	21.38%
Return on Equity %	15.60%	22.71%	25.81%	38.03%	42.65%	29.85%
Debt to Equity	0.20	0.23	0.34	0.46	1.29	

CONTACT INFORMATION:

Phone: 781-800-5000   Fax:
Toll-Free:
Address: 400 1st Ave., Needham, MA 02494 United States

STOCK TICKER/OTHER:

Stock Ticker: TRIP
Employees: 3,008
Parent Company:

Exchange: NAS
Fiscal Year Ends: 12/31

SALARIES/BONUSES:

Top Exec. Salary: $700,000   Bonus: $630,000
Second Exec. Salary: $433,177   Bonus: $211,336

OTHER THOUGHTS:

Estimated Female Officers or Directors: 4
Hot Spot for Advancement for Women/Minorities: Y

Sales, profits and employees may be estimates. Financial information, benefits and other data can change quickly and may vary from those stated here.

TRT Holdings Inc

NAIC Code: 721110

www.omnihotels.com

TYPES OF BUSINESS:

Hotels
Gymnasiums
Oil & Gas Exploration

BRANDS/DIVISIONS/AFFILIATES:

Omni Hotels & Resorts
Mokara Hotel and Spa
Gold's Gym International
Tana Exploration Company LLC
Waldo's Dollar Mart

CONTACTS: *Note: Officers with more than one job title may be intentionally listed here more than once.*

Robert B. Rowling, CEO
James D. Caldwell, Pres.
Robert B. Bean, CFO
James D. Caldwell, CEO-Omni Hotels & Resorts
Michael J. Deitemeyer, Pres., Omni Hotels & Resorts
Kevin D. Talley, Pres., Tana Exploration Company LLC
Jim Snow, Pres., Gold's Gym
Robert B. Rowling, Chmn.

GROWTH PLANS/SPECIAL FEATURES:

TRT Holdings, Inc. is a diversified holding company with interests in the lodging and hospitality, fitness and oil industries. The firm owns and franchises the Omni Hotels & Resorts chain, Gold's Gym International, an oil and gas exploration firm Tana Exploration Company, Waldo's Dollar Mart in Mexico and many investments in other companies. Omni hotels offer luxury and first-class accommodations at approximately 60 locations across North America, totaling approximately 21,000 rooms. A typical Omni hotel has over 300 rooms and offers amenities such as marble bathrooms, high-speed Internet access, gourmet dining, fitness centers, 24-hour room service and valet ordering, among other services. The hotel chain caters primarily to corporate business and upscale leisure travelers. Apart from the Omni brand, TRT has introduced the Mokara Hotel and Spa brand, which currently has one location in San Antonio, Texas. Gold's Gym International is a franchiser of more than 700 fitness centers throughout the U.S. and worldwide. Tana Exploration Company LLC is an independent oil and gas exploration firm headquartered in Dallas, Texas. The firm has working interests in a number of wells in the offshore Gulf of Mexico region, as well as in the Fort Worth basin. Waldo's Dollar Mart is a line of convenience stores with headquarters in Tijuana and Baja California, Mexico.

FINANCIAL DATA: *Note: Data for latest year may not have been available at press time.*

In U.S. $	2015	2014	2013	2012	2011	2010
Revenue						
R&D Expense						
Operating Income						
Operating Margin %						
SGA Expense						
Net Income						
Operating Cash Flow						
Capital Expenditure						
EBITDA						
Return on Assets %						
Return on Equity %						
Debt to Equity						

CONTACT INFORMATION:

Phone: 972-730-6664   Fax: 972-871-5665
Toll-Free: 800-843-6664
Address: 4001 Maple Ave., Dallas, TX 75219 United States

STOCK TICKER/OTHER:

Stock Ticker: Private
Employees: 47
Parent Company:

Exchange:
Fiscal Year Ends: 12/31

SALARIES/BONUSES:

Top Exec. Salary: $ Bonus: $
Second Exec. Salary: $ Bonus: $

OTHER THOUGHTS:

Estimated Female Officers or Directors:
Hot Spot for Advancement for Women/Minorities:

Sales, profits and employees may be estimates. Financial information, benefits and other data can change quickly and may vary from those stated here.

Trump Entertainment Resorts Inc

www.trumpcasinos.com/

NAIC Code: 531120

TYPES OF BUSINESS:

Real Estate Investment, Development & Operations
Property Management
Residential & Commercial Brokerage
Hotel, Casino & Resort Management
Golf Courses

BRANDS/DIVISIONS/AFFILIATES:

Trump Taj Mahal
Taj Mahal's Trump One

GROWTH PLANS/SPECIAL FEATURES:

Trump Entertainment Resorts, Inc. is a gaming and hospitality company that owns and operates the Trump Taj Mahal hotel and casino in Atlantic City, New Jersey. The firm was initially founded by Donald J. Trump, who is no longer involved in the company, but is now a subsidiary of Icahn Enterprises. The Trump Taj Mahal operates approximately 5,700 slot machines, 280 gaming tables and 2,700 hotel rooms. Taj Mahal's Trump One card is a free, with a valid photo ID, which provides special offers and benefits such as free show tickets, the display of account balances online, free parking, as well as opportunities to earn slot/table dollars. The firm is currently undergoing operational and debt restructuring.

CONTACTS: *Note: Officers with more than one job title may be intentionally listed here more than once.*

Robert F. Griffin, CEO
Michael P. Mellon, VP-Oper.
Donald J. Trump, Pres.
Daniel M. McFadden, CFO
Donald Trump, Jr., Exec. VP-Dev. & Acquisitions
Ivanka Trump, Exec. VP-Dev. & Acquisitions
Eric Trump, Exec. VP-Dev. & Acquisitions
Cathy Hoffman Glosser, Exec. VP-Global Licensing
Robert F. Griffin, Chmn.

FINANCIAL DATA: *Note: Data for latest year may not have been available at press time.*

In U.S. $	2015	2014	2013	2012	2011	2010
Revenue						
R&D Expense						
Operating Income						
Operating Margin %						
SGA Expense						
Net Income						
Operating Cash Flow						
Capital Expenditure						
EBITDA						
Return on Assets %						
Return on Equity %						
Debt to Equity						

CONTACT INFORMATION:

Phone: 609-449-5534   Fax:
Toll-Free:
Address: 1000 Boardwalk at Virginia Avenue, Atlantic City, NY 08401 United States

STOCK TICKER/OTHER:

Stock Ticker: Subsidiary
Employees: 5,500
Parent Company: Icahn Enterprises LP

Exchange:
Fiscal Year Ends: 12/31

SALARIES/BONUSES:

Top Exec. Salary: $ Bonus: $
Second Exec. Salary: $ Bonus: $

OTHER THOUGHTS:

Estimated Female Officers or Directors: 2
Hot Spot for Advancement for Women/Minorities:

Sales, profits and employees may be estimates. Financial information, benefits and other data can change quickly and may vary from those stated here.

TUI AG (TUI Group)

www.tuigroup.com/en

NAIC Code: 721110

TYPES OF BUSINESS:

Tours, Chartered Air Travel and Hotels
Tour Operations
Charter Flights
Travel Agencies
Cruises
Resorts
Boat Charter

BRANDS/DIVISIONS/AFFILIATES:

Hotelbeds
TUI Cruises
TUI Magic Life
TUI Hotel
Intercruises
Robinson
TUI Travel plc
TUI AG

CONTACTS: *Note: Officers with more than one job title may be intentionally listed here more than once.*

Friedrich Joussen, Co-CEO
Horst Baier, CFO
Elke Eller, Human Resources
Peter Long, Exec. Dir.-Tourism

GROWTH PLANS/SPECIAL FEATURES:

TUI AG, based in Germany, is one of Europe's largest travel and tourism groups. The company operates through two business segments: tourism and specialist travel. Tourism, the firm's core business, is further divided into three regions: the northern region, comprising the U.K., Ireland, Sweden, Norway, Finland, Denmark, Canada and Russia; the central region, comprising Germany, Austria, Switzerland, Poland and TUI Mallorca destination services; and the western region, comprising Belgium, the Netherlands and France. This segment offers hotels, resorts, cruises, inbound services, aviation services and technical services. Hotel and resort brands include Robinson, Rui, TUI Hotel and TUI Magic Life, and cruise brands include TUI Cruises, Hapag-Lloyd Cruises and Thomson Cruises. Specialist travel is further divided into two groups: the hotel beds group and the specialist group. The hotel beds division provides travel services in more than 180 countries, offering hotel accommodations, transfers, excursions, tours, meetings, events, visa outsourcing and cruise handling services. Hotel bed's main clients include tour operators, travel agencies, corporate clients and consumers. Its brands include Intercruises. The specialist group division provides a wide range of travel experiences such as private jet tours, polar expeditions and sailing excursions worldwide. In 2016, the firm agreed to sell Hotelbeds Group for approximately $1.3 billion (1.2 billion euros); and agreed to sell a collection of adventure-travel activities within its specialist travel segment, retaining only the Crystal Ski and Thomson Lakes & Mountains businesses, which help fill its U.K. fleet of aircraft in the winter months.

FINANCIAL DATA: *Note: Data for latest year may not have been available at press time.*

In U.S. $	2015	2014	2013	2012	2011	2010
Revenue	22,609,420,000	21,144,160,000	20,876,170,000	20,709,860,000	19,749,520,000	18,472,600,000
R&D Expense						
Operating Income	816,969,900	829,962,700	567,054,500	616,992,400	444,469,500	191,390,800
Operating Margin %	3.61%	3.92%	2.71%	2.97%	2.25%	1.03%
SGA Expense				1,757,654,000	1,704,666,000	1,735,397,000
Net Income	384,589,300	118,291,700	4,858,208	-17,060,220	133,544,200	128,347,100
Operating Cash Flow	893,119,400	1,214,213,000	988,927,700	925,432,200	1,226,415,000	924,302,300
Capital Expenditure	933,679,800	679,245,200	801,152,400		544,571,200	607,389,000
EBITDA	1,589,086,000	1,260,535,000	1,130,720,000	1,067,450,000	1,257,259,000	1,260,310,000
Return on Assets %	2.42%	.59%	.03%	-.11%	.17%	.72%
Return on Equity %	15.76%	3.67%	.20%	-.66%	.99%	4.63%
Debt to Equity	0.85	0.72	0.88			

CONTACT INFORMATION:

Phone: 49 5115661425   Fax: 49 5115661096
Toll-Free:
Address: Karl-Wiechert-Allee 4, Hannover, D-30625 Germany

STOCK TICKER/OTHER:

Stock Ticker: TUIFF   Exchange: PINX
Employees: 76,036   Fiscal Year Ends: 12/31
Parent Company:

SALARIES/BONUSES:

Top Exec. Salary: $ Bonus: $
Second Exec. Salary: $ Bonus: $

OTHER THOUGHTS:

Estimated Female Officers or Directors: 4
Hot Spot for Advancement for Women/Minorities: Y

Turk Hava Yollari AO (Turkish Airlines)

www.thy.com

NAIC Code: 481111

TYPES OF BUSINESS:

International Airline
Air Cargo
Aircraft Maintenance

BRANDS/DIVISIONS/AFFILIATES:

Republic of Turkey
Turkish Airlines
Miles&Smiles
Turkish Technic Inc
THY DO & CO Catering Services Inc
TGS Yer Hizmetleri AS
THY Opet Havacilik Takitlari AS
Sun Express Aviation Inc

CONTACTS: Note: Officers with more than one job title may be intentionally listed here more than once.

Temel Kotil, Gen. Mgr.
Coskun Kilic,
Cemal Sanli, Deputy Chmn.
M. Ilker Ayci, Chmn.

GROWTH PLANS/SPECIAL FEATURES:

Turk Hava Yollari AO (Turkish Airlines) is the Turkey-based operator of Turkish Airlines, a domestic and international air transport and cargo services provider. Turkish Airlines operates a fleet of 319 passenger and 11 cargo airplanes; its models include the Airbus A319, A320, A321, A330 and A340 passenger aircraft; the Boeing B737 and B777 passenger aircraft; the Embraer ERJ-195 aircraft; and the Airbus A310 and A330 cargo aircraft. The airline flies to 264 destinations both domestically and internationally. Turkish Airlines also offers cargo, technical, passenger and training services as well as online services such as Internet check-in, reservation/tariffs, electronic ticketing, schedule, cargo baggage tracking and departure-arrival data services. The firm's technical services include overhaul; periodic maintenance services; and general maintenance, such as cleaning, painting, and engineering. It also operates a flight academy. Turkish Airlines' Miles&Smiles promotional program offers frequent customers rewards such as free tickets and seating upgrades. The firm is publicly traded, and its largest stakeholder is the Republic of Turkey, which holds approximately 49.12% of the company. Subsidiary Turkish Technic, Inc. provides maintenance, repair and overhaul services for Boeing and Airbus engines, auxiliary power units, airframes, landing gear and components. Turkish Airlines also holds a 50% interest in THY DO & CO Catering Services, Inc.; TGS Yer Hizmetleri AS; THY Opet Havacilik Yakitlari AS; and Sun Express Aviation, Inc. as well as a 49% interest in P & W.T.T. Sti. Care Flight Centre Ltd. and Airlines of Bosnia & Herzegovina. The firm's destinations include several cities in countries such as the U.S., Iraq, Afghanistan, Spain and Italy.

FINANCIAL DATA: Note: Data for latest year may not have been available at press time.

In U.S. $	2015	2014	2013	2012	2011	2010
Revenue	10,522,000,000	11,070,000,000	7,154,900,000	8,503,541,248	6,598,289,408	4,703,671,808
R&D Expense						
Operating Income						
Operating Margin %						
SGA Expense						
Net Income	1,069,000,000	845,000,000	260,100,000	646,430,528	10,340,559	159,963,456
Operating Cash Flow						
Capital Expenditure						
EBITDA						
Return on Assets %						
Return on Equity %						
Debt to Equity						

CONTACT INFORMATION:

Phone: 90-212-463-63-63   Fax: 90-212-465-21-21
Toll-Free:
Address: Bldg. Ataturk Airport, Yesilkoy, Istanbul, 34149 Turkey

STOCK TICKER/OTHER:

Stock Ticker: THYAO   Exchange: Instanbul
Employees: 27,676   Fiscal Year Ends: 12/31
Parent Company:

SALARIES/BONUSES:

Top Exec. Salary: $ Bonus: $
Second Exec. Salary: $ Bonus: $

OTHER THOUGHTS:

Estimated Female Officers or Directors: 1
Hot Spot for Advancement for Women/Minorities:

Sales, profits and employees may be estimates. Financial information, benefits and other data can change quickly and may vary from those stated here.

TWC Enterprises Inc

NAIC Code: 488310

www.twcenterprises.ca/Default.aspx

TYPES OF BUSINESS:

Transportation & Environmental Svcs.
Tourist Railroad
Port Operations
Golf Courses
Resorts

BRANDS/DIVISIONS/AFFILIATES:

White Pass & Yukon Route
ClubLink

CONTACTS: *Note: Officers with more than one job title may be intentionally listed here more than once.*

K. (Rai) Sahi, CEO
Andrew Tamlin, CFO
Eugene N. Hretzay, General Counsel
Edge M. Caravaggio, VP-Oper., Golf Club & Resort Oper.
Eugene N. Hretzay, Pres., White Pass & Yukon Route
Neil E. Osborne, VP-Clubhouse Oper., Golf Club & Resort Oper.
Robert Wright, VP
K. (Rai) Sahi, Chmn.
John A. Finlayson, VP-Florida Oper., Golf Club & Resort Oper.

GROWTH PLANS/SPECIAL FEATURES:

TWC Enterprises Limited is active in the fields of tourism and golf club operations. The rail/tourism/port segment operates through wholly-owned subsidiary White Pass & Yukon Route (White Pass). White Pass operates three major port facilities in Skagway, Alaska that serve cruise ships in the spring and summer as well as a tourist railway connecting Skagway to northern British Columbia and the Yukon Territory. Construction on the railway began in response to the 1898 Klondike Gold Rush, and the railway was completed in 1900. For most of the 20th Century, the railway carried both passengers and freight, especially ore concentrates. However, during the late 1980s, changes in the local ore concentrates marketplace forced the railway to abandon its freight operations, and it has carried only passengers since 1988. Currently, White Pass owns 110 miles of track stretching from Skagway, Alaska to Whitehorse, Yukon. The golf club operations segment offers golfers a wide variety of unique membership, corporate event and resort opportunities under the ClubLink brand name. Member and hybrid golf club revenue is maximized by the sale of personal and corporate memberships that offer reciprocal playing privileges at ClubLink golf clubs as well as inter-regional play within the ClubLink and ClubCorp of America Golf Clubs. Golf resorts include three in Muskoka, Ontario: The Lake Joseph Club, Rocky Crest Golf Resort and Sherwood Inn; one in Mont-Tremblant in the Laurentian Mountains: Le Maitre Golf Community; and two in Florida, USA: Little Harbor and Heron Bay Marriott.

FINANCIAL DATA: *Note: Data for latest year may not have been available at press time.*

In U.S. $	2015	2014	2013	2012	2011	2010
Revenue			41,089,472	218,259,280	217,515,600	206,392,080
R&D Expense						
Operating Income						
Operating Margin %						
SGA Expense						
Net Income			18,331,304	14,760,600	16,483,605	11,911,085
Operating Cash Flow						
Capital Expenditure						
EBITDA						
Return on Assets %						
Return on Equity %						
Debt to Equity						

CONTACT INFORMATION:

Phone: 905-841-3730   Fax: 905-841-1134
Toll-Free:
Address: 15675 Dufferin St., King City, ON L7B 1K5 Canada

STOCK TICKER/OTHER:

Stock Ticker: TWC   Exchange: TSX
Employees: 500   Fiscal Year Ends: 12/31
Parent Company:

SALARIES/BONUSES:

Top Exec. Salary: $ Bonus: $
Second Exec. Salary: $ Bonus: $

OTHER THOUGHTS:

Estimated Female Officers or Directors:
Hot Spot for Advancement for Women/Minorities:

UB Group (The)

NAIC Code: 312120

www.theubgroup.com

TYPES OF BUSINESS:

Beverages-Breweries
Beverage Distribution
Airlines
Construction
Fertilizers
Real Estate Development

BRANDS/DIVISIONS/AFFILIATES:

United Breweries Holdings Limited
United Breweries Limited
United Spirits Limited
Mangalore Chemicals & Fertilizers Limited
UB Engineering Limited
Kingfisher

CONTACTS: *Note: Officers with more than one job title may be intentionally listed here more than once.*

Ravi Nedungadi, Pres.
Ravi Nedungadi, CFO
Ashok Capoor, Co-Pres., Spirits Div.
Sammy D. Lalla, Co-Pres., Spirits Div.
Deepak Anand, Pres., Fertilizer Div.
Kalyan Ganguly, Pres., Breweries Div.
Vijay Mallya, Group Chmn.

GROWTH PLANS/SPECIAL FEATURES:

The UB Group is an India-based conglomerate with interests in beverage distilling and marketing, fertilizers and engineering. UB Group's international division comprises United Breweries Limited and United Spirits Limited, which exports alcoholic beverages, processed foods, leather footwear and apparel from India to more than 75 countries worldwide. Kingfisher is the group's most visible and profitable alcoholic beverage brand. Mangalore Chemicals & Fertilizers Limited is a leading manufacturer of chemicals and fertilizers in India. Mangalore's products include urea, di-ammonium phosphate, potash, granulated fertilizers, micronutrients, soil conditioners and specialty fertilizers. UB Engineering Limited is the flagship company of the Group's engineering business. UB Engineering's activities encompass environmental protection projects, infrastructure, on-site fabrication of structures, installation services, testing & commissioning of electrical & mechanical equipment, and piping. UB Engineering services industrial projects such as power, refinery, steel, cement, fertilizer, petrochemical and desalination. United Breweries Holdings Limited is the parent of The UB Group. In 2014, the firm sold its Scottish distiller subsidiary, Whyte and Mackay; and ceased its Kingfisher Airlines operation.

FINANCIAL DATA: *Note: Data for latest year may not have been available at press time.*

In U.S. $	2015	2014	2013	2012	2011	2010
Revenue	635,058,972	833,949,425	830,647,276	987,716,357	763,804,187	1,290,410,000
R&D Expense						
Operating Income						
Operating Margin %						
SGA Expense						
Net Income	646,489,423	-3,014,234,568	-248,676,369	11,321,997	66,442,246	
Operating Cash Flow						
Capital Expenditure						
EBITDA						
Return on Assets %						
Return on Equity %						
Debt to Equity						

CONTACT INFORMATION:

Phone: 91-3985-6000   Fax: 91-3985-6034
Toll-Free:
Address: UB City 24, Vittal Mallya Rd., UB Tower Fl. 12-16, Bangalore, 560001 India

STOCK TICKER/OTHER:

Stock Ticker: Subsidiary   Exchange:
Employees: Fiscal Year Ends: 03/31
Parent Company: United Breweries Holdings Limited

SALARIES/BONUSES:

Top Exec. Salary: $ Bonus: $
Second Exec. Salary: $ Bonus: $

OTHER THOUGHTS:

Estimated Female Officers or Directors:
Hot Spot for Advancement for Women/Minorities:

Uniglobe Travel International LP

www.uniglobetravel.com

NAIC Code: 561510

TYPES OF BUSINESS:

Travel Agencies

BRANDS/DIVISIONS/AFFILIATES:

Charlwood Pacific Group
Century 21 Canada Limited Partnership
Century 21 Asia/Pacific
Centum Financial Group Inc

GROWTH PLANS/SPECIAL FEATURES:

UNIGLOBE Travel International LP offers travel information and products to online consumers and retail travel agencies through its web site. It has locations in more than 60 countries across the Americas, Europe, Asia/Pacific, Africa and the Middle East. The firm's website divides its offers into business travel management, travel consultants, business travel inquiry services, vacation planning and destination guides. UNIGLOBE is a subsidiary of the Charlwood Pacific Group, which also owns Century 21 Canada Limited Partnership, Century 21 Asia/Pacific, Centum Financial Group, Inc. and other interests in travel, finance and real estate.

CONTACTS:
Note: Officers with more than one job title may be intentionally listed here more than once.

U. Gary Charlwood, CEO
Martin H. Charlwood, COO
Martin H. Charlwood, Pres.
Tracy Bartram, CFO
Chiyoko Kakino, VP-Mktg.
Andrew Henry, VP-U.S. Oper. & Industry Rel.
John L. Henry, Sr. VP-Global Dev.
U. Gary Charlwood, Chmn.
Amanda J. Close, VP-Global Oper. & Regional Services

FINANCIAL DATA:
Note: Data for latest year may not have been available at press time.

In U.S. $	2015	2014	2013	2012	2011	2010
Revenue	5,000,000,000					
R&D Expense						
Operating Income						
Operating Margin %						
SGA Expense						
Net Income						
Operating Cash Flow						
Capital Expenditure						
EBITDA						
Return on Assets %						
Return on Equity %						
Debt to Equity						

CONTACT INFORMATION:

Phone: 604 718-2600   Fax: 604 718-2638
Toll-Free:
Address: 1199 W. Pender St., Ste 900, Vancouver, BC V6E 2R1 Canada

STOCK TICKER/OTHER:

Stock Ticker: Private   Exchange:
Employees: 100   Fiscal Year Ends: 12/31
Parent Company: Charlwood Pacific Group

SALARIES/BONUSES:

Top Exec. Salary: $ Bonus: $
Second Exec. Salary: $ Bonus: $

OTHER THOUGHTS:

Estimated Female Officers or Directors: 2
Hot Spot for Advancement for Women/Minorities:

Sales, profits and employees may be estimates. Financial information, benefits and other data can change quickly and may vary from those stated here.

United Continental Holdings Inc newsroom.united.com/corporate-fact-sheet

NAIC Code: 481111

TYPES OF BUSINESS:

Airline
Air Freight
Regional Airlines

BRANDS/DIVISIONS/AFFILIATES:

United Airlines Inc

CONTACTS: *Note: Officers with more than one job title may be intentionally listed here more than once.*

Oscar Munoz, CEO
Jennifer Kraft, Other Corporate Officer
Gerald Laderman, CFO
Chris Kenny, Chief Accounting Officer
Linda Jojo, Chief Information Officer
Gregory Hart, COO
Robert Milton, Director
Michael Bonds, Executive VP, Divisional
Brett Hart, Executive VP
Julia Haywood, Executive VP
James Compton, Other Executive Officer

GROWTH PLANS/SPECIAL FEATURES:

United Continental Holdings, Inc. is the holding company for United Airlines, Inc. The airline operates approximately 5,055 flights per day to 373 airports across six continents, serving 233 domestic destinations and 140 international destinations. Hubs are located in major cities around the world, including Chicago, Cleveland, Denver, Houston, Los Angeles, Newark, San Francisco, Washington D.C., Guam and Tokyo. United provided transportation to 138 million passengers in 2014. The company is a member of the Star Alliance, which has 18,500 daily flights to 1,300 airports in 190 countries through its member airlines. The firm's fleet includes 1,257 international aircraft, regional jets and turbo props, consisting of Airbus, Boeing, Bombardier, Embraer and Canadair aviation brand lines.

United offers its employees travel passes; medical, dental, vision, life, personal and business accident insurance; flexible spending accounts; a 401(k) plan and profit sharing plans; a perfect attendance program; and on-time bonuses.

FINANCIAL DATA: *Note: Data for latest year may not have been available at press time.*

In U.S. $	2015	2014	2013	2012	2011	2010
Revenue	37,864,000,000	38,901,000,000	38,279,000,000	37,152,000,000	37,110,000,000	23,229,000,000
R&D Expense						
Operating Income	5,166,000,000	2,373,000,000	1,249,000,000	39,000,000	1,822,000,000	976,000,000
Operating Margin %	13.64%	6.10%	3.26%	.10%	4.90%	4.20%
SGA Expense	11,809,000,000	11,191,000,000	10,951,000,000	9,297,000,000	9,087,000,000	5,914,000,000
Net Income	7,340,000,000	1,132,000,000	571,000,000	-723,000,000	840,000,000	253,000,000
Operating Cash Flow	5,992,000,000	2,634,000,000	1,444,000,000	935,000,000	2,408,000,000	1,907,000,000
Capital Expenditure	2,747,000,000	2,005,000,000	2,164,000,000	2,016,000,000	700,000,000	371,000,000
EBITDA	6,658,000,000	3,490,000,000	2,962,000,000	1,596,000,000	3,309,000,000	2,127,000,000
Return on Assets %	18.76%	3.05%	1.53%	-1.91%	2.16%	.86%
Return on Equity %	129.20%	42.08%	32.95%	-63.22%	47.55%	
Debt to Equity	1.15	4.46	3.66	23.35	6.32	7.22

CONTACT INFORMATION:

Phone: 872-825-4000   Fax: 847 700-2214
Toll-Free:
Address: 233 South Wacker Drive, Chicago, IL 60606 United States

STOCK TICKER/OTHER:

Stock Ticker: UAL   Exchange: NYS
Employees: 87,000   Fiscal Year Ends: 12/31
Parent Company:

SALARIES/BONUSES:

Top Exec. Salary: $261,218   Bonus: $5,200,000
Second Exec. Salary: $715,000   Bonus: $246,154

OTHER THOUGHTS:

Estimated Female Officers or Directors: 2
Hot Spot for Advancement for Women/Minorities: Y

Sales, profits and employees may be estimates. Financial information, benefits and other data can change quickly and may vary from those stated here.

Vail Resorts Inc

NAIC Code: 713920

www.vailresorts.com

TYPES OF BUSINESS:

Ski Resorts
Luxury Hotels & Lodging
Real Estate Development
Golf Courses

BRANDS/DIVISIONS/AFFILIATES:

Heavenly Mountain Resort
Colorado Mountain Express
RockResorts
Vail Marriott
Grand Teton Lodge Company
Vail Resorts Development Company
Northstar Resort
Wilmot Mountain

CONTACTS: Note: Officers with more than one job title may be intentionally listed here more than once.

Robert Katz, CEO
Michael Barkin, CFO
Mark Schoppet, Chief Accounting Officer
Kirsten Lynch, Chief Marketing Officer
John Buhler, COO, Subsidiary
Michael Goar, COO, Subsidiary
David Shapiro, Executive VP
Patricia Campbell, President, Divisional

GROWTH PLANS/SPECIAL FEATURES:

Vail Resorts, Inc. (VRI), one of the leading resort operators in North America, is organized as a holding company, operating through various subsidiaries. VRI currently operates in three business segments: mountain, lodging and real estate. In the mountain segment (79% of revenues), the company owns and operates 11 world-class ski resort properties: Breckenridge Ski Resort, Vail Mountain, Keystone Resort, Beaver Creek Resort, Park City, Heavenly Mountain Resort, Northstar Resort, Kirkwood Mountain Resort, Perisher Ski Resort and Urban & Afton Alps Ski Areas. The segment also maintains the firm's ancillary services such as ski/snowboard school, dining and retail/rental operations and lift tickets. These resorts use federal land under the terms of Special Use Permits granted by the USDA Forest Service. In the lodging segment (18% of revenues), VRI owns and operates luxury hotels under its RockResorts brand as well as other lodging properties and condominiums near its ski resorts including the Grand Teton Lodge Company (GTLC), which operates three destination resorts at Grand Teton National Park and the Jackson Hole Golf & Tennis Club; Colorado Mountain Express, a resort ground transportation company; five company-owned golf courses; and five independently flagged company-owned hotels under such names as the Vail Marriott and Mountain Thunder Lodge. Vail Resorts Development Company, a wholly-owned subsidiary, conducts the company's real estate development operations (3% of revenues). VRI's mountain business and its lodging properties at or around the company's ski resorts are seasonal in nature, with peak operating seasons from mid-November through mid-April. At GTLC and its golf courses, peak season occurs between May and October. In 2015, the firm combined Canyons Resort with Park City as one unified mountain resort named Park City; the base area will be known as Canyons Village. In March 2016, VRI acquired Wilmot Mountain, located in Wisconsin.

FINANCIAL DATA: Note: Data for latest year may not have been available at press time.

In U.S. $	2015	2014	2013	2012	2011	2010
Revenue	1,399,924,000	1,254,646,000	1,120,797,000	1,024,394,000	1,167,046,000	868,632,000
R&D Expense						
Operating Income	210,513,000	117,263,000	96,953,000	59,331,000	94,472,000	69,309,000
Operating Margin %	15.03%	9.34%	8.65%	5.79%	8.09%	7.97%
SGA Expense						
Net Income	114,754,000	28,478,000	37,743,000	16,453,000	34,489,000	30,385,000
Operating Cash Flow	303,660,000	245,878,000	222,423,000	185,419,000	267,287,000	35,950,000
Capital Expenditure	123,884,000	118,305,000	94,946,000	132,625,000	95,640,000	68,957,000
EBITDA	349,692,000	257,864,000	229,641,000	188,473,000	207,118,000	181,950,000
Return on Assets %	4.92%	1.28%	1.79%	.84%	1.78%	1.59%
Return on Equity %	13.60%	3.46%	4.64%	2.01%	4.26%	3.91%
Debt to Equity	0.96	0.76	0.96	0.61	0.59	0.66

CONTACT INFORMATION:

Phone: 303 404-1800 Fax: 303 404-6415
Toll-Free:
Address: 390 Interlocken Crescent, Broomfield, CO 80021 United States

STOCK TICKER/OTHER:

Stock Ticker: MTN Exchange: NYS
Employees: 5,200 Fiscal Year Ends: 07/31
Parent Company:

SALARIES/BONUSES:

Top Exec. Salary: $846,281 Bonus: $
Second Exec. Salary: $427,784 Bonus: $

OTHER THOUGHTS:

Estimated Female Officers or Directors: 3
Hot Spot for Advancement for Women/Minorities: Y

Sales, profits and employees may be estimates. Financial information, benefits and other data can change quickly and may vary from those stated here.

VIA Rail Canada Inc

www.viarail.ca

NAIC Code: 482111

TYPES OF BUSINESS:

Line-Haul Railroads

BRANDS/DIVISIONS/AFFILIATES:

CONTACTS: *Note: Officers with more than one job title may be intentionally listed here more than once.*

Yves Desjardins-Sciliano, CEO
Marc Laliberte, Pres.
Patricia Jasmin, CFO
Martin R. Landry, Chief Mktg. & Sales Officer
Linda Bergeron, Chief Human Resources Officer
Robert St-Jean, Chief Admin. Officer
Yves Desjardins-Siciliano, General Counsel
Denis Pinsonneault, Chief Customer Experience Officer
Jean Tierney, Sr. Dir.-Safety, Security & Risk Mgmt.

GROWTH PLANS/SPECIAL FEATURES:

VIA Rail Canada, Inc. operates Canada's national passenger rail service. It runs nearly 500 train routes per week on nearly 7,770 miles of track, of which it directly owns 140 miles, with the remainder of the track owned and managed by third-party freight train operators. Serving over 400 communities, the company transports more than 3.8 million passengers, for a total of roughly 807 million passenger miles. Its current active fleet consists of 444 passenger cars and 73 locomotives. VIA Rail trains link Ottawa and Toronto, transporting travelers between the two cities via 48 weekly departure options in each direction. Over 500,000 people travel VIA Rail trains along the Ottawa-Toronto route annually. Approximately 250,000 passengers travel on VIA Rail trains during holiday seasons. Every week the company provides 251 trains to transport travelers by rail in the busy Montreal-Ottawa-Toronto triangle. VIA Rail provides free WiFi service for the Quebec City-Windsor corridor, in which 68% of its passengers utilized. VIA Rail's inter-modal network encompasses over 20 partners that offer rail, air, motor coach and automobile connections in order to provide its passengers extended service to and from travel destinations. Additionally, the company has partnerships with more than 120,000 travel agencies worldwide that can issue VIA Rail tickets through AccessRail, a reservation system. In June 2016, the firm expanded its network by offering Maritime Bus tickets online through its viarail.ca website.

Employee benefits include health, dental and vision coverage; life and accident insurance; short- and long-term disability; an employee assistance program; career advancement programs; a pension plan; and tuition reimbursement.

FINANCIAL DATA: *Note: Data for latest year may not have been available at press time.*

In U.S. $	2015	2014	2013	2012	2011	2010
Revenue	214,229,545	200,993,405	193,937,363	263,892,186	258,735,000	258,200,000
R&D Expense						
Operating Income						
Operating Margin %						
SGA Expense						
Net Income	7,065,395	38,148,036	32,590,431	25,137,116	19,639,600	13,097,000
Operating Cash Flow						
Capital Expenditure						
EBITDA						
Return on Assets %						
Return on Equity %						
Debt to Equity						

CONTACT INFORMATION:

Phone: 514-871-6000   Fax: 514-871-6104
Toll-Free: 888-842-7245
Address: 3 Place Ville-Marie, Ste. 500, Montreal, QC H3B 2C9 Canada

STOCK TICKER/OTHER:

Stock Ticker: Government-Owned
Employees: 2,600
Parent Company:

Exchange:
Fiscal Year Ends: 12/31

SALARIES/BONUSES:

Top Exec. Salary: $ Bonus: $
Second Exec. Salary: $ Bonus: $

OTHER THOUGHTS:

Estimated Female Officers or Directors: 3
Hot Spot for Advancement for Women/Minorities: Y

Sales, profits and employees may be estimates. Financial information, benefits and other data can change quickly and may vary from those stated here.

Virgin America Inc

NAIC Code: 481111

TYPES OF BUSINESS:

Airline

BRANDS/DIVISIONS/AFFILIATES:

CONTACTS: Note: Officers with more than one job title may be intentionally listed here more than once.

Peter Hunt, CFO
Stephen Forte, COO
Donald Carty, Director
Samuel Skinner, Director
John Varley, General Counsel
C. Cush, President
John MacLeod, Senior VP, Divisional
E. Fiorillo, Senior VP, Divisional

GROWTH PLANS/SPECIAL FEATURES:

Virgin America, Inc. is a U.S.-owned and -operated airline based out of California. The company currently operates flights to and from 23 cities in the U.S. and Mexico, primarily from its focus cities of Los Angeles and San Francisco. The company has a smaller presence at the Dallas Love Field (DAL) airport. Virgin America's niche is as a low-cost carrier with a first class option along with its standard service offering. Its fleet of 60 Airbus A319 and A320 narrow-body aircraft that feature amenities such as mood-lit cabins, custom-designed leather seats, power outlets, USB ports, Wi-Fi, Ethernet jacks and seatback video touch-screens. In-flight entertainment and services include a selection of on-demand movies, 17 live television channels, videogames, seat-to-seat chat, an on-demand food ordering system, interactive Google maps to track the flight, fleet-wide in-flight internet service and an extensive MP3 library. In April 2016, Virgin American agreed to be acquired by Alaska Air Group, Inc. for $2.6 billion. The transaction was expected to close by January 2017.

Virgin America offers employees health, dental and vision coverage; a 401(k); life and disability insurance; an employee assistance program; flexible spending accounts; free and discounted flights; and other employee discounts.

FINANCIAL DATA: Note: Data for latest year may not have been available at press time.

In U.S. $	2015	2014	2013	2012	2011	2010
Revenue	1,529,584,000	1,489,967,000	1,424,678,000	1,332,837,000	1,037,108,000	
R&D Expense						
Operating Income	177,239,000	96,415,000	80,881,000	-31,733,000	-27,396,000	
Operating Margin %	11.58%	6.47%	5.67%	-2.38%	-2.64%	
SGA Expense	558,248,000	503,698,000	425,697,000	393,517,000	307,310,000	
Net Income	340,537,000	60,109,000	10,144,000	-145,388,000	-100,403,000	
Operating Cash Flow	197,519,000	135,605,000	50,603,000	-50,645,000	-28,971,000	
Capital Expenditure	254,571,000	55,160,000	41,996,000	27,184,000	38,578,000	
EBITDA	195,876,000	110,625,000	95,183,000	-20,179,000	-16,977,000	
Return on Assets %	26.51%	7.06%	11.11%	-28.45%		
Return on Equity %	53.73%	159.80%				
Debt to Equity	0.32	0.20				

CONTACT INFORMATION:

Phone: 650-762-7000   Fax: 650-762-7001
Toll-Free: 877-359-8474
Address: 555 Airport Blvd., 2nd Fl., Burlingame, CA 94010 United States

STOCK TICKER/OTHER:

Stock Ticker: VA   Exchange: NAS
Employees: 2,375   Fiscal Year Ends: 03/31
Parent Company:

SALARIES/BONUSES:

Top Exec. Salary: $667,423   Bonus: $
Second Exec. Salary: Bonus: $
$412,154

OTHER THOUGHTS:

Estimated Female Officers or Directors: 3
Hot Spot for Advancement for Women/Minorities: Y

Virgin Atlantic Airways Ltd

www.virgin-atlantic.com

NAIC Code: 481111

TYPES OF BUSINESS:

Airline
Discount Airlines

BRANDS/DIVISIONS/AFFILIATES:

Virgin Group Ltd
Delta Air Lines Inc
Flying Club

CONTACTS: Note: Officers with more than one job title may be intentionally listed here more than once.

Craig Kreeger, CEO
Philip Maher, Dir.-Technical Oper.
Tim Livett, Dir.-Finance
John Lloyd, Dir.-Cargo
Amanda Wills, Managing Dir.-Virgin Holidays Ltd.
Jill Brady, Dir.-People & External Affairs
Corneel Koster, Dir.-Safety & Security

GROWTH PLANS/SPECIAL FEATURES:

Virgin Atlantic Airways Ltd., a subsidiary of Virgin Group, Ltd. is an international long-haul airline offering service out of London's Heathrow and Gatwick airports to over 30 destinations worldwide, including locations in the Caribbean, Asia Pacific, Europe, South Africa and the U.S. The company currently owns and operates a fleet of over 40 aircraft, composed of Boeing 747 and 787, Airbus A330 and A340 aircraft. The firm is among the largest long-haul airlines in the U.K., carrying more than six million passengers annually. The airline offers amenities such as a stand-up bar, interactive entertainment systems, pre-flight champagne, complimentary ice cream during movies, in-flight beauty therapy and reclining sleep seats for travelers flying first-class. Flying Club is Virgin Atlantic's frequent flyer program, which offers discounts for flying on Virgin Atlantic and other airlines including Air Jamaica, Hawaiian Airlines, Air China, US Airways and South African Airways as well as using associate hotels and car rental companies. Virgin Atlantic has code-sharing agreements with South African Airways, Air China and Australia-based sister company Virgin Australia. Virgin Group Ltd. owns 51% of Virgin Atlantic Ltd., with the remaining 49% held by Delta Airlines, Inc.

U.S. Employees receive benefits including 401(k), tuition assistance, income protection, life insurance, paid time off, health care coverage and airshare profit sharing.

FINANCIAL DATA: Note: Data for latest year may not have been available at press time.

In U.S. $	2015	2014	2013	2012	2011	2010
Revenue	3,681,494,521	5,322,804,140	4,838,912,855	4,294,404,537	4,165,050,000	3,931,266,652
R&D Expense						
Operating Income						
Operating Margin %						
SGA Expense						
Net Income	105,959,420	19,718,045	-397,007			
Operating Cash Flow						
Capital Expenditure						
EBITDA						
Return on Assets %						
Return on Equity %						
Debt to Equity						

CONTACT INFORMATION:

Phone: 44-1293-562-345   Fax: 44-1293-538-337
Toll-Free:
Address: The Office, Manor Royal, Crawley, West Sussex RH10 9NU United Kingdom

STOCK TICKER/OTHER:

Stock Ticker: Subsidiary
Employees:
Parent Company: Virgin Group Ltd

Exchange:
Fiscal Year Ends: 02/28

SALARIES/BONUSES:

Top Exec. Salary: $ Bonus: $
Second Exec. Salary: $ Bonus: $

OTHER THOUGHTS:

Estimated Female Officers or Directors: 3
Hot Spot for Advancement for Women/Minorities: Y

Sales, profits and employees may be estimates. Financial information, benefits and other data can change quickly and may vary from those stated here.

Virgin Australia Airlines Pty Ltd   www.virginaustralia.com

NAIC Code: 481111

TYPES OF BUSINESS:

Air Transportation
Air Cargo

BRANDS/DIVISIONS/AFFILIATES:

Virgin Group Ltd
Virgin Samoa
Virgin Australia Holidays
Virgin Australia Lounge
Live2air
Velocity
Corporate Plus
Voyeur

CONTACTS: Note: Officers with more than one job title may be intentionally listed here more than once.

John Borghetti, CEO
Gary Hammes, COO
Sankar Narayan, CFO
Laurie Turner, CIO
Adam Thatcher, General Counsel
Angela Rowland, Group Exec.-Strategy & Planning
Danielle Keighery, Exec.-Corp. Comm.
Judith Crompton, Chief Commercial Officer
Merren McArthur, Group Exec.-Virgin Australia Regional Airlines
Jane McKeon, Exec.-Govt Rel.
Mark Hassell, Chief Customer Officer
Richard C. N. Branson, Chmn.

GROWTH PLANS/SPECIAL FEATURES:

Virgin Australia Airlines Pty Ltd. is a discount Virgin Group Ltd. airline that transports passengers and cargo. It offers two airlines: Virgin Australia, the flagship carrier of the group, which operates the firm's domestic and international flights as well as its long- and short- haul carrier services; and Virgin Samoa, the company's joint venture with the government of Samoa. The firm's passenger promotions include Virgin Australia Holidays, which packages flights with hotel reservations in locations like Hong Kong and Fiji; and the Virgin Australia Lounge, an Internet accessible area in the Adelaide, Brisbane, Canberra, Melbourne, Mackay, Gold Coast, Perth and Sydney airports for business travelers. The airline provides service to 54 destinations through its fleet of 124 Boeing, Airbus, Boeing, Embraer and Convair aircraft. Other offerings include Live2air, a live in-flight entertainment system available on select Boeing 737 aircraft (which are currently being phased out); Velocity points for frequent travelers; Corporate Plus, which includes priority check-in, free Lounge access, free flight changes, a bigger luggage allowance and a full money-back refund for business travelers; and Voyeur, the company's in-flight magazine. In May 2016, Chinese aviation holding company HNA Group agreed to purchase 13% of Virgin Australia, a stake which HNA intends to increase to nearly 20%. The deal will create a codeshare partnership between Virgin Australia and HNA on routes between Australia and China.

Employee benefits include performance based rewards, travel benefits, paid parental leave, an employee assistance program, study assistance program and study assistance.

FINANCIAL DATA: Note: Data for latest year may not have been available at press time.

In U.S. $	2015	2014	2013	2012	2011	2010
Revenue	3,580,341,000	3,273,890,000	3,033,932,000	2,977,404,000	2,486,534,000	
R&D Expense						
Operating Income	-86,199,030	-289,942,200	-104,001,800	46,485,090	-37,355,450	
Operating Margin %	-2.40%	-8.85%	-3.42%	1.56%	-1.50%	
SGA Expense	1,127,435,000	1,043,822,000	937,766,400	849,893,600	749,011,000	
Net Income	-84,297,020	-270,541,700	-74,634,820	17,346,320	-51,582,480	
Operating Cash Flow	165,931,200	-5,858,187	46,104,690	217,513,700	162,431,500	
Capital Expenditure	485,088,300	329,123,600	398,432,800	527,236,800	398,432,800	
EBITDA	186,396,800	-73,493,620	122,337,200	266,509,500	163,801,000	
Return on Assets %	-2.11%	-7.81%	-2.32%	.58%	-1.75%	
Return on Equity %	-10.42%	-34.05%	-9.96%	2.45%	-7.29%	
Debt to Equity	2.15	1.51	1.45	1.52	1.52	

CONTACT INFORMATION:

Phone: 61 732953000   Fax: 61 732953996
Toll-Free:
Address: 56 Edmondstone Rd., Bowen Hills, QLD 4006 Australia

STOCK TICKER/OTHER:

Stock Ticker: VBHLF   Exchange: PINX
Employees: 8,423   Fiscal Year Ends: 06/30
Parent Company:

SALARIES/BONUSES:

Top Exec. Salary: $ Bonus: $
Second Exec. Salary: $ Bonus: $

OTHER THOUGHTS:

Estimated Female Officers or Directors: 7
Hot Spot for Advancement for Women/Minorities: Y

Sales, profits and employees may be estimates. Financial information, benefits and other data can change quickly and may vary from those stated here.

Virgin Group Ltd

www.virgin.com

NAIC Code: 481111

TYPES OF BUSINESS:

Airlines
Rail
Travel Planning
Beverages
Retail, Books & Music
Telecommunications
Media
Health

BRANDS/DIVISIONS/AFFILIATES:

Virgin Atlantic Airways
Virgin Australia
Virgin Trains
Virgin America
Virgin Holiday Cruises
Virgin Radio International
Virgin Money
Virgin Hotels

CONTACTS: Note: Officers with more than one job title may be intentionally listed here more than once.

Joshua Bayliss, CEO
Ian Woods, COO
John Patrick Moorhead, CFO
Ashley Stockwell, Managing Dir.-Virgin Media Brand
Richard Branson, Chmn.

GROWTH PLANS/SPECIAL FEATURES:

Virgin Group, Ltd. is a holding company for the various Virgin operations. The firm has created over 400 branded companies, covering everything from travel, leisure, retailing, telecommunications and media to finances, publishing, health and social and environmental companies. Travel and tourism make up the majority of the group, and services offered include booking tours as well as transportation under brands such as Virgin Atlantic Airways, Virgin Australia, Virgin Trains, Virgin America and Virgin Holiday Cruises. Virgin is the largest shareholder of Virgin Atlantic Airways. In the commercial sector, the firm maintains retail locations and at-home shopping services as well as branded books, wine and beverages. Virgin offers mobile phone service and broadband Internet access in 12 countries. Virgin Media offers bundled broadband, television, phone and mobile services in the U.K. Virgin Money is the firm's financial brand, offering services in the U.K., Australia and South Africa. The group offers various products and services in the health industry, including a health mile reward program; fitness clubs in Europe, Australia and South Africa; health care providers; spa locations; and umbilical cord blood stem cell banks. Finally, the company maintains a presence in the social and environmental sectors, focusing on greenhouse gas removal solutions and investment in renewable energy and resource efficiency companies in the U.K. and the U.S. Other groups include Virgin Hotels, specializing in four-star hotels; Virgin Radio International; and Virgin Oceanic, a deep sea exploration submarine. In 2015, the firm formed OneWeb, a joint venture with Qualcomm, to build, launch and operate the satellite constellation aimed at providing Internet access and telephony to some of the world's currently unconnected locations. That April, it sold an 80% stake in Virgin Active, retaining 20% in the fitness chain. In April 2016, the firm agreed to sell Virgin America to Alaska Air Group.

FINANCIAL DATA: Note: Data for latest year may not have been available at press time.

In U.S. $	2015	2014	2013	2012	2011	2010
Revenue	20,146,500,000	26,000,000,000	25,400,000,000	24,000,000,000	22,000,000,000	19,000,000,000
R&D Expense						
Operating Income						
Operating Margin %						
SGA Expense						
Net Income						
Operating Cash Flow						
Capital Expenditure						
EBITDA						
Return on Assets %						
Return on Equity %						
Debt to Equity						

CONTACT INFORMATION:

Phone: 44-20-7313-2000   Fax:
Toll-Free:
Address: 179 Harlow Road, London, W2 6NB United Kingdom

STOCK TICKER/OTHER:

Stock Ticker: Private   Exchange:
Employees: 50,000   Fiscal Year Ends: 03/31
Parent Company:

SALARIES/BONUSES:

Top Exec. Salary: $ Bonus: $
Second Exec. Salary: $ Bonus: $

OTHER THOUGHTS:

Estimated Female Officers or Directors:
Hot Spot for Advancement for Women/Minorities:

Sales, profits and employees may be estimates. Financial information, benefits and other data can change quickly and may vary from those stated here.

Walt Disney Company (The)

corporate.disney.go.com

NAIC Code: 515210

TYPES OF BUSINESS:

Cable TV Networks, Broadcasting & Entertainment
Filmed Entertainment
Merchandising
Television Networks
Music & Book Publishing
Online Entertainment Programs
Theme Parks, Resorts & Cruise Lines
Comic Book Publishing

BRANDS/DIVISIONS/AFFILIATES:

ABC Television Network
Hulu
ESPN Inc
Fusion
A&E
Walt Disney Pictures
Touchstone Pictures
Pixar Animation Studios

CONTACTS: Note: Officers with more than one job title may be intentionally listed here more than once.

Robert Iger, CEO
Christine Mccarthy, CFO
Brent Woodford, Executive VP, Divisional
Mary Parker, Executive VP
Kevin Mayer, Other Executive Officer
Alan Braverman, Senior Executive VP

GROWTH PLANS/SPECIAL FEATURES:

The Walt Disney Company is an international entertainment company operating in five primary business segments: media networks, studio entertainment, Disney consumer products, parks and resorts and Disney interactive. The media networks segment, which operates ABC Television Network, is involved in domestic broadcast television, cable/satellite networks, international broadcast operations, television production and distribution, domestic broadcast radio and Internet operations. The company also owns interest in and/or operates numerous cable networks, including ESPN Inc., ABC Family, Hulu, Fusion and A&E. The studio entertainment segment produces and acquires feature films, direct-to-video programming, musical recordings and live stage plays. Its motion picture subsidiaries include Walt Disney Pictures, Touchstone Pictures, Pixar Animation Studios and Marvel. The Disney consumer products segment designs, promotes and sells merchandise based on the firm's intellectual property. The parks and resorts segment owns and operates Florida's Walt Disney World Resort, Disney Cruise Line, the Disneyland resort in California, Adventures by Disney and the Disney Vacation Club. It also holds interest in the Disneyland Paris and Hong Kong Disneyland resorts and licenses the Tokyo Disney Resort in Japan. The Disney interactive segment creates and delivers company-branded entertainment and lifestyle content across interactive media platforms. The segment's primary operating businesses are Disney Interactive Studios, which produces video games; and Disney Online, which produces web sites and online virtual worlds. Additionally, the segment maintains the firm's Japan-based Disney-branded mobile phone business. The company's Shanghai Disney Resort is set to open in 2016. In 2014, Disney acquired Maker Studios, a leading network of online video content on YouTube.

FINANCIAL DATA: Note: Data for latest year may not have been available at press time.

In U.S. $	2015	2014	2013	2012	2011	2010
Revenue	52,465,000,000	48,813,000,000	45,041,000,000	42,278,000,000	40,893,000,000	38,063,000,000
R&D Expense						
Operating Income	13,224,000,000	11,540,000,000				6,456,000,000
Operating Margin %	25.20%	23.64%				16.96%
SGA Expense	8,523,000,000	8,565,000,000				
Net Income	8,382,000,000	7,501,000,000	6,136,000,000	5,682,000,000	4,807,000,000	3,963,000,000
Operating Cash Flow	10,909,000,000	9,780,000,000	9,452,000,000	7,966,000,000	6,994,000,000	6,578,000,000
Capital Expenditure	4,265,000,000	3,311,000,000	2,796,000,000	3,784,000,000	3,559,000,000	2,110,000,000
EBITDA	16,487,000,000	14,828,000,000	12,161,000,000	11,719,000,000	10,319,000,000	8,796,000,000
Return on Assets %	9.72%	9.06%	7.85%	7.72%	6.80%	5.98%
Return on Equity %	18.73%	16.59%	14.40%	14.73%	12.83%	11.12%
Debt to Equity	0.28	0.28	0.28	0.27	0.29	0.27

CONTACT INFORMATION:

Phone: 818 5601000   Fax:
Toll-Free:
Address: 500 S. Buena Vista St., Burbank, CA 91521 United States

STOCK TICKER/OTHER:

Stock Ticker: DIS   Exchange: NYS
Employees: 185,000   Fiscal Year Ends: 09/30
Parent Company:

SALARIES/BONUSES:

Top Exec. Salary: Bonus: $
$2,548,077
Second Exec. Salary: Bonus: $
$1,963,541

OTHER THOUGHTS:

Estimated Female Officers or Directors: 7

Hot Spot for Advancement for Women/Minorities: Y

Sales, profits and employees may be estimates. Financial information, benefits and other data can change quickly and may vary from those stated here.

Walt Disney Parks & Resorts

disneyparks.disney.go.com

NAIC Code: 713110

TYPES OF BUSINESS:

Theme Parks
Cruise Line
Sports Complexes
Hotels & Resorts
Golf Courses
Timeshares

BRANDS/DIVISIONS/AFFILIATES:

Walt Disney Company (The)
Walt Disney World Resort
Disneyland Park
Disneyland Paris
Hong Kong Disneyland
Shanghai Disney Resort
Downtown Disney
Walt Disney Imagineering

CONTACTS: Note: Officers with more than one job title may be intentionally listed here more than once.

Jeff Smith, Deputy General Counsel
Meg Crofton, Pres., Parks & Resorts Oper., U.S. & France
Kristin Nolt Wingard, Sr. VP-Worldwide Public Affairs
Nick Franklin, Exec. VP-Next Generation Experience
Craig Russell, Chief Design & Project Delivery Exec.
Bruce Vaughn, Chief Creative Exec., Walt Disney Imagineering
Karl L. Holz, Pres., New Vacation Oper. & Disney Cruise Line
Bob Chapek, Chmn.
Philippe Gas, Pres., Euro Disney SAS

GROWTH PLANS/SPECIAL FEATURES:

Walt Disney Parks & Resorts (WDPR), a division of The Walt Disney Company, manages the Walt Disney World Resort in Orlando, Florida and Disneyland Park in Anaheim, California. The company also owns a 51% stake in Disneyland Paris, a 47% stake in Hong Kong Disneyland and a 43% stake in Shanghai Disney Resort (which opened June 2016). Additionally, the firm licenses the operations of Tokyo Disneyland. Walt Disney World is situated on approximately 25,000 owned acres and is one of the most popular tourist destinations in the U.S. In addition to four theme parks (the Magic Kingdom, Disney's Hollywood Studios, Epcot and Disney's Animal Kingdom), Disney World encompasses resort hotels, golf courses, water parks, an ESPN sports complex and a retail, dining and entertainment complex called Downtown Disney. Disneyland Resort in California includes theme parks Disneyland and Disney's California Adventure; an adjacent retail, dining and entertainment area; and company-owned hotels with 2,400 rooms among them. WDPR also oversees Walt Disney Imagineering, Disney Vacation Club, Adventures by Disney and Disney Cruise Line. Walt Disney Imagineering handles the creative design process for new theme park concepts and attractions as well as resort properties. The Disney Vacation Club offers ownership interests in resort facilities located at the Walt Disney World Resort; Disneyland Resort; Vero Beach, Florida; and Hilton Head Island in South Carolina. Adventures by Disney offers families all-inclusive guided vacation tours to more than 20 worldwide destinations. Disney Cruise Line offers Disney-themed family cruises on board its four ships: Disney Magic, Disney Dream, Disney Fantasy and Disney Wonder. Construction for Star Wars Land, a 14-acre themed land for both Disneyland park and Disney's Hollywood Studios began construction April 2016.

Walt Disney Company offers employees medical, dental, vision, life and disability insurance; employee assistance & stock options; 401(k); and paid time off.

FINANCIAL DATA: Note: Data for latest year may not have been available at press time.

In U.S. $	2015	2014	2013	2012	2011	2010
Revenue	16,162,000,000	15,099,000,000	14,087,000,000	12,920,000,000	11,797,000,000	10,761,000,000
R&D Expense						
Operating Income						
Operating Margin %						
SGA Expense						
Net Income	3,031,000,000	2,663,000,000	2,220,000,000	1,902,000,000	1,553,000,000	1,318,000,000
Operating Cash Flow						
Capital Expenditure						
EBITDA						
Return on Assets %						
Return on Equity %						
Debt to Equity						

CONTACT INFORMATION:

Phone: 714-781-4500 Fax:
Toll-Free:
Address: 700 W. Ball Road, Anaheim, CA 92802 United States

STOCK TICKER/OTHER:

Stock Ticker: Subsidiary Exchange:
Employees: 175,000 Fiscal Year Ends: 09/30
Parent Company: Walt Disney Company (The)

SALARIES/BONUSES:

Top Exec. Salary: $ Bonus: $
Second Exec. Salary: $ Bonus: $

OTHER THOUGHTS:

Estimated Female Officers or Directors: 4
Hot Spot for Advancement for Women/Minorities: Y

West Japan Railway Company

NAIC Code: 482111

TYPES OF BUSINESS:

Line-Haul Railroads
Hotels
Department Stores
Real Estate
Advertising
Travel Agencies
Convenience Stores

BRANDS/DIVISIONS/AFFILIATES:

JR Kyoto Isetan

CONTACTS: Note: Officers with more than one job title may be intentionally listed here more than once.

Tatsuo Kijima, Pres.
Shizuka Yabuki, Exec. VP
Akiyoshi Yamamoto, Exec. VP
Tatsuo Kijima, Exec. VP

GROWTH PLANS/SPECIAL FEATURES:

West Japan Railway Company (JR-West), serving approximately 52 billion passengers per year, runs the railway operations in western Japan. Its network covers approximately 3,111 miles of track and 1,197 stations and is divided into two categories: conventional lines (covering 2,606 miles and running 485 trains a day) and high-speed services, known as Shinkansen (covering 504 miles and running 354 trains a day). The Shinkansen route lies on one long track linking Osaka with Hakata, the entire course of which only takes a little over two hours, averaging 186 miles per hour. Sales from the Shinkansen line account for roughly 47% of the company's total transportation revenue, and consequently, JR-West focuses much of its effort on improving this service by increasing efficiency and introducing faster and more comfortable trains. Besides railway operations, the company provides transportation services by means of ferry and bus throughout the Hokuriku, Nagoya, Kyoto, Osaka, Kobe and Shinjuku areas. In connection with its railway operations, the company provides food and goods retail through convenience stores, specialty stores and other food and beverage establishments in and around its station buildings. This division also operates the JR Kyoto Isetan department store. Additionally, it has a real estate segment that operates shopping centers and station buildings as well as developing commercial facilities near the company's stations or underneath elevated tracks. JR-West's other businesses include travel agency operations, hotel management operations, advertising services and railway maintenance and engineering services.

FINANCIAL DATA: Note: Data for latest year may not have been available at press time.

In U.S. $	2015	2014	2013	2012	2011	2010
Revenue	13,428,960,000	13,236,860,000	12,917,570,000	12,805,850,000	12,068,200,000	
R&D Expense						
Operating Income	1,390,039,000	1,338,515,000	1,287,835,000	1,091,941,000	954,591,600	
Operating Margin %	10.35%	10.11%	9.96%	8.52%	7.90%	
SGA Expense	1,813,354,000					
Net Income	666,796,000	666,915,300	521,550,600	271,943,500	344,650,700	
Operating Cash Flow	2,223,810,000	2,364,232,000	2,366,987,000	2,050,918,000	2,219,912,000	
Capital Expenditure						
EBITDA	2,965,571,000	2,920,252,000	2,894,147,000	2,809,774,000	2,443,394,000	
Return on Assets %	2.43%	2.47%	2.29%	1.10%	1.34%	
Return on Equity %	8.41%	8.58%	8.30%	4.23%	5.15%	
Debt to Equity	0.97	0.92	0.93	0.96	1.05	

CONTACT INFORMATION:

Phone: 81 663758929   Fax:
Toll-Free:
Address: 4-24, Shibata 2-chome, Kita-ku, Osaka, 530-8341 Japan

STOCK TICKER/OTHER:

Stock Ticker: WJRYF   Exchange: GREY
Employees: 45,326   Fiscal Year Ends: 03/31
Parent Company:

SALARIES/BONUSES:

Top Exec. Salary: $ Bonus: $
Second Exec. Salary: $ Bonus: $

OTHER THOUGHTS:

Estimated Female Officers or Directors:
Hot Spot for Advancement for Women/Minorities:

Westgate Resorts

www.westgateresorts.com

NAIC Code: 561599

TYPES OF BUSINESS:

Condominium Time Share Exchange Services

BRANDS/DIVISIONS/AFFILIATES:

Central Florida Investments Inc
Wild Bear Inn

CONTACTS: Note: Officers with more than one job title may be intentionally listed here more than once.

David Siegel, CEO
Mark Waltrip, COO
Tom Dugan, CFO

GROWTH PLANS/SPECIAL FEATURES:

Westgate Resorts is a Florida-based timeshare resort. The company operates as a subsidiary of Central Florida Investments, Inc. Westgate comprises more than 13,500 villas at 28 resorts in premiere travel destinations throughout the U.S. Its resorts are located in Florida, Tennessee, South Carolina, Missouri, Utah, Nevada and Arizona, providing a diverse range of vacation experiences. Westgate owners can enjoy world-class theme parks in Orlando, relax on sandy beaches in Myrtle Beach, hike the Smoky Mountains in Gatlinburg, snow ski the slops of Park City, horseback ride on trails at a dude ranch or gamble in Las Vegas. There are vacation and budgets for every family. Each villa is furnished, features fully-equipped kitchens or kitchenettes and most offer separate living areas with sleeper sofas, leather furnishings, jetted tubs and private balconies or patios. Partners of the firm include Interval International, providing vacation owners exchange services; Westgate Cruise & Travel Collection, a premium vacation loyalty program that offers members vacation savings; Tickets2You.com, which provides discounted prices on tickets to Walt Disney World, Universal Orlando and Busch Gardens; and Enterprise, Alamo and National, each providing car rental services. In February 2016, the firm acquired Wild Bear Inn, a resort in Pigeon Forge, Tennessee, which is very close to Great Smoky Mountains National Park.

FINANCIAL DATA: Note: Data for latest year may not have been available at press time.

In U.S. $	2015	2014	2013	2012	2011	2010
Revenue						
R&D Expense						
Operating Income						
Operating Margin %						
SGA Expense						
Net Income						
Operating Cash Flow						
Capital Expenditure						
EBITDA						
Return on Assets %						
Return on Equity %						
Debt to Equity						

CONTACT INFORMATION:

Phone: 407-351-3351 Fax:
Toll-Free:
Address: 5601 Windhover Dr., Orlando, FL 32819 United States

STOCK TICKER/OTHER:

Stock Ticker: Private   Exchange:
Employees: 6,500   Fiscal Year Ends:
Parent Company: Central Florida Investments Inc

SALARIES/BONUSES:

Top Exec. Salary: $ Bonus: $
Second Exec. Salary: $ Bonus: $

OTHER THOUGHTS:

Estimated Female Officers or Directors:
Hot Spot for Advancement for Women/Minorities:

Sales, profits and employees may be estimates. Financial information, benefits and other data can change quickly and may vary from those stated here.

WestJet Airlines Ltd

www.westjet.com

NAIC Code: 481111

TYPES OF BUSINESS:

Airline
Travel Agency

BRANDS/DIVISIONS/AFFILIATES:

WestJet Encore
WestJet Vacations
AIR MILES Rewards

CONTACTS: Note: Officers with more than one job title may be intentionally listed here more than once.

Gregg Saretsky, CEO
Harry Taylor, CFO
Clive Beddoe, Chairman of the Board
Rocky Wiggins, Chief Information Officer
Cameron Kenyon, Executive VP, Divisional
Robert Cummings, Executive VP, Divisional
Mark Porter, Executive VP, Divisional
Ferio Pugliese, Executive VP

GROWTH PLANS/SPECIAL FEATURES:

WestJet Airlines Ltd. is a low-fare airline company that provides scheduled and chartered air transportation to, from and within Canada. With an average of 425 departures per day, it serves over 90 destinations in 20 countries. WestJet maintains a fleet of 118 next-generation Boeing 737 (including 737-600, 737-700 and 737-800 aircraft) and Boeing 767-300ER aircraft, with six 737-800, 25 737-MAX7 and 40 737 MAX8 on order. All aircraft offer live satellite channels on seatback TV screens as well as leather seats and increased legroom. To help keep ticket prices low, the firm uses only one type of jet to reduce maintenance costs. Complimentary snacks and non-alcoholic beverages are served on all WestJet flights, while alcohol and food products are offered for purchase on longer flights. The company owns two subsidiaries: WestJet Encore, a smaller airline which offers flights to smaller Canadian cities; and WestJet Vacations, a travel agency. The company offers a mileage reward program in conjunction with MasterCard under the name AIR MILES Rewards. In 2016, the firm launched service to London's Gatwick Airport. Beginning January 2017, WestJet will continue to serve the seasonal Edmonton-Maui, Calgary-Honolulu and Calgary-Maui flights.

WestJet offers all its employees travel discounts, an employee share purchase plan, profit sharing and flexible benefits.

FINANCIAL DATA: Note: Data for latest year may not have been available at press time.

In U.S. $	2015	2014	2013	2012	2011	2010
Revenue	3,125,496,000	3,084,607,000	2,840,762,000	2,658,637,000	2,382,590,000	2,024,001,000
R&D Expense						
Operating Income	441,956,800	368,822,300	309,899,500	291,445,600	199,006,300	192,020,400
Operating Margin %	14.14%	11.95%	10.90%	10.96%	8.35%	9.48%
SGA Expense	1,445,651,000	794,654,700	894,289,300	816,435,500	743,396,500	651,639,800
Net Income	285,092,600	220,265,100	208,447,300	188,023,200	115,348,000	106,053,600
Operating Cash Flow	679,854,300	443,403,500	471,739,000	559,770,700	392,801,500	343,854,100
Capital Expenditure	703,000,400	574,626,900	554,758,100	208,901,200	91,821,810	37,667,160
EBITDA	650,690,400	518,853,300	476,575,500	445,662,300	340,213,800	302,309,200
Return on Assets %	7.51%	6.46%	6.81%	6.71%	4.22%	3.87%
Return on Equity %	19.66%	16.86%	17.55%	17.05%	10.33%	9.44%
Debt to Equity	0.52	0.57	0.43	0.38	0.49	0.57

CONTACT INFORMATION:

Phone: 877 493-7853   Fax: 800 550-7880
Toll-Free: 877-293-7853
Address: 22 Aerial Place N.E., Calgary, AB T2E 3J1 Canada

STOCK TICKER/OTHER:

Stock Ticker: WJA   Exchange: TSE
Employees: 8,698   Fiscal Year Ends: 12/31
Parent Company:

SALARIES/BONUSES:

Top Exec. Salary: $ Bonus: $
Second Exec. Salary: $ Bonus: $

OTHER THOUGHTS:

Estimated Female Officers or Directors: 1
Hot Spot for Advancement for Women/Minorities:

Sales, profits and employees may be estimates. Financial information, benefits and other data can change quickly and may vary from those stated here.

Winter Sports Inc

www.skiwhitefish.com

NAIC Code: 713920

TYPES OF BUSINESS:

Ski Resorts
Property Management

BRANDS/DIVISIONS/AFFILIATES:

Whitefish Mountain Resort
Hibernation House
Summit House
Remedies
Outpost

CONTACTS: *Note: Officers with more than one job title may be intentionally listed here more than once.*

Daniel Graves, CEO
Daniel Graves, Pres.
Riley Polumbus, Mgr.-Public Rel.
Bill Cubbage, Dir.-Snow Sports

GROWTH PLANS/SPECIAL FEATURES:

Winter Sports, Inc. owns and operates the Whitefish Mountain Resort, a ski resort located on 3,073 acres around Big Mountain in the Rocky Mountains of Montana. The company's ski facilities include 11 chairlifts (including three high-speed quad lifts) and two T-bar lifts, which serve 93 marked trails. The ski terrain's difficulty is around 15% beginner, 35% intermediate, 40% advanced and 10% expert. The firm also operates the Hibernation House, a lodging and hotel facility; a ski rental, retail and repair shop; a ski school; the Summit House (a retail store at the mountain's peak); Remedies day spa; and the Outpost (a ski shop and services operation). Associated recreational opportunities include snowshoeing, Nordic skiing, tubing, snowmobiling, dog sledding, ice-skating and winter tours of nearby Glacier National Park. In addition, Winter Sports operates a property management business and owns over 700 acres at the base of the mountain. Nearly half of company revenues come from lease arrangements with other companies who use this land. The firm also operates on a limited basis between June and October, hosting a chairlift and gondola ride to the summit for sightseeing, hiking, mountain biking, zip lining and other recreational activities.

FINANCIAL DATA: *Note: Data for latest year may not have been available at press time.*

In U.S. $	2015	2014	2013	2012	2011	2010
Revenue						
R&D Expense						
Operating Income						
Operating Margin %						
SGA Expense						
Net Income						
Operating Cash Flow						
Capital Expenditure						
EBITDA						
Return on Assets %						
Return on Equity %						
Debt to Equity						

CONTACT INFORMATION:

Phone: 406 862-1900   Fax: 406 862-2955
Toll-Free:
Address: 3889 Big Mountain Rd., Whitefish, MT 59937 United States

STOCK TICKER/OTHER:

Stock Ticker: Private   Exchange:
Employees: 80   Fiscal Year Ends: 05/31
Parent Company:

SALARIES/BONUSES:

Top Exec. Salary: $ Bonus: $
Second Exec. Salary: $ Bonus: $

OTHER THOUGHTS:

Estimated Female Officers or Directors: 1
Hot Spot for Advancement for Women/Minorities:

Sales, profits and employees may be estimates. Financial information, benefits and other data can change quickly and may vary from those stated here.

Wizz Air Hungary Airlines Ltd

www.wizzair.com

NAIC Code: 481111

TYPES OF BUSINESS:

Regional Airline

BRANDS/DIVISIONS/AFFILIATES:

Wizz Air Holdings plc
Wizz Premium
Wizz Flex
WizzTV

CONTACTS: *Note: Officers with more than one job title may be intentionally listed here more than once.*

Jozsef Varadi, CEO

GROWTH PLANS/SPECIAL FEATURES:

Wizz Air Hungary Airlines Ltd. is a discount commercial airline that offers flights throughout eastern and central Europe. The company has more than 22 operating bases located throughout Poland, Hungary, Bulgaria, Romania, Serbia, Lithuania, Ukraine and the Czech Republic, offering service to more than 115 destinations and 410 routes. Wizz Air's fleet consists of 63 Airbus A320-200 and two A321-200 planes; with A320-200 (11), A321-200 (25) and A321neo (110) aircraft on order and deliveries scheduled from 2015-2024. The firm keeps fare prices low by flying into secondary airports and offering ticketless travel, no seat assignments, web check-in, single class leather seat configurations and on-demand catering, which allows customers to order in-flight meals for an extra fee. For an extra price, the company offers a Wizz Premium service package which includes prepaid airport check-in, front row seating, on time arrival guarantee and security fast track as well as access to Wizz Flex, an option that allows customers to change their flight without charge up to three hours before departure time. The airline maintains partnerships with online travel service sites, including Booking.com, HolidayCars and Hostelworld.com, to offer supplemental travel arrangements. Through a partnership with Tourist Mirror, the firm offers WizzTV, a channel available on WizzAir.com or social media outlets that features proprietary videos about over 85 travel destinations. The company is a subsidiary of Wizz Air Holdings plc, based in Switzerland. In 2015, parent Wizz Air completed its IPO on the London Stock Exchange under ticker WIZZ. In 2016, the firm announced plans to launch three new routes from the Macedonian capital Skopje to destinations in Europe as part of its expansion in the Balkan state; and will add Iasi International Airport, in Romania, to its list of operating bases.

FINANCIAL DATA: *Note: Data for latest year may not have been available at press time.*

In U.S. $	2015	2014	2013	2012	2011	2010
Revenue	1,287,000,000	1,136,020,600	955,290,050	859,873,300	661,181,950	
R&D Expense						
Operating Income						
Operating Margin %						
SGA Expense						
Net Income		99,906,950	33,676,500	47,147,100	-10,102,950	
Operating Cash Flow						
Capital Expenditure						
EBITDA						
Return on Assets %						
Return on Equity %						
Debt to Equity						

CONTACT INFORMATION:

Phone: 06-90-181-181   Fax:
Toll-Free:
Address: BUD International Airport Bldg 221, Budapest, H-1185 Hungary

STOCK TICKER/OTHER:

Stock Ticker: WIZZ   Exchange: London
Employees: Fiscal Year Ends:
Parent Company:

SALARIES/BONUSES:

Top Exec. Salary: $ Bonus: $
Second Exec. Salary: $ Bonus: $

OTHER THOUGHTS:

Estimated Female Officers or Directors:
Hot Spot for Advancement for Women/Minorities:

WorldHotels AG

www.worldhotels.com

NAIC Code: 561599

TYPES OF BUSINESS:

Hotel Marketing
Online Reservations

BRANDS/DIVISIONS/AFFILIATES:

IHS GmbH
WorldHotels.com
Academy (The)
Indigo Pearl
Hotel de Sers
Grand Hotel de la Minerve

GROWTH PLANS/SPECIAL FEATURES:

WorldHotels AG offers sales, marketing and distribution for over 450 affiliate hotels and resorts in 250 destinations and 65 countries around the world. Some of the firm's notable hotels are the Indigo Pearl, a 5-star resort set on Thailand's Nai Yang Beach in Phuket; Hotel de Sers, a private mansion with a large portrait gallery, located in Paris; and the Grand Hotel de la Minerve, a hotel in Rome that was originally a 17th-century palace. The firm's Internet customers can use its homepage, WorldHotels.com, to book rooms at member hotels all over the world. WorldHotels also has direct connections with travel agent terminals worldwide. Through The Academy, it offers education and training courses to staff at its affiliated hotels. The firm has partnerships with the frequent flier programs at 26 airlines as well as two car rental companies: Avis and Sixt. WorldHotels operates as a subsidiary of IHS GmbH.

CONTACTS: *Note: Officers with more than one job title may be intentionally listed here more than once.*

Dirk Fuehrer, CEO
Geoff Andrew, COO
Sven Larsen, CFO
Ingo Gurges, VP-Global Hotel Dev.
Roland Jegge, VP-Asia Pacific
Thomas Griffiths, VP-Americas

FINANCIAL DATA: *Note: Data for latest year may not have been available at press time.*

In U.S. $	2015	2014	2013	2012	2011	2010
Revenue						
R&D Expense						
Operating Income						
Operating Margin %						
SGA Expense						
Net Income						
Operating Cash Flow						
Capital Expenditure						
EBITDA						
Return on Assets %						
Return on Equity %						
Debt to Equity						

CONTACT INFORMATION:

Phone: 49-09-000-50-0   Fax: 49-69-660-561-99
Toll-Free:
Address: Unterschweinstiege 2-14, Frankfurt, 60549 Germany

STOCK TICKER/OTHER:

Stock Ticker: Private   Exchange:
Employees: Fiscal Year Ends:
Parent Company: IHS GmbH

SALARIES/BONUSES:

Top Exec. Salary: $ Bonus: $
Second Exec. Salary: $ Bonus: $

OTHER THOUGHTS:

Estimated Female Officers or Directors:
Hot Spot for Advancement for Women/Minorities: Y

Sales, profits and employees may be estimates. Financial information, benefits and other data can change quickly and may vary from those stated here.

WorldMark by Wyndham Inc

www.worldmarkbywyndham.com/

NAIC Code: 561599

TYPES OF BUSINESS:

Timeshare Resorts
Property Management

BRANDS/DIVISIONS/AFFILIATES:

Wyndham Worldwide
WorldMark The Club
Wyndham Vacation Ownership
www.worldmarktheclub.com

CONTACTS: *Note: Officers with more than one job title may be intentionally listed here more than once.*

Stephen P. Holmes, CEO-Wyndham Worldwide
Franz S. Hanning, Pres.

GROWTH PLANS/SPECIAL FEATURES:

WorldMark by Wyndham, Inc., a wholly-owned subsidiary of Wyndham Worldwide, develops and markets the vacation ownership program WorldMark, The Club. It is one of the three brands operated by Wyndham Vacation Ownership, another subsidiary of Wyndham Worldwide. Unlike traditional timeshare owners, who have access to a specific time at a specific place, WorldMark member-owners purchase annually-renewed credits, which can be spent like currency to reserve vacations in WorldMark resorts. Among other benefits, this gives member-owners flexibility over vacation dates and locations. The firm operates 60 WorldMark resorts, mostly in the U.S., with additional locations in Canada and Mexico. Most of the resorts are designed to be a short drive away from major metropolitan areas, and the remaining resorts are in exotic locations, such as those in Hawaii and Fiji. Resorts are often located near golf courses, beaches, sightseeing locations, hiking trails, romantic getaways, shopping centers, skiing slopes or family-friendly entertainment. A typical resort room includes a stocked kitchen, laundry facilities, television and video players, stereos, a fireplace, a private deck with access to swimming pools, indoor and outdoor spas, exercise rooms, arcade games and sports facilities. Its WorldMark, The Club program has over 234,000 member-owners. The Club is based in Redmond, Washington, and its website is www.worldmarktheclub.com. The firm also operates a vacation exchange partnership with Resort Condominiums International (RCI), one of the largest vacation ownership companies in the world. This partnership grants WorldMark, The Club member-owners access to thousands of resorts worldwide for an exchange fee.

Employees receive medical, dental and vision plans; a 401(k) plan; long- and short-term disability benefits; an educational assistance plan; adoption assistance; domestic partner benefits; paid time off; an employee assistance program; and discounts on va

FINANCIAL DATA: *Note: Data for latest year may not have been available at press time.*

In U.S. $	2015	2014	2013	2012	2011	2010
Revenue						
R&D Expense						
Operating Income						
Operating Margin %						
SGA Expense						
Net Income						
Operating Cash Flow						
Capital Expenditure						
EBITDA						
Return on Assets %						
Return on Equity %						
Debt to Equity						

CONTACT INFORMATION:

Phone: 425-498-2500   Fax: 425-498-3675
Toll-Free:
Address: 6277 Sea Harbor Dr, Orlando, FL 32821 United States

STOCK TICKER/OTHER:

Stock Ticker: Subsidiary   Exchange:
Employees: 27,000   Fiscal Year Ends: 12/31
Parent Company: Wyndham Worldwide

SALARIES/BONUSES:

Top Exec. Salary: $ Bonus: $
Second Exec. Salary: $ Bonus: $

OTHER THOUGHTS:

Estimated Female Officers or Directors:
Hot Spot for Advancement for Women/Minorities:

Sales, profits and employees may be estimates. Financial information, benefits and other data can change quickly and may vary from those stated here.

Wyndham Vacation Ownership

www.wyndhamworldwide.com/about-wyndham-worldwide/wyndham-vacation-ownership

NAIC Code: 561599

TYPES OF BUSINESS:

Resorts
Timeshare Resorts
Property Management

BRANDS/DIVISIONS/AFFILIATES:

Wyndham Worldwide
Wyndham Vacation Resorts Inc
Club Wyndham
WorldMark by Wyndham
Club Wyndham Asia
WorldMark South Pacific Club by Wyndham
Wyndham Club Brasil
Margaritaville Vacation Club

CONTACTS: Note: Officers with more than one job title may be intentionally listed here more than once.

Franz S. Hanning, CEO
Franz S. Hanning, Pres.

GROWTH PLANS/SPECIAL FEATURES:

Wyndham Vacation Ownership (WVO), a subsidiary of Wyndham Worldwide, is one of the world's leading time share companies. WVO primarily operates through subsidiary Wyndham Vacation Resorts, Inc. (WVR). WVR markets point-based vacation ownership units through the brands Club Wyndham, WorldMark by Wyndham, Club Wyndham Asia, WorldMark South Pacific Club by Wyndham, Wyndham Club Brasil, Shell Vacations Club and Margaritaville Vacation Club. The firm maintains 213 resort properties as well as over 24,000 individual vacation ownership units and 897,000 owners of vacation ownership interests across the U.S., Canada, Mexico, the Caribbean and the South Pacific. Domestic locations can be found in every region of the U.S., including Texas, California, Hawaii, Florida, South Carolina and Massachusetts. WVR uses a points-based internal reservation system called Club Wyndham Plus to provide owners with flexibility as to resort location, length of stay, unit type and time of year. Through the Wyndham Asset Affiliation Model (WAAM), WVO also offers a fee-for-service timeshare sales model. Vacation units are fully furnished, and many include washers/dryers, whirlpool spas, fireplaces and home entertainment systems. WVR manages the majority of property owners' associations at resorts in which it develops, markets and sells vacation ownership interests as well as at resorts developed by third parties. Additionally, the company offers travel discounts and other member specials to all vacation ownership members.

Through Wyndham Worldwide Corp., the company offers employees a variety of benefits, including medical and life insurance, short- and long-term disability, a 401(k), an employee stock purchase program, adoption assistance, educational assistance and disco

FINANCIAL DATA: Note: Data for latest year may not have been available at press time.

In U.S. $	2015	2014	2013	2012	2011	2010
Revenue	2,660,000,000					
R&D Expense						
Operating Income						
Operating Margin %						
SGA Expense						
Net Income						
Operating Cash Flow						
Capital Expenditure						
EBITDA						
Return on Assets %						
Return on Equity %						
Debt to Equity						

CONTACT INFORMATION:

Phone: 407-370-5200   Fax: 407-370-5143
Toll-Free: 800-251-8736
Address: 6277 Sea Harbor Drive, Orlando, FL 32821 United States

STOCK TICKER/OTHER:

Stock Ticker: Subsidiary   Exchange:
Employees: 16,000   Fiscal Year Ends: 12/31
Parent Company: Wyndham Worldwide

SALARIES/BONUSES:

Top Exec. Salary: $ Bonus: $
Second Exec. Salary: $ Bonus: $

OTHER THOUGHTS:

Estimated Female Officers or Directors:
Hot Spot for Advancement for Women/Minorities:

Sales, profits and employees may be estimates. Financial information, benefits and other data can change quickly and may vary from those stated here.

Wyndham Worldwide Corporation

www.wyndhamworldwide.com

NAIC Code: 721110

TYPES OF BUSINESS:

Hotels, Motels & Resorts
Property Management
Hotel Development
Vacation Property Exchange and Rental
Timeshare Resorts
Franchising
Vacation Ownership

BRANDS/DIVISIONS/AFFILIATES:

Wyndham Hotel Group
Wyndham Destination Network
Wyndham Vacation Ownership
Margaritaville Vacation Club
Baymont Inn & Suites
Wyndham Vacation Rentals
Club Wyndham
WorldMark

CONTACTS: Note: Officers with more than one job title may be intentionally listed here more than once.

Franz Hanning, CEO, Divisional
Geoffrey Ballotti, CEO, Divisional
Gail Mandel, CEO, Divisional
Stephen Holmes, CEO
Thomas Conforti, CFO
Scott McLester, Executive VP
Mary Falvey, Executive VP
Thomas Anderson, Executive VP
Nicola Rossi, Senior VP

GROWTH PLANS/SPECIAL FEATURES:

Wyndham Worldwide Corporation (WW) is a hospitality company offering individual consumers and business customers an array of hospitality products and services as well as various accommodation alternatives and price ranges through its portfolio of world-renowned brands. WW's Wyndham Hotel Group is a world renowned hotel company with 7,812 hotels and more than 678,000 hotel rooms. The group franchises in the upscale, upper midscale, midscale, economy and extended stay segments with a concentration on economy brands. It also provides property management services for full-service and select limited-service hotels, which is predominantly a fee-for-service business. Group brands include Dolce Hotels & Resorts, Wyndham Grand Hotels & Resorts, Wyndham Hotels & Resorts, Wyndham Garden Hotels, TRYP, Wingate, Hawthorn, Microtel, Ramada Worldwide, Baymont Inn & Suites, DaysInn, Super 8, Howard Johnson, Travelodge and Knights Inn. Wyndham Destination Network (formerly Wyndham Exchange & Rentals) operates more than 110,000 vacation properties worldwide under the following brands: cottages4you, Hoseasons, James Villa Hollidays, Landal GreenParks, Novasol, RCI, The Registry Collection and Wyndham Vacation Rentals. Wyndham Vacation Ownership (WVO) is a timeshare/vacation ownership business with 213 resorts and approximately 897,000 owners. WVO develops and markets vacation ownership interests (VOI) to individual consumers, provides consumer financing, as well as property management services at the resorts. WVO brands include Club Wyndham, WorldMark, Shell Vacations Club, Margaritaville Vacation Club, Club Wyndham Asia, WorldMark South Pacific Club and Wyndham Club Brasil. In January 2016, Wyndham Exchange & Rentals changed its name to Wyndham Destination Network.

The firm offers employees medical, dental, vision and life insurance; domestic partner benefits; flexible spending accounts; an educational assistance program; an employee assistance program; adoption reimbursement; and travel discounts on Wyndham propert

FINANCIAL DATA: Note: Data for latest year may not have been available at press time.

In U.S. $	2015	2014	2013	2012	2011	2010
Revenue	5,536,000,000	5,281,000,000	5,009,000,000	4,534,000,000	4,254,000,000	3,851,000,000
R&D Expense						
Operating Income	1,015,000,000	941,000,000	910,000,000	852,000,000	767,000,000	718,000,000
Operating Margin %	18.33%	17.81%	18.16%	18.79%	18.03%	18.64%
SGA Expense	1,574,000,000	1,557,000,000	1,471,000,000	1,389,000,000	1,221,000,000	1,071,000,000
Net Income	612,000,000	529,000,000	432,000,000	400,000,000	417,000,000	379,000,000
Operating Cash Flow	991,000,000	984,000,000	1,008,000,000	1,004,000,000	1,003,000,000	635,000,000
Capital Expenditure	222,000,000	235,000,000	238,000,000	208,000,000	239,000,000	167,000,000
EBITDA	1,275,000,000	1,191,000,000	1,030,000,000	945,000,000	980,000,000	903,000,000
Return on Assets %	6.31%	5.44%	4.49%	4.32%	4.52%	4.03%
Return on Equity %	55.51%	36.76%	24.31%	19.22%	16.19%	13.52%
Debt to Equity	5.21	3.81	2.83	2.08	1.69	1.20

CONTACT INFORMATION:

Phone: 973 753-6000   Fax: 973 496-7658
Toll-Free:
Address: 22 Sylvan Way, Parsippany, NJ 07054 United States

STOCK TICKER/OTHER:

Stock Ticker: WYN   Exchange: NYS
Employees: 37,700   Fiscal Year Ends: 12/31
Parent Company:

SALARIES/BONUSES:

Top Exec. Salary: $1,595,784   Bonus: $

Second Exec. Salary: $794,824   Bonus: $

OTHER THOUGHTS:

Estimated Female Officers or Directors: 2

Hot Spot for Advancement for Women/Minorities: Y

Sales, profits and employees may be estimates. Financial information, benefits and other data can change quickly and may vary from those stated here.

Wynn Resorts Limited

www.wynnresorts.com

NAIC Code: 721120

TYPES OF BUSINESS:

Hotel Casinos
Online Poker

BRANDS/DIVISIONS/AFFILIATES:

Wynn Las Vegas
Encore at Wynn Macau
Wynn Macau
Encore Theater
Palo Real Estate Company Limited
Wynn Resorts
Wynn Palace

CONTACTS: Note: Officers with more than one job title may be intentionally listed here more than once.

Stephen Wynn, CEO
Stephen Cootey, CFO
John Strzemp, Chief Administrative Officer
Linda Chen, COO, Subsidiary
Kim Sinatra, Executive VP
Matt Maddox, President

GROWTH PLANS/SPECIAL FEATURES:

Wynn Resorts Limited is a developer, owner and operator of destination casino resorts. It owns and operates two destination casino resorts: The Wynn Las Vegas on the Strip in Las Vegas, Nevada, which includes Encore at Wynn Las Vegas; and the Wynn Macau in the Macau Special Administrative Region of China. The firm's Las Vegas operations offer 4,748 rooms and suites. The 186,000 square foot casino features 232 table games, a poker room, 1,849 slot machines and a race and sports book. The resort also features 34 food and beverage outlets; three nightclubs; two spas and salons; a Ferrari and Maserati automobile dealership; wedding chapels; an 18-hole golf course; 290,000 square feet of meeting space; and a 99,000 square foot retail promenade featuring boutiques from Alexander McQueen, Cartier, Chanel and Louis Vuitton. At the Encore Theater, the company offers headlining entertainment acts from personalities such as Beyonce. The company's Wynn Macau resort operations, including Encore at Wynn Macau, features 1,008 rooms and suites, approximately 284,000 square feet of casino gaming space with 625 slot machines and 498 table games, eight restaurants, two luxury spas and 57,000 square feet of retail space. Wynn Palace is a resort development scheduled to open by mid-2016, featuring 1,700 rooms and suites, an 8-acre performance lake, air-conditioned SkyCabs, floral sculptures, gaming space, meeting facilities, spa, salon, retail spaces and fine dining.

FINANCIAL DATA: Note: Data for latest year may not have been available at press time.

In U.S. $	2015	2014	2013	2012	2011	2010
Revenue	4,075,883,000	5,433,661,000	5,620,936,000	5,154,284,000	5,269,792,000	4,184,698,000
R&D Expense						
Operating Income	658,814,000	1,266,278,000	1,290,091,000	1,029,276,000	1,008,240,000	625,252,000
Operating Margin %	16.16%	23.30%	22.95%	19.96%	19.13%	14.94%
SGA Expense	552,951,000	533,047,000	469,095,000	482,143,000	519,702,000	425,969,000
Net Income	195,290,000	731,554,000	728,652,000	502,036,000	613,371,000	160,127,000
Operating Cash Flow	572,813,000	1,098,317,000	1,676,642,000	1,185,718,000	1,515,835,000	1,057,312,000
Capital Expenditure	1,925,152,000	1,345,940,000	506,786,000	240,985,000	184,146,000	283,828,000
EBITDA	912,782,000	1,588,043,000	1,656,596,000	1,394,956,000	1,433,524,000	965,464,000
Return on Assets %	1.99%	8.38%	9.30%	7.08%	9.03%	2.24%
Return on Equity %				54.86%	28.35%	6.07%
Debt to Equity					1.34	1.45

CONTACT INFORMATION:

Phone: 702 770-7555   Fax: 702 733-4681
Toll-Free:
Address: 3131 Las Vegas Blvd. S., Las Vegas, NV 89109 United States

STOCK TICKER/OTHER:

Stock Ticker: WYNN   Exchange: NAS
Employees: 16,800   Fiscal Year Ends: 12/31
Parent Company:

SALARIES/BONUSES:

Top Exec. Salary: Bonus: $
$2,500,000
Second Exec. Salary: Bonus: $
$1,500,000

OTHER THOUGHTS:

Estimated Female Officers or Directors: 3

Hot Spot for Advancement for Women/Minorities: Y

Sales, profits and employees may be estimates. Financial information, benefits and other data can change quickly and may vary from those stated here.

Xanterra Parks & Resorts Inc

www.xanterra.com

NAIC Code: 721110

TYPES OF BUSINESS:

Hotel & Restaurant Management
Conference Center Management

BRANDS/DIVISIONS/AFFILIATES:

Anshutz Company (The)
Windstar Cruises
VBT Bicycling and Walking Vacations
Austin Adventures
Country Walkers

CONTACTS: *Note: Officers with more than one job title may be intentionally listed here more than once.*

Andrew N. Todd, CEO
Andrew N. Todd, Pres.
Michael F. Welch, CFO
Betsy O'Rourke, VP-Mktg. & Sales
Shannon Dierenbach, VP-Human Resources
Kirk H. Anderson, General Counsel
Robert T. Tow, VP-Bus. Dev.
Michael F. Welch, VP-Finance
James W. McCaleb, VP-Parks, North
Gordon R. Taylor, VP-Parks, South
Tim Schoonover, VP-Retail
Catherine Greener, VP-Sustainability

GROWTH PLANS/SPECIAL FEATURES:

Xanterra Parks & Resorts, Inc. is a parks concessions management company operating in national parks and state parks across the U.S. The company operates hotels, restaurants, cruises and adventures. Xanterra hotels offer a wide range of experiences, from conference facilities with premium golf, tennis and spa amenities, to historic park lodges & cabins. Some of the firm's hotels include Furnace Creek Resort, Grand Canyon Railway, Yellowstone's Old Faithful Inn and El Tovar Hotel. Restaurants include dozens of restaurants across the U.S., ranging from full-service to quick-service outlets and cafes. Restaurants can be found in the Grand Canyon Lodge, the Old Faithful Lodge and the Zion Lodge. Through wholly-owned subsidiary Windstar Cruises, Xanterra operates a fleet of luxury yachts and ships that cruise to 50 nations and 100 ports-of-call throughout Europe, the Caribbean and the Americas. The firm's fleet of small ships carry between 148 and 310 guests. Adventures include watching wild buffalo at Yellowstone, viewing Zion, experiencing Death Valley and exploring Crater Lake. Subsidiary VBT Bicycling and Walking Vacations offers deluxe, small group bicycling, walking and cross-country skiing tours worldwide, including destinations in Europe, Costa Rica, New Zealand, Vietnam, Thailand, Peru, Argentina, Canada and the U.S. Other experiences at select destinations worldwide include Austin Adventures tour operator, as well as Country Walkers, each providing cultural and artistic adventures. National parks include Crater Lake, Furnace Creek-Death Valley, Glacier, Grand Canyon, Mount Rushmore, Yellowstone, Rocky Mountain and Zion. Ohio state parks include Ohio State Park Lodges, Deer Creek Lodge, Geneva State Park, Maumee Bay Lodge, Mohican Lodge, Punderson Manor Lodge and Salt Fork Lodge. The firm is owned by The Anschutz Company.

Xanterra offers employee benefits including dental, vision, life, disability, AD&D and medical coverage; an employee assistance program; education assistance; and a prescription drug plan.

FINANCIAL DATA: *Note: Data for latest year may not have been available at press time.*

In U.S. $	2015	2014	2013	2012	2011	2010
Revenue	106,000,000	103,000,000	98,000,000	90,000,000	89,000,000	86,000,000
R&D Expense						
Operating Income						
Operating Margin %						
SGA Expense						
Net Income						
Operating Cash Flow						
Capital Expenditure						
EBITDA						
Return on Assets %						
Return on Equity %						
Debt to Equity						

CONTACT INFORMATION:

Phone: 303-600-3400   Fax: 303-600-3600
Toll-Free:
Address: 6312 South Fiddlers Green Cir., Ste. 600N, Greenwood Village, CO 80111 United States

STOCK TICKER/OTHER:

Stock Ticker: Subsidiary   Exchange:
Employees: 7,500   Fiscal Year Ends:
Parent Company: Anschutz Company (The)

SALARIES/BONUSES:

Top Exec. Salary: $ Bonus: $
Second Exec. Salary: $ Bonus: $

OTHER THOUGHTS:

Estimated Female Officers or Directors: 3
Hot Spot for Advancement for Women/Minorities: Y

Sales, profits and employees may be estimates. Financial information, benefits and other data can change quickly and may vary from those stated here.

XOJET Inc

www.xojet.com

NAIC Code: 481111

TYPES OF BUSINESS:

Private Jet Interval Ownership
Private Jet Operations
Private Jet Charter and Leasing

BRANDS/DIVISIONS/AFFILIATES:

XOJET
XOJET Preferred Access
XOJET Elite Access
XOJET Preferred Partner Network

CONTACTS: *Note: Officers with more than one job title may be intentionally listed here more than once.*

Bradley Stewart, CEO
Austin Schell, COO
Bradley Stewart, Pres.
Mark Long, CFO
Shari Jones, Chief Mktg. Officer
Jerry Joondeph, General Counsel
Blake Hirth, Sr. VP-Oper.
Theodore Botimer, Sr. VP-Strategic Planning & Revenue Mgmt.
Gregg Slow, Sr. VP-Sales & National Accounts
Chris DiCara, Chief Pilot
David Colbert, VP-Maintenance
Tracy Chaplin, Sr. VP-Procurement

GROWTH PLANS/SPECIAL FEATURES:

XOJET, Inc. is a private aviation firm offering customers private jet ownership, leasing and on-demand travel solutions geared specifically toward frequent business jet fliers, including fractional ownership in its fleet of super-midsized jets. The company serves 22,000 airports across five continents. The firm's fleet consists of Cessna Citation X and Bombardier Challenger 300 jets. XOJET offers on-demand cross-country flights at fixed prices or custom-priced flights that feature no restrictions. The firm does all its maintenance in-house as a quality control measure. The company also offers an XOJET Preferred Access program designed for private flyers that need on-demand access to a floating fleet of Challenger 300 and Citation X jets. XOJET Elite Access is a program of on-demand executives that can schedule a flight with 12 hours' notice. The company's XOJET Preferred Partner Network program offers access to an additional 900 aircraft of varying sizes. This network includes private jets such as the Hawker 800XP, Hawker 400XP and Gulfstream G-V, with each network operator required to hold a current ARG-US-platinum rating. Partners of the firm include Golden State Warriors, Butterfield & Robinson, Element Lifestyle, IfOnly, Yellowstone Club, Travel Management Company, Virgin Galactic, Creative Artists Agency, Savoya, Gavin De Becker and Vail Mountain & Beaver Creek Resort.

XOJET offers its employees medical, dental and vision coverage; life insurance; short- and long-term disability; flexible spending accounts; a 401(k) program, stock options; and an employee assistance program.

FINANCIAL DATA: *Note: Data for latest year may not have been available at press time.*

In U.S. $	2015	2014	2013	2012	2011	2010
Revenue						
R&D Expense						
Operating Income						
Operating Margin %						
SGA Expense						
Net Income						
Operating Cash Flow						
Capital Expenditure						
EBITDA						
Return on Assets %						
Return on Equity %						
Debt to Equity						

CONTACT INFORMATION:

Phone: 650-676-4700   Fax: 650-636-2525
Toll-Free: 888-759-6538
Address: 2000 Sierra Point Parkway, Brisbane, CA 94005 United States

STOCK TICKER/OTHER:

Stock Ticker: Private   Exchange:
Employees: 220   Fiscal Year Ends:
Parent Company: TPG Capital

SALARIES/BONUSES:

Top Exec. Salary: $ Bonus: $
Second Exec. Salary: $ Bonus: $

OTHER THOUGHTS:

Estimated Female Officers or Directors: 2
Hot Spot for Advancement for Women/Minorities:

Sales, profits and employees may be estimates. Financial information, benefits and other data can change quickly and may vary from those stated here.

Sales, profits and employees may be estimates. Financial information, benefits and other data can change quickly and may vary from those stated here.

ADDITIONAL INDEXES

Contents:

INDEX OF FIRMS NOTED AS HOT SPOTS FOR ADVANCEMENT FOR WOMEN & MINORITIES

Silversea Cruises
Singapore Airlines Ltd
SkyWest Inc
SNCF Reseau
Societe Anonyme des Bains de Mer et du Cercle des
Etrangers a Monaco
Sodexo Inc
Sonesta International Hotels Corp
Southwest Airlines Co
Spirit Aerosystems Holdings Inc
Stagecoach Group plc
Starwood Hotels & Resorts Worldwide Inc
Strategic Hotels & Resorts Inc
Sunstone Hotel Investors Inc
Supranational Hotels Ltd
Textron Inc
Thomas Cook Group plc
Trailways Transportation System Inc
Transat AT Inc
Travelzoo Inc
TripAdvisor Inc
TUI AG (TUI Group)
United Continental Holdings Inc
Vail Resorts Inc
VIA Rail Canada Inc
Virgin America Inc
Virgin Atlantic Airways Ltd
Virgin Australia Airlines Pty Ltd
Walt Disney Company (The)
Walt Disney Parks & Resorts
WorldHotels AG
Wyndham Worldwide Corporation
Wynn Resorts Limited
Xanterra Parks & Resorts Inc

INDEX OF SUBSIDIARIES, BRAND NAMES AND AFFILIATIONS

Brand or subsidiary, followed by the name of the related corporation

INDEX OF SUBSIDIARIES, BRAND NAMES AND AFFILIATIONS, CONT.

INDEX OF SUBSIDIARIES, BRAND NAMES AND AFFILIATIONS, CONT.

INDEX OF SUBSIDIARIES, BRAND NAMES AND AFFILIATIONS, CONT.

INDEX OF SUBSIDIARIES, BRAND NAMES AND AFFILIATIONS, CONT.

INDEX OF SUBSIDIARIES, BRAND NAMES AND AFFILIATIONS, CONT.

INDEX OF SUBSIDIARIES, BRAND NAMES AND AFFILIATIONS, CONT.

INDEX OF SUBSIDIARIES, BRAND NAMES AND AFFILIATIONS, CONT.

INDEX OF SUBSIDIARIES, BRAND NAMES AND AFFILIATIONS, CONT.

INDEX OF SUBSIDIARIES, BRAND NAMES AND AFFILIATIONS, CONT.

INDEX OF SUBSIDIARIES, BRAND NAMES AND AFFILIATIONS, CONT.

INDEX OF SUBSIDIARIES, BRAND NAMES AND AFFILIATIONS, CONT.

INDEX OF SUBSIDIARIES, BRAND NAMES AND AFFILIATIONS, CONT.

INDEX OF SUBSIDIARIES, BRAND NAMES AND AFFILIATIONS, CONT.

INDEX OF SUBSIDIARIES, BRAND NAMES AND AFFILIATIONS, CONT.

INDEX OF SUBSIDIARIES, BRAND NAMES AND AFFILIATIONS, CONT.

INDEX OF SUBSIDIARIES, BRAND NAMES AND AFFILIATIONS, CONT.

INDEX OF SUBSIDIARIES, BRAND NAMES AND AFFILIATIONS, CONT.

INDEX OF SUBSIDIARIES, BRAND NAMES AND AFFILIATIONS, CONT.

A Short Airline, Hotel & Travel Industry Glossary

802.11ac: An ultra-high-speed Wi-Fi standard. It operates on the 5 Ghz band and is backwards compatible with older 802.11 standards. 802.11 standards are set by the IEEE (Institute of Electrical and Electronics Engineers). This specification is capable of 1 gigabit per second data transfer speeds.

AAA: American Automobile Association.

AAAE: American Association of Airport Executives.

Accessibility: The degree to which customers can easily get into and out of a shopping center, store, home or office's various rooms and facilities. Accessibility is an issue in providing proper accommodation to the elderly and the physically challenged.

ACRA: American Car Rental Association.

ACTA: Alliance of Canadian Travel Associations.

ACTE: Association of Corporate Travel Executives.

ADA Room: A hotel room designed for a disabled person, named after the Americans with Disability Act. In the U.K. such a room is referred to as a Special Needs Accommodation.

ADR: See "Average Daily Rate (ADR)."

ADS-B: A new air traffic control system that is generating headlines is the Automatic Dependent Surveillance-Broadcast (ADS-B) which commenced service in Canada in January 2009. ADS-B uses GPS information to replace radar when tracking planes. It is more accurate and faster than radar, allowing planes to travel more closely together safely.

Adventure Tour: A tour built around a sport, such as hiking, cycling or rafting. For example, Backroads, based in Berkeley, California, is a significant operator of adventure tours involving hiking, biking and other sports.

Aeronautical Telecommunications Network (ATN): Refers to the collection of ground, air/ground and airborne subnetworks interconnected by routes that support computer-to-computer, internetwork communication and message transfer between host computers.

AGV: See "Automotrice a Grande Vitesse (AGV)."

AH&LA: American Hotel & Lodging Association (formerly the American & Motel Association).

AHMA: American Hotel and Motel Association.

Air Travel Card: A credit card, sponsored by various airlines, used only to purchase airline tickets. Also known as the Universal Air Travel Plan Card.

Airline Codes: Unique two- or three- digit alphanumeric codes that represent specific airlines. For example, CO is Continental Airlines. Also known as Airline Designators.

Airline Designator: Unique two- or three-digit alphanumeric codes that represent an air carrier. Codes are designated by the International Air Transport Association (IATA). Also known as Airline Codes.

Airlines Reporting Corporation (ARC): The domestic airlines created this autonomous corporation to perform functions including travel agent accreditation; distribution and control of tickets and ticket number assignment; travel transaction reporting and financial settlement; and other travel related services.

Airport Codes: Unique three-letter codes that represent each airport. For example, DFW is the Dallas/Ft. Worth International Airport.

All-Inclusive: Designates that one price includes all the listed elements of a tour or hotel package. For example, an all-inclusive hotel price would include meals, drinks and entertainment.

All-Inclusive Tour Package: A product that includes all essential elements, such as airfare, hotel and ground transportation, for a set price.

ALPA: Airline Pilots Association.

American Plan (AP): See "Full Board."

Amtrak: The U.S. National Railroad Passenger Corporation; the government-subsidized operator of passenger trains in the United States.

Antitrust Legislation: A set of laws that foster a competitive environment preventing unreasonable restraint of trade or unfair trade practices such as price-fixing. In the United States, antitrust laws originated with the Sherman Antitrust Act of 1890.

Apollo: A computerized reservation system used for airline, cruise, tour, hotel, car and train reservations.

ARC: Airlines Reporting Corporation.

ARR: Average Room Rate.

ARTCC: Air Route Traffic Control Center.

Asia Pacific Advisory Committee (APAC): A multi-country committee representing the Asia and Pacific region.

ASRS: Aviation Safety Reporting System, run by NASA for the FAA.

Association of Southeast Asian Nations (ASEAN): Association of Southeast Asian Nations. A regional economic development association established in 1967 by five original member countries: Indonesia, Malaysia, Philippines, Singapore, and Thailand. Brunei joined on 8 January 1984, Vietnam on 28 July 1995, Laos and Myanmar on 23 July 1997, and Cambodia on 30 April 1999.

ASTA: American Society of Travel Agents.

ATA: Air Transport Association.

ATM: Air Transportation Management.

ATME: Association of Travel Marketing Executives.

ATN: See "Aeronautical Telecommunications Network (ATN)."

ATP: Airline Tariff Publishing Company.

ATSC: Air Traffic Service Communications. Communication types include ATC, aeronautical and meteorological information, position reporting and services relating to safety and regularity of flight.

Automotrice a Grande Vitesse (AGV): A type of high speed passenger train which uses motors under the floors of passenger carriages instead of in separate locomotives at either end of the trains and can reach a commercial speed of 222 mph.

Available Rooms: The number of rooms actually available for use during a particular day in a hotel.

Available Seat Miles (ASM): A measure of the airline seating capacity available for sale. For an individual flight, ASM is the number of seats multiplied by the distance traveled. (Each ASM is one seat flown one mile.)

Available Ton Mile (ATM): A measure of air transport capacity, defined as one ton of passengers and/or cargo transported one mile.

Average Daily Rate (ADR): In hotels, room revenue divided by rooms sold.

Average Room Rate: Gross Rooms Revenue divided by the total number of rooms occupied. Complimentary rooms are excluded from rooms occupied.

Aviation Trust Fund: A measure that takes revenues from airport user taxes and uses those taxes exclusively for airport improvement.

B&B: See "Bed and Breakfast (B&B)."

Baby Boomer: Generally refers to people born from 1946 to 1964. In the U.S., the initial number of Baby Boomers totaled about 78 million. The term evolved to describe the children of soldiers and war industry workers who were involved in World War II and who began forming families after the war's end. In 2011, the oldest Baby Boomers began reaching the traditional retirement age of 65.

Back of the House: Area of a hotel separated from the guest areas, containing administrative offices, kitchens, plant, etc.

Bareboat Charter: A charter of a boat or yacht that does not include a crew. Bareboats are typically sailing yachts used by knowledgeable vacationers. Leading companies in the bareboat business include The Moorings and Sunsail.

Bays: Often the number of guest rooms in a hotel, but this differs from Keys because a suite with a bedroom and sitting room is counted as one key and two bays.

Bed and Breakfast (B&B): Typically, a privately owned lodging that includes breakfast in the price of a stay. A B&B can range from a small home with one spare room to a luxury inn.

Bed Night: A measure of occupancy in a hotel (one person for each bed per night).

Bereavement Fare: A lower fare offered by an airline to someone traveling because of a death or illness in the family.

Best Available Rate (BAR): A method of hotel room pricing that offers guests the assurance that they are paying the lowest room price available for a given night.

Boutique: A term used by often smaller and usually luxury independent hotels to differentiate themselves from larger branded hotels, but which has been applied to some chains to their design-led "lifestyle" brands, e.g. Starwood's "W" Hotels.

Boutique Hotel: A small hotel with enhanced levels of service, catering to affluent customers.

BPO: See "Business Process Outsourcing (BPO)."

Brand: A marketing strategy that places a focus on the brand name of a product, service or firm in order to increase the brand's market share, increase sales, establish credibility, improve satisfaction, raise the profile of the firm and increase profits. Also, see "Brand."

Branding: A marketing strategy that places a focus on the brand name of a product, service or firm in order to increase the brand's market share, increase sales, establish credibility, improve satisfaction, raise the profile of the firm and increase profits. Also, see "Brand."

Brigade: A kitchen term meaning the team of cooks and porters.

BritRail: Short for British Railways.

B-to-B, or B2B: See "Business-to-Business."

B-to-C, or B2C: See "Business-to-Consumer."

Bullet Train: One of the fastest passenger transportation networks in the world, topping speeds of 220 mph. Called the Shinkansen, Japan has been a long-term investor in these train systems.

Business Class: A class of airline service between first class and coach, marketed largely to business travelers. Business class features roomier seats, enhanced meals and other services not found in coach. Some airlines offer business class as their top level of service. Continental Airlines combines business and first features in its top level of services called Business First.

Business Process Outsourcing (BPO): The process of hiring another company to handle business activities. BPO is one of the fastest-growing segments in the offshoring sector. Services include human resources management, billing and purchasing and call centers, as well as many types of customer service or marketing activities, depending on the industry involved. Also, see "Knowledge Process Outsourcing (KPO)" and "Business Transformation Outsourcing (BTO)."

Business Transformation Outsourcing (BTO): A segment within outsourcing in which the client company revamps its business processes with the goal of transforming its business by following a collaborative approach with its outsourced services provider.

Business-to-Business: An organization focused on selling products, services or data to commercial customers rather than individual consumers. Also known as B2B.

Business-to-Consumer: An organization focused on selling products, services or data to individual consumers rather than commercial customers. Also known as B2C.

C&B: Conference and Banqueting.

CAA: Civil Aviation Authority (Great Britain).

CAB: Civil Aeronautics Board.

CAFTA-DR: See "Central American-Dominican Republic Free Trade Agreement (CAFTA-DR)."

Cancellation Penalty: A monetary penalty incurred when a reservation or a contract is cancelled.

Car For Hire: British term for a rental car.

Carrying Capacity: The maximum number of people allowed in a particular mode of transport, such as an airplane.

CCTE: Certified Corporate Travel Executive.

Central American-Dominican Republic Free Trade Agreement (CAFTA-DR): A trade agreement signed into law in 2005 that aimed to open up the Central American and Dominican Republic markets to American goods. Member nations include Guatemala, Nicaragua, Costa Rica, El Salvador, Honduras and the Dominican Republic. Before the law was signed, products from those countries could enter the U.S. almost tariff-free, while American goods heading into those countries faced stiff tariffs. The goal of this agreement was to create U.S. jobs while at the same time offering the non-U.S. member citizens a chance for a better quality of life through access to U.S.-made goods.

Central Reservation Office: Call center location at which reservations are taken for a travel services provider, such as a chain of hotels or car rental agencies.

Certified Travel Counselor (CTC): A travel counselor that has passed the tests required by the Institute of Certified Travel Agents.

CHRIE: The Council on Hotel, Restaurant and Institutional Education.

Chunnel: Slang name for the Channel Tunnel, the railway tunnel beneath the English Channel linking Britain and France.

Circle Trip: A trip that involves more than one destination but returns to the point of departure.

Circumnavigate: To sail or travel around something, such as an island or the world.

CITC: The Canadian Institute of Travel Counselors.

City Codes: Three-letter alphanumeric codes that represent cities and/or their airports.

City Ticket Office: An airline sales office that is not located at an airport. City ticket offices tend to be located in high-traffic business environments, such as major hotels or office complexes.

CLIA: Cruise Lines International Association.

CMI: Corporate Meetings and Incentives.

Codesharing: A practice in which two or more different airlines share the same two-letter code used to identify carriers in travel agents' reservation systems.

Commercial Airline: Any airline that transports passengers for pay.

Common Carrier: A registered and licensed truck or rail company that transports people or goods for others (also called a carrier).

Computerized Reservation System: Any computer system that allows instant access to airline schedules, tickets and fares.

Condominium: 1) In the travel industry, lodging similar to furnished, private apartments that are available to rent for days or weeks. 2) In real estate, a kind of property ownership in which the owner holds title to an individual unit in a multi-unit dwelling and shares ownership of common areas such as hallways or swimming pools.

Consolidator: An individual or a company that negotiates bulk contracts with a travel supplier, usually an airline or a hotel, and then sells that space at a discount to the general public. For example, hotels.com is a major consolidator of hotel rooms.

Consulate: A subsidiary office of a foreign government that handles visa applications and various business affairs of the government.

Convention Bureau: Usually a publicly funded organisation in the U.S. charged with the promotion of a town or region for conferences, meetings and exhibitions

Cooperative (Co-Op) Advertising: A program in which the vendor agrees to pay all or part of a retailer's ads for the vendor's products.

Corporate Rate: A reduced price for guests staying on business, sometimes through specially negotiated terms.

Cover: Each guest in food and beverage.

CRM: See "Customer Relationship Management (CRM)."

CTC: Certified Travel Counselor.

CTD: Corporate Travel Department.

CTIP: Coalition for Travel Industry Parity.

Customer Relationship Management (CRM): Refers to the automation, via sophisticated software, of business processes involving existing and prospective customers. CRM may cover aspects such as sales (contact management and contact history), marketing (campaign management and telemarketing) and customer service (call center history and field service history). Well known providers of CRM software include Salesforce, which delivers via a Software as a Service model (see "Software as a Service (Saas)"), Microsoft and Oracle.

CVB: Convention and Visitors Bureau.

CYBA: Charter Yacht Brokers Association.

Demographics: The breakdown of the population into statistical categories such as age, income, education and sex.

Destination Club: A program where wealthy travelers purchase the right to use a group of luxury vacation homes. Participants, sometimes referred to as members, purchase temporal ownership in a group of highly appealing properties. What makes this arrangement different from the standard timeshare is the fact that members buy in the right to use a variety of luxury houses (and sometimes yachts), rather than resort condos.

Destination Specialist: A person who is certified as an expert on a specific destination or region.

Domestic Airline: An airline that mainly provides service in its home country. Also known as a domestic carrier.

DOT: Department of Transportation. Generally refers to a U.S. Government agency.

Double-Occupancy Rate: The price per person for a room for two.

EATA: East Asia Travel Association.

Echo Boomers: See "Generation Y."

Ecofriendly: See "Ecotourism."

E-Commerce: The use of online, Internet-based sales methods. The phrase is used to describe both business-to-consumer and business-to-business sales.

Economy Class: Ticket class available at the lowest price. Also known as coach.

Ecotour: A tour built around the appreciation and conservation of nature.

Ecotourism: A philosophy used by a hotel in design, construction and operation, generally has goals that include: conservation of electricity, water and other natural resources; sensitivity to the surrounding natural environment, ecosystem, wildlife (and sometimes native peoples); use of organic ingredients in the hotel kitchen (which may include items from a hotel's own organic garden); and a peaceful, soothing environment throughout the hotel property (which may include such elements as extensive landscaping with native plants, running water, Zen-like gardens and areas that encourage contemplation, meditation and relaxation). Ecotourism may also be used to describe sensitivity to local ecology and native peoples in tours and excursions. "Sustainable tourism" is another phrase used to describe this sector.

Electronic Data Interchange (EDI): An accepted standard format for the exchange of data between various companies' networks. EDI allows for the transfer of e-mail as well as orders, invoices and other files from one company to another.

Electronic Reservations Service Provider (ERSP): A system that identifies airline reservations made online.

EMEA: The region comprised of Europe, the Middle East and Africa.

Enterprise Resource Planning (ERP): An integrated information system that helps manage all aspects of a business, including accounting, ordering and human resources, typically across all locations of a major corporation or organization. ERP is considered to be a critical tool for management of large organizations. Suppliers of ERP tools include SAP and Oracle.

ERP: See "Enterprise Resource Planning (ERP)."

ERSP: See "Electronic Reservations Service Provider (ERSP)."

ETC: European Travel Commission.

EU: See "European Union (EU)."

EU Competence: The jurisdiction in which the European Union (EU) can take legal action.

Eurail Pass: A train ticket that allows the purchaser unlimited train travel in several European countries for a specific number of days or weeks, very popular with students touring Europe for the summer.

European Community (EC): See "European Union (EU)."

European Union (EU): A consolidation of European countries (member states) functioning as one body to facilitate trade. Previously known as the European Community (EC). The EU has a unified currency, the Euro. See europa.eu.int.

Extended Stay: A type of hotel that has been designed to attract guests who will stay for an extended period of time. Rooms at these hotels typically resemble small apartments, with kitchens and living rooms. Other features may include outdoor grills and recreation areas.

FAA: See "Federal Aviation Administration (FAA)."

FAR: See "Federal Aviation Regulations (FAR)."

FASB: See "Financial Accounting Standards Board (FASB)."

FBO: See "Fixed Base Operator (FBO)."

Federal Aviation Administration (FAA): A U.S. Government agency that regulates and monitors airline safety regulations.

Federal Aviation Regulations (FAR): Refers to the rules, published by the FAA, under which flight operations are conducted.

Financial Accounting Standards Board (FASB): An independent organization that establishes the Generally Accepted Accounting Principles (GAAP).

Fixed Base Operator (FBO): A firm or organization that runs the business side of an airport, such as leasing hangars and selling fuel.

FL310: In flying, an abbreviation used for altitudes above 18,000 feet. For example, FL310 is an altitude of 31,000 feet.

Flag Carrier: In the airline industry, a class of air carriers authorized to operate scheduled flights over specified routes between the U.S. and foreign countries.

FMC: Flight Management Computer. Also known as FMC System or FMCS.

FMGC: Flight Management Guidance Computer.

FRA: The Federal Railroad Administration, a U.S. Government agency that regulates railroads.

Franchise: 1) A contractual agreement between a franchisor (for example, a company or organization owning all rights to a brand, type of business, retail operation, restaurant concept or sports league) and a franchisee (person or organization desiring to license the use of those rights for a specific purpose within a specific region) that allows the franchisee to operate a retail outlet or other type of business using a brand, trade secrets, formulas and format developed and supported by the franchisor. Typically, a franchisee pays an upfront fee and then continuing fees to the franchisor. 2) A generic term used to describe a very well established business or brand.

Franchisee: See "Franchise."

Franchisor: See "Franchise."

Free Port: A port free of customs duties and many other customs regulations.

Full Board: A hotel rate which includes three meals a day (also known as Full pension or American Plan (AP) in the U.S.).

GA: See "General Aviation (GA)."

GAAP: See "Generally Accepted Accounting Principles (GAAP)."

Galileo: Galileo is a major computerized travel reservation system. It is owned by Galileo International.

GDP: See "Gross Domestic Product (GDP)."

GDS: See "Global Distribution System (GDS)."

General Aviation (GA): Designates aircraft and pilots that are not part of commercial airlines or military flying. For example, business jets are part of general aviation.

Generally Accepted Accounting Principles (GAAP): A set of accounting standards administered by the Financial Accounting Standards Board (FASB) and enforced by the U.S. Security and Exchange Commission (SEC). GAAP is primarily used in the U.S.

Generation M: A very loosely defined term that is sometimes used to refer to young people who have grown up in the digital age. "M" may refer to any or all of media-saturated, mobile or multi-tasking. The term was most notably used in a Kaiser Family Foundation report published in 2005, "Generation M: Media in the Lives of 8-18 year olds." Also, see "Generation Y" and "Generation Z."

Generation X: A loosely-defined and variously-used term that describes people born between approximately 1965 and 1980, but other time frames are recited. Generation X is often referred to as a group influential in defining tastes in consumer goods, entertainment and/or political and social matters.

Generation Y: Refers to people born between approximately 1982 and 2002. In the U.S., they number more than 90 million, making them the largest generation segment in the nation's history. They are also known as Echo Boomers, Millennials or the Millennial Generation. These are children of the Baby Boom generation who will be filling the work force as Baby Boomers retire.

Generation Z: Some people refer to Generation Z as people born after 1991. Others use the beginning date of 2001, or refer to the era of 1994 to 2004. Members of Generation Z are considered to be natural and rapid adopters of the latest technologies.

GIANTS: Greater Independent Association of National Travel Services.

Global Distribution System (GDS): Refers to the reservation tool that travel agents use when making an air, hotel, car or other travel service bookings.

Global Positioning System (GPS): A satellite system, originally designed by the U.S. Department of Defense for navigation purposes. Today, GPS is in wide use for consumer and business purposes, such as navigation for drivers, boaters and hikers. It utilizes satellites orbiting the earth at 10,900 miles to enable users to pinpoint precise locations using small, electronic wireless receivers.

Globalization: The increased mobility of goods, services, labor, technology and capital throughout the world. Although globalization is not a new development, its pace has increased with the advent of new technologies.

GMT: See "Greenwich Mean Time (GMT)."

GPS: See "Global Positioning System (GPS)."

Greenwich Mean Time (GMT): The time of day at the Greenwich Observatory in the U.K. which is used as a standard point of reference in global timekeeping and navigation; the base time used for calculation of longitude in navigation.

Gross Domestic Product (GDP): The total value of a nation's output, income and expenditures produced with a nation's physical borders.

Gross National Product (GNP): A country's total output of goods and services from all forms of economic activity measured at market prices for one calendar year. It differs from Gross Domestic Product (GDP) in that GNP includes income from investments made in foreign nations.

HEDNA: Hotel Electronic Distribution Network Association.

HORECA: Hotel, Restaurant and Catering.

HSMA: Hospitality Sales and Marketing Association.

Hub (airline usage): Any airport where one airline controls much of the passenger capacity or has a significant number of connecting flights arriving and departing daily. For example, Denver is a significant hub for United Airlines and Detroit is a hub for Northwest Airlines.

Hub-and-Spoke: A system of scheduling and routing airline flights in which planes carrying passengers from smaller cities feed into a few major airports. This means that several of an airline's planes arrive at a hub at approximately the same time, and passengers then hurry from gate to gate to make connections.

IACVB: International Association of Convention and Visitors Bureau.

IAMAT: International Association for Medical Assistance to Travelers.

IAPA: International Air Passenger Association.

IATA: International Air Transport Association.

IATAN: International Airlines Travel Agency Network.

IAWT: International Association of World Tourism.

ICAO: International Civil Aviation Organization.

ICCL: International Council of Cruise Lines.

ICTA: Institute of Certified Travel Agents.

IFRS: See "International Financials Reporting Standards (IFRS)."

IFTAA: International Forum of Travel and Tourism Advocates.

IFWTO: International Federation of Women's Travel Organizations.

ILS: See "Instrument Landing System (ILS)."

IMO: International Maritime Organization.

Inclusive Tour: See "All-Inclusive Tour Package."

Industry Code: A descriptive code assigned to any company in order to group it with firms that operate in similar businesses. Common industry codes include the NAICS (North American Industrial Classification System) and the SIC (Standard Industrial Classification), both of which are standards widely used in America, as well as the International Standard Industrial Classification of all Economic Activities (ISIC), the Standard International Trade Classification established by the United Nations (SITC) and the General Industrial Classification of Economic Activities within the European Communities (NACE).

Initial Public Offering (IPO): A company's first effort to sell its stock to investors (the public). Investors in an up-trending market eagerly seek stocks offered in many IPOs because the stocks of newly public companies that seem to have great promise may appreciate very rapidly in price, reaping great profits for those who were able to get the stock at the first offering. In the United States, IPOs are regulated by the SEC (U.S. Securities Exchange Commission) and by the state-level regulatory agencies of the states in which the IPO shares are offered.

INS: Immigration and Naturalization Service, a U.S. Government agency.

Instrument Landing System (ILS): Uses precision localizer and glide-slope radio transmitters near runways to provide landing approach guidance.

Intellectual Property (IP): The exclusive ownership of original concepts, ideas, designs, engineering plans or other assets that are protected by law. Examples include items covered by trademarks, copyrights and patents. Items such as software, engineering plans, fashion designs and architectural designs, as well as games, books, songs and other entertainment items are among the many things that may be considered to be intellectual property. (Also, see "Patent.")

International Financials Reporting Standards (IFRS): A set of accounting standards established by the International Accounting Standards Board (IASB) for the preparation of public financial statements. IFRS has been adopted by much of the world, including the European Union, Russia and Singapore.

IP: See "Intellectual Property (IP)."

ISA: International Standard Atmosphere.

ISO 9000, 9001, 9002, 9003: Standards set by the International Organization for Standardization. ISO 9000, 9001, 9002 and 9003 are the highest quality certifications awarded to organizations that meet exacting standards in their operating practices and procedures.

ISTTE: International Society of Travel and Tourism Educators.

IT-Enabled Services (ITES): The portion of the Information Technology industry focused on providing business services, such as call centers, insurance claims processing and medical records transcription, by utilizing the power of IT, especially the Internet. Most ITES functions are considered to be back-office procedures. Also, see "Business Process Outsourcing (BPO)."

ITTA: Independent Travel Technology Association.

Km: Abbreviation for kilometer.

LAC: Latin America and the Caribbean.

LAT: Abbreviation for latitude.

LDCs: See "Least Developed Countries (LDCs)."

LDW: See "Loss Damage Waiver (LDW)."

Least Developed Countries (LDCs): Nations determined by the U.N. Economic and Social Council to be the poorest and weakest members of the international community. There are currently 50 LDCs, of which 34 are in Africa, 15 are in Asia Pacific and the remaining one (Haiti) is in Latin America. The top 10 on the LDC list, in descending order from top to 10th, are Afghanistan, Angola, Bangladesh, Benin, Bhutan, Burkina Faso, Burundi, Cambodia, Cape Verde and the Central African Republic. Sixteen of the LDCs are also Landlocked Least Developed Countries (LLDCs) which present them with additional difficulties often due to the high cost of transporting trade goods. Eleven of the LDCs are Small Island Developing States (SIDS), which are often at risk of extreme weather phenomenon (hurricanes, typhoons, Tsunami); have fragile ecosystems; are often dependent on foreign energy sources; can have high disease rates for HIV/AIDS and malaria; and can have poor market access and trade terms.

Limited-Purpose Card: A credit card that may be used only for travel-related expenses.

Load Factor (LF): In airlines, the percentage of seating capacity that is filled with paying passengers (RPM divided by ASM).

LOHAS: Lifestyles of Health and Sustainability. A marketing term that refers to consumers who choose to purchase and/or live with items that are natural, organic, less polluting, etc. Such consumers may also prefer products powered by alternative energy, such as hybrid cars.

LON: Abbreviation for longitude.

Loss Damage Waiver (LDW): Daily rental car insurance that covers vandalism, theft and damage caused by an accident. LDW is sold at considerable additional cost to travelers.

Maglev Trains (Magnetic Levitation): Trains that utilize powerful magnetic fields in order to float about 3/8" above their tracks. Unhindered by rail friction, they can travel at speeds up to 300 miles per hour. For example, in Shanghai, a maglev train serves passengers between the Pudong Airport and the City Center. The 19-mile trip takes eight minutes at a top speed of 310 miles per hour.

MAPTA: Metropolitan Association of Professional Travel Agents.

Market Segmentation: The division of a consumer market into specific groups of buyers based on demographic factors.

MARS (travel industry): Multi-Access Reservations System.

Meet-And-Greet Service: A service that assists travelers with baggage handling, transport and orientation upon arrival.

Millennials: See "Generation Y."

MN: Magnetic North.

MSL: Mean Sea Level.

NABTA: National Association of Business Travel Agents.

NACA: National Air Carrier Association.

NACTA: National Association of Commissioned Travel Agents.

NAOAG: North American Official Airline Guide.

NAS: National Aircraft Standard.

NASA: National Aeronautics and Space Administration.

NATA: National Air Transportation Association.

NATCA: National Air Traffic Controllers Association.

Nautical Mile (NM): A distance equaling 6,000 feet, while a statute mile equals 5,280.

NAV (in Travel): Abbreviation for navigation.

NAVAID: Navigational Aid.

NBAA: National Business Aircraft Association.

NBTA: National Business Travel Association.

NextGen: An advanced air traffic control system in the U.S.

NM: See "Nautical Mile (NM)."

North American Industrial Classification System (NAICS): See "Industry Code."

NPTA: National Passenger Traffic Association.

NTA: National Tour Association.

NTSB: National Transportation Safety Board.

NWS: National Weather Service.

OAG: Official Airline Guide.

Occupancy Rate: In hotels, the percentage of hotel rooms occupied during a certain time period.

OECD: See "Organisation for Economic Co-operation and Development (OECD)."

Onshoring: The opposite of "offshoring." Providing or maintaining manufacturing or services within or nearby a company's domestic location. Sometimes referred to as reshoring.

Opaque Inventory: Used to describe websites that offer unsold hotel room or airline seat inventory at discounted prices.

Organisation for Economic Co-operation and Development (OECD): A group of more than 30 nations that are strongly committed to the market economy and democracy. Some of the OECD members include Japan, the U.S., Spain, Germany, Australia, Korea, the U.K., Canada and Mexico. Although not members, Estonia, Israel and Russia are invited to member talks; and Brazil, China, India, Indonesia and South Africa have enhanced engagement policies with the OECD. The Organisation provides statistics, as well as social and economic data; and researches social changes, including patterns in evolving fiscal policy, agriculture, technology, trade, the environment and other areas. It publishes over 250 titles annually; publishes a corporate magazine, the OECD Observer; has radio and TV studios; and has centers in Tokyo, Washington, D.C., Berlin and Mexico City that distributed the Organisation's work and organizes events.

OTA: Online Travel Agency.

PATA: Pacific Asia Travel Association.

Point-to-Point (Airlines): A system of scheduling planes used by highly-efficient airlines Southwest and JetBlue. In this type of system, passengers are often carried in a straight line to their destinations, with possible stops en route. This differs greatly from the hub-and-spoke systems preferred by many major airlines. See "Hub-and-Spoke."

Positioning: The design and implementation of a merchandising mix, price structure and style of selling to create an image of the retailer, relative to its competitors, in the customer's mind.

Pre-Boomer: A term occasionally used to describe people who were born between 1935 and 1945. They are somewhat older than Baby Boomers (born between 1946 and 1962). Also see "Baby Boomer."

RAA: Regional Airline Association.

Rack Rate: Term for the price a hotel charges per room before any discounts have been taken into account.

Revenue Departures: In the airline industry, the number of take-offs actually performed in scheduled passenger/cargo and all-cargo services.

Revenue Passenger Mile (RPM): One paying passenger transported one mile. Sometimes referred to as passenger mile.

Revenue Per Available Room (REVPAR): A hotel performance measure that divides revenue by the number of available rooms, as opposed to the number of occupied rooms.

Revenue Ton Mile (RTM): A standard unit of demand for air transport, defined as one ton of revenue passenger and/or cargo traffic transported one mile.

Rolling-Hub: A cost-cutting system of flight scheduling in which flights are evenly spaced with regard to arrival times. Flights arrive at an airport gate, unload passengers and quickly load waiting passengers with as little gate time as possible. See "Hub-and-Spoke."

Room Block: A number of rooms in a hotel reserved by customers or set aside for a group.

Room Night: In hotels, a statistical unit of occupancy, designating one hotel room occupied for one night.

RPM: See "Revenue Passenger Mile (RPM)."

RTM: See "Revenue Ton Mile (RTM)."

SaaS: See "Software as a Service (SaaS)."

Sabre: Name of a major computerized travel reservation system. Sabre is owned and operated by Sabre Holdings Corporation, a Ft. Worth-based, NYSE-listed company.

SATH: Society for the Advancement of Travel for the Handicapped.

SATW: Society of American Travel Writers.

Seat Pitch: In passenger aircraft, the distance between any point on a seat from the same point on the seat directly in front or behind.

Select Service: A category of hotel that offers limited guest services. Typically, there are no meeting or banquet rooms, and restaurants, if any, are limited to a free breakfast service each morning. Select service hotels do not offer such luxury amenities as room service, valet parking or concierge service.

Sharing Economy: A rental practice that affords consumers the ability to rent or borrow everything from hotel rooms to cars to private homes. It is also known as collaborative consumption.

Single-Entity Charter: An airplane or other transportation vessel that is chartered to one company or group for use only by its employees or members.

SITA: Societe Internationale Telecommunique Aeronautique.

SITE: Society of Incentive Travel Executives.

Software as a Service (SaaS): Refers to the practice of providing users with software applications that are hosted on remote servers and accessed via the Internet. Excellent examples include the CRM (Customer Relationship Management) software provided in SaaS format by Salesforce. An earlier technology that operated in a similar, but less sophisticated, manner was called ASP or Application Service Provider.

SRP: Special Rate Plan.

STAG: Society of Travel Agents in Government.

Standard Industrial Classification (SIC): See "Industry Code."

STOL: In aircraft, Short Takeoff and Landing.

STTE: Society of Travel and Tourism Educators.

Subsidiary, Wholly-Owned: A company that is wholly controlled by another company through stock ownership.

Supersonic Transport (SST): Supersonic Transport (SST) refers to an airplane which is capable of exceeding the speed of sound. At one time, the Concorde was operated commercially as an SST, however it has been taken out of service.

Supply Chain: The complete set of suppliers of goods and services required for a company to operate its business. For example, a manufacturer's supply chain may include providers of raw materials, components, custom-made parts and packaging materials.

Sustainable Tourism: See "Ecotourism."

TGV: Train a Grande Vitesse. Typical TGV trains travel at 180 miles per hour, but the company has tested trains at much higher speeds. France's (TGV) has been providing high-speed rail service since 1981.

TIA: Travel Industry Association.

TIAA: Travel Industry Association of America.

TIAC: Travel Industry Association of Canada.

Time-share (Timeshare): A type of joint ownership in which a group of owners share a particular piece of property, agreeing to have use of the property only during set days each year. Typically, time-share properties are vacation properties in such areas as beach resorts or ski resorts. They typically are condominium properties in which each condominium is jointly owned by a large group of people. Each owner typically has access to one week's use per year and pays for a proportionate share of the property's upkeep, taxes and insurance as well as management fees.

Ton-Mile: A measure of output for freight transportation, reflecting the weight of the shipment and the distance it is hauled; a multiplication of tons hauled by the distance traveled.

Tour Operator: A business that creates, markets and operates group travel offerings that provide a complete travel experience for one fixed price.

Tour Wholesaler: A business that creates and markets tours and travel packages to travel agents.

Travel Agent: An agent who markets and sells travel services directly to the consumer and to corporations.

TTGAC: Travel and Tourism Government Affairs Council.

TTRA: Travel and Tourism Research Association.

UATP: Universal Air Travel Plan. See "Air Travel Card."

UBOA: United Bus Owners of America.

UFTAA: Universal Federation of Travel Agents Associations.

Upgauging: The practice among major airlines to replace smaller places with larger ones, thereby increasing capacity.

USTAR: United States Travel Agent Registry.

USTOA: United States Tour Operators Association.

USTTA: United States Travel and Tourism Administration.

Utilization Rate: In the car rental industry, the percentage of vehicles in use during a certain time period.

Value Added Tax (VAT): A tax that imposes a levy on businesses at every stage of manufacturing based on the value it adds to a product. Each business in the supply chain pays its own VAT and is subsequently repaid by the next link down the chain; hence, a VAT is ultimately paid by the consumer, being the last link in the supply chain, making it comparable to a sales tax. Generally, VAT only applies to goods bought for consumption within a given country; export goods are exempt from VAT, and purchasers from other countries taking goods back home may apply for a VAT refund.

Very Light Jet (VLJ): A type of business jet that is much lower in cost to purchase and to operate than commercial passenger jets. Typically seating six people, these lightweight aircraft cost from $1.5 million to $3 million, utilize high-efficiency, lightweight jet engines, and can be operated in the $2 to $3 per mile range. Many of these new aircraft will be used as air taxis.

VLJ: See "Very Light Jet (VLJ)."

WAPTT: World Association for Professional Training in Tourism.

WATA: World Association of Travel Agents.

World Trade Organization (WTO): One of the only globally active international organizations dealing with the trade rules between nations. Its goal is to assist the free flow of trade goods, ensuring a smooth, predictable supply of goods to help raise the quality of life of member citizens. Members form consensus decisions that are then ratified by their respective parliaments. The WTO's conflict resolution process generally emphasizes interpreting existing commitments and agreements, and discovers how to ensure trade policies to conform to those agreements, with the ultimate aim of avoiding military or political conflict.

WTO: See "World Trade Organization (WTO)."

WTO (Tourism): World Tourism Organization.

WTTC: World Travel and Tourism Council.

Lightning Source UK Ltd.
Milton Keynes UK
UKOW07f1937190317

296984UK00020B/487/P